JAPAN
ENCYCLOPEDIA

Boye Lafayette De Mente

Printed on recyclable paper

PASSPORT BOOKS
a division of *NTC Publishing Group*
Lincolnwood, Illinois USA

Acknowledgments

I am grateful to the following companies, organizations, and individuals for helping me prepare this book:

Japan Air Lines
Japan National Tourist Organization
Japan Travel Bureau
Foreign Press Center
Keizai Koho Center
Japan External Trade Organization
Nippon Steel Corporation

Morris Simoncelli
Geoffrey Tudor
Yoshio Kimura
Toshi Ikubo
Kiyoshi Hirayama
Yasuyuki Yabuki
Takashi Nagaoka
Tsutomu "Tommy" Sugiura
Shiro Hazue
Hiroshi Mitsukawa
Joel Friedman
Earle Okumura
Paul Maruoka
Frank Kawahara
Haruo Shinoda
George Pokrovsky
Masaharu Hirukawa

Library of Congress Cataloging-in-Publication Data

De Mente, Boye Lafayette.
　　Japan encyclopedia / Boye Lafayette De Mente.
　　　　p.　　cm.
　　ISBN 0-8442-8435-1 : $27.95
　　1. Japan—Encyclopedias.　　I. Title.
DS805.D355　1995
952' .003—dc20

95-1790
CIP

Cover Design: Nick Panos
Cover Photographs: Photo Network
Interior Photographs: Japan National Tourist Organization
Line Drawings: Keiko Yokoyama & Paula Weber
Mon (crest): Kiyoshi Kawamoto, from *The Elements of Japanese Design.*
　　Used with the permission of John Weatherhill, Inc.

Originally published as *Japan Almanac*, © Boye Lafayette De Mente.
Published by Passport Books, Trade Imprint of National
Textbook Company, 4255 West Touhy Avenue, Lincolnwood
(Chicago), Illinois 60646-1975.

5 6 7 8 9 VP 0 9 8 7 6 5 4 3 2 1

96163

Preface

Most Westerners will readily accept the proposition that they and the Japanese are different. Others, however, persist in the belief that while there may be surface differences, Japanese and Westerners are very much alike.

Having been intimately involved with Japan since the late 1940s, I can attest to one difference that goes beyond any facade and is a vital factor in Japan's transformation from an isolated feudal society to a major economic power in just a few decades. Immediately after Japan's doors were opened to the West in the mid-1850s, the Japanese began to stream abroad on official government-sponsored, as well as independent, study-missions, seeking to absorb and synthesize everything the West had to offer.

This activity was to continue for generations, reaching a peak in the 1950s and 1960s, when unending droves of note- and picture-taking Japanese were a common sight in the laboratories, factories, and stores of the West.

Japanese interest in what is going on in the outside world, in discovering, recording, and studying every attitude, every action—including changes in the weather—is as strong now as ever, and has become so refined that the Japanese probably have the most comprehensive and sophisticated information-gathering network ever seen. In contrast, most Westerners not only remain almost totally ignorant of Japan and things Japanese, they show little real interest in learning.

This attitude toward Japan is a handicap of enormous proportions. It has had, and will continue to have, serious economic and political implications —and must be overcome if we and the Japanese are to maintain friendly, mutually beneficial relations.

This book is designed to serve as a comprehensive introduction to Japan —in a novel and provocative way—and to encourage further study in the hope that this will lead to a better understanding and appreciation of both our differences and similarities.

Just as the Japanese have learned a great deal from us since the 1850s, there are many things we can learn from them—things that have to do with personal relations, social responsibility, aesthetics, and ethics.

It is my hope that the *Japan Encyclopedia* will serve as an exciting beginning to a firm knowledge of Japan, its people, and its culture.

Boye Lafayette De Mente

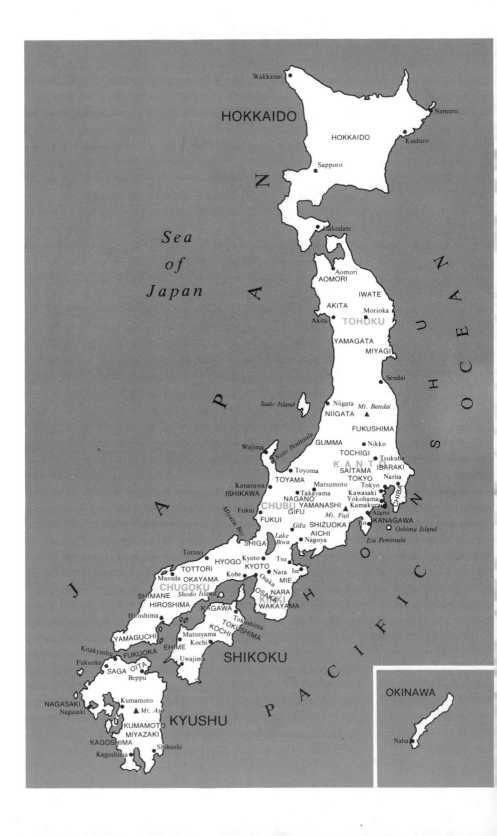

HOKKAIDO

Wakkanai

Nemuro

HOKKAIDO

Kushiro

Sapporo

*Sea
of
Japan*

Hakodate

Aomori
AOMORI

IWATE

AKITA   Morioka

Akita   TOHOKU

YAMAGATA
MIYAGI

Sendai

Sado Island   Niigata   *Mt. Bandai*
NIIGATA   ▲

FUKUSHIMA

Wajima   GUMMA   Nikko

TOCHIGI   Tsukuba

Noto Peninsula   K A N T O   IBARAKI

SAITAMA

Toyoma   TOYAMA   TOKYO   Narita

Kanazawa   Matsumoto   Tokyo

ISHIKAWA   Takayama   Kawasaki
Yokohama

NAGANO   YAMANASHI   Kamakura

GIFU   Atami

Miyazu Bay   CHUBU   *Mt. Fuji* ▲   KANAGAWA

Fukui   FUKUI   Ito

Gifu   SHIZUOKA   Oshima Island

SHIGA   AICHI   *Izu Peninsula*

*Lake
Biwa*   Nagoya

Tottori   Kyoto   Tsu

HYOGO   Ise

TOTTORI   KYOTO   MIE

Masuda   OKAYAMA   Kobe   Osaka   NARA

SHIMANE   CHUGOKU   *Shodo Island*   OSAKA   WAKAYAMA

HIROSHIMA   KAGAWA   KINKI

Hiroshima   Tokushima

TOKUSHIMA

YAMAGUCHI   Matsuyama   KOCHI

Kitakyushu   FUKUOKA   EHIME   Kochi

Fukuoka   SAGA   OITA   Uwajima   SHIKOKU

Beppu

NAGASAKI   Kumamoto
Nagasaki   ▲ *Mt. Aso*

KUMAMOTO   KYUSHU
MIYAZAKI

KAGOSHIMA   Shibushi

Kagoshima

OKINAWA

Naha

J A P A N   O C E A N   P A C I F I C

Contents

A

Abacus **1**
A-Bomb **2**
Abortion **3**
Acupuncture **3**
Adams, William **4**
Addresses **6**
Advertising Agencies **7**
Aesthetics **8**
Agriculture **9**
Aikido **10**
Ainu **11**
Airlines **13**
Air Miles **13**
Airports **14**
Ajinomoto **14**
Akasaka **14**
Akasaka Detached Palace **14**
Akasaka Prince Hotel **15**
Alcoholic Beverages **16**
Alien Registration **17**
All Nippon Airways **17**
Allowances (Employment) **17**
American/Allied Occupation of Japan **17**
American Chamber of Commerce in Japan **19**
American Contact **20**
Ando, Hiroshige (*see* Hiroshige)
Animals **22**
Antimonopoly Law **22**
Aoyama Palace **23**
Archery **23**

Architecture **25**
Area Codes **27**
Arita **27**
Armed Forces **27**
Arranged Marriages **28**
Asakusa **28**
Ashiya **29**
Associations of Foreign Wives **29**
Atami **29**
Atomic Bomb Dome **30**
Atsugi **30**
Atsuta Shrine **30**
Auto Accident Hospital **31**
Automobiles **31**
Average Life Expectancy **32**
Awa Dance **33**

B

Bamboo **34**
Banzuiin, Chobei **34**
Barbershops **35**
Barrier Gates **35**
Bar (Legal) System **36**
Baseball **36**
Basho, Matsuo **38**
Bathhouses/Massage Parlors **38**
Bathhouses, Public **39**
Bathing **40**
Beaches **40**
Beauty **41**
Beefsteaks **41**
Beer **42**

Beer Halls and Gardens 42

Benedict, Ruth 42

Bento (*see* Station Box-Lunches)

Beppu 42

Biwa 43

Black Mist 43

Blyth, Reginald H. 43

Bonenkai (*see* Forget-the-Year
    Parties)

Bon Festival 43

Bonkei 44

Bonsai 45

Bonseki 45

Bonuses 45

Book Publishing 45

Boso Peninsula 47

Boss 47

Bowing 47

Bridge of Heaven 48

Buddhism 49

Buddhist Temples 52

Budget Traveling 52

Buildings 53

Bunraku 54

Bunya Puppetry 55

Burial 55

Bush, Lewis 55

Bushido 55

Business Groups in Japan 56

Business Japan 57

Business Nippon 57

Business Publications 57

C

Cabarets 58

Calligraphy 59

Capsule Hotel 60

Carpenters 60

Castles 61

Cats 63

Ceramic Ware 63

Chamberlain, Prof. Basil Hall 64

Chanbara Movies 64

Cherry Blossoms 64

Chestnuts 65

Chiba 65

Chikamatsu, Monzaemon 65

Children's Songs 65

China Town 66

Chindon-ya 67

Chinese 67

Chinese Food 67

Chochin 68

Chopsticks 68

Christianity in Japan 68

Cinemas 69

Cities 69

Clark, Dr. William S. 71

Class Distinctions 72

Climate 72

Clinics 73

Cloisonné 74

Coffee Shops 74

Comics 75

Comic Storytellers 75

Commuting 76

Companies 76

Company Housing 77

Company-run Bars 77

Competition 77

Computers 78

Constitution Day 79

Construction Industry 79

Contracts 79

Convenience Agencies 79

Cormorant Fishing 80

Courting—Dating 81

Courts **82**
Cram Schools **82**
Credit Cards **83**
Crests **83**
Crime **84**
Cultural Affairs **84**
Cultural Medals **85**
Customers **85**

D
Daimon Temple Fire Festival **86**
Daimyo **86**
Dancing **86**
Date, Masamune **87**
Dating (*see* Courting—Dating)
Death **88**
Decision Making **88**
Dejima **88**
Deming, Dr. W. Edwards **90**
Democracy **90**
Dentsu, Inc. **90**
Department Stores **91**
Descending from Heaven **91**
Designer Clothing **92**
Desserts **92**
Dictionaries **93**
Diet Building **93**
Dining Out **94**
Diplomatic History **95**
Directory of Foreign Capital
  Affiliated Enterprises in Japan
  101
Disneyland of Tokyo **101**
Districts of Japan **103**
Divorce **106**
Doing Business in Japan **107**
Dolls **107**
Driver's License **108**

Driving in Japan **109**
Drug Abuse **109**
Dying in Japan **109**

E
Earthquakes **110**
Eastern Japan **111**
East, The, Magazine **111**
Eating **111**
Economic Information Center
  112
Economic Progress after 1868
  112
Edo (Tokyo) **114**
Edo Castle **115**
Education **116**
Eighty-Eight Sacred Places of
  Shikoku **118**
Elder Statesmen **119**
Elections **120**
Electricity **120**
Emperor **120**
Employment Agencies **122**
Encyclopedia of Japan **122**
Energy Research **122**
English Language Study **123**
Eno Island **123**
Entertainment Expense **124**
Entrance Examinations **124**
Environmental Pollution **125**
Epic Songs **125**
Eras **125**
Escalator System **126**
Etiquette **126**
Examination Hell **127**
EXPO Memorial Park **127**
Exporting **127**

F

Face **129**
Face—Hand Towel **129**
Family Crests **130**
Family Register **130**
Famous Products **131**
Famous Sights **131**
Fans **132**
Farmers **133**
Farming **134**
Fashion Apparel **134**
Fashion Models **135**
Fast Foods **136**
Fenollosa, Ernest Francisco **136**
Festivals **137**
Fireworks **142**
Fishing **142**
Flower Arranging **143**
Folk Art **144**
Folk Songs **145**
Food **145**
Food Carts **147**
Foreign Companies in Japan **148**
Foreign Correspondents **149**
Foreigners in Japan **150**
Foreign Children Born in Japan
  150
Foreign Press Center **150**
Foreign Students in Japan **151**
Foreign Workers in Japan **151**
Forests—Forestry **152**
Forget-the-Year Parties **152**
Forty-Seven Ronin **153**
Freedom of Speech **154**
Freeways **154**
Fringe Benefits **155**
Fruit **155**
Fuchu **155**
Fukuoka **156**

Funerals **156**
Furoshiki (*see* Wrapping Cloth)
Futaara-San Shrine **157**
Futon (*see* Sleeping Mats)

G

Gakushuin University **158**
Gambling **158**
Games **158**
Gangs **160**
Gardens **161**
Geisha **163**
Geta (*see* Wooden Clogs)
Ghosts and Goblins **165**
Gift Giving **166**
Gifts **166**
Gifu **167**
Ginza **167**
Gionmachi **168**
Giri **169**
Glover Mansion **169**
G-Mark Award **169**
Go (*see* Games)
Go-betweens **169**
God-Shelf **170**
Goldfish **170**
Gorges **170**
Government **171**
Government, Local **173**
Grand Masters **173**
Grandmother Throwing-Away
  Mountain **174**
Grand Ise "Sweat" **174**
Grand Shrines of Ise **174**
Great Bridge of Choshi **175**
Great Buddha of Kamakura **175**
Great Buddha of Nara **177**
Guide Services **178**

H
Hachimaki   179
Haiku   179
Hakodate   180
Hakone   180
Hakozaki-cho   182
Hall of Poets   182
Hama Detached Palace   183
Hand-clapping   183
Handicrafts   183
Haneda Airport   184
Hanging Scrolls   185
Happi Coats   185
Harakiri   186
Haramaki   186
Harmony   186
Harris, Townsend   187
Hatsu-Mairi   190
Hatsu Shima   190
Health   190
Hearn, Lafcadio   191
Hechima   191
Heian Shrine   191
Heike   192
Heike Monogatari   192
Hello Kitty   192
Hepburn, Rev. James C.   192
Hibachi   193
Hidden Christians   194
Hidden Talent   194
High-Rise Buildings   194
Hikone   194
Himeji   195
Hiroshige Ando   195
Hiroshima   195
History   196
   Historical Periods   212
   Historical Table   214
Hokkaido   217

Homes   219
Home Visits   219
Honda Motor Company   220
Honshu   221
Horie, Kenichi   221
Hors d'Oeuvres   222
Horses   222
Horyu Temple   222
Hostesses   223
Hotels   224
Hotel Services   226
Hot Spring Spas   226
Households   227
Housing   227
Human Feelings   228
Humor   229

I
Ice Sculptures   230
Ikaho   230
Ikebana   230
Ikebukuro   231
Iki Island   232
Immunization Cards   232
Imperial Family   232
Imperial Hotel   236
Imperial Palace   239
Imperial Palace (Detached)   240
Incense Burning   240
Industrial Tours   241
Inland Sea   242
Inns   243
International Christian University   244
International Marriages   245
Introductions   246
Iron and Steel   247
Ise-Shima National Park   247

Ishikawa, Goemon   **247**
Ito   **248**
Izu Peninsula   **248**

J
Japan   **249**
Japan Academy   **250**
Japan Air Lines   **250**
Japan Alps   **251**
Japan Art Academy   **251**
Japan Asia Airways   **251**
Japan Automotive News   **252**
Japan Bridge   **252**
Japan Broadcasting Corp. (*see* NHK)
Japan Chamber of Commerce & Industry   **253**
Japan Economic Journal   **253**
Japan English Books in Print   **253**
Japanese Food   **254**
Japanese Houses   **254**
Japanese Language   **255**
Japanese People   **256**
Japanese Society   **258**
Japanese Typewriters   **259**
Japanese Women   **259**
Japan Folkcraft Museum   **262**
Japan Institute for Social and Economic Affairs (*see* Economic Information Center)
Japan Letter, The   **262**
Japan National Tourist Organization (JNTO)   **262**
Japan Petroleum & Energy Weekly   **263**
Japan Prize   **263**
Japan Rail Passes   **263**
Japan Railways Group   **263**
Japan Statistical Yearbook   **264**

Japan Steel Journal, The   **265**
Japan Travel Bureau (JTB)   **265**
Japan Travel Phone   **265**
Japan Youth Hostels   **266**
JETRO (Japan External Trade Organization)   **266**
Jidai Matsuri   **267**
Jishu Kanri   **268**
Job Hunting in Japan   **268**
Jogging   **269**
Judo   **269**
Juku (*see* Cram Schools)
Juvenile Delinquency   **270**

K
Kabuki   **272**
Kagoshima   **274**
Kaiseki   **274**
Kakemono   **274**
Kamakura   **275**
Kamikaze Pilots   **275**
Kanazawa   **276**
Kanda   **276**
Kanji Characters   **276**
Kara-Oke Singing   **277**
Karate   **278**
Karuizawa   **279**
Kato, Kiyomasa   **279**
Katsura Imperial Villa   **279**
Kawana   **280**
Kawasaki   **281**
Kegon Falls   **281**
Keidanren   **281**
Keio University   **282**
Keizai Koho Center (*see* Economic Information Center)
Kendo   **282**
Kikotsu   **282**

Kimono **284**
Kinokuniya Data Bank **285**
Kiso Rapids **285**
Kita-Kyushu **285**
Kite-flying **286**
Kobe **287**
Kofu **288**
Kojiki **288**
Komuso **288**
Koraku Garden **289**
Koreans in Japan **289**
Koshi Temple **290**
Koto **290**
Kowakidani **290**
Kumamoto **291**
Kusunoki, Masashige **292**
Kyoto **293**
Kyoto University **297**
Kyushu **298**

L

Labor **299**
Labor Unions **299**
Lacquerware **300**
Lakes **301**
Land Area **301**
Language **301**
Laws **304**
Lawyers **304**
Liberal Star **305**
Literary Agencies **305**
Literature **306**
Living Treasures **311**
Loan Words **311**
Location **311**
Love & Marriage **312**
Luck **312**

M

Magazines **313**
Mahjong (*see* Games)
Mainichi Newspaper **315**
Major Japanese Companies **315**
Management **316**
Manyoshu **318**
Marriage **319**
Martial Arts **320**
Maru **322**
Marunouchi **322**
Massagers **323**
Matsushima **324**
Matsushita Electric Industrial Co. **325**
Medical Care **325**
Meetings **326**
Meiji **327**
Meiji Memorial Picture Gallery **327**
Meiji Mura (*see* Meiji Village)
Meiji Park **327**
Meiji Shrine **328**
Meiji Village **328**
Meishi (*see* Name Cards)
Mikoshi **328**
Minamoto, Yoritomo **329**
Minamoto, Yoshitsune **329**
Mining **330**
Minshuku **330**
Mishima, Yukio **331**
Missionaries **331**
Mistresses **333**
MITI (Ministry of International Trade & Industry) **333**
Mito **334**
Mitsubishi Corp. **335**
Mitsui & Company, Ltd. **335**
Miura Peninsula **338**
Miyako Hotel **338**

Miyamoto, Musashi   339
Miyanoshita   339
Mizu Shobai   339
Mochi   340
Modeling   340
Mohammedan Mosque   340
Money   340
Mongol Invasions   340
Moon Viewing   343
Morioka   343
Mountains   343
Movies   344
Mt. Aso   344
Mt. Fuji   345
Mt. Koya   347
Music   347

N
Nagasaki   350
Nagasaki Holland Village   351
Nagoya   352
Nakahama, Manjiro   353
Name Cards   354
Names   354
Nara   355
Narita   356
Nasu Spas   357
National Anthem   357
National Bird   357
National Diet Library   358
National Flag   358
National Flower   358
National Holidays   359
National Parks   360
National Stadium   362
National Theater   362
National Vacation Villages   362
Netsuke   363

New Otani Hotel   364
Newspapers   364
Newspapers in English   366
News Services   367
New Year's Call   368
New Year's Party   368
NHK (Japan Broadcasting
   Corporation)   368
Nichiren   369
Niemon Jima   370
Nightclubs   370
Niigata   371
Nikko   371
Nikko Mausolea   373
Nikko-Yumoto Spa   374
Ninja   374
Nishijin   376
Nitobe, Dr. Inazo   376
Nobel Prize Winners   376
Noboribetsu Spa   377
Nogi, Gen. Maresuke   378
Noguchi, Dr. Hideyo   378
Noh—and Other Drama Forms
   378
Noren   379
No-Shop Sales   380
Nursery Songs   380

O
O'Bon   381
Oda, Nobunaga   382
Ofuda   383
Ogasawara Islands   384
Oka, Tadasuke   384
Okayama   384
Okazaki   385
Okinawa   385
Okura Hotel   386

Onsen (*see* Hot Spring Spas)
Origami **387**
Osaka **387**
Osaka Castle **389**
Ozaki, Yukio **390**

P
Pachinko **391**
Paintings **391**
Paper Doors **392**
Patents **392**
Pearl Island **393**
Pearls **393**
Peerage **394**
People's Lodges **394**
Permanent Residency **394**
Perry, Commodore Matthew C. **395**
Personnel Management **396**
PHP Institute **396**
Poetry (*see* Literature)
Poetry-reading Party **396**
Police **397**
Police Boxes **398**
Political Parties **398**
Pollution **399**
Population **400**
Pornography **400**
Portuguese in Japan **400**
Postal Service **402**
Pottery **402**
Prefectures **403**
Preparatory Schools **403**
Press Clubs **404**
Prisons **405**
Processions of the Lords **405**
Prostitution **407**
Proverbs **408**

Public Opinion **410**
Publications in English on Japan **410**
Publishing **410**

Q
Quality **412**
Quality Control **412**

R
Race **415**
Race Relations **415**
Radio Broadcasting **416**
Railroads **416**
Rain **417**
Ranking **418**
Raw Fish **418**
Receptionists **419**
Reischauer, Edwin O. **419**
Religions **419**
Restaurants **421**
Retail Chain Stores **423**
Retirement **423**
Rice **424**
Rikugi Garden **425**
Rivers **426**
Roads **427**
Robots **428**
Ronin **429**
Roppongi **430**
Ryokan (*see* Inns)

S
Sado Island **431**
Saga **431**

Saigo, Takamori   **432**
Sake   **432**
Samurai   **433**
San Bonaventura   **434**
San Mon   **435**
Scenic Trio   **435**
Schools (*see* Education)
Science City   **435**
Seascapes   **436**
Seasons   **436**
Seating Etiquette   **437**
Seed Gene Bank   **437**
Sekigahara   **437**
Self-defense Forces   **437**
Sendai   **438**
Sen-No Rikyu   **439**
Seto   **440**
Setsubun   **440**
Seven Gods of Good Luck   **440**
Seven Isles of Izu   **441**
Severance Payments   **441**
Sex   **441**
Shikoku   **442**
Shimabara   **443**
Shimoda   **443**
Shimonoseki   **444**
Shinagawa   **444**
Shinjuku   **445**
Shinjuku National Garden   **445**
Shin Kammon Tunnel   **446**
Shinkansen (*see* Trains)
Shinto   **446**
Shiobara Spas   **448**
Ships   **448**
Shizuoka   **449**
Shochu   **450**
Shogi (*see* Games)
Shogun   **450**
Shoji (*see* Paper Doors)

Shotoku Taishi   **451**
Shrines   **452**
Shuri-ken Jutsu   **454**
Signs   **454**
Silent Language   **455**
Silk   **455**
Singing   **456**
Sister Cities   **456**
Size   **456**
Skiing   **457**
Sleeping Mats   **457**
Smoking   **457**
Snow Festival   **458**
Soaplands   **458**
Social Security   **459**
Sogoro's Sacrifice   **460**
Sokaiya   **460**
Sony   **461**
Sophia University   **462**
Space Exploration   **462**
Split-level Economy   **462**
Spring Labor Offensive   **462**
Stagecoaches   **463**
Standards Information Center   **463**
Station Box-Lunches   **463**
Stone Lanterns   **464**
Story Telling   **465**
Students   **466**
Subways   **466**
Suicide   **467**
Suicide Forest   **468**
Sumo   **469**
Supermarkets   **471**
Superstitions   **471**
Supreme Court   **471**
Sushi   **472**
Swords   **472**

T

Tachikawa 475
Taikun 475
Taira, Kiyomori 475
Takarazuka 476
Takayama 477
Tanegashima 477
Tanka Poetry 477
Tatami 477
Taxes 478
Tea 479
Tea Ceremony 480
Telephones 482
Television 482
Temple Lodgings 483
Temple Schools 483
Tempura 483
Tengu 483
Thunder God 484
Tipping 484
Tobacco 485
Tofu 485
Togo, Admiral Heihachiro 485
Togu Palace 486
Toilets 486
Tokaido 486
Tokonoma 486
Tokugawa, Ieyasu 486
Tokushima 490
Tokyo 490
Tokyo Business Today 493
Tokyo Climate 493
Tokyo Disneyland 493
Tokyo Journal 494
Tokyo Station 494
Tokyo Tower 494
Tokyo University 495
Tokyo Weekender 495
Tour Companion 496

Tourism 496
Tourists in Japan 497
Toyama 497
Toyotomi, Hideyoshi 497
Trade 500
Tradepia International 500
Trading Companies 500
Trains 501
Trappists in Japan · 502
Travel 502
Tsu Islands 503
Tsukiji Hongan Temple 504
Tsukiji Wholesale Market 504
Tsukuba (*see* Science City)
Tunnels 505
Turkish Bathhousees (*see*
  Soaplands)

U

Ueno 506
Ueno Park 506
Ueno Zoo 506
Uji Shrine 507
Ukiyo-e 507
Umeda and Umeda Underground
  Center 508
Unions 508
Universities 509
Unlucky Numbers 510
Unzen-Amakusa National Park
  510
Uraga 511
Utsunomiya 511

V

Vaccari, Mr. and Mrs. Oreste 512
Viewing Facilities 512

Visas   512
Volcanoes   513

W
Wa (*see* Harmony)
Wakayama   514
Wakkanai   514
Wandering Priests   514
Warrior Monks   515
Waseda University   515
Water   515
Water Business   516
Wax Food Models   516
Wedding Ceremonies   516
Weights and Measures   518
Winds   518
Wine   518
Women Divers   518
Women's Organizations   519
Women's Rights   519
Wood-Block Prints   520
Wooden Clogs   521
Woods Bathing   522
Word Processing in Japanese   522
Wrapping Cloth   522
Writing Japanese   523

Y
Yabuiri   524
Yakitori   524
Yakuza   524
Yamaguchi City   525
Yamanashi Prefectural Visitor
    Center   526
Yamato   526
Yasukuni Shrine   527
Yellow Pages   527

Yen   527
Yokohama   527
Yokosuka   528
Yomiuri Land   529
Yomiuri Newspaper   529
Youth Hostels   529
Youth Travel Villages   530
Yoshino   530
Yoyogi Sports Center   530
Yukata   531
Yunokawa Spa   531
Yushima Seido   531

Z
Zaibatsu   532
Zaikai   533
Zao Ski Resort   534
Zeami   534
Zempuku Temple   534
Zen   534
Zen Food   537
Zeni-Arai Benten   537
Zeniya, Gohei   537
Zenkoku Kinro Seishonen Hall
    538
Zenko Temple   538
Zentsu Temple   538
Zodiac   539
Zojo Temple   539
Zori   540
Zuigan Temple   540
Zuiryu Hill   540
Zuisen Temple   540
Zushi   541

OTHER
    ENGLISH-LANGUAGE
    SOURCES   543

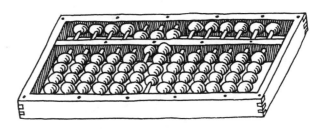

ABACUS / SOROBAN (Soe-roe-bahn)   The *soroban*, or abacus, was developed in China well over 1,000 years ago and brought to Japan in the 1500s. Just as it had in China, this marvelous calculating device was to become a vital part of Japanese life, influencing not only the conduct of business, but the manual and mental dexterity of the people.

Often described as the world's first computer, the *soroban* differs from the computer—in particular the electronic calculator—in that its use requires both physical and mental skill. The user actually does all of the calculating mentally and merely records the results on the *soroban*.

When the electronic pocket calculator became popular in the mid-1970s, it was feared that the use of the *soroban* would die out, along with the special skills that it developed. But this was not the case. There was a sudden drop-off in the number of young people signing up for *soroban* classes, but a few years later, it began to make a surprising comeback.

Now between three and four million people a year take the Japan Chamber of Commerce and Industry's annual abacus proficiency test, according to records kept by the National Abacus Education Federation (NAEF).

Interestingly enough, almost half the people who take the test each year are children, some of them as young as 12.

The Federation says the main reason so many young people are interested in the *soroban* is that it is simple to learn and operate and introduces an element of fun and personal achievement into mathematics.

Japanese teachers and educational leaders are delighted with the continuing popularity of the *soroban* because using electronic calculators requires neither manual skill nor mental agility and, as a result, has a detrimental effect on students and others who use them regularly.

For those who might believe the *soroban* is too inefficient and/or too slow to compete with computers, consider this: At a number of contests between computer and *soroban* users held in Tokyo, the *soroban* users not only held their own, they won several of the contests!

In another surprising development, it was found that people who use electronic calculators are much more prone to make mistakes than people who use the *soroban*. In the early 1980s, many Japanese companies, concerned about problems caused by operator errors, began to restrict the use of calculators in favor of the abacus.

Perhaps even more surprising, there is a Soroban Institute in the United States, at the University of Southern California in Los Angeles, founded by Dr. Leo Richards.

Dr. Richards says the abacus has value in the psychological aspects of learning. It provides youngsters with a hands-on experience of mathematical processes. He says any concept can be taught with the abacus. In fact, the user creates mathematics.

Richards adds that the *soroban* instills discipline and confidence, while the calculator, which performs all the operations itself, is alienating. Japan's NAEF agrees. It says that the *soroban* can turn a mathematical duffer into a whiz kid, removing a lot of the intimidating mystery from math.

Many Japanese companies still require proficiency with the *soroban* as a necessary qualification for employment. In 1983, the Nakano Abacus Institute in Tokyo began a program to increase the popularity of the *soroban* in Western countries.

Recommended reading: *The Japanese Abacus—Its Use & Theory*, by Takashi Kojima (Tuttle).

A-BOMB / GENSHI BAKUDAN (Gain-she bah-kuu-dahn) Japan is the only country ever to have been atom-bombed. The cities of Hiroshima and Nagasaki were destroyed by atom bombs dropped by U.S. Air Force planes on August 6 and August 9, 1945. The rationale used by the American government in making the decision to drop the bombs was that without such a demonstration of awesome power and destructive capability, Japan would not surrender, an invasion of Japan's homeland islands would be necessary to end the war, and many more lives would be lost in the process.

Besides almost totally leveling the two large cities, the bombs killed over 200,000 people, injured several hundred thousand others, and left thousands suffering from radiation ailments that did not show up until years later.

In the years following the end of hostilities between the U.S. and Japan, both Nagasaki and Hiroshima were rebuilt. Now the only physical evidence of the bombs and man's inhumanity to man are memorials erected to commemorate the events and express hope that atom bombs will never again be used. See HIROSHIMA and NAGASAKI.

ABORTION / DATAI (Dah-tie)   Article 14 of Japan's Eugenic Protection Law specifies that abortions may be performed for economic reasons. To qualify for an abortion, a pregnant girl or woman need only sign a form attesting that giving birth would result in an economic hardship. In effect, this means that abortions are virtually uncontrolled in Japan, and there is currently a movement underway to get the law changed.

Other attempts to eliminate or weaken Article 14 have failed, however, and this new movement is strongly opposed by many groups. Women's groups charge that the proposed change in the law does not reflect the views of most Japanese women, who generally insist that it is the woman's right to decide whether she should have an abortion.

Abortions have been common in Japan for several decades. In the mid-1950s, an estimated four million or so a year were performed. With economic growth and a significant improvement in the standard of living, abortions fell off drastically and are currently running between 500,000 and 600,000 a year.

ACUPUNCTURE / HARIKYU (Hah-ree-que)   The earliest known text on acupuncture is believed to have been written by China's legendary Yellow Emperor, Huang Ti, who supposedly lived from 2697 B.C. to 2596 B.C.

In any event, acupuncture has been practiced in China for well over 3,000 years. Ancient Chinese doctors learned that there are many points on the surface of the body that have a direct relationship with the various internal organs and their functions.

It was discovered that these points were well defined and constant and that they could be used to diagnose ailments as well as to relieve or cure many bodily malfunctions. It was also learned that the best way to effect such cures was to stimulate these focal points with needles.

The early Chinese reasoned that people live and function as the result of a life-force or body energy that flows through the body in a prescribed manner, from organ to organ. When this body energy is diminished or disturbed, one or more organs can no longer function properly, and the body becomes ill.

Acupuncture, the inserting of needles into the body's energy focal points, was developed as a method of redirecting and recharging the energy levels of the different organs.

The practice of acupuncture was introduced into Japan from China in the sixth century and gradually spread throughout the medical community. When Western medicine was officially introduced into Japan in 1884, acupuncture and other Chinese folk treatments were officially abandoned. But acupuncture did not disappear from the scene, and it is now more popular than ever.

Acupuncture was first introduced to the West in the seventeenth century by Jesuit priests who had been dispatched to Peking. The art/science made practically no headway in the West, however, until French sinologist and diplomat Soulie de Morant published a definitive study on the subject in the 1940s. Western doctors simply could not believe there was anything at all to the practice.

Beginning in the late 1950s, Western interest in acupuncture began to pick up, and it is now an accepted and growing form of medical treatment in most countries around the world.

In Japan, numerous clinics offer acupuncture treatments, and it is the subject of serious research in many medical centers, hospitals, and universities. According to Dr. Yoshio Manaka, a leading authority on acupuncture, the liver, spleen, and gall bladder are especially susceptible to treatment by acupuncture, as are most of the other major organs.

Recommended reading: *The Layman's Guide to Acupuncture*, by Dr. Yoshio Manaka and Dr. Ian A. Urquhart (Weatherhill).

ADAMS, WILLIAM / ANJIN MIURA (Ahn-jeen Mee-uu-rah)   William Adams was the role model for the famous *anjin* (ahn-jeen), or pilot, of Robert Clavell's novel and TV extravaganza, *Shogun* (Show-goon). Born in Gillingham, England, in 1554, Adams was a shipwright, a ship's captain, and the operator of his own trading company. In June 1598, he joined a Netherlands trading fleet of five vessels to search for a new and faster route to the East Indies.

While crossing the Atlantic Ocean, the fleet encountered a great storm. The *De Liefde*, on which Adams served as the pilot major, was the only ship to reach the Pacific and continue the voyage. On April 19, 1600, with most of the crew dead and the survivors near death from starvation, the *De Liefde* drifted into a cove on the coast of Bungo, near Oita, Kyushu, the southernmost of Japan's four major islands. Only 25 of the *De Liefde's* original crew of over 100 were still alive. The ship was towed to the harbor of Funai in Kyushu and was almost immediately thereafter visited by Portuguese Jesuits.

At first, Adams and the surviving crew members were treated kindly by the Japanese authorities. Then the Portuguese, who were in Japan as traders and missionaries, accused Adams and the sailors of being pirates, and they were immediately imprisoned by the local authorities.

Adams, apparently the ranking survivor and spokesman for the crew, and Jan Justen, a Dutch crew member, were escorted to Osaka where they were taken before Ieyasu Tokugawa, then the leading contender for political and military power in Japan. Tokugawa was so impressed with Adams that he ordered the rest of the crew freed and had Adams taken to Edo (Tokyo), his fief headquarters.

Adam's shipmates were allowed to leave Japan, but Tokugawa decided to keep Adams to oversee the construction of oceangoing vessels and to instruct him and his retainers in navigation and other Western sciences. After Tokugawa became *shogun* in 1603, Adams negotiated a trade agreement between the shogunate and the Dutch East India Company.

Tokugawa gave Adams the rank of *samurai* and a fief on Miura Peninsula, near present day Yokosuka, just south of Yokohama. Adams realized the *shogun* had no intention of letting him leave Japan, and, although he had a wife and children in Kent, he adopted the Japanese name Anjin Miura (after the Miura district, where his fief was located), married the daughter of Magome, an official in charge of Tokugawa *Shogun's* horses, and had a son and a daughter.

Adams lived for a while in Ito, where he built the first ships for the *shogun's* fleet; then he established a shipyard at Uraga and moved to Hemi, nearby. In addition to supervising the construction of at least two oceangoing vessels, Adams also gave the *shogun* lessons in gunnery, mathematics, and navigation.

Adams wrote to England, urging the East India Company to set up a trading post in Japan. In 1613, the company sent Richard Cocks and five other merchants to Japan, where they set up a "factory" on Hirado Island off Nagasaki. The post was doomed to failure, however. The English were not able to deal in the popular Chinese silk. The woolen goods they had to offer were not that much in demand. Cocks turned out to be a weak manager, and sailors off the English ships that called at Hirado caused numerous problems.

Adams was given permission to make several voyages on the ships he built—going as far as China and Siam. He was on one of these trips in 1616 when Ieyasu Tokugawa died. Ieyasu's son and successor, Hidetada, was not the man his father had been.

The Jesuits continued to stir up trouble. Hidetada frequently sent for Adams to ask his advice, but there was no friendship between the two. Hidetada eventually restricted the English to trading only through Hirado, hastening the failure of the company.

By this time, the shogunate was convinced that the Portuguese priests were a serious threat to Japan and ordered them banished from the country. The *shogun* allowed the Dutch to maintain one tiny post on a man-made island called Dejima, in Nagasaki harbor.

Anjin Miura died at the age of 66 on May 16, 1620, while on a visit to the British trading company in Hirado, where he was staying with a Japanese friend, Utaemon Kidayaji. As the only foreigner ever to have become a *samurai*—and a close advisor and friend of the founder of the great Tokugawa Shogunate—he had become something of a legend in Japan.

Just before his death, Adams told Richard Cocks, the manager of the trading house they had established at Hirado: "Ever since drifting into this country, I have enjoyed a comfortable life until now, due to the kindness of the Tokugawa *Shogun*. So bury me atop Hemi Hill and face the tomb to the East so that I may face toward Edo and my spirit guard the capital forever."

Later, Adams's ashes were buried on Tsuka Hill, part of the estate given to him by Shogun Ieyasu.

The shogunate continued to curtail the rights of the English trading post after Tokugawa Ieyasu died in 1616, and, in 1623, three years after Adams died, the post was closed down. The East India Company ordered Cocks to return to England and stand trial for mismanaging the affairs of the company, but he died at sea before reaching home.

In 1947, a monument was erected to Adams's memory two kilometers south of Ito Station, at the mouth of the Okawa River. Adjoining the monument is a stone tablet with a poetic epigram written in 1948 by the famous English poet Edmund Blunden, commemorating his visit to the monument.

The memory of the famous foreign *samurai*/pilot is celebrated on the 14th of April each year at Hemi, at the site of the Pilot Mound, which was rediscovered by an Englishman named Walters in 1872. The ceremony is attended by Japanese, Dutch, and English dignitaries. A memorial observance is also held at the Adams Monument in Ito in mid-summer each year. See HISTORY; TOKUGAWA.

ADDRESSES / JUSHO (Juu-show)   The addressing system in Japan is altogether different from the systems used in most other countries. Rather than being related to whatever street or lane the houses or buildings may be on, addresses are determined on an area basis—areas that vary in shape and size.

At first, all of the buildings in any one area had exactly the same address. As the areas became more crowded, houses or buildings were numbered in the order in which they were built. Until the late 1950s and 1960s, there were still many areas that had dozens of homes and buildings with exactly the same address.

An attempt was then made to rationalize the system by giving individual homes and buildings their own private numbers. This helped considerably, but it still causes problems because the numbers of the houses and buildings do not always follow in sequence along a given street or lane.

The problem is further complicated by the fact that most streets and lanes in Japan are not named. It was not until the 1950s that even major thoroughfares were named, although there were a few historical exceptions.

Still today, it is not common to refer to places by whatever street they might be on—again, with the exception of a few main streets in the leading cities and then only as an additional means of locating places.

Japanese addresses are backwards, as far as most Westerners are concerned, but they are understandable from the viewpoint of common sense. Addresses begin with the country; then comes the prefecture and the city, town, or village. If the address is in a city of any size, the next step down is the *ku* (kuu), or "ward" (into which cities are divided). This is followed by a smaller division that often has an area name, like Ginza, Roppongi, or Minami-Aoyama (South Aoyama).

Next comes a still smaller area called *chome* (choe-may), which might be equated with a block—although it may be much larger than a typical block, and it is not likely to be square, since most streets are not parallel or perpendicular to each other. The next division is the *ban* (bahn), or "lot number," and, finally, the *go* (goh), or "building number."

Thus, we have the following typical address (in case of mail from overseas): Japan, Tokyo, Shibuya Ku (Shibuya Ward), Harajuku (area name), 4-chome (the fourth of several *chome*), 3-12 (the twelfth house on the third lot), and the addressee's name.

Out in the countryside, the sequence would be Japan, prefecture, area name and lot or house number, and addressee's name. There are slight variations of these, in various areas, depending on the system of naming areas.

Mail addressed in English, Western style, is, of course, accepted by the Japanese postal system. There is also a growing tendency for people and businesses to put the house and lot number before the area name and *chome*, as a result of Western influence.

ADVERTISING AGENCIES / KOKOKU GAISHA (Koe-koe-kuu guy-shah)   From a dead standstill in 1945, advertising agencies in Japan grew at such a phenomenal rate that by the 1960s they were among the top economic forces in the country. Shortly thereafter, Dentsu (Dane-t'sue), the largest agency in the country, went on to become the largest advertising agency in the world (a ranking it was to hold until the mid-1980s, when the U.S.'s Young & Rubicam took over the first-place spot).

Other leading advertising agencies in Japan include Chuo Senko, Cosmo, Dai-Ichi, Daiko, Grey-Daiko, Hakuhodo, McCann-Erickson-Hakuhodo, and Young & Rubicam.

One of the outstanding features of Japanese advertising is the high quality of their production work. Just as the Japanese are fastidious about product design and appearance, agency people are fanatical about attention to detail.

Despite the many international honors won by Japanese advertising, it has its critics. Norman A. MacMaster, president of J. Walter Thompson Japan Group, says, "Japanese advertising agencies achieved their dominance by buying up huge chunks of television time and selling it off to eager advertisers. They paid very little attention to the contents of the ads they created for clients."

MacMaster adds that, since Japanese advertising agencies "abdicated the creative function," many of them failed to develop their own creative account management departments and a strong awareness of what constitutes good and bad advertising. He says that Japanese ad agencies see themselves as facilitators of advertising rather than as creators of advertising.

Advertising rates for major daily newspapers in Japan tend to startle foreign businesspeople, who are not used to publications with such large circulations. See NEWSPAPERS.

Japanese advertising agencies typically handle competing accounts without apparent friction. They manage this by keeping the accounts in separate, vertically arranged, exclusive divisions.

Advertising agencies are of special importance to foreign companies operating in Japan, since they are called upon to provide much more than just the creating and placing of ads. They act as both advertising and marketing advisors, and often get involved in product development and packaging, as well.

Among Japan's top advertisers are Nissan Motor Company, Kao Soap, Toyota Motor Sales, Lion Dentifrice Co., Toshiba, Matsushita, Daiei (supermarket chain), Shiseido, Hitachi, Honda Motor Co., Mazda, Hayakawa Denki (Sharp), Ajinomoto, and Sony.

Dentsu, Japan's largest advertising agency, is so large and engages in so many aspects and areas of product marketing that it has far more influence than the typical ad agency in other countries.

One of Dentsu's many publications is the English language *Dentsu Japan Marketing/Advertising*, which is published annually. It carries special articles on Japanese management, marketing, communications and on newspapers, magazines, television, radio, and other subjects of interest to foreign people.

The publication is available from Dentsu offices around the world (New York, Los Angeles, Honolulu, Chicago, Washington, D.C., San Francisco, London, Paris, Hong Kong, Taipei, Singapore, Bangkok, Beijing, Shanghai).

AESTHETICS / BIGAKU (Bee-gah-kuu)   In the Western world, the study and apprecation of beauty has traditionally been relegated to a few categories of people, generally professional. As a result, Western definitions and standards of beauty tend to be loose and variable, and there are no commonly known foundations for recognizing and appreciating beauty.

In Japan, some of the primary threads of the cultural fabric are pure aesthetics. By 700 A.D., members of Japan's nobility and priesthood were already making the study and appreciation of beauty a part of their daily lives.

Over the centuries, their cultural descendants created and institutionalized a number of ways to develop aesthetic ability and to exercise it. The epitome of this aesthetic impulse was the tea ceremony, which was practiced by a small minority of the population, but, as time passed, the principles taught by the tea masters became an integral part of the culture and were reflected in all the arts and crafts of the country.

After centuries of exposure to the principles and practices of a refined kind of beauty and elegance, the Japanese developed the ability to recognize and produce this quality almost instinctively.

While considerably weakened by the imperatives of an industrialized society, the aesthetic impulse is still strong in Japan. It is still a primary theme—often the dominant one—in many areas of Japanese life.

Recommended reading: *Japanese Secrets of Graceful Living*, by Boye Lafayette De Mente.

See TEA CEREMONY; IKEBANA; MOONVIEWING.

AGRICULTURE / NOGYO (No-g'yoe)   Japan was almost totally an agricultural society until the controlled advent of industrialization in the 1860s, '70s, and '80s.

Today less than one percent of the total population engages in farming as the primary activity, and less than three percent of the gross domestic product is made up of agricultural goods.

Japan is self-sufficient in the production of rice, still the staple of the Japanese diet, and raises large quantities of vegetables and fruits. But over 90 percent of its wheat and soybean needs are imported. To be more specific, some 99 percent of Japan's bread wheat is imported, as is 87 percent of its cheese, 76 percent of its shrimp, 72 percent of its sugar, and 66 percent of its seaweed.

Land reforms enacted in 1945 (after World War II) were a boon to Japanese farmers, most of whom had previously been tenant farmers. By the mid-1960s, the living standard of Japan's farmers had made them the envy of less affluent nations in Asia and the rest of the world.

Recognizing the importance of the agricultural sector, the Japanese government provides its farming population with generous protection against price fluctuations and international competition.

In the early 1980s, the government announced a three-point growth program designed to improve the efficiency of its farming industry and keep it competitive with agriculture in other advanced nations. This program is based on improving marketing procedures, continuing technical innovation, and improving the industry's competitive position internationally.

Farm land accounts for a little less than 14 percent of Japan's total land area, and it is shrinking as urbanization and industrialization grow.

Approximately 55 percent of the cultivated land is devoted to rice growing. Orchards take·up about 23 percent; meadows and pastures, about 11 percent. Rice, livestock products, and vegetables are the main agricultural products, but, overall, Japan is only about 49 percent self-sufficient in its food needs.

There are approximately 378,000 farms and a farm population of 1.7 million in Japan, and the average land holding is 1.2 hectares, or 2.8 acres. As a result of this small size and low labor productivity, only 32 percent of Japan's farming families derive all their livelihood from farming. In the majority of farm families, one or more of the members work part-time or full-time in some other industry.

The productivity of Japan's farm lands is very high, however, and, as mechanization increases, labor productivity is also rising.

AIKIDO (Aye-kee-doe)   One of the leading members of Japan's famous Minamoto family, Yoshimitsu, who lived from 1045 to 1127, is credited with founding the first school of *aiki jujutsu,* as *aikido* was then known. The secrets of the art were handed down within the Minamoto family for several generations. Then it was taken over by the Takeda family of Kai Province and eventually became the exclusive skill of the branch of the Takeda family that lived in the Aizu district.

Morihei Ueshiba (1883–1970) learned the art from Sokaku Takeda, the seventh generation of the Aizu Takedas, and developed it into the form of *aikido* that is practiced today.

Aikido was originally practiced only for learning form, and it was a martial art designed to be used without a weapon. Kenji Tomiki, a disciple of Ueshiba, developed it into the free-style method that resulted in its being reorganized as a sport.

The aim of *aikido* is to allow the practitioner to throw an opponent or disable him by attacking a weak point or applying a pain hold to pin him down. The practice of sports *aikido* develops both mental and physical control, along with physical health, since it helps keep the muscles and joints flexible.

Recommended reading: *Aikido and the Dynamic Sphere*, by Adele Westbrook and Oscar Ratti (Tuttle); *Dynamic Karate*, by Gozo Shioda, translated by Geoffrey Hamilton (Kodansha International).

AINU (Aye-nuu)   When the ancestors of the present-day Japanese first began pushing into central and northern Honshu from the south, they encountered a race of people already inhabiting the region, as well as the island of Hokkaido. These original inhabitants of Japan were a Caucasian race, larger than the Japanese in stature and with imposing features, who called themselves Ainu.

The Ainu were light skinned and had large, light brown to golden eyes. The men were exceptionally hairy and had thick black beards. Despite their formidable appearance, the Ainu were gentle in nature. The women, who were often exceptionally beautiful, customarily wore decorative tattoos around their mouths and on their hands.

As the Japanese population grew and more pressure was brought against the Ainu, skirmishes became common, and the Ainu were gradually pushed farther and farther northward. As the Japanese expanded and increased their control of the northern regions of Honshu, rebellions among the Ainu became frequent.

On a number of occasions during the first centuries A.D., the emperor appointed a *Sei-i-tai-Shogun*, or Barbarian Subduing Generalissimo, to carry out military campaigns against the Ainu.

The Ainu were primarily hunters and fishermen. The bear was one of the chief religious totems of the Ainu, and a number of their ceremonies and festivals centered on bears. Striped owls were revered as their guardian god.

By the Middle Ages, there were only a few pockets of Ainu left on the island of Honshu. They had been driven to Hokkaido or assimilated into the main Japanese population. One of the last major campaigns against the Ainu was in 1457, when an Ainu chief named Koshamain rebelled against the local Japanese overlord.

From this period on, the Ainu were prominent only on the northernmost island of Hokkaido—and both they and the island were called Ezo (Eh-zoe).

By 1900, there were only about 40,000 pure Ainu left in Hokkaido. Their numbers have continued to decrease, and there are now only about 25,000 throughout the island in some 100 villages. Most of these villages are in the Abashiri, Hidaka, Iburi, Kushiro, and Tokachi districts of Hokkaido.

Some 14,000 of the racially pure Ainu are represented by the Hokkaido Utari Association, which is seeking to protect the human rights, culture, and traditional livelihood of the Ainu. Over the years, the Ainu have lost nearly all of their land and now own title to only 1,500 hectares.

In 1984, the Hokkaido Prefectural Office and the Utari Association estimated there were over 200,000 Ainu who have been racially and socially assimilated into the general population of Japan.

The life-styles of most of the Ainu have been Japanized, except for those in a few villages, such as Shiraoi and Chikabumi, where the old ways are still followed—in part as commercial tourist ventures, much like the Polynesian Village of Hawaii.

Biratori Village, southeast of Tomakomai, in the valley of the Saru River, is one of the oldest and largest Ainu communities in Hokkaido. The Ainu of this village have retained most of their traditional culture. The racial mingling of the Japanese and Ainu is particularly noticeable in many towns and villages of the Tohoku district in northeastern Honshu. The mixtures are conspicuous because of their decidedly Caucasian appearance and especially because of their eyes, which are often exceptionlly large and luminous.

When Tohoku women who are part Ainu inherit the "Ainu eyes," they are often extraordinarily beautiful and entrancing. A number of them became popular movie stars and models in the 1950s and '60s.

Besides visiting one or more of the Ainu villages, it is worthwhile to see the Ainu Memorial Hall in Chikabumi, northeast of Sapporo. Various articles relating to the daily lives of the early Ainu are on display in the hall, and ceremonial dances are performed there on a scheduled basis. Several Ainu houses are on display in Arashima park, a few minutes west of Chikabumi Station.

The Ainu traditionally believed in a life after death. In earlier years, when a married woman died, her house and all of its contents were burned in the belief that she would need them in the other world. Now a small replica of the house is burned in a symbolic gesture.

In November 1983, after a break of 75 years, the Ainu reinaugurated an annual three-day festival in honor of the owl god.

AIRLINES / KOKUGAISHA (Koe-kuu-gie-shah)   Japan has several airlines, including Japan Air Lines, All Nippon Airways, Japan Asia Airways (the latter a subsidiary of Japan Air Lines), Toda Domestic Airlines, Southwest Air Lines (which services the Okinawa islands), and Nihon Kinkyori Airways.

Japan Air Lines (JAL), the country's flagship line, was founded in 1953 and inaugurated its first international service in 1954, between Tokyo and San Francisco.

JAL now provides service to over 30 countries and some 50 major cities around the world, and it is one of the top four airlines in the world.

All Nippon Airways (ANA) originally provided domestic service to cities throughout Japan, while Japan Asia Airways provided service to Taiwan. In 1985, new laws were passed making it possible for ANA and other domestic airlines to operate international services. See JAPAN AIR LINES and ALL NIPPON AIRWAYS.

The largest general aviation airport in the country is the Yao Airport, located eight nautical miles southeast of Osaka. It handles some 80,000 flights a year, making it the fifth or sixth busiest airport in the country.

There are some two dozen Japanese-language trade publications on the airline industry in Japan, and seven in English. These latter include the *JPE Aviation Report*, the *Japan Air Transport Handbook*, *Japan Aviation Directory*, and *Travel Journal International*.

Nearly 40 foreign airlines serve Japan, and an additional 30 countries (from Afghanistan to Zaire) have requested air treaties with Japan. See AIRPORTS.

AIR MILES   In its position off the northeastern coast of the Asian continent, Japan is distant from most of the capitals of the world. The following air miles from Tokyo to other capitals around the world reveal just how distant. From Tokyo to Seoul, 869 miles; to Hong Kong, 1,933; to Manila, 1,916; to Peking, 2,092; to Bangkok, 3,121; to Singapore, 3,448.

To Anchorage, 3,527; to Moscow, 4,986; to London, 8,041; to Paris, 8,280; to Hamburg, 7,967; to Sidney, 4,934; to Vancouver, 4,788; to San

Francisco, 5,247; to Los Angeles, 5,616; to Honolulu, 3,870; and to New York, 7,037.

AIRPORTS / HIKOJO (He-koe-joe)   All of Japan's larger cities have airports, and those serving the largest regional cities have international service. The three main international airports are Tokyo International Airport in Narita, some 70 kilometers northeast of Tokyo on Chiba Peninsula, Nagoya International Airport, and the huge 24-hours-a-day Osaka International Airport, located on a man-made island in Osaka Bay.

Haneda Airport in Tokyo was the country's primary international gateway until the opening of Narita. At this writing, the only international flights in and out of Haneda are those by China Airlines of Taiwan—a political gesture toward The People's Republic of China.

AJINOMOTO (Ah-jee-no-moe-toe)   A powdered seasoning made of monosodium glutamate, *ajinomoto* has long been popular in Japan for its food-enhancing qualities. It is now known and used around the world. Monosodium glutamate was originally extracted from seaweed but is now processed from sugar cane molasses.

AKASAKA (Ah-kah-sah-kah)   Part of the northwestern portion of Minato Ward in Tokyo, Akasaka is noted for its concentration of cabarets, nightclubs, bars, restaurants, geisha district, hotels, and shops.

Among the major hotels in Akasaka and the immediate vicinity are the New Otani, Akasaka Tokyu, the original Hilton (now the Capital Tokyu), the luxurious Okura, and the gorgeous Akasaka Prince.

Japan's government center is on a low rise overlooking Akasaka from the north, and the American Embassy adjoins it on the southeast. Akasaka Mitsuke (Akasaka Intersection) is one of the major subway terminals in the city.

AKASAKA DETACHED PALACE / GEIHINKAN (Gay-e-heen-khan) This is the magnificient structure near Yotsuya Station in Tokyo, within sight of the New Otani Hotel, that so impresses visitors to Japan. Completed in 1909 as the residence of the Crown Prince, the Palace was patterned after eighteenth-century French architectural styles and was later used as an Imperial chamber and for other purposes.

Granite and marble imported from France, Italy, Greece, and Norway were used in the construction of the palace, and oil paintings by European, as well as Japanese, masters were used to decorate its walls.

Many of its great rooms are famous for their gorgeous decorations, including ceiling motifs said to have been inspired by a *noh* play.

The palace is now Japan's official State Guest House.

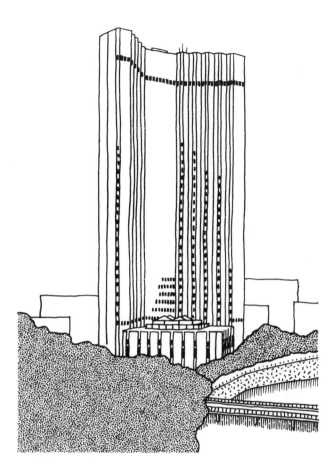

AKASAKA PRINCE HOTEL (Ah-kah-sah-kah)   Opened in 1983, the Akasaka Prince Hotel in Tokyo is one of the most spectacular high rise buildings in Japan. Designed by Kenzo Tange, the country's most famous architect, the snow-white, 40-story tower is set on a 45-degree angle from the center axis of the core of the building, so each room has a two-sided corner view of the city.

In explaining the unusual architecture of the building and vast expanses of white marble in the lobby, Tange said the design was a break from the past, intended to express twenty-first-century concepts.

Situated on a hill adjoining Japan's government center and the famous Akasaka entertainment district, the Akasaka Prince Hotel is built on the garden grounds of a former Daimyo princely estate, in what is often referred to as the "Akasaka Hotel Village," because of the number of major hotels in the immediate vicinity.

Like all of Japan's great hotels, the Akasaka Prince has numerous restaurants (12), including American, Chinese, and several Japanese; and 32 banquet rooms, including a huge Grand Ballroom, with mirrored walls, that occupies the entire second floor and will seat 1,000 dinner party guests or accommodate 2,500 cocktail reception guests.

The Akasaka Prince has both a restaurant and a cocktail lounge on the top floor of the tower, providing patrons with a magnificent view of the city below. On clear days, the splendid pinnacle of Mt. Fuji, nearly 100 miles to the southwest, is also visible.

In addition to its Western rooms and suites, the Akasaka Prince has 23 traditionally styled Japanese suites, complete with hot baths. Besides the regular facilities, the hotel also has a number of meeting rooms and lounges for businesspeople, including an Executive Service Lounge—with secretaries, telephones, typewriters, a telex, and a business reference library—on the third floor.

The Akasaka Prince is especially popular with visitors because it is within walking distance of the historically famous entertainment-restaurant-shopping area of Akasaka. It is just a two-minute walk from the Akasaka Subway Station, where the Ginza and Marunouchi Lines interconnect; two minutes from the Nagatacho Subway Station on the Yurakucho Line; and only five minutes from the Kojimachi Subway Station, also on the Yurakucho Line.

Other Prince hotels in Tokyo are the venerable Tokyo Prince in Shiba Park, next to the Tokyo Tower; the beautiful Takanawa Prince and adjoining New Takanawa Prince, also on the grounds of a former princely estate, near Shinagawa Station; and the Roppongi Prince, in the internationally famous Roppongi entertainment-restaurant district, only a short distance from Akasaka.

See ARCHITECTURE.

ALCOHOLIC BEVERAGES / NOMI MONO (No-me moe-no)   On a national average, the Japanese are not big drinkers compared to the French, West Germans, Italians, Australians, Canadians, British, and Russians (in that order). With the French at the top, consuming an average of well over 15 liters of pure alcohol a year, the Japanese average is a little over five liters.

This is certainly contrary to the popular conception, because there are so many drinking establishments in Japan (over 225,000, plus thousands of other places where drinks are served), and most of them are jammed with drinkers most evenings. The reason for the disparity is that most alcoholic drinks in Japan are consumed by men between the ages of 22 and 52, and primarily by those in white-collar jobs.

The most popular alcoholic drink in Japan is beer, followed by *sake*, whiskey and brandy, *shochu* (a much stronger version of *sake*, originally favored by laborers but now an upscale drink), wine, *mirin* (a sweet *sake*), and liqueurs.

Japanese-made beer is popular in many places around the world for its mellow and refreshing taste. The top brands are Kirin (Kee-reen), Asahi

(Ah-sah-he), and Sapporo (Sop-poe-roe). Japan is also famous for its Scotch whiskey.

ALIEN REGISTRATION / GAIJIN TOROKU (Guy-jeen Toe-roe-kuu) All foreigners intending to stay in Japan for more than 90 days must register with the local ward or district office where they live (even if they are on a tourist visa and staying in a hotel). Upon registration, they receive a *Gaijin Toroku Shomeisho* (show-may-e-show), or Alien Registration Certificate, a small identification booklet, which must be carried at all times.

ALL NIPPON AIRWAYS (Neep-pone)   Founded in 1952 as the Japan Helicopter & Aeroplane Transport Company, All Nippon Airways (ANA) changed its name in 1957 and in 1958 merged with Kyokuto Airlines. Other mergers followed in the 1960s, and, by the 1980s, ANA was Japan's biggest airline in terms of fleet size and passengers carried—and the seventh largest airline in the world.

ANA presently operates over 70 routes throughout Japan, with around 500 daily flights. The airline has several wholly owned and partly owned subsidiary and affiliated companies, including a trading company, a restaurant chain, and a tour wholesaler. New laws passed in 1985 made it possible for ANA to inaugurate international service, and it is expected to become one of the world's major international carriers.

ANA also joined with Nippon Yusen Kaisha, the huge shipping company, in 1985, to establish Nippon Cargo Airlines (NCA), which competes internationally with the world's largest cargo carriers.

ALLOWANCES (EMPLOYMENT) / TEATE (Tay-ah-tay)   Japanese companies generally pay their employees allowances of one kind or another, in addition to their regular base wages. These allowances cover such expenses as housing, child care, trips, transportation, weddings, and funerals. They also compensate for dangerous work.

The most important of these allowances is usually the housing allowance, which is not taxable. Larger Japanese companies also often provide housing for their executives and dormitories for their single factory workers. They also sometimes guarantee low-cost loans for the construction of housing.

Allowances, like bonuses, are an important part of the overall income of Japanese employees, and they are a significant factor in the cost of labor in Japan.

AMERICAN / ALLIED OCCUPATION OF JAPAN   World War II ended with the surrender of Japan to the Allied forces on August 15, 1945. Four days later, on August 19, a Japanese surrender mission went to Manila to receive instructions from General Douglas MacArthur, who was to be the Supreme Allied Commander in the Military Occupation of Japan.

Between August 25 and 27, American planes made reconnaissance flights over the country to make sure all planes had been disarmed and grounded (one group had taken off following the surrender announcement, and it was the 23rd before they were talked into surrendering).

The first contingent of American forces arrived by air at Atsugi Airbase, southwest of Yokohama, on August 28, with General MacArthur, unarmed and without a tie, leading the way. The whole group drove to Yokohama. And thus began a seven-year military occupation that was to be one of the most extraordinary experiments and experiences in history.

The Occupation of Japan was officially an Allied affair, but for all practical purposes it was American. All Occupation forces were under the command of General MacArthur, who, with his aides, was to be the primary architect and enforcer of Occupation policies.

Japan officially surrendered to the Allied powers on September 2, 1945. The signing of the surrender documents took place aboard the battleship *USS Missouri* in Tokyo Bay.

The first American troops did not arrive in Tokyo until September 8th.

In the meantime, the decision had been made to retain Japan's Emperor Hirohito as the symbolic head of the nation and to govern the country through its elected and appointed officials.

Over the next several months, Japan's social and political structures were reorganized according to democratic principles, setting the stage for the dramatic recovery Japan was to make in the next decade. The Allied Military Occupation of Japan ended in May 1952.

The story of the American Occupation of Japan, to my knowledge at least, has never been fully told. It was a drama of such scope and depth that it virtually defies telling in more than a cursory manner.

It was made up of the interaction of literally millions of Japanese with hundreds of thousands of Americans, on every level of human activity. That it was almost totally a peaceful experience, following a protracted war of extraordinary intensity and violence, serves as a monument to both the Americans and Japanese who survived the fighting and went on to work together for peace and a new order of things that would remake Japan.

The Occupation certainly ended the old belief that East and West could never meet on common ground—at least in a romantic sense. Much of the real story, in fact, is the story of hundreds of thousands of romantic liaisons between American men and Japanese women—a phenomenon that played a fundamental role in both the character and quality of the Occupation's success in eliminating feudalism from Japanese society and introducing Western social concepts.

In 1952, the year the Occupation ended, the Ministry of Health and Welfare (MHW) estimated that there were some 70,000 prostitutes, popularly called "pan-pan," keeping the occupying forces busy. The true number was probably well over that estimate. The MHW also estimated that the pan-pan earned around $200 million a year in hard cash—which is also probably a very low estimate, because a great deal of the money that exchanged hands would have been impossible to trace.

One American writer who succeeded in giving a glimpse of what life was like for many people in Occupied Japan is Donald Richie. His book *This Scorching Earth* (Tuttle) is recommended.

AMERICAN CHAMBER OF COMMERCE IN JAPAN   Established in Tokyo in the early 1950s, immediately following the end of the military Occupation of Japan by the Allied powers, the American Chamber of Commerce in Japan (ACCJ) was little more than a social club during the first several years of its existence.

It was not until the early 1960s—by which time Japan was well on its way to becoming a world economic power and much of the Occupation mentality had dissipated—that new directors and new members of the Chamber began to see it as something other than a club.

Another decade was to pass, however, before the combination of Japan's growing economic strength and a new generation of American business-people in Tokyo were to develop the Chamber into a useful and influential organization.

Today the ACCJ plays a vital role in the conduct of business in Japan by American companies and in ongoing economic and political relations between Japan and the U.S.

The specific role of the ACCJ is to promote measures calculated to benefit and protect the interests in Japan of companies and citizens of the U.S.; to represent, express, and give effect to the opinions of the business community regarding trade, investment, commerce, finance, industry, and related questions; and to collect, evaluate, and disseminate among its members statistical and other information concerning commerce or other undertakings of interest to the members.

The ACCJ sponsors briefing breakfasts for newcomers and visitors; has an active speakers program that brings in leading American and Japanese business, government, and academic leaders; holds regular seminars on a wide variety of trade topics; and publishes a monthly journal, a newsletter, position papers, and a number of books of special interest to its members and the foreign business community in Japan.

All Americans interested in doing business in Japan are strongly urged to contact the ACCJ and to become members. It is one of the best investments any company could possibly make to help ensure its success in the highly competitive Japanese market.

The ACCJ has two offices in Japan—one in Tokyo and one in Osaka. The Tokyo office, very near the American Embassy, is in the Fukide Building No. 2 (7th Floor), at 1-21, 4-chome, Minato-Ku, Tokyo 105 Japan. The Kansai (Osaka) office is in the Nihon Seimei Imabashi Bldg., 4th Floor, 3-12-1 Imabashi, Higashi-ku, Osaka 541 Japan.

AMERICAN CONTACT   The first American of record to have contact with Japan was a Captain John Kendrick, whose ship, the *Lady Washington*, took shelter in the Kii Channel of Japan's Inland Sea in 1817. Five years before this, however, another American ship captain, David Porter, wrote a letter to President Madison urging him to begin trade and diplomatic negotiations with Japan.

In his letter, Porter said, "The time may be favorable and it would be a glory beyond that accomplished by any other nation, for us, a nation of only forty years standing, to beat down their rooted prejudices, secure to ourselves a valuable trade, and make that people known to the world."

President Andrew Jackson in 1835 tried to send a letter to the Emperor of Japan (in which he said the U.S. was probably the only nation that could bring about the opening of all of Japan's ports to foreign trade), but the envoy carrying the letter, Edmund Roberts, died suddenly in Macau before he could make arrangements for the message to be delivered.

In 1837, W. C. King, an American businessman with a company in Canton, tried to return seven shipwrecked Japanese fishermen who had been picked up by American vessels. His ship, the *Morrison*, was fired on by shore batteries when he anchored off of Uraga, a port near the tip of Miura Peninsula, which was the official inspection station for barges entering Tokyo Bay. King then sailed to Kagoshima, where an official came aboard, provided him with a pilot, and told him a senior government official would arrive to discuss the matter with him the following day.

Warned by a friendly Japanese boatman that all the men aboard the vessel were to be arrested, King began making preparations to sail out of the harbor. The ship immediately came under cannon fire from the shore, but was able to escape unharmed and return to China with the Japanese fishermen still aboard.

When the news of this incident reached the U.S., there was a great deal of indignation, but the situation in Japan was even worse. A number of Japanese who criticized the actions of the government were imprisoned, forced to commit suicide, or ostracized.

In 1845, another American vessel, the *Manhattan*, under the command of Captain Mercator Cooper, arrived at Uraga with some Japanese fishermen who had been picked up adrift in the Pacific. This time, the Japanese were allowed to disembark because they had not been aboard the ship when it left port. Cooper sailed away without incident.

The following year, U.S. President James K. Polk, acting in accordance with a resolution passed by Congress, sent Commodore James Biddle and two ships to Japan with a letter addressed to the emperor, requesting that diplomatic and trade relations be established. Biddle's ships arrived at Uraga, the entrance to Tokyo Bay, in the summer of 1846.

His ships were immediately boarded by *samurai*, who treated him and his men with arrogance and finally demanded that he leave his vessel and wait on a Japanese ship for an answer to his letter. Mistaking the ship he was to board, Biddle was struck by a *samurai* and knocked backward into his own boat.

The Japanese authorities apologized to Biddle and offered to punish the *samurai*, but Biddle declined. Shortly thereafter, he received an unofficial message saying that his request had been denied and that he and his ships were to leave Japan immediately and not return.

News of this incident aroused some anger in the U.S., and in 1849, when Commander Glynn of the *USS Preble* sailed into Nagasaki to demand the release of American castaways being held by the Japanese, he went prepared to fight. After making his initial demand, he waited for three days, and then delivered what amounted to an ultimatum if the men were not released within the following three days.

Before the deadline expired, the Japanese delivered 13 American castaways to the *Preble*, and Glynn sailed away. In 1851, Glynn met President Millard Fillmore as the representative of several groups interested in opening Japan to foreign trade, and warned him that, if the U.S. did not act soon, Russia, England, or some other nation might be the first to establish relations with Japan. The American consul in Singapore had already suggested that the U.S., Great Britain, and France send a joint expedition to Japan to force its doors open.

In the meantime, the ferment within Japan was increasing, as those who opposed the shogunate and favored the opening of Japan became more active and gained support. A few Japanese were already studying English (some of them taught by a man named MacDonald, who had been turned over to Commander Glynn in 1849), and the Japanese were feverishly trying to learn as much as they could about the U.S.

Besides the Dutch traders in Nagasaki (see HISTORY; DEJIMA; TOKUGAWA; PORTUGUESE; ADAMS), Japan's primary source of information about the United States was a man named Manjiro Nakahama, whose fishing boat had gone down in the Pacific when he was a boy and who had been rescued by an American whaling ship, which took him to Fairhaven, Massachusetts. There he learned English, was converted to

Christianity, and returned to Japan nine years later aboard the whaler *Sarah Boyd*. See NAKAHAMA, MANJIRO.

In June 1851, an expedition under the command of Commodore Aulick set sail for Japan, intending to stop over in Hong Kong to pick up 17 Japanese castaways and return them to their homeland. But Aulick was recalled to Washington from China because of some other matters, and Commodore Matthew C. Perry was picked to replace him.

Perry left Norfolk, Virginia, in November 1852, sailed to Shanghai on the frigate *Mississippi*, and took command of the squadron Commodore Aulick had left there. Leaving Shanghai, he first went to the Ryukyu Islands, south of Kyushu, Japan's southernmost main island, and arrived in Tokyo Bay on July 8, 1853.

The Japanese had been warned of Perry's expedition, as well as the preparations being made by other nations to force Japan to open its doors to the outside world. Still, the shogunate was not prepared to take this bold step. After some very stiff formalities, the Japanese agreed to talk to Perry at Kurihama, south of Edo (Tokyo).

After delivering his letters to the representatives of the shogunate (the Americans still did not know that the *shogun* was not the emperor), Perry sailed back to China, telling the *bakufu* (bah-kuu-fuu), or shogunate government, officials he would return the following July for their answer.

Thus it was in July 1854 that the stage was set for the beginning of diplomatic and trade relations between Japan and the United States and for the United States to play the leading role in bringing Japan into the community of nations. See HISTORY; PERRY; HARRIS; ADAMS.

ANIMALS (WILD)/YASEI NO DOBUTSU (Yah-say-e no doe-boot-sue) Because most of Japan is mountainous, covered with forests, and basically uninhabited, there are still many animals in the wild, despite the dense population.

There are three distinct types of wild animals in Japan, depending on the region. Hokkaido, at the northern end of the island chain, is known for its brown bears, sables, and northern foxes.

The other three major islands of Honshu, Kyushu, and Shikoku are home to wild boars, deer, raccoon dogs, monkeys, bears, weasels, mandarin ducks, and pheasants.

The southern islands of Okinawa and Amami have fauna similar to that found in Taiwan and India, along with an indigenous snake (*habu*), and the Amami hare.

ANTIMONOPOLY LAW / DOKUSEN KINSHI HO (Doe-kuu-sin keen-she hoe) Following the end of the Pacific War in 1945, the American forces occupying Japan fostered the passage of laws prohibiting private monopolies, to prevent the concentration of excessive economic power, such as had been wielded by the notorious *zaibatsu* combines (see ZAIBATSU).

With the growing Cold War with the Communists, the American attitude toward Japan changed rather rapidly, however, and in 1949 the anti-monopoly laws were altered to permit intercorporate stockholding and interlocking multiple directorates.

When the Occupation of Japan ended in 1952, the Japanese government further changed the law, to permit the formation of depression and rationalization cartels and to relax even more the controls on stock ownership, multiple directorates, and mergers.

The revision of these laws made it possible for the reappearance of huge industrial combines reminiscent of the prewar *zaibatsu*, but primarily owned by stockholders, instead of a few privileged families.

Among the mergers that took place as a result of these new laws was the one that combined the Yawata and Fuji steel companies into Nippon Steel Corporation, which became the world's largest producer of steel.

In the mid-1980s, the Japanese government tried to strengthen the anti-monopoly laws somewhat in an effort to protect weaker companies from takeover bids and to guarantee the interests of the public. See MITSUI; MITSUBISHI; ZAIBATSU.

AOYAMA PALACE (Ah-oh-yah-mah)   In the northern section of Tokyo's huge Minato Ward, the Aoyama Palace, which adjoins the Akasaka Detached Palace, is where the late Empress Dowager Teimei lived, as did the late Prince Chichibu. Before the fall of the Tokugawa Shogunate in 1868, the grounds were part of the mansion estate of the Kii branch of the Tokugawa family.

ARCHERY / KYUDO (Que-doe)   It is not known if archery developed on its own in Japan or if it was introduced from the Asian mainland. It was already in wide use for hunting and fighting by the early centuries and was promoted as a martial art as early as the eighth century A.D.

Over the generations, the Japanese developed a bow that was much longer and much more powerful than those generally seen in Asia and Europe. It is recorded that a warrior who happened to catch the enemy in ranks was able to kill three of them with the same arrow, so great was its penetrating power.

In the Middle Ages, Japanese pirates foraging along the coasts and islands of Southeast Asia were especially feared because of their extraordinary prowess with swords and bows.

As with other martial arts, *kyudo*, or "the way of the bow," became imbued with Zen Buddhist and Confucian principles, and Zen concepts were used in its practice. Japanese history is replete with the exploits of archers who achieved incredible skill as a result of strict Zen discipline.

With the advent of prolonged peace in 1603, archery became more of a mental and spiritual exercise, but it was kept alive by the *samurai* emphasis on such training and by annual contests held in many places around the country.

Kyudo contests, still popular in Japan, are generally sponsored by a particular temple and staged during festivals. The most popular of these contests are those that take place from horseback and are known as *yabusame* (yah-buu-sah-may).

Originally a Shinto rite that began in the sixth century to ensure good harvests, and later a ceremony performed by courtiers at the Butokuden Palace in Kyoto, *yabusame* is now performed as part of Culture Day (Bunka-no Hi) at Meiji Shrine in Tokyo and at several other shrines around the country in the fall. During the early centuries, an archer who missed the target was obliged to commit suicide. To help prevent the loss of otherwise skilled warriors, Minamoto-no Yoritomo (1147–1199) enlarged the targets and ringed them with a garland of flowers, which, if touched, counted as a hit.

From the beginning of *yabusame*, only three families—Miura, Ogasawara, and Takeda—were authorized to teach it. The Ogasawara family dropped out in 1882. The *yabusame* demonstration at the Meiji Shrine grounds in Tokyo in 1984 was led by Ietaka Takeda, the thirty-sixth direct lineal descendant of the founding family.

Basically, *yabusame* consists of archers on horseback racing at full gallop down a prescribed path and firing their arrows at special targets. It was originally a form of divination, in which horses' hoofprints and the position of arrows on the target had different meanings.

Today the ceremony in Tokyo is presided over by the Great Japan Traditional Horsemanship and Great Japan Archery and Horsemanship associations. A dozen or more horsemen, dressed in colorful period costumes, race down a 217-meter-long track, shooting at targets erected on both sides.

ARCHITECTURE / KENCHIKU (Kane-chee-kuu)   Traditional Japanese architecture is distinctive in that the only building material used was wood, regardless of the purpose, size, or ornateness of the structure. As a result, most buildings are simple in design, but they often reveal a subtlety that makes them the epitome of refinement and elegance.

The best examples of pure Japanese architecture can be seen in Shinto shrines, the form of which dates back to the dawn of Japan's history. These buildings have crossed rafters at the end to hold the ridgepoles, crosspieces to hold the roof-thatch in place, and gabled ends.

Temples that were built after the introduction of Buddhism into Japan in the sixth and seventh centuries incorporated many Chinese concepts, including the use of huge pillars placed on granite foundation stones, tile roofs, hipped roofs, projecting eaves, and red paint on the exteriors. The pagoda-style building was another import from China.

As the decades passed, more and more mansions and palaces were built —the mansions following the form and pattern established by Shinto shrines, and the palaces patterned after splendid buildings popular in China at that time.

One of the temples built in Nara in the seventh century, the Horyu, still stands and is regarded as the oldest wooden building in the world. The Todai Temple in Nara, built in the eighth century, is the world's largest wooden building.

Most ordinary buildings in Japan that came after the Nara Period were refined combinations of shrine and temple architecture.

Japan's golden age of castle building occurred in the fifteenth and sixteenth centuries. Before 1576, the castles in Japan, built in mountainous areas that were difficult to approach and easier to defend, were little more than forts. In this year, Nobunaga Oda built a castle out in the open at Azuchi, adjoining Lake Biwa. With a central tower seven stories high, a soaring copper-rust roof, and white walls, it was designed and furnished to be both a castle and a villa.

Hideyoshi Toyotomi, who followed Oda as the most powerful military leader in Japan, also followed his example and built similar castles at Fushimi and Osaka. Thereafter, it became customary for the *daimyo* (dime-yoe), or "provincial lords," to build their castles on the plains and to emphasize architectural beauty, as well as luxurious interior decorations.

The best existing example of these great castles is the one at Himeji, on the Inland Sea, southwest of Kyoto and Osaka.

Up to this time, the mansions of the nobles of Japan were based on Zen Buddhist temple architecture, but when the feudal lords began building luxurious residential castles that in effect were palaces, the nobles also began to build splendid palaces for themselves.

These great mansions had dozens of rooms separated by sliding screen doors. The walls and ceilings were profusely decorated with rich paintings in white and black on gold backgrounds. The transoms were embellished with ornate carvings, and metal fittings were everywhere.

The greatest sobering force during these exciting decades was Zen Buddhism. It maintained a strict simplicity, which is epitomized in the structures built, especially for the tea ceremony.

The practice of building elaborate mansions continued in the Edo Period (1603–1868), when the Tokugawa *Shogun* made it mandatory that all the feudal lords in the country build mansions in Edo (Tokyo) and leave their families there. There was a strong competitive element among the lordly *daimyo*, and those who could afford the expense outdid themselves in building palatial mansions in the environs of Edo Castle.

Much of the architecture of early Japan still exists in hundreds of temples and shrines around the country, as well as in private residences, palaces, and castles. Kyoto, the Imperial capital of Japan from 784 to 1868, is a treasure trove of outstanding architectural examples and a must on the itinerary of most visitors to Japan.

Following the opening of Japan to the West in the 1850s and '60s, the government commissioned foreign architects to design and build government and public offices. Among the first of these buildings were the Osaka Mint in 1871, Shimbashi Station in 1872, and Yokohama Station, also in 1872.

The British architect J. Condor was engaged to teach architecture at the Tokyo Imperial University, which graduated its first four Western-trained Japanese architects in 1879. The first steel-frame building was erected in Tokyo in 1909 by Toshitaka Sano, for the Maruzen Co. Ltd.

From 1914 on, the construction of ferro-concrete buildings became common—although their height was limited to eight stories because of the danger from earthquakes.

The famous American architect Frank Lloyd Wright was commissioned in 1916 to design and build a new Imperial Hotel, construction of which was completed in 1923. When the Great Kanto Earthquake struck in 1923, leveling much of Tokyo and Yokohama, the Imperial Hotel was one of the few buildings to survive virtually undamaged—not only proving the durability of Western-style architecture, but also making both Wright and the Imperial Hotel world famous.

Contemporary Japanese architecture, a blend of Western and traditional concepts, came of age in the 1960s, when rapid economic development resulted in a building boom that was to continue for decades. The appearance of earthquake-resistant building techniques in the 1960s resulted in the abolition of the 31-meter-height limitation, and the construction of Japan's first super high rise in 1968—the 36-story Kasumigaseki Building, near the government center in Tokyo.

Japan now has almost as many high rise buildings as it does towering volcano mountains, with some of the largest and most spectacular in the Shinjuku section of Tokyo.

Probably the best known of Japan's architects during the immediate postwar decades was Kenzo Tange, whose buildings include the National Indoor Athletic Hall and the adjoining gymnasium built for the 1964 Tokyo Olympics, as well as the spectacular Akasaka Prince Hotel.

Born in 1913 in Imabari, Shikoku, Tange attended Tokyo University, worked for a few years, and then returned to the university for graduate study and the academic life of a professor of architecture.

His design of the Hiroshima Peace Center in 1949 brought him international attention, and during the next decade he became recognized as one of the world's leading architects.

Recommended reading: *The Classic Tradition in Japanese Architecture— Modern Versions of the Sukiya Style*, by Teiji Ito (Weatherhill); *Early Buddhist Architecture in Japan*, by Kokichi Suzuki (Kodansha Int'l).

AREA CODES   Japan has nine telephone area codes:
01 (Hokkaido, Aomori, Iwate, and Akita prefectures)
02 (Miyagi, Yamagata, Fukushima, Niigata, Nagano, Ibaragi, Tochigi, and Gunma prefectures)
03 (the 23 wards of metropolitan Tokyo)
04 (the Tokyo suburbs, Saitama, Chiba, and Kanagawa prefectures)
05 (Yamanashi, Gifu, Shizuoka, Aichi, and Mie prefectures)
06 (metropolitan Osaka)
07 (Osaka suburbs, Toyama, Fukui, Shiga, Kyoto-Fu, Hyogo, Nara, and Wakayama prefectures)
08 (Tottori, Shimane, Okayama, Hiroshima, Yamaguchi, Tokushima, Kagawa, Ehime, and Kochi prefectures)
09 (Fukuoka, Saga, Nagasaki, Kumamoto, Oita, Miyazaki, Kagoshima, and Okinawa prefectures)
The international telephone code for Japan is 81.

ARITA (Ah-ree-tah)   The small town of Arita, 96 kilometers from Fukuoka on the Sasebo Line, is noted as the place where white porcelain was first produced in Japan. A Korean potter with the Chinese name of Li-sang P'ing brought the art to Arita in 1616. Porcelain made in Arita is now an important export industry.

ARMED FORCES   At the end of World War II in 1945, all of Japan's armed forces were demobilized. All arms were confiscated, and the new constitution, promulgated in 1947, renounced the nation's right to use war as a means of settling international disputes.

This did not mean that Japan had renounced the right to defend itself, and in 1950 a National Police Reserve (NPR) was established. In 1952, when sovereignty was returned to Japan, the NPR was reorganized as the Peace Preservation Corps.

The present-day Self-Defense Force (SDF) grew out of the Peace Preservation Corps and consists of three branches: the Ground Self-Defense Force (army), the Maritime Self-Defense Force (navy), and the Air Self-Defense Force (air force).

The prime minister is the chief commanding officer of the SDF, but the armed forces are administered by the director of the Defense Agency, who has the rank of a minister of state.

Service in the three branches of the armed forces is on a volunteer basis. At present, there are fewer than 300,000 members in the combined forces.

ARRANGED MARRIAGES/MIAI KEKKON (Me-aye keck-kone)   Until the end of World War II, nearly all marriages in Japan were arranged— either by a friend or employer of the bride or groom or by professional marriage go-betweens called *nakodo* (nah-koe-doe).

With the elimination of the feudal family system at the end of the war, young Japanese men and women were free to make their own choices. Still today, however, some 20 to 30 percent of the marriages in Japan are arranged.

In the *miai* system, eligible young men and women are introduced to any number of prospects, usually at a restaurant or coffee shop, until they both agree to the match.

Love plays no part in these matches, but the individuals concerned are almost never forced to marry anyone whose looks or personalities are disagreeable to them.

Once the marriage is agreed to, the couple normally have several days or weeks to get to know each other before the wedding takes place.

The success of arranged marriages is as good as, if not better than, love matches, in part because the couples concerned are not emotionally involved and are therefore less susceptible to disappointment. See MARRIAGE.

ASAKUSA (Ah-sock-sah)   In the northeastern part of Tokyo's Taito Ward, Asakusa is a major railway terminal for northern and eastern cities (including Nikko). It is also a nationally famous entertainment, shopping, and wholesale district.

For several generations, Asakusa had one of Japan's most famous entertainment quarters, the Yoshiwara (Yoe-she-wah-rah), which closed in 1956.

Among the major attractions in Asakusa today are the Asakusa Hongan (Hone-gone) Temple, the famous Asakusa Kannon (Khan-noan) Temple, and a covered shopping street known as Nakamise (Nah-kah-me-say), which leads to the temple.

The Kannon Temple, which dates from the seventh century, is one of the most popular in the country, drawing huge crowds on New Year's Day. There is a major festival in the area on May 17–18.

While Asakusa's hundreds of restaurants, theaters, bars, and night spots attract people from all over Tokyo, it is best known as a mecca for people who live in the prefectures adjoining Tokyo on the north and east.

ASHIYA (Ah-she-yah)   The Beverly Hills of the Hanshin (Osaka-Kobe) district, Ashiya is one of the most prestigious residential areas in Japan. A picturesque community on the foot of Mt. Rokko between Osaka and Kobe, Ashiya offers a commanding view of the surrounding countryside and is equally famed for its mild climate. It is 19 kilometers from Osaka and 10 kilometers from Kobe.

ASSOCIATIONS OF FOREIGN WIVES   Foreign women who marry Japanese men are still unusual enough that they have formed an association in Tokyo and hold regular meetings. Notice of such meetings appears in local English-language newspapers. There is also an organization in Tokyo called Kokusai Kekkon wo Kangaeru Kai, which literally means, more or less, Association of Those Thinking About a Foreign Marriage, but which is referred to in public notices as the Group of Japanese Women Married to Non-Japanese.

The Allied Military Occupation of Japan from 1945 to 1952—and subsequent contacts on a major scale—resulted in thousands of marriages between Western men and Japanese women. During these early years, marriages between Western women and Japanese men were rare, however.

As time went by, the number of Western women marrying Japanese men increased and, in a surprising turnabout, surpassed the number of Western men-Japanese women marriages in 1975—a trend that has continued.

This development is surprising because of the traditional customs in Japan that separate men and women, not only in the home, but in the workplace and in the huge world of entertainment, as well.

The problems facing most such marriages, generally including the couple's inability to communicate well with each other, are formidable, and they require extraordinary adjustments on the part of most of the foreign wives. (In the case of Western men marrying Japanese women, most of the adjustments are left to the Japanese wife.) See INTERNATIONAL MARRIAGES.

ATAMI (Ah-tah-me)   One of the most popular hot spring resorts in Japan, Atami is situated on the northeast neck of Izu Peninsula, which juts out into the Pacific Ocean about 100 kilometers south of Tokyo (55 minutes by Kodama Express Train).

The name of the city, which means Hot Sea, is derived from an old legend about a hot geyser that suddenly appeared in the sea just offshore, killing the fish in the area. A Buddhist priest, famed for having conquered the nine-headed dragon of Lake Ashi (Hakone), came to the area in 749 and prayed for the geyser to move, which it did—onto the beach.

Also one of the most spectacular resorts in Japan, Atami is perched on the steep wall of a great volcanic crater, half of which collapsed and fell into the sea ages ago. The volcanic nature of the surrounding hills accounts for the large number of hot springs in the area, many of which have proven medicinal value.

The hot spring inns of Atami begin on the waterfront and spiral upward, offering scenic views of the oceanfront and offshore islands. The area abounds in equally scenic drives. One drive climbs the crater wall to Jukkoku (Juke-koe-ku), or Ten Province Pass, en route to Lake Hakone; and another, Izu (Ee-zoo) Skyline Parkway, runs along the ridge of mountains that forms the backbone of Izu Peninsula.

Views from the Izu Skyline Parkway include snowcapped Mt. Fuji and Suruga Bay, celebrated in wood block prints for their extraordinary beauty. A sea-road, cut in the cliffs, runs along the coast from Atami toward Ito (Ee-toe), another seaside hot spring resort to the south.

There are many historical sites and attractions in Atami, including the famous Atami Plum-Tree Garden and Atami Art Museum (which is in the hall of the headquarters building of the Church of World Messianity, on a hill overlooking Atami Station).

Farther up along the slopes of the collapsed crater is a golf course, one of the most rugged and spectacular in the country (where I played my very first game of golf in 1950).

ATOMIC BOMB DOME   On the morning of August 6, 1945, one of the most beautiful buildings in Hiroshima was the Industry Promotion Hall, whose majestic dome framed the skyline of the former castle town.

At precisely 8:15 A.M. that morning, an atom bomb exploded over the hall, completely devastating everything within a three-kilometer radius. Only the gutted steel frame of the dome was left etched against the smouldering sky.

After World War II ended and reconstruction began, it was decided to leave the atomic-bomb-ravaged dome as a grim reminder of the bombing. Later consecrated as the Atomic Bomb Dome, it is now a special memorial that is visited by hundreds of thousands each year.

ATSUGI (Aht-sue-ghee)   Famous since 1945 as the site of an American air force base and the place where the first American Occupation troops and General Douglas MacArthur first set foot on the Japanese mainland, Atsugi, near Yokohama, is now a major industrial center.

ATSUTA SHRINE / ATSUTA JINJA (Aht-sue-tah jeen-jah)   Near Atsuta Station in Nagoya, the Atsuta (hot field) Shrine is the second most important Shinto shrine in Japan because it is the repository of the Sacred Sword that, together with the Mirror at Ise Jingu and the Jewels at the Imperial Palace, make up the Three Regalia of the Emperor.

Founded in the third century, the shrine was totally rennovated in 1955. Its annual festival is on June 5.

According to legend, the Sacred Sword, called Kusanagi-no Tsurugi or Grass-Mowing Sword, was presented to Prince Takeru Yamato, the son of Emperor Keiko, by Princess Yamato when he visited the Ise Jingu Shrines before starting out on an expedition against rebels in the east.

During the expedition, the enemy set fire to the grass surrounding the prince, whereupon he used the sword to mow the grass down. The prince then left the sword hanging in a mulberry tree, and it was later carried away by Princess Miyazu.

The princess placed the sword in a cedar tree, but it shone so brightly that it set the tree on fire. The tree fell and set the field around it ablaze — thus the name Hot Field.

AUTO ACCIDENT HOSPITAL / JIDOSHA JIKO TAISAKU (Jee-doe-shah Jee-koe tie-shah-kuu)   In February 1984, the world's first hospital exclusively for automobile accident victims opened in the city of Chiba, northeast of Tokyo. The hospital offers round-the-clock care for patients with brain or spinal column injuries, admitting only those who are living a "quasi-vegetable life in the aftermath of road mishaps."

AUTOMOBILES / JIDOSHA (Jee-doe-shah)   In 1980, Japan bypassed the United States as the world's leading producer of automobiles, in what has to have been one of the industrial upsets of the century.

Wheeled vehicles in the form of carts for transporting goods were in use in Japan in ancient times. There was an officer in charge of *kuruma* (wheels or wheeled vehicles) at the Imperial Court when the great historical chronicle *Nihon Shoki* was published in 720 A.D. The first modern automobile, driven by a steam engine, was imported into Japan in 1897 by a foreigner.

At the turn of the twentieth century, Japan was only a few decades away from a feudal society made up of peasants, artisans, shopkeepers and sword-carrying warriors. It was thus several decades behind the U.S. and Europe in starting an automobile manufacturing industry.

The first steam car was manufactured in Japan in 1904, when a man named Torao Yamaha, in Okayama Prefecture, succeeded in building one. World War I provided the impetus for the development of an automobile industry in Japan, when the Japanese observed the role of trucks and other vehicles in the conduct of modern warfare.

The Ford Motor Company built an automobile assembly plant in Japan in 1925 and was followed a year later by General Motors. This resulted in a lag in the development of the domestic industry, and in 1931 the Japanese government got involved in designing and promoting the manufacture of vehicles by Japanese companies. War with China in 1931 provided another boost for the auto industry, and in 1936 the government passed an Automobile Production Enterprise Law to support large-scale auto production.

Then Japan's automakers had to start over from scratch at the end of World War II in 1945.

Japan's largest automobile manufacturers are Toyota Motor Company, Nissan Motor Company, Mitsubishi Motor Company, Toyo Kogyo Company, and Honda Motor Company. (By the way, Honda is pronounced HONE-dah, not Hahn-dah; and Datsun is not a real Japanese word. It was made up from the initials of the three men who developed it—D.A.T.— plus son.) See individual listings.

AVERAGE LIFE EXPECTANCY   In 1901, the average life expectancy of Japanese males was 39.4 years. The average for women was 49.5 years.

By the 1980s, Japan had one of the longest life expectancies in the world —78.8 years for women and 73.3 years for men. By the mid-1990s these figures had passed 82 years for women and 76 years for men, and now appear to be holding fairly steady. This is about four years longer than the projected life expectancy for American men and women. (Longevity in Japan is attributed to a diet that emphasizes rice, vegetables, and seafood products.)

Currently the major causes of death in Japan are malignant neoplasms, heart diseases, cerebrovascular diseases, pneumonia and bronchitis, accidents (with motor vehicle accidents the leading cause of accidental deaths), senility, suicide, nephritis, cirrhosis of the liver, and diabetes, in that order.

AWA DANCE / AWA ODORI (Ah-wah oh-doe-ree)   One of the most picturesque and popular of Japan's folk dances, the *awa odori* is also one of the major attractions of the city of Tokushima, on Shikoku Island, the smallest of the four main islands of Japan.

The dance, which originated in the mid-1600s, is performed in the streets of the city from August 15 through 18 every year. The dancers wear colorful *yukata* (yuu-kah-tah) robes and distinctive hats, and dance through the streets to the accompaniment of flutes, drums, and *shamisen* (shah-me-sane) music.

The festival attracts a large number of visitors from the other islands of Japan, as well as from abroad. It is also highlighted on national television.

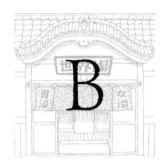

BAMBOO / TAKE (Tah-kay)   It has often been said, seriously, that the Japanese might not have developed their high form of civilization without bamboo. A partial listing of just some of its more important uses just begins to suggest its importance in the past. These include water pipes, fan ribs, chopsticks, lantern frames, food, flower vases, baskets, scoops, rulers, wind and sun screens, eating bowls, serving trays, furniture, fencing swords, garden fences, insect cages, flutes, wind chimes, doors, and handbags.

Bamboo is said to have been introduced into China and Japan from India. There are more than 600 varieties of the plant, but only about a dozen of these are used regularly for utilitarian and aesthetic purposes. These types are selected because of their form, size, and natural beauty. They include a long-jointed type that has amazing plasticity, a type that has unusually beautiful patterns on its bark, a type that is multicolored, and one that is almost black.

Over the centuries, the Japanese developed something of a cult surrounding the use of bamboo. Certain types were always used to make certain items, but never others. One type of bamboo was appropriate for one purpose, while another was not. Bamboo generally was regarded as a symbol of virtue, fidelity, and constancy, but only certain types of bamboo were used to convey this symbolism.

The most conspicuous use of bamboo in Japan today is for decorative purposes, both by itself and in the form of functional objects, such as latticework, sun blinds, corner posts, planters, and vases and in the interiors of homes and inns.

It has a distinctive texture and charm that adds significantly to Japanese life.

Recommended reading: *Bamboo*, by Robert Austin and Koichiro Ueda (Weatherhill).

BANZUIIN, CHOBEI (Bahn-zoo-een, Choe-baye)   Japan had its Robin Hoods—or, as such persons were known in Japan, its *kyokaku* (k'yoe-kah-kuu), which translates as Hosts of Heroism.

The *kyokaku* were common men (not *samurai*) of extraordinary courage and martial skills, who became famous during the early decades of the Tokugawa Period (1603–1868) for championing the rights of the ordinary people against corrupt officials of the military Bakufu government and arrogant—often murderous—*samurai* who were legally permitted to kill anyone who broke the law or insulted them.

The *kyokaku* were generally members of Japan's traditional underworld of gamblers and gangs who operated outside the establishment, but were often considered heroes by the lower classes, who had no rights other than those given to them by their feudal lords.

The most famous of these *kyokaku* was a man named Chobei Banzuiin, born in 1640. Among the many celebrated exploits of Chobei, none caught the popular imagination more than his saving the life of a swordsmith named Gonpachi Shirai, who later became a notorious criminal in order to get money to redeem the girl he loved from a life of servitude in a brothel.

Gonpachi was caught and crucified, and his lover committed suicide on his grave.

In 1657, when he was 37, Chobei became the victim of a trick arranged by Jurozaemon Mizuno, a senior retainer of the *shogun*, and was killed. He was buried at Genku Temple in Higashi Ueno, in Tokyo's Taito Ward. His life and exploits have since been immortalized in songs, plays, and films.

BARBERSHOPS / TOKO YA (Toe-koe yah)   Japan is rightly famous for its barbershops, which dispense far more than a haircut and a shave. The typical Japanese barbershop carries on the traditions of special service that have been an integral part of life in Japan since ancient times.

The normal barbershop session lasts for 30 minutes to an hour and includes a meticulous haircut—and shave, if desired—along with a head and shoulder massage. It is a thoroughly relaxing experience that makes a visit to a barbershop something more than just getting a haircut.

BARRIER GATES / SEKI SHO (Say-kee show)   During much of Japan's early history, and in particular during the Tokugawa Shogunate from 1603 to 1868, the *daimyo* (dime-yoe) feudal lords and *shogun* maintained barrier gates on the roads leading into their fiefs. The barriers were, in effect, border inspection stations at which travelers had to present identification papers to guards and give their reason for traveling.

One of the most famous of these barriers was in Hakone on the shore of Lake Ashi, which controlled traffic on the Tokai Do, the great road that connected Kyoto and Edo (Tokyo). This barrier was erected in 1618 and manned until 1868. An exact replica of the Barrier Guardhouse, built across the road from the old site in 1965, is now a popular tourist attraction.

Near the present Barrier Guardhouse is the Hakone Historical Materials Museum (Hakone Shiryo-Kan), which houses weapons, documents, and other items mainly connected with the Barrier.

The Hakone Museum, across the street from the Hakone Hotel, also has numerous artifacts relating to the Barrier and to the life-style of the times.

Many of Japan's most popular plays and folk songs make references to these barriers because they played such a vital role in the lives of people over many centuries.

BAR (LEGAL) SYSTEM   Japan's first regulation concerning lawyers was passed in 1876, and a Lawyer Law went into effect in 1895. But the bar association was under the direct supervision of chief prosecutors attached to district courts.

The present Lawyer Law was passed in 1949, and Nichibenren (Nee-chee-bane-rane), the Japan Federation of Bar Associations, was founded on the same day. The law guarantees the independence of the association and sets standards for lawyers.

Persons who pass the national bar examination or have taught law as a university professor for at least five years, as well as foreign lawyers who have been screened by Nichibenren, are eligible to practice law in Japan.

Nichibenren, headquartered in Kasumigaseki, the government center in Tokyo, has 52 local branch offices, including one in each prefecture. All lawyers are required to register with their local branch office and the main office of Nichibenren. Lawyers are required to have offices, and they must follow guidelines set by the bar association in charging fees.

Most of Japan's 17,000-plus lawyers are in Tokyo and Osaka. Fewer than 500 of Japan's lawyers are women.

BASEBALL / YAKYU (Yah-que)   It is often said that baseball is more popular in Japan than in the United States, where it was invented. In any event, it is one of Japan's most popular sports.

Baseball, introduced into Japan in 1873, quickly became popular among university students and nonprofessional company teams. Professional baseball made its debut in Japan in 1934, but did not really flourish until after World War II.

There are two leagues, the Central League and the Pacific League, each with six teams. As in the U.S., the two league winners compete in a playoff—the Japan Series—at the end of the season.

The teams in the Central League are the Yomiuri Giants (Tokyo), the Hiroshima Carps (Hiroshima), the Hanshin Tigers (Osaka), the Yakult Swallows (Tokyo), the Chunichi Dragons (Nagoya), and the Taiyo Whales (Yokohama).

In the Pacific League are the Hankyu Braves (Osaka), the Kintetsu Buffaloes (Osaka), the Lotte Orions (Tokorozawa), the Nankai Hawks (Osaka), and the Nippon Ham Fighters (Tokyo).

Each team plays 130 games per season, which runs from April through October.

There are over 10,000 baseball and softball fields in Japan, including 4,203 owned by companies, 3,181 that are public, and 1,759 that belong to elementary, junior, and senior high schools.

The leading home run hitter of all time is a Japanese—Sadaharu Oh, who had 868 homeruns to his credit when he retired in 1980. Other top Japanese batters are Isao Harimoto (504 home runs), Masahiro Doi (465 home runs), and Katsuya Nomura (657 home runs), along with Katsuo Osugi, Shigeo Nagashima, and Koichi Tabuchi, all of whom hit over 400 home runs in their careers.

Still today, competition between Tokyo's Big Six university baseball teams (Waseda, Keio, Meiji, Hosei, Rikkyo and Tokyo) is fierce, as is that between Japan's high school teams.

Japan also has a nonprofessional, intercity baseball tournament, representing teams from various commercial companies. One of the most successful of these teams is the Japan Steel Corporation team, which has won four All-Japan championships in recent years.

Each of Japan's professional baseball teams is allowed to have two foreign players on the parent team and one on the farm team. Over the years, many of the American baseball players picked up by Japanese teams have become national heroes.

But the cultural difference between Japanese and American baseball is enormous, as most of the American players who have attempted to make the transition have discovered to their chagrin.

Baseball as it is played in Japan may look like American baseball, but it has been Japanized to the point that some Amercian players have said it is not baseball at all.

Japanese baseball is, in fact, a microcosm of Japanese culture, with all of its emphasis on the suppression of individualism, team spirit, rigid hierarchical ranking among players and management, and the absolute requirement for *wa* (wah) or harmony.

In Japan's world of baseball, managers treat players more like children than responsible adults, controlling virtually every aspect of their behavior on and off the field.

Training, both physical and mental, is far more intense than in baseball in the U.S., and it lasts longer. Players are routinely required to practice until they are exhausted.

Individualistic behavior and displays of pride and arrogance—both hallmarks of Americans—are taboo in Japanese baseball. The more talented and successful a player, the more humble he is expected to be.

Japanese baseball is regularly used as a metaphor for how business as well as politics are conducted in Japan.

Recommended reading: *You Gotta Have Wa*, by Robert Whiting.

BASHO, MATSUO (Bah-show Mot-sue-oh)   Regarded as the father of modern *haiku* poetry, Basho Matsuo (1644–1694) and his disciples elevated the previously low-class *haikai* (hie-kie) to the level enjoyed by Chinese poetry and by Japan's ancient *renga* (rane-gah) style poetry.

Basho infused his *haiku* with an elegance and freshness that made them eternal and as new as each day's morning dew. His work and that of his 10 most famous disciples, known as the Juttetsu (Jute-tate-sue), or Ten Great Disciples, was collected in a book called *Shichi Bushu* (She-chee Buu-shuu), which is prized as the sacred book of *haiku*. See HAIKU.

BATHHOUSES / MASSAGE PARLORS   So-called Turkish-style bathhouses have been popular in Japan for centuries, and massage parlors are the successors to bathhouses found in the licentious entertainment quarters, which flourished until the mid-1950s.

Today's massage parlors, now called "Soaplands," are not the elegant inns which for many generations were both the inspiration and center for much of the literature and theater for which Japan is now famous.

Some of the bathhouses are very large and ornate, but they are essentially massage parlors that cater primarily to a male clientele looking for more than a bath and a massage. A number of those catering to foreign clientele have lounges stocked with copies of the *Wall Street Journal*, *Fortune* magazine, and other amenities. One of the largest bathhouses in Osaka has a floor reserved exclusively for women.

In 1984, Turkish nationals began protesting to the Japanese government about the practice of referring to such bath and massage parlors as "Turkish baths." In early 1985, the bathhouse operators agreed to find a substitute name for them and to remove all signs referring to Turkish baths. The new name the operators finally decided on was "Soaplands."

BATHHOUSES, PUBLIC / SENTO (Sin-toe)   Not only has nude communal bathing suffered a setback in image-conscious Japan since the mid-1950s, but public bathhouses, as well, are losing ground.

A traditional and vital part of rural and urban life in Japan since ancient times, Japan's hot public bathhouses are losing out to growing affluence, new life-styles, and rising costs—at least in the major cities.

In Tokyo, where over six million people a day went to the public baths in the early 1970s, only about three million people now use the city's 2,300 public bathhouses.

The head of the Tokyo Public Bath Owners' Union blames the steady disappearance of the *sento* on the fact that approximately two-thirds of the households in Tokyo now have their own baths.

To bolster their income, Tokyo's *sento* operators are now offering such extras as coin-operated laundry machines, saunas, and adjoining coffee shops and supermarkets. A new approach is to add game rooms, reading rooms, and facilities for practicing such traditional arts as flower arranging and the tea ceremony.

In earlier years, there were *yuna* (you-nah), or water women bathhouses, as well as regular *sento*. In the *yuna*, attractive young women scrubbed the backs of patrons, served drinks, and were available for various sensual pleasures as well—an area now served by massage parlor/bathhouses.

The normal water temperature in Japan's *sento*, between 105 and 108 degrees F., is guaranteed to take the kinks and strains out of tired bodies.

BATHING / MIZU WO ABIRU (Me-zoo oh ah-bee-rue) Very early in their history as a people, the Japanese developed the custom of bathing regularly in hot water as part of their religious life. Unlike Westerners, who ordinarily wash themselves while they are in the bathtub (a very unsanitary habit, if one stops to contemplate it), the Japanese thoroughly scrub themselves before entering the bath and are therefore able to enjoy soaking in clean, hot water—at the same time, making it possible for several people to use the same water.

It was also customary for the Japanese to bathe together in larger private and public baths, without the slightest sexual connotation to the practice. This custom continued in public bathhouses until the 1950s, when, as a result of pressure from female members of the Diet (Japan's Parliament), a few Christian religious leaders, and some Westernized wives of prominent men, a law was passed requiring that all public baths be sexually segregated.

This required that walls be built, separating the large common baths into two sections. Until such walls were built, many bath operators strung a rope across the bath to distinguish the sections.

After the walls were built, the attendants, sometimes male and sometimes female, sat between the two sections on a rise that provided them with an unobstructed view of bathers in both male and female areas. When paying their fees, taller bathers could also peer into the other sections, if they so desired.

In their homes and in hot spring spa baths, the Japanese still enjoy the healthy practice of mixed bathing. While not overtly sexual, bathing is still a very sensual activity in Japan. The Japanese have recognized since ancient times the lustration effect of water—the fact that bathing not only washes away dirt, but spiritual and emotional grime, as well. A good scrubbing followed by a relaxing soak in a hot tub has the effect of returning one to a virginal state of mind.

Recommended reading: *Bachelor's Japan*, by Boye Lafayette De Mente (Tuttle).

BEACHES / BICHI (Be-chee) With one of the longest coastlines in the world, Japan has literally thousands of sand-covered beaches, large and small, in easily accessible areas, and in tiny coves and inlets that can be reached only by an overland hike or by boat.

Until the 1950s, the Japanese were not great beach-goers. The young did not date and did not engage in the kind of individualized free-for-all fun that is typical of beach behavior today. Married couples did not go out together for such public forms of recreation. Most men preferred the more traditional forms of entertainment at hot spring spas and in the great entertainment districts, and sunbathing was not the custom.

With the personal freedoms and improved standard of living that followed the ending of the Pacific War in 1945 and the example set by huge numbers of young American members of the Occupation forces, the Japanese began flocking to the beaches by the millions.

Today there are hundreds of beaches around the country that are crowded from late spring to early fall. Those in the vicinity of Tokyo and Yokohama, on Chiba, Miura, and Izu peninsulas, are especially crowded during the summer months.

They include Kujukuri and Byobugaura beaches on Chiba Peninsula and Enoshima, Fujisawa, Chigasaki, and Oiso, along Sagami Bay (formed by Miura and Izu peninsulas).

BEAUTY / UTSUKUSHISA (Uut-sue-kuu-she-sah)   The Japanese are the only people I know who developed specific standards of beauty that were taught and practiced and became an integral part of the culture.

The principles of beauty in Japan, which evolved from Shintoist concepts of purity and simplicity, were refined and codified by Zen Buddhists. This standard of beauty, described by the words *shibui* (she-buu-e) and *shibumi* (she-buu-me), is based on naturalness and a highly refined elegance that is found in the epitome of simplicity. Both *shibui* and *shibumi* mean astringent, simple, natural—the opposite of gaudy or extravagant.

The principles of *shibui* beauty are exemplified in traditional Japanese architecture, handicrafts, the tea ceremony, flower arranging, and other arts.

Recommended reading: *Japanese Secrets of Graceful Living*, by Boye Lafayette De Mente.

BEEFSTEAKS / BIFU SUTEKI (Bee-fuu su-tay-kee)   It is somewhat surprising, at least to the cattle ranchers and beefsteak eaters of Western America, that many beefsteak gourmets say that the best steaks they have ever eaten were served up by steakhouses in Japan.

This reputation derives from the fact that beef raised in the Matsutaka area of Kobe, for the country's leading steakhouses, gets very special treatment, resulting in both incredibly tender and very tasty meat.

This treatment consists of a special diet that includes beer. In addition, according to the popular story, the cattle are massaged by the farmers (and of course the farmers' daughters), who first spray the pampered cattle with high-grade O'sake from their own mouths.

Having witnessed this latter treatment a number of times in years past, I believe there might be something to it.

Among Japan's most famous steakhouses are those in the Suehiro (Sway-he-roe) chain. The beef served in these restaurants is called Kobe beef or Matsutaka beef.

BEER / BIRU (Be-rue)   The brewing of beer was among the technologies imported into Japan from the West when its doors were opened to foreign trade in the 1850s and '60s. Since that time, the Japanese have become world-renowned masters of the art.

Beer is now the leading alcoholic beverage consumed in the country, having outstripped the traditional *O'sake* (Oh-sah-kay) many times over. Among the popular brands are Kirin (Kee-reen), Asahi (Ah-sah-he), Sapporo (Sop-poe-roe), and Suntory.

Japanese beer is noted for its mellow taste—and for coming in both small (*ko-bin*) and large-sized (*o-bin*) bottles. See ALCOHOLIC BEVERAGES.

BEER HALLS and GARDENS   Beer halls and gardens, many of them European styled, are popular in Japan. Those that are European in style usually feature some kind of entertainment, ranging from singing to elaborate floor shows.

During the summer months, the rooftops of several buildings in Tokyo and other cities suddenly blossom into beer gardens.

For names and locations, see current editions of *Tour Companion* (a visitors' guide) and the *Tokyo Weekender*.

BENEDICT, RUTH   Ruth Benedict was the author of *The Chrysanthemum and the Sword* (Tuttle), one of the most famous books ever written about Japan.

An American anthropologist who had never been to Japan, Benedict was asked in the early 1940s by the U.S. government to research and write a cultural/psychological profile of the Japanese that could be used as guidelines during the expected Military Occupation of the country following the end of World War II.

Most of Benedict's research consisted of interviews with Japanese-Americans living in the U.S. The study played an important role in the manner in which General Douglas MacArthur set up and conducted the Occupation of Japan.

The book also greatly influenced many of the postwar studies and books on Japan, and it continues today to be a popular title on the country.

BEPPU (Bape-puu)   One of the most unusual of Japan's hundreds of hot spring resorts, the Beppu district on the northeastern shore of Kyushu has eight spa resort areas, with dozens of *ji goku* (jee go-kuu), or "hell springs," which are boiling mud ponds that detonate loudly, burping hot mud several inches into the air.

The mud ponds come in different colors and different temperatures. Many of them have been developed into mudbaths. The entire *ji goku* circuit is 20 kilometers and a two-and-a-half-hour bus trip.

There are some 3,795 hot springs in the Beppu area, with nine different types of water. Dozens of them have been developed as spas since the dawn of Japan's history. One of the most popular spas among foreign visitors is the Takegawa (Tah-kay-gah-wah), which includes hot sand baths on the beach. Excursion ships from Osaka and Kobe call at Beppu daily.

BIWA (Bee-wah)   The *biwa* is a four- or five-stringed, pear-shaped lute that was originally introduced into Japan from China in the seventh and eighth centuries—the first version (*muso-biwa*) was primarily used by blind priests, and the second version (*gaku-biwa*) was used for court music.

The earliest type was used by Buddhist priests when chanting sutras; the latter, by court musicians when performing for court functions.

In the thirteenth century, storytellers began using the *biwa* as accompaniment, and, in the sixteenth century, ballad singers took up the instrument. These traditional, epic-like ballads were known as *jouri* (joe-uu-ree) and were later accompanied by the *shamisen*. Modern forms of music for the *biwa* were developed during the late 1800s and early 1900s.

BLACK MIST / KUROI KIRI (Kuu-roy kee-ree)   The Japanese love euphemisms, and "black mist" is one that is popularly used in reference to scandals, usually those involving business or government figures.

BLYTH, REGINALD H.   Born in London in 1898, Reginald H. Blyth went to India when he was in his early twenties. There he developed an interest in Oriental literature and philosophy and decided to go to Korea to study and teach. He remained in Korea until 1940, at which time he moved to Japan, where he was to remain until his death in 1964.

Blyth continued his studies in Japan, becoming renowned as a teacher, scholar, and writer. After teaching at several colleges and universities, including the Peers' School, he was appointed tutor in English to Crown Prince Akihito.

Among Blyth's many books are: *Japanese Humor, History of Haiku, Zen and Zen Classics*, and *Haiku* (four volumes).

BON FESTIVAL / BON MATSURI (Bone mot-sue-ree)   Held in Japan in mid-July since the seventh century, this Buddhist celebration is one of the nation's most important annual events. Often called the Festival of the Dead or the Festival of Lanterns, it is similar to All Souls' Day observed in Catholic countries.

The purpose of O'Bon is to perpetuate the memory of ancestors and to inspire filial piety by reminding everyone of the debt they owe their ancestors.

While the occasion is solemn, the festival is primarily a joyful one. People clean their homes and family graves and prepare offerings for the spirits, which are believed to return to their former homes at this time.

On the eve of July 13 in the more traditional families, the pious go to the family graves, burn incense, and then invite the spirits to return home, lighting the way for them by carrying lanterns (or, in some mountainous districts, torches).

At home, the spirits are treated as if they were still alive. On the 15th, the last day of O'Bon, special farewell rice dumplings (*okuri-dango*) are presented to the spirits. On the following day, the traditionalists still light bonfires in front of their homes, to help guide the spirits back to the world of the dead.

Many communities celebrate O'Bon with dances—*Bon Odori* (Bone Oh-doe-ree)—usually held on the precincts of the local shrine or temple. The dances, to the tune of drums and flutes, often last until near dawn.

Bon Odori that are national attractions include those in Kiso, Nagano Prefecture; Sado Island, off the coast of Niigata; Tokushima City, on Shikoku; and Shiraishi Island, in the Inland Sea.

BONKEI (Bone-kay-e)   *Bonkei* is a miniaturized landscape on a dish or a tray that may be made of just about any natural material: stones, pebbles, moss, plants, etc., combined with something manmade—a house, gate, or bridge, etc. *Bonkei* are sometimes called *hako niwa* (hah-koe nee-wah), or garden boxes.

Recommended reading: *Bonkei Tray Landscapes*, by Jozan Hirota (Kodansha International).

BONSAI (Bone-sigh)   The art of cultivating dwarf trees, or *bonsai*, was originated in Japan in ancient times and is now a popular pastime around the world.

The primary attractions of *bonsai* are the art itself and the fact that one's handiwork, if properly tended, may last a lifetime and even bring pleasure for several centuries.

Basically, the art of *bonsai* consists of planting a tree in a ceramic pot, and then controlling its growth and shape through periodic transplanting, root trimming, regulating the water and fertilizer, and other techniques.

Bonsai may be sculptured into any number of shapes, depending on the desires of the bonsai artist. Pine trees are probably the most popular subjects for *bonsai*, but other ones also commonly used include fruit trees and various evergreens.

Recommended reading: *Bonsai with American Trees*, by Masakuni Kawasumi (Kodansha International).

BONSEKI (Bone-say-kee)   *Bonseki* is a dry, miniature landscape that consists of rocks and white sand arranged on a black lacquer tray, representing mountains, rivers, or the ocean. *Bonseki* developed as an art in the Muromachi Period (1392–1573), the same period that saw the development of the tea ceremony and flower arranging.

A popular traditional handicraft, it is sold in department stores as a decorative item.

BONUSES / BONASU (Boe-nah-sue)   In addition to regular monthly wages, Japanese companies generally pay their employees seasonal bonuses, in June and December, which are regarded as a basic, integral part of their income.

The amount of the bonuses, usually based on the equivalent of one or more months' pay, varies considerably from company to company and industry to industry. Companies that are very profitable may pay the equivalent of three or four months' wages on each of the two bonus-paying occasions.

When companies suffer financial reverses, they often borrow money to pay bonuses rather than let their employees go without.

Most Japanese families save a significant percentage of their bonuses. The two annual bonus-paying periods also coincide with major gift-giving and shopping periods during the year.

BOOK PUBLISHING / HON NO SHUPPAN (Hone no shupe-pahn) Book publishing in Japan grew more slowly than magazine publishing. In the mid-1920s, low-priced editions of collected works of four or five volumes each became very popular. This was followed in 1926 by the One Yen books, of which some 200 titles were published. The next year, Iwanami Bunko

(E-wah-nah-me Boon-koe) introduced its series of inexpensive pocket books, featuring classics from all over the world.

The first successful postwar book was *Nichi-Bei Kaiwa Techo* (Nee-chee-bay-e Kie-way Tay-choe), or *Handbook of English Conversation*. It came out in September 1945, one month after the war ended, and sold 3.6 million copies.

Another significant early postwar success was the *People's Encyclopedia*, published by Heibonsha (Hay-e-bone-shah) in 1961.

Today there are over 4,000 book publishers in Japan, but fewer than 100 of them are sizable. Some 1,300 of them have fewer than 10 employees, and 4,000 of them publish fewer than two titles a year.

The three biggest book publishers in Japan—Kodansha (Koe-dahn-shah), Shogakkan (Show-gock-khan) and Shuei-Sha (Shuu-a-shah)—account for around 20 percent of the industry's total sales of both books and magazines.

Most books in Japan are distributed through commissioned agents. The two largest distributors are Tohan (Toe-hahn) and Nippan (Neep-pahn), which together handle 70 percent of the industry's sales of books and magazines. Two well-known publishers who do not use commission agents are Iwanami (Ee-wah-nah-me) and Miraisha (Me-rye-shah). They distribute directly.

As in the U.S., the book industry in Japan is facing serious problems, including rising costs and complaints that the distribution and retailing of books is grossly inefficient.

Japanese book publishers now average printing only about 6,000 copies of a first edition—not nearly enough to go around to all bookstores. One advantage that authors have in Japan: Many publishers pay royalties on the basis of print runs, not sales, and they pay shortly after the printing.

An early 1980 development in Japan was the appearance of super book-stores carrying as many as one million books.

Each year, between 2,500 and 3,000 foreign books (not counting children's books and reference books) are translated and published in Japanese. Altogether, about 40,000 titles are published annually.

The 10 leading book publishers in Japan are Kodansha, Shogakkan, Shuei Sha, Kadokawa Shoten, Iwanami Shoten, Chuo Koron Sha, Shincho Sha, Hayakawa Shobo, Bungei Shunju, and Meiji Tosho Shuppan.

In 1984, 25 leading Japanese publishers set up a company to translate and export Japanese books to other countries. The company, called the Japan

Foreign-Rights Centre, took over the business of the former Kurita-Bando Literary Agency, an exclusive Japanese copyright exporter in Tokyo.

BOSO PENINSULA (Boe-soe)   This is the large peninsula that juts out into the Pacific in a southeasterly direction from Tokyo and incorporates Chiba Prefecture, with Tokyo Bay on the west and the Pacific Ocean on the east.

Like virtually every other region of Japan, Chiba is dotted with historical places—temples, shrines, etc. It is also the location of the New Tokyo International Airport, which is on the outskirts of the city of Narita, 68 kilometers from central Tokyo. It also boasts two quasi-national parks (Suigo-Tsukuba and Minami Boso).

The peninsula, part of the Keiyo (Tokyo-Chiba) Industrial Zone, is also a major agricultural area, frequently called the Kitchen of Tokyo because of its peanuts, soybeans, vegetables, fish, dairy products, and natural gas.

There are several popular beaches along the peninsula, but its most famous attraction is Tokyo's Disneyland.

BOSS / OYABUN (Oh-yah-boon)   In feudal Japan, the operators of certain kinds of businesses, as well as gang leaders, were called *oyabun*, and their employees or followers were called *kobun* (koe-boon). *Oya* means parent and ko means child, which is an indication of the relationship that existed between the two.

In many businesses, the *kobun* lived on the premises in their own rooms or in dormitories, depending on their status. They were expected to be totally loyal to their master—to obey him as would a dutiful son.

In return for such loyalty, the boss was expected to accept complete responsibility for the welfare and interests of his *kobun* and their families. This same attitude and a similar relationship still exists today, although in diluted form, between employers and workers.

The word is still very much a part of the vocabulary (and psychology) of modern day Japanese.

BOWING / OJIGI (Oh-jee-ghee)   Bowing, the traditional Japanese way of greeting people and saying farewell, as well as showing respect, is one of the most important aspects of Japanese culture—far more meaningful and important to the Japanese than the handshake or wave in Western cultures.

The bow, done at the right time and in the right way, is important to the Japanese because their social etiquette is much stricter and more demanding than the etiquette of most other countries.

In feudal times, failing to bow or bowing incorrectly was a very serious offense, which, in the case of a commoner, could and often did mean immediate death at the hands of a haughty *samurai*.

Generally speaking, the lower the bow and the longer it is held, the stronger its implications. The higher the rank of the person receiving the bow, the lower the bow tends to be. When the bow is in the form of a supplication or apology, the trunk of the body may be bowed as low as a 90-degree angle.

The best way to learn how to bow properly is to observe the Japanese in different situations.

BRIDGE OF HEAVEN / AMANOHASHIDATE (Ah-mah-no-hah-she-dah-tay)   On the Japan Sea coast, west of Kyoto and a short distance from Nishi Maizuru, Amanohashidate, or Bridge of Heaven, is so beautiful that it has been renowned since ancient times as one of the three most scenic spots in Japan (the other two are Matsushima, near Sendai, and Miyajima, in the Inland Sea).

The spot consists of a pine-tree covered sandbar, which projects out into the Bay of Miyazu and forms a lagoon and a slender island, all connected to the coast by bridges. There are a number of viewing spots in the area, plus the Nariai Temple (twenty-eighth in the string of 33 holy Kannon temples that make up a popular pilgrimage in Western Japan), in the vicinity.

The area around Amanohashidate is a fashionable summer vacation resort for people from Kyoto, Osaka, and Kobe.

BUDDHISM / BUKKYO (Buke-yoe)   Buddhism, founded by Sakyamuni Gautama in India in the fifth century B.C., is a religion in which the ultimate goal is to attain enlightenment and in which one is spiritually free and has an understanding of the relationship between man and the cosmos.

Gautama was called Buddha, or the Awakened One, by his followers.

Bukkyo teaches that the way to reach nirvana—the divine state of release from physical pain and sorrow—is through correct living and self-denial. Over the centuries, various techniques for speeding up this process have been developed and taught by innovative priests. One such method is asceticism (*aragyo*), in which practitioners fast for several days and splash cold water on themselves in winter—or stand under waterfalls—while chanting sutras.

It has been found that such shock treatments will sometimes result in a separation of the mind and body and in the attainment of a holy state.

Buddhism was introduced into Japan from Korea and China in the sixth century A.D., but it made very little impression until the beginning of the seventh century, when Crown Prince Shotoku, one of the most famous persons in Japan's history, became a patron of the new religion and worked diligently to spread the belief among the aristocracy.

When Buddhism was introduced into Japan in the middle of the sixth century, the government was controlled by two powerful clans, the Soga family and the Mononobe family. The Soga clan advocated the acceptance of Buddhism, while the Mononobe opposed it.

The Mononobe held that Buddha was a foreign god and was incompatible with the native Shinto beliefs of the Japanese.

Buddhism was inextricably bound up with China's highly advanced culture, and the acceptance of one meant at least the partial acceptance of the other. But as both the tenets and physical aspects of Buddhism flowed into Japan, both were repeatedly modified to fit the unique Japanese environment.

Despite opposition from the Shinto traditionalists, Buddhism and its highly sophisticated culture gradually permeated the Imperial Court and ruling families. With strong Court backing, the new religion eventually developed into a national cult, alongside of Shintoism.

By the mid-700s, the foreign origins of Buddhism were virtually forgotten, and it was held up as the guardian faith of the nation. Many of the emperors and princes of sixth, seventh, and eighth centuries were dedicated scholars of Buddhism, along with such reknowned priests as Saicho (767–822), also known as Dengyo Daishi, and Kukai (774–835), known as Kobo Daishi.

The great priest-teachers Dengyo and Kukai introduced the doctrine that the native Shinto gods were manifestations of the various Buddhas, thus making it possible for the two religions to exist side by side. They differed in other doctrinal matters, however, and the two sects they established became great rivals—the Tendai sect headquartered on Mt. Hiei, northeast of Kyoto, and the Shingon sect on Mt. Koya, south of Osaka.

These two famous monasteries became the twin fountains of Buddhist learning in Japan, but the more powerful they became, the more secular and corrupt they became, giving rise in the thirteenth century to four new sects, all reformist in their aims.

Prince Shotoku (537–621) had set up schools to teach Buddhism and began a program of constructing temples around the country that was to continue for several centuries. Emperor Kotoku, who reigned from 645 to 655, decreed that Buddhism was a legitimate religion.

Thus, between the sixth and twelfth centuries, Buddhism, along with the architecture and arts and crafts of China, were totally Japanized and became an integral part of the mainstream of Japanese culture.

With the founding of the first shogunate in Kamakura in 1192, Japanese religious leaders began changing Buddhism even more, formulating their own doctrines that were closer to the hearts of the Japanese and better fitted the times. The four leading Buddhist sects that made their appearance at this time were Jodo, founded by Honen; Jodo-Shinshu, founded by Shinran; Zen, taught by Eisai and Dogen; and Hokke, founded by the irrepressible Nichiren.

The internal strife that characterized this period in Japanese history, along with the invasions by the Mongols of China, made the Japanese ripe for the propagation of new religions that offered salvation to the common people, as well as the elite, with no more effort than a profession of belief and prayer.

Zen, which taught a very strict system of mental and physical discipline aimed at total self-control and willpower, became the religion of the new class of samurai warriors and was to play a leading role in the country for the next 600 years.

Soon after Buddhism became a religion of the masses, corruption set in. As in other mass religions around the world, formalities and ceremonies became more important than keeping or teaching the faith.

The abuse of power became rife among most of the Buddhist sects, and the faith of the common people weakened. Thus, when Christianity first appeared in Japan in the mid-1500s, there were many who listened to this new message.

But the political and financial machinations of the Portuguese priests who brought Catholicism to Japan resulted in their expulsion, and shortly after the beginning of the Tokugawa Shogunate in 1603, it was decreed that all common Japanese would register as Buddhists at their neighborhood temple and thereafter become regular donors to the temple.

The degeneration of Buddhism had gone too far, however, and, for most Japanese, membership in a local temple was little more than a kind of taxation. As the hedonistic decades of the Tokugawa period went by, more and more people began to question the legitimacy of Buddhism as a state religion.

Scholars went back to the early history of Japan and discovered that Buddhism had usurped the native religion of Shintoism. These same scholars also found that the shogunate was similarly illegitimate, having usurped the power of the emperor.

Public sentiment began to swing in favor of Shintoism and the emperor in Kyoto and helped to bring the downfall of the shogunate in 1868. Almost immediately thereafter, Buddhism was officially declared a heresy and banned. Shintoism was elevated to the status of a state religion.

Too much a part of Japanese culture to be wiped out by a ban, however, Buddhism survived the nationalistic fever of the next 78 years and remains today an important influence in the lives of the Japanese.

There is no god in the Buddhist faith. Adherents believe that the ultimate state is self-enlightenment, which is achieved by a total recognition of the true essence of life and reality. A primary goal of Buddhists is to rid themselves of the idea that everything is everlasting and to eliminate feelings of jealousy and hate through infinite love. Tolerance and equality are the hallmarks of the Buddhist faith.

Even though most Japanese are not religious in the strict sense of the term, Buddhism exercises an important influence in their lives. They go to temples on special occasions and are buried according to Buddhist rites.

Over the centuries, Buddhism has permeated every part of Japan's culture, molding their way of thinking and their architecture, art, literature, and morality.

Recommended reading: *Introducing Buddhism*, by Kodo Matsunami (Tuttle); *Religions in Japan*, edited by William K. Bunce (Tuttle); *Buddhism: Japan's Cultural Identity*, by Stuart D. B. Picken (Kodansha Int'l).

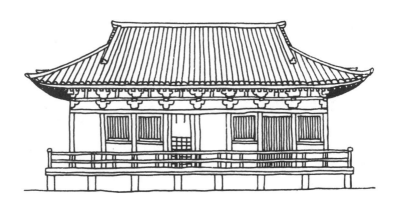

BUDDHIST TEMPLES / BUKKYO NO OTERA (Buke-yoe no oh-tay-rah)
Soon after the introduction of Buddhism into Japan in the early centuries,
Buddhist priests began traveling all over the country, seeking out places
that were sublime in their scenic beauty as sites on which to build temples.

As a result of this religious compulsion, which lasted for many centuries,
thousands of temples were built—some of them on a scale so large and
grand that they are startling even today.

Still today, there are over 100,000 Buddhist temples in Japan. See KYOTO;
NARA; etc.

BUDGET TRAVELING   It is possible to travel in Japan for extended periods of time and be comfortable and well fed and thoroughly enjoy yourself,
without spending the kind of money required at luxury hotels and exclusive
restaurants.

In fact, the Japan National Tourist Organization (JNTO) has prepared
special guides and other literature for people interested in budget traveling
These guides include places to stay (hotels, inns, lodges, youth hostels, etc.)
and tips on less expensive bus and train travel and dining in nontourist
restaurants.

Japan has a large number of Western-style hotels below the luxury class
that are comfortable, as well as interesting. Many are first class, but cost
about one-half or one-third as much as the name luxury hotels. Even those
that would be considered second class are comfortable and perfectly safe
for someone who is really economizing.

Food, always a major concern of travelers, presents no such problems in
Japan. There are thousands upon thousands of restaurants serving Western-
style dishes or Japanese and Chinese dishes that may sound different and
look different but still consist of meat, vegetables, and seafoods. Small
convenience markets selling cookies, crackers, candies, nuts, breads, canned
goods, and other familar items are plentiful and welcome touring visitors.

You can buy enough food in such shops to make three full meals for as
little as what you would pay for a snack in a popular tourist-type restaurant.

To take advantage of budget travel opportunities in Japan, check with the
nearest JNTO office (see OTHER SOURCES), and once you are in Japan
buy a copy of *Eating Cheap in Japan*.

Another important point: You do not have to be concerned about the
sanitary conditions in small, inexpensive-looking, neighborhood-type restaurants that cater to local residents. Their standards of cleanliness are among
the highest in the world.

You can categorize budget-priced Japanese restaurants by their location,
as well as their type: department store dining rooms, office building restaurants, special lunch menus at first-class hotels and restaurants, shopping
center restaurants, back-street restaurants, fast-food and franchised places,
and coffee shops with so-called morning service.

Japan's department stores have large dining rooms that are primarily operated for the convenience of their customers, rather than for profit. They usually have several choices of Japanese, Chinese, and Western dishes, along with soft drinks and beer—and they are good. Hours are generally 10:30 A.M. to 5:30 P.M.

Restaurants in office buildings—the general type, not the sushi or tempura specialty shops—are also moderately priced and serve various rice, noodle, and meat dishes.

Many first-class restaurants and hotel dining rooms have daily business-men's lunches or quick lunches during the week that are priced well below their regular menu choices.

Restaurants in underground shopping centers and clustered around rail-way stations, which cater primarily to younger people and ordinary workers, are budget-priced—especially for lunch and continental-style breakfast.

Back-street restaurants is a broader category, but basically these are small restaurants—in the basements or on the first and second floors of small buildings—that do not advertise in foreign-language media.

Foreign fast-food chains—all low priced—which abound in larger cities in Japan, include Dairy Queen, Denny's, Dom Dom, Doughnut Art, Kentucky Fried Chicken, Lottelia, McDonald's, Mosburger, Mr. Doughnut, Peter Pan, Sant Ole, and Wimpy.

Popular Japanese chains, which have extensive menus but are still moder-ately priced, include Fujiya, Morinaga, Lion, Coc d'Or and Benihana (which is not a specialty *teppan-yaki* steak house, as it is in the U.S., but a general menu restaurant).

Many coffee shops offer a special morning service that consists of a light breakfast for the price that one often pays in similar establishments for just a cup of coffee. There are also stand-up counters at train terminals where you can get coffee or tea, toast, and a boiled egg for a very moderate price.

All of the above categories of restaurants are in central downtown loca-tions. They do not have service charges, and tipping is not customary. Virtu-ally all have menus in English, as well as Japanese. Most have wax models of their dishes on display, and in many of them some of the staff speak enough English to get by.

If you are adventurous to any degree, you won't have any problem finding a clean, modestly priced restaurant wherever you are in Japan. In Tokyo, for example, there are some 90,000 of them!

BUILDINGS / BIRUDINGU (Bee-rue-ding-goo)   Except for castles, stor-age towers, and a few other special structures, all buildings in Japan were constructed of wood until the nineteenth century. Wood was plentiful and inexpensive. Japanese carpenters were masters at using it in aesthetically pleasing ways. It was practical in the humid climate of the country, and the Japanese long ago devised construction methods that made wooden buildings fairly earthquake resistant.

Both the world's oldest wooden building and the world's largest wooden building are in Japan. The former is the Horyu Temple in Nara, which was built in the latter half of the seventh century. The world's largest wooden structure, the Todai Temple, also in Nara, is 48.6 meters (159.45 feet) high, 57.3 meters (188 feet) wide; and 50.4 meters (165.35 feet) deep. Inside the Todai Temple is one of the world's largest statues of Buddha.

Because of the constant threat of earthquakes, Western-style brick and concrete buildings were limited to 31 meters in height until 1960, when new technology was introduced. Now there are high-rise buildings in most major Japanese cities. Several buildings in Tokyo are over 50 stories high, and they are a prominent feature of the skyline.

Since the appearance of high-rise buildings in Japan, there have been no major earthquakes to test their durability.

BUNRAKU (Boon-rah-kuu)   One of the three classical forms of theater in Japan, *bunraku*, or "puppetry," has been popular since the seventeenth century. Each of the puppets is manipulated by three puppeteers, who wear black robes with flaps covering their faces, even though they are generally not visible to the audience.

One puppeteer works the puppet's head and right hand, another one manipulates the left hand, and the third one works the feet—on male puppets. Female puppets have no feet, and the third puppeteer manipulates the skirts of female puppets to simulate walking and other leg movements.

Bunraku puppets perform stories that are told in special chants called *jouri* (joe-oou-ree), to the accompaniment of *shamisen* (shah-me-sane) music.

Puppet dolls consist of a head, trunk, hands, feet (on male dolls), and costume. They range in size from about one meter to a meter and a half.

Altogether, there are about 60 different puppet heads or characters, of which some 40 may play more than one role. Some *bunraku* puppets have moving eyes, eyebrows, mouths, and fingers.

Experienced puppeteers become masters at expressing emotions by subtle movements that make the dolls appear to be alive.

Osaka is considered the *bunraku* capital of Japan, and the *bunraku* theater there (the Bunraku Za) is regarded as its headquarters.

Developed at the same time as Japan's more famous *kabuki* (kah-buu-kee), *bunraku* deals with the same themes and was a more popular medium for playwrights than *kabuki*. Many of *kabuki's* most famous plays were originally written for the puppet theater.

Monzaemon Chikamatsu (1653–1724), who is often described as the Shakespeare of Japan, wrote many *bunraku* plays that were later adapted for *kabuki*. See CHIKAMATSU, MONZAEMON.

Recommended reading: *Bunraku—The Art of the Japanese Puppet Theater*, by Donald Keene (Kodansha International).

BUNYA PUPPETRY   *Bunya* is a style of puppetry that was originated in feudal Japan by a wandering minstrel named Bunya Okamoto. Later, another minstrel introduced the art to the island of Sado, in the Japan Sea, 35 miles off the coast of Niigata, in northwest Honshu.

The art took root there, and the island came to be regarded as its center. After World War II, *bunya* almost disappeared, but in 1971 it was designated an Important Intangible Cultural Property by the government and has since undergone a revival.

There are now 10 *bunya* troupes on Sado Island. They stage performances for local residents, as well as visitors, and tour the rest of the country.

BURIAL / MAISO (My-soe)   It is the law in Japan that the bodies of the deceased be cremated. The ashes may then be placed in a tomb or buried or kept wherever the survivors wish. Burial services are usually Buddhist in nature, but may be Shintoist. It was traditional for someone to stay up all night with the deceased on the first night after death.

See DYING IN JAPAN.

BUSH, LEWIS   An Englishman who went to Japan to lecture on literature at the Hirosaki and Yamagata high schools in 1934, Lewis Bush became an avid student of things Japanese and published his first book, *Japanalia*, in 1938. Bush was still in Japan when war broke out between Great Britain and Germany in 1940. He joined the Royal Naval Volunteer Reserve and was serving as a sub-lieutenant with an MTB flotilla in Hong Kong when he was captured by Japanese forces on Christmas Day in 1941.

Bush spent the remainder of the war years as a prisoner, first in Hong Kong and then in Omori, Tokyo, and Yokohama. From 1947 to 1954 he represented British film interests in Japan and then worked for the Japan Broadcasting Corporation (NHK) for several years. He was also a columnist for *The Japan Times*.

His postwar books include *Clutch of Circumstance*, which details the years he spent as a prisoner of war in Hong Kong and Japan; revisions of the original *Japanalia*; and *New Japanalia*, published in 1977.

In 1964, Bush was awarded the Order of the Rising Sun Third Class for his contributions to British-Japanese relations.

BUSHIDO (Boo-she-doe)   During Japan's Kamakura Period (1185–1333), the *samurai* warrior class that came into power based its personal and professional codes on Confucian concepts that eventually came to be identified as *bushido*, or the Way of the Warrior.

In *bushido*, loyalty to one's superior is the paramount morality, followed by an overwhelming sense of self-sacrifice, martial spirit, honor, justice, refined manners, frugality, purity, and modesty.

Death was the ultimate test of the *samurai's* adherence to *bushido*, and the *samurai* and their families were taught that it was their duty to make this final sacrifice for their clan lord. Death in battle and self-destruction on other occasions thus came to be glorified.

But a willingness to die for the sake of their lord and honor was not the only trait that distinguished the *bushido*-steeped *samurai*. The code demanded that its followers pursue both physical and spiritual training of the highest order and thus resulted in the development of a class of people who were extraordinarily disciplined and accomplished.

After the beginning of the Edo Period in 1603 and over two centuries of peace, much of this rigorous training in the precepts of *bushido* was gradually channeled into more constructive pursuits, such as art, architecture, literature, and various aspects of graceful living.

Recommended reading: *Bushido: The Soul of Japan*, by Inazo Nitobe (Tuttle).

BUSINESS GROUPS IN JAPAN   A key characteristic of the world of big business in Japan is the existence of several very large so-called Industrial Enterprise Groups made up of dozens of companies that regard themselves more or less as members of what might be called families or clans and cooperate with each other in various ways.

There are six major industrial groups and ten lesser ones. The major groups are Mitsubishi (made up of 139 companies); Sumitomo (108 companies); Mitsui (110 companies); Dai-Ichi Kangyo (117 companies), which has three subgroups: Furukawa (10 firms), Kawasaki (4 firms), NKB (16 firms); Fuyo (64 companies); and Sanwa (84 companies).

The lesser groups are: Tokai Bank (25 firms), Industrial Bank (23), Hitachi (38), Nippon Steel (40), Toyota (30), Nissan (27), Matsushita (25), Toshiba-IHI, Tokyu, and Seibu.

The six largest of the groupings are the offspring of the pre-1945 *zaibatsu*, which were totally controlled by individual families and were broken up during the Allied Military Occupation of Japan following the end of World War II.

It is often pointed out that if the Mitsubishi group were a conglomerate (which it certainly resembles), it would be over 40 percent larger than Exxon, the world's largest company.

Another primary characteristic of the economic structure of Japan is the existence of nine giant general trading companies (Sogo Shosha), along with dozens of smaller ones.

The nine giants of the industry are Mitsubishi Shoji, Mitsui & Co., C. Itoh & Co., Marubeni Corporation, Sumitomo Corp., Nissho Iwai, Toyo Menka,

Kanematsu-Gosho, and Nichmen—each of which is associated with one of the huge industrial enterprise groups. See TRADING COMPANIES.

BUSINESS JAPAN   A monthly magazine published by the Japan Industrial Newspaper (Nihon Kogyo Shimbun), *Business Japan* carries articles on Japanese management, technological developments, and relevant economic and political subjects. Contributors are both foreigners and Japanese, and it is one of the more interesting and useful English-language magazines on Japan. See OTHER SOURCES for address.

BUSINESS NIPPON   "Business Nippon" is a series of 30-minute TV programs, produced by Japan Cable Television Ltd. and distributed by the Keizai Koho Center (Japan Institute for Social and Economic Affairs), on business in Japan.

The programs, on ½- and ¾-inch videotape cassettes, cover management, industrial enterprises, marketing, energy, and international relations. All of the cassettes, except the industry films, are available for purchasing or borrowing from the KKC. See OTHER SOURCES.

In the management series are "Japan's Employment System," "Quality Control," "How a Japanese Company Trains Its Employees," "Industrial Robots & Labor Problems," "Japan's Wage Mechanism," "Job-Hunting System in Japan," and "Labor-Management Relations."

In the marketing series are "Japan's Distribution System," "How to Penetrate the Japanese Market," "Why Are the Prices of Imported Goods So Expensive?" "How to Invest in Japan," "Why Not Let the Sogo Sho-sha Solve Your Business Problems?" and "Manufacturing Enterprises and Their Retailers."

The tapes may be borrowed for use in Japan only and must be picked up in person and returned within two weeks.

BUSINESS PUBLICATIONS   Among the top weekly and monthly Japanese-language business publications in Japan are the weekly *Economist*, which is published by the giant Mainichi Newspaper Company: *Jitsugyo No Nihon (Industrial Japan)*, published by a company by the same name; *Nikkei Business*, a management-oriented biweekly, published by Nikkei-McGraw Hill; *Nikkei Mechanical*, a biweekly aimed at mechanical engineers, also published by Nikkei-McGraw Hill.

Also: *President*, a monthly that is affiliated with *Fortune* magazine of the U.S., with some 20 percent of its contents translated from *Fortune; Shukan Diamond*, a weekly for businesspeople who are concerned about both domestic and international problems; *Shukan Toyo Keizai (Oriental Economist Weekly)*; and *Zaikai*, a biweekly that caters to the top-level financial community in the country. See ZAIKAI.

CABARETS / KYABARE (K'yah-bah-ray)   To most Westerners, a cabaret and a nightclub are more or less synonymous, and the words are used interchangeably. But in Japan that is not the case. They are two quite different types of establishments.

The Japanese-style cabaret is a club or lounge or bar that features hostesses who are automatically assigned to all customers who come in. If the customer has a choice, he may request a specific hostess. Otherwise, he takes whoever is sent to his table.

The hostesses in cabarets may wear either Western-style dress or kimono. In some cabarets, kimono is the prescribed costume for all the hostesses, and in others dresses or gowns are the uniform of the day.

In cabarets, it is also automatic that individuals or groups are immediately served a plate or tray of peanuts, tiny *sembei* rice crackers, or some other kind of snack food—called *tsumami* (t'sue-mah-me)—that goes with drinking. And there is a charge for the *tsumami*, as well as for the hostesses.

Another characteristic of Japanese cabarets is that when business is slack, the hostesses—usually with the understanding and permission of customers—rotate, so that one group of customers ends up being entertained by two or three groups of hostesses, all of whom are charged for at separate, set rates. Not knowing anything about these established practices, foreign visitors who wander into cabarets often get very upset when they are billed for snacks and hostesses they didn't order.

Cabarets in Japan are used primarily by company managers or executives entertaining customers or customer-prospects at company expense. Bills are sent to their companies for payment.

Since most cabaret entertainment is charged, it is necessary for would-be patrons to first establish credit with the cabarets they want to patronize—another factor that foreign customers must also take into consideration.

Some of the more exclusive cabaret/lounges do not have menus or posted prices. Regular customers know approximately what their bill is going to be from the number of guests they have, how many hostesses are assigned to them, and how long they stay at the cabaret.

For this system to function effectively and smoothly, a great deal of goodwill and faith are necessary.

Every city and town of any size in Japan has its cabarets, varying in size from small lounges with three or four hostesses to huge theaterlike places with 500 or more hostesses.

The larger the cabaret, the more likely it is to have live entertainment (and to serve full meals). Some feature elaborate Las Vegas-type shows, with imported, as well as local, talent.

Another characteristic of Japanese cabaret patrons is that they like to visit more than one place during an evening; so it is common to see customers, already tipsy, going from one place to another.

Japanese cabarets are usually concentrated in well-known entertainment districts, and there may be a dozen or more in one district in the larger cities—and dozens of such districts in the major cities.

The legal definition of a cabaret in Japan is a club or bar that employs hostesses. See NIGHTCLUBS; MIZU SHOBAI.

CALLIGRAPHY / SHODO (Show-doe)   Calligraphy, the art of beautiful handwriting, has been practiced in the West for many centuries. But because of the nature of the ideograms with which the Japanese (and Chinese) write their languages, calligraphy there is a far more demanding art and has achieved far greater heights of artistic expression.

Skill in calligraphy has been a highly prized art in Japan for well over a thousand years, and for one long period in the history of the country, a person's character was equated with his or her ability with the writing brush.

Drawing the complicated *kanji* (khan-jee) characters with which Japanese is written forces all Japanese to spend a great deal of time practicing the art during their early school years. The aim of those who go on to develop skill as calligraphers is to imbue the strokes with a living personality of their own, expressing beauty, refinement, discipline, and an appreciation for the metaphysical and spiritual side of life.

It is customary for devotees of calligraphy to write auspicious words and poems on January 2 each year in an observance that is called First Writing of the Year, or *Hatsu Sho* (Hot-sue show).

Calligraphy has been a major art in Japan since the seventh and eighth centuries—or shortly after the *kanji* style of writing was introduced into Japan from China. *Shodo* is written—or drawn, rather—with a brush, using a dark, Japanese-style India ink (*sumi*), which is made from soot and glue.

The beauty of the drawing is an integral part of the message. The key to *shodo*, masters say, is that it must be done with the whole body and mind working in perfect unison—not just the hand.

Many of Japan's great figures of the past are known for their calligraphy, as well as their achievements in religion, education, statesmanship, and other fields.

Examples of calligraphy, printed on silk and paper scrolls, are traditionally displayed in the *tokonoma* (toe-koe-no-mah) of Japanese homes. See TOKONOMA.

CAPSULE HOTELS   Leave it to the Japanese to miniaturize hotels. Going after businesspeople and travelers who couldn't afford or didn't want to bother with regular hotels, entrepreneurs in the early 1980s introduced the "capsule hotel" to Tokyo and Osaka.

The capsule hotels, which offer sleeping berths and the use of a shower room, have been compared to railroad sleeping cars. The berths are lined up along aisles, and guests have to climb ladders to reach berths above the floor level.

Each capsule room is six feet long, three feet wide, and three feet high (just high enough for a small person to sit up in) and contains a bunk, a television set, a radio, a clock, and a reading light. The rooms are made of heat-resistant, molded plastic.

Some of the capsule hotels have sauna baths available, and some of them set aside some of their rooms for women. The rooms are also rented by the hour to people who want to take short naps. The capsule hotels have from 70 to 240 rooms. Rates are from one-fourth to one-third of what regular hotels charge.

Addresses and price lists for the capsule inns are available from Japan National Tourist Organization offices around the world.

Indications are that the capsule hotel concept will become another successful Japanese export—for airports, recreational camps, and possibly even prisons.

CARPENTERS / DAIKU (Die-kuu)   Since the civilization of Japan was virtually built on wood, carpentry has traditionally been one of the country's

leading professions. From earliest times, the profession was based on a master-apprentice system, in which young, preteenaged boys were assigned to master carpenters for many years before they could become journeymen.

Most carpenters belonged to *gumi* (guu-me), or "groups," headed by an *oyabun*, or "boss." Some of these *gumi* were quite large and controlled all carpentry work in designated areas.

The *daiku* of Old Japan were—and still are today, in many respects—a distinctive breed of men who took pride in their work. They dressed in sandals, leggings, and short *happi* jackets that were a mark of their trade, and they had a code of their own that set them apart from other tradesmen.

Throughout much of Japan's early history, the building of great temples, villas, castles, and palaces was an ongoing event—now in this part of the country and then in another. It was thus common for crews of *daiku* to travel about the country, and often stay away from their homes for years when engaged in huge projects like the shrines of Nikko.

One of the very special, but tragic, reasons for the importance of carpenters in early Japan was the incidence of fires. With fatal regularity, Japan's cities of wood and paper were swept by conflagrations that reduced great areas of them to ashes.

Such fires were so common in Edo (Tokyo) during the Tokugawa Shogunate (1603–1868) that people would gather at night on the low hills of the city to watch them—a practice that came to be known as viewing the Flowers of Edo.

CASTLES / SHIRO (She-roe)   The first castles in Japan, simple forts known as *ki* (kee), were in use by the first century B.C. As the centuries passed, these forts became more elaborate and more permanent.

These earliest castles were built entirely for defensive purposes, and were located in places that were the easiest to defend—in rugged passes and so on.

It was not until near the end of the fourteenth century that castles began to take the form that is known today—large edifices of stone and wood, but still primarily in mountain passes and other places difficult for enemies to approach.

With the appearance of Nobunaga Oda and Hideyoshi Toyotomi on the scene in the mid-1500s, when they began to consolidate the feudal fiefs under their military rule, the nature of warfare changed from basically single combat or combat in small groups to battles between large armies.

This led to the construction of larger and more formidable castles on plains and low hills surrounded by plains, which afforded the defenders a wide view of the countryside. These new castles, which were built to function as places of residence as well as forts, were usually surrounded by one or more moats, with high stone ramparts along the inner bank.

There were high wooden or stone walls along the ramparts, with spaced holes through which the defenders could fire upon attackers. The center of each castle was called the Hon Maru or Center Circle and featured a high tower.

When the Tokugawa Shogunate came under attack by Imperialists in 1867, there were 182 such castles throughout Japan. Among the most famous were the ones in Hikone, Inuyama, Kokura, Himeji, Iwakuni, Komabi, Hiroshima, Kanazawa, Kumamoto, Inaba, Kochi, Matsumae, Maruoka, Matsue, Matsuyama, Niji, Okezaki, Osaka, Sendai, Wakayama, and Uwajima.

The Nagoya Castle, built in 1611 by Kiyomasa Kata, was regarded as one of the finest castles in the country. Its walls were 15 to 18 feet thick. Its five-story *donjon* (tower) was 144 feet high. The roof was made of copper, and the scales of decorative dolphins at the ends of the roof were made of pure gold. (One of these dolphins was loaned to an exhibit in Vienna in 1863. The ship returning it to Japan sank off the coast of Izu Peninsula, and it was six months before the gold dolphin was recovered and returned to the roof of the castle.)

Some 150 of these castles were destroyed in the fighting that precipitated the fall of the shogunate and the restoration of the emperor to power in the late 1860s. Others, including the Nagoya Castle, were destroyed during the bombing raids of World War II.

After the war, several of the greater castles were completely or partially restored and now serve as impressive reminders of Japan's feudal age. These include the Hikone Castle and the castles in Himeji, Hiroshima, Inaba, Inuyama, Iwakuni, Kanazawa, Kochi, Kokura, Komaki, Kumamoto, Matsumae, Maruoka, Matsue, Matsuyama, Niji, Okazaki, Osaka, Sendai, Wakayama, and Uwajima.

See individual listings. Recommended reading: *Feudal Architecture Of Japan (Castles & Mansions)*, by Kiyoshi Hirai (Weatherhill).

CATS / NEKO (Nay-koe)   Cats have a long history in Japan and are interwoven into the culture. They are often depicted as having magical powers and being both ungrateful and evil. At the same time, they were highly prized at the Imperial Court in ancient times—a practice also imported from China.

Because cats with long tails were generally regarded as more likely to possess supernatural powers, short-tailed cats were preferred (and those born with tails often had them snipped off).

The best-known cats in Japan include the *Nemuro Neko* (Nay-muu-roe Nay-koe), or *Sleeping Cat*, at the entrance of Ieyasu Tokugawa's mausoleum in Nikko, carved by one of Japan's greatest sculptors, Hidari Jingoro (Left-Handed Jingoro); and statues of *maneki-neko* (mah-nay-kee nay-koe), or "beckoning cats," often found in front of shops in *geisha*-house districts, where they are used to entice customers.

CERAMIC WARE / SETO MONO (Say-toe moe-no)   The Japanese word for ceramic ware literally means "Seto things" or things from Seto, because the area around Seto City, in the Chubu district near Nagoya, has been a ceramic ware center since the thirteenth century.

The manufacture of ceramic ware has been important in Japan since prehistoric times—two of the country's major prehistoric periods are named after earthenware associated with these ages (*jomon* and *yayoi*).

But it was in the fifth and sixth centuries, following the importation of new techniques from Korea and China, that Japanese potters began turning out beautiful, high-quality artistic ceramics. As the generations passed, they developed their own unique techniques and styles.

Among the best-known name categories of ceramics today are *oribe-yaki* (oh-ree-bay-yah-kee), *kyo-yaki* (k'yoe-yah-kee), *shino-yaki* (she-no-yah-kee), and *raku-yaki* (rah-kuu-yah-kee). Famous Japanese porcelain styles include *kutani-yaki* (kuu-tah-nee-yah-kee), *arita-yaki* (ah-ree-tah-yah-kee), and *kiyomizu-yaki* (k'yoe-me-zoo-yah-kee).

Note: The difference between ceramics and porcelain is in the materials, as well as the firing temperatures. The main ingredient in ceramics is clay, and ceramics are fired at about 1,000 degrees centigrade. Porcelain is made out of a mixture of crushed kaolin, quartz, and feldspar stone, and it is fired at temperatures beginning at about 1,300 degrees centigrade and up. Porcelain is still sometimes referred to as China, because China was originally its main source.

Recommended reading: *The World of Japanese Ceramics*, by Herbert H. Sanders, with Kenkichi Tomimoto (Kodansha International).

CHAMBERLAIN, PROF. BASIL HALL   One of the best known of the foreign scholars who went to Japan shortly after the fall of the Tokugawa Shogunate in 1868, Prof. Basil Hall Chamberlain taught for many years at the Imperial University of Tokyo, but is primarily remembered because of two popular-styled books he wrote about Japan—*Things Japanese* and *A Handbook for Travellers in Japan*—the latter borrowing heavily from a book called *Handbook for Central and Northern Japan*, written by Sir Ernest Satow and Lt. A.G.S. Hawes, which was published in 1881.

CHANBARA MOVIES (Chan-bah-rah)   These are historical movies depicting events that took place during Japan's early days and later feudal periods, especially during the period from 1192 until 1868, when the country was ruled by *daimyo* lords and sword-carrying *samurai*.

Chanbara refers specifically to action movies, in which the heroes and villains battle it out with swords. The word refers to the sound swords make when several are clanged together.

This genre of movies has its popular stars (Toshiro Mifune was one during his early years), and it is one of the most popular movie forms in Japan. The movies are often based on the lives of real persons and on true historical events.

The *chanbara* are an excellent medium for getting a feel for what Japan was like in its prefeudal and feudal ages because the settings and manners of the times are very accurately portrayed.

CHERRY BLOSSOMS / SAKURA NO HANA (Sah-kuu-rah no Hah-nah) Cherry blossoms have been the national flower of Japan since ancient times —apparently because of the extraordinary beauty of the blossoms, as well as their fragility and short lifetime.

The custom of cherry blossom viewing is also an old one, and it is still today an aesthetic pursuit that each year attracts millions of people to well-known groves of cherry trees.

The *samurai* of feudal Japan were especially attracted to cherry blossoms, seeing a close similarity in the tenuous short life of the beautiful blossoms and their own obligation to die for their lord at a moment's notice.

There are over 100 varieties of cherry trees in Japan, and they bloom at different times in the spring, depending on their location and type. The first to burst forth are in Okinawa sometime in February. Some trees in southern Kyushu begin blooming in late March. The season then gradually spreads northward, reaching Hokkaido in the middle of May.

Virtually every area in Japan has its well-known spots for cherry blossom viewing. Among those that have been nationally famous for centuries are Mt. Yoshino, near Kyoto and Nara; Ueno, in Tokyo, and Hirosaki, in Aomori Prefecture.

CHESTNUTS / KURI (Kuu-ree)   Roasted chestnuts, a popular snack item in Japan for centuries, have traditionally been sold by two kinds of vendors —one in a regular shop and the other selling the tasty nuts from a wheeled pushcart.

Both types of vendors take advantage of the same advertising technique —they let the distinctive aroma of the roasting nuts herald their presence.

Chestnut stores can be found on busy shopping streets and in centers around commuter terminals. The pushcart vendors prowl the streets of entertainment and shopping districts, especially in the wintertime, when the hot nuts are particularly delicious.

CHIBA (Chee-bah)   Chiba is both a prefecture and a city of nearly 600,000 that serves as its capital. The prefecture encompasses Boso Peninsula, which adjoins Tokyo on the east and forms the northeastern shore of Tokyo Bay.

Chiba has been settled since very early times, first as an agricultural area and, since the 1960s and '70s, as a major industrial zone—with most of the industrial development along the coast of Tokyo Bay on reclaimed land.

The prefecture has numerous historical sites and contemporary recreational areas, including swimming beaches, the Funabashi Health Center (one of the largest recreational centers in Japan), and the Tokyo Disneyland, or Magic Kingdom.

The prefecture has several famous temples, including the Chiba Temple, founded in 709 by Priest Gyoki. See DISNEYLAND.

CHIKAMATSU, MONZAEMON (Chee-kah-mot-sue, Moan-zie-moan) Japan's greatest playwright, who is often compared with Shakespeare, Monzaemon Chikamatsu was born in 1653 to a *samurai* family in the service of the Lord of Mori.

Rather than take up the arts of fighting, Chikamatsu entered a Buddhist temple and later went to Kyoto, where he went to work for a high court noble named Ichijo.

Chikamatsu later left the service of Lord Ichijo to devote himself to writing *kabuki* and *bunraku* puppet plays and *joruri* dramatic poetry full-time. Chikamatsu's writings (of which there are many) are said to reflect the great insights into human nature that are characteristic of works by Shakespeare. He died in 1724.

Some of Chikamatsu's most popular plays have been translated into English by Prof. Asataro Miyamori.

CHILDREN'S SONGS / KODOMO-NO UTA (Koe-doe-moe-no uu-tah) Children's songs, most of them passed down for generations, are especially popular in Japan and are a distinctive part of the lives of all children.

One of the most popular of the numerous songs is about the legend of the Badgers of Shojo Temple, who listened to the chief priest teaching songs to the local children and learned how to keep time with the music by beating on their protruding bellies. The only problem was that they became so enthusiastic some of them beat themselves to death. They were buried by the kindly priest, who later won a rich lottery and was able to refurbish the temple.

The badgers song, composed by Ujo Noguchi in honor of the legend, is known by virtually everyone in Japan. It goes like this:

Sho, sho, Shojoji
Shojo no niwa wa,
Tsun, tsun, tsukiyo da
Minna dete koi, koi, koi.
Oira no tomodachi
Pon, poko, pon no pon

In the garden of Shojoji
Under the harvest moon,
Come, everyone,
For our friends
Are beating their drums
Pon, poko, pon!

CHINA TOWN   Internationally known for its 70-odd Chinese restaurants, numerous bars, cabarets, teahouses, and shops selling Chinese foodstuffs and souvenirs, China Town is one of the most popular districts in Yokohama.

It is located about 500 meters south of Yamashita Park, near where one of the first foreign communities in Japan was situated (behind a great barrier fence).

The attractions of China Town draw people from Tokyo and neighboring cities throughout the week.

CHINDON-YA (Cheen-doan-yah)   *Chindon-ya* are street musicians who are hired by businesses and others to promote openings and public events. They wear period costumes and usually have a drum beater, along with flute and *shamisen* players.

They carry banners and other signs and make a colorful procession as they parade through the streets, playing their instruments and engaging in comic routines.

The sound of the *chindon-ya* (whence the name comes) is very distinctive, and it is bound to attract the children of a neighborhood and bring a smile to the faces of adults.

CHINESE / CHUGOKU-JIN (Chuu-go-kuu-jeen)   There are some 55,000 Chinese who are permanent residents of Japan, primarily in the Tokyo and Yokohama areas. Virtually all of the Chinese who work are engaged in one kind of business or another or work for foreign companies; Japanese companies do not hire them. See FOREIGN WORKERS IN JAPAN.

Most self-employed Chinese are in the restaurant business or operate import-export companies.

CHINESE FOOD / CHUGOKU RYORI (Chuu-go-kuu rio-ree)   There are an estimated 55,000 Chinese restaurants in Japan, including several nationally known chains. Most of them are the small neighborhood-type restaurant that the average Westerner would not recognize as Chinese.

Regular Chinese restaurants, or those that offer menus similar to Chinese restaurants in China, Hong Kong, Taipei, and other Asian centers, number in the several hundred and cater to the more affluent.

While the neighborhood *Chugoku ryoriya* mainly offer noodle and rice dishes that have been somewhat Japanized over the decades, the international-class restaurants boast the same dishes one expects to see in a first-class Chinese restaurant, regardless of its location.

All of the first-class Chinese restaurants are run by Chinese, and a number of them import their chefs from Hong Kong or Taiwan. Some of the best Chinese restaurants in Tokyo are the Jade Garden, Tokyo Dai Hanten, Akasaka Hanten, Mandarin Palace, and the Nan-Goku Shukka in Harajuku.

CHOCHIN (Choe-cheen)   *Chochin*, the beautiful paper lanterns that accompany many Japanese festivals and announce the presence of bars and traditional-style restaurants, are made of thick, oiled paper stretched over bamboo frames.

Chochin are most often red but also come in other colors, such as white, black and yellow. They are a distinctive and nostalgic reminder of traditional Japan, adding a special ambience to the contemporary scene.

CHOPSTICKS / O'HASHI (Oh-hah-she)   Chopsticks, as primary eating utensils, were already in use in China around 2000 B.C., and made their first appearance in Japan sometime in the early centuries A.D. The ease in making them and their utter simplicity appealed to the Japanese, and they were soon adopted as the only eating utensil—soups were sipped from the bowl, and larger pieces of meat, seafood, and vegetables were chopped up in the process of preparation.

There are several kinds of *o'hashi*, including metal ones for cooking. In homes, they are usually made of ivory, bamboo, or plastic. In less expensive restaurants, they are usually made of soft wood and are still attached at the top, so that diners will know they have never been used.

These restaurant chopsticks are called *waribashi* (wah-ree bah-she), or half-split chopsticks.

It takes only a short while to become adept at using *o'hashi*, if you start out holding them the right way—the bottom one in the crook of your thumb and hand and held with a slight amount of pressure against your ring finger, and the top one held between the thumb and the first two fingers. The bottom stick is kept stationary. You move only the top one, in a grasping motion.

A set of ivory chopsticks makes a much-appreciated gift. (In exclusive Chinese restaurants, the chopsticks are almost always long and heavy and made of plastic or ivory. They are more difficult to handle than the lightweight *waribashi* or Japanese-size plastic versions.)

CHRISTIANITY IN JAPAN   Francis Xavier, a Catholic missionary belonging to the Society of Jesus, is credited with introducing Christianity to Japan in 1549, upon his arrival in Kagoshima, Kyushu, from Macau.

Used to dealing with overlords, Xavier soon made friends with members of Japan's ruling class, who were primarily interested in Western technology and science and gave him permission to teach the Catholic faith in exchange for gifts and some of his knowledge of the outside world.

With the blessings of a number of clan lords and other high personages, Christianity spread rather rapidly in Southern Japan, and by the early 1600s there were an estimated 750,000 converts. The peasants liked the human rights ideals of the Catholic religion.

By this time, missionaries from other Christian sects had arrived in Japan and, as was their wont, soon became involved in political intrigue and machinations against each other.

Fearing that the growing influence of the foreign missionaries might endanger the feudal government, *Shogun* Hidetada Tokugawa banned Christianity in 1613. Most of the foreign missionaries in Japan were banished from the country, and, for several decades thereafter, Japanese Christians were vigorously persecuted.

In their final stand against the *shogun's* forces, several thousand converts, having taken refuge in a castle on Shimabara Peninsula, were besieged and slaughtered. See SHIMABARA.

The feudal government's campaign to completely rid Japan of Christians of whatever nationality resulted in the renunciation of the faith by most Japanese converts, but a few thousand of them continued to practice their beliefs in secret and eventually came to be known as the *Kakure* (Kah-kuu-ray), or Hidden, Christians.

In 1859, shortly after Japan's feudal government started breaking up and the country began to establish diplomatic relations with the U.S. and Europe, missionaries once again began flocking to the islands.

At present, there are an estimated 490,000 Protestants and 370,000 Catholics in Japan—a very significant sign that given a free choice, the Japanese are not particularly attracted to Christianity.

There are several Christian-run universities in Japan, the best known being International Christian University (ICU) and Sophia University, or Jochi Daigaku (Joe-chee Die-gah-kuu), both in Tokyo.

Japan's first Catholic cardinal, Tatsuo Doi, was appointed in 1960.

CINEMAS / EIGAKAN (Aa-e-gah-khan)   There are presently about 550 movie theaters in Japan, most of them owned by the country's two largest entertainment conglomerates, Toho (Toe-hoe) and Shochiku (Sho-chee-kuu). The theaters show Japanese as well as foreign films, the latter usually with subtitles.

CITIES / SHI (She)   Despite its small size, Japan is second only to the U.S. in number of large cities. The reason for this exceptional number of populous cities is the clan-feudal system that existed for several centuries. There were some 270 clans in the country prior to 1868, each with its own boundaries and each, to a considerable extent, self-sufficient.

Each of the clans had its own headquarters, usually centered around the castle of the *daimyo* (die-m'yoe), or lord. As the long decades of the Muromachi (1392–1573) and Tokugawa eras (1603–1868) passed, these headquarters grew into cities.

Most of the earliest of these castles were built in mountainous areas for strategic purposes. With the coming of peace, many of the lords abandoned their old castles and had new ones built in plains areas, where most of the people lived. They required their warrior retainers and the leading merchants to move into the vicinity of their new castles, which resulted in the rapid development of new communities.

Some of the best known of these *joka machi* (joe-kah mah-chee), or "castle towns," are Odawara, built around the Hojo clan's Odawara Castle; Kai-Fuchu, built around the Takeda clan castle; Suruga-Fuchi, built around the Imagawa clan castle; and Yamaguchi, built around the Ouchi clan castle. Osaka, Fushimi, and Sendai are pure castle towns. Tokyo and Nagoya are also *joka machi*.

More than half of every castle town was reserved for the homes of *samurai* families, which were built in circles around the castle. Outside of this circular area were the commercial districts, where the merchants lived and worked. Immediately beyond the merchant district were the homes and shops of craftspeople and artists. Furthest out was the temple area, which was intended to be the first line of defense in case of an attack.

Each castle town was surrounded by a moat or a high dirt embankment. All the streets were built in a labyrinthine layout, so that none of them led directly to the castle.

The main castle towns (all of which are cities today) were Ueno, Tsu, and Matsusaka, in Mie Prefecture; Hikone and Nagahama, in Shiga Prefecture; Maizuru, Miyazu, Kameoka, and Fukuchiyama, in Kyoto Prefecture; Osaka, Kishiwada, Ibaraki, and Ikeda, in Osaka Prefecture; Miki, Himeji, Tatsuno, Ako, Sumoto, Toyo-oka, Itami, and Amagasaki, in Hyogo Prefecture; and Yamato-Koriyama, in Nara.

Also: Wakayama, Tanabe, and Shingu, in Wakayama; Tottori, in Tottori Prefecture; Matsue and Hamada, in Shimane; Okayama, Tsuyama, and Takahashi, in Okayama; Hiroshima, Miyoshi, and Mihara, in Hiroshima; Hagi, Iwakuni, and Tokuyama, in Yamaguchi; Tokushima, in Tokushima; Takamatsu, in Kagawa; Saijo, Imabari, Matsuyama, and Ozu, in Ehime; Kochi and Sukumo, in Kochi; Fukuoka, Kurume, and Yanagawa, in Fukuoka; Saga, Kashima, and Karatsu, in Saga; Fukue and Omura, in Nagasaki; Kikuchi, Uto, Hitoyoshi, and Yatsushiro, in Kumamoto; Oita, Nakatsu, Hita, Kitsuki, and Usuki, in Oita; Nobeoka and Saito, in Miyazaki; and Kagoshima, in Kagoshima Prefecture.

In addition to Japan's castle towns, there were five other types of towns, many of which grew up to be cities. These include *Shukuba Machi* (shuu-kuu-bah mah-chee), or Inn Towns; *Monzen Machi* (moan-zen mah-chee), or In Front of Temple Gate Towns; *Jinai Machi* (jee-nie mah-chee), or Towns Within Temples; *Ichiba Machi* (ee-chee-bah mah-chee), or Market Towns; and *Minato Machi* (me-nah-toe mah-chee), or Port Towns.

Inn Towns were towns that developed as way stations for travelers along feudal-age roads. They became especially important during the Tokugawa Period, when all the *daimyo* lords were required to spend every other year in Edo (Tokyo), making it necessary for them to march to and from their fiefs, with large numbers of retainers, in alternate years. See PROCESSIONS OF THE FEUDAL LORDS.

To accommodate these privileged travelers, these stopover towns developed elaborate inns for the lords and their closest retainers, called *honjin* (hone-jeen) or "headquarters." Less ostentatious inns called *waki honjin* (wah-kee hone-jeen), or "backup headquarters," were built for the other members of the lords' entourage. *Chaya* (chah-yah), or "restaurant-entertainment houses," grew up around these two types of inns.

Among the more famous of these Inn Towns that are now cities are Nabari, Otsu, Moriyama, Moriguchi, Himeji, Gojo, Ibara, Otake, and Takeo.

In Front of Temple Gate Towns are towns that grew from restaurants and shops that lined the approaches to famous temples. Those that became cities include Ise, Yawata, Osaka, Yao, Nishinomiya, Gobo, Shingu, Soja, Kasaoka, Tokushima, Zentsuji, Kanonji, and Okinawa.

Towns Within Temples began in the compounds of temples—mostly Shinshu sect temples, because this sect built huge compounds to ward off attacks by other sects and had its followers establish their homes and businesses inside the compounds. The biggest of these compounds was around the Ishiyama Hongan Temple, which enclosed six towns that finally merged to form Osaka, one of the great cities of the world.

Beginning on the southernmost island of Kyushu, Japan's major cities include Kagoshima, Fukuoka, Hiroshima, Kita-Kyushu, Kobe, Osaka, Kyoto, Nagoya, Yokohama, Kawasaki, Tokyo, Sendai, and Sapporo. In addition, there are literally dozens of smaller cities that have been and still are of special importance in Japan. These include Nara, Kamakura, and Nikko. See individual listings.

Japan has 19 cities with populations over half a million, 10 of which are well above the million mark: Kawasaki, Kita-Kyushu, Fukuoka, Kobe, Sapporo, Kyoto, Nagoya, Osaka, Yokohama, and Tokyo.

CLARK, DR. WILLIAM S.   A chemist and botanist who was born in Massachusetts in 1826, studied in Germany, taught at Amherst College, and then became the president of Massachusetts Agricultural College, Dr. William S. Clark was invited by the Japanese government in 1876 to establish an agricultural college in Sapporo, Hokkaido, and serve as its first dean.

Although Clark taught at the new college for only one year, he left an extraordinary legacy, and his memory is still honored by the Japanese. When he left Sapporo his students rode with him on horseback to Shimamatsu, 24 kilometers south of Sapporo. His parting words to them were: "Boys, be ambitious!" and this has since been accepted as the motto of millions of young Japanese boys. Several of Clark's students went on to become celebrated scholars.

In 1960, the city of Sapporo built the Clark Memorial Hall to honor his memory.

CLASS DISTINCTIONS   Prior to the end of World War II, Japanese society had a privileged upper-class aristocracy made up of former Imperial princes and clan lords, along with a number of immensely wealthy families, mostly *zaibatsu* owners, whose wealth gave them aristocratic standing. At the end of the war, all class distinctions were legally abolished, except for those pertaining to the Imperial family.

With two more conspicuous exceptions, Japan is now virtually classless. Even great wealth does not grant or guarantee special privileges. The two exceptions are the Imperial family and a fairly large group of people formerly known as Eta (Eh-tah), not counted in the general population, who are the descendants of a caste that was associated with the slaughter of animals and working with animal by-products.

Over the centuries, these people came to be discriminated against, segregated in certain areas, and prohibited from changing their occupation or marrying outside their group.

There are occasional public indications that not all of the prejudice against this group has disappeared.

The Japanese, in fact, have been conditioned during centuries of isolation and insularity to distinguish immediately and completely between themselves and anyone who is not racially Japanese. Being a Japanese is not just a matter of nationality—it is racial first, ethnic second, and political third, with the last two not counting, except in the legal sense.

Generally speaking, social status in Japan is determined by one's own ability, ambition, and success in any professional field.

CLIMATE / KIKO (Ke-kooh)   One of the best ways to understand and appreciate Japan's climate is to equate it with the climate on the east coast of the United States, from Bangor, Maine, to Jacksonville, Florida.

Japan's four main islands stretch some 3,000 kilometers (1,860 miles) in a north-southwest direction. The northernmost island of Hokkaido is in the subarctic zone, and the southern end of the southernmost main island of Kyushu is in the subtropic zone.

The next most important factor in Japan's climate is ranges of high, rugged mountains that run nearly the full length of the country, effectively dividing it into two conspicuously different climatic zones.

The Japan Sea or Asian continent side of Japan is buffeted by cold winter winds from Siberia, Korea, and Northern China, bringing regular heavy winter snows that have resulted in the common reference to the Niigata Prefecture area as *Yuki Guni* (You-key Goony), or Snow Country.

At the same time, the famous *Kuroiso* (Kuu-roy-soh), or Black Current, that comes up from the South Pacific bathes the Pacific side of Japan, keeping the temperatures moderate.

(Some Japanese authorities believe that the famous Kuroshio Current was responsible for bringing both people and various agricultural products to Japan long before the beginning of recorded history.)

All of Japan, except for Hokkaido (and mountainous highlands), has hot, humid summers and a pronounced rainy season, called *baiu* (by-you), which usually begins in early June and lasts until mid-July. Some inland areas of Honshu and Shikoku tend to be very dry, except during the annual rainy season and when typhoons hit the islands.

On the Pacific side of Honshu, the largest and most heavily populated of the four main islands, winters range from mild to relatively cold. Dry, clear days, sometimes with wind, are common in the winter months.

On the Japan Sea side, there is very little rain in the summer, and the winters are marked by an abundance of snow. The mountainous areas of the islands are cool in the summer and cold in the winter, with varying amounts of snow. The further north and west you go, the more snow you get.

Hokkaido, the northernmost island, is cool in the summer and very cold in the winter. It has a great deal of snow in the winter but gets very little rain in comparison with the islands to the south.

Japan's famous Inland Sea area—the sea separating Shikoku, Honshu, and Kyushu—is noted for its relatively mild winters.

Japan's typhoon season usually begins in late summer and may last as late as November. While very important to Japan's rice crop and its other water needs, the annual typhoons are responsible for considerable wind and flood damage virtually every year.

The four seasons are distinct in Japan and have played fundamental roles in the development of Japanese culture, influencing virtually every aspect of life, from housing, wearing apparel, food, and arts and crafts to the appreciation of nature in general and to aesthetics in particular.

See individual cities for local weather information.

CLINICS / KURINIKU (Kuu-ree-nee-kuu)   Because of the closed nature of Japan's hospitals, which generally do not allow outside doctors to bring their patients in for any purpose—which also prevents hospital doctors from earning higher incomes—there are a very large number of clinics in the country that, for all practical purposes, are small private hospitals.

These thousands of clinics are owned and operated by doctors who are in private practice, often without any kind of relationship with university and public hospitals. Doctors who are on the staffs of various hospitals also sometimes own or are in partnership with private clinics.

Many Japanese clinics and some hospitals do not have emergency rooms and may refuse to accept patients brought in on an emergency basis. In such cases, it is usually necessary to call ahead and make arrangements.

CLOISONNÉ / SHIPPOYAKI (Sheep-poe-yah-key)   First introduced into Japan from Persia and Europe through China in the eighth century, the art of cloisonné flourished for a while and then died out. It was reintroduced from Korea in the seventeenth century and has been very popular since the nineteenth century, following numerous improvements in the technology.

Cloisonné refers to a style of decorating ceramic, glass, and various metals by baking onto them designs created from vitreous enamels.

Japan is especially known for high-quality personal ornaments and craftworks decorated in this style. The Japanese word *shippoyaki* means something like "Seven Precious Stones Baked Ceramic."

Some cloisonné artists use wire to outline their designs.

COFFEE SHOPS / KISSATEN (Kees-sah-tane)   Coffee shops have played a special and important role in Japanese life since they first appeared in the 1920s—a role that became even more important following World War II.

The first coffee shops in Japan were founded by Japanese who had spent several years abroad, mostly in France, and wanted to recreate some of the ambience of Paris's famous cafés.

These first shops eventually ran into trouble with the prewar militaristic government and were closed down. Following the Pacific War and the revolutionary changes that were introduced into the lives of the Japanese, the coffee shops came back in a new form and were an immediate success.

These new postwar coffee shops were short-order restaurants that also served coffee, tea, and, later, carbonated drinks. Their patrons were businesspeople, who needed a place to meet and talk to customers, and the millions of young Japanese men and women, now with a modest amount of discretionary money to spend, who found the coffee shops ideal places to meet their friends and dates. See COURTING.

As time went by, several different kinds of coffee shops developed— usually classified by the kind of recorded music they offered. There were jazz coffee shops, chamber music coffee shops, folk-song coffee shops, etc. There were also *bijin* (bee-jeen), or "beautiful girl" coffee shops—so-called because their waitresses were picked for their beauty.

Tokyo also usually has a number of coffee shops that cater especially to unmarried foreign patrons—as an attraction for Japanese who want to meet foreigners.

There are at least 10 different categories of coffee shops in Japan today, and while they are now less used by businesspeople as extensions of their offices, they are as popular as ever as meeting places and for light snacks. Altogether, there are more than 132,000 coffee shops in Japan.

COMICS / MANGA (Mahn-gah)   Comics apparently have a universal appeal, but it is difficult to imagine a country where they are more popular than they are in Japan. Having been a highly sophisticated people for many centuries, the Japanese have long had an intense interest in oral narratives with a humorous slant, humorous writing, and comic entertainment.

Wood-block prints with humorous and often ribald themes were popular during the middle and later years of the long Tokugawa Shogunate Period (1603–1868). This impulse was generally stifled during the early nationalistic decades of the 1900s, but, with the coming of an open society and affluence after the end of the Pacific War, cartoons and cartoon books proliferated.

By the mid-1960s, there was a flood of comic magazines and books on the market, some of them achieving a circulation of well over a million copies a month in very short periods.

Now a major part of the publishing industry, they range in subject matter from the exploits of superheroes and space adventures to historical themes featuring *samurai* or *ninja* (neen-jah) characters. Many of the *manga* are overtly sexual, often with strong macho and masochistic themes.

In 1983, Frederik Schodt, an American graduate of a Japanese language school, published a book called *Manga! Manga!* (*Comics! Comics!*) in Japanese, which became a controversial popular seller. In the book, Schodt defended comics, saying they provide needed escape and fantasy for young Japanese who are burdened by heavy social pressures.

Schodt says it is television, not *manga*, that causes negative reading habits among school-age Japanese.

See NINJA; PUBLISHING; LITERATURE.

COMIC STORYTELLERS / RAKUGO (Rah-kuu-go)   One of the special categories of traditional entertainment in Japan is that of the *rakugo*, or "comic storyteller." Dating back to feudal times, the *rakugo* specialize in long, anecdotal monologues that are characterized by many twists and turns, numerous puns, and surprise or witty endings.

These professional raconteurs appear regularly on nationwide television shows and are among the most celebrated artists in Japan. There have been two foreign *rakugo* artists in Japan—one of them an American named Robert Strickland, who is known as the operator of a steak house in Kyoto that employs orphaned, mixed-blood youngsters. The other man was an Englishman named Black.

The language skills and cultural knowledge necessary to become a recognized *rakugo* artist are formidable, even for a Japanese. That Strickland and

Black were able to achieve such an accomplishment is testimony to their fluency and knowledge.

COMMUTING   With over 80 percent of Japan's limited land area mountainous and with inadequate housing in the central portions of its major cities, commuting from 30 minutes to two hours or more is a way of life for millions of Japanese. It is not uncommon for people to commute two hours each way going to and from work.

Most people commute by public transportation—trains, subways and buses—since existing roadways and streets cannot accommodate more than 10 percent or 15 percent of the commuting public, and parking space is not available for more than 5 percent to 10 percent.

As a result, Japan's commuter transportation system is among the most crowded in the world. Its trains and subways are so jammed during rush hours that extra platform attendants are sometimes hired to help push people into coaches, so the doors will close.

In the wintertime, when people wear heavy coats, the crowding is even worse because the extra bulk from the coats means less room for people. Train and subway coaches carrying four times their rated capacity are commonplace.

Despite this extraordinary strain on the commuter systems in Japan, they are incredibly efficient, keeping split-second schedules that are the envy of much of the world.

COMPANIES / KAISHA (Kie-shah)   There are some six million recorded enterprises or business establishments in Japan—not including farmers, fishermen, or proprietary forest workers. Of this huge number, approximately 70 percent are unincorporated.

In manufacturing industries, over half of the companies have fewer than five employees. Only about half of one percent, or some 4,000 companies, have 300 employees or more. Among 840,000 manufacturing companies, 434,000 have 1–4 employees, 190,000 have 5–9 employees, 149,000 have 10–29 employees, 31,000 have 30–49 employees, 21,000 have 50–99 employees, and 12,000 have 100–299 employees.

In the wholesale/retail trades in Japan, there are 2,868,000 enterprises. Of them, 2,176,000 have 1–4 employees, 434,000 have 5–9 employees, 192,000 have 10–29 employees, 26,000 have 30–49 employees, 13,000 have 50–99 employees, 5,000 have 100–299 employees, and 1,000 have 300 or more employees.

There is a very large gap between the fringe benefits, pensions, and wages paid by the smaller enterprises (those with fewer than 300 employees) and those paid by the larger firms. Wages at smaller enterprises are anywhere from 30 percent to 40 percent less than what they are in large companies.

This disparity accounts for the overwhelming ambition among Japanese youths to get an education and go to work for a major enterprise.

COMPANY HOUSING   Many of Japan's larger companies provide or subsidize housing for their employees. Before industrialization, it was common for employees of restaurants, shops, and other types of businesses to live in. After industrialization in the latter part of the nineteenth century, when many factories and mines were in distant locations, it was necessary for employers to provide housing in order to attract workers.

As time went by, it became customary for Japanese companies to transfer employees regularly from one location to another as part of their on-the-job training. Company-provided housing became an important part of this program.

Larger factories almost always provide dormitory-type housing for unmarried employees. Executives in companies are often provided housing at low rents or at no cost as part of their compensation.

The giant Nippon Steel Corporation, for example, owns close to 30,000 housing units and provides housing for some 35 percent of its married employees. Dormitories are available for single employees who do not live near their work.

COMPANY-RUN BARS   A growing number of Japanese companies operate bars on their premises for employees. The in-house bars help to strengthen the sense of corporate identity among employees by "improving communication" among them and also save them money.

It is a traditional practice for middle managers to treat their subordinates to drinks after working hours to boost company morale and heighten their sense of loyalty to the company. One company spokesperson also said it was easier for female employees to stop in for a drink before going home.

Although the savings to company employees who like to patronize bars but are not on expense accounts is substantial, not all of them like the idea of doing their drinking on the premises. Said one, "All of your superiors are there! How can you relax in a place like that?"

COMPETITION / KYOSO (K'yoe-so)   The Japanese did not have a word for competition until the latter part of the 1800s, when the term *kyoso* was coined by famed educator Yukichi Fukuzawa.

The reason there was no such word is because the concept of competition as it is used in the West did not exist in Japan prior to the modern era—although there was competition in some sports and certainly between clans and groups and even individuals.

In all group efforts, however, the primary Japanese principle has always been cooperation—trying to get along, by compromising, so that no one loses and all gain.

During feudal days, travelers on the road were expected to apologize and ask permission to pass slower walkers to avoid giving the suggestion of aggressive impropriety.

In Japan today, competition in business is still primarily a group, as opposed to an individual, matter. In fact, the individualist is the oddball in Japan and has no place in most companies.

COMPUTERS / KOMPYUTA (Kome-pyu-tah)   In the 1960s, the Japanese government, in concert with various research institutions and electronics companies, made the decision that the rapid development of the computer industry in Japan would be a primary goal.

The joint program of research and development has made Japan a leader in the computer field, further advanced in some areas than the United States. Until 1980, IBM (Japan) was the top computer company there in terms of sales. Since that year, Fujitsu has been number one.

Other leading Japanese computer manufacturers are Hitachi, NEC, Oki, Mitsubishi, and Toshiba.

Until the early 1980s, all Japanese computer software was written in English. Now much of it is written in the Japanese language in a mixture of *kana* (kah-nah) and *hiragana* (he-rah-gah-nah). See JAPANESE LANGUAGE for an explanation of these terms.

In the spring of 1984, the Tokyo Metropolitan Police Department began using computers to control traffic in Chuo and Chiyoda wards, the main downtown areas of the city. Besides changing the signals on the basis of traffic volume, the computers use a voice synthesizer to give drivers traffic information via car radio.

But mid-1980 predictions that Japan would be the first country to achieve virtually complete computerization of its industry and life-style were premature. Japan now significantly lags behind the U.S. in the dissemination of computers for both business and personal use.

The failure of Japan's computer industry to fulfill its earliest expectations was not caused by technological, manufacturing, or marketing problems per se, but because it encountered unyielding cultural barriers.

The impersonal, direct communications and transfer of data by computer ran counter to the very core of the Japanese way of doing things, which was based on team consensus, team effort, face-to-face exchanges of information, and a highly personalized approach to every aspect of business and professional relationships.

Japan's computer manufacturers and software companies are now very much aware of the cultural handicaps they face, and all have devised various strategies for overcoming them. But the traditional way of doing things is so deeply ingrained in the psyche of most Japanese that it will take at least one and possibly two or more generations for this problem to disappear.

The personal computer in Japan has been abbreviated to *paso-kon.*

CONSTITUTION DAY / KEMPO KINENBI (Kim-poe kee-name-bee)
This May 3rd national holiday commemorates the promulgation of Japan's
constitution on May 3, 1946 (it went into effect one year later).

CONSTRUCTION INDUSTRY   There are some half million construction
companies in Japan, but only a few of these are major enterprises operating
on a national and international basis. The Big Five are Kajima Corp.,
Ohbayashi Gumi, Shimizu Construction Co., Taisei Corp., and Takenaka
Komuten Co.

Japan ranks second only to the U.S. in the scale of its construction industry and since the 1960s has become increasingly active abroad.

One of the special reasons for the success of Japan's construction industry is the fact that so many of the building sites are on reclaimed land and in
earthquake-prone areas that it was necessary to develop special technology
and skills to overcome these handicaps.

The industry has also benefited from a high degree of automation.

CONTRACTS / KEIYAKU (Kay-e-yah-kuu)   Traditionally in Japan, contracts were based on verbal agreements, and among the *samurai*, in matters
of consequence, the commitment was total—a matter of life and death.

The conclusion of agreements in Japan was generally marked by toasts
and by the formalized clapping of the hands three times in rapid unison, a
practice known as *te-uchi* (tay-uu-chee). This practice was also used to mark
the end of a special party.

Written contracts, particularly between foreign interests and Japanese,
are common today, but the Japanese still feel that, if there is enough mutual
trust and confidence to make an agreement in the first place, a signed
contract is superfluous.

The Japanese are also uncomfortable with written contracts that are
based on hard, specific absolutes, pointing out that circumstances change
and that arrangements between two parties should be flexible enough to
allow for periodic adjustments arrived at by mutual agreement.

Western executives who are used to formal, binding contracts that have
little or nothing to do with personal feelings, often find it difficult to negotiate
deals with Japanese companies and, once such contracts are signed, encounter more problems in working effectively with their Japanese counterparts.

Recommended reading: *Japanese Etiquette and Ethics in Business*, by
Boye Lafayette De Mente (Passport Books). Also: *How to Do Business in
Japan*, by the same author.

CONVENIENCE AGENCIES / BENRI-YA (Bane-ree Yah)   A type of
agency that developed in the late 1970s, the *benri-ya* are odd-job services
that perform such tasks as housework, shopping, yard cleanup, moving

heavy objects—and spying on students suspected of not studying and on spouses suspected of infidelity.

Women often use the *benri-ya* to help them win divorce cases and to fill in when they need a man around the house.

The first *benri-ya* was the Ukon Service Company, founded by Katsuyoshi Ukon in 1979. Two dozen of the companies that cropped up soon afterward were founded by ex-Ukon employees who went out on their own as soon as they learned the business.

CORMORANT FISHING / UKAI (Uu-kie)   One of Japan's most popular tourist attractions is fishing with trained cormorants, primarily on the Nagara River near Gifu, southwest of Nagoya.

The large, pelicanlike birds are controlled by a cormorant fishing master, who has them on individual leashes. A cord ring is placed around their necks to keep them from swallowing fish above a certain size.

Cormorant fishing takes place at night. Torches are lighted and held out over the water from boats to attract the fish. The huge birds are then sent splashing into the river. When their pouches are full, they are pulled into the boat and relieved of their catch.

A cormorant fishing master can handle up to a dozen of the large sea birds. From July 1 to August 31, cormorant fishing is demonstrated on the Uji River in Kyoto's Arashiyama Park.

Cormorant fishing is mentioned in the *Kojiki* (Koe-jee-kee), a record of Japan's early history that was compiled in 712. The birds used for this kind of fishing are caught in winter off the coast of Ibaraki Prefecture and on Shino Island in Mikawa Bay.

The birds stand about 60 centimeters high when full-grown and weigh two to three kilograms. The first bird is caught by placing bird lime on the rocks where they ordinarily land, and this bird is then used as a decoy to attract others.

The cormorants are kept in large, bamboo lattice baskets. When being used, they are controlled by thin, 3.6-meter-long leashes attached to the cords around their necks.

The birds are given about two weeks of individual training and then are put into the water with cormorants that are already trained. Each cormorant boat has four crew members: a steersman, the fishing master, and two assistants.

The fishing master stands in the bow of the boat, controlling 12 birds at the same time. The two assistants, amidship, each manage two birds. The steersman is in charge of the decoy fire, which is kept burning in an iron grate at the bow.

Boats, gaily lighted with lanterns, usually go out in groups of five or seven, either before the moon rises or after it sets because fish are not attracted to the fires on bright nights.

Each time a cormorant is put into the water, it catches from two to four fish, and on a good night catches from 40 to 50. Individual boats can accommodate from 8 to 30 sightseeing passengers.

The fish the cormorants go after are called *ayu* (ah-you), a trout-like fish with very sweet meat that is found all over Japan.

Emperor Daigo (885–930) was especially fond of *ayu* caught by cormorants, as was Yoritomo Minamoto, who established Japan's first shogunate in Kamakura in 1192. In fact, Yoritomo liked the fish so much he had them delivered to him regularly. The presentation of cormorant-caught *ayu* to the *shogun* became a formal custom that was continued into the Tokugawa Period that began in 1603.

Ayu from Gifu's Nagara River also remained a favorite of Japan's emperors. In 1890, three sections of the river were set aside as the private *ayu* preserves of the Imperial Court and placed under the charge of special cormorant masters.

COURTING—DATING / DETO (Day-toe)   Until the 1950s, Western-style courting or dating was not part of Japan's social scene. Virtually all marriages were arranged, and, with few exceptions, unmarried men and women did not date in the usual sense of the word.

Following an arranged meeting between a prospective bride and groom, the two were usually allowed to meet a few times before the wedding took place, but these were get-acquainted dates, not courting dates.

In the prewar feudal family system, unmarried daughters especially were subject to the wills and preferences of their fathers. The old family system was abolished in 1945, but it was not until the late 1950s that young Japanese men and women began to date and choose their own spouses.

The Allied Military Occupation of Japan from 1945 to 1952 by several hundred thousand young American and other Western men had a lot to do with the rapid assimilation of dating and courting customs in Japan. Within months after the end of the war in 1945, a significant percentage of the younger GIs had Japanese girlfriends.

It wasn't too long before young Japanese men adopted the custom, beginning a revolution in Japanese society that was to change traditions that had endured for nearly 2,000 years.

COURTS / SAIBAN (Sie-bahn)   There are five categories of courts in Japan: the Supreme Court, high courts, district courts, family courts, and summary courts. In addition, there is a court of impeachment in the Diet to try judges whose dismissal is sought.

The Supreme Court nominates judges for all of the lower courts, and the Cabinet makes the final appointments.

There are 15 justices on the Supreme Court. They are subject to review by popular vote at the first House of Representatives election following their appointment. A majority of votes against a particular justice results in dismissal.

High courts are located in eight cities—Tokyo, Nagoya, Osaka, Hiroshima, Takamatsu, Fukuoka, Sendai, and Sapporo. There are 50 district courts and 50 family courts—four each in Hokkaido and one each in the 46 other prefectural capitals.

Family courts handle civil cases involving domestic matters, such as divorce, inheritance, and juvenile delinquency. (In Japan, anyone under 20 is considered a juvenile.)

Summary courts handle initial trials involving monetary claims of 300,000 yen or less and minor offenses, such as gambling or organizing a gambling establishment. Other cases, civil as well as criminal, are initially tried in district courts.

Trial procedures are similar to those in the U.S., but a larger number of suspended sentences are handed down—around 60 percent of all short-term sentences.

CRAM SCHOOLS / JUKU (Juu-kuu)   Millions of Japanese children between the ages of 6 and 15 attend *juku*, or "cram schools," to give themselves an extra edge in the struggle to get into a name university. During any summer, 60 percent of the youngsters in this age group attend *juku* instead of taking vacations.

A recent survey revealed there were 180,000 cram schools just for primary and junior high students, with an enrollment in excess of 5 million.

The cram school business is so big (approaching $300 million a year) that all kinds of entrepreneurs are getting into it. The third largest *juku* chain in the country, Kawai Juku, has teamed with the Nagoya Railroad Company to build new schools on land owned by the railway company near its stations.

In addition to the private *juku*, there are thousands of private tutors who teach children in their homes.

There are also some 200 *yobiko* (prep schools) in Japan—all of them well attended. See PREPARATORY SCHOOLS.

CREDIT CARDS/KUREJITO KADO (Kuu-ray-jee-to kah-doe)   Despite their traditional fondness for cash transactions, the Japanese took to the credit card system with considerable alacrity. Over 70 million cards are in circulation.

But because the Japanese are unaccustomed to the responsibilities that go along with credit buying, the credit-card delinquency rate is so high that it has become a national problem—approaching 10 percent, according to industry estimates.

Most of the credit cards in Japan are issued by banks, and all of the bank-affiliated card companies are tied in with Visa, MasterCard, and Amex of the U.S., so that the cards can be used abroad.

CRESTS / MON (Moan)   Japan's famous Fujiwara clan, whose lords were the de facto rulers of Japan from the eighth to the eleventh centuries, are credited with popularizing the practice of using emblems to identify high-ranking courtiers. From there, the custom spread to lords of clans and their retainers.

At first, the *mon* were used only on costumes worn for official occasions—one in the center of the back, and one on each sleeve.

These first family crests were elegantly designed and featured such popular symbols as the crane, wisteria, peony, and other flowers.

The *samurai* warrior clans that came into power at the end of the twelfth century used *mon* on their banners, flags, weapons, and other paraphernalia, as well as on their clothing. Only the immediate members of the *samurai* lord's family were allowed to wear his crest, but their retainers were allowed to use a variation.

During the age of wars in the fifteenth century, when it was very important for the warring clans to be able to identify their own soldiers, especially during combat, the crests of the clans were simplified and made easier to recognize.

Following the establishment of the Tokugawa Shogunate in 1603 and the beginning of a long period of peace, the *mon* became more refined and elegant, and it became the custom to enclose them in a circle.

Up to this time, only the privileged *samurai* had their own crests, but from this period on, merchants and other successful common people began to create and wear their own family *mon*.

In 1868, when the emperor was restored to power, the use of any form of chrysanthemum was reserved exclusively for the Imperial family. By this time, there were some 500 basic *mon* designs in Japan, with several thousand variations. See FAMILY CRESTS.

CRIME / HANZAI (Hahn-zie)   Japan is rightfully noted for being one of the safest countries in the world. The incidence of violent crimes against people—assault, armed robberies, rape, murder and so on—is one of the lowest, if not the lowest, in the world.

That is not to say that all Japanese are totally law-abiding. At present, one and a half million criminal cases are reported to the police each year.

But the overwhelming majority of these cases concern nonviolent crimes —thefts (approximately 86 percent) and fraud and embezzlement (about 7 percent). Well under 4 percent of these cases involve intimidation and/or assault, and vicious crimes (murder, armed robbery, and arson) account for only one half of one percent. See JUVENILE DELINQUENCY.

CULTURAL AFFAIRS / BUNKA (Boon-kah)   With its long history and powerful traditions, the Japanese are very cognizant of the importance of culture to the quality and continuity of a society. Since 1968, the country has had an Agency for Cultural Affairs (ACA).

The ACA is in charge of administrative affairs relating to the preservation and utilization of cultural properties and the promotion and dissemination of culture, including religious matters.

The country's national museums, the national museums of modern art, the National Museum of Western Art, the National Language Research Institute, the National Research Institutes of Cultural Properties, and the Japan Art Academy come under the jurisdiction of the Agency for Cultural Affairs.

One of the most laudable things the ACA does each year is to select outstanding men and women to receive the Order of Cultural Merit and to designate Persons of Cultural Merit (who are regarded as national treasures). The Agency holds special ceremonies for the presentation of these awards on Culture Day (*Bunka no Hi*), November 3.

In addition, the Agency sponsors an annual Japan Art Festival and awards prizes in such fields as theater, broadcasting, and cinema every fall.

The ACA regularly adds to its list of designated cultural properties and in the early 1980s began a program to preserve rows of old homes and portions of the country's old pedestrian highways. See TOKKAIDO.

Recommended reading: *Appreciation of Japanese Culture*, by Donald Keene (Kodansha International).

CULTURAL MEDALS In 1937, the Japanese government instituted the practice of honoring men and women who made extraordinary contributions in the fields of arts and sciences by awarding them Cultural Medals.

Since 1973, recipients of the annual awards have also received annuities.

Only a few people are deemed worthy of the Cultural Medal, as the standards are very high. Each year, five people receive the Order of Culture Award, and 10 people are designated Persons of Cultural Merit.

Recommended reading: *The Living Treasures of Japan*, by Barbara Adachi (Kodansha International).

CUSTOMERS / O'KYAKU-SAN (Oh-k'yack-sahn)   The Japanese have long been famous for the extra special respect and care with which they treat customers. That this practice is an integral part of their culture is revealed by the fact that the word *o'kyaku* is used for both customer and guest.

The tradition of not distinguishing between guest and customer is bound up in their custom of personalizing every relationship, of putting everything into a human perspective, including business.

This basic impulse is just the opposite of what most Americans and many other Westerners are taught, particularly where business is concerned. We say that business is business, meaning personal concerns should not be allowed to play any role in business dealings.

Since these two concepts are diametrically opposed, it is not surprising that the Japanese and American ways of doing business are quite different.

Recommended reading: *Japanese Etiquette and Ethics in Business*, by Boye Lafayette De Mente (Passport Books), and *How to Do Business with the Japanese* (NTC Business Books), by the same author.

DAIMON TEMPLE FIRE FESTIVAL / DAIMON JI YAKI MATSURI
(Die-moan jee yah-kee mot-sue-ree)   A major annual spectator event in
Hakone, a mountain resort southwest of Tokyo, the Daimon Temple Fire
Festival is held on August 16 on the slopes of Mt. Myojo. Torches arranged
in the outline of a huge Chinese *kanji* character—*dai*, meaning "great"—
are set afire to mark O'Bon, the Festival of the Dead.

The purpose of the bonfires is to light the way for the spirits of the dead
to return to Buddhist paradise after a few days of visiting with their living
relatives.

The crossbar of the *dai* ideogram is 108 meters in length, which gives an
idea of the overall dimensions of the figure.

DAIMYO (Dime-yoe)   During the long Tokugawa Shogunate, Japan was
divided into fiefs presided over by feudal Lords known as *daimyo*—literally,
"great name." The *daimyo* were divided into two groups based on their
relationship with Ieyasu Tokugawa, the founder of Japan's last great feudal
house. In the first group were those who had been allied with Ieyasu before
the Battle of Sekigahara in 1603. The second group was made up of those
who had opposed him or were neutral.

There were also three ranks of *daimyo*, depending on the revenues of
their fiefs and whether or not they owned a castle. These three classes were
kokushu (koe-kuu-shu)—provincial lords whose fiefs produced at least
300,000 *koku* (koku = 4.96 bushels) of rice, *joshu* (joe-shu) or castle-owning
lords whose annual income was 100,000 to 300,000 koku of rice, and *ryoshu*
(rio-shu), or lords without castles, with incomes from 10,000 to 100,000 *koku*
of rice.

The *daimyo* were responsible to the Tokugawa Shogunate for upholding
the policies of the central government and were restricted in matters having
to do with the security of the shogunate, but within their domains their power
was absolute. See SOGORO'S SACRIFICE; PROCESSIONS OF THE
LORDS; DATE, MASAMUNE.

DANCING / ODORI (Oh-doe-ree)   There are three types of traditional
Japanese dancing—one associated with *kabuki* (*odori*), one associated with
noh (*mai*), and folk dancing.

Mai is described as a more static dance form, in keeping with *noh*, while *odori* is more dynamic. Both very stylized forms of dancing, they are generally seen today in the *kabuki* and *noh* theaters, among small groups of devotees, and among *geisha* entertainers.

Folk dancing, which is very common in Japan, is also stylized but can be very robust and lively. It is common at festivals (of which there are thousands around the country every year) and on television.

There are a number of different schools of dancing in Japan today, each teaching some variation of *mai, odori*, or folk dancing. Among the better known of these schools are *nishikawa, hanayagi, fujima*, and *wakayagi*.

All forms of popular Western-style dancing are just as popular in Japan, and all have their heydays.

DATE, MASAMUNE (Dah-tay, Mah-sah-muu-nay)   Masamune Date, one of the most important feudal lords in Japan during the wars that marked the end of the Ashikaga Shogunate (1336–1598) and the founding of the Tokugawa Shogunate in 1603, played a key role in the history of Sendai in northeastern Japan and in the introduction of Christianity into the country.

Born in 1566, Date was a minor provincial *daimyo* until he allied himself with Hideyoshi Toyotomi, who became the military ruler of Japan in the 1580s, and then joined forces with Ieyasu Tokugawa, who succeeded Hideyoshi and went on to establish the Tokugawa Shogunate.

When the second Tokugawa *Shogun* began persecuting Christians in 1613, Date had Franciscan Father F. Luis Sotelo released from prison and brought to his fief headquarters. There he had Sotelo tutor him on the outside world and gave him permission to preach in the province.

Later, Date sent one of his retainers, Tsunenaga Hasekura, and Sotelo on a mission to Spain and Rome. When Date died in 1636, his fief was the largest one north of Edo (Tokyo).

DEATH / SHI (She)   Cancer, cerebral hemorrhage, and heart disease are the three major causes of death in Japan. Other significant causes of death are pneumonia, bronchitis, disasters, and accidents. Cancer is the leading cause of death, accounting for around 23 percent of the total.

DECISION MAKING   Generally speaking, the Japanese way of making decisions is to arrive at a consensus among all those concerned. When two opposing groups cannot reach a decision, it is traditional to bring in an outside advisor or consultant to help resolve the issue.

The outsider then attempts to help the two sides work out a compromise on which both can agree. If a compromise cannot be reached, which is rare, then the advisor tries to persuade the minority view to accept the majority opinion. This outside consultant/advisor is often referred to as *ten-no koe*, or "the voice of heaven."

The golden rule of any confrontation in Japan is compromise, since the Japanese regard rule by the major faction as tyranny of the majority.

Many of Japan's larger companies use a system called *ringi seido* (reen-ghee say-e-doe) in making management decisions. In this system, proposals for management action are written up, usually by lower management, and then circulated up and down the managerial ladder for comments and approval.

If the proposal is not approved but comes back with suggestions for changes, it may be revised and circulated again. If the reaction is conspicuously negative, it is usually dropped. To avoid having a proposal turned down, it is customary for it to be unofficially circulated first, to pretty much pin down what the response is going to be.

Recommended reading: *Japanese Etiquette and Ethics in Business*, by Boye Lafayette De Mente (Passport Books).

DEJIMA (Day-jee-mah)   In 1639, when Iemitsu, the third Tokugawa *Shogun*, decreed that all foreign missionaries would be expelled from Japan, he also expelled the Portuguese traders who had been the first to open the country up to trade with the Western world. This left only a few Dutch traders in the country, since the English and Spanish had already been squeezed out. See PORTUGUESE; HISTORY; ADAMS.

At the same time, *Shogun* Iemitsu banned all travel to and from Japan, with the exception of the Dutch and a few Chinese and Korean traders. But to minimize the influence the Dutch could have, he ordered that a small islet be constructed in Nagasaki harbor and that the Dutch trading company be confined to that one tiny isolated and guarded spot.

When the island was completed in 1641, it was named Dejima, which literally means Exit Island. Holland maintained a small company of traders on Dejima for the next 213 years, providing the only window Japan had to the outside world.

Diaries and notes left by some of these Dutch traders over the generations make fascinating reading—especially accounts of the few times when one or more of their party were allowed to go ashore for some special purpose.

Probably the most famous foreign resident of the island during this long period was Dr. Phillip Franz von Siebold, a German, who first served as a surgeon with the Dutch Army Medical Corps in Java and then was assigned to accompany the newly appointed General Trade Agent to Dejima in 1823, when he was 27 years old. Almost refused entrance to the tiny, closely guarded outpost because he could not speak Dutch well, Siebold went on to impress the Japanese with his medical and general knowledge. He was given permission to visit the mainland regularly and was allowed to buy a small estate, where he grew herbs, plants, and trees. He also married a young Japanese woman. In contrast to the treatment extended to Siebold, when other members of the trading company were granted permission to leave the island and go ashore for brief visits, they were accompanied by an entourage of *samurai* guards, interpreters, servants, and a paymaster who paid for all their expenditures.

Every four years, the Dutch traders at Dejima were required to go to Edo to pay homage to the *shogun*. Siebold accompanied the group in 1826, later expressing shock at the lascivious life-style he witnessed in the hundreds of inns and restaurants along the way.

Siebold became famous in Japan and was sought after as a physician by many Japanese, often accepting handicrafts and art objects in lieu of cash payment for his services. These objects became the basis for a large collection that was later purchased by the Dutch government and is now in the National Museum of Ethnology in Leiden. Siebold set up a medical school at his estate and taught many young Japanese students the principles and practices of Western medicine, conferring degrees on them.

Siebold's first parting with Japan was to be an unpleasant affair, however. When the ship he boarded in 1827 to return to Holland was grounded by a typhoon, some maps of Japan that he had received from a friend were found in his luggage. He was accused of being a spy, arrested, and two years later put on trial. Found guilty, he was banned from Japan for life and forced to leave his wife and two-year-old daughter, Ine.

Returning to Holland, Siebold wrote several books about his experiences in Japan that were the definitive works on the country for several decades. After years of effort, he finally got the ban lifted and returned to Japan in

1859 as a representative of a Dutch trading company. He lived for three years at his old estate in Nagasaki but did not like the new changes that were taking place in Japan following the opening of its doors to the outside world by the United States. He died in 1866, at which time a son by a second marriage sold the rest of his extensive Japanese collection to museums in Munich, Leipzig, and Vienna.

Siebold's Japanese daughter became a doctor when she grew up.

DEMING, DR. W. EDWARDS   Dr. W. Edwards Deming, an American most Americans never heard of, is something of a legend in Japan. In 1950, he was invited by the Union of Japanese Scientists and Engineers (JUSE) to give a series of lectures in Japan on quality control.

The lectures were so popular that Dr. Deming was invited back to Japan several times. To commemorate Dr. Deming's contribution to quality control in Japan and to further its development, the JUSE shortly thereafter established the Deming Prizes to be presented each year to the Japanese firms that demonstrated the most outstanding advances in quality control.

As Sumitomo Metals once announced in a large advertisement that ran in the *Asian Wall Street Journal*: "The Most Famous Name in Japanese Quality Control is American." See QUALITY.

DEMOCRACY / MINSHUSHUGI (Meen-shu-shu-ghee)   The modern political concept of democracy was introduced into Japan, in part, in 1889 when the first constitution was promulgated. It was not until 1945, however, following the end of World War II, that representative government became a significant reality.

But the Japanese concept of democracy differs from the typical Western concept. Very broadly speaking, the Western view of democracy is that it provides for rule by the majority. The Japanese, on the other hand, feel that it is undemocratic for a simple majority to rule over the minority.

Their approach, in principle at least, is that government by compromise, which takes into consideration all viewpoints, is the most democratic form of government.

To the average Japanese, the most important thing that democracy has brought to Japan is individual freedom and the protection of their personal rights.

DENTSU, INC. (Dane-sue)   Dentsu is Japan's largest advertising agency. The company controls some 25 percent of the domestic advertising in Japan and has offices in many countries abroad.

The company often refers to itself as a total marketing service, because its activities go far beyond advertising.

Dentsu has joint ventures and tie-ups with a number of agencies around the world, and it is aiming for a global network offering conventional advertising services, as well as special functions, to both Japanese and foreign clients. See ADVERTISING.

DEPARTMENT STORES / DEPATO (Day-pah-toe)   The department store concept was invented in Japan in the 1700s, during the feudal Tokugawa era, and the Japanese have remained leaders in the field ever since. To say that leading Japanese department stores are large and carry a wide range of merchandise does not do justice to them.

Besides being just very large department stores, typical Japanese *depato* offer dozens of other services to customers, from restaurants and financial services to miniature zoos and recreational parks on their rooftops. All of them sponsor several different kinds of cultural and art shows each year that are free to the public.

One of the most extraordinary departments in a Japanese department store is its food floor (or floors), which are usually below ground level. Besides dry goods, fresh produce, seafood, breads, pastries, and the like, the departments also offer various cooked and ready-to-eat items.

Any visitor to Japan who fails to visit a name department store is missing one of the experiences of a lifetime. There are more than 20 leading department store chains in the country. In the order of their sales, they are: Mitsukoshi, Daimaru, Takashimaya, Seibu, Matsuzakaya, Tokyu, Marui, Hankyu, Isetan, Sogo, Yokohama Takashimaya, Kintetsu, Odakyu, Marui Imai, Tenmaya, Hanshin, Tobu, Matsuya, Keio and Meitetsu Hyakkaten.

The main categories of merchandise sold in *depato* are clothing, foodstuffs, household utensils, sundries, personal effects, and services.

Several Japanese department stores have overseas branches. Mitsukoshi, one of the most active, has branches in Paris, Rome, London, Dusseldorf, Frankfurt, New York, Honolulu, Singapore, and Hong Kong.

DESCENDING FROM HEAVEN / AMA KUDARI (Ah-mah kuu-dah-ree) *Ama Kudari* refers to a well-established practice in which high-ranking bureaucrats in Japan's government ministries join major companies (as high-ranking executives) after they step down from their lofty positions— retire from government service.

Given the nature of the personal relationships and obligations that develop between ministry officials and those they groom to succeed themselves, such lifelong ties become a very valuable asset to commercial firms.

Some 80 percent of all public corporation executive posts are occupied by former ranking government officials. Most such ex-officials retire from the public corporations after an average of four years, with very substantial retirement payments.

DESIGNER CLOTHING   On the whole, the Japanese are probably more interested in what they wear and more concerned about their appearance than any other people. The reason for this is that during the country's very long feudal period, wearing apparel was closely related to social class and occupation.

During the last great shogunate dynasty (1603–1868), the shogunate went to the extreme of designating what type of clothing each class should wear — even specifying by law when people had to change from summer to winter attire and back again in the spring (regardless of how hot or cold it might be on the date specified).

Wearing the right apparel therefore went beyond just being important. It was vital to the personal security of the individual, and, in extreme cases, it was a matter of life and death. Any commoner, for example, who might have been tempted to dress up as a *samurai* put his life and the security of his family in jeopardy.

This concern for appearance has carried over into modern times and helps make the Japanese especially conscious not only of styles, but of name brands, as well.

All these factors combined have resulted in the development of a thriving apparel industry made up of a large number of designers, thousands of boutiques that specialize in designer clothing, and a market for designer apparel that is second to none.

In the late 1950s, when I was editor of *The Importer* magazine in Tokyo (at that time the leading English-language journal covering Japanese-made consumer products for export), I began predicting that within a decade Japanese fashion designers would be on a par with those in Paris, Rome, and New York.

I was about one decade early, but I firmly believe that the cultural traditions of Japanese fashion designers give them a significant advantage that will eventually take them to the top of the world of fashion.

DESSERTS / DEZATO (Day-zah-toe)   Sugar was not known in Japan until the sixteenth century. Prior to this period, the only desserts available were fruits and other naturally sweet foods. With the introduction of sugar, cakes and buns stuffed with sweetened bean paste became popular, and, by the early years of the eighteenth century, close to 400 different varieties of cakes and confections were being made.

Today there are thousands of different confections available in Japan, including dozens of varieties of cakes and pastries that are baked in single-serving sizes and sold in bakeries and coffee shops in virtually every neighborhood.

Traditional Japanese meals are generally followed by a fruit in season, instead of a prepared dessert — or nothing sweet at all.

Ice creams, sherbets, and yogurts are big sellers in Japan as snack items.

DICTIONARIES / JIBIKI (Jee-bee-kee)   Language dictionaries are very important in the study of Japanese, and some very good ones are available —including ones in which the Japanese is in Roman letters (*Roma-ji*) for those who cannot read the *kanji* (kahn-jee) ideogram characters.

One of the best series is published by the Sanseido Press in Tokyo. For English-speaking students of the language, I recommend *Sanseido's New Concise English-Japanese Dictionary* and the Japanese-English edition of the same series.

My favorite over the years has been the *English-Japanese Conversation Dictionary*, by Mr. and Mrs. O. Vaccari, which gives sample sentences with each word entry. See VACCARI, ORESTE.

DIET BUILDING / KOKKAI GIJIDO (Koke-kie ghee-jee-doe)   The National Diet Building of Japan is on a hill near the Imperial Palace, in the Nagato-cho area of Tokyo, overlooking Japan's other primary government buildings (clustered around it) and the downtown area, which is only a short distance away.

The building was completed in 1936 after 17 years of frequently interrupted construction. It has one basement and three floors above ground, plus a central tower that is nine stories high. There are 449 rooms in the central block of the Diet Building.

The Kokkai Gijido is built of white granite and marble, with ornately carved fine woods in the interior. The left wing is the House of Representatives, and the right wing is the House of Councillors. The central hall is used only when the emperor visits the Diet on the day the newly elected legislators report for their first session. This is the only occasion when the central gate is opened.

There is a special chamber on the third floor, called the *Gokyusho* (Go-que-show), or "place of rest," that is reserved for the exclusive use of the emperor and his family. It is a magnificient room, with lacquered cedar and pure gold fittings.

In the spring and summer tourist seasons, visitors line up in the hallway outside the chamber to peer through a glass panel at the redolent decorations on the inside.

The Diet Building is located in the Nagato-cho area of the Kasumigaseki district. The official residence of the prime minister, a low yellowish brick building, is behind the Diet Building. Other government buildings in the immediate area are the Diet members' office buildings, the Diet Press Club, Diet Library, headquarters of the Liberal Democratic Party and the Japan Socialist Party, and the official residences of the speaker of the House of Representatives and the president of the House of Councillors.

The term Nagata-cho is often used to mean the government or the prime minister or government policies.

For security reasons, members of the Diet have been required since 1903 to wear special lapel pins to identify themselves. The same law was applied to House of Councillor members in 1953.

The pins for the two Houses differ, and they have been changed several times. Today both pins depict an 11-petaled chrysanthemum. The Lower House pin has a maroon border, and the Upper House pin has a deep blue border.

Numerous other government officials who are in and out of the Diet Building regularly also wear pins to identify themselves.

DINING OUT   There are probably more restaurants in Japan than in any other country in the world. In fact, there are more restaurants in Tokyo alone than in most countries. This, of course, indicates that the Japanese dine out a great deal, which they do.

Dining out in Japan is an old custom that apparently derived from several factors. Because houses were constructed of wood, with paper interiors, and charcoal braziers were used for cooking, it was impractical to cook very much or very many complicated dishes and dangerous to cook inside the house because of smoke and the threat of fire.

Thus, because the Japanese were unable to cook more than basic dishes at home and because they love food in both variety and volume, the appearance of a large number of restaurants in Japan was a natural development. The traditional forms of entertainment, as well as travel, also contributed to the proliferation of restaurants.

Today, on a nationwide basis, the Japanese spend approximately 15 percent of their food budget in restaurants. Families in which the head of the household is 24 years old or under, spend 24 percent of their food budget dining out. Those between 25 and 29 spend close to 16 percent of their food money in restaurants, and those between 30 and 49 spend between 14 percent and 15 percent.

DIPLOMATIC HISTORY (1853–1994)

1853, July 8: America's Commodore Matthew C. Perry and his fleet of Black Ships arrive at Uraga—the opening wedge in convincing Japan to reopen its doors to the outside world.

1854, Mar. 31: The first Japan-U.S. treaty of friendship signed.

1855, Feb. 7: Japan-Russia treaty signed at Shimoda, setting the northern boundary between the two countries at midway between the Kurile Islands of Etorofu and Urup.

1875, May 7: Japan-Russia treaty signed, giving Sakhalin to Russia and the Kurile Islands to Japan.

1894, July 25: Beginning of the Sino-Japanese war.

1895, April 17: Sino-Japanese peace treaty signed at Shimonoseki.

1902, Jan. 30: Anglo-Japanese Alliance signed.

1904, Feb. 10: Russo-Japanese War begins.

1905, Sept. 5: Russo-Japanese Peace Treaty signed at Portsmouth in the U.S., with U.S. acting as mediator.

1910, Aug. 22: Japan annexes Korea.

1914, July 28: World War I begins (Germany declares war on Russia August 1).

1914, Aug. 23: Japan enters World War I on the side of the Allies.

1915, Jan. 18: Japan issues 21 Demands to China.

1919, June 28: Treaty of Versailles and League of Nations Covenant signed.

1920, Jan. 10: Japan joins the League of Nations.

1922, Feb. 6: Five-Power Naval Disarmament Treaty signed in Washington, D.C., setting parity at U.S. 5, Britain 5, Japan 3.

1925, Jan. 20: Japan-USSR Treaty signed, restoring diplomatic relations.

1931, Sept. 18: Manchurian Incident occurs, marking the start of Japan's expansion into China.

1932, Mar. 1: Japan takes over Manchuria and establishes the state of Manchukuo.

1933, Mar. 27: Japan withdraws from the League of Nations.

1934, Dec. 29: Japan cancels Washington naval treaty.

1936, Nov. 25: Japan signs Anti-Comintern Pact with Germany.

1937, July 7: Clash at Marco Polo Bridge between Japanese and Chinese troops marks the beginning of full-scale war between Japan and China.

1940, Sept. 27: Japan, Germany, and Italy sign the Tripartite Pact.

1941, April 13: Japan and USSR sign a neutrality agreement.

1941, Dec. 8: Japan attacks Pearl Harbor and declares war on the U.S.

1945, Aug. 6: U.S. drops atom bomb on the city of Hiroshima.

1945, Aug. 8: Russia declares war on Japan.

1945, Aug. 9: U.S. drops atom bomb on the city of Nagasaki.

1945, Aug. 14: Japan surrenders unconditionally.

1945, Aug. 15: Emperor Hirohito makes his first radio broadcast to the nation, announcing that Japan has surrendered to the Allied powers.

1945, Sept. 2: Japan signs the documents of surrender aboard the U.S. battleship *Missouri* in Tokyo Bay.

1951, Sept. 8: Peace treaty between Japan and the Allies and a Japan-U.S. Security Treaty is signed in San Francisco.

1952, April 28: San Francisco peace treaty goes into effect. Japan-Taiwan peace treaty signed.

1954, Nov. 5: Japan-Burma peace treaty and other agreements signed.

1955, Sept. 10: Japan joins General Agreement on Tariffs and Trade (GATT).

1956, May 9: Japan-Philippines reparations agreement signed.

1956, Oct. 19: Diplomatic relations restored with Russia.

1956, Dec. 18: Japan admitted to the United Nations.

1960, Jan. 19: New Japan-U.S. security treaty signed in Washington; goes into effect on June 23.

1963, Aug. 14: Japan signs partial nuclear test ban treaty.

1964, April 1: Japan accepts International Monetary Fund (IMF) Article 8, regarding currency regulations.

1964, April 28: Japan joins the Organization for Economic Cooperation and Development (OECD).

1965, June 22: Japan establishes diplomatic relations with the Republic of Korea, signs other agreements.

1966, April 6: First Southeast Asia Development Ministerial Conference opens in Tokyo.

1968, April 5: Agreement with U.S. for the return of the Ogasawara Islands to Japan, effective June 26.

1969, Nov. 21: Japan signs joint statement with the U.S. on return of Okinawa to Japanese sovereignty.

1970, June 22: Japan announces the automatic renewal of the Japan-U.S. Security Treaty.

1971, June 17: Treaty signed with the U.S. for the return of Okinawa, effective May 15, 1972.

1971, Aug. 27: Japan floats the yen, following August 15 dollar defense measures announced by the U.S.

1972, Sept. 29: Japan, China renew diplomatic ties.

1973, Oct. 20: Oil crisis leads Cabinet to change Middle East policy, demand that Israel withdraw troops from occupied territories.

1974, Nov. 18: U.S. President Gerald Ford makes the first visit to Japan by an incumbent president.

1975, Jan. 16: USSR proposes good-neighbor, cooperation treaty.

1975, Sept. 30–Oct. 14: Emperor Hirohito pays state visit to the U.S.

1975, Nov. 15: Prime Minister Takeo Miki attends the first summit conference of advanced industrial nations at Rambouillet, near Paris.

1976, June 8: Japan ratifies the Nuclear Non-Proliferation Treaty.

1976, June 16: Japan-Australia treaty of friendship and cooperation signed.

1976, June 27: Prime Minister Miki attends the second summit conference of advanced industrial nations, in San Juan, Puerto Rico.

1976, Sept. 6: Soviet MiG-25 plane lands at Hakodate Airport in Hokkaido, and the pilot defects.

1977, May 7: Prime Minister Takeo Fukuda attends the third summit conference of advanced industrial nations, in London.

1977, May 27: Japan-USSR provisional fishery treaty signed subsequent to Soviet declaration of a 200-mile economic zone.

1977, July 1: Japan begins enforcing 12-mile territorial waters and 200-mile economic zone.

1977, Aug. 6: Prime Minister Fukuda announces a new Southeast Asian policy.

1978, June 22: Instruments of ratification of the Japan-Republic of Korea continental shelf agreement exchanged.

1978, July 16: Prime Minister attends the fourth summit conference of advanced industrial nations, in Bonn.

1978, Aug. 12: Japan-China Treaty of Peace and Friendship signed in Beijing.

1979, May 9: Prime Minister Masayoshi Ohira attends the Fifth United Nations Conference on Trade and Development, in Manila.

1979, June 28: The fifth summit conference of advanced industrial nations is held in Tokyo.

1979, Oct. 2: Foreign Affairs Vice Minister Masuo Takashima lodges a protest with the Soviet Ambassador to Japan over Soviet military build-up on Kunashiri and Etorofu and its new deployment of military forces on Shikotan.

1980, Feb. 1: Japan protests Soviet invasion of Afghanistan and later decides to boycott the Moscow Olympic Games (July 19–Aug. 3).

1980, June 22–23: Due to the death of Prime Minister Masayoshi Ohira, Foreign Minister Saburo Okita represents Japan at the sixth summit conference of industrial nations, in Venice, Italy.

1980, July 9: Fifty nations send special representatives to the official funeral for Prime Minister Ohira, including U.S. President Jimmy Carter, Chinese Premier Hua Guofeng, and Australian Prime Minister Malcolm Fraser. Fifty-three other nations were represented by their ambassadors to Japan.

1981, May 8: Prime Minister Zenko Suzuki meets U.S. President Ronald Reagan in Washington. A disagreement between Suzuki and Foreign Minister Masayoshi Ito over the wording of a joint communiqué following the summit leads to Ito's resignation on May 16.

1981, July 20–21: Prime Minister Suzuki attends the seventh summit conference of advanced industrial nations, in Ottawa, Canada.

1982, April 14–18: French President François Mitterrand visits Japan.

1982, May 31–June 5: Chinese Premier Zhao Ziyang visits Japan.

1982, Sept. 17–22: British Prime Minister Margaret Thatcher visits Japan.

1982, Sept. 26–Oct. 1: Prime Minister Suzuki visits China.

1983, Jan. 11–12: Prime Minister Yasuhiro Nakasone visits South Korea.

1983, May 29–June 2: Prime Minister Nakasone attends ninth summit conference of advanced industrial nations, in Williamsburg, Virginia.

1983, Oct. 31–Nov. 4: West German Chancellor Helmut Kohl visits Japan.

1983, Nov. 9–12: U.S. President Reagan visits Japan.

1983, Nov. 23–30: Chinese Communist Party General Secretary Hu Yaobang visits Japan.

1984, June 7–9: Prime Minister Nakasone attends tenth summit conference of advanced industrial nations, in London.

1984, Sept. 6–8: South Korean President Chun Doo Hwan makes first visit to Japan by an incumbent South Korean president.

1985, March 12–14: Prime Minister Nakasone visits Moscow to attend funeral of soviet President Konstantin Chernenko.

1985, May 2–4: Prime Minister Nakasone attends eleventh summit conference of advanced industrial nations, in Bonn.

1986, May 2–6: Twelfth annual summit conference of advanced industrial nations, held in Tokyo, attended by leaders of the free world.

1987, Nov. 6: Veteran politician Noboru Takeshita replaces Yasuhiro Nakasone as Prime Minister of Japan.

1988, April 22: Cabinet Minister Seisuke Okuno creates an international furor by claiming that Japan was not the aggressor nation in the invasion of China in the early 1930s, and in World War II.

1989, March 22: U.S. agrees to help Japan build its own version of the highly advanced FSX fighter jet in a controversial decision widely opposed by American trade experts and business leaders.

1990, October: Nelson Mandella, vice-chairman of the African National Congress, visits Japan.

1991: Japan is slow in responding to the U.S.'s call for aid during the Gulf War against Iraq, resulting in acrimonious debate about the U.S.-Japan relationship, and Japan's overall international role, with critics claiming that Japan is not living up to its responsibilities as a major industrial power dependent on foreign markets and foreign oil supplies.

1991, October: Japan lifts wide range of restrictions on private sector business ventures in South Africa. U.S. continues to pressure Japan to further open its own markets and reduce its huge trade surplus with the U.S.

1991, November 5: Veteran politician Kiichi Miyazawa replaces Toshiki Kaifu as prime minister, and shortly thereafter visits the U.S. for trade talks with President George Bush.

1992: The Japanese Diet passes a bill authorizing the government to send contingents of Japanese troops abroad to aid in peace-keeping operations —the so-called Bill of PKO. The bill was "rammed" through the Diet by the Liberal Democratic Party, whose members had to use physical force to keep opposition members from blocking the voting process.

1992, January: Japan resumes bilateral diplomatic relations with South Africa; welcomes visit from President F.W. de Klerk in June.

1993, September: Prime Minister Morihiro Hosokawa makes the clearest statement to date that Japan was the aggressor against Korea, China, and other nations of Southeast Asia in World War II, admitting that Japan brought unbearable suffering to millions of Asians.

1994, January: Japan lifts all remaining restrictions on trade with South Africa.

1994, February: U.S. and Japan "summit" trade talks between Prime Minister Morihiro Hosokawa and President Bill Clinton fail when Japan refuses to accept the idea of "numerical targets" on imports from the U.S.

1994, May: Newly appointed Minister of Justice Shigeto Nagano claims that the "Rape of Nanking" massacre of Chinese civilians by Japanese troops during World War II did not happen, resulting in a storm of criticism from China, and setting back Japan's efforts to improve its global image. Nagano, a former military officer who fought in China, is forced to resign.

1994, May: Japan and U.S. trade negotiators make compromises, agree to restart stalled talks on procedures to further open Japan's markets, particularly for automobiles, auto parts, telecommunications products, medical equipment, and insurance.

1994, June: Japan continues to seek a permanent seat on the Security Council of the United Nations.

1994, July: Japan participates in annual seven-nation economic summit in Naples, Italy.

DIRECTORY OF FOREIGN CAPITAL AFFILIATED ENTERPRISES IN JAPAN Revised annually, this directory of foreign firms in Japan includes the company's name, line of business, address, Japanese investors, date of establishment, percentage of foreign capital, and capitalization. It is compiled and published by Business Intercommunications, Inc. See OTHER SOURCES.

DISNEYLAND OF TOKYO Japan's own Disneyland, also known as the Magic Kingdom, opened in April 1983 in the town of Urayasu, on Chiba Peninsula, about half an hour from downtown Tokyo.

The Japanese Disneyland, owned and operated by Oriental Land Company (which is a subsidiary of Mitsui Real Estate Development Company and the Keisei Railway Electric Company), was the first Disneyland park to be built outside the U.S.

With 115 acres, the Tokyo Disneyland is slightly larger than the original California and Florida versions, but the park is a faithful reproduction of the many attractions of the American originals.

Because it rains a lot in the area, however, many of the Magic Kingdom attractions are covered. And because the winters are colder, the jungle is provided with heaters.

The entrance to the park is Main Street, modeled after old Americana. It is covered with a skylight roof and lined with shops and restaurants. The street leads to a plaza in front of Cinderella's Castle, from which Tomorrowland, Adventureland, Westernland, and Fantasyland are accessible via bridges.

The park has the same kind of live and animated entertainment that proved so successful in California and Florida. Many of the familiar characters and cartoon figures are played by young foreign boys and girls, hired locally for the parts.

The Japanese Disneyland cost over 650 million dollars to build—all of it financed by the Japanese partners, who bought the rights to use the name and the technology from Disneyland Productions of the U.S.

Among the special features and services of Tokyo Disneyland are a Lost Children Center, Baby Center, Coin Locker, Pet Club, Picnic Rest Area, and guided tours. There are 95 public telephones.

The park has a staff of 2,000 full-time employees and some 4,500 part-time workers, including 300 professional actors, musicians, and dancers. Several dozen foreigners, mostly Americans, work at the park.

During the peak seasons of its first year, the park was forced to close its gates 19 times because too many people were trying to get in.

DISTRICTS OF JAPAN   Japan is divided into eight districts according to geographical location, topography, and historical precedent. These regions (from the north) are Hokkaido, Tohoku, Kanto, Chubu, Kinki, Chugoku, Shikoku, and Kyushu. These divisions are used in reference to many social and economic variables, from climate and industrial development to population and regional dialects.

HOKKAIDO (Hoke-kie-doe): Japan's northernmost main island, Hokkaido makes up 22.1 percent of the country's land area but has less than five percent of the population. The island has several spectacular mountain ranges, high peaks, and two large plains. Its distance from the center of Japan's cultural and economic activity over the centuries, plus the rigorous climate, kept it isolated and undeveloped until the 1960s and '70s. Dry-field farming and dairy farming are major industries in Hokkaido, as are fishing, pulp, paper, beer, *sake*, sugar, and cement.

TOHOKU (Toe-hoe-kuu): On the northern end of Honshu, the Tohoku region includes six of Japan's 47 prefectures: Aomori, Akita, Iwate, Yamagata, Miyagi, and Fukushima. Another area that has been in the backwash of economic development, the Tohoku region has 17.7 percent of Japan's land, and just over 8 percent of the population. It is broken up by three mountain ranges that run parallel north and south, with plains and basins in between. The Kurile Current coming down from the north on the Pacific side of Tohoku keeps it cool in summer and cold in winter. The Japan Sea side is warmed by the Tsushima Current coming up from the south. Both sides have heavy winter snowfalls, particularly in the mountains.

Tohoku produces 25 percent of Japan's rice and 70 percent of its apples. Fishing is also important, as the meeting of warm and cold currents of the Pacific, plus many coastal bays, gives the region rich fishing grounds. Large-scale industry is limited in Tohoku, but the region is noted for its handicrafts, such as ironware and *kokeshi* dolls, along with dairy farming and horse raising.

Tohoku was once a stronghold of the Ainu (Aye-nuu), Japan's indigenous race of Caucasian people, many of whose descendants—mostly mixed with Japanese—still live in the region. The Tohoku area is famous for its beautiful women (*tohoku bijin*) and for the Texas-type attitudes and behavior of its horse-loving men.

KANTO (Kahn-toe): The primary cultural and economic hub of Japan, the Kanto region includes the prefectures of Ibaraki, Tochigi, Gunma, Saitama, Chiba, Kanagawa, and Tokyo. While it has only 8.6 percent of the land area, it has approximately 30 percent of the population. The northwestern portion of Kanto is characterized by numerous mountain ranges. The Kanto Plain, Japan's largest, makes up most of the southeastern portion of the region.

Farming is a major activity in the Kanto region, as is fishing (one-fifth of the nation's total). Choshi, in Chiba Prefecture, is famous as a deep-sea fishing port. The Kanto region is also Japan's largest industrial center. With the exception of textiles, all of Japan's major industries are represented in the sprawl that incorporates and surrounds Tokyo, Tokyo Bay, Yokohama, and Chiba Prefecture.

CHUBU (Chuu-buu): The historical crossroads between Kyoto and Tokyo, Chubu is made up of nine prefectures: Shizuoka, Yamanashi, Nagano, Niigata, Toyama, Ishikawa, Fukui, Gifu, and Aichi. It has 17.7 percent of the land area and approximately 17 percent of the population—the only region where these two figures are well matched.

Because it sprawls across the waist of Honshu from east to west, Chubu is subdivided into the Tokai district on the Pacific side and the Hokuriku district on the Japan Sea side. The two districts are separated by central highlands with several peaks above 3,000 meters. The Tokai area owes much of its viability to the Nobi Plain. The Japan Sea side of Chubu experiences heavy winter snowfalls, as do the central mountains. The eastern or Tokai area climate, influenced by the warmer waters of the Pacific, has mild winters.

Farming, primarily rice, is a major industry on the west side of Chubu. Shizuoka Prefecture is famous for mandarin oranges and tea, and Yamanashi is noted for its grape industry. Lumbering is big in the central highlands (one of the forests in this area, Kiso, is regarded as being one of the three most beautiful forests in Japan).

Shizuoka, on the eastern coast, is a major deep-sea fishing port, and its Hamana Lagoon is famous for its artificial breeding of eels. Nagoya is the largest city in Chubu and the hub of a major industrial area (called Chukyo for economic, marketing, and other purposes), in which heavy industries and textile spinning are prominent. There is a huge oil-refinery complex in nearby Yokkaichi. Hamamatsu is noted for its output of musical instruments (Yamaha, etc.). Toyota is an automobile manufacturing center. Fuji is big in paper, and Suwa is a center for the production of precision machinery.

KINKI (Keen-kee): The great cities of Kyoto, Osaka, and Kobe are in the Kinki region, which is the cradle of Japanese civilization. It consists of the prefectures of Mie, Shiga, Kyoto, Nara, Osaka, Wakayama, and Hyogo. Encompassing 8.7 percent of Japan's land area, it has over 18 percent of the population.

The northern portions of Kinki are mostly mountainous. The central portion has numerous hills and some mountains, but also the large Osaka Plain and numerous small basins. Lake Biwa, the country's largest lake, is in Kinki. See LAKES. The weather in Kinki is similar to that in the rest of Honshu—lots of winter snow in the north and on the west side, lighter snows in the lower central regions, and milder winters along the Pacific coast.

Fruit and vegetable farming are important industries in Kinki. The Uji district of Kyoto is famous for its tea. Wakayama is noted for its oranges. Fishing is also important, with ports on both the east and west coasts, as well as in Lake Biwa. The combined areas of Osaka and Kobe (called Hanshin), are Japan's second largest industrial area, with both heavy and light industries, including textiles, highly developed.

CHUGOKU (Chuu-go-kuu): With 8.4 percent of Japan's land space and only a little over 6 percent of its population, Chugoku is lightly populated when compared with Kinki, Chubu, and Kanto, primarily because there are few plains and basins in the area.

The west side of Chugoku fronts on the Inland Sea (Seto Naikai), which separates Honshu, Shikoku, and Kyushu, and has been a traditional waterway between Kyushu and central Japan. The massive Chugoku Mountain Range runs east-west through this district, again creating two vastly different climatic regions. The Japan Sea side (called San'in) has very few basins or plains of any significant size and is noted for its huge sand dunes. The east, or Inland Sea, side (called San'yo) is also characterized by hilly and broken terrain that prevents large-scale farming. While the San'in area has the usual heavy wintertime snows, the Inland Sea district has mild winters with many sunny days.

Western Chugoku, which has numerous terraced fields and irrigation ponds, is popular for its pears, peaches, and rice. Okayama Prefecture is especially noted for its peaches. Fishing is still an important industry on both of Chugoku's coasts, but the volume of fish caught in the Inland Sea has dwindled with the increase in pollution from coastal industrial plants and huge land reclamation projects. The major industries strung out along the Inland Sea coast include petrochemicals, textile spinning, and cement. The area is also noted for its cottage industries, producing traditional, as well as contemporary, items.

SHIKOKU (She-koe-kuu): The smallest of Japan's four major islands, Shikoku was out of the mainstream of economic development in Japan until the 1960s and '70s. With 5 percent of the nation's land, Shikoku has less than 4 percent of the population, which puts it well below the average in population density. Central Shikoku is mountainous, and there are small plains scattered along the coastlines. The mountains and the plains provide a natural division of the island into four sections, which from early times developed culturally, politically, and economically independent of each other. The island was under the control of four feudal lords. Each clan had its own castle, around which a town and then a city developed.

Northern Shikoku has a mild climate that is typical of the Inland Sea area. The southern portion of the island, exposed to the Pacific Ocean, has the typical oceanic climate of this region—muggy, hot summers, mild winters, spring rains, and fall typhoons. Shikoku's southern plains, once a popular rice-growing area, are now primarily devoted to providing vegetables for the population centers of Osaka, Kobe, and Kyoto. A number of fishing fleets are stationed in Shikoku, some of them concentrating on bonito in the nearby Japan Current. Others are primarily tuna fleets that fish in distant waters.

The island's major industrial activity includes petrochemical plants along the Inland Sea and paper and pulp plants in the southern area, where forests and electrical power are plentiful.

KYUSHU (Que-shuu): This is the southwesternmost of Japan's four main islands, and, during much of the early history of the country, it was the gateway between Japan and the Asian mainland. The port of Fukuoka is only 120 miles from Korea's port city of Pusan. Kyushu is about half the size of Hokkaido, with 11.8 percent of the total land area but with over 12 percent of the country's population.

Like all the other islands, Kyushu is very mountainous (Mt. Aso, a huge volcanic cone with an impressive crater, is its most famous mountain), but it is blessed with a number of fairly large plains, with Tsukushi (T'sue-kuu-shee) and Kumamoto (Kuu-mah-moe-toe) being the largest. Kyushu is hot in the summer (the southern portion of the island is far enough south to be semitropical) and has very mild winters. Rainfall is abundant, and typhoons (which bring even more rain) are an annual fall event.

The island is famous for its sweet potatoes and other vegetables, oranges, wheat, rice, tobacco, and dairy farming. Fishing is a major industry in Kyushu, with Nagasaki noted as a center for trawling operations. Industry in Kyushu is headed by coal mining, the manufacture of iron and steel, and shipbuilding. Cottage industries of many kinds have also been highly developed since the early centuries.

DIVORCE / RIKON (Ree-kone)   Still low by international standards, Japan's divorce rate has been climbing steadily since 1963. It is now approximately 23 percent of all marriages, as compared to 7.3 percent in 1963.

Most divorces in Japan occur during the first few years of marriage, when the women are in their mid to late twenties, and the men are in their early to mid-thirties.

In early feudal days, women did not have the right of divorce and were totally subject to their husbands' wills. As a result, it eventually became accepted that if a wife could escape from her home and make her way to special temples, she would be given sanctuary.

A man could divorce a wife, however, simply by having her name removed from his family register at the local district office.

In Japan today, divorces are handled by special family courts and generally do not involve lawyers or any substantial expense.

DOING BUSINESS IN JAPAN   For most non-Japanese businesspeople, doing business in Japan is a very special challenge. As I pointed out in my third book on Japan (*How to Do Business in Japan—A Guide for International Businessmen*), first published in 1962, even the goals of Japanese and foreign executives are often diametrically opposed to each other.

To summarize, management in Japan, along with the entire business structure, is based on historical patterns of thought and experience that are different in varying degrees from the Western way of looking at and doing things.

Japanese management and business relations are personalized and primarily based on hierarchical relationships among people within groups. Decision making is based on consensus within each group and normally goes up, instead of down.

With the exception of small and so-called one-man companies, in which decisions tend to be made by the owner/manager, most proposals in Japanese companies originate in the lower levels of management and are then circulated upward for the approval or disapproval of top executives.

Unlike many American companies, for example, in which the president or chairman of the board runs the company in a literal sense, top Japanese executives generally are more concerned with long-range planning and with nurturing managerial talent within the ranks of the company. They leave the proposals and decision-making to the people who are actually doing the work.

Well over 80 percent of the American companies that have tried to do business in Japan have failed because they refused to accept the idea that it is necessary to adapt to the Japanese way of doing things.

The batting average has improved somewhat in recent years, but it is still much lower than it should be, again because of cultural differences that the foreign companies ignore. See CONTRACTS; DECISION MAKING; MANAGEMENT.

Recommended reading: *Japanese Etiquette and Ethics in Business; How to Do Business with the Japanese* (Passport Books).

DOLLS / NINGYO (Neen-g'yoe)   Dolls have played an important role in Japanese life since long before any known contacts with Korea or China. As in China, however, clay figurines, called *haniwa* (hah-nee-wah), have been unearthed from ancient burial mounds.

Throughout the history of Japan, clay and wooden dolls have been an integral part of religious observances, festivals, the theater, and home life.

Warrior dolls are a central theme during Boy's Day. *Hina* (he-nah), or Imperial Court dolls, are traditionally displayed during Girl's Day.

So-called *hakata* (hah-kah-tah) dolls, made of fired clay and then painted, from the Hakata area of Fukuoka Prefecture in Kyushu, are sold throughout

Japan as traditional handicraft items and are known worldwide by doll lovers and collectors.

The dolls—made in the form of *kabuki* actors, beautiful women from around the world, fishermen, and old men and women—are noted for their finely detailed realism.

The manufacture of female wooden dolls called *kokeshi* (koe-kay-she) has been a traditional winter industry in northeastern Japan for centuries. The *kokeshi* have cylindrical bodies and round heads turned out on lathes. Two or three colors are used to draw girls' faces on the dolls and decorate them with various abstract and pictorial designs.

Recommended reading: *Haniwa: Arts of Japan* by Fujio Miki (Weatherhill).

DRIVER'S LICENSE / JIDOSHA-UNTEN MENJO (Jee-doe-shah-uun-tane Mane-joe)   For a Japanese, getting a driver's license is an expensive and formidable undertaking. The driving test is strict, and the written test requires applicants not only to know the rules and regulations of driving, but also to have a rather extensive knowledge of the engine and other mechanical parts and to be able to repair them.

Before taking the tests for a license, most Japanese attend special—and expensive—driving schools. It is common for applicants to fail the test from one to three or four times before they are able to achieve a passing score.

Foreigners in Japan who do not have an International Driver's License or a regular driver's license issued in their own country, must take the same test. With a regular license, a foreign visitor or resident is required to fill out various forms and show the valid foreign license.

It is advisable for the foreign applicant to have an official translation of the foreign license if the application is being made in any city other than Tokyo. Such translations are available from the Japan Automobile Federation.

The booklet to study before approaching the license office is *Rules of the Road*, published by the auto federation and available at license offices.

Another important point about driving in Japan: You must present proof that you have an off-street parking place for a car before you can be issued license plates.

DRIVING IN JAPAN   In Japan, driving is on the left side of the road and requires considerably more expertise than is generally seen in the U.S. Most streets in Japan are narrow and apt to contain numerous obstacles (besides pedestrians) because they were originally designed as footpaths and walking lanes and do not have sidewalks.

Despite the rigid requirements for obtaining a driver's license, driving in Japan is kind of a free-for-all insofar as turning corners, switching lanes, and pulling out of parking areas and alleys. It is the responsibility of the individual driver to avoid collisions, regardless of what the other driver may do.

Another factor is the number of new, inexperienced drivers on the roads at any one time (not to mention trucks, bicycles, scooters, etc.). The authorities recognize this problem by requiring all drivers with less than a year's experience to identify their vehicles with a green and yellow decal.

Japan uses uniform International Traffic Signs on its roads and highways, and they are outstanding, since their meaning is generally clear, regardless of the language. But most other road and highway signs are in Japanese only, and unless you can read them or really know your way around, driving from one place to another can be a mattter of luck.

Recommended: *Reading Your Way Around Japan—A Sign For Every Occasion*, by Boye Lafayette De Mente.

DRUG ABUSE/MAYAKU JOSHU (May-yah-kuu joe-shuu)   Japan's laws against the manufacture, import, possession, sale, and use of unprescribed drugs are strict and harshly enforced. Despite this, drug abuse has been increasing in recent years. Narcotics arrests have been going up as much as 9 percent a year, exceeding 24,000 cases in 1994.

DYING IN JAPAN   In Japan, it is against the law to move a dead body for any reason (unless a doctor is present) until it has been examined by a medical examiner and a release has been issued.

If a doctor is not present, call a doctor, then the police, and then your embassy.

Another point to keep in mind: An ambulance may not be used to transport a body, which can be done only by an authorized undertaker's vehicle.

In the event of the death of an American in Japan, someone should call the American Embassy and ask for the American Citizen Services Branch of the Consular Section. There are companies that specialize in transporting the bodies of deceased foreigners to their home countries.

EARTHQUAKES / JISHIN (Jee-sheen) Earthquakes are so common in Japan that hardly a day goes by without an earthquake occurring somewhere in the islands. Fortunately, most of these quakes are very minor and detectable only by a seismograph. But every year there are usually a few that are strong enough to make themselves known to everyone in the area.

Japan lies on top of one of the earth's largest and most active faults, which accounts for its earthquakes and its large number of active and dormant volcanoes.

Since the beginning of recorded history, Japan has been struck by many earthquakes that left death and destruction in their wake, primarily from fires and tidal waves that followed the quakes.

The fact that homes and other buildings in Japan were traditionally built very close together and made of wood and paper and that open fires were used for cooking, heating, and lighting made them especially susceptible to fires caused by earthquakes.

The most destructive earthquake of modern times struck the Tokyo and Yokohama areas just before noon on September 1, 1923. The force of the quake toppled several hundred thousand homes and buildings, and the fires that followed caused even more damage. Over 100,000 people died in the conflagrations that followed this great quake.

On January 17, 1995, at 5:46 A.M., a devastating earthquake struck Kobe, a major port city 280 miles southwest of Tokyo, killing over 5,000 people, injuring approximately 24,000 more, destroying or severely damaging 44,000 building, leaving over 300,000 homeless, and collapsing a long stretch of the elevated Hanshin Freeway.

The Tokyo Metropolitan Government had prepared various disaster-prevention and relief measures to be taken in the event of a serious earthquake, but the destructiveness of the Kobe quake over-whelmed the government's capacity to respond and shattered the Japanese belief that the high technology they had developed in the previous three decades had made much of the county earthquake-proof. See IMPERIAL HOTEL; NEWSPAPERS.

EASTERN JAPAN References to eastern and western Japan are often confusing to foreigners who visualize the Japanese islands as being in a more or less straight north-south line and think of Kyoto, Osaka, and other major cities of western Honshu as being south of Tokyo.

The island chain actually is curved like a crescent. The curve in Honshu, the longest and largest of the islands, is especially pronounced—going from latitude 142 to 131—with the result that the lower half of the island is almost due west of the Tokyo area.

When viewed from Kyoto, Japan's Imperial capital for over a thousand years, Tokyo and all the prefectures north of it are in the east—thus the name Tokyo (Eastern Capital).

EAST, THE, **MAGAZINE** Founded in 1963, *The East* magazine is intended for people interested in both historical and contemporary Japan. Its articles cover history, traditional culture, geography, industry, society, celebrities, and the arts.

It often runs excerpts from classical Japanese literature and pieces on the Japanese language—generally all from a sociological point of view. Well done and recommended, it is available in the U.S. from The East, P.O. Box 2640, Grand Central Station, New York, NY 10164. Or directly from The East Publications, 3-19-7 Minami-Azabu, Minato-ku, Tokyo 106 Japan.

EATING / MESHIAGARU (May-she-ah-gah-rue) Over the centuries, eating in Japan became imbued with religious and aesthetic practices and was stylized to a meticulous degree. Great significance was attached to the appearance and arrangement of food, as well as to the utensils used.

Beauty and harmony were the hallmarks of a well-prepared and well-served meal, and it was important to observe a carefully prescribed dining etiquette. Learning how to eat properly was therefore an important part of the education of every Japanese child.

Eating etiquette is considerably less demanding in modern-day Japan, but it is still a distinctive feature of Japanese life, and in formal situations the traditional ways are still followed. The biggest difficulty foreigners have in adapting to the Japanese way of eating is in manipulating chopsticks and sitting on the floor for long periods of time. The only solution for this challenge is practice.

When eating a Japanese-style meal in a Japanese setting, you should at least try to follow Japanese etiquette and custom in sitting and handling your chopsticks and the various small saucers and bowls.

It is customary to pick up bowls and small dishes and bring them up near and under the mouth when eating, especially in the case of small soup or noodle bowls and rice bowls, to help avoid spilling or dropping anything. The soup is sipped, and the rice is often more or less shoveled into the mouth.

Before beginning to eat, whether a snack or full meal, it is important to say, *"Itadakimasu"* (Ee-tah-dah-kee-mahss), which is a form of thanks and appreciation for the food you are about to eat. When you finish eating with someone else who is the host, it is equally important to say, *"Gochisosama"* (Go-chee-so-sah-mah), the institutionalized expression for thanking him or her for feeding or treating you.

ECONOMIC INFORMATION CENTER / KEIZAI KOHO CENTER (Kay-e-zie koe-hoe)   Established in 1978 by the Japan Federation of Economic Organizations, the country's most powerful and prestigious business group, the Economic Information Center (KKC) is charged with developing and disseminating information about Japan's ecomony.

In 1982, the KKC undertook a new program—a direct-mail promotional campaign, aimed at the U.S. and Europe, to help explain the position and trade policies of Japan's major corporations.

The KKC's mailing list, consisting of high-level business leaders, academics, and political leaders, originally was made up of some 10,000 names. In 1983, an additional 2,000 leaders in Southeast Asia were added to the list. See OTHER SOURCES for KKC's address.

The Center researches and publishes, in English, articles, monographs, and books on social and economic subjects and aids in the production and dissemination of video films and cassettes on matters relating to Japan's economy and way of doing business.

Two publications of special interest are *Economic Eye—A Digest of Views from Japan* and *Speaking of Japan*, a digest of major speeches given by Japanese and foreign experts on various Japanese topics. For a listing of other major publications, see OTHER ENGLISH-LANGUAGE SOURCES.

The KKC is subtitled Japan Institute for Social and Economic Affairs.

ECONOMIC PROGRESS AFTER 1868   Following the resignation of the last Tokugawa *Shogun* and the restoration of Imperial power in 1868, Japan began a systematic program to totally remake the industrial base of the country.

The first industrialization project launched by the new Meiji government was the export of raw silk and use of the foreign currency earned to start a small-scale cotton-spinning and weaving industry. This pattern of development was quickly expanded to include a wide range of light and heavy industries, including shipbuilding and military arms manufacturing. The government subsidized many of these industries and later turned them over to private interests, contributing to the appearance and growth of huge industrial conglomerates known as *zaibatsu* (zie-bot-sue). See ZAIBATSU.

Annual growth was only about 3 percent until the advent of World War I. But, at a safe distance from the main action of the war, Japanese industry became a large-scale supplier to the warring nations. Its machinery industry in particular made great progress.

The economic benefits of the war encouraged a strong expansionist element in Japan's armed forces, however, eventually resulting in Japan's invasion of China, Southeast Asia, the South Pacific, and finally the attack on Pearl Harbor in 1941—which ended in utter defeat for the Japanese empire in 1945.

With its foreign colonies gone, its home economic base virtually wiped out by massive bombing raids, and over six million demobilized soldiers and civilians suddenly returned to a starving Japan in 1945, the country was at the lowest point ever in its long history.

With generous support from the United States and demonstrating an almost unbelievable degree of cooperation, hard work, and sacrifice, the Japanese began the task of rebuilding their devastated economy.

Domestic purchases by the American occupying forces made a significant contribution during the first five years of Japan's struggle to overcome its gravest crisis. An even more important factor was the outbreak of the war in Korea. The U.S. began to use Japan not only as a staging area for carrying on the war in Korea, but also as a major supply source.

Primarily as a result of the economic impetus provided by the Korean War and the new American policy of helping Japan become an economic bastion in Asia, the Japanese regained their prewar economic level by 1955 —only 10 years after suffering total defeat.

For the next 18 years, fueled by massive infusions of new technology and a worldwide demand for Japanese-made consumer merchandise, Japan's economy grew at the incredible rate of 9.9 percent to 11.8 percent. Its GNP passed the $100 billion mark in 1966.

The international monetary crisis that developed in 1971—triggered to a considerable extent by American reactions—followed by the first oil crisis in 1973, slowed the mighty Japanese industrial engine down to more modest growth rates, but it continued to expand.

In 1978, when the second oil crisis came, the Japanese were prepared and weathered the storm better than most of the other advanced nations. In that same year, its GNP surpassed the one trillion dollar mark.

Despite the fragility of an economy based almost entirely on importing massive amounts of raw materials from around the world and then exporting, in turn, huge amounts of finished products, the Japanese managed to balance the economic and political factors involved, going from war-time devastation in 1945 to being one of the three major economic powers in the world by 1970.

However, by the end of the 1980s, Japan's economic blitzkrieg had over-extended itself, and the bubble finally burst. Banks and stock companies incurred enormous losses. By 1990 the mad rush to invest overseas had ended, and for the first time in the post–World War II years, many of Japan's world-famous manufacturing and exporting giants reported dramatic drops in profits and, in some cases, outright losses.

But this startling setback did not undermine the basic strength of Japan's economy, and although the recession caused by the bursting of the "bubble economy" was still being felt in the mid-1990s, Japan's leading enterprises once again took advantage of adversity to initiate management reform programs, streamlining their operations, cutting costs at home, and shifting more of their manufacturing overseas.

Another significant factor to emerge from the dust and debris of the bubble economy of the 1980s was an acute awareness among Japan's industrial leaders that the only way they could continue to survive and grow within the world economy was to form strategic alliances with compatible foreign enterprises on a global basis—a concept that was subsumed in the term *kyosei* (k'yoe-say), which means symbiosis, or in this new sense, "living in cooperative harmony with the rest of the world."

Japan is now the world's second largest economy—a development that was so unexpected, so extraordinary, that it continues to defy all conventional wisdom.

Recommended reading: *Miracle by Design: The Real Reasons Behind Japan's Economic Success*, by Frank Gibney (Times Books).

EDO (Eh-doe)   Edo (also spelled Yedo), which means "estuary," is the old name of Tokyo. It began as a tiny fishing-farming village at the head of Edo (Tokyo) Bay and was first mentioned in history at the end of the twelfth century when Taro Shigenaga Edo, a member of the famous Taira clan, was appointed political agent in charge of the province of Musashi (where the village was located) by *Shogun* Yoritomo Minamoto, head of the Taira clan.

But Edo was to remain in the backwater of history until 1457, when warrior/poet Dokan Ota, a high-ranking retainer of the Uesugi clan, which then controlled the area, chose the site for a castle fortress.

One hundred and forty-three years later (1590), the soon-to-be famous Ieyasu Tokugawa was given the eight provinces on the Musashino Plain (Kanto) by Hideyoshi Toyotomi, whom he had helped become the military leader of the country.

Ieyasu made Edo his fief capital, and its population immediately began rising. When he replaced Hideyoshi and became *shogun* in 1603, Edo became the headquarters of the shogunate government. All of Ieyasu's 80,000 retainers and soldiers and their families moved to Edo.

The small town was turned into a sprawling city in just a few weeks' time. One can just imagine the great hustle and bustle as these new residents built homes and businesses and went about providing for themselves and the needs of the Shogunate Court.

In 1605, Ieyasu retired from the formal position of *shogun*, and turned the post over to his son, Hidetada. The new *shogun* immediately commissioned Toda Takatora, the most famous castle architect of the day, to design and build a new Edo Castle that would be the best fortified in the land.

Hundreds of thousands of workmen took part in the great building project, which was not completed until April 1640.

In 1635, Edo received another great boost in population when the third Tokugawa *Shogun*, Iemitsu, decreed that all the 270 *daimyo* (feudal lords) in Japan would build mansions in Edo, leave their families there (well attended by servants and retainers) at all times, and spend every other year in Edo in attendance at the *shogun's* court.

This shogunate order resulted in another great burst of building in Edo. Large areas of the shallow bay were reclaimed, and a number of lagoons and marshes were filled in so that the mansions of the *daimyo* could be built in the vicinity of the *shogun's* castle (known as the Edo or Chiyoda Castle).

Despite moves to widen the city's major streets—usually after major fires, such as an unusually destructive one in 1657—Edo remained a city made up of hundreds of communities grouped around the different *daimyo* estates, with little rhyme or reason to its overall layout, a legacy present-day Tokyoites must still contend with.

The heyday of the Edo Period was from 1688 to 1704, known as the *genroku* (gane-roe-kuu) era. There was a general relaxation of political control, economic conditions were good, and the arts and other endeavors flourished.

Many businesspeople amassed wealth, and those who could afford it lived extravagantly, dressing in beautiful silk *kimono*, attending popular playhouses, and treating themselves to sumptuous banquets.

The quality of the shogunate leadership fluctuated. The fortunes of the *samurai* class declined as the financial power of the merchant class grew and money began to replace rice as the primary medium of exchange.

Scholars studying Japanese history began to question the right of the shogunate to govern Japan. News of the growing power and activities of foreign nations continued to seep into Japan, raising the question of national defense.

In 1792 and again in 1804, Russia sent envoys to Japan, demanding that the country open its doors to trade. In 1808, an English warship pursued a Dutch vessel right into Nagasaki Bay and left only after members of the crew had caused a furor. Many Japanese expected the country to be invaded at any time, and the shogunate went to special lengths to fortify Hokkaido against possible Russian intrusions.

Several of the largest clans, particularly those in Kyushu, set up strong coastal defenses.

By 1731, Edo had a population of 562,000, not counting the *shogun's* thousands of retainers and the families of all the feudal lords. Just 56 years later (1787), Edo had a population of 1,368,000, making it one of the largest cities in the world.

When the Tokugawa Shogunate fell in 1868, the Imperial Court was moved from Kyoto to Edo, which was then renamed Tokyo, or Eastern Capital. See HISTORY; TOKUGAWA; MEIJI; TOKYO.

EDO CASTLE   The forerunner of today's Imperial Palace in Tokyo was Edo Yakata, or Edo Mansion, built on a hill overlooking Hibiya Inlet by the warrior/poet Ota Dokan in 1457. At that time, the castle had three parts (an inner, middle, and outer compound) and was known as the finest castle in the Kanto district. Surrounding streams were converted into moats.

Following Ota's death, the city of Edo returned to its former role as an unimportant village in an out-of-the-way place.

In 1590, Ieyasu Tokugawa, who was to establish Japan's last great feudal shogunate in 1603, ordered the remodeling of the castle. Work was carried on intermittently for several years but it was not until 1605, after Ieyasu had turned the title of *shogun* over to his son, Hidetada, that full-scale construction began.

Hidetada retained Takatora Toda, the greatest castle architect of the time, to make Edo Castle the finest and best fortification in the country. The building project was one of the largest ever undertaken up to that time, involving civil engineers from all over Japan and thousands of workers assigned to the project by their clan lords.

When completed, Edo Castle was one of the great sights in the land. Its roof tiles—which, from a distance, appeared to be white—were made of lead to withstand strong winds and rain. The view of the castle from afar was often compared to the view of the snow-tipped crown of Mt. Fuji.

In 1637, Iemitsu, the third Tokugawa *Shogun*, ordered the inner keep of the castle remodeled again. It was completed in 1640 and remained unchanged up to modern times.

EDUCATION / KYOIKU (K'yoe-e-kuu)   Japan's educational system is based on six years of elementary school, three years of junior high school, three years of senior high school, and four years of university.

Some children are enrolled in private kindergartens as early as the age of three, but elementary school starts at six. In elementary schools, one teacher generally teaches all subjects in each class. Primary emphasis is first given to teaching the young students how to read and write the relatively simple *hiragana* (he-rah-gah-nah) and *katakana* (kah-tah-kah-nah) characters, which are phonetic representations of the syllables making up the Japanese language. Then the students go on to the much more complicated *kanji* (kahn-jee) characters, borrowed from China over a thousand years ago.

The first nine years of school in Japan are compulsory, and the rate of attendance is normally 100 percent. From junior high school on, individual subjects are taught by different teachers, and students are introduced to the study of English.

In order to get into senior high school, junior high school students must pass rigorous entrance examinations. In addition to general academic subjects, senior high students usually also take such vocational subjects as engineering, agriculture, commerce, and fishing.

The entrance examinations for universities in Japan are tougher still. The competition to get into name universities is surely the toughest in the world. See EXAMINATION HELL.

The current annual nationwide preliminary achievement test that is given for state and public universities was introduced in 1979. The tests are administered on a weekend in January at some 280 places around the country.

The test begins a two-month period during which all Japanese students who want to pursue higher education must sit for examinations, for private, as well as public, schools.

Degrees in medicine and dentistry require six years. A master's degree requires two years, and if sought, a Ph.D. requires an additional three years. A start-to-finish doctoral program takes four years.

Japan has both private and public (national) universities, but fewer of the latter. There are also junior colleges with two-year curriculums and specialized vocational high schools with five-year terms.

Prior to 1872 and during most of the long Tokugawa Shogunate Period (1603–1868), the children of *samurai* families were taught in *han* (hahn), or clan, schools operated by the ruling *samurai* authorities. In these schools, the emphasis was on moral, martial, and cultural subjects designed to prepare the young, privileged students to assume the duties of their class.

In addition to these *han* schools, there were some 20,000 *tera koya* (tay-rah koe-yah), or temple, schools for the children of farmers and townspeople. Attendance at these temple-run schools was not compulsory, and there were no age limits. It is estimated that some 40 percent of the common people studied at these schools. One of the most popular subjects was how to use the *soroban*, or abacus.

The lecture format is the usual method of instruction in Japanese universities, and, because of limited facilities and a shortage of professors, up to 500 or more students may attend individual lectures.

Ambitious students wanting direct, personal guidance by their professors may attend seminars conducted on an ongoing basis.

The academic year in Japan, which runs from April to March, is divided into two semesters—from April to September and from October to March.

During the 1960s and 1970s, many Japanese students became involved in political movements, through which they were able to influence national policies. The number of students participating in such activities has declined significantly in recent years.

Since 1970, Japan has had the highest literacy rate of any country in the world—well over 99 percent. Interestingly enough, only Korean students spend more time studying after school than the Japanese do. Almost 20 percent of Japanese students study more than three hours a day at home, 30.9 percent study from two to three hours, and 32.9 percent study from one to two hours.

More and more Japanese parents are enrolling their children in kindergarten to give them a headstart in the uphill struggle to get into the more desirable universities. Some parents engage private tutors for their children before they are old enough for kindergarten.

The percentage of children going to kindergarten jumped from 28.7 percent in 1960 to 64.4 percent in 1980 and is still climbing.

There are over 15,000 kindergartens, over 25,000 elementary schools, close to 11,000 junior high schools, and well over 5,000 senior high schools in Japan.

Besides these regular schools, there are 72 schools for the blind, 110 schools for the deaf, and 695 schools for the handicapped in Japan.

Japan has over 18,000 public and private research institutions, 16,452 public halls, 1,200 libraries, 493 museums, 709 national and public children's and youth centers, 89 women's halls, and 690 audiovisual centers and libraries.

In addition, approximately 50,000 social-education classes and lectures are offered annually by boards of education, with nearly three million people enrolled. There are also close to 200,000 Boy Scout troops, well over 200,000 facilities for physical education and sports, including 1,915 athletic fields, 10,297 baseball and softball fields, 30,911 swimming pools, 4,946 outdoor basketball courts, 1,911 golf courses, 850 ice skating rinks, and 769 ski areas. Public cultural facilities include 548 cultural halls, 11 archaeological activities centers, and 264 historical and ethnological museums.

In recent years, Japanese schools have come under increasing criticism for their failure to imbue students with a strong sense of curiosity and creativity. The annual dropout rate has continued to creep up, and there has been an increase in the problem of *ijime* (ee-jee-may), or bullying, in schools. See CRAM SCHOOLS; PREPARATORY SCHOOLS.

EIGHTY-EIGHT SACRED PLACES OF SHIKOKU   During the peaceful centuries of the Tokugawa Shogunate era (1603–1868), various religious pilgrimages around Japan became very popular. Written accounts of some of these trips indicate that they were undertaken as much for pleasure as for religious reasons and sometimes lasted for several months.

One of the most popular and longest of these pilgrimages was a visit to each of the Eighty-Eight Sacred Places of Shikoku—88 temples of special renown, along a circuitous route around the island. Among the temples on the route that are still notable are Hotsumi Saki, Kokubun Ji, Kongofuku Ji, Kakurin Ji, Shido Ji, and Tatsu Ji.

A full list of the 88 temples is available from the Japan National Tourist Organization (see listing).

Recommended reading: *Japanese Pilgrimage*, by Oliver Statler (Morrow). Using his own temple pilgrimage as a starting point, Statler weaves the history of Japan into this fascinating account.

ELDER STATESMEN / GENRO (Gane-roe)   Japan has a long history of regents, retired emperors, *shogun*, and influential politicans advising and sometimes directing the government from the background. In the modern era, the most famous of these advisors were the *genro*, appointed to the position by the young Emperor Taisho when he ascended the throne in 1912, after the death of his illustrious father, Emperor Meiji.

Those appointed to the position of *genro* were Princes Yamagata, Oyama, Katsura and Matsukata, and Marquis Inoue. The sixth and best known of the *genro*, was Prince Kimmochi Saionji, appointed to the position in 1921, when he was 70, to replace Field Marshal Yamagata, who had died.

Prince Saionji is one of the most interesting figures in Japan's modern history. Raised at the Imperial Court in Kyoto, he was a favorite of Emperor Komei and a playmate to Prince Mutsuhito, who was to become Emperor Meiji.

At 19, Saionji was made a commander in the Imperial army and took part in an important battle. He was later appointed governor of Echigo, then studied French in Nagasaki, and in 1871 sailed abroad with a large entourage, some still wearing their full *samurai* regalia.

In Washington, D.C., Saionji was introduced to society by President Ulysses S. Grant. From there he went to New York, London, and Paris, where he studied law. Returning to Japan nine years later, Saionji wrote a book about his travels, founded a liberal newspaper, and lectured at Meiji Law School. A very controversial figure who continuously criticized corruption in the Satsuma and Choshu clans—the ones responsible for the Restoration of Emperor Meiji—and scandalized his family and friends by appearing in public with *geisha*, Saionji was appointed Minister to Austria in 1885 and to Germany and Belgium in 1887.

Back in Japan in 1889, Saionji became a member of the Privy Council, leader of the Seiyukai political party in 1903, and president of the Privy Council and prime minister in 1906. He again served as prime minister in 1911.

As a former prime minister, Saionji continued to serve the government in various ways, including representing Japan at the Peace Conference at Versailles, following the conclusion of World War I.

Between 1921—when he became a member of the *genro*—and 1925, all the other elder statesmen died, leaving only Saionji. From that time on, until his own death in 1940 at the age of 91, he was one of the most revered and influential men in Japan.

Saionji was a direct descendant of Emperor Seiwa (859–876), whose son Shinno Sadazumi took the name Minamoto and founded one of the country's greatest families. The story of the family was told in the famous novel,

Genji Monogatari (Gane-jee Moe-no-gah-tah-ree), or *Tale of Genji*, written in the eleventh century by Lady Murasaki Shikibu.

ELECTIONS / SENKYO (Sen-k'yoe)   Japan's election campaigns are apt to be noisy affairs, with candidates riding around in vehicles equipped with public address systems, broadcasting their views to all within a several block distance—or with their staff playing recordings of their appeals over and over.

Since 1945, both women and men who have reached the age of 20 have the right to vote. Voters write the name or names of the candidates of their choice on ballots. House-to-house canvassing is prohibited by law, as are especially noisy methods of getting the public's attention, but the latter, it seems, is not strictly enforced.

Members of Japan's Diet (Parliament), prefectural governors, and assemblymen, along with city, town, and village mayors and assemblymen, are chosen by direct election. The assemblymen who run Tokyo's 21 wards are also elected by direct vote.

ELECTRICITY / DENKI (Dane-kee)   A difference in electrical voltage between eastern and western Japan makes it neccesary to be careful about buying household appliances or recreational equipment in one part of the country and using it in another.

The electricity in eastern Japan (The Tokyo-Yokohama area and everything north) is 50 cycles and 100 volts. In western Japan (Kyoto-Osaka-Kobe and everything west and south), it is 60 cycles and 100 volts. U.S.-made appliances will work in the Tokyo area but at reduced efficiency. Voltage regulators are available.

EMPEROR / TENNO (Tane-no)   Although there is some doubt about the date of Japan's first emperor, the tendency, unofficially, is to accept the year 660 B.C. as accurate. With this as a starting point, Emperor Hirohito (He-row-he-toe), who ascended the throne in 1926, was the 124th emperor. He and his wife, Nagako, had two sons and three daughters. His oldest son, Akihito (Ah-kee-he-toe), who succeeded him on January 9, 1989, is the 125th occupant of the Chrysanthemum throne.

Except for the earliest years, for which records are questionable, plus brief periods in later centuries, Japan's emperors have not actually been the rulers of their country. Until 1868, when the Meiji Restoration placed power in the hands of a constitutional monarchy, real control was exercised by various members of the nobility, and, from the twelfth century on, their successors, the *samurai* warrior class and several *shogun* dynasties.

Despite the fact that for over 1,000 years real power was in the hands of the nobility and various military dictators, the Imperial system was continued, and each of these governments in turn based its authority on the sovereign right conferred upon it by the reigning emperor.

Living emperors are generally not referred to by their given names and are given a posthumous name upon their death. The late Emperor Hirohito reigned for a total of 63 years, far longer than any of his ancestors. An accomplished biologist, he wrote 14 books on the subject.

The present emperor, Akihito, was born in 1933 and attended Gakushin University in Tokyo, where he studied politics and economics. The first member of the Imperial family to be raised more or less as an ordinary child, Akihito had an American tutor, Ms. Elizabeth Vining, for several years, and is known to have gone out drinking with his school friends. In 1959 he married a commoner, Michiko Shoda, the daughter of an old and successful business family. They have three children, including Crown Prince Naruhito.

Prior to 1945, the emperor was officially regarded as divine and, to a degree, was treated as a living god. When he left the Imperial Palace and traveled about the city or country, people were not permitted to gaze upon him directly, especially from a position above the ground level. Those who were out in the open had to prostrate themselves on the ground as his entourage passed.

Today the emperor has no governmental power. He is treated as the head of state in diplomatic and ceremonial functions. The constitution declares that he is the symbol of the state and that he derives his position from the will of the people.

The Japanese have ambivalent feelings toward the Imperial family. In a recent survey, 44 percent said they felt affection toward the emperor, empress, and their family, but 45 percent said they felt nothing at all. Only six percent of those surveyed said they thought the emperor's status should be elevated, while 82 percent said it should remain the same. Eight percent said the system should be abolished.

Emperor Akihito's brother, Prince Hitachi, is involved in Red Cross and other volunteer activities. One of his sisters, Princess Suga, is married to the scion of the famous Shimadzu family, one of Japan's most powerful clans during the Tokugawa period.

For more personal details about the present emperor and his family, see IMPERIAL FAMILY.

EMPLOYMENT AGENCIES   Lifetime employment is still the rule in larger Japanese corporations, as well as in the many city, prefectural, and federal government offices and agencies. And, although municipal governments have traditionally maintained job placement operations, commercial employment agencies are still limited in number and in the scope of their activities.

Generally speaking, major Japanese companies seldom, if ever, make use of the services of employment agencies. The agencies that do exist—and there are only a dozen or so—cater primarily to foreign-owned or foreign affiliated companies in Japan.

Executive "head hunting" for foreign clients is an especially delicate business in Japan because of the deep and pervasive relationship that exists between the Japanese and their employers—and because there is a strong tendency for Japanese executives to be extremely cautious about the stability, longevity, and reliability of foreign companies.

Among the best known of the employment agencies in Tokyo are Beststaff Japan Inc., Cambridge Corporation, ECI Inc., International Management Consultants Association Inc., Nippon Manpower Company Ltd., and Tokyo Executive Search Company Ltd.

ENCYCLOPEDIA OF JAPAN / NIHON NO HYAKKAJITEN (Nee-hone no h'yack-kah-jee-tane)   Published in the fall of 1983 by Kodansha Ltd., the Kodansha Encyclopedia of Japan is a nine-volume English-language encyclopedia that covers over 10,000 topics and is the most comprehensive source on Japan ever compiled.

The compilation of the work was directed by Professor Gen Itasaka of Harvard University and the reference department of Kodansha. Some 1,400 scholars, specialists, and writers—half of them Japanese and half foreign—contributed to the project.

Produced in an 8½-by-11-inch format, with some 1,000 illustrations, eight volumes of the handsome set have 352 pages each, and the ninth volume (index to the other eight) is 288 pages.

In 1993 Kodansha published a two-volume *Japan: An Illustrated Encyclopedia*, based on the original 1983 series. The new two-volume series—with 1,964 pages, 12,000 entries, 4,000 color illustrations, 20 pages of maps and a 14-page bibliography of major works on Japan—is both an update and an addition to the original work.

Japan: An Illustrated Encyclopedia is available internationally through Kinokuniya bookstores, OCS bookstores, and Maruzen.

ENERGY RESEARCH   The almost complete lack of domestic oil supplies, making it necessary for Japan to import a significant percentage of its energy needs, is a primary factor in Japan's energy-related research and development programs.

The Organization for General Development of New Energy is responsible for carrying out research in nuclear power, coal, coal gas, solar heat, geothermal heat, and alcohol.

Research is also being conducted in the use of biomass, wind power, wave power, ocean temperature differentials, and in small and medium-size hydroelectric systems.

ENGLISH LANGUAGE STUDY   The Military Occupation of Japan by the U.S. from 1945 to the spring of 1952, along with the subsequent emergence of Japan as an international economic and political power, set the stage for the adoption of English as Japan's second language.

This might suggest that most Japanese speak very good English, which is not the case. The majority of Japanese speak very little or no English, but the number who are studying English and the time and energy they devote to it may dramatically change this situation in the years ahead.

Most Japanese study English in high school, and literally millions make an effort to learn it on their own or in special language schools or from private tutors. But there are not enough good teachers to go around, especially with conversational fluency. The language is hard for the Japanese to learn, and the majority have very little opportunity to practice it on English-speaking foreigners.

In 1984, Japanese schools in Tokyo set a precedent by hiring 30 native English speakers to teach in the city's school system. The new system was adopted by the Tokyo Education Board as a step toward teaching students practical English conversation as a supplement to their regular formal studies.

The first English teacher to take up her duties under the new system was Anne Marian Newell from England, who took over her class at Adachi Nishi Senior High School in Adachi Ward on April 9, 1984.

In contrast to this late beginning by the public educational system in Japan, virtually every major company in Japan has or has had—in some cases, since the early 1950s—some kind of English teaching program in which native-born teachers are hired to conduct classes for employees. It is common for senior Japanese executives, including those who are in their sixties and seventies, to attend such privately held classes. (The author conducted such classes for the Japan Travel Bureau in 1953–54.)

The head office of Nippon Steel in Tokyo regularly offers some 30 courses in English and other foreign languages to its employees.

In addition, there are hundreds of privately run English-language schools for Japanese of all ages, some of them quite large. There are also a number of television shows that teach English, German, and French, usually in the mornings.

ENO ISLAND / ENO SHIMA (Eh-no she-mah)   A tiny islet connected to Katase Beach by a long bridge, Eno Shima is one of several seaside resorts on Miura Peninsula, about an hour's train ride south of Tokyo, that is famous for its shrines, temples, and recreational facilities. Actually, when people say Eno Shima, they generally mean the Katase beach area, with its mile after mile of beachfront hotels and restaurants.

In the summer months, the Katase/Eno Shima area is jammed with beach-goers, with as many as a million people littering the sands, from the island causeway to the adjoining Kugenuma Beach.

During the Kamakura Period (1192–1333), Katase Beach was the shogunate's official execution grounds. It is the spot where Kublai Khan's envoys were beheaded in 1275, when they demanded that Japan pay tribute to China. The great priest Nichiren, founder of the sect bearing his name, would have been executed there, but the executioner's sword broke when he tested it. The incident was taken as an omen that the priest should not be killed, and his execution was canceled.

ENTERTAINMENT EXPENSE / SHAYO (Shah-yoe)   Japan is famous for its nightlife (see MIZU SHOBAI and WATER BUSINESS), which centers on a larger number of bars, cabarets, and nightclubs per capita than in any other country in the world—not to mention massage-parlor baths, hot spring spas, *geisha* inns, and other types of entertainment that are unique to Japan.

Much of the several billion dollars a year that is spent on nighttime entertainment in Japan comes from the expense accounts of company executives, managers, and salespeople, entertaining themselves, their colleagues, and customers at company expense.

Such expense accounts vary from a few hundred dollars to several thousand dollars a month. In a few cases, the expense account is paid directly to the company employee. In most cases, the clubs, restaurants, inns, and other establishments bill the company directly.

The more the members of the *shayo zoku*, or "expense account tribe," are authorized to spend, the more and better service they and their guests get.

This system makes it very difficult for foreign executives living in Japan or visiting there to keep up with their Japanese colleagues on the entertainment front. See NIGHTCLUBS; CABARETS.

ENTRANCE EXAMINATIONS / NYUGAKU SHIKEN (Nyu-gah-kuu she-kane)   In Japan, getting a white-collar job with a large company or in the more desirable agencies, bureaus, and ministries of the government depends almost entirely on one's education—and on the particular schools one attended.

Since there are not enough openings in the more desirable schools (from kindergarten on up!), entrance into these schools is based on competitive examinations.

While the kindergarten, grade school, and high school one attends is important, the critical jump is from high school into college, because many of the most desirable employers in Japan hire only from, or primarily from, certain schools (usually the ones their top executives graduated from).

As a result, the entrance examinations for Tokyo University, Keio, Waseda, and the other top universities are extremely difficult. Well over half the students who take them each year fail—because the exams are hard and because there are not enough openings to go around.

The trial of preparing for these examinations is a serious strain on the mental and physical health of many students, and is often referred to as the Examination Hell.

Students who fail the examinations and are thus not admitted (until they can try again the following year) are often called *ronin* (roe-neen), or masterless *samurai*, after feudal-age warriors who lost their lord and were left on their own. See RONIN.

ENVIRONMENTAL POLLUTION By the early 1960s, Japan was suffering from serious pollution problems as a result of rapid industrial development. Laws intended to prevent and control pollution were passed as early as 1949, but it was 1970 before Japan had a comprehensive legal system for protecting the environment and began a crash effort to do something about its problems.

The situation was so bad in the early and mid-1960s that traffic police officers at major intersections had to work in short shifts, alternately breathing oxygen from special tanks provided for that purpose. Tokyo was almost permanently shrouded in smog that was so thick it was said that children four and five years old had never seen the stars at night.

There were also incidents of poisonings from industrial wastes, resulting in a national outcry that something be done. Something was done, and Japan is now noted for its stringent pollution controls and for the progress it has made in cleaning up its environment.

EPIC SONGS / NANIWABUSHI (Nah-nee-wah-buu-she) A very popular genre of epic folk songs, *naniwabushi* tell stories of the rise and fall of Japan's great feudal families, the triumphs of the weak over the powerful, and the inevitability of justice. The songs are rendered in a high-pitched, formalized style of recitation to the accompaniment of *shamisen* music.

ERAS / JIDAI (Jee-die) From ancient times in Asia, it was the practice to count years according to the reign of an emperor or an imperial line. This custom of reckoning years by eras was adopted in Japan in the seventh century. From that time until the nineteenth century, the reigning emperor decided when one era ended and another began.

Under the current system, adopted following the ascension of Emperor Meiji in 1868, the era begins the day an emperor ascends the throne and continues until his death. Thus the Meiji era began in 1868 and lasted until 1912 and was followed by the Showa era. The present era, Heisei, began in 1989 with the accession of Crown Prince Akihito to the throne.

Currently, official documents are dated according to the era, and many older people still reckon years by the system for both personal and business affairs, but the Western calendar is by far the most common system for recording and keeping track of dates.

ESCALATOR SYSTEM The Escalator System refers to the system of promotion in Japanese companies and other organizations. Japanese companies and organizations generally hire only at the entry level, selecting the new employees they want each year from classes graduating from high schools and colleges.

Thereafter, promotion up the ladder of success is primarily based on seniority and occurs only after the employees concerned have spent a certain number of years in grade—as in the military.

People who joined the company the same year tend to be promoted at the same time, at least until they reach the managerial or executive level, at which time the most able are singled out for further advancement.

The concept of the escalator comes from the fact that unless employees commit some kind of serious offense, they will not be fired, their income will gradually go up, and they will be automatically advanced in rank.

Those who prove to be inept are still carried along by the system and often end up in the position of manager. This is not as serious as the Westerner might think because the Japanese hiring system precludes the employment of complete incompetents in white-collar jobs, and, once employees are hired, the system of continuing job-rotation assures that they will learn a great deal about how the company operates and what its needs are.

Futhermore, the higher a Japanese employee rises in the company, the less specialized expertise he or she is expected to have. Generalized knowledge, a broad and long view, the ability to get along with people, and a knack for keeping everything working smoothly are the traits the manager must have to succeed in Japan.

ETIQUETTE / SAHO (Sah-hoe) In Japanese society, all things, including people, are ranked in a superior/inferior system. Because of the importance of maintaining the relationships established in this system in accordance with the exacting standards developed by the Imperial nobility and continued by the feudal *samurai* class, the Japanese created an etiquette system that was the most comprehensive, the most specific, and the most demanding the world has ever seen.

Until the end of the Tokugawa Shogunate in 1868, virtually every move or action a Japanese might make or take was prescribed in exact detail. This included sleeping, sitting, walking, eating, dressing, and working. How well one learned and followed this etiquette was equated with both one's education and one's morality.

In feudal days, failure to follow the prescribed manner in many actions was a serious and sometimes fatal offense. The role models and guardians of the system were the sword-carrying *samurai*, and they were very strict disciplinarians, indeed.

The legal sanctions and *samurai* standards that made etiquette a matter of life or death during Japan's long feudal period have long since gone, but a very carefully prescribed and detailed etiquette is still an important part of life in Japan.

Much of the etiquette is bound up in the language and requires different levels and styles for different occasions, making it difficult or impossible for Westerners to do as the Japanese do, unless they speak the language very, very fluently.

The most that the average non-Japanese can do is learn the physical aspects of traditional Japanese etiquette—in greetings, partings, dining, drinking, and so forth—and just be polite in his or her native tongue.

EXAMINATION HELL / JIGOKU SHIKEN   (Jee-go-kuu she-kane) The entrance examinations of Japan's ranking universities are so difficult and so competitive that the process of preparing for and taking them is known as Examination Hell. Only a small percentage of the high school graduates who take the examinations each year get passing marks.

It is not uncommon for students to suffer physical and mental breakdowns as a result of their efforts to get into the more desirable universities. See ENTRANCE EXAMINATIONS; RONIN.

EXPO MEMORIAL PARK   At Suita City, between Osaka and Kyoto, the EXPO Memorial Park is the site of a World Exposition held in 1970. After the exposition ended, the grounds and buildings were turned into a huge recreation and amusement center, which opened in 1972.

The park includes a Japanese Garden, the Japan Folk Art Museum, EXPO Memorial Hall, EXPO Land, and numerous other attractions on a 264-hectare (652-acre) site.

EXPORTING / YUSHUTSU (You-shute-sue)   The Japanese are currently among the most successful exporters in the world. They achieved this extraordinary position because of a number of very specific factors.

First, the Japanese are a proud and ambitious people. They think of themselves (as do many other nationalities) as among—if not the—best, most talented, and hardest-working people in the world.

They have a very strong desire to be the best in the world and an extraordinarily competitive spirit that drives them unmercifully. They are very nationalistic and, more often than not, put the interests of their country above their personal interests.

With an insatiable appetite for learning, the Japanese drive themselves to learn all they can about things of importance to them—especially knowledge about foreign affairs, politics, and economics.

Furthermore, all Japanese are acutely aware that the great industrial economy they have developed depends entirely on the importation of huge amounts of raw materials, from oil to iron, and they all know that the only way they can pay for these imports is to export a lot.

Japanese manufacturers, no matter how small or insignificant their operation, are likely to be export minded. The great export boom that began in Japan in the 1950s was not just the doing of large companies. It was also the work of thousands upon thousands of small and medium-size companies whose employees worked 10 to 12 hours a day, six and seven days a week.

Few of these manufacturers/exporters could speak any foreign language. Almost none of them had ever been abroad. But they persevered, and if they were not able to export directly, they went through trading companies. Today, hundreds of these companies are large, internationally known firms.

Another of the major reasons for Japan's success as an exporting nation is the insatiable appetite of American and other Western importers, wholesalers, and retail chain store operators for making money—regardless of its economic, political, or social implications—along with the appetite of Western consumers for buying goods at bargain prices.

Then there was American procurement of supplies in Japan during the Korean War. The boost this gave the Japanese economy was significant, to say the least.

Despite their nearly 250 years of exclusion from most of the world, from the early 1600s to the mid 1850s, the Japanese have had centuries of experience at exporting and importing. The same year that the seclusion-minded Tokugawa Shogunate fell (1867), the Japanese attended a foreign trade show in Paris, exhibiting handicrafts, prints, fans, ceramics, swords, paper products, agricultural tools, armor, and two small boats. They had a larger selection of goods on display at a trade show in Vienna in 1873. See HISTORY; ECONOMIC PROGRESS AFTER 1868.

FACE / KAO (Kah-oh)   As a tightly knit, group-oriented society in which people are not free to move from one job to another, discard old friends and make new ones, or move away and start over when they have problems or fail, the Japanese are very much concerned about their face—their reputation.

The loss of face during feudal times often had fatal consequences, and even today there are people who take their own lives to redeem a sullied reputation.

Maintaining one's face in Japan is still of vital importance, although the sanctions imposed by society are far less severe than they were in feudal times. It is especially important in both social and business situations that one be equally careful about not causing someone else to lose face.

In a Japanese company, every employee has a face that goes with his or her person and job. Because of the group orientation and consensus approach to management, the face of each person is inextricably linked to that of his co-workers on all levels and to the face of the company.

People must know and maintain the face that is proper for their position. If they step out of bounds, they endanger their own face, as well as that of co-workers.

Foreign executives dealing with the Japanese should be aware that some of the things foreigners say and do—all perfectly common and acceptable in their own countries—may be seen as a threat to the face of the Japanese and their company.

See *Japanese Etiquette and Ethics in Business*, by Boye Lafayette De Mente (Passport Books).

FACE—HAND TOWEL / OSHIBORI (Oh-she-boe-ree)   The *oshibori* is a small, dampened face/hand towel, cooled in the summer and heated in the winter, given to customers by many businesses in Japan, including Japanese-style restaurants, some bars and cabarets, inns, and Chinese-style restaurants.

Some places of business impregnate their *oshibori* with jasmine scent or some other delightful aroma that adds a very special touch to the ambience of their place of business.

Whether one is sweaty from the heat of summer or bitten by the cold of winter, the *oshibori* is one of the most refreshing and relaxing customs ever invented—and one that I believe should be adopted by every country.

FAMILY CRESTS / MON (Moan)   In feudal Japan, all clan lords had their individual family crest, which they put on their formal *kimono*, lanterns, and banners. The practice of establishing a family *mon* then spread to *samurai* families who served the clan lords and finally to merchant families.

A *mon* may consist of a plant, a stylized bird, or Chinese character, or some other motif that struck the fancy of its creator. In the days of the Tokugawa *Shogun*, when clan lords and large numbers of retainers had to march to and from Edo (Tokyo) every other year, the *mon* were of vital importance in identifying the various processions as they traversed the country's great walking roads. See PROCESSIONS OF THE LORDS.

Formal *kimono* bearing the family crest are known as *montsuki* (moan-ski), or bearing a crest.

After the breakup of the Tokugawa Shogunate in 1868, many ordinary Japanese families and businesspeople created crests for themselves, but nowadays they are seldom used.

Recommended reading: *The Elements of Japanese Design—A Handbook of Family Crests, Heraldry & Symbolism*, by John W. Dower (Weatherhill). See CRESTS.

FAMILY REGISTER / KOSEKI (Koe-say-kee)   In the seventh century, the government of Japan, as well as Buddhist temples, began keeping registers of the families making up villages, towns, and clans. These family registers included records of birth, schooling, marriage, divorce, death, and any criminal acts committed.

The registers were used for tax purposes, recruiting labor for public works, and so on. When a man married and set up his own household, a new register was started in his name.

The *koseki* system was made into a national law in 1870, making it mandatory that everyone in the country (including foreign residents) be registered with the appropriate village, town, or city office. No birth, marriage, divorce, or death is officially recognized until it is entered in the official family register.

In Japan, a copy of the family register (*koseki tohon*) is the ultimate identification and is required on many occasions.

The family registration law has been a principal legal barrier to the acquisition of Japanese citizenship by foreigners and the offspring of Japanese-foreigner marriages. Under the original law, the children of a Japanese mother and a foreign father can neither obtain Japanese citizenship nor have their names entered in the mother's family register.

In 1984, the Minister of Justice recommended that the law be changed to reflect the equality of paternal and maternal family relationships, one effect of which would be the legal recognition of the children of mixed marriages when the mother is Japanese. It took several years but the law was finally passed, making it possible to put foreign names in family registers.

The children of Japanese mothers and foreign fathers are now able to get free education, welfare benefits, a driver's license, and a passport.

FAMOUS PRODUCTS / MEIBUTSU (May-e-boot-sue) Over the centuries, many areas in Japan have become famous for particular local products referred to as *meibutsu*, or famous products, which are much sought after by visitors to these areas. Among the most famous of these areas and their products are:

ARITA: Porcelain ware of the finest quality.
BEPPU: Bamboo and wooden items for kitchen and household use.
KAGOSHIMA: Silk fabrics and Satsuma-yaki porcelain ware.
KANAZAWA: Porcelain ware known as Kutaniyaki, lacquerware, silk, kaga dolls, and toys.
KOBE: Silk and silk goods, bamboo ware, tortoiseshell ware.
KYOTO: Brocades (especially Nishijin silk embroidered), wood-block prints, cloisonné, damascene, lacquerware, screens, fans, curios, porcelain ware, and dolls.
NAGASAKI: Coral ware, tortoiseshell ware, *koga* folk dolls.
NAGOYA: Lacquerware, porcelain of many types, cloisonné, curios, fans, and toys. Nagoya is Japan's porcelain ware center.
NAHA: Lacquerware, *tsuboya-yaki* porcelain, *bingata* cotton, linen and silk cloth dyed in paper patterns, and cloth made of banana fiber (*bashofu*).
NIKKO: Wooden ware, lacquerware, curios.
OSAKA: Silks, toys, curios, old and new works of art.
SAPPORO: Ainu-made wooden and textile handicraft items.
SENDAI: Folk dolls, bamboo ware, wooden ware, silk fabrics, lacquerware.
TAKAMATSU: Parasols, wooden and bamboo ware, lacquerware, engravings.
TOKYO: Pearls, books, cloisonné, silver ware, brocades, ivories, wood-block prints, fans, toys, handmade paper, porcelain, cameras, lacquerware, electronic items of all kinds, curios.

FAMOUS SIGHTS Japan has more identified and cataloged famous sights than any other country—a circumstance that derives from the existence of so much scenic beauty and a culture in which the recognition and appreciation of natural beauty has traditionally been an important part of the lives of a large segment of the population.

While each area of the country invariably has its famous scenic spots, natural beauty is also ranked on a national level. For hundreds of years, Japan's Scenic Trio have been Amanohashidate, on the Japan Sea coast, north of Kyoto; Itsuku Island, in Hiroshima Bay; and the pine-clad islands of Matsushima Bay near Sendai on northeastern Honshu. See individual listings.

(Suizen Garden, Kumamoto)

FANS / SENSU (Sane-sue) also **UCHIWA** (Uu-chee-wah)   Fans have played an extraordinary role in Japan since their introduction from China in the sixth and seventh centuries. The fans first imported from China were the flat, rigid kind (*uchiwa*) and not only were used for cooling one's self during the humid summer months, but also became an integral part of court and later formal wear.

The making of fans became a handicraft art, which led to the invention by a Japanese fanmaker of the ribbed folding fan, called *sensu*.

The folding fan was first used for strictly functional purposes, but, under the influence of Court dilettantes, it became an accessory that was essential in proper etiquette, personal as well as ceremonial. Folding fans made of cypress slats first appeared in Japan's Imperial Court in the seventh century and, by the eighth century, were an indispensable part of Court attire. These first *sensu* were thin sticks held together by ribbons. Paper covering was added later.

As the centuries passed, fans began to play a similar role in religious ceremonies, dancing and the theater, particularly in *kabuki* and *noh*.

As more time went by, fans became an integral part of the formal dress of the privileged classes, representing not only a symbol of this class, but a symbol of cultural achievement and good manners. They were used as an accessory to speech and became an important part of nonverbal communication in formal, as well as informal, settings.

The ladies of the Imperial Court in Kyoto became especially adept at carrying on surreptitious communications with their fans.

Fans also became an essential ingredient in the aesthetic ritual of the tea ceremony that developed in the fifteenth century, and were a highly valued gift.

The making of *sensu* folding fans is still a major handicraft industry in present-day Japan, and they are still an important part of the ensemble of a man or woman dressed in formal Japanese attire. They are also still popular gifts, especially for someone who is going on a trip or has become engaged to be married.

Flat, rigid *uchiwa* fans, used for fanning, come in many designs and colors, ranging from simple natural tones of bamboo to colorful landscapes, portraits, and *kanji* characters with auspicious meanings.

FARMERS / NOFU (No-fuu) As late as 1960, nearly 17 percent of all Japanese were farmers. Today that number is less than 2 percent—or 1.7 million people.

Land reforms instituted in Japan in 1945 by the Allied Occupation forces revolutionized the country's farming industry. Most of the arable land in the country was owned by nonfarming landlords. This land was bought up and given to the tenants who actually worked it.

This step, plus the introduction of more and more technology, resulted in amazing increases in production—despite the rapid loss of land to industrialization. This increase in production, plus government-subsidized prices for rice, beef, and pork, allowed the incomes and living standards of farm families to keep pace with those of industrial workers.

Many Japanese farmers became wealthy by selling off their lands to major industrial companies seeking sites for factories. For several years in a row from 1960 to 1980, Japan's top money earners included one or more farmers.

FARMING / NOGYO (No-g'yoe)   Japan's main agricultural products are rice (see RICE), vegetables, fruit, wheat, barley, rye, soybeans, beef, pork, chickens, eggs, milk, and cheese.

Vegetable production (radishes, tomatoes, cabbage, onions, etc.) just about matches demand, primarily because of the widespread use of hot-houses that make year-round cultivation possible.

The most popular fruit in Japan is the mandarin orange (*o'mikan*), the growth of which is now controlled by the government to prevent over-production. Apples, peaches, pears, plums, and persimmons are also raised and consumed in great quantities.

One of the most delicious of all of Japan's fruits is a hybrid pear/apple called twentieth-century pear, or *niju seki nashi*.

Japan's production of wheat, barley, rye, and soybeans meets less than 10 percent of the national demand. The shortfall is made up through massive imports from the U.S., Canada, Australia, etc.

Because of Japan's economic vulnerability, the government has an on-going policy of self-sufficiency in food, but the policy is not enforced. The number of farms and the farming population in Japan have been decreasing since 1960. There are now some 378,000 farms in the country with a farming population of 1.7 million—a drop of more than 50 percent in the last 10 years.

In the interim, Japan has become the world's largest importer of agricul-tural products. Major import items include wheat, beans, fruit, vegetables, meat (beef, pork, chicken), milk and other dairy products, and potatoes.

About the only major food product in which Japan has continued to be self-sufficient is rice, but inclement weather in 1993 resulted in such a shocking shortfall that rice had to be imported in large volume to meet the demand.

The Japanese government controls the production of rice by planting allocations, and the price of rice by buying the entire production from farmers and reselling it at a highly subsidized price—making rice produced in Japan up to five times more expensive than rice produced abroad.

See RICE.

FASHION APPAREL   Fashions in Japan were primarily prescribed by one's position in the social hierarchy (royalty, *samurai*, farmers, towns-people) prior to the downfall of the Tokugawa Shogunate in 1868. From that period until the 1950s, the fashion industry as such was small and of little consequence.

During the 1950s, thousands of sewing schools sprang up all over Japan, encouraging young women to make their own Western-style clothing. This movement resulted in the appearance of design schools by the hundreds, and the fashion industry was on its way.

By the mid-1960s, there were thousands of designers in Japan and thou-sands of boutiques featuring their designs. It was not until the mid-1970s, however, that the influence of Japanese designs and designers began to make a substantial impression abroad.

The most successful of Japan's early designers was Hanae Mori, who turned a successful boutique into a multimillion dollar a year conglomerate, with offices around the world.

Recognizing the importance of the fashion industry to Japan's economy, the Ministry of International Trade and Industry in 1984 authorized the establishment of a foundation to promote the creation of high-quality fashion.

The members of the foundation are the Hanae Mori Group and 10 other fashion-related companies, including the Isetan Department Store and Unichika Ltd., a leading synthetic fiber maker.

Other well-known fashion designers in Japan are Kansai Yamamoto, Issey Miyake, Yuki Torii, and Mitsuhiro Matsuda.

FASHION MODELS Fashion modeling, now an important industry in Japan, grew apace with the ready-made apparel industry from the mid-1950s on. Apparently in imitation of the world of fashion in Paris and New York, the industry preferred tall, lean models with a Western look.

In the early years, virtually all of the manikins in Japanese boutiques and department stores were made in the image of Caucasian Westerners—providing both a cosmopolitan and exotic air.

Because of this predilection for the Western/exotic, a number of Western women living in Tokyo became well-known as fashion models. By the mid-1960s, extraordinarily beautiful young women of Japanese-Caucasian parentage began entering the field.

These young women were especially popular as models because they were both Japanese and foreign at the same time, and in most cases they were fluent in English, as well as Japanese.

It was also during these early years that a number of mixed Japanese-Ainu girls broke into modeling and became stars. (See AINU.) Some of them were even more beautiful and exotic than the Japanese-Western mixtures, particularly those who had what I call Ainu Eyes—eyes so large, so luminous, and so magnetic that they have a hypnotizing effect on viewers.

By the early 1980s, Japan's world of fashion modeling had matured, and, as in the U.S., it is dominated by a few companies that exercise considerable influence over the industry.

Foreign models are even more popular in Japan today than they were in the early stages of the industry. At any one time, some 2,000 foreign models are available from the various agencies, and a fairly large number of them work regularly.

Succeeding as a foreign model in Japan is not nearly as easy as some might think, however. The Japanese like their models young (20 is "old"), and they like them with a fresh, innocent, cute look.

Models in Japan are worked a lot harder than their counterparts in New York and elsewhere. They have to be healthy and strong and willing to work under the most uncomfortable and inconvenient conditions and maintain a bubbly, spirited attitude about everything.

Once models sign up with one agency, other agencies generally do not employ them. The problem of communication is also serious, as most of the models do not understand Japanese, and many of the clients cannot speak English or any other foreign language.

There are also a number of free-lance foreign models in Tokyo, including tourists and students, who are more likely to find jobs with minor publications—some of which feature nudity.

Among the better-known model agencies are Satoru Model Management, Cinq Deux Un, Folio Modeling Agency, and Office Miyama International. Foreign models working in Japan are limited to visas good for only two months. If they want to continue working, they must leave the country to obtain a new visa.

FAST FOODS   Many Westerners were surprised when foreign-style fast-food restaurants caught on in Japan in the 1960s. They shouldn't have been. Fast-food restaurants have been popular in Japan since the Middle Ages (if not before)—Japanese-style, of course.

The biggest-selling fast-food item in Japan is not McDonald's hamburgers (which are number two). It is *sushi*—slices of raw fish and other seafood on little buns of slightly vinegared and sweetened rice.

Sushi restaurants and stands have been going strong in Japan since early times, but what is new is the appearance in the 1970s of take-out *sushi* chains. The largest *sushi* chain, Kozozushi Hombu, racks up sales in excess of 65 billion yen a year.

Besides McDonald's hamburgers, other popular fast-food items in Japan include fried chicken, noodles, *gyu-don* (*sukiyaki*-style beef on rice), and *yakitori* (barbecued chicken on skewers).

One of the earliest take-out fast-foods in Japan was *nigiri* (nee-ghee-ree) or *nigiri-meshi* (may-she), meaning hand-made riceballs. Riceballs were already a popular food among the nobility of eleventh-century Japan (the common people at that time mostly ate millet), who customarily ate them outside, when traveling and on picnics. (See STATION BOX-LUNCHES).

Among the more popular varieties of riceballs are *nori-musubi* (wrapped in seaweed); *umeboshi* (a pickled plum embedded in a ball of rice); *sansai* (rice mixed with vegetables); *sekihan* (rice and red beans); and *shake-nori* (a riceball with a chunk of salmon in the center and wrapped in seaweed).

FENOLLOSA, ERNEST FRANCISCO   An American art critic, Ernest Francisco Fenollosa went to Japan in 1879 and taught at Tokyo Imperial University. He became a great admirer of Japanese art, and his books and lectures did much to make it known around the world.

Fenollosa also studied Buddhism, converted to that religion, and when he died in London in 1908 left instructions that he was to be buried at the Miidera Temple close to Lake Biwa, near Kyoto.

FESTIVALS / O'MATSURI (Oh-mot-sue-ree) Having two major religions as an integral part of its culture (Shintoism and Buddhism), with both religions emphasizing group ceremonies and celebrations, Japan is blessed with many festivals. Every major shrine and temple around the country—and there are thousands—has an annual festival.

The festivals are street processions of parishioners of particular Buddhist temples and Shinto shrines, held to honor the tutelary deity of the temple or shrine.

Most of them include a *mikoshi* (me-koe-she), which is a portable shrine in which the spirit of the deity can be moved about. Carrying the *mikoshi* through the streets was thought to spread the purifying power of the deity and neutralize any evil in the vicinity.

Eight of the largest and most important of these festivals have been institutionalized into national holidays.

Ganjitsu (Gahn-jeet-sue) is the first day of the New Year, when people visit shrines, relatives, and friends, drink *sake* and eat special New Year dishes. Children play special card games, shuttlecock, battledore, and fly kites. The homes (of some) are decorated with sacred straw ropes and pine boughs, the latter symbolizing trees by which the gods may descend from heaven.

All businesses are closed down for at least the first three days of the new year, a period called *sanga-nichi* (sahn-gah-nee-chee), and some remain closed for five or more days.

At the stroke of midnight on New Year's eve, the great bells of many nationally known temples are rung 108 times to symbolize the elimination of as many bad things during the past year, so that everyone may enter the new year with a clean slate.

The clappers in some of the huge bells consist of immense logs suspended from the ceiling by stout ropes. Young men, usually warmed up by *sake*, take turns swinging the log against the bell—a ceremony that is televised nationwide from a number of locations.

Hina Matsuri (He-nah Mot-sue-ree), on March 3, also called Girls' Day, honors young girls and wishes them future happiness. Besides displaying dolls dressed in the costumes of ancient court ladies, along with peach blossoms, a sweet drink called *shirozake* (she-roe-zah-kay) is served.

Nowadays, young girls are also likely to get gifts and be taken out for dinner.

Tango No Sekku, (Tahn-go no sake-kuu), on May 5, is the annual festival for boys and symbolizes the hopes of parents that their sons will grow up to be healthy and strong. Warrior dolls are displayed, iris leaves are placed under the eaves of homes to ward off evil, and large banners shaped like carp are flown on poles over homes in which young boys live. These latter streamers are what most people associate with Boys' Day—the carp symbolizing their perseverence in their attempts to swim upstream against whatever odds.

Tanabata (Tah-nah-bah-tah), the Star Festival, on July 7, celebrates the meeting of two lovers, the stars Altair, personified by a cowherd, and Vega, as a weaving girl, separated by the Milky Way the rest of the year.

Poems celebrating the story are written on pieces of paper and attached to bamboo poles set up in the garden. Special food offerings are made, and young girls hope that they will be as skillful in their cooking and other home duties as Vega was reputed to be.

Obon (Oh-bone), celebrated in mid-August in the countryside and in July in major cities, is one of Japan's major festivals. This is the time when people visit and clean up the graves of their ancestors, and those who have moved to cities return to their birthplaces.

Usually translated as Festival of the Souls, Obon includes the preparation of special foods to be offered to the spirits of dead ancestors, hanging up lanterns so the spirits may find their way back to their former homes, and praying for their repose.

This is also the season for the *bon-odori* (bone-oh-doe-ree) or *bon* dances, which are staged outdoors, usually in the precincts of shrines, villages, and towns all over the country. People dress in light summer *yukata* and dance, watch, and stroll around, enjoying the cool of the evening.

Vendors usually set up stalls at such festivals, selling knicknacks and snack items.

Tsukimi (T'sue-kee-me), held on nights of the full moon in August, literally means "moon viewing," and that is what people do, while drinking *osake*, eating *dango* (dahn-go), a dumpling—and, if they are moved by the muse, composing poetry celebrating the beauty of the moon.

Higan (He-ghan) is celebrated twice a year during the spring and autumn equinox, over a period of seven days on each occasion. During Higan, families attend Buddhist rites, recall their ancestors, and visit family graves.

Shichi-Go-San (She-Chee-Go-Sahn), on November 15, is still one of Japan's most popular festivals. This is the occasion when parents take children who are three, five, and seven to shrines to pray for their future. These odd numbers are chosen because they are considered lucky. The children are dressed in their most colorful attire—the girls usually in bright *kimono*. It is naturally one of the most popular picture-taking days of the year.

As mentioned earlier, local festivals abound in Japan. Among the most popular are the following.

The Kamakura Festival, held during the New Year holidays in Akita Prefecture, is for children. Adults help children build snow igloos, called *kamakura* (kah-mah-kuu-rah), into which are put altars dedicated to the God of Water. At night, children gather in the *kamakura*, eat rice cakes, and drink *amazake* (ah-mah-zah-key), a sweet wine.

The *kamakura* festival grew out of an ancient custom in which adults in the central and eastern portions of Japan built small huts for use during the New Year period as part of a purification ritual. They lived in the huts for a few days, without eating or drinking, to purify themselves.

Sapporo's annual Snow Festival has received international publicity in recent years. Held from the first Friday in February through the following Sunday, it is part of a popular Winter Carnival.

The snow festival consists of a large number of snow sculptures in the form of animals and figures from legends and mythology. It is held in Odori Park.

The *Dontaku* (Doan-tah-kuu) Festival is held in Hakata, Fukuoka Prefecture, from May 3 to 5. It is marked by spectacular parades of floats and participants made up to represent deities riding on horseback. Children in *kimono* ride on the floats.

One of Kyoto's most popular events, the *Gion* (Ghee-on) Festival sponsored by the Yasaka (Yah-sah-kah) Shrine, originated in the ninth century as a supplication to ward off a plague. It begins on July 1 and lasts until the 29th.

The big days of the festival are the 16th and 17th. On the evening of the 16th, lanterns are hung from the eaves of homes in the old section of the city. Special blue curtains are hung in doorways. Flowers are set out on cloth spreads, and decorative wind screens are displayed.

Floats, gaily lighted with lanterns and accompanied by music, make their way through the streets. On the 17th, the highlight of the festival, the brilliantly decorated floats are carried through the city streets.

Each year, the Gion Festival attracts thousands of foreign tourists who coordinate their trips so they will be in Kyoto on this occasion.

Akita City's *Kanto* (Kahn-toe) Festival, August 5–7, is held to drive away the demon of drowsiness that afflicts people at work during the year.

A *kanto* is a long bamboo pole with numerous crossbars on which are hung from 46 to 48 lanterns. The highlight of the festival comes when groups of young men dance through the streets to the accompaniment of drums, vying with one another in balancing the poles on their hands, shoulders, and heads.

Tokushima's *Awa Odori* Dancing Festival, from August 15–18, also attracts international interest. Residents dance in the streets in a celebration that dates back to the end of the sixteenth century, when their new lord moved into the city's castle.

Men and women of all ages, dressed in light, colorful *yukata* and sometimes traditional hats, dance the evening away to music provided by *shamisen*, flutes, and drums.

The *Okunchi* (Oh-kune-chee) Festival of Nagasaki features Chinese-style dragon dances from the 7th to the 9th of October. Staged by the Suwa Shrine, the festival is designed to bring good luck to participants and viewers. The dragon concept was apparently imported from China when Nagasaki was the only Japanese port open to the outside world.

One of the most spectacular and the most interesting of Kyoto's many festivals, as far as history buffs are concerned, is the *Jidai Matsuri* (Jee-die Mot-sue-ree), on October 22, sponsored by the equally famous Heian Shrine. It features a unique procession of men and women clad in authentic costumes representing each of the 10 centuries during which Kyoto was Japan's Imperial capital.

The parade, in effect, gives one a glimpse of one of the most fascinating periods in the history of the country and attracts foreign visitors by the thousands.

Jidai Matsuri can be translated as Festival of the Ages. See JIDAI MATSURI.

One of the most unusual of Japan's popular local festivals is the *Namahage* (Nah-mah-hah-gay) Matsuri on Oga Peninsula, in Akita Prefecture. Aimed at frightening the laziness out of laggards, the December 31 event involves young men dressed as demons and carrying papier-mâché knives, clubs, and paper bags, going from house to house, and warning sluggards to mend their ways.

The term *namahage* is a corruption of *namamihagi*, the treatment used for getting rid of calluses caused by sitting close to a fire for a long time.

While Japan's numerous *matsuri* began as part magical, part religious rites to attract a particular god or goddess down from heaven to ensure bountiful harvests and to gain the favor of the spirits in warding off bad luck or natural disasters, they have evolved with the times.

Over the centuries, the *matsuri* retained their religious significance but also came to be popular just for the fun of them, as a time to eat, drink, and be merry. Some of the festivals are pure Shintoist; others are Buddhist. Some are a subtle mixture of both.

Some of the more unusual of Japan's festivals are the one for silkworms at the Mie Temple in Gifu on January 31; the seaweed festival at the Mekari

Shrine in Moji (founded by the Empress Jingu in the fourth century); and the Laughing Festival of Nagahama in Shiga Prefecture, held to celebrate the gift of a large sum of money from Hideyoshi Toyotomi on the birth of his son.

There are dozens of others, among which are those that have to do with phallic worship. One of the most important of these fertility festivals is the Honen Matsuri, held each spring at the Oagata Shrine in Inuyama and the Taagata Shrine in Komaki, both in Aichi Prefecture.

The theme of these ritual celebrations is that the sexual joining of male and female elements is necessary to produce abundant crops. The festival at Taagata centers around the male symbol, represented by replicas of the penis in varying sizes, including ones carved out of huge logs.

During this festival, a *mikoshi* (portable shrine) bearing a large replica of the male organ is carried through the streets, while young men shout encouragement and young women vie to get lucky sexual charms.

The *Oagata* Festival centers around symbols of the female organ. A portable shrine bearing a wooden representation of the vulva is carried through the streets, followed by a procession of decorated horses and men carrying banners. A second *mikoshi* carries a large clam and good-luck rice cakes, which are thrown to the crowd.

Several of the most fascinating of Japan's festivals are held each year in Kyoto. They include the *Gion Matsuri* held by the Yasaka Shrine in July, the *Jidai Matsuri*, or Festival of the Ages, held by the Heian Shrine in October, and the *Aoi Matsuri* held in May by the Shimogamo and Kamigamo shrines.

The *Aoi Matsuri*, or Festival of the Hollyhock, dates from the seventh century, when rites were held to propitiate the gods after a series of great storms. The festival consists of a procession that includes an Imperial messenger and his entourage of warriors, pages, and others going from the old Imperial Palace to the Shimogamo Shrine, where leaves of the hollyhock are offered to the gods.

The procession then proceeds to the Kamigamo Shrine where a similar ceremony is held, after which it returns to the palace.

All of the people participating in this ancient *matsuri* are dressed in authentic costumes of the period.

One of my favorite festivals is the great *Sennin Gyoretsu*, or One Thousand People Procession in Nikko, held each year on May 17 and 18 to commemorate the day in 1617 when the remains of Ieyasu Tokugawa, founder of Japan's last great shogunate (and the model for the television special "Shogun"), were moved from Shizuoka to Nikko, accompanied by 1,000 people.

Now the festival includes *mikoshi* symbolizing the spirits of Ieyasu, along with two other great Japanese heroes—Hideyoshi Toyotomi and Yoritomo Minamoto—which are conveyed to the astoundingly elaborate Futarasan Shrine in Nikko.

The procession recreates the original, with a thousand men and women dressed in costumes of the early Tokugawa Period, passing along a road lined by 8,000 cedars planted by Masatsune Matsudaira, one of the *daimyo* (provincial lords) responsible for constructing the shrine.

Iemitsu Tokugawa, the grandson of Ieyasu and the third Tokugawa *shogun*, had the mausoleum built for his grandfather. The project took 12 years to complete, and was done by 12,000 artisans and 7,000 laborers who were sent from all over Japan by their lords.

A similar shrine was built in Nikko for Iemitsu 18 years later, with the various *daimyo* contributing to the project.

FIREWORKS / HANABI (Hah-nah-bee)   Fireworks were introduced into Japan from China in 1543, but, as in so many other instances, the Japanese quickly made revolutionary improvements that far exceeded anything ever seen in China.

The manufacture of *hanabi* became a hereditary craft passed on within families that became famous for their distinctive products. Fireworks displays were staged for the *shogun* at Yedo (Edo) Castle, but were eventually banned because of the danger of fires.

It then became an annual summer event to stage a fireworks display on Sumida River, on the edge of Edo, to mark the opening of the river for sweet trout fishing—*kawabiraki* (Kah-wah-bee-rah-kee). This event gradually took on religious overtones as a Buddhist ceremony to console the victims of a great famine and epidemic.

As more time passed, it became an annual festival at which the fireworks makers competed for prizes and honor. One of the famous stories connected with the *hanabi* involved a master of the craft who witnessed a murder. Fearing for his life if he publicly revealed the identity of the murderer, he recreated the scene of the homocide in fireworks and during the next *hanabi* shot them into the sky where the killer was revealed for all to see.

After 223 years, this great annual celebration ended in 1956, because of the congestion from buildings and traffic.

In July 1977, the annual fireworks tradition was revived and has been going strong ever since. An average of 15,000 fireworks are shot into the sky during each display, and well over a million people are on hand to enjoy the event.

Other fireworks displays are held at other locations in Japan today, and the descendants of the families that began the industry are still in business, shipping their merchandise around the world.

FISHING / GYOGYO (G'yoe-g'yoe)   Fishing has been a primary part of Japanese life since the dawn of the people, and seafood has been and still is one of the Big Three in the Japanese diet, along with rice and noodles.

In the early years, Japan's fishing was confined to coastal waters, but, as the population and demand grew, its fleets began expanding their ranges. By the end of the 1960s, they were fishing in waters as far away as the Atlantic.

The establishment of a 200-mile coastal economic zone by many nations in the mid-1970s was a serious blow to the Japanese fishing industry. As quickly as possible, Japan negotiated fishing rights with the U.S., Russia, Canada, New Zealand and other countries to allow its fleets to continue operation within the restricted zones.

But the problem was far from solved. While the demand for seafood in Japan continued to grow, the areas where the Japanese could fish were gradually reduced.

To help compensate for this, the Japanese fishing industry and government began promoting aquaculture, with which they have had significant success in the growing of shrimp, yellowtail fry, scallops, and oysters. They are now experimenting with farming other types of seafood as well.

In the mid-1970s, it was felt that the problem of fulfilling the national demand for seafood was gradually becoming less of a challenge, as the diets of younger Japanese were moving away from such traditional fare, and the overall consumption of fish was declining.

But by the early 1980s this trend began to reverse itself, as people became more health conscious and began to choose fish over meat for their daily diet.

By the mid-1990s, however, the world's diminishing stock of fish had begun to have a dramatic effect on Japan's fishing industry. The downsizing of fishing fleets had put thousands of fishermen out of work, but Japan's annual fish catch still accounted for some 11 percent of all the fish harvested in the world, and in the interim Japan had become the world's largest importer of marine products.

The largest exporters of fish to Japan are the United States, Korea, China, and Taiwan.

In keeping with the rising scarcity and cost of marine products and the changing tastes of Japan's younger generations, the per capita consumption or fish is now slowly declining.

FLOWER ARRANGING / IKEBANA (E-kay-bah-nah)   The word *ikebana* literally means "living flowers" and refers to the idea of arranging flowers so that they look alive and embody the principles of heaven, earth, and humans.

Broadly speaking, *ikebana* is an exercise in aesthetics, in recognizing and achieving harmony with nature, and in developing good character and therefore morality.

The art of *ikebana* originated in the fifteenth century, apparently in the tearoom of the Silver Pavilion of the Jisho Temple in Kyoto (which was built for the eighth *shogun* of the Ashikaga family, Yoshimasa).

With the beginning of the Tokugawa Shogunate in 1603, the practice of *ikebana* became widespread, and many schools developed—some advocating the formal (*rikka*), or standing, style; others, a natural style known as *nage-ire*, or thrown in. The formal school gave birth to the heaven-earth-man (*ten-chi-jin*) principle, which all schools now follow.

Flower arranging was once popular with both men and women, but it is now practiced primarily by women and is considered a vital part of the upbringing of all young girls, several million of whom take lessons in it each year.

There are over 20 well-known *ikebana* schools in Japan today, plus numerous offshoots and branches. Among the best known are *Sogetsu-ryu, Misho-ryu, Saga-ryu, Ohara-ryu, Ikenobo, Kyofu-ryu, Ko-ryu, Enshu-ryu, Adachi-shiki,* and *Nakayama Bumpo-kai.*

Recommended reading: *Fun with Flowers*, by Martha and Marvin Neese (Weatherhill). Also: *Ikebana: A New Illustrated Guide to Mastery*, by Wafu Teshigahara (Kodansha International).

FOLK ART / MINGEIHIN (Meen-gay-e-heen)   During all of its early history, Japan was divided into literally hundreds of distinct regions and areas by its mountains, rivers, long distances, and political subdivisions.

For most of these centuries, each of these districts had to be pretty much self-sufficient in most things. Thus, each area had its own artisans who produced the majority of items they needed for their livelihood, as well as specialty folk art items.

These folk arts ranged from dolls and cast-iron kettles to bark work (*kaba zaiku*), made in Akita Prefecture for use in boxes and other containers.

These traditions of folk art have been continued down to the present time and are well-known products of these areas. Besides the cast-iron kettles of Iwate Prefecture and the bark work of Akita, there are the snow boots (*yuki gutsu*) of Yamagata; lacquered tableware from Aizu-Wakamatsu; wooden horses from Miharu; *kokeshi* dolls from Akita, Yamagata, Miyagi, and Fukushima; Mashiko pottery from Tochigi; lacquerware and *magemono* woodwork from Nagano; copperware from Toyama; pottery and porcelain from Aichi; and tea utensils and other pottery items from Shiga.

The best way to see and buy folkcraft products from all over Japan is to visit the prefectural trade promotion offices in Tokyo, in the Kokusai Kanko Building on the Yaesu side of Tokyo station.

Recommended reading: *Folk Traditions in Japanese Art*, by Victor and Takako Hauge (Kodansha International). Also: *Folk Arts of Japan*, by Hugo Munsterberg (Tuttle).

FOLK SONGS / MINYO (Meen-yoe)   Popular in Japan since ancient times, folk songs are usually associated with the districts in which they originated. They include work songs, drinking songs, play songs, and sacred songs.

Most of the folk songs popular among the Japanese today are based on work songs that first became popular in the sixteenth and seventeenth centuries and eventually became associated with entertainment or religion.

Following the industrialization of Japan in the late 1800s, many work songs became party and festival songs. In more recent years, several folk songs have become popular hit tunes on various record labels.

The Japanese love to sing, and virtually every party brings on a songfest —including solo performances at cabarets, where patrons often carry on despite the noise and other competition. See SINGING.

FOOD / TABEMONO (Tah-bay-moe-no)   Like that of many people around the world, the traditional diet of the Japanese consists of a mixture of vegetables, grains, fruits, seafood, chicken, and, after 1868, small quantities of meat—usually pork, until recent times. Prior to 1869, Buddhist religious taboos forbade the consumption of meat from any four-legged animal.

Also like other native diets, Japanese food is distinguished by the manner of its preparation, plus the various items the Japanese eat that are not common in other countries.

The main characteristics of Japanese dishes include preservation of the natural appearance of the food, minimal use of gravies, heavy use of soy sauce, pickling, and eating many foods raw.

In a typical Japanese meal, the main dish is boiled rice, and all the other foods that go along with the main course (of rice) are side dishes. Or various vegetables, seafoods, and other tidbits are mixed in with rice to make a rice dish.

About the only category of traditional Japanese food that does not include rice as the main dish is the various *soba* and *udon* noodle dishes.

In a traditional Japanese meal, the appearance and manner of serving food is as important as what is served. Like virtually all other areas of life, the Japanese developed the preparation and serving of food into a highly refined art—an art that was designed to nurture the spirit, as well as the body.

The various items of food are arranged on the dish or tray in such a way that perfect harmony is obtained in color and size. Slices of a colorful fish, for example, may be served in a deep black lacquered bowl or tray. Roe of sea bream with peas in the pod may be served on a curving slab of stoneware.

A clear soup containing two or three white beans, a slice of red ginger cut in the shape of a starfish, two pieces of twisted kelp, an ear-shell, and a sliver of pink fish may be served in a lacquered bowl with a milk-white bottom fading rapidly into a soft russet, tinged with brown and cream. The lid, decorated with a pattern of wild grain sprigs, may be a fusion of gold and russet.

An accompanying petal-size saucer for sauce may be a brilliant vermilion with only a hint of a pattern extending down one side, toward the center.

Other dishes follow suit, all artistically placed on pottery, lacquerware, bamboo trays, or woven straw. When served by a *kimono*-clad waitress in a typical Japanese setting—a room with a *tatami* reed-mat floor, a *tokonoma* (beauty alcove), and a picture window looking out on a valley scene or a tree-clad mountain—the atmosphere is one of serenity and restfulness that is literally out of this world.

Traditional Japanese food is different enough that a taste for it must be acquired over a period of time. Because food is very much a part of our psychological profile and has a direct bearing on our physical and mental well-being, any introduction to Japanese food should be voluntary and gradual.

The Japanese have the same problem adapting to Western foods. When a Japanese who is not already conditioned to eating Western food goes abroad, he or she must be very careful to avoid becoming quite ill. When they have no choice but to eat unfamiliar dishes, especially heavy meat dishes and dishes with lots of oil or butter, their health suffers.

Rice has traditionally been the main dish of all Japanese meals. Other traditional dishes include soups; boiled vegetables; fish or vegetables cooked in soy sauce; fried foods; broiled foods; fish, shellfish, and vegetables served with vinegar; vegetables and seafood cooked in pots; grilled eel; pieces of raw fish, and pickled vegetables.

Special items include rice cakes (*mochi*), a thick broth containing *mochi* (*zoni*), vegetables and seafood cooked *tempura*-style (covered with batter and deep-fried in oil), steamed egg custard with chicken and vegetables, grilled beef and vegetables, and numerous noodle and macaroni-type dishes. See individual listings.

Traditional Japanese dishes are not about to disappear, but the diet of the young urban Japanese had already changed significantly by the mid-1970s. They eat less than half the amount of fish consumed by their parents and grandparents and far more meat and breads.

Recommended reading: *Japanese Secrets of Graceful Living*, by Boye Lafayette De Mente (Phoenix Books); *Eating Cheap in Japan*, by Kimiko Nagasawa and Camy Condon (Shufunotomo); *The Book of Miso*, by William Shurtleff and Akiko Aoyagi (Ten Speed Press).

FOOD CARTS / YATAI MISE (Yah-tie me-say)   One of the most traditional and nostalgic sights in Japan are the *yatai mise*, or wheeled food carts with roofs, that appear around dusk in popular station and entertainment areas.

Each cart specializes in a particular kind of traditional food, ranging from baked sweet potatoes and boiled corn (in season) to a style of cooking called *oden* (oh-dane), which consists of seafood, vegetables, chicken, and rice bread boiled in a special stock.

The *yatai mise* that specialize in hot foods are particularly popular in the winter months, especially among those who have been out late and are on their way home.

The *yakimo-ya*, or baked sweet potato vendor, is another of the most popular of these *yatai mise*. The sound of the potato vendor's horn and his cry of *Yaki-moohh*! echoing through the streets in the evening is one of the special sounds of Japan that is sure to touch the heart of Japanese and foreigners raised there.

FOREIGN COMPANIES IN JAPAN There are currently some 4,000 foreign companies with their own operations, or with affiliated operations, in Japan. American-owned companies make up approximately 40 percent of this total, followed by Germany, Britain, Switzerland, Hong Kong, France, the Netherlands, and Sweden. Germany, which is second, has some 400 companies in Japan.

Of the the U.S.'s top 200 companies, over 100 have branch or affiliated operations in Japan.

Among the industrial categories represented by the foreign-owned companies in Japan are foods, chemicals, oil, rubber goods, nonferrous metals, general machinery, electrical machinery, and other manufacturing and service companies. The only category in which these foreign firms have a significant percentage of Japan's market is oil (approximately 48 percent).

The secret of success for a foreign company in Japan is being able to adapt to the local environment—a concept that is difficult for many Western businesspeople to grasp. A number of the larger American companies that have succeeded in Japan did so only because they were big enough and rich enough to survive their early mistakes.

The smaller foreign companies now thriving in Japan had to work "smarter" to get where they are. Among these smaller firms are some with extraordinary stories. One example: E-Z Trading Company and E-Z Ware Company, founded by Mike Solomko, a former baseball player who spent six years with the Hanshin Tigers and then set up his own business rather than leave Japan. E-Z Trading Company, which Solomko later sold, specialized in cookware.

Another example is International Business Information (IBI), founded by C. Tait Ratcliffe, which now has 25–30 percent of the English language annual report business in Japan. Ratcliffe first visited Japan with a glee club.

From the 1950s to the 1970s, one of the main problems facing larger foreign firms in Japan was attracting qualified job applicants and managers. The best high school and college graduates preferred to go with Japanese organizations for reasons ranging from trust to concern about getting along in a foreign enterprise.

It was also rare for a competent, experienced manager to quit a Japanese company to go with a foreign firm (something that is still unusual in Japan, although some mobility has developed in the electronics industry among young engineers who are frustrated by the seniority system in Japanese companies).

For the most part, foreign companies recruiting in Japan must depend on disenchanted employees of Japanese firms, on women (who often prefer working for foreign companies because they are paid more and treated more equally), and on the pool of Japanese, who for one reason or another (often schooling abroad), did not become a part of the corporate establishment immediately upon graduation from a Japanese high school or university—and generally cannot get in at a later date.

The Ministry of International Trade and Industry estimates that around 380,000 Japanese work for foreign and foreign-affiliated firms in Japan. Of this number, some 170,000 are women.

FOREIGN CORRESPONDENTS / GAIKOKU SHIMBUN-KISHA (Gie-koe-kuu shim-boon-kee-shah)   There are a large number of foreign correspondents stationed in Tokyo, representing the various wire services (Associated Press, United Press International, Reuters, Tass, etc.), and many of the world's larger magazines, newspapers, and special publications, including newsletters.

In pre–World War II days, foreign reporters in Japan were likely to be regarded as intelligence agents—probably because most of their foreign reporters were. Following the war, they were officially welcomed, but unofficially they were not held in very high esteem because it was felt that they would not interpret the Japanese scene in a way that would benefit the country.

Part of this fear was well founded. Virtually none of the foreign correspondents stationed in Japan during the late 1940s, '50s, and '60s could read, write, or speak Japanese (the exceptions were a few Japanese-Americans), with the result that the reporters had to depend on secondary materials and sources for their information.

Most correspondents hired Japanese assistants or used their Japanese girlfriends as interpreters and translators and got most of their news from the Japanese press and English-language handouts.

During these years, the activities of foreign correspondents were a frequent target of the more sensational weekly and monthly Japanese-language magazines, which gave the public the impression that the Foreign Correspondents' Club in downtown Tokyo was the proverbial den of iniquity.

In the 1970s, the situation changed. The quality of the average correspondent—especially those from European countries—went up significantly. Many of the newer, younger correspondents had studied Japanese, and some of them were quite fluent in the language.

This resulted in a gradual improvement in the reputation of foreign correspondents in Japan—and in the Foreign Correspondents' Club. Ranking Japanese politicians and business leaders now appear regularly as speakers at club functions, and the club is one of the most popular luncheon places in Tokyo.

FOREIGNERS IN JAPAN   All residents of Japan who are not racially Japanese are counted as foreign, regardless of their citizenship. On this basis, the largest group of foreign residents is Korean (some 670,000), followed by Chinese (approximately 55,000)—most of whom are Japanese citizens or have permanent resident status. Other groups—American, English, French, Australian, etc.—range from a few hundred to a few thousand and are primarily in Japan as executives, diplomats, students, entertainers, and so on. The activities of foreigners in Japan is strictly controlled by immigration measures and is determined by the individual's visa status. See VISAS.

Most foreigners in Japan live in Tokyo, Yokohama, Osaka, and Kobe, but there are little pockets and sprinkles of foreign residents throughout most of the islands. Certain residential areas in the major cities are favored by foreigners (because the housing has been designed for Western-style living).

The first and only exclusively foreign settlement in Tokyo was established in the Tsukiji district, just east of the Ginza, in 1870, when the government gave foreigners permission to establish residences there. Prior to this, foreigners were not allowed to live in Tokyo. The American legation was opened in the settlement soon after (on property that is now the garden of St. Luke's Hospital).

An estimated 160,000 foreigners live in the Tokyo area, making this the largest foreign community in the country, by far.

There are English-language newspapers and magazines, clubs, restaurants, and other facilities that cater specifically to the foreign communities in Japan.

Recommended reading: *Living in Japan* (American Chamber of Commerce in Japan).

FOREIGN CHILDREN BORN IN JAPAN   A child born in Japan of foreign parents must be registered as a foreigner within 60 days, at the local ward or city office. Prior to this, the parents must obtain a passport for the child from their embassy in Japan.

FOREIGN PRESS CENTER   The Foreign Press Center, located on the sixth floor of the Nippon Press Center Building, 2-2-1 Uchisaiwaicho, Chioyda-ku, Tokyo (about a five-minute walk south and west of the Imperial Hotel), is maintained as a source of information, primarily in English, for foreign correspondents and writers stationed in or visiting Japan.

The Center maintains a collection of books, pamphlets and papers put out by the government and other organizations, on political, social, and economic topics. Some of the periodicals are mailed out free to qualified news organizations.

FOREIGN STUDENTS IN JAPAN Since the 1970s, Japan has become increasingly popular with students seeking to study abroad, but the number of foreign students in Japan has remained relatively small—fewer than 50,000—because of inadequate housing, cultural and language problems, and the overall cost of living.

Recognizing the political, economic, and cultural implications of this disparity, Japan's Ministry of Education and the Japan International Education Association have implemented programs to increase the number of foreign students in Japan to a minimum of 100,000.

At this writing, there are only about 1,000 people teaching the Japanese language to foreign students in Japan, and efforts are underway to raise this number to around 11,000 by the end of the century.

In the past, few Japanese universities have had any kind of program for accepting and handling foreign students. Most of those studying in Japan have done so privately, paying their own way.

FOREIGN WORKERS IN JAPAN Japan's Immigration Control Act prohibits foreigners from entering the country to find work. In order to qualify for a work visa to enter Japan as a temporary resident, one must have a job contract and a guarantor (an employer may also act as guarantor) beforehand.

The period of stay allowed is determined by the type of work one is engaged to do and ranges from a few months to five years. Businesspeople, educators, missionaries, foreign correspondents, and technical specialists invited to Japan normally receive five-year visas. Students, artists, and others in skilled professions generally get one-year visas. Sports people and entertainers are normally limited to three to six months.

Temporary residents who are in Japan under any visa category may apply for an extension at least one time, and most—with the exception of tourists and other short-term residents—may extend their periods of stay any number of times, as long as they remain in good standing with Japanese authorities.

Until the 1980s, major Japanese companies seldom, if ever, employed any non-Japanese in Japan. The exceptions were part-time English teachers and other specialists who were brought in for temporary periods—such as copywriters for advertising agencies.

This policy was so strictly adhered to that in 1981, when a major department store chain announced that it would hire several young foreign men and women to work in its Tokyo stores, the event made the national news and was the talk of the town for several weeks.

The department store announcement noted that the reason larger Japanese firms had not hired foreigners in the past was because of the language problem and because they did not believe foreigners could adapt to the Japanese way of doing business.

It was also big news when the Oriental Land Company, the owner and operator of Japan's Disneyland, began advertising for foreign job applicants in 1982.

By the mid-1990s this situation had changed dramatically. Particularly in the construction and service industries, which employed over 400,000 foreigners—mostly illegal entrants from the Philippines, Thailand, Iran, and Iraq.

FORESTS—FORESTRY / SHINRIN (Sheen-rene)   Nearly two-thirds of Japan's total land area is covered by forests, but the demand for lumber products is so great that Japan is able to produce less than 30 percent of its annual needs. The balance is imported.

To help overcome this deficiency, the Japanese government has an ongoing 20-to-50-year range forestation program in the national forests (which account for a third of the country's forested areas). So far, the program has not been able to keep up with the growing demand.

Although Japan's wooded land is sizable, there are a number of fundamental factors that limit the forestry industry. A significant percentage of the forested areas is on steep slopes, forest roads are undeveloped, the majority of the trees are young, and many of the forests are in national park areas, where lumbering is not permitted.

Lumber imports account for some 5 percent of Japan's total imports. Some 40 percent of this total is in the form of logs. The largest suppliers of lumber to Japan are the U.S., Malaysia, Russia, Canada, New Zealand, and Papua New Guinea, in that order. The U.S. accounts for around 35 percent of the total, with Malaysia next at 29 percent.

FORGET-THE-YEAR PARTIES / BONENKAI (Boe-nane-kie) From around mid-December until near the end of the year, it is customary for the Japanese to hold *bonenkai*, or "forget-the-year parties," as a formal way of forgetting all the bad things that happened during the year and getting ready to start the new year off with a clean slate.

The parties may be held at home, in company offices, in restaurants, or in carbarets or clubs. The main objective is to let go of old grudges, bad memories, and other negative thoughts, and forgive others for their transgressions.

FORTY-SEVEN RONIN / YONJU SHICHI NO SAMURAI (Yoan-juu she-chee no sah-muu-rie)   The story of the 47 *ronin* (masterless *samurai*) of the Province of Harima is probably the best-known story of the valor and ideals of Japan's famous *samurai* warriors.

In 1701, two young *daimyo* (provincial lords), Naganori Asano, the Lord of the Castle of Ako in Harima Province, and Munehara Date, Lord of Sendai, were appointed by the shogunate to act as hosts during the forthcoming visit of a member of the Imperial Court in Kyoto.

Because the lords were inexperienced at entertaining high-born guests, the shogun appointed an elderly high official named Yoshinaka Kira to assist them. Kira, whom history describes as greedy and conceited, became very angry at Lord Asano for not presenting him with expensive gifts (to show appreciation, etc.) and became very abusive and insulting toward Asano.

Finally unable to take the insults, Asano drew his sword (itself a capital offense when done inside Edo Castle) and attempted to kill his tormentor. He succeeded only in wounding the arrogant official and was quickly seized by guards.

That very same day, the shogunate ordered Asano to commit *harakiri*, which he did. The shogun also ordered that Asano's fief be confiscated.

When Yoshio Oishi, Lord Asano's chief councillor in Ako, heard the tragic news, he immediately called a meeting of Asano's retainers. The decision was made to petition the *shogun* to reestablish the House of Asano with Lord Asano's younger brother, Daigaku, as its head. It was also resolved by the key retainers that, if the petition was refused, they would refuse to turn the castle over to the *shogun's* agents and defend it to the death.

In the next few days, while the *shogun's* agents were on the road en route to Ako, all of the Asano *samurai* who had opposed the petition deserted the castle, leaving only 60 loyal men behind. Before the *shogun's* men could reach the castle, Daigaku Asano sent a letter to the chief retainer, Oishi, asking him to obey the orders of the *shogun* and hand the castle over.

Oishi and the 59 other *samurai* accepted Daigaku's request as binding on them as the word of Lord Asano himself, but before they quit the castle they made plans to take revenge against Kira, whose un-*samurai*-like character had brought their lord and house to such a tragic end.

The men split up to conceal their plans from Kira, who naturally suspected that Asano's retainers would try to get revenge against him. Oishi went to Yamashina, a suburb of Kyoto, and spent his days in apparent idleness and his evenings sporting with prostitutes in the gay quarters—always under the watchful eyes of spies sent from Edo by Kira.

The shogunate, also concerned that the affair might not be ended, arrested Daigaku Asano and sentenced him to confinement in the main villa of the Asano family, thus ending any remaining hope that the House of Asano might be reestablished.

At a secret meeting, Oishi and his men decided that the time had come to move against Kira. But Oishi would allow only 47 of the men to participate in the attempt. He sent the other men back home to their families.

One by one, Oishi and his men infiltrated Edo, and on the snowy night of December 14, 1702, they attacked the mansion of Kira, in Honjo. Kira's *samurai* guards fought fiercely, but when Oishi and his men gained access to the mansion, Kira hid himself in a small outhouse on the grounds.

Oishi and his men searched the house and then came to the place where Kira was hiding. Without knowing for sure he was in the outhouse, they ran a spear through it. The spear pierced Kira, but did not kill him. He quickly wiped the blood from the spear as it was withdrawn from him.

The ruse did not work, however. Oishi dragged Kira out into the open and beheaded him. He then dispatched the youngest member of the band to Ako to inform the wife of Lord Asano that he had been avenged. They then took Kira's head to their lord's grave and presented it to his spirit, asking him to again strike the head with his own sword that he might rest in peace.

Oishi then sent word to the Magistrate of Edo, informing him of what had been done and telling the official that he and his men would be at the Sengaku Temple in the Takanawa area of Edo, awaiting orders from the shogunate.

After many days of deliberation—for the incident immediately became a highly controversial matter—the shogunate ordered Oishi and 45 of his men to commit suicide. The youngest one, who had been sent to Ako with the news of Kira's death, was exempted from the sentence.

The rest of the men were divided into four groups and handed over to four different *daiymo*, who were ordered to supervise and witness their *harakiri*. When all had killed themselves in the manner prescribed for *samurai*, they were buried on the grounds of the Sengaku Temple in Edo.

Still today, thousands of Japanese visit the grave of the 46 *ronin* each year, and the story is mentioned and retold as an example of the spirit of Japan.

FREEDOM OF SPEECH   Japan's constitution guarantees freedom of speech, including freedom of the press. There is no censorship. Individuals and organizations are free to publish newspapers and magazines as they wish and to publish any article that does not violate the penal code or other laws. Even when a publication infringes on a law, it cannot be closed down.

Television and radio broadcasters must obtain a license from the government and must operate within the range of the wavelengths assigned to them. But the Broadcast Law leaves all programming and program content to the broadcasters.

Citizens are free to assemble and to express their views without fear of repression or censorship. Japan is thus one of the world's freest societies.

FREEWAYS / KOSOKUDORO (Koe-soe-kuu-doe-roe)   Japan's first freeway (or expressway, as they are generally called) was the Meishin Expressway from Nagoya to Kobe, which was completed in 1965. This was soon followed by the Tomei Expressway connecting Tokyo and Nagoya. Then came the Chuo and other expressways.

The chain of mountainous islands now has over 3,000 kilometers of expressways, including several that dissect Tokyo. A government program initiated in 1954 calls for a national network of 24 arterial expressways.

One innovative feature of Japanese freeways that may eventually be adopted by other countries: Instead of having motorized police patrolling the highways to catch speeders, the Japanese have installed combination radar and camera devices that clock the speed of passing cars. If they are exceeding the speed limit, the cameras take photographs of their license plates, and a few days later they receive a ticket in the mail.

FRINGE BENEFITS Fringe benefits make up an important part of the income of most Japanese workers. By law, companies must provide their employees with health insurance, welfare annuity insurance, employment insurance, and labor hazard insurance.

Companies with five or more employees must participate in the government's health insurance and welfare annuity insurance programs. All must join the employment insurance and labor hazard insurance programs.

Companies and employees share the cost of health and welfare annuity insurance premiums (with the company paying the larger share). All of the cost of labor hazard insurance is paid by the employer.

Other fringe benefits that are common in larger companies include low-cost or free meals, low-cost dormitory housing, free or low-cost accommodations at resorts, and annual, expense-paid company trips to resort areas.

FRUIT / KUDAMONO (Kuu-dah-moe-no) Fruit has been an important part of the Japanese diet for a long time. The two most popular fruits are mandarin oranges (*mikan*) and apples (*ringo*). Peaches, melons, pears, and persimmons are also popular. A special treat is a hybrid apple-pear called 20th-century pear (*ni-ju seki nashi*).

Various tropical fruits such as bananas and papaya are imported— bananas in large volume.

FUCHU (Fuu-chuu) A satellite city of Tokyo, 20 minutes northwest of Shinjuku Station by the Keio Line, Fuchu played a significant role in the history of the Kanto Plains area. In ancient times, it was the capital of the province of Musashi and is noted for the Okunitama Shrine, believed to have been founded in 111 A.D.

The shrine was a favorite of Ieyasu Tokugawa, founder of the great Tokugawa Shogunate in 1603. In 1614, he had *keyaki* trees planted along the approach to the shrine. Most of them are still there.

Following World War II, Fuchu became the site of an American airbase. It is now best known as a residential community and as the site of the Tokyo Race Track, regarded as one of the finest racing tracks in the country.

The Kurayami Festival held by the Okunitama Shrine on May 5–6 each year attracts substantial crowds from the surrounding areas.

FUKUOKA (Fuu-kuu-oh-kah)   The capital of Fukuoka Prefecture and Japan's tenth largest city, Fukuoka is on the Japan Sea side of northwestern Kyushu, facing the Asian mainland.

Fukuoka is divided into two parts—Hakata and Fukuoka proper—by the Naka River. The Hakata side of the city has been an important port since ancient times, and it was the focal point of the two attacks against Japan by Kublai Khan's Mongol fleet in 1274 and 1281.

Following the first attack, which was driven off by a typhoon that sank most of the Mongol ships, the feudal lords (*daimyo*) of Kyushu cooperated in building a 15-foot-high stone wall along Hakata Bay, from Hakozaki to Imazu. When the Mongols arrived the second time, very few of them ever got over this wall. And, soon after the attack began, another typhoon struck, again devastating the invasion fleet.

The commercial, shopping, and entertainment centers of Fukuoka are mostly on the Hakata side of the river. Prefectural government and other public offices are mostly in Fukuoka proper.

In addition to serving as a foreign trade port, Fukuoka has several industries of note—electrical appliances, foodstuffs, silk textiles, machines, tools, and *hakata ningyo*, or *hakata* dolls, a handicraft speciality of the area that has been famous for centuries. The pottery dolls take their theme from nature, depicting people, places, and things with such reality that they are regarded as works of art.

Here again, there are dozens of extraordinary places of interest, including the usual ancient temples and shrines (Sumiyoshi Shrine, Shofuku Temple, Kinryu Temple, Dazaifu Shrine, and Kanzeon Temple); the entertainment district of Higashi Nakasu; Higashi Park, which contains a monument commemorating the Mongol invasions and numerous sports facilities; and the remnants of Fukuoka Castle.

One of the most important shrines in the city is Hakozaki Hachiman, which was established in 923 and includes several parts that have been designated Important Cultural Properties. The shrine sponsors two popular festivals a year.

Within a short distance from Fukuoka are numerous other places and things, including hot spring spas, that attract visitors the year round.

FUNERALS / SOSHIKI (So-she-kee)   Most funerals in Japan are conducted according to Buddhist rites. Traditionally, a Buddhist priest is called to read sutras over the body of the deceased, which is then placed in a coffin with the head turned to the north. Twenty-four hours or more later, the body is taken to a crematorium in a hearse. In earlier years, relatives and friends followed the hearse. Men carried real flowers, and others carried artifical flowers, an incense burner, banners, and long-handled silk parasols.

Today such processions are rare; people follow the coffin to distant crematoriums in cars. The funeral takes place in a temple or a funeral hall of the cemetery. Priests recite sutras to the accompaniment of bells, gongs, and hollow wooden blocks and pray for the souls of the dead. All present then pay their respects to the dead by burning incense before the coffin.

Most families also erect a *butsudan* (boot-sue-dahn), or family altar, in their homes and place on it a picture of the deceased, along with a mortuary tablet and other sacred articles. Incense is burned on the altar, and members of the family pray before it.

Shinto funeral rites are similar to the Buddhist rites, but the head of the deceased is turned to the east; offerings of fish, fowl, and vegetables are made, and instead of burning incense, the mourners offer strips of white paper and twigs of the sacred *sakaki* tree.

The Shinto priest offers prayers and reads an account of the life of the deceased. The spirit tablet used in Shinto funeral ceremonies is made of plain wood, while Buddhist tablets are lacquered and gilded.

Families traditionally mourn their dead for 49 days and then mark the first, third, seventh, and thirteenth anniversaries by engaging a priest to perform a prayer service for the dead.

FUTAARA-SAN SHRINE (Fuu-tah-ah-rah-sahn) The Futaara-San, or Three Shrines of Futaara, in Nikko, are among the most revered in Japan. The Futaara shrines are dedicated to three Shinto deities—Okuninushi, his consort Princess Tagori, and their son, Prince Ajisukitakahikone—who were renowned for their virtues and for bringing prosperity to Japan.

The deities were closely associated with Mt. Futaara (now Mt. Nantai). The first of the three shrines, Oku-Miya, or Inner Shrine, was built on the summit of the mountain in 784 by Priest Shodo. Because many people could not ascend the mountain to worship at the shrine, a second one, Chugushi (Middle Shrine), was built on the shore of Lake Chuzenji at the foot of the mountain.

The third shrine, Honsha (Head Shrine), was built on the banks of the Daiya River, a short distance from Nikko's famous Toshogu Shrine, which memorializes the great Ieyasu Tokugawa, first of the Tokugawa *shogun*.

GAKUSHUIN UNIVERSITY (Gah-kuu-shu-een)   Near Mejiro Station on Tokyo's Yamanote Line, Gakushuin University is the former Peers' School, established after the fall of the Tokugawa Shogunate in 1868 as a private school for the sons of the nobility.

The young Crown Prince Akihito attended this school. His route to school each day took his chauffeured limousine by Shinjuku 2-chome, a popular red light district. A high, wooden fence was built along the street to block the prince's view of the area.

GAMBLING / KAKEGOTO (Kah-kay-go-toe)   Gambling has been a popular pastime and profession in Japan from early times. Nearly 2,000 years ago, *sumo* matches were popular betting events. These were eventually followed by cockfights, dogfights, and bullfights and, in more recent years, horse racing, bicycle racing, and other types of sporting events.

Various kinds of card games, as well as *go* and *mahjong* (see GAMES), have also been popular betting events for a long time. During the long feudal age—and, in particular, during the Tokugawa era (1603–1868)—professional gamblers abounded.

These gamblers were a conspicuous breed who developed their own style of dress and speech, had a well-defined code of honor, and often became heroes to the common people, whom they frequently defended against unscrupulous *samurai*.

GAMES / YUGI (You-ghee)   The three most popular indoor adult games in Japan are *go* (goh), *shogi* (show-ghee), and *mahjong. Go* is played on a square board that is divided into 361 squares. Players—limited to two—alternately place small button-like stones on the board in such a way as to surround as much area as possible. The player who encloses the largest area is the winner. There are two sets of stones, one black and the other white.

The player recognized as being the best gets the white stones. Black always moves first. Various handicaps make it possible for two players with different skills to play a more evenly matched game. Handicaps are achieved by allowing Black to place a certain number of stones on the board before the White begins.

158

Go, which originated in China, was first introduced into Japan in the eighth century, and it quickly became popular among the aristocracy. It did not begin to become popular among the common people until the thirteenth century and has since become a national pastime, played regularly by hundreds of thousands of people.

The first foreigner to pass the very difficult test to become a professional *go* player was a 17-year-old American, Michael Redmond, from Santa Barbara, California. Redmond became interested in the game at the age of 13, after watching his father play it with friends. Impressed with the idea that winning was a matter of skill rather than luck, Redmond was soon the champion *go* player of Los Angeles. When he was 14, he went to Japan for three years of apprenticeship with *go* player Yusuke Oheda, becoming a certified professional three years later.

Shogi, also imported from China in the eighth century, is also played by two players on a board, but in this case there are only 81 squares. This game is sometimes compared to chess because the object is to immobilize the other player's king and capture him.

Each *shogi* player has 20 pieces that have eight different ranks. A skillful player may remove one or more pieces from the board at the beginning of the game to give the other person a handicap.

Like *judo* and *karate* practitioners, *go* and *shogi* players are ranked in grades (*dan*) from one through nine. There is another grading system for novices, called *kyu* (que). The less skillful, the higher the kyu number, which is just the opposite of the *dan* system).

When *go* and *shogi* players win tournaments, they are awarded various titles, including *meijin* (may-e-gene), *kisei* (key-say-e), and tenth *dan*.

Both *go* and *shogi* are played professionally, and the competition and skill involved are just as intense as they are in chess. *Go* and *shogi* are more likely to be played by intellectuals and well-educated people.

Mahjong, more of an average person's game, is also more likely to be played for the fun of it—or as a gambling game. A *mahjong* set consists of 136 tile-shaped ceramic pieces, each of which is identified by a Chinese *kanji* (kahn-jee) character on its face—usually in an attractive color.

At the start of a game, each player (there are usually four) gets a hand of 13 pieces, called *pai* (pie) in Japanese. The remaining 84 pieces are placed, face down, in the middle of a table. Players take turns picking up *pai* from the pile, discarding unwanted pieces as they try to build up various combinations. The first player to meld wins the hand and receives a certain number of points determined by the combinations he or she has built up.

Mahjong is relatively new to Japan, having been introduced in the 1920s by Japanese returning from visits to China and the U.S. (where it was played by Chinese-Americans). The game really became popular after World War II, and there are now *mahjong* parlors all over Japan.

One of the oldest home games in Japan is a card game based on 100 famous *waka* (wah-kah) poems and developed in the thirteenth century.

Each *waka* poem consists of 31 syllables arranged in three lines of five, seven, and five syllables each.

To begin the game, all cards that have only the second part of a *waka* are laid down face up, with the players sitting around in a square or circle. As the *waka* that can be seen are read out loud, the players try to pick up the matching card. The one who picks up the most cards is the winner.

To become an expert at this game you have to memorize all of the 100 *waka* poems, and be able to quickly link the right parts. Besides being played in the homes by old and young alike, there are factory and regional tournaments, especially during New Year celebrations.

There are a number of similar card games for children, with proverbs and popular sayings on them, that have been played in Japan for centuries.

Recommended reading: *The Game of Go* by Arthur Smith (Tuttle). Also: *Shogi: Japan's Game of Strategy.*

GANGS / GUMI (Guu-me) Organized gangs operating outside the law have been a significant aspect of Japanese society since early feudal days. The gangs were not the kind that robbed and killed but were traditionally engaged in such businesses as gambling, sporting events, nighttime entertainment, and prostitution.

During the feudal period, these gangs often acted as protectors of the common people against abuse by shogunate authorities and unprincipled *samurai.*

The gangs and many of their traditions have continued into modern times and are now known as *yakuza* (yah-kuu-zah). The gang leaders and their members are known to police authorities, but remain in business by operating behind legitimate fronts.

On occasion, when the activities of a gang in a particular area become conspicuous, authorities round up as many as 200 or 300 gang members in a series of coordinated raids. But most of them are soon back on the streets.

When members of the gangs are involved in violence, it is usually connected with intergang rivalry over territorial rights. On some of these occasions, gang members battle it out with swords, knives, and guns.

The world of the *yakuza* is often featured in Japanese movies and television dramas and has been the theme of a number of American movies.

In 1984, the number of gangsters in underworld organizations dropped below 100,000 for the first time since the mid-1960s, according to a report by the National Police Agency (NPA). In 1963, there were 5,216 gangs and 184,094 members.

The decline was attributed to the difficulty in recruiting new members because young men were no longer as attracted to the idea of operating roadside stalls, and the merging of several organizations into larger groups.

The latest NPA reports say there are now approximately 2,000 gangs in Japan with a membership of around 75,000, but the annual decrease in numbers has slowed down.

GARDENS / NIWA (Nee-wah) The art of landscape gardening in Japan goes back to at least the sixth century. During the reign of the Empress-Regent Suiko (554-628), gardens with beautifully designed artificial hills and ornamental ponds were already popular.

The aim of Japanese landscape gardening is to create in miniature a scenic landscape that suggests something on a large scale and looks completely natural.

Such gardens were an integral part of landscaping by the time Japan's Imperial capital was moved from Nagaokakyo to Kyoto in 794, where a garden of immense size called Shin Sen En, or Sacred Fountain Garden, was a centerpiece in the new city. The introduction of Zen Buddhism into Japan during the Kamakura Period (1185-1336) had a significant influence on garden landscaping. Gardens became less decorative and were designed to impart a sense of tranquility and happiness. The Zuisen Temple in Kamakura is an example of the hundreds of gardens designed during this period.

It was also during the Kamakura era that two of Japan's most famous books on landscape gardening were published—*Emposho* (*Book of Gardens*), written by the priest Zoen, and *Sakuteiki* (*Book of Garden Planning*), written by Nagatsune Fujiwara. Both books are still regarded as authoritative.

Kyoto abounds in gardens dating back to this and the following Muromachi Period (1392-1573), including those of the famous Silver Temple Pavilion and the Gold Pavilion Temple. So-called flat gardens (*hira niwa*), using only stones and trees arranged in a flat area, also became popular during the Muromachi era.

Between 1573 and 1615, during the wars that culminated in the consolidation of the Tokugawa Shogunate, both landscaping and architecture increased in scale and grandeur, taking on the heroic spirit of the age. Gardens designed during these years tended to be more colorful and vigorous.

At the same time, this was also the age of several of Japan's greatest tea masters, who designed some of the country's most renowned gardens. Among the most famous of these garden designers were So-ami, Mon-ami, Zen-ami, and the great Sen-no Rikyu (1521–1591). Rikyu was the leading tea master of his day and created many gardens, including one at the noted Chishaku-in Temple in Kyoto. See RIKYU, SENNO, for the story of this remarkable man's untimely end.

Another of the great tea masters who also gained fame for his garden designs was Enshu Kobori (1579–1647), whose most outstanding work is the celebrated garden of the Katsura Imperial Villa in Kyoto. He also designed the garden of the Kohoan of the famous Daitoku Temple in Kyoto, as well as the gardens at the equally famous Nanzen and Chion-in Temples.

The beautiful gardens of Nijo Castle, the Shugakuin Palace and the Hompo Temple in Kyoto were designed by Koetsu Hon-ami. Altogether, there are more than 50 outstanding gardens in Kyoto that have been preserved and are open to the public today.

After Ieyasu Tokugawa established his shogunate in Edo (Tokyo) in 1603 and his grandson later passed the decree that all the nation's 270 feudal lords would build mansions there, Edo became the new center of garden landscaping activity, and the designing of such gardens gradually passed out of the hands of the tea masters and priests to professional gardeners.

The wealthier feudal lords vied to make the gardens of their Edo mansions into works of art and constructed gardens of great beauty around their fief estates. Among the more famous ones that may still be enjoyed are the Kenrokuen in Kanazawa, the Ritsuen in Takamatsu, and the Korakuen in Okayama.

Only a few of the great gardens constructed in Tokyo by the feudal lords of the Edo era remain today. Among them are Kyosumien at Fukagawa, Rikugien in Komagome, Korakuen in Koishikawa, Chinzanso in Mejiro, Shiba-Rikyu Onshi in Shiba, Tokaiji in Shinagawa, and the Akasaka Rikyu Garden in Moto-Akasaka.

Unlike most gardens in the West, which generally create an artificial landscape, Japanese gardens strive to symbolize a large natural landscape in a small, concentrated area. The materials used by Japanese gardeners are all natural—shrubs, rocks, trees, and water—with the emphasis on harmonious spatial beauty, instead of geometric forms favored by Westerners.

The underlying philosophy of Japanese gardening is a combination of Shintoism, which reveres nature, Buddhism, which reveres life, and Zen, which seeks to perceive the fundamental reality in all things and abide by the laws of nature.

Generally speaking, there are three styles of Japanese gardens: the *tsukiyama* (t'sue-kee-yah-mah), or pond-sea-hill; the *karesansui* (kah-ray-sahn-sue-e), or dry water and waterfall; and the *shakkei* (shock-kay-e), or water-mountain-woods.

The *tsukiyama* style uses a central pond to symbolize the sea and banks of earth and rocks to represent mountains. The *karesansui* uses white sand to represent the sea and blue rocks to represent waterfalls. The *shakkei* uses all the above, plus the views of surrounding natural mountains and woodlands.

The Tenryu (Tane-ree-you) and Saiho (Sie-hoe) Temple gardens in Kyoto are famous examples of *tsukiyama* style gardens. The Ryoan (Rio-on) and Daisen-In (Die-sin-een) gardens, also in Kyoto, are noted examples of the *karesansui* style. Two of the most famous *shakkei* gardens in Japan are those surrounding the Katsura (Kot-sue-rah) Imperial Villa and the Shugaku-In (Shuu-gah-kuu-Een) Villa in Kyoto.

Recommended reading: *The Garden Art of Japan*, by Masao Hayakawa (Weatherhill). Also: *Japanese Gardens for Today*, by David H. Engel (Tuttle); *Japanese Courtyard Garden Landscapes for Small Spaces*, by Shigamori Kanto (Weatherhill); *Imperial Gardens of Japan*, by Teiji Ito (Weatherhill); *A Japanese Touch for Your Garden*, by Kyoshi Seike, Masanobu Kudo, and David H. Engel (Kodansha International).

GEISHA (Gay-e-shah)   During the 1600s in Edo (Tokyo), women entertainers who were skilled at playing the *shamisen* and singing gradually came to be known as *geisha—gei* meaning art and *sha* meaning person.

In those days especially, such entertainment usually took place in licensed quarters or in *ryokan* (inns) and *ryotei* (restaurants) where prostitution was practiced. Thus, *geisha* came to be regarded by many as courtesans who were also skilled entertainers.

As the decades passed, the profession of *geisha* grew in stature. The training became more formalized and strict. With the deterioration of the large, elaborate, licensed entertainment quarters following the downfall of the Tokugawa Shogunate in 1868, the social status of professional prostitutes began to drop and that of *geisha* to rise. Within a few decades, their positions were completely reversed—*geisha* were the most elite of public women, and prostitutes were the lowest. Well-to-do executives and politicians began to vie with each other to make the most famous *geisha* their mistresses. Their training included lessons in etiquette, grace, flower arranging, singing, dancing, the tea ceremony, and in how to be a stimulating conversationalist. While lower-class *geisha* were generally available as prostitutes, those of extraordinary talent and beauty were sought after as entertainers and, before and after the turn of the twentieth century, as wives.

Given the social system in which wives did not participate with men in business or politics—and therefore could not act as hostesses for their husbands under any circumstances—*geisha* came to perform valuable functions not only in dressing up business and political meetings held in inns and restaurants, but also in helping these meetings run smoothly.

Apprentice *geisha*, who often start their training before they are in their teens, are called *maiko* (my-e-koe), a term that originated in Kyoto. (In pre-1945 days, apprentice *geisha* in Tokyo were called *hangyoku*.)

Today, many waitresses and barmaids who wear *kimonos* and elaborate wigs are often passed off as *geisha*. But true *geisha* are members of very tightly run associations and, for the most part, are simply too expensive for the average person to afford.

Most *geisha* live in or near the districts where they work, and they can be seen in the evenings going to and from the various *ryokan* and *ryotei* that utilize their services—some still by *jinrikisha* (man-powered vehicle).

It is these clusters of *ryotei* that are known as *geisha* houses and *geisha* districts. Three of Tokyo's best-known *geisha* districts are Shimbashi, Akasaka, and Yanagibashi.

One of the most celebrated stories about a Meiji-era man who bought a *geisha* had its beginnings in the city of Shimonoseki in the 1860s. The city's leading gay quarter was a favorite playground of several of the country's most daring young revolutionaries, who were then plotting to overthrow the feudal Tokugawa government.

Among these revolutionaries was a man named Ito. His favorite house of recreation was the Hayashiya, which was presided over by a well-known madam named Toku. Like all the young men who frequented the Hayashiya, Ito had his regular courtesan. Then he broke the rules by taking up with a *geisha* named Ume, who was the mistress of a merchant.

One night, Ito's courtesan caught him and Ume in a compromising situation and immediately reported him to the council of elders responsible for handling such breaches of conduct. A famous gang boss of the period tried to persuade the courtesan to forgive Ito and the *geisha*, but she was adamant.

According to the code of the entertainment quarters, the only way Ito could redeem himself was to buy his freedom from the courtesan and also buy Ume from her patron. This required more money than Ito had.

Finally, Toku, the madam of the Hayashiya, gave Ito the money he needed. Ito then married the *geisha* and went on with his revolutionary activities, eventually becoming one of Japan's outstanding prime ministers and the foremost statesman of the Meiji era—known to the world as Prince Hirobumi Ito.

In 1882, Ito was sent to Europe by Emperor Meiji to study the constitutions and codes of laws of various countries. On his return to Japan, he and several others drew up the country's first constitution, which was promulgated on February 11, 1889.

After an outstanding career in government, Ito was appointed Resident-General of Korea in 1905 and served in that capacity until 1909. In October of that year, while visiting in Harbin, he was assassinated by a Korean dissident.

Many foreigners are fascinated by the institution of the *geisha* but only one has gone as far as writer Liza Dalby. An anthropologist who spoke Japanese well, Dalby became a *geisha*, named Ichigiku, lived and worked in the elite Pontocho *geisha* community in Kyoto, and then wrote a book on the profession.

In her book *Geisha*, Dalby scrutinizes the real world of the *maiko* (apprentice *geisha*) and the licensed professionals—who usually do not engage in prostitution but are likely to have "patrons" who support them and enjoy their favors.

Recommended reading: *Geisha*, by Liza Dalby (Kodansha International).

GHOSTS and GOBLINS / YUREI and BAKE MONO (You-raye and Bah-kay moe-no)   Ghosts and goblins played a major role in the legends and myths of Japan, and until the mid-1900s, they were an important aspect of folklore. In ancient times, goblins were said to have originally been deities who became depraved and were banished from heaven. There were many different kinds of *bake mono*, or goblins, associated with rivers, mountains, valleys, and other areas. Ghosts were also plentiful and came in different forms.

Ghosts and goblins are still popular themes in Japanese movies, TV films, plays, and literature, and dozens of such stories are known by all Japanese.

Recommended reading: *Kwaidan*, by Lafcadio Hearn (Tuttle).

GIFT GIVING   Gift giving has traditionally been a very important part of life in Japan—more important than in most countries. In earlier times, the practice was so important—and so formalized and institutionalized—that the guidelines for gift giving would fill a large book.

The type of gift appropriate for specific occasions, the materials in which it was to be wrapped, and even the manner of wrapping were prescribed. The act of presentation was also meticulously detailed. In upper-class families, there was often a member who was responsible for making sure these guidelines were followed.

Such formalities are not nearly as strict today, but gift giving is still important—on the usual festive occasions, as well as to establish or maintain relations with doctors, teachers, employers, benefactors, etc.

The two biggest gift giving seasons in Japan are *Chugen* (Chuu-gain) in the summer and *Seibo* (Say-e-boe) at the end of the year.

Chugen gifts are given to express appreciation for daily services and favors received from individuals, as well as from professionals (superiors, teachers, good customers, doctors, lawyers, accountants, etc.). These gifts are not necessarily expensive.

O'Seibo gifts at the end of the year serve the same purpose as *Chugen* gifts and are also given to superiors, good customers, and other people to whom one feels a special obligation. Year-end gifts tend to be more costly than mid-year gifts.

The Japanese also customarily give gifts to someone leaving on a trip (usually money) and to people who do them favors while they themselves are traveling. These parting gifts, called *senbetsu* (sin-bate-sue) nowadays are usually limited to people leaving on long trips.

Senbetsu gifts carry with them the strong obligation for the receiver to bring back presents or souvenirs of their travels for each person who gave a parting gift—often requiring the recipient to keep a list of the names of the people involved.

Giving the right gift at the right time can be a very important matter in both personal and business situations, and the foreigner who is not familiar with the intricacies of gift-giving Japanese style would be well advised to consult with a Japanese friend or contact.

GIFTS / OMIYAGE (Oh-me-yah-gay)   Since gift giving has been a very important part of social and business life in Japan for many centuries, the manufacture and sale of gift items is a major industry.

In addition to art, folkcrafts and various handicrafts, other popular gift items include fruit, cakes, traditional accessories and decorative items, seaweed, *sembei* rice crackers, *mochi* rice cake, tea, and *sake* and other alcoholic beverages.

The custom of gift giving as a vital part of social and business obligations very early led to highly refined packaging that in itself is often a work of art, ranging from wrapping paper to wooden boxes.

Visitors to Japan are often taken aback by the variety, quality, and price of gift items in department stores.

GIFU (Ghee-fuu)   Thirty kilometers northwest of Nagoya, at the foot of Mt. Inaba on the Nagara River, the city of Gifu came into Japanese history as a castle town on the famous Nakasen Highway.

The castle was occupied by feudal *Daimyo* Nobunaga Oda in 1564 and was passed on to his son Nobutada and, later, his grandson Hidenobu. After the Battle of Sekigahara in 1600, Ieyasu Tokugawa's forces captured the castle, and it was given to the Owari Clan.

Gifu grew into a thriving farming and cottage industry center during the Tokugawa Shogunate. In 1891, most of the city was destroyed by an earthquake and great fire, but it was quickly rebuilt.

The city is now noted for the scenic beauty of the surrounding area; cormorant fishing (*ukai*), paper umbrellas, lanterns and fans, handmade paper, persimmons, the Zuiryu Temple, and the Shoho Temple, with its 13.6-meter image of Buddha.

GINZA (Gheen-zah)   The Ginza in Tokyo is Japan's best-known shopping and entertainment district. Measuring about a mile in length and half a mile in width, the Ginza extends north-south from Kyobashi to Shimbashi and east-west from Tsukiji to Marunouchi, Yurakucho, and Uchisaiwaicho in downtown Tokyo. The name comes from a silver mint (*ginza*) established in the area in 1612, shortly after the beginning of the Tokugawa Shogunate (1603–1868), when the land was reclaimed from Tokyo Bay. (The earth to fill in the Ginza and Marunouchi areas was dug from Kudan Hill by 10,000 men, provided by the country's 200 feudal lords, and carted to the area.)

Shops, restaurants, and drinking establishments grew up around the mint, and, by the late 1700s, the Ginza was one of the liveliest and most colorful areas in Edo. The intersection at Ginza 4-chome, where Ginza Dori, the main north-south avenue, crosses Hibya Dori, the main east-west thoroughfare, was to become one of the main crossroads of the city.

Ginza Dori was the first street in Japan to be paved and to have sidewalks (of stone blocks), following the construction of brick buildings along the avenue in 1873.

The first electric lights on the Ginza were installed in 1879, quickly replacing the wax candle lanterns that had been in use for generations. Soon thereafter, strolling the Ginza (*Ginbura*/Gheen-buu-rah) became a fashionable pastime of the city.

In 1882, horse-drawn trolley cars were introduced to the Ginza, going from Shimbashi to Ueno. For a brief period around the turn of the century, the Ginza was the equivalent of London's famous Fleet Street, with more than 30 newspaper companies lining the avenue.

There are numerous other huge shopping-entertainment districts in Tokyo today, but the Ginza retains its drawing power. Its hundreds of shops, boutiques, bars, lounges, restaurants, and huge department stores give it an ambience that is magnetic to Japanese and foreign visitors alike. On Sundays, Ginza Avenue is closed to traffic and becomes a bazaar of food stalls and stands selling gift and novelty items, attracting thousands of strollers and shoppers.

GIONMACHI (Ghee-own-mah-chee)   One of the most famous of Japan's traditional *geisha* quarters, Gionmachi is a section of Kyoto on the east bank of the Kamo River. In addition to the traditionally styled *geisha* inns, the area also boasts the country's oldest theater, the Minami Za, founded in the early 1600s, where all-star *kabuki* performances are staged every year in December.

Also in Gionmachi is the famous Kaburenjo Theater, noted for its spring Miyako Odori (Cherry Dance festival).

GIRI (Ghee-ree)   *Giri* refers to the very strong feelings of obligation and responsibility the Japanese have for doing what is expected of them in all areas of life. What is expected of them is to obey and abide by traditional customs regarding education, marriage, gifts, parties, work, and so on.

Basically, upholding the demands of *giri* is upholding one's honor and reputation by doing what is expected, even though it may be unpleasant or result in unhappiness. In earlier days, when the demands of *giri* could not be reconciled with a person's own wishes, suicide was often the way out.

Even today, among older Japanese, there are many who are *giri-gatai*— or very strict in their observance of *giri*.

GLOVER MANSION   The Glover Mansion, originally called the Glover House, is a large residence built on a prominence overlooking Nagasaki Harbor by a British trader before the turn of the twentieth century. The mansion is believed to be the original setting for the story on which the famous opera *Madame Butterfly* is based.

In Japan, the word "butterfly" (*cho-cho*) has long been used to describe a person—especially a man—who is not content with one woman and flutters like a butterfly from one to another.

G-MARK AWARD   In 1958, Japan's Ministry of International Trade and Industry (MITI) established an annual competition for companies to vie for best product-design awards in certain categories.

Winners in the competition are given a G-MARK, which is recognized as the most authoritative and prestigious award in the field of industrial design.

In 1983, the rules governing the competition were changed to allow foreign manufacturers to participate by applying through importers in Japan or directly to the Japan Industrial Design Promotional Organization, Annex 4th Floor, World Trade Center Building, 2-4-1 Hamamatsucho, Minato-ku, Tokyo, Japan.

Among the product categories eligible for the competition are audiovisual equipment, electric home appliances, optical equipment, air-conditioning equipment, automobiles, communications equipment, kitchen utensils, and stationery and accessories.

In a recent year, 2,973 products were entered in the competition, and MITI chose 854 of them for the coveted G-MARK award.

GO-BETWEENS / NAKODO (Nah-koe-doe)   The use of go-betweens, in arranging marriages and even in handling personal and business matters where there is ill will or the likelihood of conflict, is a tradition in Japan.

The reasons for this custom are simple: First, a third party who is not personally or emotionally involved in a matter is more likely to act rationally and fairly. Second, the custom provides a way for both parties to avoid putting their reputations on the line.

GOD-SHELF / KAMI-DANA (Kah-me-dah-nah)   Until recent times, nearly all homes in Japan had a miniature Shinto shrine that was placed on a special shelf, the *kami-dana*, along with various religious articles. On special occasions—such as memorial services—offerings of food, consecrated twigs, etc., are placed on the shelf.

Many homes, particularly in rural areas where religious observances are more common, still have the *kami-dana*.

GOLDFISH / KINGYO (Keen-g'yoe)   Japan is now synonymous with beautiful goldfish that come in all sizes and color combinations. Goldfish were introduced into Japan from China in the early 1600s, and there were later infusions from the Netherlands and Hawaii.

The Chinese goldfish were quickly adopted as pets by the aristocracy in the Imperial capital of Kyoto. Japanese goldfish breeders both developed old varieties and introduced new varieties, and keeping goldfish gradually became a national pastime. Goldfish peddlers, pushing their bowl-laden carts, became a familiar sight on the lanes and streets of towns and villages. Their cry of "Keeeennnng-yohhhhhh!" soon became one of the most familiar sounds of the country.

Kingyo vendors are still seen in Japan, especially around temples and shrines during festival time and at resort beaches.

GORGES / KYOKOKU (K'yoe-koe-kuu)   With its mountainous terrain and high rainfall, Japan has an exceptionally large number of mountain streams that over the eons have carved out thousands of gorges, many of which have been famous for centuries for their incredible beauty.

Among the best-known gorges in the country are Tachikue, near Izumoshi on the west side of Honshu, and Takachiho, in the Sobo-Katamuki Quasi-National Park, near Kumamoto in Kyushu.

GOVERNMENT / SEIFU (Say-e-fuu)   Japan's government is composed of a legislative branch called the Diet, an administrative branch, which includes the prime minister and his cabinet, and a judiciary branch.

The Diet, made up of a House of Representatives and a House of Councilors, is the highest organ of state power and the sole lawmaking body. Members of both Houses are elected by popular vote.

In addition to the power to pass laws, the Diet also designates the prime minister (usually the leader of the most powerful party or faction), approves budgets and treaties, and has the power to impeach judges and amend the constitution.

In administering the country, the prime minister and cabinet ministers are collectively responsible to the Diet. Altogether, there are 12 ministries, each of which is headed by a cabinet minister.

The prime minister has discretionary power to dismiss cabinet ministers; the prime minister may be removed from office by a vote of no-confidence by the majority of the Diet.

The judiciary consists of the Supreme Court and a number of lesser courts, including high courts, district courts, family courts, and summary courts. The prime minister and cabinet appoint all of the judges of the courts, including the chief judge of the Supreme Court.

There are a total of 763 Diet members, 511 of them in the House of Representatives and 252 in the House of Councilors. The House of Representatives outranks the House of Councilors. Business in the Houses can be conducted only if at least one-third of the membership is present. All matters are decided by a simple majority vote or, in special cases, by a two-thirds majority.

Members of the House of Representatives are elected from prefectural electorates for four-year terms that may be terminated by the cabinet if it decides to dissolve the House. Members in the House of Councilors are elected from both national and prefectural constituencies. Their term of office is six years. Half of the membership comes up for election every three years, and the House of Councilors is never dissolved.

The 12 ministries are Justice, Foreign Affairs, Finance, Education, Health and Welfare, Agriculture, Forestry and Fisheries, International Trade and Industry, Transport, Labor, Construction, and Home Affairs.

Besides these ministries, there are nine administrative agencies attached to the Office of the Prime Minister—the Administrative Management Agency, Hokkaido Development Agency, Defense Agency, Economic Planning Agency, Science and Technology Agency, Environment Agency, Okinawa Development Agency, National Land Agency, and National Public Safety Commission.

Each of Japan's 47 prefectures is administered by a popularly elected governor, as is the metropolis of Tokyo.

Ostensibly, Japan's government policies are set by the party in control of the Diet, and administered by officials of the ministries and agencies. But much of party politics in Japan is a facade, and both policies and administration are primarily controlled by the top ministry bureaucrats.

One of the reasons for this situation is that since the introduction of the parliamentary system of government in Japan the leading "parties" have consisted of groups of politicians who join together in factions that are fairly fluid, gaining and losing members in a constant struggle for administrative posts and political influence.

The faction with the largest number of members and coalition votes controls the House of Representatives. Its head invariably becomes the prime minister who then, with the advice and consent of faction leaders, appoints all of the cabinet ministers.

Since the 1950s most political power in Japan, on both a national and provincial level, has been wielded by individuals within these factions who had access to the most money, raised from business circles, and were the most effective in using the money to support the faction members of their choice. These individuals did not necessarily have a high post in the government, but their power was such that they could name and remove prime ministers at will.

Japan's government was totally dominated by the Liberal Democratic Party (LDP) from 1955 until August 1993, when it was finally toppled from power as a result of a long series of financial scandals involving huge amounts of money and the leadership of the party.

Diet member Morihiro Hosokawa, formerly a governor of Kumamoto Prefecture on the southern island of Kyushu—and the scion of one of Japan's most famous clan families who ruled in that area for more than 300 years—bolted from the Liberal Democratic Party in May 1992, formed the Japan New Party, and rode the popular revulsion to all of the LDP scandals to the premiership on August 9, 1993.

Hosokawa's new reform-oriented administration was to be short-lived, however, falling victim to behind-the-scenes power plays in April 1994, when he was replaced as prime minister by Tsutomu Hata, a veteran politician who had allied himself with another faction that called itself *Shin Sei To* (sheen say toe), which is short for "New Made-in Japan Party."

But Hata and his faction did not have a majority in the House of Representatives, and were seen as an interim group by the power brokers who continued to maneuver behind the scenes.

The basic structure of Japan's government is not likely to change in the foreseeable future, but evolving domestic as well as international circumstances will inevitably force reforms to diminish the role of "money politics" and the ongoing cycle of scandals.

In the meantime, it is also likely that Japan's powerful bureaucracies, particularly the Finance Ministry, the Ministry of International Trade and

Industry, and the Foreign Ministry, will continue to control most of the policy and all of the day-to-day activities of the government.

See POLITICAL PARTIES.

GOVERNMENT, LOCAL   Since 1947, Japan has had a Local Autonomy Law that guarantees the right of local communities to govern themselves by popular vote. Anyone 30 years of age or older may run for governor of a prefecture. The mayor of a village, town, or city must be at least 25 years old. Tenure in all cases is four years.

Each village, town, and city in the country has its own unicameral assembly, which is empowered to enact and abolish ordinances, approve budgets, and authorize expenditures. Local residents have the right of a wide range of appeals, including the demand that ordinances be abolished, that the assembly be dissolved, or that the chief executive officers and assembly members be recalled.

Prefectural and municipal governments share the functions and responsibilities of administration with the national government. The local governments are responsible for most functions regarding land preservation and development, disaster prevention, pollution control, labor, education, social welfare, and health problems.

Local taxes account for about 30 percent of the revenues of municipal and prefectural governments, with the national government making up the balance through tax transfers and allocations, plus reimbursement for work done under national programs.

GRAND MASTERS / IEMOTO (E-eh-moe-toe)   One of the most distinctive and important aspects of life in Japan is the so-called *iemoto* system in such fields as martial arts, performing arts, aesthetic pursuits, and *sumo*.

Iemoto is generally translated as "grand master," but its root meaning is "house founder."

In the early decades of the Tokugawa era (1603–1868), different schools developed in all of the above disciplines, each one founded by a man or woman who became its *iemoto*, or grand master, and exercised virtually absolute authority over the activities of the schools and their graduates.

The position of grand master was hereditary or passed to the favorite disciple, who continued the system. The grand master has the exclusive right to issue graduation certificates and grant teaching licenses to former students— for which the grand master or head school receives what amounts to franchise fees.

Despite criticism of the system, especially in the years following the end of World War II, the system has not only persisted, it has gained in strength and importance and must be reckoned with in any dealings with these various disciplines.

It is particularly important in flower arranging, the tea ceremony, and *sumo*.

GRANDMOTHER THROWING-AWAY MOUNTAIN / OBASUTE YAMA
(Oh-bahh-sue-tay yah-mah)   Some 21 kilometers south of Nagano, on the slopes of Mt. Kamuriki, is an area known as Obasute or Grandmother Throwing-Away.

It is said that in ancient times, nearby poor villages developed the custom of taking old women who could no longer work or take care of themselves to the mountainside and leaving them there to die of exposure.

The area is now known as a popular place for viewing the moon when it is reflected in the water of hundreds of rice paddies terraced onto the slopes of the mountain.

GRAND ISE "SWEAT"   Ise (E-say), south of Nagoya, is famous for the Ise Training Center, which is a kind of spiritual and physical training camp for employees of Japanese companies. The Center holds two four-day training sessions each month, putting its recruits through a training program that would daunt most would-be commandos.

Companies do not require their employees to go to Ise, but many of them strongly encourage it, and pay all tuition costs.

The regimen includes strenuous physical workouts, intensive lectures on social roles and obligations to children and parents, group singing and dancing, and—in winter—a dip in the icy waters of the Isuzu River.

The purpose of the Center is to teach team spirit and team achievement in the proper social context and, as the director says, to help the trainees empty out their old selves and become new people. Part of the uniform at the Center is a headband imprinted with the *kanji* characters for love and sweat, which is a good description of the Japanese approach to business.

There are a number of other such training camps for company employees and managers around Japan. In some of them, the training is more stren-uous than the regimen at Ise. One, on the waist of Mt. Fuji, quite literally aims at breaking the individual's ego and remaking him or her into the perfect team player.

GRAND SHRINES OF ISE (E-say)   The most venerated spot in Japan, where the spirits of all past emperors are enshrined, Ise is on the Pacific Ocean side of Shima Peninsula, south of Nagoya in Mie Prefecture.

The city of Ise is actually made up of two towns, Uji and Yamada, that were joined to form one municipality. The area was selected as a site for the Imperial Jingu shrines because of the incredible beauty of the area and because it was regarded as holy ground by the ancient Shinto leaders who chose it.

The Ise Jingu Shrines are actually made up of two extensive complexes that are 6.2 kilometers apart—the Naiku, or Inner Shrine, and the Geku, or Outer Shrine.

The Outer Shrine, dedicated to the Goddess of Farms, Harvest, Food, and Sericulture (silk making), consists of nine major buildings, including an Imperial House of Sojourn, where the emperor rests when he visits the shrine; the Place of Assembly, where other members of the Imperial family rest; a sacred dance pavilion; the Hall of Worship; and the Main Hall.

The grounds of the Outer Shrine, surrounded by a great grove of ancient Japanese cedars, covers an area of 89 hectares (219.6 acres). The shrine was originally located in Manai, in what is now Kyoto Prefecture. But it was moved to Ise in 478 by Emperor Yuryaku, following a revelation from Amaterasu O-Mikami, the Sun Goddess.

The Inner Shrine (Naiku), which dates from about 288 A.D., is where the Three Sacred Treasures that make up the Three Regalia of Japan's Imperial Throne—a mirror, sword, and jewel—were originally kept.

According to Japanese mythology, the mirror was given by the Sun Goddess to her grandson Ninigi-no Mikoto when he came down to earth to reign (on the spot now occupied by the Outer Shrines of Jingu). The mirror was first kept in the Imperial Palace in Yamato, as instructed by the Sun Goddess. But in 92 B.C. it was moved to a shrine in Kasanui, near Nara, because of the fear that close contact with too many people might desecrate it.

Apparently this same fear resulted in its being moved again around 288 A.D. to what was then distant Ise.

There are eight major structures in the Inner Shrine, similar to the main buildings in the Outer Shrine. The shrines are constructed of Japanese cypress (*hinoki*), one of the most beautiful of woods, obtained from a national forest in the Kiso Mountains. Their architecture is pure Japanese, dating back to before the introduction of Buddhism and Chinese influences into Japan.

The Grand Shrines of Ise are as fresh today as they were over a thousand years ago because from early times it has been the custom (called *sen-gu-shiki*) to rebuild them completely every 20 years. The last such rebuilding was done in 1993.

There are several annual festivals held at the Jingu Shrines. The most important are held in May, October, and November.

GREAT BRIDGE OF CHOSHI / CHOSHI OHASHI (Choe-she oh-hah-she)   The Great Bridge of Choshi, spanning the Tone River at its mouth on Boso Peninsula, which joins Tokyo on the northeast, is the longest river bridge in Japan. It is 1,450 meters in length and links Choshi City and Hasaki Town in Ibaraki Prefecture.

GREAT BUDDHA OF KAMAKURA / KAMAKURA DAIBUTSU (Kah-mah-kuu-rah Die-boot-sue)   Cast in the year 1252 by either Goroemon Ono or Hisatomo Tanji, both famous casters of that period, the great bronze image of Buddha in Kamakura is one of the world's most impressive sights.

Sitting in the precincts of the Kotoku-in Temple in a narrow valley that is close to a mile from the sea, the *Great Buddha* is 11.4 meters high and 29.4 meters wide at the base and has a face that is 2.3 meters in length. A silver boss on the Buddha's forehead weighs 13.6 kilograms, and, altogether, the image weighs over 93 tons. A spiral staircase inside the statue leads up to the shoulder level.

The expression on the *Great Buddha's* face is one of passionless calm, and over the centuries it has inspired millions of worshippers and sightseers, including Rudyard Kipling, who made the image known to millions of readers in one of his poems.

After the *Great Buddha* was cast and completed, a great hall was built around it. In 1369, a typhoon severely damaged the large wooden building, and in 1495 a tidal wave entered the valley from the distant ocean and carried the huge hall away. Since that time, the *Great Buddha* has sat out in the open.

One of the first foreigners to visit the *Great Buddha* was an Englishman named John Saris, a ship's captain. In 1613, he entered the statue and carved his name and the date into its inner wall.

After British poet Rudyard Kipling visited Kamakura in the late 1890s, he wrote a poem entitled "Buddha at Kamakura." Three of the most quoted verses in the poem are:

O ye who tread the Narrow Way
By Tophet-flare to Judgement Day,
Be gentle when the heathen pray
To Buddha at Kamakura.

Yet spare us still the Western joke
When joss-sticks turn to scented smoke
The little sins of little folk
That worship at Kamakura.

A tourist show, a legend told,
A rusting bulk of bronze and gold,
So much, and scarce so much, ye hold
The meaning of Kamakura

Recommended reading: *Sculpture of the Kamakura Period*, by Hisashi Mori (Weatherhill).

GREAT BUDDHA OF NARA The Great Buddha (*Daibutsu*) of Nara is the centerpiece of Todai Temple, which was erected between 745 and 752 and is still the largest wooden building in the world. The great bronze statue was commissioned by Emperor Shomu, and work on it was first begun in 743 at Shigaraki Palace, south of Lake Biwa.

This effort ended in failure, but it was started again in Nara in 745 and was completed in 749 after eight attempts.

The seated figure is 16.2 meters in height, and its face is 4.8 meters wide. A total of 437 tons of bronze, 75 kilograms of mercury, 130 milligrams of pure gold, seven tons of vegetable wax, and an unrecorded amount of charcoal and other materials were used in the casting of the image.

The dedication ceremony for the Great Buddha, held in 752, was attended by the Empress Regent Koken and her parents, the ex-Emperor and Empress Shomu, all the court dignitaries, and over 10,000 priests and nuns.

In 855, an earthquake shook the Great Buddha's head off, but it was replaced in 861. In 1180, after a fire melted the head and right hand of the statue, they were replaced. Again, in 1567, the head was lost in a fire. It was 1692 before it was completely repaired—and it has been kept in repair since.

The Great Buddha of Nara is one of the most popular visitor attractions in Japan.

GUIDE SERVICES   With tourism and international business so important to the Japanese economy, Japan is one of the few countries that has a Guide-Interpreter Business Law. The law requires anyone who wants to engage in the guide/interpreting business to pass a national examination conducted by the Ministry of Transport and obtain a license from the governor of the local prefecture.

There are over 2,000 such guides in Japan, over half of whom belong to the prestigious Japan Guide Association (JGA). The rates charged by the guides are controlled by the JGA. Among the languages spoken by the guides are English, French, German, Russian, Chinese, Italian, Spanish, and Portuguese.

H

HACHIMAKI (Hah-chee-mah-kee)   This is the headband the Japanese have traditionally worn when engaged in strenuous physical work, participating in some festival activity, or engaging in some kind of labor or political demonstration.

A very old custom in Japan, the wearing of the *hachimaki* is said to have developed in ancient times as part of Shinto religious ceremonies. It is both a practical and picturesque custom that adds to the colorful ambience of life in Japan.

HAIKU (Hie-kuu)   A highly stylized and refined form of poetry that fascinates both Japanese and Westerners, *haiku* was developed in the middle of Japan's Edo Period in the late seventeenth century by the famous poet Basho Matsuo.

Basho took the opening verse (*hokku*/ hoke-kuu) of the long-established *haikai-renga* (hie-kie rane-gah), a linked verse form, and made it into an independent form. It was not until the end of the nineteenth century that Masaoka Shiki made the name *haiku* the generic term for this form of poetry.

Haiku poetry consists of 17 syllables (the Japanese language is made up of syllable sounds), arranged in three lines of five, seven, and five syllables each, respectively.

This style of poetry traditionally deals with nature and life in a highly austere, elegant way that distills the essence of a thing, presenting a clear but fleeting glimpse of what the author has seen or felt.

It is also traditional to use a "seasonal" word in every *haiku* — referring to a plant, animal, event, or custom in a particular season, thus evoking mental images of spring, the mountains, the brevity of life, and so on.

Here is one of the most famous of Basho's *haiku*:

Yagate shinu	The cicada's cry
Keshiki wa miezu	Gives no sign
Semi no koe	It is about to die

Recommended reading: *A Haiku Journey*, by Basho Matsuo, translated by Dorothy Britton (Kodansha International). Also, *The Japanese Haiku*, by Ken Yasuda (Tuttle).

HAKODATE (Hah-koe-dah-tay) The third largest city on Hokkaido, Japan's northernmost main island, Hakodate (Box Castle) owes its origin and name to the Kono clan, which built a box-shaped castle there in the fifteenth century.

The gateway to Hokkaido, Hakodate is located at the neck of Hakodate Peninsula, which extends out into the Straits of Tsugaru and has a spectacular mountain at its tip.

Hakodate first became of special importance in the history of Japan when it was designated as a coaling station for foreign ships in 1855 under the terms of the Kanagawa Treaty, which was negotiated by the American, Townsend Harris.

Then on July 1, 1859, Hakodate became one of five ports opened to foreign commerce (the others were Yokohama, Kobe, Nagasaki, and Niigata), but it was so far away from the population and industrial centers that it did not enjoy the rapid growth experienced by the other ports.

Hakodate is now a major fishing port and a center for food processing and shipbuilding. There are dozens of points of interest in the Hakodate area, including Hakodate Park, famous for its cherry blossoms in the late spring; the Hakodate Museum, which is Japan's oldest local museum; and the Goyokaku, which was the country's first Western-style military fort (completed in 1864) and the site of one of the last major battles surrounding the downfall of the *Shogun* in 1868.

The famous Yunokawa Spa, which boasts over 100 inns and restaurants set among hot springs that have an average temperature of 66 degrees C., plus a Trappist convent, is near Hakodate.

HAKONE (Hah-koe-nay) Situated in the mountains southwest of Tokyo and adjoining Mt. Fuji, Hakone is one of the most beautiful and popular resorts in all of Japan. The heart of the Hakone district is a huge volcanic crater that is 40 kilometers in circumference and includes a beautiful lake (Ashino Ko, popularly known as Lake Hakone) and 12 hot spring spas that have been known and used since ancient times.

These spas, several in picturesque gorges whose beauty is beyond words, are Yumoto, Tonosawa, Miyanoshita, Dogashima, Sokokura, Kowakidani, Giga, Gora, Ubako, Sengokuhara, Ashinoyu, and Yunohanazawa.

The oldest of these spas is Yumoto. The three most famous (especially among foreign visitors to Japan) are Miyanoshita, Gora, and Kowakidani.

Hakone is served by bus and train lines, and is a popular overnight and weekend trip by car from the Tokyo and Yokohama areas. Besides its superb scenery and dozens of hotspring inns (whose waters are classified according to their mineral content and effects on various ailments), the cool summer weather makes Hakone doubly popular in the summer months.

The most famous tourist attraction in Hakone is the annual reenactment of one of the great *Daimyo* Processions of the Tokugawa Period, when all the feudal lords had to march to the capital at Edo every other year to attend the *shogun's* court. The event usually takes place on November 3, but may vary by a day or so.

The Procession begins at Yumoto, goes to Tonosawa in the morning, and returns to Yumoto in the afternoon.

There are dozens of historical sites in the Hakone area, including a replica of one of the famous Barrier Gates that were erected along the great walking roads that led to Edo. During the long period of the Tokugawa Shogunate, Hakone was one of the largest and most important of the post stations that lined the old Tokaido Highway.

Some of the huge Japanese cedars that lined the Tokaido along the shores of Lake Hakone are still alive, making it easier to visualize the passing of one of the great *Daimyo* Processions (some of which consisted of over 1,000 warriors and retainers, all in their official regalia). See PROCESSIONS OF THE LORDS.

HAKOZAKI-CHO (Hah-koe-zah-kee-choe)   This is the location of Tokyo International Airport's city terminal. It is the station for limousine buses that arrive from and leave for the airport in Narita, 60 kilometers away, every few minutes. Several airlines, including Japan Air Lines, have check-in facilities at the City Terminal. Hakozaki-cho is in Chuo Ward about 15 minutes from central Tokyo. The Suitengumae subway station on the Hanzomon line is located beneath the city air terminal.

HALL OF POETS / SHI SENDO (She sane-doe)   One of the most beautiful examples of Japanese architecture and gardening is the famous Hall of Poets in Kyoto. A short distance north of the noted Temple of the Silver Pavilion, the *Shi Sendo* was founded in 1631 as a retreat by Jozan Ishikawa, a famous poet and scholar of that period.

The temple takes its name from the *Shi Sen*, or Poet Room, where the portraits of 36 famous Chinese poets line the walls. The temple is also known for the exceptional beauty of its white-sand garden, lined with azaleas that have been sculptured into numerous shapes and surrounded by a grove of maple trees.

HAMA DETACHED PALACE (Hah-mah) Originally a villa of the Tokugawa *Shogun's* family, the Hama Detached Palace in Tokyo was taken over by the Imperial Household in 1871 and was frequently used as a State Guest House. American President U.S. Grant stayed there when he visited Japan after leaving office.

The site was given to the city of Tokyo in 1945 and has been open to the public since 1946. The 25-hectare (60-acre) grounds include a tidal pool spanned by three bridges that lead to an islet in the heart of the landscaped garden.

The buildings and garden give an impressive insight into the way the feudal lords of Edo lived. The area is especially attractive in the early spring, when the cherry trees on the grounds are in bloom.

The garden is only a short walk from Shimbashi Station in downtown Tokyo.

HAND-CLAPPING AT SHRINES / KASHIWADE (Kah-she-wah-day) Worshippers at Shinto shrines clap their hands to concentrate their own attention on their prayers and to attract the attention of the deity of the shrine.

HANDICRAFTS / MINGEIHIN (Meen-gay-e-heen) Japanese historians have traced the country's famous handicraft industries to metal work that was already in evidence in the seventh century. Several thousand items on display in the Shosoin Repository in Nara were first presented to the Todai Temple in 756. They include swords, mirrors, ornaments, musical instruments, and other items.

During the Heian Period (794–1185), great progress was made in both metal and lacquerware handicrafts. With the rise of the warrior class, swordsmiths proliferated, and over 20,000 of their names were recorded. The three best known of the great swordsmiths of this period were Yoshimitsu, Masamune, and Yoshihiro.

Metalware, pot-metal casting, lacquerware, ceramics, glassware, and cloisonné continued to make significant progress during these centuries and really flowered during the long, peaceful Tokugawa Period (1603–1868), which preceded the reopening of Japan to the outside world.

The secret of the quality and beauty of Japanese-made handicrafts can be found in the master-apprentice system and in the fundamental concepts of beauty that grew out of Shintoism and Zen Buddhism. This was a classic beauty that emphasized the natural essence of the material. See BEAUTY; QUALITY.

The master-apprentice system was already well entrenched in Japan by the seventh century. Under this system, boys were apprenticed to tradesmen when they were as young as seven or eight and learned a craft from the bottom up over a period of many years. In some of the more demanding crafts, the period of apprenticeship lasted for up to 30 years or even longer —sometimes until the master died.

It was almost always at least 20 years before an apprentice was permitted to go out on his own and set up his own shop. Thus, the products that came out of Japan's handicraft industries were routinely of a quality that has not been surpassed in any country.

Interestingly, traditional Japanese woodworking tools are now popular among a growing number of American and other Western handicraft artists, as is the spiritual kinship that exists between wood workers and their tools.

Recommended reading: *Famous Ceramics of Japan Series* (Kodansha International); *The Arts of Japan Series* (Weatherhill); *Japanese Cloisonné— History, Technique & Application*, by Lawrence A. Cohen and Dorothy Ferster (Weatherhill); *Japanese Woodworking Tools: Their Tradition, Spirit and Use*, by Toshio Odate (Taunton Press).

HANEDA AIRPORT/HANEDA KUKO (Hah-nay-dah kuu-koe) Tokyo's original international airport—located only 15 to 20 minutes by taxi from downtown Tokyo—Haneda is now the city's domestic airport, but it still has one international client: China Air Lines.

As a result of a diplomatic arrangement with Taiwan, CAL was allowed to continue using Haneda when all other international operations were moved to the new international airport in Narita. See AIRPORTS.

HANGING SCROLLS / KAKEJIKU (Kah-kay-jee-kuu)   The focal point of the main room or guest room in a Japanese house, inn, or mansion is the *tokonoma* (toe-koe-no-mah), a recessed alcove designed for the express purpose of displaying a flower arrangement, a hanging scroll, or some other work of art.

Kakejiku are long, vertical scrolls of silk or paper bearing a painting or a choice selection of calligraphy, or both. The painting or calligraphy is often selected for display on the basis of the season it fits.

Kake means "hanging," and *jiku* means "axis" or roller," and, together, they refer to the wooden rollers at the bottom (and sometimes the top) of the scrolls, which allow them to be easily rolled up when not in use.

Kakejiku are also called *kakemono*, or "hanging things."

The custom of building *tokonoma* into Japanese homes and other buildings is an ancient one. It began as a private Buddhist altar where an incense burner, flowers, and a Buddhist scroll were hung. It then developed into an integral part of the aesthetic practices that are a distinctive part of Japanese culture—practices that derive from Shintoistic themes that celebrate nature and humanity's relationship with the cosmos, and from Taoist and Buddhist teachings that the appreciation of nature and beauty is necessary for the whole person. See IKEBANA; TOKONOMA.

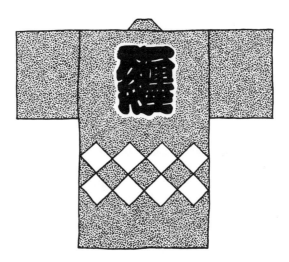

HAPPI COATS (Hop-pee)   The *happi* is a short, *kimono*-styled, slipover-type jacket worn by workers and *daimyo* retainers since early times—and also worn by youths and men as a sort of costume when they participate in many festivals. It is also called *hanten* (hahn-tane).

While strictly a common worker's jacket, as far as the Japanese were concerned, foreign residents and visitors in Japan in the late 1940s and 1950s picked up on the *happi* coat as casual wear, and it became a popular gift item. The Westerners were probably misled by the word *happi*, which they pronounced "happy," and took it to mean that the jacket was for recreational wear.

Regular *happi* coats traditionally had the name or crest of the wearer's employer on the back.

HARAKIRI (Hah-rah-kee-ree)   The Japanese word *harakiri* is widely recognized around the world—though it is invariably mispronounced as something like "harry-kerry"—because of the sensational nature of ritual suicide.

An understanding of the cultural and social role that *harakiri* played in Japanese life for so many centuries is one of the most fascinating facets of Japanese history, and it is a key to understanding that history. See SUICIDE; SAMURAI.

HARAMAKI (Hah-rah-mah-kee)   The *haramaki*, or "stomach band," is a long band of cloth, usually woolen these days, that was traditionally wrapped around the abdomen by Japanese men—especially working-class men and especially during winter but often during other seasons, as well.

The custom is still followed by many laborers who work outside (and some older men). Its purpose is to prevent the abdomen from getting chilled. The practice goes back to the ancient concept that the solar plexis is the center of one's life-force.

HARMONY/WA (Wah)   One of the primary aspects of any society or social system is the various customs and laws that are designed to maintain harmony all—or, at least, most—of the time among the members of the society.

In Japan, this harmonious state has traditionally been referred to as *wa*, a term that is simple enough in itself but has very broad implications when used in its Japanese context.

It goes back to one of the primary principles of Shintoism—that peaceful, harmonious relations must exist among human beings and between humans and nature in order for everything and everybody to stay in balance, prosper, and fulfill their purpose.

The ultimate goal of *wa* permeates and colors every facet of Japanese culture and the Japanese social system, from the way the language is constructed and used to the customs and rules that apply to behavior in personal relationships.

Wa does not have anything to do with equality. Its essence is that everything and everybody has a proper place and a proper role and must conform to this place and role in order to stay right with the world.

All of the many artifices that make up the Japanese social and business system—the bow, the use of respectful language, introductions and go-betweens, the consensus approach to decisions, the role of cabarets and drinking, and so on—are aspects of maintaining harmony.

HARRIS, TOWNSEND   Following the success of his trade and diplomatic mission to Japan in 1853–1854, Commodore Matthew C. Perry recommended that Townsend Harris, a merchant with extensive experience in the South Pacific and Orient, be appointed the U.S.'s first consul to Japan.

Harris's appointment was made in August 1855, and on August 21, 1856, he arrived at the small fishing town of Shimoda, near the the tip of Izu Peninsula, south of Edo (Tokyo), which had been designated as the site for the first American consulate and trading post. Harris was 45 years old at this time.

Just before arriving in Shimoda, Harris made the following entry in his diary: "I shall be the first recognized agent from a civilized power to reside in Japan. This forms an epoch in my life and may be the beginning of a new order of things in Japan. I hope I may so conduct myself that I may have honorable mention in the histories which will be written on Japan and its future destiny."

Harris was accompanied by a 24-year-old Dutchman named Henry Heusken, whom he had hired as his secretary-interpreter. Heusken, a former trader, had studied Japanese and could speak the language fairly well.

Harris soon recognized that Shimoda was useless as a trading port. His primary goals were thus to conclude a treaty with Japan providing for freedom of trade, the opening of additional ports, and moving the American consulate from Shimoda to the shogunate capital of Edo.

The Gyokusen Temple, located in Kakisaki Village about two kilometers east of Shimoda on the harbor road, was assigned to Harris as his residence. According to his descriptions, it was a dilapidated and uncomfortable place.

Harris immediately requested permission to travel to Edo to present his credentials to the *shogun*—but was told he would have to hand them over to the local governor, who would forward them to Edo. Harris recognized this as a delaying tactic and rejected it. In November 1857, after more than a year of frustrating negotiations, Harris was permitted to travel from Shimoda to Edo to officially announce his presence and begin his work.

The majority of Japan's feudal lords were bitterly opposed to opening the country to foreign trade and diplomatic relations, no doubt recognizing the threat to their positions.

During Harris's trip to Edo, which he made in a palanquin, a form of travel reserved for the ruling class, an attempt was made to assassinate him, but the would-be killers were caught and jailed.

Harris was courteously received by *shogun* Iemochi Tokugawa. A tentative agreement was reached, and he returned to Shimoda in March 1858. The following month he returned to Edo for the *shogun's* reply.

The reply was not ready. Harris returned to Shimoda in June and in July was summoned to Kanagawa (now part of Yokohama), where the treaty was signed. *Shogun* Iemochi had consulted with his strongest supporters among the feudal lords before agreeing to sign the new treaty, which opened the ports of Yokohama, Kobe, and Nagasaki to trade; allowed religious freedom in Japan; permitted Japan to build ships in the U.S.; and appointed the U.S. as mediator in the event of disputes between Japan and European countries. The treaty was signed on July 20, 1858, but did not go into effect until July 4, 1859.

This new treaty divided the country into two factions—those who agreed with the *Shogun* that the country should be opened to the outside world and the traditionalists who believed that the *shogun* and his allies had betrayed the country by opening it up to barbarians.

Soon after the new treaty was signed, *shogun* Iemochi became ill, and Lord Kamon Ii of Hikone was appointed prime minister (Tairo). Lord Ii was in favor of the treaty and thus became the leader of the forces working toward elimination of the exclusion policy. The opposition group was headed by the Lord of Mito, who was a member of the Tokugawa family, but a strong traditionalist.

While enroute to the *shogun's* castle in Edo on March 23, 1860, Lord Ii was attacked by Mito *samurai*. His head was cut off and taken to Mito where it was exhibited in public. The *samurai* then surrendered to the shogunate authorities, saying they had killed Ii because he had gone against the wishes of the emperor in signing the treaty with Harris.

The following year, Harris's secretary, the Dutchman, was murdered, and in July of the same year a group of foreigners from the British Legation were set upon by *ronin samurai*. Two of the Englishmen were wounded, and several of their guards were killed.

The shogunate was alarmed by these attacks, fearing that they would provoke the foreign powers into declaring war on Japan. All foreign residents of Edo were escorted to Yokohama, where they would be safer in the foreign compound.

The U.S. Senate approved Harris's appointment as Minister to Japan in January 1859, and on July 7 he established the American Legation in Edo in the Zempuku Temple, said to have been founded by the famous Kobo Daishi in the ninth century. Harris continued as the American minister in Japan until 1861, when he retired from government service. He died in 1878 and was buried in Brooklyn, New York.

The Zempuku Temple was to continue to serve as the American Legation in Edo until 1869, by which time the *shogun* had stepped down and a new government had been formed by Emperor Meiji. A new legation was opened in the Tsukiji district, just east of the Ginza.

In 1936, the American-Japan Society erected a stone monument at the Zempuku Temple to commemorate the legation's history in Japan-U.S. relations. The monument was inlaid with a bronze disk bearing Harris's likeness and an inscription, which reads, "On this spot Townsend Harris opened the first American Legation in Japan, July 7, 1859."

On the back of the monument, in Japanese, is a handwritten note by Baron T. Matsuda that says, "The site of the residence of early American envoys."

During the three years he stayed in Shimoda, Harris was kept under close watch by local and shogunate authorities and was not allowed to leave the town, except on his two official trips to Edo. He greatly resented being isolated in this manner and lodged numerous protests with the Japanese authorities.

Hoping to both mollify and distract Harris, the authorities assigned a *geisha* named Okichi to him as a woman servant. While Japanese records indicate that Harris carried on an affair with the maid, he wrote in his diary that he was too ill from an unsatisfactory diet and various ailments to notice her. Heusken was provided with a girl named Ofuku.

One can imagine how the women felt. The two men smelled of meat and butter, which the Japanese of that time found nauseating; bathed once a week, if that often; had heavy beards; wore their shoes inside their dwelling; and otherwise behaved like "hairy barbarians."

According to Japanese records, Harris later carried on another affair with a young Japanese girl after he moved from Shimoda to the shogunate capital of Edo. Records kept by a priest who lived in a temple near Harris's Edo residence in what is now Azabu say that Harris told the temple clerk he would like to have a massage. The temple arranged for a 17-year-old girl named Rin to give the massage. The priest wrote that Harris "fell in love with the girl overnight," asked for her regularly for the next several months, and showered her with clothes and money.

In the 1920s, Edgar A. Bancroft, the American ambassador to Japan, Viscount E. Shibusawa, and Prince Iesato Tokugawa (then president of the American-Japan Society) had the Gyokusen Temple, Harris's first place of residence in Japan, renovated and a granite tablet erected commemorating the event. The tablet bears an inscription from Harris's diary in which he recounts the raising of the first American flag in Japan, his problems with huge mosquitoes and lack of sleep, and grave reflections about the omnious changes he foresaw for Japan.

Underneath this note is the inscription: In memory of Townsend Harris, American Consul-General, who by the Treaty of Yedo, July 29, 1858, opened Japan to the world, and on this spot, September 4, 1856, raised the first Consular flag in this Empire and here resided until November 23, 1857. Erected by Viscount E. Shibusawa, Edgar A. Bancroft and Henry M. Wolf of Chicago, September 4, 1927."

On the back of the granite slab is a glowing tribute to Harris in Japanese, written by Viscount Shibusawa.

Inside the temple is a framed portrait of Harris and a glass case containing a number of mementos from his days there. The most valuable artifact in the temple is an eight-volume diary in Japanese detailing Harris's life in the village, written by the elder of the village on orders from the authorities.

HATSU-MAIRI (Hot-sue my-ree)   Literally "first visit," *hatsu-mairi* refers to the traditional custom of visiting a Shinto shrine or Buddhist temple immediately after the beginning of the new year. For millions of people, this means staying up late New Year's Eve and visiting the temple or shrine of their choice just after midnight.

Some people travel long distances to keep this popular tradition at a nationally famous shrine or temple. At the latter, there are often nationally televised ceremonies of ringing out the old year and ringing in the new— with huge bells that have giant logs for clappers.

Young men take turns swinging the logs (suspended on stout ropes) against the temple bells.

The most popular *hatsu-mairi* place in Tokyo is the great Meiji Shrine near Harajuku Station, just outside the city's inner loop.

HATSU SHIMA (Hot-sue she-mah)   This is an island that can be seen from the famous hot springs resort of Atami, on Izu Peninsula. It is 10 kilometers off the coast, about three kilometers in circumference, and a popular campsite for young people during the summer months. It is 40 minutes by boat from either Atami or Ito (the next seaside resort south of Atami).

HEALTH / KENKO (Kane-koe)   Although health services in Japan often appear to be well below Western standards—most of its some 9,250 hospitals are old and decrepit and extremely crowded—the Japanese have one of the longest life-expectancies in the world.

In addition to the hospitals, there are 165,000 family doctors who generally run small clinics—many of them out of their homes. These doctors are barred from working in hospitals and cannot take their patients to hospitals for more complicated treatments. All they can do is refer them to hospitals. Most of these family doctors also act as pharmacists and earn a great deal of their income from selling drugs to their patients.

Patients going to hospitals take their own personal toilet articles, as well as their own eating implements, towels, and soap.

A revised health insurance law that went into effect on August 1, 1984, abandoned the principle of free medical aid for participants in the public health insurance system, and everyone is now required to pay 10 percent of the medical expenses they incur. Retired persons and their dependents must pay premiums and 20 percent of their medical expenses.

Japanese employers are required to provide health insurance for workers. At the age of 60, retired persons generally transfer to the national health insurance system.

The fees doctors can charge patients are controlled, and they are very low by American standards. As a result, patients routinely give their doctors monetary gifts and other favors that go unreported.

HEARN, LAFCADIO   Lafcadio Hearn, probably the best known of the earlier writers on Japan, was born in the Ionian Islands in 1850, the son of a British army surgeon and a Greek mother. He was educated in England and France. Following the death of his father, which reduced the family to poverty, he migrated to the U.S. when he was 19.

In the U.S., Hearn held many jobs, ranging from dishwashing to hack-writing. He then moved to the French West Indies and later wrote a book, *Two Years in the French West Indies*, that was quite popular. In 1890, Harper & Row, his publisher, commissioned him to go to Japan and write a series of articles on the Japanese islands.

Once in Japan, Hearn was so delighted with the country, he accepted a position teaching English at the Matsue Middle School and severed his relationship with Harper & Row.

Hearn later said the next two years were the happiest of his life. He married a Japanese woman named Koizumi and began studying and writing about Japan. He was then invited to teach at the Kumamoto Higher School and began writing for the *Japan Chronicle Newspaper* in Kobe.

In 1896, Hearn was invited to become a lecturer in English literature at Tokyo Imperial University, the most prestigious university in the country. He was to stay there until two years before his death in 1904.

In the intervening years, Hearn published many books about Japan, became a naturalized citizen, and adopted the name Yakumo Koizumi, after his wife. He also translated the works of several famous French writers and wrote a number of literary critiques that are still highly regarded.

Hearn achieved some notice before he died, but he was not to become world-famous as an interpreter of Japan until well after his death. Among his best-known books—which are still in print—are *Glimpses of Unfamiliar Japan, Japan: An Attempt at Interpretation, Kokoro (Heart), Gleanings from Buddha Fields,* and *Kwaidan*.

HECHIMA (Hay-chee-mah)   The *hechima* is a washing sponge made from a long, cucumber-shaped gourd. In use in Japan for centuries, it not only gets one clean but also provides a stimulating massage.

HEIAN SHRINE (Hay-e-on)   One of the most famous of Kyoto's Shinto treasures, the Heian Shrine, in Okazaki Park, is dedicated to Emperor Kammu, who founded Kyoto (Heian) in 794, and to Emperor Komei, the last emperor who reigned in Kyoto before the capital was moved to Tokyo following the Meiji Restoration in 1868.

The Heian Shrine, built in 1895 to commemorate the 1,100th anniversary of Kyoto, consists of two main halls, a Great Hall of State, two pagodas, a huge Main Gate, and a *torii*. All of the buildings are exact replicas, except on a reduced scale, of the palace of the founder, Emperor Kammu, built in 794.

The shrine sponsors two of Kyoto's most popular festivals, one on April 15 and the other on October 22. The latter one, the famous *Jidai Matsuri*, or Festival of the Ages, attracts spectators from around the world. See FESTIVALS.

HEIKE (Hay-e-kay) Heike is another name for the famous Taira clan, which began its rise to power in the 1100s, when Kiyomori Taira, a leading member of the new *samurai* warrior caste that had appeared in the previous two centuries, became the paramount military force in the land and usurped most of the power from the reigning emperor. See TAIRA, KIYOMORI.

HEIKE MONOGATARI (Hay-e-kay moe-no-gah-tah-ree) The *Heike Monogatari*, or Tale of Heike, is a famous war narrative that recounts the rise and fall of the Taira clan in the twelfth century. The long story, like other chronicles written during this period, is characterized by strong Buddhist concepts: for example, that the lives and fortunes of men are in the hands of fate and that the mighty will fall. See TAIRA, KIYOMORI.

HELLO KITTY Hello Kitty is a cartoon character created by the Sanrio Company as a trade name that has become one of the most successful in the history of mass-market merchandising.

The trademark now appears on dozens of different lines of merchandise, from leisure wear to stationery. It was first used in the U.S. by the publisher Random House on a line of children's books and was subsequently franchised to manufacturers of toys, T-shirts, and other products in the U.S.

HEPBURN, REV. JAMES C. The Portuguese traders who arrived in Japan in the mid-1500s were the first to attempt to establish a uniform system of writing the Japanese language in Roman letters. The Dutch and other nationalities, who came soon after the Portuguese, also came up with their own systems.

As a result, there were so many ways of spelling individual words that none of the systems became established. As each new nationality arrived and began its own system, the Romanization of Japanese became even more complicated and was often virtually unintelligible to everyone except its creators.

An American missionary and doctor named James C. Hepburn brought order out of the chaos and thus made a profound and lasting contribution to the entry of Japan into the community of nations.

Hepburn spent many years studying the Japanese language and translating the Bible into Japanese. In the process, he developed a system of spelling Japanese that came to be known as the Hepburn System (and is the one used in this book).

Hepburn also founded Meiji Gakuin, one of Tokyo's best-known schools today, as well as the predecessor of Ferris' Girl School in Yokohama. In 1905, Emperor Meiji conferred the Order of the Rising Sun, Japan's highest award, upon Dr. Hepburn, who was then 90 years old, in recognition of his contributions to the country. He died in 1911 at age 96, one of the most honored of the many foreigners who devoted their lives to Japan.

During the subsequent periods of strong nationalism, there was a concentrated attempt by militaristic government leaders to substitute a made-in-Japan system for the Hepburn System. But the system approved by the government was incomprehensible to most foreigners, and it was dropped in 1945.

Probably the most famous story about the use of the government-approved system involved the passenger ship *Chichibu Maru*, which became *Titibu Maru* when spelled according to government edict. Foreign passengers missed the ship because they didn't recognize the name, and Titibu became the subject of salacious jokes.

HIBACHI (He-bah-chee)   A brazier or firebox in which charcoal is burned, the *hibachi* was traditionally the Japanese cook stove and source of heat in the winter.

Foods were boiled, broiled, and fried by most Japanese over open *hibachi* in kitchens that were open to the outside—until after World War II, when natural-gas plates, stoves, and electric ranges were introduced on an increasingly mass scale.

The *hibachi* used for heating were either in a room at floor level or were placed inside a pit (*kotatsu*) in the floor and then covered by a table over which a large cloth was spread to keep the heat in. To take advantage of the heat, you sat with your legs extending into the pit and the cloth draped over your lap.

These traditional *kotatsu* were an effective way to keep one's feet and legs warm, and they brought people close together, but it was necessary to wear several layers of clothing to keep the upper part of the body from freezing. There was also the added danger of carbon monoxide poisoning from the burning charcoal.

The kitchen *hibachi* and the *kotatsu*—both open flames inside homes made of paper, wood, and straw—were the cause of so many disasterous fires in Japan that fires were equated with earthquakes and typhoons, both of which have struck Japan with unfailing regularity since the birth of the islands.

Kotatsu are still popular in Japan because they are so much a part of the social interaction of the people. But, instead of open charcoal flames, they are warmed by especially designed electrical heaters.

Hibachi are also still in common use—but for outside barbecue purposes and by many restaurants that specialize in such charcoal-broiled delicacies as *yaki-tori* (barbecued chicken).

HIDDEN CHRISTIANS / KAKURE KIRISHITAN (Kah-kuu-ray kee-ree-she-tahn)   When the practice of Christianity was forbidden by the Tokugawa Shogunate in the early 1600s, a group of Japanese converts to the Christian faith continued to practice Christian rituals in secret.

The group passed their beliefs and rituals on to their descendants for the next 200 or so years—until freedom of religious choice was again granted in 1873. When their presence was discovered in the 1870s, they were given the name Hidden Christians.

HIDDEN TALENT / KAKUSHI GEI (Kah-kuu-she gay-e)   The Japanese have traditionally developed a particular skill (such as singing, solo dancing, or doing imitations), that they keep quiet about—thus the sobriquet "hidden talent"—knowing it is going to come in handy.

At parties, dinners, and other social gatherings, it is common for the participants to be called on to perform some kind of entertainment act. Having a *kakushi gei* prevents them from being embarrassed and allows them to demonstrate their skill.

Many foreign residents of Japan—and others just visiting there—have been put on the spot at such gatherings and, because they do not have a hidden talent, are unable to perform. Their hosts and friends were not trying to embarrass them, however, as they have been conditioned to take it for granted that everybody has at least a little *kakushi gei*.

HIGH-RISE BUILDINGS   The first high-rise building in Japan was the 36-story Kasumigaseki Building in Tokyo, which was completed in 1968. The building, based on new earthquake resistant technology and designed by Toshiro Yamashita and the Mitsui Real Estate Development Company, was put up by the Kajima Corporation and Mitsui Construction Co.

Prior to this, the highest building in Japan was 18 stories. Now there are dozens of high rises in Japan's major cities, particularly in Tokyo.

HIKONE (He-koe-nay)   The headquarters city of the famous Ii clan, Hikone is noted for the Ii (Hikone) Castle, the Villa and garden of the Ii family, the Taga Shrine, a popular beach, and textile industries.

Hikone Castle was constructed in 1603 by Naokatsu Ii immediately after he returned home from the Battle of Sekigahara—as a result of which Ieyasu Tokugawa became the new shogun. In the mid-1800s, Naosuke Ii was the chief minister of the Tokugawa Shogunate and was active in helping open Japan to the Western world.

The Ii clan castle is an Important Cultural Property and one of the Eight Views of Lake Biwa.

HIMEJI (He-may-jee)   An hour from Kobe by train, on the coast of the beautiful Inland Sea, Himeji is one of the best known of Japan's many castle towns.

Now the leading industrial and commercial center of the surrounding Harima Plain, Himeji became important in Japan's history in 1581, when Hideyoshi Toyotomi had a castle built there to control the area. In 1600, the castle was taken over by Terumasa Ikeda, one of Hideyoshi's generals, who remodeled its main tower. The castle was enlarged to its present grand size during the Genna era (1615–1624).

The castle, registered as a National Treasure, is regarded as the best in design and architectural technique ever built in Japan. It is called the Hakuro Jo, or Egret Castle, because its white-plastered walls suggest this popular rice-field bird.

From the tower of the castle, there is an equally grand view of the Inland Sea and Ejima Islands, as well as the surrounding countryside.

Himeji has a Sister City relationship with Phoenix, Arizona.

HIROSHIGE ANDO (Ahn-doe, He-roe-she-gay)   Probably the best known of Japan's great *ukiyoe* (ou-key-yoe-eh), or wood-block print, artists, Hiroshige was born at Yaesu in Edo (Tokyo) in 1797, the son of an official of the Tokugawa Shogunate fire department. After failing to become a student of Hokusai, the most famous *ukiyoe* artist of his day, Hiroshige studied under Toyohiro Utagawa, another popular artist.

Hiroshige is primarily known for his landscape paintings, especially the *Fifty-Three Post Stations of the Tokaido*, which made him famous at the age of 30. Among his other popular series of prints were *Noted Places of Edo, Eight Landscapes of Edo Suburbs, One Hundred Scenic Spots of Edo,* and *Eight Scenes of Omi.*

Hiroshige inherited his father's position as a fire department official, but soon handed the position over to his young son so he could devote all his time to painting. He died in 1859, during a great cholera epidemic in Japan and was buried at the Tokaku Temple in the Asakusa district of Tokyo.

HIROSHIMA (He-roe-she-mah)   Famed in contemporary history because it was the first city ever to be atom-bombed—at 8:15 A.M. on August 6, 1945 —Hiroshima dates from 1593, when feudal lord Terumoto Mori built a castle there and named it Hiroshima Jo, or Broad Island Castle. The village that grew up around the castle gradually came to be known as Hiroshima.

During the Sino-Japanese War from 1894 to 1895, Hiroshima Castle was used by the Emperor Meiji as his headquarters, while the city itself, facing

("Floating Shrine" of Miyajima, near Hiroshima)

the Inland Sea, became a major port. By the beginning of World War II, it had a population of 344,000 and was a major industrial center.

The single atom bomb that was dropped on Hiroshima that fateful day in 1945 leveled the city in a flash of light that was followed by a windstorm and great fires. Over 100,000 of the inhabitants of the city were killed outright, and, in the days and months that followed, thousands more died in agony.

With peace returned in 1945 and the Law for the Construction of a Hiroshima Peace Commemoration City passed in 1949, the rebuilding of the city picked up pace. Today, it is more than twice as large as it was in 1945.

Once again a major industrial area, Hiroshima is also a popular tourist destination. Each year, hundreds of thousands of people go to see the Atomic Bomb Dome, Peace Memorial Park, Peace Memorial Hall, and the Memorial Cenotaph for A-Bomb Victims.

Other places of interest are the famous Shukkei-En Garden, designed by feudal lord Nagaakira Asano in 1620 and now a registered Scenic Place, the restored Hiroshima Castle (the original was totally destroyed by the atom bomb), and the Memorial Cathedral for World Peace (built following an appeal by the Rev. Hugo Lassalle, a German Jesuit priest who was in Hiroshima when the bomb fell).

HISTORY / REKISHI (Rake-shi)   Legend says that Japan's first emperor, Jimmu Tenno (Jeem-muu Tane-no), ascended the chrysanthemum throne in 660 B.C. (*jimmu* means "divine warrior" and *tenno* means "heavenly"). But written records indicate that in the first century A.D., Japan was still a collection of over 100 independent little kingdoms in various parts of the islands.

Some of these tiny fiefdoms had diplomatic contacts and surely some trade relations with the Later Han Dynasty in China.

By the fourth century A.D., one of the larger kingdoms in the Kansai (Khan-sigh) area, where Osaka, Kobe, and Kyoto are now located, had absorbed the smaller groups in the vicinity and fairly quickly thereafter expanded its rule over the western half of Honshu (Hone-shuu), the northern half of Kyushu (Que-shuu), and all of Shikoku (She-koe-kuu).

The Yamato family that ruled this kingdom during its final stages of consolidation became Japan's Imperial family, whose descendants now occupy the throne. In some records, this country is referred to as the Kingdom of Yamato (Yah-mah-toe), which figuratively means Great Peace or Great Harmony, but is generally translated as meaning Japan. *Yamato* is also used when referring to the soul or heart of Japan—*yamato damashii* (yah-mah-toe dah-mah-shee).

Two ancient and famous chronicles, the *Nihonshoki* (Nee-hone-show-kee) and the *Kojiki* (Koe-jee-kee), both written in the eighth century, say very explicitly that Emperor Jimmu, Japan's first emperor, began his reign on February 11, 660 B.C., and this is the date that is celebrated as Japan's National Foundation Day.

The first inhabitants of Japan are believed to have been a Caucasian race who call themselves Ainu (Aye-nuu) and probably came to the islands when they were still part of the Asian mainland. See AINU.

It is believed that Japan was still connected to the Asian mainland until around 200,000 years ago. After the separation took place, it was far enough away to be safe from invasion, but close enough for immigration and infusions of culture from Korea and China.

As for the Japanese people, it is generally agreed that they are an Asian Mongoloid race (most Japanese babies are born with a blue mark at the base of the spine, known as the Mongoloid Spot). It is also generally agreed that most of the ancestors of the present-day Japanese came to the islands from different parts of Asia, primarily from Korea, China, and Southeast Asia.

The dates of the very first migrations are unknown, but it is known that the Japanese islands were inhabited 10,000 years ago by people very much like modern Japanese.

Before the arrival of the Asian ancestors of the present-day Japanese, the southern part of the islands was inhabited by people who had come up from the South Pacific and Southeast Asia, and the northern third of the islands was populated by the Ainu, who were Caucasian in their racial features.

The earliest inhabitants of the south were eventually merged in with the new arrivals from Asia, but the Ainu resisted assimilation and were gradually driven further northward. As the centuries passed, however, the Ainu, as well, were gradually assimilated into the main body of the population. Today fewer than 20,000 of them remain.

In the Tohoku region of northern Honshu and in Hokkaido, the mixing of the two races is very evident in the Caucasian look of great numbers of the people. These Ainu/Japanese mixtures are responsible in part for the reputation the Tohoku area has for exceptionally beautiful women.

Archeologists have named the time from around 10,000 B.C. to the third or second century B.C. as the Jomon Period, from the type of pottery left by the people. This was followed by the so-called Yayoi Period, which lasted until about the third century A.D., during which time the Japanese mastered the technique of rice cultivation and gradually established the family or clan system and patterns of social and economic life that were to endure down to the nineteenth century.

The paramount leader among the various clans was called *okimi*, or "great prince." Some time in the sixth century this title was changed to *tenno* (tane-noh), or "emperor."

There is other evidence to support the belief that Japan was a recognized nation prior to the fourth century A.D.. A gold seal, unearthed in what is now Fukuoka Prefecture in the eighteenth century, is mentioned in Chinese records as having been presented by Emperor Kuang Hsu to a ruler in Kyushu in the first century A.D..

Other records show that in the third century the Queen of Yamatai (Yah-mah-tie) sent an envoy to China and received a Chinese envoy in her Court. The first officially recorded government-level contacts between Japan and Korea were in the fourth century, although unofficial contacts with that country had undoubtedly been frequent for a long period.

With the emergence of one paramount kingdom, trade and cultural relations with Korea and China flourished. The Japanese imported the Chinese writing system, Buddhism, Confucianism, and many arts and crafts. The Imperial family and the court nobles also adopted many of the customs and manners of the Imperial Court in China.

From the end of the sixth century to the beginning of the eighth century, the capital of Japan was located in the Asuka region, south of present-day Nara. The capital was moved to Nara in 710 and then to Kyoto in 794.

The first major political figure in Japanese history—of whom there is a record—was Prince Shotoku, who acted as regent for Empress Suiko, whose reign extended from the latter part of the sixth century to the early years of the seventh century. He initiated a series of reforms that established a political system based on the authority of the emperor, and codified them in a seventeen-article constitution. Following the death of Prince Shotoku, the Soga clan gained dominance in Japan, and continued contacts with Korea and China.

In the year 645, Prince Nakano (who later became Emperor Tenchi) joined with clan leader Nakatomi-no Kamatari, founder of the famous Fujiwara dynasty, to crush the Soga clan.

The then-dominant Fujiwara clan, along with Emperor Tenchi, embarked on a new series of political reforms, using the Tang government of China as their model. In 702, these reforms were published in the so-called Taiho Code. The codes stipulated the organization of both central and regional governments, divided the country into 62 provinces, and required the central government to assign a governor to each of the provinces.

The Taiho Codes also declared that all agricultural land belonged to the state and that fixed areas were to be allotted to the people for cultivation, in return for which they were to pay taxes in the form of grain, textiles, and labor.

Just before he died, Emperor Tenchi rewarded Nakatomi by giving him the highest status in the Court and the new family name of Fujiwara. Thereafter, the Fujiwara family took over the government by providing the Imperial line with consorts and regents and controlling who became emperor.

This new system of government lasted for about 100 years. Then the leading clan families once again began usurping the state's power, taking possession of both the land and the peasants on it, and creating wealthy and powerful provinces of their own. These estates, known as *shoen* (show-inn), were the forerunners of the great feudal fiefs or provinces that were to last until 1868.

These family clans, mostly relatives of the Imperial family, maintained their own armed forces to protect their territories and to keep the peasants under control. As time passed, the soldiers formed a distinct hereditary class of professional warriors.

The peak of the Nara Period was the reign of Emperor Shomu (724–749). A firm believer in Buddhism as a way of warding off natural disasters and ensuring the wealth and prosperity of the country, he ordered the construction of branch monasteries and nunneries in the 62 provinces. He also ordered the construction of the Todai Temple in Nara, the largest wooden building ever built, and had a 16-meter-high, seated image of the Buddha cast and installed inside it.

In the intervening centuries, the great Todai was burned and seriously damaged several times, but it was restored each time and still stands today as one of the wonders of early Japan. In a wooden storehouse next to the Todai Temple are preserved many items donated to the temple by the empress after the death of Emperor Shomu.

The power of the Fujiwara family continued to wane during the ninth and tenth centuries, and in the eleventh century they began to lose control of the country to the rising warrior clans. They were to maintain their influence at the Imperial Court until 1868, however, and one of their direct lineal descendants, Prince Konoe Fumimaro, served as the prime minister of Japan just before and during part of the second World War.

The introduction of Confucianism and Buddhism from Korea and China resulted in profound changes in Japan. In the seventh century, large numbers of Japanese envoys and scholars went to China. The new knowledge and technology they brought back from the mainland was to further revolutionize the Japanese way of life.

These exchanges continued during the eighth, ninth, and tenth centuries, but in the latter part of the tenth century, Japan entered a period of near isolation that lasted for some 200 years. During this long period, the Japanese were literally consumed by the cultural and political changes taking place in their own country.

By the ninth century, the powerful regional clans—with their own trained armies of professional, mounted warriors armed with swords and bows and clad in armor—were already an important political force. Provincial governors, as well as court nobles, also began retaining their own *samurai*, and as time passed the size of these private armies grew, became hereditary, and formed a new privileged class.

The leaders of these warrior families were descendants of the Imperial family or court nobles who had been appointed governors of provinces, but did not return to the capital when their tenure was complete and made their position hereditary.

The two most powerful of these warrior clans were the Taira and Minamoto, both descended from the Imperial House. As the power of the central government declined and revolts occurred in the provinces, it was these new warrior lords who put them down.

The power of the Minamoto clan was greatly expanded in the latter half of the eleventh century, when it put down revolts in the Kanto (Tokyo) region and thereafter had close connections with the clans in that area.

In the meantime, the Taira clan was extending its power in the western end of Japan and, in the latter part of the twelfth century, seized political power from the Fujiwara family in Kyoto. In the first clashes between the two great *samurai* clans, the Taira won and further consolidated their power by marrying into the Imperial family. The head of the Minamoto clan was executed and his oldest son, Yoritomo, was exiled to what is present-day Shizuoka.

A few years later, Yoritomo, with the aid of his younger brother, Yoshitsune, enlisted the help of the *samurai* of the Kanto plains and, in the famous sea battle in the straits of Danno-ura, totally destroyed the Taira clan.

At the battle of Danno-ura, the first great sea battle in Japan, the Heike (Taira clan) suffered total defeat. The boy emperor, his mother, grandmother, and many court ladies were aboard one of the Heike vessels. When they saw that the battle was lost, the emperor's grandmother took him in her arms and, together with many of the other women, jumped into the sea. Only the emperor's mother was saved.

In 1185, Yoritomo set up a military government called *bakufu* (bah-kuu-fuu) in present-day Kamakura, then a small coastal village south of what is now Yokohama. His main purpose in picking such an out-of-the-way place was to avoid the weakening influences of Imperial Kyoto.

In 1192, the reigning emperor officially awarded the title of *shogun* to Yoritomo, beginning a government system that was to endure for most of the next 700 years.

The Kamakura Shogunate lasted for 140 years, although Yoritomo's line died out in less than 30 years. Power thereafter was in the hands of the Hojo family, which had served as advisors to the first three Minamoto *shogun*.

The Imperial Court tried to wrest control from the Hojo regents in the Jokyu War, but the Hojo were to remain in power until 1333, when then-Emperor Godaigo allied with clan leaders Masashige Kusunoki and Takauji Ashikaga to end the Kamakura Shogunate.

Takauji then turned against Masashige, defeating him and forcing Emperor Godaigo to flee into the mountains of Yoshino. Takauji set up a relative of the emperor in Kyoto and had himself named *shogun*. The two courts and their allies battled for 60 years, after which the Ashikaga clan emerged the victor and began the Ashikaga Shogunate, which was to last for 240 years.

The Ashikaga *bakufu* was not as powerful as its predecessor, and distant *samurai* clan leaders, now called *daimyo* (dime-yoe), or "Great Names," began building up their power. The period degenerated into a series of clashes between contending *daimyo*, who gained control of all of the provincial estates that were still in the hands of court nobles.

These powerful *samurai daimyo* built castles and encouraged the construction of temples and shrines, many of which became the nucleus for new villages and towns. See CITIES.

In Kyoto, the Ashikaga Shogunate adopted the manners and practices of the Imperial Court, which was heavily influenced by Zen Buddhism. The seventh Ashikaga *Shogun*, Yoshimitsu, had the Temple of the Golden Pavilion built. His successor, Yoshimasa, built the Silver Pavilion—both major attractions of modern-day Kyoto.

Relations with China were gradually restored in the twelfth century, but they were infrequent and minor until the next century. Two major events during the thirteenth century were successive attacks on Japan by the Mongols of China. Kublai Khan demanded that Japan become a vassal state within his empire. The Japanese refused, and, in 1274 and 1281, Mongol forces with Korean allies invaded northern Kyushu.

In the first invasion, the Chinese used massed cavalry attacks and catapults that threw gunpowder missiles against the Japanese warriors, who were used to single combat. But a typhoon struck, sinking many of the Mongol ships, causing them to abandon the attack.

The second invasion involved a fleet of ships said to be five times as large as the Spanish Armada that attacked England in 1588, making it the largest naval force in history. But once again a typhoon struck, wreaking havoc on the fleet and saving Japan from probable disaster.

This was the last the Japanese were to see of the Mongols, and in gratitude they begin to call the typhoons *kamikaze*, or "divine winds," and to believe that Japan had divine protection and could not be invaded or conquered—a feeling that persisted until the 1940s.

Europe first heard of Japan from Marco Polo, that intrepid Italian adventurer who went to China as a boy and became a favorite of Genghis Khan. In the *Book of Marco Polo*, published in 1298, Polo referred to Japan as Zipangu.

The first recorded contact between Europeans and Japanese occurred in 1543, when a Chinese junk, with several Portuguese traders aboard, was blown off course by a typhoon and landed on the island of Tanega, south of Kyushu.

Among the things these Portuguese visitors introduced to the Japanese were gunpowder, firearms, tobacco, and venereal disease. Soon thereafter, Japan was visited regularly by traders and missionaries from Spain and Portugal and by traders from Great Britain and Holland.

The 1500s saw the rise to power of Nobunaga Oda, Hideyoshi Toyotomi, and Ieyasu Tokugawa. In 1573, Nobunaga came into conflict with the Asnikaga *Shogun* and drove him out of Kyoto. To complete his conquest, he crushed the power of the militant Buddhist monks in the Kyoto area and was friendly toward the spread of Christianity as a means of diluting the power of the Buddhist temples. He also supported free trade and promoted the abolition of powerful guilds that controlled such commodities as salt, vegetable oils, textiles, and paper.

Before Nobunaga could consolidate his power, however, he was turned on by a trusted retainer, Mitsuhide Akechi, and forced to commit suicide.

Another of Nobunaga's retainers, Hideyoshi Toyotomi, who had been born a peasant instead of a *samurai* but had risen to the rank of a general in Nobunaga's army, attacked and destroyed Mitsuhide's forces, thus becoming heir to political control of the country.

By 1550, Japanese ships of up to 800 tons were plying trade routes to South China, Siam, the Philippines, and other Southeast Asian countries. Among the Japanese entrepreneurs who became involved in this flourishing trade was Hideyoshi Toyotomi, who had replaced Nobunaga as the military ruler of Japan. By 1592, ships bearing his vermilion seal were carrying such commodities as silver, copper, iron, and sulfur, and exchanging them for silk, sugar, leather, and lead. Hideyoshi did not become *shogun* (he was named *kanpaku*, or prime minister, instead). He had the nation surveyed to determine the amount of arable land and its productivity and then awarded fiefs to his supporters on this basis. He took all weapons away from the common people, clearly defined the class differences between commoners and the *samurai*, and promoted foreign trade. He also built the great Osaka Castle.

Up to this time, the *samurai* had engaged in agriculture, but Hideyoshi's program separated them from the land and brought them into castle towns, where they lived on fixed incomes provided by the *daimyo* they served.

Fearing that Christianity might become the ideological basis for attempts by the *daimyo* of Kyushu to challenge his authority, Hideyoshi outlawed the teaching of Christianity and ordered the deportation of all Christian missionaries. Little was done against the missionaries and their converts for the first 10 years; then the campaign against them was stepped up. Several Japanese and a number of foreign priests and monks were crucified in 1597.

The first Spanish vessel arrived in Japan at Tosa in 1596, and Spanish traders set up their first company in Japan in 1602. The first Dutch ship arrived in 1609 and established a trading post at Hirado.

With his power over Japan complete, Hideyoshi decided to invade and conquer China. He ordered Korea to allow his armies to pass through on their way to China. The Koreans refused, and on two occasions Hideyoshi sent large armies to Korea, where they fought combined Korean and Chinese forces. The conflict raged on, but in 1598 Hideyoshi died of illness, and the Japanese forces were withdrawn from Korea.

With Hideyoshi dead, Ieyasu Tokugawa, who had been his most powerful ally, defeated several contenders for power, eliminated Hideyoshi's other close allies, including Hideyoshi's young son by his favorite mistress, and in 1603 established the Tokugawa Shogunate, destined to be Japan's last great feudal dynasty.

Ieyasu had begun as a minor *daimyo* who allied himself with Nobunaga Oda and extended his power in south-central Honshu. When Hideyoshi came to power, Ieyasu fought him at first and then joined him, and it was Hideyoshi who ordered Ieyasu to move his domain to the Kanto (Tokyo) region, where he established his headquarters in Edo Castle.

The Tokugawa Shogunate took direct control of more than one-quarter of Japan's land area, including the most important cities, ports, and mines. In order to ensure the obedience of the country's other *daimyo*—whose numbers ranged between 245 and 295 during the Tokugawa Period—Ieyasu devised a system under which the *daimyo* would be required to leave their families in Edo at all times and themselves spend every other year in Edo, in attendance on the *shogun*.

This system, called *sankin kotai* (sahn-keen koe-tie), was not put into effect until the mid-1630s, however, after Ieyasu's grandson became *shogun*. It was to have profound economic, social, and cultural effects on Japan. It cost a great deal for the *daimyo* to travel back and forth between their fiefs and Edo and to maintain their families in Edo in impressive circumstances. In order to afford such expenses, the *daimyo* had to encourage the progress of agriculture and other industries in their fiefs. This constant coming and going of great numbers of people, who traversed Japan on foot in great processions, resulted in the rapid development of inns and towns along the national roads leading to Edo and spread the culture of Edo throughout the country.

The *sankin kotai* system was aimed not only at keeping the fief lords under the *shogun's* thumb, but also at keeping them from amassing enough wealth to offer a threat to the shogunate. The system lasted for nearly 250 years. (For more about this amazing phenomenon, see PROCESSIONS OF THE LORDS.)

The Tokugawa system of government was known as *baku-han*, from *baku* (the Japanese word for the shogunate), and *han*, the word for a feudal domain. The *han* were ostensibly independent and the *baku-han* had no authority to collect taxes from them. But, in reality, the shogunate levied heavy taxes on them to finance public works, castle building, and other projects.

During the early years of the Tokugawa Period, Ieyasu and his successors favored foreign trade. But as trade increased, so did the number and influence of Christian missionaries. The preachings of Christianity were incompatible with the philosophy and policies of the shogunate, and the continued activities and growing power of the missionaries and their converts frightened the government.

When the third Tokugawa *shogun*, Iemitsu, took over in 1623, measures against Christians became severe. In 1635, all Japanese were forbidden from going abroad, and those already overseas were forbidden from returning home.

In 1637, Christians in Shimabara Peninsula and on the Amakusa Islands south of Kyushu rebelled against this religious persecution and heavy taxation. The shogunate sent an army of 100,000 men to crush the rebellion. In 1639, the shogunate outlawed the propagation of Christianity and expelled all foreign missionaries.

The Shogunate then prohibited Spanish and Portuguese ships from coming to Japan. The English had not been active in missionary work but were losing out to Dutch competition in trade; so they also withdrew from Japan.

The third Tokugawa *shogun* in 1639 broke off all relations with foreign countries, prohibited travel from or to Japan, and closed the country off— with one minor recognized exception—for more than 200 years.

Thousands of Japanese had been dispatched to overseas trading posts. In 1639, when the Tokugawa Shogunate closed the country, none of the Japanese traders and their families who were abroad at that time were allowed to return home and had to live out their lives in exile.

In the city of Hirato in Kyushu, one can see and read letters written by a girl named Oharu, who was among these unfortunate people, expressing her anguish at not being able to return to her homeland.

During this long period, the Dutch were allowed to keep a small trading post in operation on a tiny man-made island (called Dejima, or Exit Island) in Nagasaki Bay. The few men who manned this outpost over the generations were not allowed to set foot on the mainland, except on very special, guarded occasions. Thus, the isolation of most Japanese from any foreign product, technology, or idea was virtually total.

The Dutch were permitted to land one ship a year at Dejima and were required to present a document to the shogunate authorities in Nagasaki covering political events in the rest of the world. The Soshi clan, on Tsushima, an island midway between Japan and Korea, engaged in some trade with Korea and indirectly with China. This system was to prevail for more than 200 years, during which time Japan was left behind by the technological developments in Europe and the United States.

The power of the Tokugawa Shogunate made this the longest period of peace in Japan's history. During these long and quiet decades, agriculture was the main occupation of most people, but gradually, as cities grew up around the castle headquarters of the *daimyo*, manufacturing and commerce became increasingly important.

At first, the Tokugawa *shogun* actually ruled, but as time went by they tended to become figureheads, as were most of their predecessors in the past. Real power shifted to the hands of shogunate bureaucrats. The same situation developed in the domains of the *daimyo*. Having to be in Edo half the time and on the road for up to several months the rest of the time (it took several weeks for the *daimyo* from the most distant domains to reach Edo), there was no way the *daimyo* could directly run their fiefs.

During the long Tokugawa Period, Japan's population remained stable at about 30 million people. The privileged *samurai* warrior class made up seven percent of the population. Below them were the townspeople, or *chonin* (choe-neen), and the peasant farmers. Legally, merchants were the lowest class in the country.

Many of the *samurai* eventually gave up the way of the warrior for the way of the bureaucrat and the scholar, dedicating themselves to the study and practice of Confucianism and Zen Buddhism.

By the middle of the Tokugawa era, the rice-based economy had broken down. Economic power was in the hands of the merchant class, many of whom had amassed great fortunes. The shogunate made three major attempts at economic reform, but the Confucian principles on which the reforms were based were no longer suitable for the times.

Many *samurai* married into the merchant class; others became *ronin* (masterless *samurai*), roaming the country and getting into mischief. Rebellions broke out among peasants who resented the growing burden of taxes needed to support the unproductive *samurai*.

The study of Confucianism lost ground to native Japanese scholarship, and what was called *kokugaku*, or native learning. These scholars learned that the shogunate was not the legitimate holder of power in the country and that the *shogun* had usurped the power of the emperor centuries earlier.

When foreign ships began knocking on Japan's doors in the early 1800s, there were many, especially those in the more distant *daimyo* fiefs, who were ready to end Japan's isolation.

As the urban populations increased and businesspeople prospered, money began to replace rice as the medium of exchange. Since the *samurai* families of all the clans, including the Tokugawa, were paid in allotments of rice, their situation grew steadily worse.

By 1800, many *samurai* families were in desperate straits. More and more of them were reduced to poverty and had to give up their privileged status or arrange for their sons and daughters to marry into merchant families—something that had been unthinkable in former times.

By this time also, many Western nations were on the move in Asia, seeking new markets and, wherever possible, military hegemony over territories they could take by force or guile. Several nations, including Russia, England, and the United States, began making overtures to Japan about opening its ports to foreign trade and the establishment of diplomatic relations.

By sheer luck, the U.S.'s Admiral Matthew Perry and his Black Ships arrived in Japan in 1853, beating the Russians out by a few months.

After a great deal of intense debate and consternation, the feudal government of Japan decided to resume trade and limited relations with the outside world. The position of the Tokugawa Shogunate went from bad to untenable. Powerful *daimyo*, especially in Kyushu, the most distant from Edo, began a campaign to topple the shogunate and restore the emperor to power.

Long outmoded and unable to contend with the economic and political ferment sweeping the country, Japan's once great and all-powerful *bakufu* government leaders realized they could no longer run the country.

Finally, in 1867, the *bakufu* relinquished power to the emperor, and the following year a new government was formed under Emperor Meiji.

In the next 20 years, the Japanese changed their country from a feudal, cottage industry/agricultural nation of Imperial courtiers, sword-carrying warriors, peasants, and plebians to a modern industrial power—presaging the Japanese miracle that occurred after World War II.

The Japanese achieved this first miracle by importing foreign technology, by inviting foreign technicians and experts in various fields in to guide them, and by an extraordinary demonstration of cooperation between government and industry.

In 1895, Japan went to war against China, winning important concessions on the Asian mainland and the island of Taiwan. Then, in 1905, hostilities broke out between Japan and Russia. In this war, as well, the Japanese emerged the winners, gaining an additional foothold on the Asian mainland.

By 1929, the military in Japan had gained the upper hand in the government, subsequently leading the Japanese on a series of territorial conquests that culminated in their attack on Hawaii in 1941, the war with the United States, and, finally, rebirth as a democratic nation and one of the world's top industrial powers.

The foreigners who made invaluable contributions to Japan's transformation from a feudal society to a modern power in the late 1800s included Gustave Emile Boissonade, a French specialist in law and legal education; Erwin von Baelz, a German medical educator; William Smith Clark, an American expert in agriculture and education; Edmund Morell, an English railroad engineer; and Gustav Toppe, a German engineer who helped set up Yawata Steel Mill, one of the predecessors of the Nippon Steel Corporation. Altogether, 45 Italians, 619 French, 913 Germans, 2,764 Americans, and 6,177 Britons were retained by the new Japanese government between 1881 and 1898 to virtually remake the country's economic and political system.

All of the supporters of the *shogun* did not voluntarily relinquish power. In 1868, the peasant army of the new Imperial government defeated the *samurai* supporters of the *shogun* in battles at Toba and Fushimi, south of Kyoto. Then the two forces reached a compromise, avoiding a battle for Edo that could have destroyed the city. Edo Castle was turned over to representatives of the Imperial government in Kyoto, and arrangements were made for the emperor to move into the castle.

France supported the shogunate, while England supported the Imperial forces. Fortunately, the Japanese refused these offers of help.

With the Restoration complete, the new government appointed a number of the more capable shogunate officials to high positions in the Imperial government. The last of the *shogun*, Yoshinobu Tokugawa, was designated a prince in a peerage system the new government established.

Most of the new government leaders were from the *samurai* clans of Satsuma and Choshu in Kyushu—those that were the farthest away from Edo and had retained most of their independence during the Tokugawa Period. Their goal was to transform Japan into a modern nation in two stages —first, to establish a unified and centralized government under a strong monarchy and, second, to develop a modern industry.

The new Meiji government abolished the system of the feudal *han*, or *daimyo* fiefs, and created a new system of prefectures and governors. All feudal classes were also abolished, but all members of the Imperial family and ranking *daimyo* became titled peers (princes, counts, barons) in the new system.

Growing pressure from more democratic-minded Japanese finally forced the Meiji government to institute a parliamentary system, and, after years of study and compromise, a constitution was adopted on February 11, 1889, and a parliament (called a Diet) was formed, consisting of a House of Representatives and a House of Councilors.

Under the new constitution, only adult males who paid a certain amount of taxes could vote, which limited suffrage to about 4.5 percent of the population. Further, for the next several decades, the government continued to be primarily controlled by a small group of elder statesmen, later called *genro* (gane-roe), who had been among the leaders of the Meiji Restoration. In addition, the Cabinet was supervised by the Privy Council, which also had to ratify all laws passed by the Diet.

At this time, Korea was still closed to the outside world and was known abroad as the Hermit Kingdom. In 1876, Japan coerced Korea into opening its doors to trade by threatening to invade the country. The Japanese immediately began making economic and political inroads in the country.

China regarded Korea as a vassal state and opposed the Japanese intrusion. This led to the outbreak of war between Japan and China. The Japanese won an overwhelming victory and not only continued their forays into Korea, but were ceded the Liaotung Peninsula, the Pescadores Islands, and Taiwan.

After the peace treaty with China, however, Russia, France, and Germany forced Japan to return the Liaotung Peninsula to China. Almost immediately thereafter, both Germany and Russia acquired major concessions in China and Manchuria. Russia then took advantage of the Boxer Rebellion in China to occupy Manchuria and began to bring pressure against Korea.

With both Japan and Russia vying for domination in Korea and Manchuria, war between the two nations broke out in 1904. Japan won quick, decisive victories on both land and sea. With American President Theodore Roosevelt as the mediator, a peace treaty between Russia and Japan was signed in 1905 at Portsmouth, New Jersey.

Japan got the southern half of Sakhalin, its primacy in Korea was recognized, and Russia had to give up its concessions in China. In 1910, Japan annexed Korea and turned it into a colony.

In 1914, Japan allied itself with the U.S., England and France against Germany and, as a result, was awarded all of Germany's concessions in Shantung and the mandate over Germany's Pacific island colonies. In 1921, Japan forced China to accept 21 demands regarding territorial rights, of which 11 were later dropped because of American pressure.

In 1918, during the Russian Revolution, Japan sent an army to Siberia in an attempt to bring this huge land mass into its sphere of influence. But the effort failed, and the army was withdrawn in 1922.

In the late 1920s, Japan renewed its encroachment on China and in 1931 invaded and occupied Manchuria, setting up a puppet state called Manchukuo. Other attacks against China followed, and undeclared war between the two countries dragged on.

The Great Depression that struck the U.S. in the 1930s also hit Japan, and there was a series of assassinations of moderate government leaders by fanatics who wanted a military dictatorship. The ultrarightists got what they wanted, and Japan began to prepare for all-out war. Nationalism ran rampant. Civil liberties were suppressed, political parties were disbanded, the Diet became completely powerless, and the course of the nation was set by the military, through General Hideki Tojo, who was prime minister when the Pacific War began.

In the grips of expansionist fever, Japan's military-controlled government signed pacts with Germany and Italy in 1940 (the Axis Alliance) and a neutrality pact with Russia in 1941. Taking advantage of the predicament of England, France, and the Netherlands in Europe, the Japanese invaded French Indochina.

Negotiations with the U.S. had been going on for some time, but came to a virtual standstill when the U.S. demanded that Japan withdraw from all the territories it had occupied since the Manchurian Incident. The war in China was also deadlocked.

To break this impasse, the Japanese attacked Pearl Harbor in Honolulu on December 7, 1941. Japan's military leaders believed that, following a devastating attack on the naval base at Pearl Harbor and their invasion and occupation of other western Pacific island outposts, the U.S. would agree to a negotiated settlement of the hostilities. Even the most rabid Japanese nationalist did not believe that Japan could invade and conquer the U.S.

Before the U.S. could recover from the attack on Hawaii and mount counterattacks, the Japanese seized Hong Kong, Malaysia, Burma, the Philippine Islands, the Dutch East Indies, and several other areas in Southeast Asia and the South Pacific.

In mid-1942, the U.S. initiated its military campaign against Japan, and, piece by piece, began winning back the territories Japan had conquered. From the end of 1944, the U.S. Air Force conducted continuous bombing raids on the home islands of Japan. After a bitter battle in June 1945, American forces captured the island of Okinawa and began massing for an invasion of the four main islands. In July, the terms for Japan's surrender were detailed in the Potsdam Declaration. Japan's leaders ignored the ultimatum.

Knowing the ferocity with which the Japanese fought and their custom of fighting to the death rather than surrender, the U.S. decided to use the atomic bomb to shock the Japanese into surrendering without the need for an invasion of the main islands.

On August 6, 1945, the U.S. Air Force dropped an atomic bomb on the city of Hiroshima. On August 8, Russia declared war on Japan. On August 9, the U.S. dropped a second atomic bomb on the city of Nagasaki. Both of these two large cities were virtually pulverized.

On August 15, the Japanese government notified the U.S. that it would accept the terms of the Potsdam Declaration. Fearful that the Japanese armed forces and the civilian population might not accept the idea of surrendering, moderate forces in Tokyo prevailed upon Emperor Hirohito, who had played no role in the conduct of the war, to make an unprecedented radio broadcast informing the people that Japan had surrendered and asking the military forces to cease fighting and lay down their arms.

For the first time in their long history, the Japanese had suffered a devastating defeat. Some 2,300,000 servicemen and 800,000 civilians had died in the long, drawn-out war, and most of the country's industrial capacity was in total ruins.

American Occupation forces began arriving in Japan 13 days later, and the documents of surrender were signed on September 2, aboard the battleship *USS Missouri* in Tokyo Bay. General Douglas MacArthur took over as Supreme Commander of the Allied Powers (SCAP), setting up his headquarters in the Dai Ichi Insurance Building, across from the Imperial Palace.

The Soviets, who had entered the war on virtually the last day, demanded that they be allowed to occupy Hokkaido. The U.S. refused, preventing Japan from being partitioned, as Germany and Korea were.

The Japanese expected brutal treatment by the Occupation forces. Before the first American servicemen arrived, large numbers of women and children were sent into the countryside. They were shocked to find themselves not only treated kindly, but generously, by the predominately American occupying forces.

Rather than set up a military government to rule Japan, SCAP, under the inspired leadership of MacArthur, elected to implement the policies of the Occupation through the Japanese government—exercising indirect control. These policies were divided into three major categories: demilitarization, democratization, and reconstruction.

In the first two years, Japan was divested of all of its overseas colonies, and over 6,500,000 Japanese living overseas were repatriated. All Japanese military forces were disbanded, and some 180,000 people who had been in senior positions in the political and economic structure of the country were removed from their jobs.

The International Military Tribunal for the Far East tried 25 of Japan's top leaders who were charged with being responsible for atrocities committed during the war and for the war itself. Five military men, along with former prime ministers Hideki Tojo and Koki Hirota, were found guilty and hanged.

The state religion of Shintoism was abolished. The emperor renounced his claim to divinity on January 1, 1946. A new constitution was drafted under the direction of SCAP and promulgated on November 3, 1946. The new constitution renounced war as a means of settling international disputes and guaranteed the people individual freedom, equality of the sexes, the right to organize and engage in collective bargaining, and the right to be educated.

The great economic combines (*zaibatsu*) were broken up, making room for the development of thousands of new companies. Farm lands were bought from absentee landlords and sold to farmers at low prices, and the educational system was reformed along democratic lines.

By the end of 1947, the fundamental goals of the Occupation had been achieved, and the process of transferring decision-making authority back to the Japanese government was begun. As the so-called Cold War between the U.S. and Russia intensified, the American policy in Japan changed dramatically. The U.S. began an all-out campaign to help Japan rebuild its industrial base as rapidly as possible.

The outbreak of the war in Korea in 1950 provided an enormous boost to the Japanese economy. The U.S. military began procuring all kinds of supplies from Japan, and these special procurements made a significant contribution to Japan's miraculous recovery.

Immediately after the outbreak of the Korean War, SCAP ordered the Japanese government to create a self-defense force, originally called the Police Reserve Force.

On September 8, 1951, in San Francisco, the U.S. and 47 other nations signed a peace treaty with Japan. The following year, on April 28, 1952, Japan regained its independence.

Thus ended one of the most extraordinary experiences in the history of any country—an experience that was to change totally the social and political structure of Japan, to alter forever the course of its culture, and to catapult it into a leadership role in the world that went far beyond the wildest dreams of its earlier expansionist military leaders.

The American Military Occupation of Japan was one of the most dramatic stories of the century, far exceeding in scale any similar event of the past, and it is still to be told. The human drama of the meeting of two such diverse peoples, who were able to work together despite profound differences, is as inspiring as the greatest of plays.

Soon after the formal ending of the Military Occupation of Japan in 1952, a new kind of army invaded the country. This time it was droves of American and European importers and buyers from major retail chain stores, carting samples that they wanted duplicated by Japan's highly skilled—and cheap— work force.

The great prewar *zaibatsu* combines, epitomized by Mitsui and Mitsubishi, reemerged immediately after Japan regained its sovereignty, with the only significant difference being they were no longer owned outright or managed by single families. Dozens of other prewar and postwar companies such as Sony, Hitachi, Toyota, and other now famous names began building their own conglomerates that would eventually equal the power and prestige of the old *zaibatsu*.

By 1958, only six years after the end of the Occupation, Japan surpassed its highest levels of prewar productivity.

By the end of the 1960s, without the financial burden of maintaining a large military establishment, with free access to the huge American and European consumer markets, and building on a flood of virtually free American and European technology, Japan was well on its way to becoming an economic superpower.

Taking advantage of its cultural traditions of group behavior, hard work, extraordinary dedication to quality, government guidance and support—and government protection from international competition in its own home market—the Japanese developed the most advanced and efficient "export economy" the world had ever seen.

By the end of the 1970s, Japan was the world's second largest economic power in terms of gross national product, and in the 1980s Japan surpassed the United States in terms of per capita income.

As a result of their new-found wealth, individual Japanese and Japanese corporations began a frenzy of overseas investing in the 1970s, buying up prime office buildings, hotels, golf courses, ski resorts, and other properties, particularly in the United States. The Japanese government also replaced the United States as the top donor of aid to less developed countries.

But Japan's frenzied rush toward economic supremacy came to a sudden stop in 1990. Banks, stock companies and dozens of the country's leading manufacturers had overextended themselves to the point that their financial "bubble" abruptly burst.

At the same time, international pressure on Japan to open its home market had continued to increase, American manufacturers had made significant progress in reforming their management and increasing their ability to compete with the Japanese, and such countries as South Korea, Taiwan, Singapore, and China had become major exporters of product lines once monopolized by the Japanese.

The collapse of Japan's "bubble economy" was not a death bell, however, and was seen by many as a blessing. It slowed everything down, rekindled the traditional conservatism of the Japanese, and provided a powerful incentive for Japanese corporations to reform their own policies and management practices. By the mid-1990s there were indications that these reforms were making Japanese corporations even more formidable players on the global scene.

In addition to motivating the Japanese to move more of their manufacturing plants overseas, the debacle of the bubble economy also resulted in a rush by Japanese companies to form strategic alliances with foreign corporations, further enhancing their ability to compete worldwide.

On the international political front, Japan continued to keep a low profile, participating in major events more as an observer than anything else —despite a growing crescendo of criticism that it was not living up to its responsibilities as a leading economic power.

HISTORICAL PERIODS NARA PERIOD, 710–784: This was a revolutionary time in Japan's history. The massive imports of Chinese culture, Buddhism, Confucianism, and other powerful social and political ideas from the Asian mainland were being assimilated and adapted to fit the distinctive indigenous Japanese way. The period coincides with the years the Imperial capital was located at Nara, which became a center for the new arts and religions.

A distinctive architecture, sculpture, painting, and other cultural forms that had been nurtured during earlier decades began to flower during these years. (The capital was located at Nagaokakyo from 784 to 794.)

HEIAN PERIOD, 794–1185: In 794, the Imperial capital was moved from Nara to Heiankyo (now Kyoto), after large-scale civil engineering and construction projects were undertaken to build a new metropolis. The city was laid out in grid fashion (following Chinese patterns), with broad thoroughfares and a system of canals that served as both a water supply system and waterways.

One of the architectural masterpieces of that time is the Phoenix Hall of Byodo Temple, which includes an image of Buddhist paradise. Buddhism, as well as other Buddhist-inspired arts, flourished during this period.

During these four centuries, Japan's contacts wlth Korea and China were considerably lessened as the Japanese developed their own aristocratic culture based on Chinese concepts but with a decidedly Japanese flavor.

The power of the ancient noble families that had dominated the government and life of the country since its founding continued to wane and was eventually usurped completely by the new warrior class that had grown up under the nobles as their military forces.

KAMAKURA PERIOD, 1185–1333: This period marks the beginning of the ascendancy of the *samurai*, or warrior class, and the establishment of a military government (*bakufu*) at Kamakura, about 50 miles south of present-day Tokyo, by Yoritomo Minamoto, who was officially designated as *shogun* by the reigning emperor in 1192.

Because Zen Buddhism provided much of the philosophical and practical underpinnings for the *samurai* and was therefore under their patronage, it flourished. Many of Japan's greatest Zen temples, including Kencho and Enkaku in Kamakura, were built during this period.

It was also during this period that the Great Buddha of Kamakura was cast—a masterpiece of Buddhist sculpture that stands today as a monument to the power and glory of thirteenth-century Buddhism. See GREAT BUDDHA OF KAMAKURA.

In 1274 and 1281, the Mongols of China mounted two attacks against Japan and each time were defeated by the divine intervention of a great typhoon.

MUROMACHI PERIOD, 1333–1573: In 1333, with political power now in the hands of the Ashikaga *samurai* clan, Japan's administrative capital was moved back to Kyoto, where the rough *samurai* came under the influence of the effete culture that had been developed over the centuries at the Imperial Court.

The third Ashikaga *shogan*, Yoshimitsu, built the Kinkaku Ji (Temple of the Golden Pavilion), now one of the great treasures of Kyoto. Landscaping and gardening in general reached its zenith during this period.

The latter half of this period was one of political intrigue and turmoil among the feudal *samurai* clans, the larger of which were continually jousting for power.

During the latter decades of this period, Japan had its first recorded contacts with Westerners and was introduced to cannons, rifles, tobacco, Catholicism, and venereal disease.

MOMOYAMA PERIOD, 1573–1600: The Momoyama Period began with the victory of Nobunaga Oda and his assumption of power over the other clans. Upon his death, the reins of power were seized by Hideyoshi Toyotomi, who had been one of his most successful generals.

Under both Nobunaga and Hideyoshi, trade with Southeast Asia and Europe flourished. Many of the castles built during this period had donjons, patterned after European castles. Merchants engaging in foreign trade amassed great wealth, and were instrumental in spreading culture in Japan to the common people.

The tea ceremony became popular and inspired a new type of architecture called *sukiyazukuri*, used for the construction of rooms and cottages specifically for the tea ceremony. The manufacture of ceramic teacups and other items used in the ceremony also flourished.

By the end of this period, the government of Japan was already trying to purge the country of the influence of Catholic missionaries and to keep European powers at arm's length.

EDO PERIOD, 1600–1867: In a final series of great battles, Ieyasu Tokugawa defeated the forces of Hideyoshi Toyotomi and, in 1603, established what was to become Japan's last feudal shogunate.

Ieyasu set up his military government in Edo, a small town at the head of what is now Tokyo Bay, and in the next few decades the town grew into one of the world's great cities. One of the primary reasons for Edo's extraordinary growth was the fact that the third Tokugawa *Shogun* required that the lords of all of Japan's 270 clans build residences in Edo, keep their families there all year round, and themselves spend every other year in Edo in attendance at his court.

With approximately half of the country's *daimyo* lords in Edo at all times —and all of them requiring large numbers of retainers and *samurai* in their retinue—Edo became the site of powerful and a bustling commercial center almost overnight.

With the power of the Tokugawa Shogunate nearly absolute and the military strength of the other clans kept strictly limited, Japan entered its longest period of internal peace.

During the 265-year-long Edo Period, when most contact with the outside world was cut off, Japan's own unique culture matured. The arts and the theater flourished. Villages became towns, and towns became cities, as the clan headquarters—mostly in castles—required a growing number of services.

The constant traveling between the clan headquarters and Edo by great processions involving up to 10,000 people helped spread both economic benefits and culture throughout the country and thus played a major role in binding the people and the provinces into a national unity. See PROCESSIONS OF THE LORDS.

HISTORICAL TABLE

YEAR	JAPAN/ABROAD
660 B.C.	Mythical date of the ascension of Japan's first emperor, Jimmu.
300–645A.D.	YAMATO PERIOD
476	End of the Roman Empire
538–552	Introduction of Buddhism from Korea
581–618	Sui Dynasty in China
593–622	Regency of Prince Shotoku
607	First envoy sent to China
618–907	Tang Dynasty in China
645	Downfall of the Soga clan, rise of the Fujiwara
702	Promulgation of Japan's first constitution
710–784	NARA PERIOD
712	Publication of *Kojiki* (*Record of Ancient Matters*)
720	Publication of *Nihon Shoki* (*Chronicle of Japan*)
752	Dedication of the Great Buddha of Todai Temple in Nara
771–814	Reign of Charlemagne
794–1185	HEIAN PERIOD
894	Sending of envoys to China abolished
995–1027	Heyday of the Fujiwara clan
1002–1019	The great novel *Genji Monogatari* written
1169–1181	Heyday of Kiyomori Taira
1180–1185	War between the Taira and Minamoto clans
1185–1333	KAMAKURA PERIOD
1192	Founding of the Kamakura Shogunate
1215	Magna Carta signed
1260–1368	Yuan Dynasty in China
1274	First Mongol invasion of Japan
1275	Marco Polo leaves Italy for China
1281	Second Mongol attempt to conquer Japan
1333	Kamakura Shogunate falls
1334	Emperor Godaigo temporarily regains power

1333–1573	ASHIKAGA (or MUROMACHI) PERIOD
1338	Founding of the Ashikaga Shogunate
1467–1477	Onin War, between contending clans
1492	Columbus discovers New World
1498	Vasco de Gama reaches India
1543	Portuguese ship lands on Japanese island of Tanega
1549	Catholic missionary, Francis Xavier lands in Kagoshima

1568–1600	AZUCHI-MOMOYAMA PERIOD
1568	Nobunaga Oda seizes Kyoto
1582	Nobunaga assassinated
1585	Hideyoshi Toyotomi appointed civil dictator
1592	Hideyoshi sends army to invade Korea
1600	Ieyasu Tokugawa wins battle of Sekigahara

1600–1867	TOKUGAWA (or EDO) PERIOD
1602	Founding of Dutch East India Company
1603	Founding of the Tokugawa Shogunate
1615	Tokugawa *Shogun* captures Osaka Castle, eliminates Hideyoshi's heirs
1637–1638	Christians of Shimabara rebel
1639	Japan closed to outside world, except for a Dutch trading post
1776–1787	American Revolution and Independence
1789	French Revolution
1853	Commodore Perry arrives at Uraga, Japan
1854	Japan signs Treaty of Kanagawa with U.S.
1858	Treaty of Friendship & Commerce with U.S.
1867	Tokugawa Shogunate gives up power
1868	Emperor Meiji ascends throne, assumes power

1868–1912	MEIJI PERIOD
1868	Feudal clan system abolished; industrialism started
1877	Rebellion of Satsuma province quelled
1889	First real constitution promulgated
1894–1895	Japan goes to war against China
1902	Japan forms alliance with England
1904–1905	Japan goes to war against Russia
1910	Japan annexes Korea

1912–1926	TAISHO PERIOD
1914	Japan sides with Allies in war against Germany
1915	Japan demands major concessions from China
1918	Japan's first parliamentary cabinet formed
1923	Great earthquake devastates Tokyo and Yokohama

1926–1989	SHOWA PERIOD
1931	Japan seizes Manchuria
1933	Japan leaves League of Nations
1933	War against China continues
1940–1941	Japan expands war into Southeast Asia
1941	Japan bombs Pearl Harbor
1945	Japan surrenders, Pacific War ends
1945–1952	Allied Forces occupy Japan, institute political, social, and economic reforms
1952	Japan regains independence, begins rise to position of economic leadership
1958–1970	Japan achieves economic superpower status, second only to the United States. Japanese corporations establish hundreds of plants overseas, buy out large numbers of American and other foreign companies, and engage in a frenzy of investments abroad, concentrating on prime commercial properties. Government removes restrictions on foreign travel in the mid-1960s, resulting in huge numbers of Japanese traveling abroad each year and spurring remarkable growth in the travel industry worldwide.
1964	The Shinkansen "Bullet Train" begins operation. The Olympic Games are held in Tokyo, heralding Japan's postwar debut on the international scene.
1965	Government signs peace treaty with South Korea.
1970	World Exposition held in Osaka.
1971	U.S. returns island of Okinawa to Japan.
1972	Japan follows U.S. move and normalizes relations with the People's Republic of China.
1973	Middle East war causes rapid escalation of oil prices and Japan's first "oil crisis."
1976	Former Prime Minister Kakuei Tanaka is accused of accepting a bribe from Lockheed in the purchase of planes, and is arrested.
1978	The New Tokyo International Airport is opened in Narita, some 60 kilometers northeast of Tokyo on Chiba Peninsula, eight years after it was built. The opening was delayed by opposition from local farmers who were supported by militant university students.
	A Peace and Friendship Treaty is signed with China.
1986	Takako Doi, elected head of the Socialist party, becomes the first woman ever to lead a political party in Japan.
1988	The "Recruit Scandal" erupts. Leaders of the ruling Liberal Democratic Party are accused of accepting stock and cash bribes from Recruit Co., a personnel recruiting and publishing conglomerate.

1989–	HEISEI PERIOD
1989	Emperor Hirohito dies after the longest reign in the history of the country, and is replaced by Crown Prince Akihito. *Heisei*, which means "Peace and Prosperity," is adopted as the new "reign name."
	For the first time since 1955, the Liberal Democratic Party loses its majority in the Diet's Upper House.
1990	Japan's so-called "bubble economy" collapses, brought down by speculation in domestic real estate, stocks, overpriced overseas investments, and foreign pressure to force the value of the yen upward. Economy begins a period of belt-tightening and retrenching.
1991	Factional infighting brings down Prime Minister Toshiki Kaifu and his cabinet. He is replaced by Kiichi Miyazawa.
1992	A controversial bill that allows Japan to send troops abroad on peace-keeping missions is passed—the so-called PKO Bill.
1993	The Liberal Democratic Party is ousted after ruling since 1955. Morihiro Hosokawa, who had broken with the old guard in May 1992, and formed a new party called the Japan New Party, becomes prime minister.
1994	In April, Prime Minister Hosokawa is ousted and replaced by Tsutomu Hata, former foreign minister, as political infighting among the factions continues.

HOKKAIDO (Hoke-kie-doe)   Japan's northernmost and second largest island, Hokkaido is still regarded by many Japanese as a frontier. Separated from Honshu by the Tsugaru Straits, and from Sakhalin by the Soya Straits, bounded on the east by the Sea of Okhotsk and on the west by the Sea of Japan, Hokkaido is as different from the southern islands of Japan as Alaska is from the lower United States.

Populated by the Ainu, a hairy Caucasian race, when the Japanese first began arriving in the islands, Hokkaido (then known as Ezo) is first mentioned in Japanese records in 658, when Hirafu Abe went there to meet with the Ainu (also called Ezo) after he had defeated an indigenous tribe called Emishi in the Tohoku (northeastern) region of Honshu.

It is not known when the first Japanese settled in Hokkaido, but it is presumed that there were Japanese living along the southern coastline from shortly after the period of Hirafu Abe.

In any event, there were numerous Japanese in Hokkaido by the Middle Ages—so much so that they had replaced the Ainu as the dominant group. In 1457, an Ainu chieftain named Koshamain led a rebellion against this Japanese encroachment, but the revolt was put down by Nobuhiro Takeda, who went on to subjugate the entire island. See AINU.

The Takeda family was to control Hokkaido for the next several generations, but in 1599 the family changed its name to Matsumae, built a castle at a location by that name, and allied themselves with Ieyasu Tokugawa, who was on the verge of establishing the Tokugawa Shogunate.

Hokkaido was to remain in the backwater of Japanese history during the long Tokugawa Period. Under the Treaty of Kanagawa, signed with the U.S. in 1854, Hakodate was made an open port. Two years later, the government was moved to the Ainu village of Sapporo, and in 1869 the name of the island was changed from Ezo to Hokkaido (Northern Sea Route). In 1871, Sapporo was laid out—American style—as a city and made the capital of the island.

It was not until 1950 that the Japanese government passed a Hokkaido Development Law and established a Hokkaido Development Agency to spur economic growth on the island.

Hokkaido, which includes the Habomai Islands lying off the eastern tip of the main island and the Kurile Islands to the northeast, has 22 percent of the land area of Japan, but only about 5 percent of its population.

Like the rest of Japan, Hokkaido is a wonderland of scenic beauty— volcanic mountains, stunning gorges and valleys, thick forests, rolling plains, and many lakes and rivers. Several huge areas on the island are so outstanding that they have been designated national parks, which are characterized by towering mountains, smouldering volcanoes, deep valleys, primeval forests embracing caldera lakes in their bosom, vast expanses of plains, and rare flora and fauna.

There are five such national parks in Hokkaido, along with eight prefectural parks on a smaller scale but of similar beauty.

Hokkaido's climate is similar to that of central Europe—very cold winters, with deep snows, especially in the mountain regions. Spring does not begin until May, and fall is underway by mid-September.

The island is now connected with Honshu by an undersea tunnel, making it possible to go from Tokyo to Sapporo by train in less than six hours. Its economy began to boom in the 1960s and '70s.

The leading industries in Hokkaido include fishing, lumbering, paper and pulp, agriculture, dairy farming, oil refining, cement making, iron and steel, foodstuffs, and brewing various alcoholic drinks.

Sapporo, which looks more foreign than any other Japanese city, is the seventh largest metropolis in the country and is especially famous for its annual Snow Festival, held from February 1–5, which centers around huge figures carved in snow. It also has a Lilac Festival in May, a Hokkaido Shrine Festival in June, a Summer Festival in August, and a Chrysanthemum Festival in the fall.

Sapporo's most famous foreign resident was Dr. William S. Clark, who was invited to Japan by the government in 1876 to establish the Sapporo Agricultural College. He lived in Sapporo and taught at the new school for one year, but made a lasting impression on the Japanese. See CLARK, WILLIAM.

Among Sapporo's other major attractions are the Ainu Museum, dedicated to the Rev. John Batchelor, who lived in the city for 40 years and became an authority on the Ainu; two underground shopping centers (Pole Town and Auroa Town) that are especially popular in the frigid winter months; and the Susukino entertainment district, where there are over 3,000 bars, cabarets, restaurants, and overnight inns.

Within 20 to 45 minutes of Sapporo are some of the best ski resorts in Japan. The famous Jozankei Spa on the Toyohira River is just 26 kilometers from the city.

HOMES / IE (E-eh) Japan has one of the highest rates of home ownership of any country in the world—well over 60 percent and climbing steadily—a situation that is a relatively recent phenomenon.

In the mid-1970s, the Japan Housing Corporation and the Housing Loan Corporation, both government agencies, launched a program to help promote the development of good, low-cost housing.

The program was called House 55 Project, in reference to its target completion date in 1980, which was the 55th year of the Showa Era (the reign of Emperor Hirohito). The goal of the project was to get commercial companies involved in the design and building of prefabricated houses.

More than 40 companies took part in the program, and three of them—Misawa Homes; Shimizu Construction; and a combine of Nippon Steel, Takenaka Komuten (a construction company), and Matsushita Electric Works—came up with winning designs and received government grants to build them.

The combine's winning design, called TOPS and put on the market at the beginning of 1982, is a two-story structure that is fabricated in sections that measure 2.5 meters by 4 meters and consists of light materials in a honeycomb-type of construction over a steel framework.

A special feature of the Misawa House 55 is a heating system built into the floor, which, claim the makers, has a heat insulation factor 10 times as high as that of a cement floor.

By mid-1992, prefabricated houses accounted for some 90 percent of all the houses being built in Japan, and the percentage was edging upward. By this time, several other major Japanese companies had jumped onto the prefabricated house bandwagon and had become active in overseas markets.

Despite this progress, the average home in Japan is still very small by most standards, and many homes are old and in need of repair.

HOME VISITS It is not customary for the Japanese to entertain casual friends or business contacts in their homes. There are several reasons for this. Japanese homes have traditionally been small, with enough room for only the immediate members of the family. It has also been, and still is, customary for Japanese to keep their business life and private family life totally separated.

Business entertainment, as well as personal entertaining, has also traditionally included drinking and eating at public places designed to cater to this type of business. In fact, specific segments of Japan's huge public entertainment business cater primarily to businesspeople—the cabarets, lounges, *geisha* houses, and private *ryotei* restaurant-inns depending almost entirely on the patronage of well-heeled and expense-account executives. See individual listings for CABARETS; GEISHA; WATER BUSINESS.

Because of the interest among foreign visitors in the way the Japanese live, however, the Japan Travel Bureau and other travel services in Tokyo and other Japanese cities have made arrangements with some Japanese families to invite tourists into their homes for brief stays.

HONDA MOTOR COMPANY (Hone-dah)   The Honda Motor Company, one of the world's leading automobile and motorcycle manufacturers, epitomizes the special insight, skills, and dedication that have characterized Japanese industry since 1945.

In 1946, a young engineer named Soichiro Honda (pronounced HONE-dah, not Hahn-dah) began attaching small engines to bicycles. In transportation-starved postwar Japan, the motorbike was an immediate success.

However, the limited supply of ready-made engines was soon used up. So, Honda decided to build his own, and in 1948 he founded the Honda Motor Company with an investment of $2,700.

By 1949, Honda had stepped up from motorbikes to motorcycles. Two years later he and his even younger engineering staff introduced the now-historic 146cc, four-stroke Dream motorcycle.

The engineer who put the motorcycle through its first grueling test was Kiyoshi Kawashima, who was destined to become president of the company. Honda sold nine million of the revolutionary, light, easy-to-operate motorcycles.

By the early 1960s, Honda Motor Company was not only the world's largest manufacturer of motorcycles—it made the best motorcyles in the world.

At this time, Soichiro decided to begin making cars, using the same innovative, high-tech, high-quality approach that had made the company so successful with motorcycles.

The company began tooling up to manufacture a line of small, hardy, inexpensive, fuel-efficient cars that would meet the transportation needs of most people around the world. The first Honda car—the Honda Civic—drove off the assembly line in 1972, one year before the great energy crisis began.

In 1975, Honda introduced an almost pollution-free engine called the CVCC, getting another jump on other automakers who were plagued by rising pollution problems.

Next came larger and more luxurious motorcycles and cars, to meet the continuing market demands for these products. By 1982, Honda had grown into an international enterprise with over 33,000 employees and annual sales in excess of $8 billion.

Honda's extraordinary success is attributed to several factors, including timing, correctly perceiving the needs of the market, emphasis on engineering excellence and quality, and a team concept that eventually came to be known as the Honda Way.

The Honda Way refers to management Japanese style, which is more personally oriented and based on a very high level of manager-worker cooperation, quality consciousness, consensus, and company loyalty.

By the mid-1990s, Honda had twenty manufacturing plants in the U.S., Brazil, and thirteen other countries, and technical tie-ups with automobile and motorcycle manufacturers in more than a dozen other countries. Annual sales were in excess of $34 billion.

In 1994, Honda began a program to establish motorcycle manufacturing plants and marketing organizations throughout Asia to take advantage of that huge market.

HONSHU (Hone-shuu)   This is Japan's largest and main island. Comprising 61.1 percent of the total land area of Japan, it is in the middle of the chain, with the island of Hokkaido just off its northern tip and Shikoku and Kyushu at its southwestern end.

Honshu curves from east to west and is shaped somewhat like a boomerang. Like all the other islands of Japan, it is extremely mountainous, with well-defined geographical regions.

The mountainous areas are characterized by extinct volcanic peaks, huge craters, lakes, gorges, ravines, narrow valleys, and a great number of hot springs.

Honshu is divided into five regions: Tohoku, Kanto, Chubu, Kinki, and Chugoku. The bulk of Japan's population and industry are on Honshu. Its major cities include Tokyo, Yokohama, Nagoya, Kyoto, Osaka, Kobe, Hiroshima, Nagasaki, Kawasaki and Sendai.

HORIE, KENICHI (Hoe-ree-eh, Kane-ee-chee)   A world-class adventurer, Kenichi Horie, born in Osaka in 1938, became the first Japanese to sail across the Pacific alone, in 1962. He then sailed around the world on a nonstop voyage in 1974, and between 1978 and 1982 became the first person to complete a longitudinal solo voyage around the globe.

After returning to Japan in 1962 following his crossing of the Pacific, Horie was immediately arrested and jailed. He was charged with leaving the country without official permission.

The story of Horie's accomplishment made worldwide news, and his arrest made him even more of a celebrity. Horie was soon released from jail, at least partly because of the favorable publicity he received and the strong criticism the authorities received.

The official reason given for dropping the charges against Horie was that he apologized and showed regret for having caused so much trouble.

HORS D'OEUVRES / TSUMAMI (T-sue-mah-me)   There are several kinds of hors d'oeuvres in Japan. *Tsumami* are the kind that accompany alcoholic drinks and are most likely to be served in bars and cabarets. They generally consist of nuts, small *sembi* rice crackers wrapped in seaweed or dipped in a cayenne pepper-laden soy sauce, or shredded cuttlefish.

In a Japanese inn, hors d'oeuvres are likely to be small squares of sweetened bean jam. At a reception or party, hors d'oeuvres run the gamut of tidbits of seafood, vegetables, cheeses, and meats.

HORSES / UMA (Uu-mah)   Horses were brought into Japan from the Asian mainland some time before recorded history began, but their use was restricted to official government and military pursuits.

In any event, the type of agriculture practiced in Japan did not lend itself to the use of horses as draft animals, and common people were prohibited from using them for riding.

Restrictions governing the use of horses continued in Japan until the fall of the Tokugawa Shogunate in 1868, but the situation really did not change very much then. Farming methods had not changed, and there was no room or need for horses in most of the country.

The exceptions to this were the Tohoku district of northern Honshu and Hokkaido, where horses had traditionally been raised for the *shogun* and lords of feudal Japan. There, in the plains areas, horses became increasingly important, both for work and military use.

Today these areas are noted for their race horses, as well as draft animals, and there is a modest, but growing, use of horses for recreational purposes.

The Tohoku district, in fact, has been compared to the state of Texas in the U.S. because of the popularity of horses, the expansive attitudes of the people, and their habit of claiming that everything in the region is bigger and better than it is anywhere else.

HORYU TEMPLE/HORYU JI (Hoe-ree-you)   The oldest existing temple in Japan and one of the oldest wooden structures in the world, the Horyu, near Nara, was founded in 607 by Prince Shotoku Taishi at the command of Empress Suiko, his aunt.

Considered one of the Seven Great Temples of Nara, the fountainhead of Japanese culture, the Horyu Temple is the headquarters of the Shotoku sect of Buddhism.

The temple is divided into two sections and, altogether, includes 45 important buildings, 31 of which are registered as National Treasures and the rest as Important Cultural Properties. There is so much to see in the temple

complex—and so much to learn—that a sojourn of a week or more would not be enough to cover it all. The barest description of its treasures would take many pages. The best idea is to go and see it.

HOSTESSES / HOSUTESU (Hoes-tay-sue)   When used in this sense, hostess refers to the young women who work in the hundreds of thousands of lounges, cabarets, and nightclubs in Japan that are authorized to employ women to act as partners or companions for customers.

The official count of the total number of nightspots with hostesses varies, but since there are well over 30,000 in Tokyo alone, the overall figure is no doubt in excess of 100,000. It has been estimated that from three to five million people are employed in the entertainment trades throughout the country.

In any event, the world of nightclub hostesses in Japan is a big one, and it is one of the most fascinating aspects of everyday life.

The hostess clubs attract some of the most beautiful and intelligent women in Japan, which is one of the reasons for their popularity.

The size of the hostess clubs range from tiny cubby holes with two or three women to large ones with over 100 hostesses—the huge ones with as many as 1,000 female attendants having disappeared in the mid-1980s. The cost of enjoying the company of hostesses also varies considerably, but on the average it is high by non-Japanese standards. It is not uncommon for the posher clubs in Tokyo's Ginza and Akasaka districts to charge from 60 to 100,000 yen per person for two or three hours of eating, drinking, dancing, and conversing with their hostesses.

Virtually all of the clients of the more expensive hostess clubs in Japan are on generous company expense accounts. The bills are sent directly to the companies, which normally pay them without question.

The National Tax Administration Agency says Japanese corporations spend billions of yen each year on nighttime entertainment for their managers and clients.

Hostesses may earn from 3,000 to 10,000 yen an hour, depending on the number of big-spending patrons they have—and the more successful ones often get bonuses and other considerations to prevent them from moving to other clubs and taking their steady customers with them.

It is fairly common for more successful hostesses to be wooed away by competing clubs, with cash bonuses of $20,000 and above.

At any one time, there are sprinklings of foreign women working as hostesses in Tokyo and other key cities.

The profession of nightclub hostess is not a casual job, particularly in the larger, name clubs. There are specific rules and regulations. The women are divided into groups, with leaders, and are ranked according to their longevity and expertise in handling customers—including encouraging them to spend money.

The more attractive, talented, and successful hostesses with well-to-do clients are often given expensive gifts and taken on overseas trips by their customers. Many women in the profession regard themselves as being on the same level as actresses and other professionals in the entertainment business.

HOTELS / HOTERU (Hoe-tay-rue)   The first Western-style hotel in Japan was the Edo, built in 1868 and boasting 102 rooms. It was located in the Tsukiji district of Tokyo, just east of the Ginza shopping and entertainment area. Second was the Club Hotel in Yokohama, which opened in 1869.

The third hotel was the Seiyoken, which opened in Tsukiji in 1871 and was followed rapidly by the Hyogo Hotel in Kobe, the Grand Hotel in Yokohama, and the Tokyo Hotel in Tokyo. These were followed by smaller, tourist-type hotels in such scenic and historic places as Nikko, Kamakura, Hakone, Karuizawa, and Kyoto.

The first of the famous Imperial Hotels, backed by the government, which saw the need for a world-class hotel for visiting foreign dignitaries, opened on November 3, 1890. The Imperial had 70 rooms and was to set the standard for Japan's hotel industry until well into the 1960s.

Actually, the luxury hotel, with its numerous amenities, was invented in Japan—although it was, of course, Japanese style. In the early 1600s, the Tokugawa Shogunate decreed that all of the country's feudal lords, known as *daimyo* (die-m'yoe), or "great names," spend every other year in Edo, the *shogun's* headquarters.

This meant that the nearly 300 *daimyo* throughout the long island chain had to march, with hundreds to thousands of retainers, from their fiefs to Edo in alternate years. These great processions had to have places to stay at night, so three categories of accommodations were built at specified intervals along the country's great walking roads. These three categories or classes of inns were known as *honjin* (hone-jeen), *waki-honjin* (wah-kee-hone-jeen), and *hatago* (hah-tah-go).

The *honjin*, reserved for the lords and their closest retainers, were beautifully styled and richly decorated, befitting the elite status and tastes of their special guests. The *waki-honjin*, or "branch *honjin*," were designed to accommodate the lesser retainers of the *daimyo*, and were less pretentious. The foot soldiers, horse grooms, sandal keepers and other lower-class members of the processions stayed in the *hatago*, which were also open to ordinary travelers.

Thus, when European travelers and travelers from other parts of the world were being put up in basic inns, the elite *samurai* and nobles of Japan —with the former spending a major portion of their lives on the road—had the advantage of accommodations that were rich, to say the least. See PROCESSIONS OF THE LORDS.

With this long tradition of providing travelers with the finest possible accommodations, it is not surprising that Japan's Western-style hotels today are among the finest, if not *the* finest, in the world.

The larger and best known of the hotels in Tokyo, for example, have a variety and quality of services and amenities that make leading hotels in New York, London, and Paris pale by comparison. It is common for them to have anywhere from half a dozen to two dozen restaurants with a variety of cuisines.

The Imperial Hotel, for example, has a large shopping arcade, a post office, a bookstore, a drugstore, a wrapping and forwarding service, an executive's work lounge, a travel office, and several dozen business offices on its premises. See IMPERIAL HOTEL.

Beginning in the early 1970s, business hotels began to proliferate in Japan. These hotels are generally smaller than the name luxury hotels and offer fewer special amenities. But they are in convenient locations, most would rank as first class, and they are significantly less expensive than the huge luxury hotels.

There are some 1,000 Western-style hotels in Japan. Tokyo alone has over 400 hotels. All are members of the Japan Hotel Association.

Direct tipping is forbidden in most Japanese hotels. Instead, a service charge of 10 percent to 15 percent is automatically added to the bill. There is also a 10 percent tax on meals and room charges that are above specified amounts.

Leading hotels in major cities include the following:

TOKYO: Imperial, Hilton, Okura, New Otani, Akasaka Prince, Takanawa Prince, Keio Plaza, Century Hyatt, New Takanawa Prince, Palace, and Grand Palace.

NAGOYA: Nagoya Castle, International, Meitetsu Grand, Nagoya Kanko, Nagoya Miyako, Nagoya Terminal, and Castle Plaza.

KYOTO: Holiday Inn, Fujita, International, Kyoto Grand, Kyoto, Kyoto Station, and Miyako.

OSAKA: International, New Hankyu, Osaka Airport, Osaka Grand, Plaza, Toyo, and Royal.

HOTEL SERVICES   A special feature of leading hotels in Japan is the variety of services they provide visiting foreign businesspeople. These services, contracted out, include translating and interpreting, secretarial help, photocopying, research, and appointment making.

Several hotels have Executive Service Lounges, a service pioneered by the Imperial Hotel in Tokyo. The Imperial's lounge has private work cubicles, typewriters, telephones, and a library of publications on Japanese industry. It is staffed by bilingual employees whose sole duty is to aid foreign executives who are guests at the hotel.

A special feature of the Okura Hotel's Executive Service Salon are 30-minute English-language tapes on various business topics, from management to robots.

HOT SPRING SPAS / ONSEN (Own-sen)   The volcanic nature of the Japanese islands has blessed them with dozens of thousands of hot springs in virtually every region of the country. Several thousand of these springs have been developed into spas. Hundreds of them have been in use and famous for over a thousand years.

Just some of the more popular hot spring spas whose names begin with A include Akiu, Aone, Arifuku, Arima, Asama, Asamushi, Aso, Asobara, Asozu, Atagawa, Atsumi, Awara, and Awazu.

Other famous ones include Bandai-Atami, Fukiage, Kaminoyama, Noboribetsu, Numa Jiri, Toyako, Unzen, Yoshina, and Yunokawa. Kusatsu, some three hours from Tokyo by express train, is one of the oldest and most famous hot spring spas in Japan. In use since ancient times, it was made nationally famous in the twelfth century as a result of several visits by Yoritomo Minamoto, who founded Japan's first shogunate at Kamakura in 1192.

Yoritomo was attracted to the spa because of the reputation its sulfuric, iron, alum, and arsenic waters had for relieving rheumatism, gout, skin diseases, and other ailments.

The main public bath at Kusatsu, called *Netsuno Yu*, or Heat Bath, is so hot that bathers generally enter the water in unison—200 or so at a time—to shouted commands from a bath master. Attendants first stir up the water with long boards to reduce its temperature.

Once the bathers are in the water—for three or four minutes—they remain absolutely motionless to keep the heat at a minimum. The bath master counts off the time and shouts encouragement to the bathers. At the end of the period, the bath master always yells for the bathers to get out of the water slowly—but most of them get out as quickly as they can.

There are more than 130 inns centered around the town square of Kusatsu, which is surrounded by a forest of pine and larch trees. The sulfur content of the water is so high that it is processed, and the collected sulfur is sold commercially.

Above Kusatsu, on mountain slopes that range from 1,200 to 1,700 meters in altitude, is one of Japan's most famous ski resorts.

There are hot spring spas in or very near virtually every city and town in Japan. In hundreds of cases, the whole town is one huge spa, with dozens to hundreds of inns featuring large and small mineral baths. See individual listings. For a directory of the leading spas in the country, contact the Japan National Tourist Organization.

HOUSEHOLDS / KATEI (Kah-tay-e)   Japan has approximately 40 million households, with an average of 3.25 persons per household. In Tokyo, the average household size is only 2.70 persons—the lowest in the country. Nuclear households (couples without children and parents with only their own children) now account for over 60 percent of all households in Japan.

HOUSING   Japan has the world's most advanced home building industry. By the early 1980s, a significant percentage of the industry had been computerized, robotized, and automated. Computers draft designs and print out blueprints, keep track of all inventory, order parts as they are needed, and handle marketing.

Builders produce up to 85 percent of their housing units in factories, where cutting, welding, nailing, and gluing are done on an assembly line—partly by robots adapted from those used in auto industry. A typical house is ready for assembly in 40 minutes, and the entire house can be put together on site by a small crew in four hours.

Many of the innovations characterizing Japan's housing industry were pioneered by Sekisui Heim and Misawa Homes, two of its leading home builders.

American home builders have described what Japanese home builders are doing as mind-boggling.

In 1984, Chiyoji Misawa, president of Misawa Homes Company, predicted that houses that were completely self-sufficient in energy would be on the market by the early 1990s. He also predicted that housing designs in the future would have positive psychological influences on the occupants, and would also contribute to the health and longevity of the occupants by controlling the quality of the air.

One of the space-age materials developed by Misawa for his homes is called PALC, for precastable autoclaved lightweight ceramics, which is similar to the ceramic shield used on the U.S. space shuttle.

Western-style housing available for foreign businesspeople and their families (and for foreigners in other categories) is still at a premium in Japan, however.

Renting a house in Japan may involve several fees or payments besides the monthly rent. Most landlords require the payment of *shikikin* (she-kee-keen), or so-called key money, which may amount to the value of several months' rent. Eighty percent of the key money is returned when the renter vacates the premises. Key money may be negotiable, but the lower it is, the higher the rent tends to be—primarily because in Japan the law protects the renter, not the owner.

In apartments and condos, there are usually manager's fees to be paid (*kyoeki*) for cleaning hallways and stairs, etc., as well as parking fees.

In Japan, first-class Western-style condominiums and apartment buildings are called mansions (mahn-shon).

Recommended reading: *The Elegant Japanese House—Traditional Sukiya Architecture*, by Yukio Futagawa (Weatherhill).

HUMAN FEELINGS / NINJO (Neen-joe)   Japan's strict traditional code of ethics and morality, in which the individual gave up many personal rights for the benefit of the family, the feudal lord, and often the country, has often resulted in fundamental clashes between their duties (*giri*) and personal feelings (*ninjo*). See GIRI.

These clashes between *giri* and *ninjo* were therefore an integral part of Japanese life and were uppermost in their minds from a very young age until death. Not only did the words and all their implications play a vital role in the daily lives of the Japanese, they became the central themes in literature and theatrical arts.

The concepts of *giri* and *ninjo* are still very important in modern day Japan, although the words themselves appear to be less frequently used in personal and business conversations. The Japanese are especially sensitive about their individual and human rights—most of which they did not have until the end of the feudal family system in 1945.

HUMOR / YUMOA (Yuu-moe-ah)   Those who do not understand the language or culture of another people often seem predisposed to presume that they do not have a sense of humor. This has especially been the case among many Westerners who were not familiar with Japan.

In actuality, the Japanese have a highly developed sense of humor that ranges from the base and bawdy to a level so refined that only the most sophisticated and educated can understand and apprecrate it.

Oral and visual humor in Japan have traditions that go back as far as any record and are no doubt as innate in the Japanese as they are in most homo sapiens. See COMIC STORYTELLERS.

Humor plays a vital role in the lives of most Japanese. In fact, it may be more vital than it is to many other people around the globe—because the Japanese have traditionally been more restricted in their behavior than most other people.

With a highly refined and constraining etiquette that prevents the Japanese from being themselves most of the time, humor has been and still is a valuable safety valve that allows them to let off steam.

The Japanese language, with its built-in ambiguities, allusions, and double meanings, more easily lends itself to humor than does English or, perhaps, any other language. See JAPANESE LANGUAGE.

ICE SCULPTURES Ice carving for decorative and festive occasions is a highly advanced art in Japan. Decorative ice carvings are the specialty of ice chefs in many of Japan's leading hotels, who use them to set off huge banquets.

The most spectacular cold sculptures in Japan are those done in snow for the Sapporo Snow Festival in Hokkaido in winter. See SNOW FESTIVAL.

IKAHO (E-kah-hoe) Ikaho is one of Japan's most celebrated hot spring spas. Located about two train-and-bus hours from Tokyo's Ueno Station, it is built on a series of terraces on the northeast slope of Mt. Haruna in Niigata Prefecture.

The whole town of Ikaho consists almost entirely of inns built around hot springs that are approximately 50 degrees centigrade and have an iron and sulfur content (recommended for stomach ailments).

Ikaho is also noted for the beauty of the surrounding hillsides, which are covered with wild flowers from June to September and with snow in the winter months. The best view of the area is from the grounds of Ikaho Shrine, which overlooks the town.

IKEBANA (Ee-kay-bah-nah) By the mid-1500s, *ikebana*, or flower arranging, was flourishing in Japan as a popular art, with the emphasis on the use of natural materials and the re-creation of natural forms. *Ikebana* literally means living flowers.

As time went by, *ikebana* became imbued with metaphysical meanings. The primary goal was to arrange the sprays in such a way as to signify the sky, earth, and humans, and to serve as a strict aesthetic and moral discipline. Three basic sprays were developed to portray the harmonious balance of nature.

Flower arranging was primarily seen as a feminine skill. Young girls were expected to study the art as part of their preparation for marriage and adulthood.

While still a national custom, as well as a profession supported by numerous schools and affiliated exhibitions, *ikebana* is now divided between the traditionalists and a post–World War II school that uses lifeless materials

(iron, glass, plaster) to give the impression of life through the vitality of the form.

The basic techniques of traditional *ikebana* differ with the particular school, but all include specific ways of cutting, pruning, and caring for the flowers. Both traditionalists and avant-garde ikebanists practice the art for interior decoration purposes on a commercial basis, as well as for personal reasons.

In homes, *ikebana* arrangements are displayed in the *tokonoma* (toe-koe-no-mah), a special alcove in the living room designed specifically for the exhibit of flowers and hanging scrolls. See FLOWER ARRANGING.

IKEBUKURO (E-kay-buu-kuu-roe)   One of Tokyo's busiest districts, Ikebukuro is in Toshima Ward northwest of downtown. The center of the area is Ikebukuro Station, which is a main stop on the Yamanote Loop Line that encircles the heart of Tokyo. It is also the terminal for four major commuter lines that serve outlying areas. The Marunouchi Subway Line that begins here curves through downtown Tokyo and then runs westward to Ogikubo.

Until the 1970s, Ikebukuro was regarded as provincial and served primarily as a shopping and entertainment center for people who came in from rural areas to the north and west.

Then a building boom began in the area, highlighted by a huge Sunrise Building, which became a popular office and shop location and helped attract other businesses.

Ikebukuro now draws shoppers and pleasure seekers from other parts of Tokyo, as well as the countryside beyond.

IKI ISLAND / IKI JIMA (E-kee jee-mah)   A small island (139 square kilometers), 16 kilometers off the northern coast of Kyushu, Iki is part of Nagasaki Prefecture and has 45,000 residents who are mostly engaged in farming and fishing.

The island was in the path of the first Mongol fleet that tried to invade Japan in 1274 and was laid waste by the invaders. The governor of the island at the time was Kagetaka Taira, a member of the famous Taira clan. He and his men were killed in their defense of the island.

The Shinjo Shrine in the village of Shinjo is dedicated to Kagetaka. Near the town of Gonoura are the ruins of a castle built there on orders from Hideyoshi Toyotomi, in connection with his campaign to conquer Korea in the 1590s. See TOYOTOMI, HIDEYOSHI.

IMMUNIZATION CARDS   At present, visitors to Japan are not required to show evidence of immunization unless they are coming from an area known to be infected (usually with smallpox or cholera). There may, however, be temporary periods when such cards are needed; so it is best to check with a travel agent or a Japanese embassy or consulate abroad before departure.

IMPERIAL FAMILY / KOSHITSU (Koe-sheet-sue)   Japan's Imperial family is the world's oldest reigning dynasty. According to the *Kojiki* (*Record of Ancient Matters*), published in 712, the first emperor of Japan was enthroned in 660 B.C., but this is disputed by some Japanese historians.

Chinese records make references to Japan in later centuries, and there is no doubt that a large area of the country in the Nara-Kyoto-Osaka region was unified under the rule of the Imperial family by 300 A.D.

The head of the Imperial family at that time was named Hatsukunishirasu Sumera Mikoto, who was later referred to as Jimmu Tenno, or Emperor Jimmu.

Following the introduction of the Chinese system of writing into Japan in the fifth and sixth centuries, records of the reigning emperors and empresses are complete and in detail.

During the earliest centuries, the emperor was both the religious and secular leader of Japan. From around 600 to the death of Emperor Saga in 842, there were many emperors who were outstanding scholars, noted for their wisdom and accomplishments in many fields.

But in the mid-800s, the Fujiwara family, which had intermingled with the Imperial family for some 200 years, gradually took over real political power, first through the office of prime minister and then as regent to the emperor.

From this period until 1868, with only a few brief exceptions, the emperors reigned, but did not rule. As more and more of the political and administrative power was usurped by the Fujiwaras, less and less attention was paid to governing the country. The nobles and their families and retainers lived in luxurious splendor, spending their days in aesthetic, artistic, and recreational pursuits.

The provincial governors, most of whom were relatives of the Imperial family and the Fujiwaras, began to act on their own and became more and more independent. They began to maintain their own elite armed forces.

Emperor Gosanjo (1034–1073), aware of what was happening, tried to weaken the power of the Fujiwara regents and rule personally. His successor, Emperor Shirakawa (1053–1129), tried a new tack—retiring from the throne and trying to exercise influence over the administration of the country unofficially.

Subsequent emperors followed suit, but this resulted in weakening the central government further, and a series of civil wars broke out among the powerful provincial clans contending for power.

Kiyomori Taira, the scion of one of the new military families that had grown up in the provinces, fought on behalf of the Imperial Court and emerged the winner in these conflicts. The grateful emperor rewarded him with one promotion after another, until he finally became the prime minister.

Just like the Fujiwaras before him, Kiyomori claimed the power of the emperor for himself, but he was careful to see that the Imperial family was not threatened.

The glory of the Taira family was to be shortlived, however; some 20 years later, in 1185, the clan was totally destroyed by Yoritomo Minamoto.

As the new supreme military power in Japan, Yoritomo obtained permission from the emperor to set up a new administrative system for the provinces—a system made up of *shugo* (guards) in charge of military and police affairs and *jito* (squires), who were in charge of running the economic affairs and collecting the annual rice tax.

Yoritomo appointed his own family members and retainers to these posts, thus eliminating the final vestiges of Imperial power. In 1192, Yoritomo succeeded in having the emperor appoint him *Sei-t-Tai-Shogun* (Say-e-e-tie-sho-goon), or General for the Subjugation of Eastern Barbarians (an old title given to generals sent against the aboriginal Ainu tribesmen of northern Japan centuries earlier).

Yoritomo then set up a military government, called *bakufu* (bah-kuu-fuu), or camp office, in Kamakura. He then contrived to make the position of *shogun* hereditary and passed it on to his sons, first to Yoriie and then to Sanetomo. But Sanetomo was assassinated in 1219 by a nephew who was a member of the Hojo clan (who hid behind a tree that still stands in Kamakura).

And this ended the days of glory of the Minamoto clan—after only 27 years in power.

The Kamakura Shogunate was to continue in the hands of the Hojo clan, in the guise of regents, who also guaranteed the continuity of the emperor as the titular head of the country.

Furthermore, the system of *shugo* and *jito* that Yoritomo established was to prevail until 1868—the *shugo* becoming known as *samurai* and the *jito* becoming feudal lords known as *daimyo*. See SAMURAI; HISTORY.

The defense of Japan against the Mongol invasions in 1274 and 1281 (see HISTORY) seriously weakened the Kamakura Shogunate. In Kyoto, Emperor Godaigo (1288–1339) and his nobles plotted to overthrow the *bakufu* government and regain real power for the throne.

Spies reported the plotting to the shogunate, which exiled the emperor to the island of Oki in the Japan Sea in 1332. He escaped the following year, however, and with the help of four famous *daimyo*-generals—Nagatoshi Nawa, Masashige Kusunoki, Yoshisada Nitta, and Takauji Ashikaga— defeated the forces of the shogunate.

Back in power for the first time in centuries, the Imperial Court angered the generals by being more generous in its rewards to the various nobles than to the warriors and by compelling the provincial *daimyo* to pay for the cost of building new palaces in Kyoto.

Takauji Ashikaga led the warriors against Kyoto and captured the city. Emperor Godaigo fled to the mountains of Yoshino and set up his court there. Back in Kyoto, Takauji enthroned a new emperor (a relative of Godaigo's) and established the Ashikaga Shogunate.

For the next 57 years, the country had two emperors. In 1392, the Yoshino court merged with the Kyoto court, but real power was still in the hands of the Ashikaga Shogunate.

Takauji's successors fell victim to the soft life of Kyoto and became involved in the arts, leaving the running of the country to subordinates. Once again, the provincial lords began to compete for power. Interclan warfare broke out between the Hosokawa and Yamana families in 1467, and, for the next 130 odd years, the feudal lords kept the country in a state of war as they battled among themselves for supremacy.

In the intervening years, the Imperial Court in Kyoto flourished or waned, depending on the amount of support it got from the Ashikaga *bakufu* government. One emperor after another succeeded to the chrysanthemum throne, in a line that remained unbroken—though sometimes bent.

When the great Ieyasu Tokugawa emerged the winner in this age of civil strife in 1603 and founded Japan's last great *shogun* dynasty, he was even more supportive of the Imperial Court than his predecessors had been.

After establishing his *bakufu* in Edo (Tokyo), Ieyasu divided the country into four hereditary classes—the *kuge*, or court nobles; the *buke*, or *samurai* warriors; farmers; and *chonin*, or townspeople. While the emperor and court nobles had the most exalted rank in the land, they had no real administrative power.

The Tokugawa Shogunate was to provide one of the longest periods of peace in Japan's history. As the decades went by, many in the *samurai* class became scholars and learned that in the early history of the country the emperor had actually ruled.

As new economic and social forces began to weaken the shogunate, these scholars and others began talking and writing about restoring the emperor to his rightful place. During these same decades, the Western powers and Russia began pressuring Japan to open its doors—closed since 1639—to the outside world.

Imperialist sentiment continued to grow in Japan when it became obvious that the Tokugawa Shogunate could not deal with these new forces coming in from the outside. Thus, once again, it was a revolt against the *bakufu* by dissatisfied provincial *daimyo* that brought the downfall of the Tokugawas and returned Emperor Meiji to power in 1868.

Emperor Meiji was to be an enlightened ruler, as emperors go, but the new concepts of democracy and constitutional government that poured into Japan from the 1850s on were to set the stage once again for a drastic change in the position of the emperor.

Voluntarily reacting to pressure from many sources, as well as to his own inclinations, the emperor approved the promulgation of a constitutional form of government in 1889.

Emperor Meiji was to remain a potent force in Japan's government until his death in 1912, but soon thereafter real power was in the hands of the prime minister and his cabinet—a situation that was to prevail until the end of World War II, at which time the position of the emperor was constitutionally prescribed to be that of a symbol of the state, with no political or administrative powers—a position that the Imperial family had held for nearly 1,000 years.

When Emperor Meiji died in July 1912, he was succeeded by his son, who became Emperor Taisho. Never of robust health, Emperor Taisho died in 1926 and was, in turn, succeeded by his son Prince Hirohito, whose reign was given the name of Showa.

The late Emperor Hirohito was born April 29, 1901. His empress, Nagako, born on March 6, 1903, was the daughter of the Kuni family, a branch of the Imperial family. Their first son, Akihito, the present emperor, was born on December 23, 1933, and in April 1959 married Michiko Shoda, the commoner daughter of the president of the Nisshin Flour Milling Company, whom he met on the tennis courts at the Karuizawa summer resort northwest of Tokyo.

This was the first time that a crown prince of Japan had married outside the nobility, and it was a popular choice among the people.

During the first decade of their marriage, Crown Prince Akihito and Princess Michiko had three children: Crown Prince Naruhito, born on February 23, 1960; Prince Akishino, born on November 30, 1965; and Princess Nori, born on April 18, 1969.

Unlike previous Imperial families, Akihito and Michiko chose to raise their children themselves, instead of turning them over to palace chamberlains as had been the tradition since ancient times.

Crown Prince Naruhito attended Gakushuin University (the Peers' school), earning a doctorate in literature. He then studied history at Oxford in England.

In another break with the past, Prince Akishino married before his older brother, Crown Prince Naruhito. In a highly publicized romance that had all of Japan atwitter, Akishino courted Kiko Kawashima, the beautiful commoner daughter of Tatsuhiko Kawashima, a professor at Gakushuin University, and married her on June 29, 1990. They had a baby girl, Mako, in October 1991.

Prince Naruhito's Ceremony of Investiture as the Crown Prince was held on February 23, 1991, creating a new flurry of excitement about when he would also take a bride. This happy event took place on June 9, 1993, after a remarkable courtship that was the top story in Japan.

Following in the footsteps of both his father and younger brother, Crown Prince Naruhito married a commoner, Mariko Owada, born December 9, 1963, the daughter of Hisashi Owada, a high government official in the Foreign Ministry.

Prince Naruhito courted Mariko for several years before she finally consented to join the Imperial family. A thoroughly modern woman who had spent years abroad in countries where her diplomat father was stationed, Mariko attended Belmont High School in Massachusetts, graduated from Harvard in 1985, attended Tokyo University in 1986, passed the entrance examinations for the Foreign Ministry the same year, and joined the Ministry in 1987.

In 1988, the Foreign Ministry sent Mariko to Oxford for two years of advanced studies in international relations. She was then assigned to the Second North American Division of the Ministry, which handles negotiations with the United States.

In addition to being perfectly fluent in Japanese and English, Mariko also speaks French and German well. Prior to marrying Crown Prince Naruhito, she participated in numerous meetings between Japan's leaders and other heads of state and dignitaries, as a Ministry official and interpreter.

Mariko consented to marry Crown Prince Naruhito only after he promised to protect her from the often heavy-handed control of the Imperial Household chamberlains—a promise that he repeated several times on public television prior to the wedding.

But there were some unhappy events in the lives of the Imperial family in 1993. Criticism of the family by some elements of the Japanese press became so virulent that it was said to have contributed to the Empress Michiko's becoming seriously ill and losing her voice for several months.

In the spring of 1994, Emperor Akihito and Empress Michiko made a highly successful goodwill tour of the United States. See HISTORY; SHOGUN.

IMPERIAL HOTEL / TEIKOKU HOTERU (Tay-e-koe-kuu hoe-tay-rue) Japan's Imperial Hotel is world-famous for many reasons—not the least of which is its tradition of service fit for royalty. The story of the Imperial Hotel is part of some of the most important and dramatic events in the history of the country.

When the Tokugawa Shogunate was dissolved in 1868, the emperor moved from the ancient Imperial capital of Kyoto to Edo, which was renamed Tokyo, or Eastern Capital. During the next several decades, the country underwent an extraordinary change, transforming itself from a feudal society with an agricultural-cottage industry economy to a modern industrial power.

During these exciting years, the many world statesmen, international businessmen, and other foreign notables who came to Tokyo had to be put up in plush but traditionally styled Japanese inns, where guests sat and slept on floor mats.

Recognizing the need for accommodations more suited to the customs and preferences of the growing number of distinguished foreign visitors, the Imperial Household Authority, Foreign Minister Viscount Inouye, and industrial leaders Count Shibusawa and Baron Okura in 1890 sponsored the construction of a large, Western-style hotel and named it the Imperial.

For the first several years of its existence, the new Imperial Hotel was anything but a rousing success. By 1906, however, it became necessary to add an annex. Patronage continued to increase, and in 1910 it was decided to replace the building altogether with a larger structure. (This was also the year that the first packaged tour—the Clark World Tour Party, with 500 people—visited Japan, staying at the Imperial Hotel.)

This was a period of great political upheavals around the world, however, and there was a delay in beginning the new Imperial. Eventually the young, but already famous American architect, Frank Lloyd Wright was engaged to design and supervise the construction of the second Imperial Hotel, which finally got underway in 1917.

The first section of the Mayan-like new Imperial Hotel opened on July 4, 1922. The completed hotel was officially open to the public on August 31, 1923.

The following day, at precisely 11:58 A.M., September 1, 1923, the Tokyo and Yokohama areas were struck by the worst earthquake on record, leaving over 100,000 people dead and vast sections of the two great cities burned-out rubble.

Among the few modern structures that escaped the holocaust with only minor damage was the brand-new Imperial Hotel. With a stroke of insight, Wright had floated the pilings of the Imperial Hotel in the spongy subsoil covering the solid strata further down. As a result, his unique creation literally rode out the giant earthquake tremors the way a ship moves with the waves at sea.

As one of the few surviving buildings in central Tokyo with large kitchen facilities, a water supply, and at least some food, the Imperial Hotel in a matter of minutes became a combination hospital, field kitchen, and general headquarters for relief measures taken to help the thousands left homeless and hungry. It also became the temporary headquarters for dozens of journalists and diplomatic personnel whose offices and homes had been demolished.

Order was restored to Tokyo in a few weeks, and, with it, the Imperial assumed a major role in Japan's affairs with the outside world—not only as the preeminent hotel in the nation, but often as a national guest house for state visitors and as a cultural and recreational center for foreign residents.

After World War II ended in August 1945, the first foreign visitor of note to step into the distinctive foyer of the famous Imperial Hotel was General Douglas MacArthur, Supreme Commander of the Allied Powers (SCAP), who was destined to rule Japan for the next four years, very much like the Tokugawa *Shogun* had in the centuries before.

The famous general landed in Japan at Atsugi Airbase on August 30, 1945, and went first to Yokohama, while quarters were prepared for him in Tokyo. On the morning of September 11, he was driven to the American Embassy in Tokyo, where he was to live for the next four years.

Before leaving Yokohama, MacArthur had someone call the Imperial Hotel and ask that a luncheon be prepared for him and the senior members of his staff. He left the Embassy early and arrived at the Imperial shortly after 11:00 A.M.

MacArthur asked Tetsuzo Inumaru, who had been general manager of the hotel since it opened, to show him some of the rooms. He then asked Inumaru to take him on a 30-minute tour of the bombed-out city.

MacArthur then requisitioned the hotel as a billet for senior officers and ranking civilians working at his headquarters, which were in the Dai-Ichi Insurance Building just two blocks away.

Rather than being disheartened by the turn of events, Inumaru, who had received his hotel training at Claridge's in London, the Ritz in Paris, and the Waldorf-Astoria in New York, called his staff together and told them that they were to take advantage of the opportunity to learn all they could and that they were to provide the same high level of service to the members of the Occupation forces as they had previously done for regular guests.

The Imperial Hotel was returned to its owners in March 1952 and opened for business on April 1, 1952—exactly four weeks before the Allied Occupation of Japan officially ended.

On December 1, 1954, an East Annex was opened behind the original Imperial. Only two years later, a second annex—this time a nine-story tower—was added. By 1967, however, it was obvious that the old Frank Lloyd Wright structure, its floors and walls gradually shifting and sinking as other builders in the area pumped out underground water, had outlived its span of years.

On November 16, 1967, after many a tearful farewell party, the famed old Imperial closed its doors for the last time. A gleaming new Imperial—the third in its history—made its debut in March 1970.

As the decade of the 1970s went by, it once again became obvious that the new T-shaped highrise building was not enough. The older East Annexes were demolished, and work began on a new 31-story Imperial Tower.

This new Imperial Tower, which has guest rooms from the twentieth to thirty-first floors, a sauna and swimming pool on the nineteenth floor, and offices on the fifth to eighteenth floors, with a shopping plaza, meeting rooms, and other facilities on the lower floors, opened in March 1983.

With this latest tower, the Imperial is again in the forefront of Japan's most outstanding hotels. It is, in fact, much more than a hotel, being, in addition, a major business, recreation, and cultural complex.

The Imperial is 300 meters from the southeast corner of the Outer Moat of the Imperial Palace. It fronts on the city's major thoroughfare, and it is across the street from Hibiya Park, formerly the private garden of a *daimyo* feudal lord.

The philosophy that has made the Imperial Hotel what it is today was summed up once by an assistant sales manager. He said: "We do not work for money alone. We work for the satisfaction, the pleasure, and the pride that comes from doing better than just a good job and being accepted and trusted by our top management."

IMPERIAL PALACE / KYUJO (Que-joe)   Known as both the Chiyoda Castle and Edo Castle during the Tokugawa Period (1603–1868), the Imperial Palace is the centerpiece of Tokyo. Located in what is now Chiyoda Ward on the western edge of the downtown district, the Imperial Palace covers an area of 1,150,000 square meters. Its central portion is surrounded by a wide moat, a high pine-clad embankment, and stone walls.

The residence of the Tokugawa *shogun* for 265 years, the original Palace was circled by three wide moats. Now only the inner moat remains, and the grounds are secluded behind high stone walls atop the moat ramparts.

During the days of the shogunate, the castle consisted of the main area (Hon Maru), where the residence and staterooms of the *shogun* were located; the Western Keep (Nishi-no Maru), where the heir apparent lived; the Second Keep (Ni-no Maru); the Northern Keep (Kita-no Maru); and the Third Keep (San-no Maru).

During the reign of the Tokugawa *shogunate*, there were five great gates leading into the castle grounds—Sakurada Mon, Sakashita Mon, Ote Mon, Hirakawa Mon, and Hanzo Mon. Today, the main gate to the Palace grounds is on the east side, where there are two bridges, one of stone and one of steel, crossing the moat. These bridges are popularly called *Niju Bashi* (Nee-juu Bah-she), or Double Bridge. The parklike plaza in front of this entrance, called the Imperial Palace Plaza, is a popular place for office workers from the nearby Marunouchi financial and business district to eat box lunches and wile away the noon hour.

The palace buildings located in the Western Keep were burned down during World War II, and a new palace was built for the present emperor in 1968 in front of the site. While built of ferro-concrete, the new palace is traditional Japanese in style and has about 4,000 square meters of floor space.

There are two palaces within the grounds—the Fukiage Palace, where the emperor and empress live, and the New Palace, where public functions are held. The residence of the Crown Prince is also located within the palace grounds, as is the Imperial Household Agency.

The main entryway to the palace is Niju Bashi, which is used a few times a year by the emperor and by ambassadors, ministers, and other foreign guests calling on the emperor. Ordinary citizens are allowed to enter the Imperial grounds only on January 2, to extend New Year's congratulations to the emperor, and on the emperor's birthday.

The eastern half of the Imperial Palace grounds is taken up by a garden, the Kokyo Higashi Gyoen, or Imperial Palace East Garden, and is open to the public, except on Mondays and Fridays. The garden was remodeled from an old garden that was at the center of Chiyoda Castle.

IMPERIAL PALACE (DETACHED) / OHAMA GOTEN (Oh-hah-mah Go-ten) Now known as Hama Rikyu, the Imperial Detached Palace began in the early years of the Tokugawa Period as a preserve for falcons, and then became the site for a seaside villa built around 1650 by Tsuneshige Matsudaira, the Lord of Kofu.

In the early 1700s, Ienobu Tokugawa had the villa expanded, adding teahouses, a temple, a shrine, a duck preserve, and other attractions.

The first member of foreign royalty to be received by the Emperor of Japan, the Duke of Edinburgh, son of Queen Victoria, was housed in the Detached Palace in 1869. In 1879, ex-President Ulysses S. Grant also stayed at the Ohama Goten, where he had a long meeting with Emperor Meiji.

The Detached Palace was donated to Tokyo in 1945 and has been open to the public as a park since 1946. It is about a 10-minute walk from Shimbashi Station in Tokyo.

INCENSE BURNING / KOH-DO (Koe-doh) Incense burning as a religious ritual to calm the mind, expand the senses and achieve spiritual awareness developed in Japan soon after the introduction of Buddhism in the

sixth century. It very quickly became popular at the Imperial Court, and with the country's famous *samurai* warrior class after it rose to prominence in the tenth and eleventh centuries.

The aristocratic courtiers and nobles amused themselves by "listening to the fragrances" to help them create imaginary scenes for their poetry and plays. From the fourteenth century, warriors perfumed their helmets and armor with incense to create a mood of elegance and sophistication and to demonstrate their cultural achievements.

The popularity of incense appreciation reached its heyday in Japan during the seventeenth and eighteenth centuries, when it spread from the Court and *samurai* to the upper and middle classes.

Altogether, there are some 500 kinds of incense available in Japan, but usually only a few dozen of these are regularly used by *koh-do* devotees. Most of them are manufactured by Nippon Kodo, the country's leading incense stick-maker.

A full incense-burning ceremony lasts up to 90 minutes and includes "listening" to the various scents, as well as enjoying their aroma. Sometimes such ceremonies include contests in which the participants try to create literary themes related to the scents of two or more kinds of incense—a practice known as *kumi-koh* (kuu-me-koh).

The Oie-Ryu School of Incense Appreciation in Tokyo, currently headed by grand master Sanenori Sanjonishi, a nephew of the empress, is regarded as the center of the art.

INDUSTRIAL TOURS   One of the most practical and enjoyable ways of getting a good introduction to various aspects of Japan's business world is to take an industrial tour—something the Japanese have been offering to foreign businesspeople and regular tourists for decades.

There are regularly scheduled tours in Tokyo, Nagoya, Osaka, and other major cities. Several travel agencies, including the huge, national Japan Travel Bureau, handle such tours. In Tokyo, for example, there are two one-day tours each week, on Tuesdays and Fridays. They go to such places as a computer laboratory, a camera factory, and a distillery. The cost is minimal and includes lunch.

The Japanese companies that cooperate with the tours take them seriously and assign some of their best employees to brief visitors.

Many Japanese companies welcome industrial tours by consumers and business leaders as part of their overall public and community relations.

Tours of traditional handicraft industries have been popular since shortly after Japan opened its doors to trade in the 1850s. Tours of modern industrial factories date from the 1950s and have since been an important function of the travel industry in cooperation with business and the government.

Several organizations besides the Japan Travel Bureau, including the Tourist Information Centers of the Japan National Tourist Organization and the Trade and Tourist Sections of the Tokyo, Nagoya, and Osaka governments, conduct regular tours of factories and industrial sites.

Your travel agent can arrange such tours for you.

INLAND SEA / SETO NAIKAI (Say-toe Nie-kie)   The great body of water that separates the islands of Honshu, Shikoku, and Kyushu is called Seto Naikai, or the Sea Within Channels. Actually a chain of five small seas linked together, the Inland Sea is so beautiful that it has been described since ancient times as "A Sight Fit for the Eyes of a King."

The Inland Sea measures 64 kilometers at its widest point and 6.4 kilometers at its narrowest. The sea is shallow, seldom reaching more than 40 meters in depth. The Straits of Naruto, between Awaji and Shikoku islands, are notorious for their giant whirlpools caused by riptides.

The Inland Sea is dotted with jewel-like islands, and its heavily indented coastlines are ringed by pine trees and white-sand beaches. The larger islands in the sea are inhabited, and they are famous for various products, ranging from oranges, peaches, and olives, to granite.

The sea is noted for its marine life, and has been a favorite fishing area since the arrival of the first inhabitants. In the spring, sea bream, a favorite fish in Japan, enter the sea from the Pacific Ocean to spawn.

From time immemorial, the Inland Sea has played a vital role in the history of Japan not only as a source of food and as a waterway, but also as a source of spiritual contentment. It was designated a national park in 1934.

The two largest islands in the Seto Naikai are Awaji and Shodo. Awaji has an area of 593 square kilometers and is densely populated. Bunraku, Japan's traditional puppet theater, originated on this island. Shodo covers only 155.5 square kilometers and is best known for its olives, soy sauce, and quarries.

The scenic highlight on Shodo is known as Kankakei, or Cold and Misty Gorge, which is a serrated series of rocky peaks, two kilometers wide and eight kilometers long, in a valley that is filled with azaleas, and maple and pine trees and, in the fall, is one of the most colorful sights in Japan.

Recommended reading: *The Inland Sea*, by Donald Richie (Weatherhill).

INNS / RYOKAN (Rio-khan)　By 1700, Japan had a network of inns around the country that was unequaled in the world—the result of an edict by the Tokugawa Shogunate requiring all feudal lords to travel to its headquarters in Edo every other year and to bring a prescribed number of retainers with them. See PROCESSIONS OF THE LORDS.

There are still over 100,000 *ryokan* in Japan, of which over 2,000 are approved by the Ministry of Transportation as Tourist Inns—meaning that their facilities and standards are sufficiently high to meet the needs and expectations of most foreign visitors.

Ryokan are usually one- to three-story wooden structures that look very much like ordinary houses, but there are many ferro-concrete high rise structures in popular tourist resorts that are furnished and operated like inns (and called *ryokan*).

The distinguishing features of *ryokan* is that they are Japanese style—that is, they have *tatami* reed-mat floors, only Japanese-type furnishings—a low movable table, cushions for sitting, and *ofuton* (oh-fuu-tone) floormats for sleeping. They also have hot baths that guests share or take turns using and mostly Japanese-style meals served in the guests' rooms.

The atmosphere and service in the typical *ryokan* is family style—very personal and intimate—and visiting a *ryokan* is one of the best possible ways of getting acquainted with traditional Japanese-style living. Shoes are exchanged for house slippers at the *genkan* (gane-khan) entrance. The slippers are worn only in the passages and corridors—not inside the rooms. The dress of the day is the *yukata* (you-kah-tah), a light, *kimono*-style robe that is also used as a sleeping garment. One scrubs oneself outside the bathtub and gets in only after a thorough rinsing, to luxuriate in the hot water. All sitting is on the *tatami* floor (back supports are available in most *ryokan*).

Since most areas of Japan are cold in the winter, and the central and southern lowland areas are hot and humid in the summer, the visitor might want to choose a *ryokan* that has central heating or air-conditioning, depending on the season. In any event, they are meant to be enjoyed in a way that is not possible in a hotel.

For guests who do choose to stay in unheated *ryokan* in the winter, thickly padded *kimono* called *tanzen* (tahn-zen) or thick *kimono* coats called *dotera* (doe-tay-rah) are provided.

The Japan National Tourist Organization (JNTO) has free directories of the approved tourist *ryokan* in the country. See JNTO listing for addresses of its offices.

INTERNATIONAL CHRISTIAN UNIVERSITY (ICU)   Well known around the world, Tokyo's International Christian University (ICU) was founded in 1953 as a place to educate young people in Christian, as well as democratic, principles.

Near Mitaka Station on the Chuo Line west of Tokyo, ICU has the largest campus—119 hectares—of any university in Japan.

The school is particularly noted for its Japanese-language course, in which students study only the Japanese language for 8–10 hours a day for nine months. A number of well-known foreign scholars and linguists, including Professor Ray Moore and Leonard Welch, took their language training at ICU.

One prominent student at ICU during the 1960s was Jay Rockefeller.

INTERNATIONAL MARRIAGES / KOKUSAI KEKKON (Koke-sie keck-kone)   The Japanese refer to marriages between Japanese and foreigners, especially non-Asians, as international marriages and generally speaking, do not wholly approve of them.

The first marriages between Japanese and Westerners took place soon after the first Westerners arrived in Japan. The famous ships' pilot Will Adams, who was the model for Anjin-San in the novel and TV extravaganza *Shogun*, married a Japanese woman in the early 1600s. The famous writer Lafcadio Hearn, who arrived in Japan nearly 200 years later, also married a Japanese woman, and the list goes on.

The phenomenon that led to thousands of *kokusai kekkon* was the American and Allied Military Occupation of Japan from 1945 to 1952. Within two years after the Occupation began, the American and other foreign embassies in Tokyo were flooded with applications from members of the Occupation forces for marriage certificates.

Many of these romances began in bars and less savory places and involved young, uneducated, and unsophisticated GI's who did not speak Japanese and had no affinity or even appreciation of things Japanese, but were strongly attracted to their Japanese girlfriends.

At the same time, their prospective brides were often at the bottom of the social scale and were primarily seeking a way out of their terrible economic predicament caused by the war. The overall result was that the image of international marriages suffered a great deal.

By the late 1950s, East-West marriages in Japan had slowed down considerably, but the people involved were more likely to be middle class, and the relationships were more solidly based on mutual understanding and compatibility.

Up to this period, most international marriages had been between Western men and Japanese women. Then the percentage of marriages between Japanese men and Western women began to rise and in 1975 exceeded the number of Western men-Japanese women marriages—a trend that has since continued. At present, approximately 70 percent of all international marriages in Japan involve Japanese men and foreign women.

A particularly noticeable trend was the increase in the number of Japanese businessmen returning with foreign wives after periods of working abroad. In 1965, American men made up 51 percent of the foreign husbands marrying Japanese women. That has dropped to around 20 percent. Korean men now account for 55 percent of the foreign husbands involved in international marriages in Japan each year.

A high percentage of the East-West marriages that took place in Japan in the late 1940s and early 1950s failed for obvious reasons—especially when the groom took his new, non-English-speaking, still very Japanese bride home with him.

The success rate of such marriages in later years is as good as, if not better than, typical marriages in most Western countries, despite basic cultural differences that are often extreme.

Western women who marry Japanese men generally have the most difficult time adapting to these cultural differences—unless the man has become very Westernized and behaves toward her in the manner to which she is accustomed, in which case it is not really an East-West marriage. See ASSOCIATIONS OF FOREIGN WIVES.

The most interesting and promising results of the many East-West marriages are the children of mixed-blood parentage. They are very special. Usually bilingual, often beautiful, they have a remarkable sensitivity to cross-cultural and racial problems that can make them valuable bridges between the two different cultures.

INTRODUCTIONS / SHOKAIJO (Sho-kie-joe)   The age-old customs that control relationships among Japanese, whether they are personal or business, make introductions very important. Their importance derives from the fact that Japanese society is based on groupings that are exclusive and not open to casual entry by outsiders.

It is therefore vital to the Japanese that they know as much as possible about anyone they meet as quickly as possible because they do not automatically accept people at face value. An introduction from someone they know helps span this otherwise formidable barrier.

Generally, the only way one can get into a particular group (of whatever kind) is to enter it at the bottom in a formal, institutionalized way. The only acceptable way to deal with a group as an outsider is through an introduction that not only identifies you, but, in effect, acts as a guarantee of your character and reliability.

Japanese groups, as well as individual Japanese, are automatically wary of strangers who come to them without credentials or without an introduction from a mutual friend or business contact.

In business, the more important the potential relationship, the more vital it is that a visitor approach a Japanese company with an effective introduction—meaning one that comes from someone or some other group well known to and respected by the Japanese company concerned.

See *Japanese Etiquette and Ethics in Business*, by Boye Lafayette De Mente (Passport Books).

IRON AND STEEL   Beginning almost at zero in 1945, Japan's iron and steel industry produced a total of 119 million tons in 1973, making Japan one of the top steel manufacturers in the world.

Several factors played a vital role in the growth of Japan's iron and steel industry, including the rapid introduction of the latest technology, huge investments in plants and facilities, and the corresponding expansion of the country's domestic economy and export industries.

Most of the iron ore Japan uses comes from Australia, Brazil, and India. Most of the coal it uses in the industry comes from Australia, the U.S., and Canada.

Japan's top five integrated steel manufacturers are Nippon Steel Corporation (the world's largest steel maker), Nippon Kokan, Kawasaki Steel Corporation, Sumitomo Metal Industries, and Kobe Steel.

ISE-SHIMA NATIONAL PARK (E-say she-mah)   The Ise-Shima National Park, which takes up a large portion of the Ise and Shima districts at the south end of Mie Prefecture, is primarily a sea park, with some of the most gorgeous seascapes in the world, but it is most famous for the Ise Jingu Shrines and Pearl Island in Toba Bay. (See PEARL ISLAND and GRAND SHRINES OF ISE.)

The best of the seascapes are in and around the bays of Matoba, Ago, Gokasho and the Kumano Nada Sea, which are bejeweled with dozens of pine-clad islets and whose shores are thick with a variety of subtropical plants.

ISHIKAWA, GOEMON (E-she-kah-wah, Go-eh-moan)   A robber chief who lived in the sixteenth century and became a folk hero because of his practice of helping common people in their struggle with oppressive *daimyo* and ruthless *samurai*, Goemon Ishikawa is often referred to as the Robin Hood of Japan.

Geomon's life did not have a happy ending, however. Reputedly hired by Hidetsugu, the nephew of Hideyoshi Toyotomi, to assassinate the latter (who was then the supreme military power in Japan), Goemon was caught and boiled to death in a cauldron of oil when he was 37 years old.

Even today, bathtubs that have iron bottoms and are heated from beneath are often referred to as *Goemon-buro*, or "Goemon baths."

ITO (E-toe)   On Izu Peninsula, 16.9 kilometers south of the famous hot springs resort city of Atami, Ito is also a noted seaside spa, with dozens of *ryokan* featuring hot spring mineral baths. Ito is also a port for ferry boats going to and from the volcanic island of Oshima in Tokyo Bay.

IZU PENINSULA (E-zoo)   Extending deep into the Pacific Ocean from the curved coastline of Honshu, south of the Tokyo area, Izu Peninsula (originally called Yu Izu, or Hot Water), is like something out of a travel brochure — unbelieveably beautiful coastlines indented by hundreds of tiny coves and ringed by picturesque islets, tree-covered mountains and hills; gorges and ravines traversed by swift-flowing streams, and over two thousand hot springs.

Among the most famous hot spring resorts on Izu Peninsula are the cities of Atami, Shuzenji, Nagaoka, Ito, and Atagawa, along with Inatori Spa, Imaihama Spa, Yatsu, Mine, Yugano, and Rendaiji, to name just a few. The spas are categorized according to their mineral content. One at Yoshina is famous for helping make barren women fertile.

Noted spots on the peninsula are Ito, where Anjin (Pilot) Will Adams built what is believed to have been Japan's first oceangoing vessel for the first Tokugawa *Shogun*; Shimoda, where the U.S.'s first envoy to Japan, Townsend Harris, lived for 15 months; Kawana, which boasts one of Japan's most popular golf courses; and Shuzen Temple, founded by the famous priest Kobo Daishi between 806 and 810.

Among the famous incidents that took place at the temple are the imprisonment there and subsequent murder of Noriyori Minamoto by his elder brother Yoritomo Minamoto (who founded Japan's first shogunate at Kamakura), and the assassination in 1215 of Yoritomo's son, Yoriie, by Tokimasa Hojo, who then seized power from the Minamoto clan.

There are numerous other historical places on the peninsula, including a memorial to Townsend Harris at Gyokusen Temple, where he first lived, just outside of the village of Shimoda.

Okichigafuchi Cliff, near Shimoda, at the tip-end of the peninsula, has a dubious claim to fame. It is recorded that after Harris left the area and moved to Tokyo, Okichi, the ex-*geisha* who had been given to him as a maid (or as a mistress, according to some authorities) committed suicide by throwing herself onto the rocks below. Having associated intimately with a foreigner, she was an outcast with no place to go.

Train and bus lines from the Tokyo and Yokohama area make the hot spring spas, historical sites, and picturesque beaches of the Izu Peninsula easily accessible to large numbers of vacationers, and its mild winter climate assures its popularity all year round.

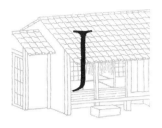

JAPAN / NIPPON (Neep-pone)   The word Japan is believed to have derived from the English pronunciation of the Chinese word *jipen*, which in Chinese is written with ideographs meaning "source of the sun." In Japanese, these characters are pronounced *nippon* (neep-pone) or *nihon* (nee-hone) and have the same meaning as they do in Chinese—thus, the use of the sun as the symbol of Japan.

Other sources credit the seventh century's famed Prince Shotoku with using Nippon (Place From Where the Sun Rises) as the name of the country in a letter sent to China. The northern Chinese called Japan *Jihpenkuo*, and some believe the English word Japan came from Portuguese attempts to pronounce this word. In early Portuguese literature, it appears variously as Zipangu and Jipangu. The southern Chinese called Japan *Yatpun*, and the Dutch pronunciation of this word closely resembles the word Japan.

Until 200,000 years ago, Japan was not entirely a chain of islands. It was connected to Siberia in the north and to Korea in the south. There is also evidence to indicate that even earlier it was connected to the Philippines and to Java, and the Sea of Japan was a huge lake.

Fossils of elephants from India, mammoths from Siberia, as well as lions and leopards, have been found in Japan. The oldest human remains found in the country also date back that far.

In addition to the four main islands of Hokkaido, Honshu, Shikoku, and Kyushu, Japan has 3,918 smaller islands, with a combined total area of 337,682 square kilometers, which makes it a little larger than Norway, Italy, or Malaysia, and a little smaller than Iraq, or Morocco.

Honshu (Hone-shuu), the largest island, is divided into five regions known as Tohoku (Toe-hoe-kuu), the northern portion of the island; Kanto

249

(Khan-toe), the Tokyo-Yokohama area; Chubu (Chuu-buu), the Nagoya plain and adjoining area; Kinki (Keen-kee), the Kyoto-Osaka-Kobe area; and Chugoku (Chuu-go-kuu), the southwestern area.

Administratively, the country consists of 47 prefectures, of which Hokkaido is one. The Tohoku district includes the prefectures of Aomori, Akita, Iwate, Yamagata, Miyagi, and Fukushima. The Kanto region consists of Ibaragi, Tochigi, Gunma, Saitama, Chiba, Tokyo, and Kanagawa prefectures.

The Chubu region is made up of Shizuoka, Yamanashi, Nagano, Niigata, Toyama, Ishikawa, Fukui, Gifu, and Aichi prefectures. Kinki consists of Mie, Shiga, Kyoto, Nara, Osaka, Wakayama, and Hyogo prefectures.

Chugoku is made up of Tottori, Okayama, Hiroshima, Shimane, and Yamaguchi prefectures. The island of Shikoku is divided into four prefectures: Kagawa, Tokushima, Kochi, and Ehime. And Kyushu has eight prefectures: Fukuoka, Saga, Nagasaki, Kumamoto, Oita, Miyazaki, Kagoshima, and Okinawa (which is a separate island 360 miles south of the tip of Kagoshima).

Topographically, 71 percent of Japan is mountainous, with the remainder made up of basins and plains. The long chain of mountains that traverses Japan from the north to the south divides the country into two distinct regions —one facing the Japan Sea to the west, and the other facing the Pacific Ocean to the east.

The Pacific Ocean side—which has the largest plains and is the most densely populated—has one of the most irregular shorelines in the world, with many large bays, thousands of inlets, and numerous offshore islets. There are only a few sandy beaches on the Pacific side of Japan.

The Japan Sea coast side on the west, which has higher and rougher waves, is less irregular and has a larger number of sandy beaches. See MOUNTAINS; DISTRICTS OF JAPAN.

JAPAN ACADEMY   The Japan Academy, formerly known as the Imperial Academy, is an honorary organization made up of a maximum of 150 members who have been recognized for making distinguished contributions to the arts and sciences. Members are voted into the Academy by organizations of their peers.

JAPAN AIR LINES / NIHON KOKU (Nee-hone koh-kuu)   The visitor heading for Japan may begin to enjoy some of the pleasures and the ambience of the country while still halfway around the world simply by flying Japan Air Lines (JAL), the nation's flag carrier.

Each of JAL's planes is a microcosm of the subdued charm and seductiveness that characterizes Japanese culture. This special quality, from the meticulous hospitality extended to guests to the attractive young cabin attendants who epitomize the traditional etiquette for which the Japanese are famous, is in fact the hallmark of Japan Air Lines.

Japan Air Lines was founded in 1951 while the post–World War II military occupation of the country was still in progress. It began with one leased aircraft that was operated by crews from Northwest Airlines.

Later that same year, the fledgling company introduced its own planes and Japanese crews. Two years later, the company was reorganized under the Japan Air Lines Law, which gave the government 50 percent ownership in the airline.

Over the next 30 years, Japan Air Lines grew to be one of the largest airlines in the world, serving over 30 countries around the world and winning numerous awards for reliability and service.

JAL, as the airline is popularly known, pioneered special services for business travelers in the early 1970s, introducing its Executive Service in 1973.

Among the services offered to executives under this program was the printing of bilingual business cards and a number of books and booklets designed to help them do business in and enjoy Japan and the Orient.

In addition to a number of guide and reference books, JAL also has both Japanese and Chinese language cassettes available at minimal cost. Another special service JAL offers to regular executive travelers is membership in its Global Club and the use of private Sakura Lounges in airports around the world.

JAPAN ALPS   The name Japan Alps has been given to three lofty mountain ranges that extend north to southwest through the central part of the main island of Honshu. Except for Mt. Fuji, all of Japan's highest mountains are in these three ranges—which are divided into the Southern, Central, and Northern Alps.

The name Japan Alps was first used in 1881 by William Garland, an English mining engineer who worked on the Osaka Mint. It was then popularized by a book called *Mountaineering and Exploration in the Japan Alps*, written by the Rev. Walter Weston in 1896.

The proper Japanese names for these mountain ranges are, from the north, Hida (He-dah), Kiso (Kee-so), and Akaishi (Ah-kie-she).

The Japan Alps National Park, regarded as the foremost mountain park in the country, encompasses all the major peaks in the Hida range and extends into the four prefectures of Nagano, Gifu, Toyama, and Niigata.

JAPAN ART ACADEMY   The Japan Art Academy (JAA), formerly the Imperial Art Academy, is an honorary organization with a maximum of 120 members. Members of the JAA receive annuities in recognition of their work and contributions to art.

JAPAN ASIA AIRWAYS   In 1974, Japan Air Lines began taking steps to establish service to the People's Republic of China, as a result of which Taiwan revoked JAL's right to serve that market. Following negotiations, Taipei agreed to allow another Japanese airline to reestablish service to the island.

Both All Nippon Airways and Toa Domestic Airlines applied to provide the service to Taiwan, but ultimately the franchise was awarded to Japan Asia Airways (JAA), a wholly owned subsidiary of Japan Air Lines, set up for that purpose. JAA began its service to Taiwan in September 1975.

JAPAN AUTOMOTIVE NEWS   The trade journal of Japan's automobile industry, the monthly *Japan Automotive News* covers new product and service news, industry trends, and statistics, plus political developments. It is published by Automotive Herald Co., Ltd. See OTHER SOURCES.

JAPAN BRIDGE / NIHONBASHI   (Nee-hone bah-she) In the center of Tokyo, in one of the leading financial districts of the city, the Japan Bridge was built in 1603, the year Ieyasu Tokugawa took over the country as *shogun*. When the bridge was built, the river it spans was much wider than it is now, the water was clear, tall pine trees lined both sides, and the third Tokugawa *Shogun*, Iemitsu, used to go swimming in it when he was a boy.

A year after the bridge was built, the shogunate officially designated it as the point from which all distances in the country would be measured, and a stone was erected on the spot to mark the center of the country. Immediately thereafter, milestones (*ichirizuka*) were placed at one-*ri* intervals along all of the main roads in the country. (A *ri* (ree) equals about two and a half miles.)

Nihon Bashi quickly developed into the business and public center of Edo. All journeys started from the bridge. All public notices were posted there, and criminals were put on display there as part of their punishment.

In more modern times, an iron post was inserted into the ground near the north end of the bridge to mark the point from which all distances were measured during the Tokugawa Period.

This area, now called Nihonbashi, was once called Muromachi 1-chome, and a nearby area was called Anjin-cho, after the English pilot Will Adams, who lived there during the early, exciting days of the Tokugawa Shogunate, when he was under the direct patronage of the *shogun*.

A monument erected on the spot in 1930 reads: "In memory of William Adams, known as Miura Anjin, the first Englishman to settle in Japan, coming as a pilot on board the *Charity* in 1600, who resided in a mansion built on this spot, who instructed Ieyasu, the first Tokugawa shogun, on gunnery, geography, mathematics, etc., rendering valuable service in foreign affairs, and who married a Japanese lady, Miss Magome, and died on May 16, 1620, at the age of 66 years."

The Japan Bridge, at which so much of the pageantry and drama of the extraordinary Tokugawa era began, now has an expressway running over it. The main thoroughfare that links Shimbashi, the famous Ginza, Kyobashi and Nihonbashi crosses over the bridge, and three of Tokyo's leading department stores (Tokyu, Takashimaya, and Maruzen) are nearby.

JAPAN CHAMBER OF COMMERCE & INDUSTRY / NIHON SHOKO KAIGISHO (Nee-hone Show-koe Kie-ghee-show)   The Japanese Chamber of Commerce & Industry (JCCI) is one of Japan's most important business organizations. It serves to coordinate the interests of the business community and also acts as one of several key bridges between industry and government.

The president and other principal officers of the JCCI are always top business leaders in the country, giving it considerable clout.

The Chamber engages in a wide range of ongoing research in trade and industry, sponsors workshops and seminars, and maintains a large publishing division. One of its publications that is of special interest to the foreign business community is the English-language monthly, *Japan Commerce and Industry (JCI)*.

JCI conducts in-depth studies on Japan's business system, the various industries, and other matters relating to management, manufacturing, labor, and trade.

The Japan Chamber of Commerce & Industry is headquartered at 2-2 Marunouchi, 3-chome, Chiyoda-ku, Tokyo 100, Japan (across from the Imperial Palace).

JAPAN ECONOMIC JOURNAL / NIHON KEIZAI SHIMBUN (Nee-hone Kay-e-zie Shim-boon)   The *Nihon Keizai Shimbun* is Japan's leading business newspaper, similar to the *Wall Street Journal* but with a larger circulation. A weekly edition of the paper is published in English.

The newspaper was founded as a weekly in 1876 and became a daily in 1885. An evening edition was added in 1925. In 1969, the newspaper's publisher, Nikkei, established a joint venture with McGraw-Hill of the U.S. (Nikkei-McGraw-Hill, Inc.). It opened its own news bureau in the U.S. in 1970.

Nikkei is now an economic information systems conglomerate, printing newspapers, newsletters, magazines, and books; providing computer data bank services; broadcasting on both radio and television; conducting marketing and cultural research; and staging exhibitions and seminars.

The company employs over 3,500 people and has offices around the world.

JAPAN ENGLISH BOOKS IN PRINT   A catalogue of some 3,000 English-language books published in Japan, the *Japan English Books in Print*, is the most comprehensive directory of its type. Each book is listed by title, author, subject, and publisher. The catalogue also includes a list of some 600 booksellers and subscription agencies outside Japan that deal in books imported from Asia, along with some 100 Japanese publishing houses that buy Japanese language rights to books.

The catalogue is published by Intercontinental Marketing Corporation, C.P.O. Box 971, Tokyo 100-91 Japan. The same company also publishes a catalogue of English-language magazines produced in Japan (*Japan English Magazine Directory*).

JAPANESE FOOD   Japanese cuisine is distinctive in its own right, having been developed within the islands over thousands of years. For close to 2,000 years, it centered on seafood, vegetables, and rice. (Meat was a fairly common staple in the Japanese diet before the introduction of Buddhism in the fifth and sixth centuries but was then almost totally eliminated on religious grounds.)

It is the preparation, of course, that makes traditional Japanese food unique. The first principle is that the ingredients should retain their natural appearance and taste as much as possible. The second is that they should be compatible with rice and *sake*.

In traditionally prepared dishes, therefore, most Japanese foods are raw, pickled, boiled, or grilled. When seasonings are used, the primary aim is to enhance the natural flavor of the food.

Another important factor in Japanese cuisine was—and still is—in the preparation. Great care is taken to see that the food items harmonize in shape, size, and color.

See individual listings for such dishes as SUSHI; SASHIMI; SUKIYAKI; TEMPURA; UDON; and SOBA. Also see RESTAURANTS.

Recommended reading: *Japanese Cooking: A Simple Art*, by Shizuo Tsuji (Kodansha International). Also *The Book of Tofu* and *The Book of Miso*, both by William Shurtleff and Akiko Aoyagi (Ten Speed Press).

JAPANESE HOUSES / NIHON NO IE (Nee-hone no e-eh)   The traditional Japanese house is a masterpiece of compromise with nature. The houses are usually small, built on raised footings so the air will circulate beneath them, and constructed of wood, plaster, and paper.

Floors consist of straw mats called *tatami* (tah-tah-me), which measure three feet by six feet and are two and a half inches thick. (These measurements differ somewhat in western Japan.) Rooms are constructed and measured according to this *tatami* size—a 4-mat room, 6-mat room, 8-mat room, and so on.

Rooms are separated by thick sliding panels called *fusuma* (fuu-sue-mah), made of paper over wooden frames, or by *shoji* (show-jee), very thin squares of rice paper pasted over latticed wooden panels. Nowadays, sliding glass doors provide access to any garden.

For protection against inclement weather, all windows and outside glass doors have sliding wooden doors called *amado* (ah-mah-doe), which cover them from the outside.

There is a *genkan* (gain-khan) entryway at the front of each house, where one removes shoes (and raincoats) before stepping up on a polished wooden landing.

The main room in a Japanese house invariably has a *tokonoma* (toe-koe-no-mah), a recessed alcove designed for the display of art, flowers, or hanging scrolls called *kakemono* (kah-key-moe-no).

Furnishings are sparse in a traditional Japanese room. During the day, the main room typically has little more than a low table and sitting cushions, or *zabuton* (zah-buu-tone). Other rooms usually have chests of drawers and a dresser, along with a few other personal items.

Today, all rooms in Japanese homes tend to be jam-packed with television sets, stereos, and numerous other possessions.

Traditionally styled Japanese houses tend to be very drafty, and, except when it is raining or the wind is blowing hard, the windows are usually opened during the day to help prevent mildew from the humidity. Heating is provided by kerosene, propane gas, and electric space heaters.

Many homes also have a *kotatsu* (koe-tot-sue), which is a bathtub-size pit in the floor in the center of the main, or family, room. A table, covered by a heavy cloth or quilt that drapes to the floor on all sides, stands over the *kotatsu*.

In winter, members of the family and visitors sit around the table, with their feet dangling into the pit beneath, with the table cover draped over their laps to keep them warm.

In earlier days, charcoal-burning *hibachi* (he-bah-chee) were put in the *kotatsu* to warm them up. Nowadays specially designed electric heaters are used—making a very cozy and intimate place for people to gather, sip hot tea, read, talk, or watch TV.

Japanese who live in traditional houses or apartments with *tatami* reed-mat floors generally sleep on the floor on layers of thin mattresses called *futon* (fuu-tone). The futon are kept in closets during the day (except when airing outside) and are spread out at night, when needed. This way, rooms are used for various other purposes during the day and can be converted into bedrooms within seconds at night—accommodating several people when necessary.

Virtually all houses and apartments built in Japan since the 1960s have been totally or partly Western in style.

JAPANESE LANGUAGE / NIHONGO (Nee-hone-go)   The Japanese language appears to be a mixture of the Altaic languages of northern Asia and the Malaysian-Indonesian-Polynesian languages of Southeast Asia.

In Japanese, there is no difference between singular and plural. There is no gender. There are no definite or indefinite articles. Changes in order are expressed by postpositional particles. Adjectives and adverbs are placed in front of nouns and verbs, and the normal grammatical order is subject, object, verb.

Present-day Japanese is based on five vowels (ah, ee, uu, eh, oh) and one additional sound, n. Words are made up of syllables that are always open—they never end in consonants—which is why the Japanese have difficulty pronouncing English.

There are numerous words in Japanese that have virtually the same pronunciation but different meanings, which often cause problems. It is sometimes necessary even for the Japanese to write out the *kanji* character for a particular sound to clarify their meaning.

A survey of 90 publications by the National Language Institute in 1956 revealed that 30,000 words were used, and that, of these, Chinese words accounted for 48 percent, Japanese words for 37 percent, and foreign words for 10 percent. The rest were mixtures of different languages.

It is now estimated that words adopted from Western languages, primarily English, make up around 20 percent of the words used by the Japanese. The Japanese language is changing so rapidly that some things written less than a 100 years ago cannot be read and understood even by educated people.

The Japanese often say their language is not a tool for transmitting clear, concise thoughts. They say words are containers for transporting feelings that cannot be expressed by words.

There are four ways of writing Japanese—the complicated Chinese ideograms called *kanji* (kahn-jee), the two *kana* (kah-nah) syllabaries called *hiragana* (he-rah-gah-nah) and *katakana* (kah-tah-kah-nah), and Roman letters, or *Roma ji* (Roe-mah jee).

The two *kana* syllabaries were derived from the *kanji* Chinese characters —*katakana* from the radical or component parts of *kanji*, and *hiragana* from the characters themselves. Kibi-no Makibi, an eighth-century scholar-statesman is credited with having invented the *katakana* way of writing Japanese, possibly as a result of having studied Sanskrit.

In addition to being used to transcribe most of the foreign words written in Japanese, in earlier times *katakana* were also always used for sending Japanese-language telegrams.

The first Japanese-language word processor was introduced in 1978 by Toshiba. Now 30 of the top electronic manufacturers produce word processors for the domestic market.

Recommended study: *The Japanese Language* by Haruhiko Kindaichi, translated by Umeyo Hirano (Tuttle); *Japanese Made Easy*, by Tazuko Ajiro Monane (Tuttle); *A Japanese Reader*, by Roy Andrew Miller (Tuttle); and *Japanese in Action*, by Jack Seward (Weatherhill).

JAPANESE PEOPLE/NIHON-JIN (Nee-hone-jeen)   The people of Japan do not all look alike, despite this frequent complaint by visitors from abroad.

Most Japanese have black or dark auburn hair. Nearly all of them have black or dark brown eyes. Most have the same or similar skin coloring, and most are primarily of Mongolian descent.

But within these general guidelines, the facial features of the Japanese are all different, all unique, and all distinguishable. What bothers Western newcomers to Japan is that they have been conditioned to distinguish people on the basis of far wider differences—in hair, eye, and skin color, in body size, and in extraordinary extremes in individual facial features.

It takes anywhere from a few hours to a few days or weeks for newcomers to learn how to pay attention to the finer differences that distinguish the Japanese.

There are, in fact, distinct regional differences in the Japanese—in their height, skin coloring, and overall appearance. People from the south tend to be shorter and darker and to show signs of Southeast Asian influence. Those from the north tend to be taller and lighter skinned. Some of these differences are environmental. Others are racial.

Particularly in northern Honshu and Hokkaido, there is substantial evidence of mixing between the Japanese and the Caucasian Ainu, who inhabited the northern and eastern portions of the island chain when the Mongolian Japanese arrived. See AINU.

But racially speaking, the Japanese are far less mixed than Americans and many other Westerners.

In the cultural area, the Japanese are among the most homogenized people on earth. Living on relatively small islands that were isolated from the rest of the world for most of their history, having a common religious heritage, and having been conditioned by the same economic, social, and political systems for many generations, the Japanese—despite many substantial differences—are more alike than the people of any other major nation.

There are strong linguistic differences in various regions of Japan. Some of the regional dialects are close to being separate languages. But all Japanese today also understand and are able to speak what is called standard Japanese.

The Japanese are inscrutable only to those people who don't speak their language or understand their beliefs and customs. Being a thoroughly homogenized people, the Japanese behave in a more institutionalized and predictable way than most Westerners.

Problems arise simply because of lack of knowledge and ability to communicate and because of the inherent differences in the way Japanese and others approach things. The solution to these problems is equally obvious.

On a personal level, the Japanese are among the world's most likable people. They are famous for their kindness, politeness, and goodwill. There is something special about the Japanese and their culture that attracts many Westerners like a magnet.

This special appeal is a combination of the character and customs of the people, the distinctive food, the traditional dress, the Japanese style of living, the arts and crafts, and so on. But I have also known dozens of Westerners who did not appreciate any of these characteristics and yet stayed on in Japan for many years, unwilling to leave, despite their many dislikes.

While it would be easy to dismiss this particular group as being attracted to Japan only because of the cultural emphasis on sex and the sexual permissiveness in which they are able to participate, this would not be the whole truth and would be unfair to both my friends and acquaintances, as well as the Japanese.

For there is actually a great deal more than sexual pleasures involved in the relationships these people have with Japan, and one way or another, it can be traced to the traditional character, personality, and manners of the people.

Recommended reading: *Exotic Japan—The Land, the Climate, the People, the Pleasures*, by Boye Lafayette De Mente (Phoenix Books); *Introducing Japan*, by Donald Richie (Kodansha International); *The Inland Sea*, by Donald Richie (Weatherhill); *The Japanese*, by Jack Seward (Lotus Press); and *More about The Japanese*, by Jack Seward (Lotus Press).

JAPANESE SOCIETY / NIHON SHAKAI (Nee-hone shah-kie)   The key to understanding Japanese society and understanding and dealing with individual Japanese lies in understanding the vertical nature of the society, says social anthropologist Dr. Chie Nakane.

By vertical society, Dr. Nakane is referring to the inferior-superior structure of Japanese society—all people fall into a specific lower-higher relationship with everyone else, based on their sex, age, schooling, employment, family, and so on.

And, Dr. Nakane continues, it is this relationship that controls or colors the functioning of Japanese society in all areas—in basic behavior, in language use, and in conducting social and business matters.

Superimposed over this vertical structure of Japanese society is an overwhelming tendency to form groups or cliques that are exclusive and take precedence over the individual. These groups encompass virtually every area of Japanese life, but are of particular importance in business and the professions.

Anyone who is not a member of one of these groups is an outsider and cannot deal with the individual members of the group as if they were individuals. Responsibility within many of these groups, especially in a company setting, is collective.

With the grouping system in Japan, all members are ranked (the higher-lower principle), whether they are people, companies, or things. The privileges, rights, and responsibilities of the individuals within these groupings are determined by their rank in relation to everyone else.

Meeting and dealing effectively with one of these groups (and individuals within the groups) requires a considerable amount of knowledge of their makeup and psychology, along with experience in the kinds of behavior that are acceptable.

While individual competition within groups is taboo, the groups compete fiercely against each other—which is the reason you find little or no contact between different Japanese professional groups that are in the same field.

The overwhelming drive within every group within Japanese society is to be as self-sufficient as possible—not to have to depend on outsiders. This syndrome is especially obvious in Japanese companies.

Recommended reading: *Japanese Society*, by Chie Nakane (University of California Press); *Japanese Etiquette and Ethics in Business*, by Boye Lafayette De Mente (Passport Books); *The Japanese;* and *More about the Japanese*, by Jack Seward (Lotus Press).

JAPANESE TYPEWRITERS   At first sight, early Japanese-language typewriters are apt to remind one of a very simple, tiny printing press, which is basically what they are. The first such typewriter was invented in 1915.

The typewriter consists of a tray of some 3,000 metal *kanji*, *hiragana*, and *katakana* characters, a scanner, a hand lever, and a roller or platten. The desired character must first be located in the tray or on a scanning plate, the hand-lever moved into a position over the character, and then the lever pressed, as a result of which the character is picked up and slammed against the roller.

Typing on a Japanese-style typewriter is thus a laborious and time-consuming chore, and this is one of the reasons why typing letters and documents has been the exception rather than the rule in Japan. Generally, only official documents and business papers were typed in this manner.

Nowadays word processors capable of writing in Japanese are common, and there are also modern-style typewriters in use in virtually all companies.

In 1984, Brother Industries introduced a word-processor-typewriter that will instantly convert Romanized Japanese (*Romaji*) into *kanji* (Chinese) ideographs, with which the language is normally written. The only catch at this point is that you have to specify the *kanji* you want. It is then automatically written out for you. The machine has a *kanji* vocabulary of 2,965 characters.

This first *Romaji-Into-Kanji* typewriter also writes the two syllabic scripts, *hiragana* and *katakana*. The word processor is called Picoword, and weighs 2.7 kilograms.

Canon, the camera company, earlier introduced an electronic *kanji* dictionary, which takes some of the drudgery out of learning the *kanji*. Computers with *kanji* ability were commonplace in Japan by the early 1990s.

JAPANESE WOMEN / NIHON-NO ONNA (Nee-hone-no own-nah) Foreign men in Japan often comment that Japanese women and Japanese men seem to belong to different cultural groups, so great is the difference in their attitudes and behavior.

In Japan, women were considered more or less traditionally to be "property." They had practically no legal rights and were regularly married off, abandoned, or divorced to suit the convenience and caprice of men.

During the long Tokugawa era (1603–1868), a popular saying was "*Danson johi*" ("Respect the male; despise the female").

Four years after the fall of the Tokugawa Shogunate, the Japanese government opened the Tokyo Girls' School, but closed it five years later because of opposition from men who did not like the idea of women being educated.

Later schools established by Western missionaries were also attacked for "introducing the idea of romance" into Japan. Romantic behavior between men and women was considered licentious and destructive to the family system.

The traditional family system in Japan remained in full sway from 1868 until 1945, and women were a major component of the cheap labor force that helped Japan become industrialized in the early decades of this period.

The feudal family system was abolished following the ending of World War II, on orders from the Allied forces occupying Japan. Japanese women voted in a Diet (Parliament) election for the first time on April 10, 1946.

With the exception of gaining voting rights, the world of Japanese women was slow to change, however, and once again they played a leading role as cheap labor in the rebirth of Japan following the devastation of World War II.

Outside the economic sphere, the progress Japanese women made in the years immediately following abolition of the old family system was considerable. They began flocking to schools by the hundreds of thousands. They began dating and marrying husbands of their own choice.

By the 1960s, with the exception of the economic area, Japanese women were almost totally free of the old feudal constraints that had bound them for ages. In the workplace, however, there were and still are various barriers that prevent them from being able to take full advantage of their legal rights and their education.

In general, a young woman goes to work immediately after graduating from high school or college at a salary well below that of her male co-workers. She is often expected to perform various maid or waitress functions and to do basic clerical work for several years. When she marries, many companies, especially larger ones, expect (or require) her to quit work.

As of 1995, approximately 65 percent of the female work force in Japan was married—but over 20 percent of this figure consisted of part-time workers who did not qualify for the benefits of full-time employment and could be let go at any time.

Beginning as early as the 1960s, there have been a growing number of examples of breakthroughs by women, some founding their own companies and others joining the lower ranks of male executives, but the numbers are still very small.

Women comprise over 40 percent of the work force in Japan, but their salaries amount to only 53 percent of what men get, and there are still many companies that will not hire female college graduates because "they are overeducated for the jobs open to them."

In 1980, Japan signed the U.N. treaty that guarantees equal rights for women, but it will surely be several decades, if not longer, before women are actually treated even half equal to men in the world of Japanese business.

The primary male stronghold is that of marketing, where women simply are not accepted—in part because marketing in Japan is closely tied in with the nighttime entertainment business, where female company employees are not welcome.

For the most part, Japanese men find it difficult to conceive of dealing with women on a high executive level, and it will be a long time before this conditioned response disappears.

Some Japanese women prefer to work for foreign-operated companies in Japan, because they find less discrimination and more opportunity for advancement.

Many Japanese men rationalize the position of women by saying that their primary duty is to have children and make a home for them. Most Japanese husbands turn their paycheck over to their wives and let them handle all household and family expenditures other than their lunch and pocket money, which they get in the form of an allowance. They frequently point to this custom as proof that Japanese women are on a par with men.

A trend that was already significant by the early 1980s was the number of middle-aged women, their children married and gone, who were anxious to go back to work, but were unsuccessful in their attempts to find employment or were relegated to part-time, low-paying jobs. Large numbers of these women have no choice but to take up some cultural hobby that also provides a social outlet.

There are now numerous "culture centers" catering to this segment of the female population in Japan. Just one of them, The Asahi Culture Center (founded by the giant *Asahi Newspaper*), has an enrollment in excess of 65,000 at its two branches in Tokyo and Yokohama.

There is an expanding body of literature aimed at this age group of Japanese women. One such book, *Wives in the Autumn of Life*, by journalist Shigeo Saito, was a best-seller.

Outside of the workplace, Japanese men consider Japanese women the best wives and mothers in the world and take special pride in their attributes of femininity, sincerity, loyalty, patience, and willingness to work hard.

Not surprisingly, Japanese wives are becoming less and less subservient to their husbands. Some of them are going out at night, rather than sit at home and wait for their husbands to return from their company drinking sprees. There are a growing number of clubs and other places catering especially to women whose husbands are out of town on company business or involved in company affairs until late at night.

The divorce rate in Japan is growing rather rapidly and is approaching that of France and other European countries. Most divorce actions are initiated by the wives. One indication of the changing attitude of Japanese women is the term *sodai*, which some of them use to describe their husbands. The word means something like "big trash."

In mid-1985, the Japanese Diet passed a law mandating that women are to be given equal consideration and treatment in hiring, pay, and promotions, but no one expects the law to be followed or enforced within this generation.

JAPAN FOLKCRAFT MUSEUM / NIHON MINGEI KAN (Nee-hone Meen-gay-e Khan)   A short walk from Komaba Station on the Inokashira Line in Tokyo, the Japan Folkcraft Museum was founded by the famous art critic Muneyoshi Yanagi. Its exhibits include old and new ceramics, dyed and woven fabrics, wood products, and various other items gathered from all over Japan and Korea. The exhibit is more of a private collection and is not intended to be comprehensive.

JAPAN LETTER, THE   One of the oldest, most authoritative and useful newsletters on Japan, *The Japan Letter* is published twice a month by Asia Letter Ltd., a Hong Kong company with branches in Japan, Los Angeles, and Singapore. The letter synthesizes political and economic trends and predicts future developments in these areas. It also keeps tabs on unusual cultural and social trends.

Contact: The Japan Letter, P.O. Box 33477, Sheungwan Post Office, Hong Kong, or P.O. Box 54149, Los Angeles, CA, 90054.

JAPAN NATIONAL TOURIST ORGANIZATION (JNTO) / KOKUSAI KANKO SHINKO KAI (Ko-ke-sie Khan-koe Sheen-koe Kie)   Founded in 1959 under the Ministry of Transport, the Japan National Tourist Organization (JNTO) is financed by the government and local contributions from the tourist industry. It is Japan's most important tourism organization.

The primary function of the JNTO is to produce and disseminate information about Japan as a tourist destination, including brochures, films, and books; to advertise Japan around the world; and to otherwise publicize Japan's tourist attractions.

The JNTO presently maintains three Tourist Information Centers in Japan (in downtown Tokyo, at the Tokyo International Airport, and in Kyoto), and operates a number of information offices in the U.S. and other countries.

The JNTO is especially helpful to individual travelers and small parties of two or three who are on low budgets and want to get off the tour-group trail and experience Japan on their own.

One of the most useful of the publications designed specifically for this category of traveler is Pamphlet MG-085, entitled "Reasonable Accommodations in Japan."

The half-tabloid sized pamphlet features listings of some 200 business hotels and inns (most located in the country's 50 largest cities) that cost between one-third and one-fifth of the regular inn and hotel rate, but have been judged acceptable by international standards, and have had experience accommodating foreign guests.

There are also numerous tips for budget travelers in a JNTO publication called "Your Traveling Companion."

The JNTO maintains overseas offices in major cities in the following countries: Australia, Brazil, Canada, England, France, Germany, Hong Kong, Korea, Mexico, Switzerland, and Thailand.

JAPAN PETROLEUM & ENERGY WEEKLY   This letter-sized publication carries news of the activities of Japan's petroleum and energy companies, articles about the government's energy policies, industry news briefs, and statistics on oil and energy in Japan. It is published by Japan Petroleum Consultants, Ltd. See OTHER ENGLISH-LANGUAGE SOURCES.

JAPAN PRIZE   The Japanese government sponsors an annual international award called the Japan Prize that goes to two people who have made outstanding contributions in the field of applied sciences—generally in fields not covered by the Nobel Prize program.

The Japan Prize consists of a cash award in excess of $200,000, plus other honors. A spokesperson for the government said the prize is one way in which Japan can repay some of its scientific and technological debt to the West.

JAPAN RAIL PASSES   The Japanese Railways (JR) version of the Eurailpass, the Japan Rail Pass (JRP), inaugurated in 1981, has become increasingly popular with foreign visitors. Holders of the JRP are entitled to travel freely throughout JR's extensive network—including the famous Bullet Train lines or Shinkansen (Sheen-Khan-sin).

The Rail Pass is also valid for travel on JR-operated ferry and bus lines where such service is available. Unlike its European counterpart, the Japan Rail Pass offers the travelers the option of either first class (Green Cars) or regular class. The passes are good for one-, two-, or three-week periods.

Foreign travelers heading for Japan can buy Rail Pass vouchers at overseas offices of the Japan Travel Bureau, Nippon Travel Agency Pacific offices, and Japan Air Lines ticket offices in the U.S. After arrival in Japan, the vouchers are exchanged for Rail Passes.

Used to its fullest extent, the JRP can result in 60 percent to 70 percent savings on travel in Japan.

JAPAN RAILWAYS GROUP / NIHON TETSU (Nee-hone tate-sue)   In 1906 the Japanese government decided to nationalize all the important railway lines in the country, and 17 lines then being operated privately were bought by the government. In the following years, other lines were added, and in 1949 the government-owned railways were reorganized under a public corporation called Japanese National Railways (JNR).

In the spring of 1987 the Japanese government privatized JNR, breaking it up into 11 companies based on their geographic service areas. Collectively the new system is known as Japan Railways (JR) Group, and altogether has some 200,000 employees.

The 10 busiest stations in the country are Shinjuku (Tokyo), Ikebukuro (Tokyo), Tokyo Central Station, Shibuya (Tokyo), Osaka Station, Yokohama Station, Shimbashi (Tokyo), Tennoji (Osaka), Ueno (Tokyo), and Takadanobaba (Tokyo).

JR also operates ferry services between the four main islands and to islands in the Inland Sea, along with bus service on some 16,000 kilometers of routes throughout the country.

In addition to the famous Bullet Trains (*Shinkan Sen*) that leave Tokyo Central Station every few minutes, the JR operates 700 limited express trains and 1,200 ordinary express trains on its main lines. To supplement these, the corporation also operates a network of intercity rapid services and over 16,000 local trains.

Trains in the JR system are classified according to their speed, the number of stops they make, and their accommodations. They include rapid express, limited express, ordinary express and regular trains.

Long-distance limited-express trains have dining cars, sleepers, and coaches with reclining seats. Both Western- and Japanese-style meals are served on the trains, and vendors are constantly passing up and down the aisles of the coaches, offering various drinks and snacks.

There are two classes of accommodations on JR trains, first class, in which the coaches are labeled Green Cars, and second, or ordinary, class. First-class cabins on JR ferries are called Green Cabins.

All of the famous Bullet Trains and limited-express trains, as well as most ordinary express trains, are air-conditioned. Trains that are not air-conditioned have overhead fans in the summer and steam heat in the winter.

Japan's railway service is world-famous for its efficiency and punctuality.

JAPAN STATISTICAL YEARBOOK / NIHON TOKEI NENKAN (Nee-hone Toe-Kay-e Nane-khan)   The *Japan Statistical Yearbook*, with statistics from the Prime Minister's Office and edited by the Japan Statistical Association and the Mainichi Newspaper Company, is a comprehensive reference book covering population, economy, business, finance, living standards, and cultural matters.

The yearbook is available through the Japan Publications Trading Company (JPTC). See OTHER SOURCES.

JAPAN STEEL JOURNAL, THE   *The Japan Steel Journal* is a daily (weekdays) newsletter covering the international activities of Japan's steel makers. It also contains listings of Japanese market prices and import and export prices of steel. Publisher is the Japan Iron and Steel Journal Co., Ltd. See OTHER SOURCES.

JAPAN TRAVEL BUREAU (JTB) / NIHON KOTSU KOSHA (Nee-hone Koat-sue Koe-shah)   The largest travel agency in Japan (300 domestic offices and 11 offices abroad), Japan Travel Bureau (JTB) was founded in 1893 as the Welcome Society. The founders were young, highly educated and cultured Japanese who wanted to help visiting travelers get to know and understand the country.

A few years later, the organization was renamed the Japan Tourist Bureau and in 1945 became the Japan Travel Bureau. Northwest Orient Airlines began regular flights to Tokyo in 1947, and the same year American President Lines resumed its Far East cruises—all contributing to the rapid postwar growth of JTB.

Other events that contributed to JTB's growth: the return of Haneda International Airport to Japanese control in 1952, the beginning of Japan Air Lines service to San Francisco in 1954, the 1964 Olympics in Tokyo, and the lifting of the government ban on overseas sightseeing the same year.

JTB has a large publishing division and is noted for its many books on cultural subjects and history, as well as on travel.

The agency's Overseas Travel Division annually sends several hundred thousand tourists abroad.

JAPAN TRAVEL PHONE   Japan's well-organized travel industry has a special telephone number for tourists to call when they need English-language assistance or travel information.

The service is sponsored by the Japan National Tourist Organization (JNTO) through its Travel Information Centers (TIC) and is available from 9:00 A.M. to 5:00 P.M. daily throughout the year.

Outside the Kyoto and Tokyo areas, the traveler dials 106 and tells the operator in English: "Collect call, T.I.C." (pronounced Tee-Aye-She). Private phones, as well as yellow and blue public phones (but *not* red public phones), may be used. When one uses a public phone, it is necessary to insert a 10-yen coin, but the coin is returned.

In Tokyo and Kyoto, the traveler dials the number of the local Tourist Information Center directly. In the Tokyo area, that is 3502-1461. In Kyoto, it is 371-5649. When one uses public phones to call these two numbers, the charge is 10 yen per three minutes.

Several dozen major Japanese companies provide funds for the operation of the Japan Travel Phone.

JAPAN YOUTH HOSTELS   There are dozens of youth hostels in Japan, and they are located in some of the most scenic and desirable travel destinations in the country. The accommodations are basic—usually dormitory style—but they are often not crowded and one sometimes has them entirely to oneself.

Bathing and laundry facilities, along with substantial, hearty food, are part of the bargain. For more information, contact Japan Youth Hostels, Inc., 1-2 Ichigaya, Sadohara-cho, Shinjuku-ku, Tokyo, Japan. In the U.S.: American Youth Hostels, 132 Spring St., New York, New York 10012.

JETRO (Japan External Trade Organization)   Probably the best known of Japan's trade organizations, JETRO was founded by the Ministry of International Trade and Industry in 1958 to promote trade. At that time, there were already several government and private sector organizations engaged in trade promotion, but their efforts were not coordinated and were inefficient.

The new organization was charged with seven areas of responsibility: to research foreign trade and publish the results, to publicize Japan's export industries and products abroad, to provide services to facilitate international trade, to publish and distribute printed materials on Japan's exports, to sponsor and participate in trade fairs, to coordinate government efforts to expand trade, and to do whatever else it could do to promote Japan's international trade.

In 1980, because of Japan's success in promoting its foreign trade, JETRO was given new responsibilities, primarily aimed at heading off growing criticism of Japan and its successes abroad. The role of JETRO was expanded to include the promotion of mutual understanding among trading partners, to encourage and facilitate the export of goods to Japan, to help emerging countries develop their overseas trading capability, and to act as a liaison between small and medium-size industries in Japan and their counterparts overseas.

JETRO presently has some 30 local and regional offices in Japan and 78 branch offices in 59 countries around the world. These offices act as information collection centers and as information dissemination centers for both Japanese and foreign executives.

The organization regularly sponsors import and export seminars for both Japanese and foreign businesspeople and carries on an extensive publishing program, along with producing educational films. Its publications include a series on marketing in Japan (*Doing Business in Japan, Rights in Japan, Planning for Distribution in Japan, Role of Trading Companies in International Commerce*, etc).

JETRO also publishes *Focus Japan*, which features articles on business, trade, labor, employment, overseas investments, and other issues of special interest; *Tradescope*, which is designed to provide developing countries with international trade information; and a *Now in Japan* series, which covers problems faced by the Japanese economy (*Productivity and QC, The Japanese Experience, The Promotion of Small and Medium Enterprises in Japan*).

Other publications include *The JETRO China Newsletter, The JETRO Arabic Newsletter, The Japan Industrial and Technological Bulletin*, an annual *White Paper on International Trade, Keys to Success in the Japanese Market*, etc.

Among the films available from JETRO are *The Japanese Economy Now; The Door is Open; Kacho—A Section Chief and His Day;* and, *Bridges and Barriers—Americans in Japan*.

JETRO maintains large libraries of trade information and materials in its headquarters building in Tokyo and in its Osaka office. All of its domestic and overseas offices maintain collections of key publications and directories.

In the U.S., JETRO has offices in New York, Chicago, Houston, Los Angeles, and San Francisco. JETRO's headquarters in Tokyo are located across the street from the American Embassy, at 2-5 Toranomon, 2-chome, Minato-ku, Tokyo 105, Japan. Tel. 3582-5511.

JETRO invites foreign business leaders to view or rent videocassettes on Japan's business world at its International Lounge on the sixth floor of its headquarters building in Tokyo. Two new tapes are to be added each month for some time.

Among the cassettes now available are: *Direct Foreign Investment, How a Japanese Company Achieves High Productivity, Point Men for Foreign Business in Japan, Are the Japanese Really Unique?*

The Lounge is open weekdays from 9:30 A.M. to noon and 1 P.M. to 4:30 P.M.

JETRO publishes a number of special reports that are available to the public, including: JETRO Marketing Series, *Your Market in Japan*, Business Information Series, and *Access to Japan's Import Market*.

Books published by JETRO include: *Nippon, Handy Facts on U.S.–Japan Economic Relations*, and *Setting Up a Business in Japan*. Directories available from JETRO include: *Japan Trade Directory*, and *Japanese Affiliated Companies in U.S.A. and Canada*.

JIDAI MATSURI / FESTIVAL OF THE AGES   One of the most elaborate and culturally interesting festivals in Japan is the annual Festival of the Ages, staged at the Heian Shrine in Kyoto in late October.

The event marks the day when Emperor Kammu moved his capital to Kyoto from Nagaoka, some distance away, in the eighth century.

The pageant, about two kilometers long, and involving nearly 3,000 participants clad in the costumes of the various epochs, begins with the Meiji Restoration (when the *shogun* returned power to the emperor) in 1868.

This group is followed in order by processions depicting a lordly procession during the Edo Period, the court ladies of the Edo era, the son of Hideyoshi Toyotomi visiting the emperor in the late 1500s, and so on, back to the Enryaku Period (782-805).

The rear of the long pageant is brought up by a company of archers, representing men from the two wards in the city who were outstanding bowmen and escorted the emperor from Nagaoka to Kyoto in 794.

JISHU KANRI (Jee-shuu Khan-ree)   Jishu Kanri are the Workers' Volunteer Activity Groups in Japanese companies. Generally abbreviated as JK and associated with Japan's quality control system, small groups of workers, from three to ten, voluntarily form their own group, independent of management, to make sure they maintain the highest possible standard of quality and continuously strive to improve technology so even higher standards can be achieved.

Centered around the senior employees involved, the JK groups are typical of the strong group approach that characterizes Japanese behavior. These groups may also be called ZD circles, or zero defect circles.

JOB HUNTING IN JAPAN   Finding a job in Japan has a number of features that are unique to the country. Generally speaking, larger companies in Japan hire only once a year, at a time that is coordinated with high school and college graduation. These companies do not have employment offices, and there is no way for job seekers to come to them directly and apply for work at other times during the year.

College seniors scheduled to graduate in the spring are prohibited by law from calling on prospective employers until October 1 of their last year. This law was enacted because many companies were recruiting students during their junior year, following which both the students' work and class attendance fell off.

In reality, most male students of leading universities do not have to go out and look for jobs because their professors generally negotiate with the more desirable employers for them—often without consulting the students.

The relationships between these companies and professors is very strong and generally takes precedence over other factors. In many cases, the professors receive research funds from the companies concerned.

There are frequent instances in which the students would prefer to work for some company other than the one chosen by their professors, but few are willing or able to go against the wishes of their teachers.

The smaller the company in Japan, the more likely it is to recruit its employees via newspaper ads, personal recommendations, and connections. There are also a growing number of employment agencies, especially on the executive level, at which people may sign up for placement.

Cities also operate employment services, primarily for placing middle-aged and older people in part-time and temporary positions.

A great deal has been made of the practice of lifetime employment in Japan, but, generally, this applies only to larger firms. There is a considerable amount of job switching among people who work for small firms, particularly in the retail and wholesale industries, where there are hundreds of thousands of firms with fewer than nine employees.

Approximately 40 percent of Japan's entire labor force work for companies that are classified as small—under 100 employees.

JOGGING Jogging is a popular form of recreation in Japan, and it is common to see both men and women on the streets and in the parks of major cities in all kinds of weather. A favorite place to jog in Tokyo is along the inner moat of the Imperial Palace, which circles the Palace grounds. Foreign executives staying in downtown hotels, particularly the Imperial, often jog in Hibiya Park (which was originally the villa garden of a *daimyo* feudal lord).

JUDO (Juu-doe) *Jujutsu* (jew-jute-sue), the forerunner of judo, was developed into a formidable martial art by Japan's professional warrior class, the *samurai*, from the twelfth century on.

Most fighting in early Japan was on a one-on-one basis, in which individual skill, with and without weapons, was crucial. The *samurai* were always concerned about being attacked when they were unarmed and unprepared, and *jujutsu* was primarily a series of highly developed techniques for unarmed defense—disarming an opponent and disabling or killing him or her with the bare hands or feet.

In addition to jabbing and hitting, *jujutsu* included throwing, holding, strangling, and breaking.

With the ascendancy of the Tokugawa Shogunate in 1603, *jujutsu* became an even more important part of the training of the *samurai* because they had no wars to fight. Several rival schools developed, and so fierce was the competition between these schools that tournament matches often ended in serious injury or death.

The two most important of these *jujutsu* schools were the Tenshin Shin-yo and the Kito.

Modern *judo* grew out of *jujutsu*. Educator Jigoro Kano, who founded Tokyo's famous Kodokan (Koe-doe-khan) in 1882, is credited with being the father of this modern form. Jigoro (1860–1938) first mastered the Tenshin Shin-yo and Kito styles and then modified and refined them into his own system. He eliminated the martial aims of *jujutsu* and developed a scientific system of training based on modern athletic principles. He called his new system Kodokan *judo* (Koe-doe-khan juu-doe).

In Kano's system, *judo* was divided into three major areas—grappling, throwing, and attacking vital points. It was made a part of Japan's educational curriculum in the early 1900s, from middle school onwards, and has played a significant role in shaping the character of the Japanese ever since.

Following the end of the Pacific War in 1945, *judo* became popular throughout the world. The World Judo Federation was established in 1952. The first World Judo Championship Tournament was held in Tokyo in May 1956, and it was designated an Olympic sport in 1964.

The practice of *judo* has three phases: form (*kata*), free-style exercise (*dandori*), and competitive matches. In *judo* matches, only grappling and throwing are allowed.

There are two ranking systems in *judo—kyu* (que) and *dan* (dahn). The *kyu* class is for beginners, with the lowest being fifth kyu and the highest first kyu. The *dan* class of ranking begins with first *dan* and goes to tenth *dan*, the highest grade.

Japan's Kodokan Judo Hall, at 1-16 Kasuga, Bunkyo-ku, Tokyo, is the mecca of the *judo* world. *Judo* is also taught at the Nippon Budokan Hall's Budo Gakuen, 2-3 Kitanomaru Park, Chiyoda-ku, Tokyo.

The primary aim of *judo* today is to discipline and train the mind and body —not to defeat an opponent in battle. It is a popular sport in most countries of the world, and it is gradually being recognized for its value as a spiritual, as well as physical, training exercise.

Judo is named after the principle expressed in the saying *Ju yoku go o seisu*, or "Softness overcomes hardness." *Ju* means soft or gentle.

An official *judo* ring is nine meters square (50 *tatami* mats). Participants wear loose-fitting trousers, jackets, and belts and try to throw each other using various grappling, tripping, and flipping techniques.

The various ranks are indicated by the color of the belts the judoists wear. Beginners wear blue belts (and have no ranking). Fifth and fourth *kyu* grades wear white belts. Third to first *kyu* ranks wear brown belts.

In the senior *dan* rankings, first to fifth *dan* judoists wear black belts, sixth to eighth *dans* wear red and white belts, and ninth and tenth *dans* wear red belts.

Recommended reading: *Best Judo*, by Isao Inokuma and Nobuyuki Sato (Kodansha International); *Judo Formal Techniques*: *A Complete Guide to Kodokan Randori no Kata*, by Donn Draeger and Tadao Otaki (Tuttle); and *Judo for the Gentlewoman*, by Ruth B. Gardner (Tuttle).

JUVENILE DELINQUENCY   A democratic form of government and individual freedom have been trade-offs for Japan. The country had virtually no juvenile delinquency problem prior to 1945, but crimes by juveniles have since been on the rise.

While it is still less of a problem than in the U.S. and other Western countries, the rate of offenses by juveniles has been climbing rapidly since 1973, and the tendency for delinquency to begin at a younger age has continued.

Offenses by juveniles are divided into five major categories—grave offenses, acts of violence, larceny, intellectual offenses, and moral offenses. Larceny is the leading category, followed by acts of violence, intellectual offenses, grave offenses, and moral charges.

The total number of juvenile delinquency offenses was still less than one million in 1994.

The number of grave offenses, such as murder and armed robbery, were less than 3,000 the same year.

All juveniles in Tokyo who get into trouble are first sent to the Tokyo Juvenile Classification Home in Hikawadai, on the western outskirts of the city. From here, young men between the ages of 18 and 20 who have committed serious crimes are sent to the Kurihama Reform Training School south of Tokyo, on Izu Peninsula.

Others, after classification, are released on probation, kept at the Home for varying periods of time, or sent to other institutions. The emphasis at both of the centers is on rehabilitation. The educational and training programs are individualized for each inmate and range from Zen and arts to crafts and sports.

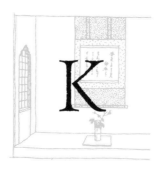

KABUKI (Kah-buu-kee)   A maid-servant at the Izumo Taisha Shrine in Kyoto is credited with having originated *kabuki* in 1603. O-Kuni, as this lady was called, was obviously an extraordinary woman for her time. In a program to raise funds for the repair of the shrine, she got a troupe of performers together and put on a show in the precincts of the famous Kitano Shrine.

Dressed like a man and carrying a sword, O-Kuni pretended to be meeting a sweetheart on the sly and acted out the story with her troupe in a series of comic routines. The act caught on and soon came to be known as *Kabuki Odori*, or Kabuki Dance, a corruption of the word *kubuku*, which refers to unseeming, ill-mannered behavior.

Rivals soon appeared on the scene, with the lead roles played by professional prostitutes. The shows became so lewd and disrespectful that the Tokugawa Shogunate banned women from appearing in the *kabuki* plays. Their place was taken by handsome young boys and men.

This change, however, resulted in a rapid increase in the practice of pederasty, which had been common among warriors and the clergy as well. In 1651, the *shogun* banned *kabuki* performances, but two years later granted permission for the *kabuki* theaters to reopen on condition that all parts in the plays, female, as well as male, be performed by adult men.

The *kabuki* plays became more sophisticated and stylized, and great actors and playwrights arose. *Kabuki* reached its zenith by 1700, and was thereafter to be one of the most important dramatic arts in Japan. *Kabuki* actors who became national heroes included Tojuro Sakata (1647–1709), Ayame Yoshizawa (1673–1729), Danjuro Ichikawa (1660–1704), and Shichisaburo Nakamura (1662–1708).

In the decades before the Tokugawa Shogunate fell in 1868, the popularity of *kabuki* declined. Around the beginning of the Meiji Period (1868), some of the leading *kabuki* actors of the day initiated a revivalist movement that resulted in the creation of a number of new works that were much more traditional in form—mostly dance-dramas inspired by *noh* themes.

Some of the plays written during this period have survived the test of time, and are among the most popular fare performed today.

Kabuki continues today as one of the very special arts of Japan, and its stars are among the most respected artists in the country. Principal *kabuki* theaters include the Kabuki Za, Meiji Za, Kokuriku Gekijo, and Shimbashi Embujo in Tokyo; the Shin Kabuki Za in Osaka; and the Minami Za in Kyoto.

Stylized and formalized to the highest degree, *kabuki* features only male actors who play both male and female roles, dressed in very elaborate, traditional costumes. There are two categories of *kabuki* plays: those depicting the lives and fortunes of the noble class and warriors of early Japan and those based on the lives of common people of an earlier age.

The plays are performed to the accompaniment of traditional Japanese melodies played on the *shamisen* (shah-me-sane), a three-stringed, lutelike instrument, flutes, and other Japanese musical instruments.

The actors perform the dialogue in a set, formalized pattern, making great use of gestures, body movements, and costume changes to tell the story. Masks are also commonly used.

Many costume changes take place on stage in full view of the audience, but the actors are aided by assistants dressed totally in black who are so skillful that they seem to be almost invisible to the experienced audience caught up in the story.

Kabuki theaters have revolving stages, making set changes possible in just seconds. They also have a long walkway running from the back of the theater to the stage, a device that allows the actors to have close contact with the audience when they enter and leave the stage.

The profession of *kabuki* actor is generally passed from father to son, and training begins early. Accomplished actors become nationally renowned, receiving generous sums of money and gifts from well-to-do admirers.

English-language programs are provided for foreign visitors who want the experience of viewing a *kabuki* play. Schedules of the plays appear regularly in such English-language publications as *The Japan Times*, *Tour Companion*, and the *Tokyo Weekender*.

Recommended reading: *Kabuki*, by Masakatsu Gunji (Kodansha International); *The Traditional Theater of Japan*, by Yoshinobu Inoura and Toshio Kawatake (Weatherhill).

KAGOSHIMA (Kah-go-she-mah)   The city of Kagoshima at the southern tip of Kyushu began as the castle headquarters of the famous Satsuma clan, which played a leading role in the fall of the Tokugawa Shogunate in 1868 and the restoration of power to the Imperial throne.

The city and its inhabitants have also played other eventful roles in Japan's history, particularly during the years when foreign nations were vying with each other to force Japan to open its doors to trade and diplomatic relations with the West.

One of these events involved the killing of an Englishman by *samurai* in 1862. On September 14, 1862, C. L. Richardson and some companions were out riding on the Tokaido Road near Nammugi when they met the Procession of the Lord of Satsuma. The *samurai* escorts of the Lord of Satsuma cut Richardson down and wounded two of his companions when they failed to yield the right of way to the *daimyo's* procession. Richardson was apparently not aware that everyone was required to move off the road and bow down while a feudal lord and his entourage were passing. The survivors of the outing accused the Satsuma *samurai* of attacking them without justification.

The following year, British naval forces bombarded Kagoshima, inflicting heavy damage on the city, in retaliation for the death of Richardson.

Other foreigners who ran afoul of belligerent *samurai* during the 1850s and 1860s were also cut down when they left the protection of the enclaves established for foreign residents.

Today, Kagoshima is a thriving port city that retains much of the charm of the past, with many old buildings and picturesque streets that date from the Middle Ages. It is a favorite departure point for Okinawa, to the south.

KAISEKI (Kie-say-kee)   The very simple food that is often served with the tea ceremony, as well as in temples, is called *kaiseki*. It is usually vegetarian.

Recommended reading: *Kaiseki—Zen Taste in Japanese Cookery*, by Kaichu Tsugi (Kodansha International).   •

KAKEMONO (Kah-kay-moe-no)   Literally a "hanging thing," the *kakemono* is a hanging scroll, made of silk or heavy paper, with a roller at the bottom, which the Japanese hang on a wall or in a special alcove called a *tokonoma* (toe-koe-no-mah). A *kakemono* may be a painting, usually a still-life, or calligraphy, and its subject is customarily chosen to fit the season. See HANGING SCROLLS.

KAMAKURA (Kah-mah-kuu-rah)   Now a popular tourist spot and elite residential community, Kamakura seems an unlikely place to have played an important role in Japan's history. Located at the neck of the Miura Peninsula in a narrow valley facing Sagami Bay, about an hour by train southeast of Tokyo, Kamakura was no more than an isolated but picturesque village when feudal lord Yoritomo Minamoto became the paramount military leader of Japan and established his military government there in 1185.

Yoritomo is said to have selected this remote spot, many days march away from Kyoto, to avoid the intrigues and weakening influences of the effete way of life that had developed in the Imperial Capital.

It was Yoritomo who established Japan's first shogunate military government (in 1192), after being given the title of *shogun* (which means something like generalissimo and had not been used for several centuries) by the emperor.

Kamakura was to remain the seat of the shogunate government for the next 151 years, during which time some of the country's most important temples and shrines were built there.

Of course, the most famous of its historic artifacts is the great bronze image of Buddha (*Dai Butsu*, or *Great Buddha of Kamakura*), which was cast in 1252 by Goroemon Ono or Hisatomo Tanji—both renowned casters of that time. See GREAT BUDDHA OF KAMAKURA.

Among the great temples at Kamakura are the Kencho Ji and the Engaku Ji. Its shrines include the famous Tsurugaoka Hachiman Gu. Other points of special interest include the Kamakura Museum and the Tomb of Yoritomo. See GREAT BUDDHA OF KAMAKURA; HISTORY; MINAMOTO, YORITOMO; SHOGUN; SAMURAI; etc.

KAMIKAZE PILOTS / TOKKOTAI (Toke-koe-tie)   When World War II began to go badly for the Japanese, the Imperial Army and Navy established special air attack forces whose mission was to sink Allied ships by crashing their bomb-laden planes into them.

Young pilots, some of them still in their teens, were recruited and trained for these one-way suicide flights, which caused considerable damage to the American fleet before the war ended.

The young airmen were popularly called *Kamikaze* (Kah-me-kah-zay), or Divine Wind, pilots in reference to the typhoon winds that saved Japan from great Mongol invasion fleets that attacked the country in 1274 and 1281. See HISTORY; SHOGUN.

They were also called Thundergods, in reference to their becoming divine spirits following the thunderous explosion of their planes.

Recommended reading: *The Thundergods*, by Hatsuho Naito; translated by Mayumi Ichikawa; edited by Boye Lafayette De Mente.

KANAZAWA (Kah-nah-zah-wah)   On the Japan Sea side of Honshu, west of Nagoyo, Kanazawa is the capital of Ishikawa Prefecture. It is noted for having retained much of the look of Old Japan and for having one of the three most beautiful gardens in Japan (Kenroku-En).

Kanazawa was headquarters for the famous Maeda clan during the Tokugawa Period—one of Japan's largest and most powerful clans. It is said that when the Lord of Maeda made his every-other-year trip to the *shogun's* capital of Edo, he took over 10,000 servants, retainers, and warriors with him. See PROCESSIONS OF THE LORDS.

The Maeda *Daimyo's* great castle, which once stood in the center of the city, was almost totally destroyed by fire in 1881, but a number of buildings are preserved, and the famous garden that adjoined the castle is intact. It was designed and built by Narihiro Maeda in 1819 while he was the lord of the clan (it is considerably larger than the two other most famous gardens in Japan—the Kairaku-En in Mito and the Koraku-En in Okayama).

KANDA (Khan-dah)   One of the most famous districts in Tokyo, Kanda used to be a ward in itself, but it is now part of Chiyoda Ward (which incorporates much of central Tokyo, the Imperial Palace grounds, and Government Hill).

Famed in history as one of the centers that bred the true *Edokko* (Eh-doak-koe), or Edo-ite, Kanda is now noted for being the home of many universities and schools and for having the largest concentration of new and used bookshops in the country.

The most important annual event in Kanda is the Kanda Matsuri (Festival), held from May 12 to 15 by the Kanda Myojin, a Shinto shrine that dates from the eighth century.

KANJI CHARACTERS (Khan-jee)   The ideograms with which the Japanese and Chinese write their languages were developed in China sometime before 1000 B.C. They grew out of the use of signs and pictograms and were gradually standardized and institutionalized over many generations of daily practical use.

The Japanese imported the *kanji* system of writing in the fifth and sixth centuries A.D. and gradually assimilated it to meet their own need for a script —but without changing the pronunciation of their own language.

As a result of this, most of the *kanji* used in Japan today still have two readings: the Chinese reading (the *on* reading), and the Japanese, or *kun*, reading. Which reading or pronunciation is used depends upon the particular word and usage over the centuries.

Altogether, there are around 50,000 of the Chinese characters, but in Japan only about 3,000 are common, and of this number, 1,945 have been designated by the government for daily use, meaning that no more than this number should be used for ordinary purposes.

Besides *kanji*, there are three other systems for writing Japanese. See JAPANESE LANGUAGE; CALLIGRAPHY.

In 1984, Toshiba introduced a word processor/typewriter that would convert Romanized Japanese into written *kanji* at the touch of a key. The first Japanese-language word processor was introduced in 1978.

KARA-OKE SINGING (Kah-rah-oh-kay) For centuries, the Japanese have been raised on lullabies and folk songs and have learned how to sing as a natural part of growing up. Everybody is expected to join in the singing at festivals, and, at parties and other kinds of gatherings, it is customary for individuals to take turns singing.

In the 1970s, electronic firms began to sell and promote home microphone systems for people to plug into their stereo sets and entertain themselves by singing on the air. This self-entertainment was dubbed *kara-oke*, which means "empty orchestra."

Soon thereafter, many bars and clubs began offering their patrons the opportunity to perform *kara-oke* in public, and "empty orchestra" singing swept the country.

All was not happy, however. Too many *kara-oke* stars began turning the sound of their stereo sets way up, disturbing neighbors and bringing on many complaints.

One of the biggest critics of *kara-oke* was Juro Kato, a sociology professor at Beppu University. He founded the Japan Tin Ear Society to champion the rights of nonsingers and tone-deaf people to resist the badgering of *kara-oke* advocates. And how do the members of the society begin each of their meetings? With a song, of course, lamenting their sad state.

KARATE (Kah-rah-tay)   *Karate* literally means "empty hands." Originally, it was a form of self-defense developed in China around the seventh century, when ordinary people were not allowed to bear arms. It consisted of highly refined techniques of striking an opponent with the bare hands or feet in especially vulnerable areas and taking advantage of the added power achieved by delivering blows with extraordinary speed and concentration.

Karate was introduced into Okinawa in the fourteenth century, but it was to be several more centuries before it made its way to the mainland of Japan —which is surprising, given the extraordinary interest the *samurai* class and *ninja* had in all martial arts.

Today, *karate* is known and practiced in most countries of the world, especially in Europe and the U.S., primarily as a means of developing physical, spiritual, and moral strength.

There are two kinds of *karate* contests—*kumite* (kuu-me-tay) and *kata* (kah-tah). In a *kata* contest, the contestant performs a series of prescribed, formalized movements—as if defending or attacking—and is judged on the correctness and quality of these drills. The contestant is also judged on the quality of his or her *kiai* (kee-aye)—the shout that accompanies thrusts or kicks.

In a *kumite* contest, two opponents spar with each other, going through a variety of movements to demonstrate their skill. The winner is decided on the basis of which opponent had the best form, the best mental attitude, and more likely would have won if the contest had been for real.

Gichin Funakoshi (1870–1957) was the Okinawan who introduced *karate* to mainland Japan and probably had more influence on the sport than any other man.

In Japan, the art was substantially improved, with several schools developing, including Shotokan, Goju, Rembukan Shito, and Wado.

Karate training includes the basic form (*kata*) and various punches, jabs and, kicks (*kumite*), which are designed to be practiced by two people, as in real combat.

The concentration of energy, both physical and mental, is such that an experienced *karate* adept can shatter between 10 and 15 roof slates or five 1.5-centimeter boards laid on top of each other, with one explosive blow.

Recommended reading: *Karate's History & Traditions*, by Bruce A. Haines (Tuttle); *The Karate Experience—A Way of Life*, by Randall G. Hassell (Tuttle); *Karate: The Art of Empty-hand Fighting*, by Hidetaka Nishiyama and Richard C. Brown (Tuttle); *Dynamic Karate*, by Masatoshi Nakayama (Kodansha International); and *Karate-Do: My Way of Life*, by Gichin Funakoshi (Kodansha International).

KARUIZAWA (Kah-rue-e-zah-wah) A picturesque mountain town in the highlands of Niigata, some two hours from Ueno Station in Tokyo via limited express, Karuizawa was first made popular as a resort by Archdeacon A. C. Shaw and a Professor Dixon, then of Tokyo University, who began spending their summers there in 1886.

At an altitude of nearly 1,000 meters and surrounded by tall pines, Karuizawa has a permanent population of only about 15,000, but in July and August this swells to over 100,000. There are some 6,000 private summer cottages in the vicinity of the town and a number of facilities for conventions and other business meetings. The area also has several golf courses.

During the war years in the early 1940s, Karuizawa was used as an internment camp for civilian prisoners of war, many of whom were stateless persons who lived permanently in Japan.

KATO, KIYOMASA (Kah-toe, Kee-yoe-mah-sah) A celebrated general of the sixteenth century who served under Hideyoshi Toyotomi, Kiyomasa Kato was in charge of Hideyoshi's war against Korea (1592–1598). When Hideyoshi died in 1598 and the war was called off, Kato allied himself with Hideyoshi's successor, Ieyasu Tokugawa, and became the *daimyo* of Higo Province.

It is said that after Ieyasu became *shogun* in 1603, he was uneasy about having such a popular, capable, and ambitious general on his flank and contrived to have Kato poisoned during a tea ceremony.

A flamboyant character, Kato wore a helmet that was three feet high and, when on the road or in battle, always carried a banner that was inscribed with the sacred formula of Nichiren Buddhism, *"Namu myoho renge kyo."* There are two Nichiren temples in Kumamoto, Kyushu, that are dedicated to Kato.

KATSURA IMPERIAL VILLA (Kot-sue-rah) One of the showplaces of Kyoto, the Katsura Imperial Villa was commissioned by the Tokugawa

Shogunate in 1620 for Prince Toshihito, the brother of Emperor Goyozei, and was completed in 1624.

The villa adjoins the Katsura River and is 4.8 kilometers from Kyoto Station. The buildings and garden of the villa were designed by the famous landscape architect Enshu Kobori and built by his two brothers under the guidance of Prince Toshihito and his son.

A story has it that Kobori would not accept the commission until the *shogun* agreed to three things—that there would be no limit set on the cost of the villa, that he would not have to hurry the work, and that no one would see the villa and garden until they were completed.

Under the jurisdiction of the Imperial Household since 1883, the villa has been preserved as it was during the Tokugawa Period. The villa consists of three apartments in the main building (which includes a veranda especially designed for moon viewing), a hall for Imperial visits, a tea room, several other apartments in the garden, and another building with 10 rooms.

The garden is a strolling garden, and it is designed in such a way that no matter where the viewer stands he or she appears to be looking at the garden from the front. It contains a pond and several teahouses overlooking it, along with several groves of trees.

The main building and other structures contain paintings by famous masters and other works of art that are considered national treasures. Permission to enter the villa must be obtained in advance from the Kyoto Office of the Imperial Household Agency.

Recommended reading: *Edo Architecture—Katsura and Nikko*, by Naomi Okawa (Weatherhill).

KAWANA (Kah-wah-nah)   Near the seaside resort of Ito, on the Izu Peninsula southwest of Tokyo, Kawana is noted as a golf resort for the rich and famous. Its two golf courses are reputedly the best in the Orient. Guests stay at the equally famous Kawana Hotel.

KAWASAKI (Kah-wah-sah-kee)   Japan's eighth largest city, Kawasaki is often literally overlooked because it is sandwiched in between Tokyo and Yokohama, along the southern bank of the Tama River.

Originally a Post Station on the famed Tokai-Do Highway that travelers walked between Edo and Kyoto, Kawasaki is now a major industrial complex representing the biggest names in Japan's chemical and heavy industries.

Besides its importance as an industrial center, Kawasaki is noted for the Heigen Temple, founded in 1128 and dedicated to the great Kobo-Daishi, who founded the Shingon doctrine of Buddhism; the Mukogaoka (Playground) Park, especially designed for children; the Inada-Zutsumi cherry-tree grove; the Ozenji Atomic Power Research Center; Yomiuri Land, a gigantic recreational area (see YOMIURI LAND); and a second famous temple, Ozen, which was once officially designated as the temple for Imperial prayers.

KEGON FALLS / KEGON TAKI (Kay-goan tah-kee)   Probably the most famous waterfall in Japan, Kegon Taki, in Nikko, is the outlet for Lake Chuzenji, the high volcanic caldera that towers over the town of Nikko, the famous Tokugawa Mausolea, and the shrines of Nikko.

A few minutes drive from Nikko town, the falls are 100 meters high, and a sheer drop-off turns the water into a lacey white curtain. The whole area is one of the most scenic in all of Japan. See NIKKO; TOKUGAWA.

KEIDANREN (Kay-e-dahn-rane)   The Keidanren, or Federation of Economic Organizations, is regarded as the most important and most powerful business organization in Japan. It is made up of representatives from virtually every major firm and industry in the country.

The Keidanren acts as a liaison between firms and the various industries and as a spokesperson for industry in general, particularly in making the views of business leaders known to the government.

The Keidanren maintains a large staff that researches economic areas and problems and writes position papers that are submitted to the government agencies concerned and made available to industry and the public.

The president of Keidanren is always one of the country's most respected and influential executives.

KEIO UNIVERSITY / KEIO DAIGAKU (Kay-e-oh Die-gah-kuu)   The oldest university in Japan, Keio is located in the Mita district of Tokyo and is famous for its faculties of law, economics, literature, commerce, medicine, and engineering and for its baseball team.

Founded by famed educator Yukichi Fukuzawa in 1858, Keio is always counted among the top five universities in the country and celebrated for its sports rivalry with Waseda, Todai (Tokyo University), and other major schools.

KENDO (Ken-doe)   One of the most popular martial arts of Japan, *kendo* is sword fighting or fencing with a kind of stave made of strips of bamboo tightly bound together.

Kendo originated in the seventh or eighth century, but it was around the sixteenth century that it became a vital part of the training and exercise of the *samurai* warrior class. In those days, solid wooden staves were used in training and tournaments, and in the hands of a skilled kendoist they could be almost as deadly as a sword.

While used by the *samurai* to hone and maintain their sword-fighting skills, *kendo* stressed the spiritual and moral aspects of the art, as exemplified by Zen Buddhism and Confucianism.

The use of the flexible bamboo staves and protective gear, such as face-masks, torso guards, and gauntlets, dates from the 1700s.

Kendo contests today consist of three bouts or rounds, with the winner determined by the number of times the contestants are able to strike their opponents in specifically prescribed places, such as the face, hands, body, and throat. Attacks are usually accompanied by loud shouts designed to fluster the opponent.

KIKOTSU (Key-kote-sue)   Just as the *samurai* class of feudal Japan had its *Bushido*, or Way of the Warrior codes and philosophy, the common people of Japan, particularly as the long decades of the Tokugawa Shogunate unfolded, developed a moral code of their own, which is usually described as incorporating *kikotsu*—a special kind of spirit.

Recommended reading: Modern Bujutsu and Budo,
by Donn F. Draeger (Weatherhill)

During the early feudal age, common people were considered chattel by the *samurai*—quite literally, property that was owned by them. With such power over ordinary farmers and townspeople, it is not surprising that many *samurai* developed an attitude of arrogance that was often translated into callous and brutal behavior.

This situation led to the development of a class of spirited commoners who resented the bullying and depredations of the unprincipled *samurai* and defended themselves and other common people against them.

These people called themselves Men of Men and were called *kyokaku* (K'yoe-kah-kuu), or "hosts of heroism," by the common people. Their moral code was based on *kikotsu*, or the spirit that gave them the courage to defy and rebel against injustice and oppression.

This spirit gradually permeated the whole population of Japan in varying degrees, and it was the foundation for the strong sense of justice and compassion for others that has long been characteristic of the common people.

In the Tokugawa Period, the leaders of the *kyokaku* formed societies called Otokodate (Oh-toe-koe-dot-tay), which basically means If You Are a Man. Similar societies formed by and for the common people were called Machi Yakko (Mah-chee Yack-koe) or Town Men.

Even the lower-ranked *samurai*, who were at the mercy of their superiors, developed a comparable society in an attempt to protect themselves during the Tokugawa era. Their societies were known as *Hatamoto Yakko* (Hah-tah-moe-toe Yack-koe), or Banner Men.

These societies became quite powerful after a number of generations and began to abuse their power. They were finally suppressed by the shogunate.

KIMONO (Key-moe-no)   The *kimono* (kee-moe-no), one of the most elaborate and attractive national costumes of any country, was introduced into Japan from China as an undergarment in the seventh century. Between the twelfth and thirteenth centuries, the Court nobility began making it of highly decorative materials and wearing it as an outer garment.

When the warrior class began replacing the ancient noble families as the rulers of the country in the Kamakura (1192–1333) and Muromachi periods (1338–1573), the *samurai* also adopted the dress of the nobles, establishing the *kimono* as everyday wear.

The voluminous trousers that had been part of the original Chinese costume were inconvenient for life outside the court, however, and the *samurai* wore them only on ceremonial occasions.

The female version of the *kimono* was also transformed over the centuries, especially during the Edo Period of peace and prosperity, when the use of expensive, colorful, gorgeously decorated silks became common among the well-to-do. This was also the period when the long, wide *obi* (oh-bee) sash became an integral part of the female *kimono*.

The shogunate passed laws prohibiting the common people from wearing luxurious clothing and living in an ostentatious manner, but the feisty Edoites were not to be denied.

The families of prosperous merchants, *geisha*, and other popular entertainers first began to wear expensive undergarments and, behind walls, to lavishly furnish and decorate their homes. Thus, as the decades passed, these laws became more difficult and finally impossible to enforce.

With the coming of industrialization to Japan in the latter 1800s and a fast-paced life revolving around factories, trains, and streetcars, the *kimono* became very impractical and lost ground to Western-style dress. Following the end of the Pacific War in 1945, it seemed that the *kimono*, traditionally made of silk, would disappear completely.

But with the gradual return of prosperity and the appearance of less expensive silks and other materials, the *kimono* made a miraculous comeback in the late 1950s and early 1960s, and, while primarily worn today for special occasions, it is nevertheless once again very much a part of the traditional beauty and charm of Japan.

In Japan today, *kimono* are generally worn on two occasions—for special events and as casual wear to relax in around the house or in a *ryokan* (riokhan), or inn.

There are several types of *kimono* for women, in different designs and colors, depending on their age and marital status and the occasion for which they are to be worn. Women often wear *kimono* during the New Year holidays and at receptions, graduations, funerals and other special days.

The most common *kimono* seen in Japan is the informal, cotton *yukata* (you-kah-tah), which is used as casual wear and as a house or bath robe. *Yukata* are especially popular in hot spring spas and other vacation spots, where they are often worn as the uniform of the day—and night.

Recommended reading: *The Book of Kimono*, by Norio Yamanaka (Kodansha International); *Kimono Masterpieces—The Nomura Collection*, by Tetsuro Kitamura, translated by Junko Pollack (Kodansha International).

KINOKUNIYA DATA BANK SERVICE   In addition to being one of Japan's oldest and largest booksellers, Kinokuniya is also one of the country's largest computer-based information brokers. The company's data bank went on line in Japan in 1971 and linked up with some dozen American information services in 1980.

At present, Kinokuniya has several hundred Japanese clients, including large manufacturing companies, universities, and government agencies. More than 90 percent of the information now being accessed from its data bank concerns developments in chemistry and engineering.

Kinokuniya's present project: feeding on-line information about Japan to foreign clients abroad.

KISO RAPIDS (Kee-soe)   Rapids shooting is as popular in Japan as in the American West, and the Kiso River, which begins at the southern end of the Japan Alps in central Honshu and flows through the Nobi Plain near Nagoya, is regarded as the finest river to shoot.

The lower section of the Kiso Rapids, one of the most scenic river areas in Japan, is known as the Japan Rhine. The boat ride down the rapids— thrilling but not particularly dangerous—lasts about two hours.

Nagoya and Gifu serve as major gateways to the Rapids of Kiso. Public boats operate on the river. But one may also hire private boats—and have the option of stopping along the way.

KITA-KYUSHU (Kee-tah-Que-shuu)   At the northern end of Kyushu, across from Shimonoseki, on the tip of Honshu, Kita-Kyushu (North Kyushu) is the seventh largest city in the country and ranks as one of Japan's four great industrial centers (the others being Keihin in the Tokyo-Yokohama area, Chukyo in the Nagoya area, and Hanshin in the Osaka-Kobe-Kyoto area).

Kita-Kyushu is unique in that it was once five important cities—Kokura, Moji, Tobata, Yahata, and Wakamatsu—which were merged in the 1960s to form one giant municipality, with the former cities being reduced to the status of wards. Each of the former independent cities retains many of its old physical characteristics, as well as its commercial and industrial specialities, but the cities are otherwise well integrated.

The port of Kita-Kyushu is divided into three parts—Moji Port, which handles foreign trade; Kokura Port, which handles both foreign and domestic trade; and Dokai Port, which is an industrial port.

Kita-Kyushu owes much of its early industrial success to vast coal fields in the Chikuho area and trade with Asia. When oil began to replace coal as the primary energy source, the area went into a decline and did not begin to pull out of it until all the resources of the area were combined.

Leading industrial products of the Kita-Kyushu area include iron and steel, metal ware, machinery, tools, electrical machines, oil and chemical products, items for the publishing and printing industries, and packaged foods.

Traditional industries that are still important include bamboo ware, paper, dolls, cutlery, seaweed, and ink stones.

The area is noted for several festivals, the largest of which are the Mekari Shinji, held by the Mekari Shrine, on January 1; Minato Matsuri, or Port Festival, in May in the port district of Moji; the Gion Daiko Festival, which includes over 100 floats, a drum-beating contest in front of Kokura Castle, and a folk-dance festival called Numagaku that is held on May 7—an event that has been designated an Intangible Cultural Property.

The lineup of places of special interest in Kita-Kyushu includes the unusual, as well as the usual—the Kammon Bridge, which links Kyushu with Honshu and is the longest bridge in the Orient; the Shin Kammon Tunnel, which links the two islands; the Sembutsu Limestone Grotto; Nippon Steel Corporation's Yawata Iron Works, the largest steel producer in the world; and the Hirodai Limestone Bed, which is partly under water.

The more usual attractions are the Mekari Shrine, founded by Empress Jingu in the third century, and Kokura Castle, which was built in 1602 by *Daimyo* Tadaoki Hosokawa. In its original glory it had a central tower, 148 secondary towers, and 48 gates and encompassed an area of 12,300 square kilometers that were surrounded by a stone wall 18 meters high.

Most of the castle was destroyed in the fighting that occurred during the time of the Meiji Restoration in the 1860s, but impressive portions of it have been restored.

KITE-FLYING / TAKO-AGE (Tah-koe-ah-gay)   Kite-flying has been a traditional sport in Japan for a long time, and kites come in a number of distinctive shapes and designs. The most popular kite-flying season is New Year's, but they are flown throughout the year.

One category of Japanese kite is very large and, in a stiff breeze, has enough pull on the line to support the weight of a person. In earlier years, it was common to stage kite competitions, in which the aim was to force competing kites down.

Recommended reading: *The Art of the Japanese Kite*, by Tal Streeter (Weatherhill).

KOBE (Koe-bay)   The capital of Hyogo Prefecture and Western Japan's leading seaport, Kobe has been known as an international city since the early days of Meiji, following the fall of the Tokugawa Shogunate. But it was engaged in foreign commerce as early as the fourth century.

Originally known as Muko-no Minato, or the Port of Muko, Kobe was even the administrative capital of Japan for a brief period (six months) in the twelfth century, when Kiyomori Taira (1118–1181) tried to develop the country through foreign trade.

While the area did not last long as the capital, its port—then called Hyogo—continued to prosper, especially in the fifteenth and sixteenth centuries. Kobe was then a suburb of Hyogo.

When Japan was opened to trade with the West, there was strong opposition to making Hyogo a foreign trade port; so, in a typically expeditious move, the suburban area of Kobe was designated as the port, and it was opened to trade on January 1, 1868.

The newly designated foreign trade port grew rapidly, and in 1889 officially absorbed Hyogo. The port city, now the sixth largest metropolis in Japan, is famous for its foreign flavor, ranging from its architecture to its selection of international restaurants.

Kobe now handies about 20 percent of Japan's exports and around 10 percent of its imports. It is also a major industrial area, big in iron and steel, shipbuilding, industrial vehicles and rolling stock, foodstuffs, flour milling, chemicals, rubber, and the distilling of *sake*. Over 10,000 ships call at the port each year.

Kobe is hemmed in by mountains. Its business district is concentrated around the port area, and its residential areas extend up the slopes of the adjoining mountains—giving it a picturesque atmosphere and a mild climate that has made it popular with foreigners for centuries.

Leading annual events in Kobe include the Opening Ceremony of the Hot Spring Bath at Arima Spa on January 2, the Festival to Drive Away Evil Spirits at Nagata Shrine on February 3 or 4, the spring festival of the

Ikuta Shrine, the Nanko Festival at Minatogawa Shrine on May 24–26, the Kobe Festival on the third weekend in May, and the Hot Spring Festival at Arima Spa on November 2–3.

Kobe was struck by a severe earthquake on the morning of January 17, 1995, that killed over 5,000 people, injured over 24,000 others, and virtually destroyed the center of the city. See EARTHQUAKES.

KOFU (Koe-fuu)   The capital of Yamanashi Prefecture, about two train-hours west of Shinjuku Station in Tokyo, Kofu was long famous as the headquarters of the Takeda clan during Japan's *daimyo* days.

In a basin surrounded by spectacular mountains, including Mt. Fuji, Kofu is now noted for its silk spinning and weaving and the production of crystalware and wine.

Among the historical attractions of the city is the famous Takeda Shrine, situated on the grounds of Takeda Castle, which was built in 1527 by Nobutora Takeda, father of Shingen, the most famous of the Takeda *daimyo*. Another is the Zenko Temple, built by Shingen and patterned after the celebrated temple of the same name in Nagano Prefecture.

The city also has a noted hot spring spa district, in which all of the *ryokan* (inns) are supplied with hot water bubbling up from the ground.

The famous Shosenkyo Gorge on the Arakawa River is just 30 minutes from Kofu.

KOJIKI (Koe-jee-kee)   The *Kojiki* is a narrative chronicle of the history of Japan, based on Shinto religious legends, that in earlier times was memorized by specially appointed Memory-Historians. The narrative began with the mythological origin of Japan and came down to 628 A.D.

In 712, a man named Yasumaro Ono wrote down in Chinese characters the entire story as recited by Hiyeda-no Are. See LITERATURE. Recommended reading: *Kojiki: Record of Ancient Matters* (Tuttle).

KOMUSO (Koe-muu-so)   During Japan's feudal age, thousands of Buddhist priests called *komuso* made a vocation of traveling about the countryside, wearing deep straw hats that covered their faces entirely. Tiny slits in the hats allowed them to see. Some of them were blind and wore the hats to hide their eyes.

Many of the *komuso* were *ronin* or masterless *samurai*, and were frequently employed by the various *daimyo* or the shogunate to act as spies. See WANDERING PRIESTS.

KORAKU GARDEN / KORAKU EN (Koe-rah-kuu een)   One of Tokyo's most celebrated gardens, Koraku En was designed in 1626 by Yorifusa Tokugawa, the eleventh son of the illustrious Ieyasu, who founded the Tokugawa Shogunate, and was the patriarch of the famous Mito branch of the Tokugawa family.

The garden was remodeled by Yorifusa's son Mitsukuni, whom history ranks as one of the greatest of the Mito Tokugawas. He was advised on the remodeling by Chu Shun-shui, a noted Chinese scholar, who was then a refugee in Japan and under Mitsukuni's patronage.

The third Tokugawa *Shogun*, Iemitsu, was also to have a hand in the garden. He designed its lake, in which there is an island with a small temple.

The garden is only a few minutes from downtown Tokyo and a five-minute walk from both Suidobashi Station on the Chuo Line and Korakuen Station on the Mita Toei Subway Line.

KOREANS IN JAPAN / KANKOKU JIN (Khan-koe-kuu Jeen)   Koreans make up the largest community of so-called foreign residents in Japan, numbering approximately 700,000. Most of them are citizens of Japan descended from Koreans who came to Japan—or were brought there—during the period from shortly after the turn of the century to 1945, when Korea was a Japanese possession.

In earlier years, there was considerable discrimination against Koreans in Japan, particularly in the areas of employment and housing. While their situation has improved significantly in recent decades, many Koreans in Japan still complain about racial and ethnic barriers and incidents.

About half the Koreans in Japan support the Communist-run People's Republic of North Korea and are therefore virtually stateless. Beginning in 1959, about 100,000 Koreans in Japan moved to North Korea, but now only 200 a year return to the land of their ancestors. It is said that many of those who went to North Korea in earlier years now regret their decision because of harsh political controls in the country and the difficulty in making a good living.

Korean residents in Japan lost their Japanese citizenship in 1952, when the treaty ending World War II stripped Japan of its overseas colonies. Koreans who were former citizens of the Empire of Japan—and those born in born in Japan since—do not automatically receive Japanese citizenship. They must apply for naturalization and go through a lengthy process.

There are 150 Korean primary, junior high, and senior high schools in Japan. Largest is the Korean High School in Tokyo, which has an enrollment of 1,200 students. There is also one Korean university in Tokyo.

The schools that are run by North Koreans in Japan teach the same courses that are taught in North Korea, including the political orientation.

KOSHI TEMPLE / KOSHI JI (Koe-she jee)   On the slopes of Asahi Hill in the outskirts of Kyoto, the Koshi Temple was built in 1233 by the famous priest Dogen, who founded the Soto sect of Buddhism after returning from a trip to China.

Dogen lived at the temple for 11 years as its abbot, before moving to Echizen Province (now Fukui Prefecture), where he built the even more famous Eihei Temple.

During June, July, and August, the ancient sport of cormorant fishing is demonstrated in the nearby Uji River.

KOTO (Koe-toe)   The *koto*, one of the four most popular traditional musical instruments in Japan (the other three being the flute, *shamisen*, and drums), dates from before the beginning of the Nara Period in 710.

A semicylindrical zither, the first *koto* apparently had five strings and was about three feet long. A sixth string was added during the early years of the Nara era, and later in the same period a 13-string *koto*, modeled after a Chinese instrument, was introduced. This new *koto* was six feet long and rested on the floor while being played. At first, it was used only by court musicians, but, from the fifteenth century on, it became popular among entertainers.

The *koto* has movable bridges for each string, and players continuously tune it while playing, in order to get more tones out of the instrument.

KOWAKIDANI (Koe-wah-kee-dah-nee)   One of the most famous hot spring spas in the Hakone district, about an hour and a half from Tokyo, Kowakidani (Valley of Lesser Boiling), also known as Ko Jigoku, or Little Hell, gets its name from sulfur fumes coming out of a cave in the vicinity.

Besides the efficacy of its hot mineral baths (against skin diseases, anemia, and nervous disorders), Kowakidani is noted for its scenic veiws of the Hayakawa Valley, the cherry tree- and azalea-covered hills, and a gorgeous waterfall known as Chisuji-no Taki, or Fall of 1,000 Threads.

KUMAMOTO (Kuu-mah-moe-toe)   The capital of Kumamoto Prefecture and Kyushu's third largest city, Kumamoto was chosen as a southwestern headquarters by the Tokugawa Shogunate (1603–1868) because of its central position on the island.

Today the city is known as an agricultural trading center and as the home of five colleges and universities, including the national Kumamoto University. Its traditional products include pottery, bamboo ware, rice gluten, and inlay work.

Kumamoto is also the home of one of the three most famous castles in Japan (the other two: Nagoya and Osaka). The castle, on a hill two kilometers northeast of Kumamoto Station, was built in 1601–1607 under the supervision of Kiyomasa Kato (1562–1611), who was lord of the area (then called Higo Province).

The castle was razed during a brief rebellion against the Imperial forces in 1877, but it has since been partially restored (in ferro-concrete). The donjon (main tower) now houses a museum. The whole area is a Place of Special Historical Importance, and the original remnants are Important Cultural Properties. Cherry trees line the ascending approach to the castle.

Other outstanding attractions: several parks (one the former garden of Lord Hosokawa's villa), Buddhist temples, and Shinto shrines (including the Fujisaki Hachiman, which dates back to the third century and was dedicated to Emperor Ojin and his mother, the Empress Jingu). There are also a number of spas in the vicinity.

KUSUNOKI, MASASHIGE (Kuu-sue-no-kee, Mah-sah-she-gay)   One of Japan's great feudal-age heroes, Masashige Kusunoki was born in 1294 and lived at the Hino-Zan Monastery in Yamato (near Nara) until he was 15. There he studied military strategy and became so proficient that his superiors feared for the country and tried to have him murdered.

The clever Kusunoki escaped, and went on to become a renowned general in the struggle between Emperor Godaigo and the Hojo clan that then controlled the shogunate through regents.

Takatori Hojo deposed the emperor, forced him into exile, and then attacked Masashige's forces with an army of 28,000 horsemen. Caught unprepared, Masashige and his army were besieged in a hastily constructed fort.

Masashige had a large funeral pyre built, placed the bodies of enemy soldiers on it, set it afire, and then escaped under the cover of darkness, spreading the word that he and his men had committed suicide. The Hojo general was deceived by the ruse and withdrew, leaving only a small detachment to hold the fort. A spy sent into the fort by Masashige learned that a convoy of supplies was coming in. He intercepted the convoy, captured it, and secreted his men in the wagons.

Masashige easily regained the fort. The garrison left behind by Hojo switched sides and swore loyalty to him. He and his men then went to the Tenno Temple in Osaka, where he had caused a fake message to be placed among the writings of the great Shotoku Taishi, who lived in the sixth century.

Masashige had an oracle read the message, which predicted that he would be victorious against the emperor's enemies. In 1333, he won a decisive victory over the Hojo forces, ending a shogunate that had lasted since 1192.

The famous general then besieged and captured Kyoto, but was not able to guarantee the emperor's safety and advised him to go to Mt. Hiei. The emperor's courtiers persuaded him to ignore the general's advice, and Masashige withdrew from the city.

A short time later, the combined forces of the enemy attacked Masashige at Minatogawa (now in Kobe) and virtually annihilated his army. Masashige, his brother Masasue, and their closest aides retreated to a nearby farmhouse. There, when Masasue took off his armor, he found that he had been wounded 11 times.

Knowing they were doomed, Masashige and his brother sat facing each other and ran each other through with their swords. Before killing themselves, Masashige asked his brother: "What shall we do after death?"

Masasue replied, "I pray that I may be reborn into human life seven times in order to destroy the rebels."

"That," said Masashige, "is exactly my desire."

At that time, Masashige's son, Masatsura, was prevented from joining his father and uncle in death, and, in 1348, when he was 23, he raised an army of 1,000 men and captured Chihaya Castle, which was defended by 13,000 men. He then attacked Kyoto, forcing the last Ashikaga *Shogun* to flee.

Only the next year, Masatsura and his own young brother were defeated in a battle at Shijo Nawate, and, like their father and uncle before them, they killed each other rather than submit to capture. Thus ended the attempts of the famous Kusunoki family to help the emperor regain the power lost by his ancestor some 200 years before.

(Golden Pavilion, Kyoto)

KYOTO (Ke-yoe-toe)   From ancient times to the year 709, Japan's capital was moved each time a new emperor ascended the throne. That year, a permanent capital was built at Nara, but in 784 it was moved to Nagaokakyo and then in 794 to a new place some distance away called Uda.

The new city was laid out according to Chinese concepts, with nine wide streets running from east to west, and a series of broad north-south avenues intersecting these streets in grid fashion.

Construction of the new city was completed in 805, and it was named Heian Kyo, or Capital of Peace. Later, this was changed to Miyako (Imperial Capital), and finally this was shortened to Kyoto, which means Capital City.

Kyoto was built on a sloping plain adjoining a river, making it possible to construct a network of canals through the city and divert water into them. As a result, it was one of the best organized and most attractive cities in the world.

Kyoto was to remain the Imperial Capital of Japan for over 1,100 years, becoming the source of arts and crafts and customs that were to distinguish Japanese culture from all others. Nestled among picturesque mountains, it was to become the religious center of Japan, as well, with an array of imposing shrines and temples dotting its landscape and the surrounding hills, along with several castles and palaces.

Over the centuries, Kyoto was often ravaged by fires and political strife. When Nobunaga Oda entered the city with his conquering forces in 1569, he found it nearly destroyed. He immediately began a program to rebuild it which was continued by his successor, Hideyoshi Toyotomi.

During World War II, a number of Americans who were acquainted with the cultural value of the city successfully lobbied to have Kyoto designated an open city and thus saved it from bombing.

Today Kyoto still boasts over 1,500 Buddhist temples and over 220 shrines, along with a number of palaces and castles.

Like all of Japan's large cities, Kyoto is divided into wards—nine of them —and covers an area of 610 square kilometers. In addition to being the nation's repository of cultural treasures, it is also a major commercial, industrial, and educational center.

It is particularly noted for its Nishijin silk weaving, dyeing, embroidery, porcelain, lacquerware, cloisonné, folding fans, screens, machinery, and metal industries, plus *sake* brewing and large-scale cookie and pastry baking.

Kyoto has major annual events every month of the year, including a number that draw visitors from all over the world. See FESTIVALS.

There are so many places of interest in Kyoto that it would take several months time to see them all. For this reason, many visitors go back to the city again and again. Among the most famous of the sights are Kyoto Imperial Park (where princes once lived), Kyoto Imperial Palace, Shokoku Temple, Nishijin (the silk-weaving district), Kitano Shrine, the Temple of the Golden Pavilion, the Daitoku Temple, the Shugakuin Imperial Villa, the Temple of the Silver Pavilion, Nanzen Temple, Nijo Castle, Yasaka Shrine, Gion Corner, Chion Temple, Kiyomizu Temple, Nishi-Hongan Temple, and the Katsura Imperial Villa.

There are also dozens of places of special interest in the vicinity of Kyoto, ranging from the Rapids of Hozu and the Byodo Temple (originally the villa of Prime Minister Michinaga Fujiwara (966–1024) to Mt. Hiei, on whose cypress-covered summit is the great and famous Enryaku Temple, founded in 788 by Dengyo Daishi as headquarters for the Tendai sect of Buddhism.

The temple and monastery buildings grew into a massive complex that housed thousands of priests who became professional warriors in the fifteenth and sixteenth centuries. Clad in armor, they made frequent raids on Kyoto. Nobunaga Oda finally destroyed the temple and monastery in the mid-1500s, killing many of the warrior-monks and dispersing the rest.

The monastery was restored during the reign of Hideyoshi Toyotomi, Nobunaga's successor, and was greatly enlarged by Tokugawa *Shogun* Iemitsu, but later generations of monks did not resume the warlike ways of their predecessors.

From the pavilion of Enryaku Temple, one has a magnificent view of Kyoto, Lake Biwa, and the surrounding mountains.

There are over 40 annual events of special significance in Kyoto, some of them lasting for several days.

These include:

JANUARY 1: Otera Mairi at Yasaka Shrine, a ceremony to ward off illness during the new year.

JANUARY 8–12: Toka Ebisu, a festival to honor Ebisu, the patron deity of business.

JANUARY 9–16: Hoonko, memorial services to honor the founder of the Shinshu sect of Buddhism, Priest Shinran.

JANUARY 14: Hadaka Odori, the so-called Nude Dance, held at the Hokai Temple by boys and young men.

JANUARY 15: Toshiya, an archery contest in which archers see who can shoot the most arrows the length of a great hall. The record holder is Daihachiro Wasa, a *samurai* of Kii Province who, in one day, in 1696, loosed 13,053 arrows, 8,153 of which went the full length of the range.

JANUARY 21: A service at To Temple in honor of Kobo Daishi, founder of the Shingon sect of Buddhism.

FEBRUARY 3 or 4: Setsubun, the bean-throwing, good-luck ceremony that marks the last day of winter.

FEBRUARY 25: Baikasai, or Plum Blossom Festival, at Kitano Shrine in honor of the shrine deity.

MARCH 1–3: Hina Matsuri, or Doll Festival, at Hokyo Temple.

APRIL–MAY 15: Miyako Odori, also known as the Cherry Dance, at the Kaburenjo Theater in Gion.

APRIL, second Sunday: Yasurai Matsuri, a demon festival to placate the spirits that cause plagues.

APRIL 21–29: Mibu Kyogen, pantomime farcical dances performed since medieval times at the Mibu Temple.

MAY 15: Aoi Matsuri, the reenactment of an Imperial Procession that dates back to the sixth century.

JULY 16–24: Gion Matsuri, one of the three greatest festivals in Japan, consisting of a great parade, floats, and other events.

AUGUST 23–24: Matsu-Age, in which people toss burning torches onto baskets of wood suspended on high poles.

SEPTEMBER 21–27: Higan-E, services at all Buddhist temples to mark the equinox.

OCTOBER 12: Ushi Matsuri, or Bull Festival, a ceremony at the Koryu Temple that began in the ninth century.

OCTOBER 22: Jidai Matsuri, or Festival of the Ages, sponsored by the Heian Shrine and one of the most spectacular annual events in Japan.

NOVEMBER, second Sunday: Momiji Matsuri, or Maple Festival, a recreation of the games and activities of the nobles of tenth-century Kyoto.

DECEMBER 1–26: Kao-mise, or all-star *kabuki* performances, at the Minami-Za Theater.

DECEMBER 25: Shimai Tenjin, the final celebration of the year in honor of Tenjin, the patron deity of scholars.

There are over 200 listed places of special interest in Kyoto, including shrines, temples, palaces, castles, gardens, and other historical and cultural treasures. Large sections of the city are in effect museums of the past, and there is virtually no end to things that attract the historical buff.

Among the dozens of major attractions:

KYOTO IMPERIAL PARK: Formerly, the park was occupied by residences of Imperial nobles and other high court officials. The Kyoto office of the Imperial Household Agency is now in the park.

KYOTO IMPERIAL PALACE (Kyoto Gosho): Originally built in 794 and rebuilt many times since, the palace is a huge complex of gates, gardens, official greeting rooms, private rooms, sanctuaries, guard houses, and offices. It gives an impressive image of the grand life-style of the emperors and their courtiers.

SHOKOKU TEMPLE: Second among the five chief temples of the Rinzai sect of Buddhism, the Shokoku was originally erected in 1393 on orders from the emperor. On the grounds are the tombs of Yoshimasa Ashikaga, the eighth Ashikaga *Shogun*, and Seika Fujiwara (1561–1619), a famous scholar in Chinese classics.

KINKAKU TEMPLE: The famous Gold Pavilion, first designed as the villa of a court noble named Kintsune Saionji, was later renovated by Yoshimitsu Ashikaga, the third Ashikaga *Shogun*, who lived there after his retirement.

DAITOKU TEMPLE: One of the chief temples of the Rinzai sect of Buddhism, Daitoku Temple was founded in 1324. Its main gate was designed and built by the famous tea master Sen-no Rikyu, in 1589. The garden of the temple was designed by the equally famous Enshu Kobori. It is one of the largest temple complexes in Kyoto.

SHUGAKUIN IMPERIAL VILLA: Located at the foot of Mt. Hiei, the first two of these three magnificent villas were built in the 1650s by the Tokugawa Shogunate for ex-Emperor Gomizuno-o. The third villa was added later for his daughter. The villas are separated from each other and have their own gates and gardens, along with summer houses.

GINKAKUJI TEMPLE: Built in 1482 by Yoshimasa Ashikaga as a country villa, this is the famous Silver Pavilion. After Yoshimasa's death, it was converted to a temple. Its garden was designed by the great Soami.

HEIAN SHRINE: This shrine commemorates the founding of Heian (Kyoto) in 794 by Emperor Kammu. It sponsors several events each year including the Jidai Matsuri, or Festival of the Ages.

NANZEN TEMPLE: There are actually 13 temples on the precincts of the Nanzen Temple, which was founded in 1293. It is the headquarters of the Nanzen school of the Rinzai sect of Buddhism, and has several gardens designed by Japan's most renowned masters and many other cultural treasures.

NIJO CASTLE: Built in 1603 by Ieyasu, founder of the Tokugawa Shogunate to serve as his residence when he visited Kyoto, the castle became the temporary seat of government in 1868, when the last Tokugawa *Shogun* resigned. The large complex has to be one of the most fascinating places in all Japan. Its great rooms, chambers, and halls echo with the color and pageantry of the past. With only a little imagination, one can see the great Tokugawa *Shogun* holding court in one of the richly decorated halls or making his way down one of the polished wooden corridors.

YASAKA SHRINE: Popularly known as the Gion Shrine, because it is at the east end of the Gionmachi entertainment district, this shrine is dedicated to one of Japan's ranking mythological deities, Susano-o Mikoto, his consort, and their sons, whose representations were transferred to the shrine in 876. Several parts of the shrine are registered as cultural treasures.

CHION-IN TEMPLE: One of the largest and most famous temples in Japan, the Chion-in is the headquarters of the Jodo sect of Buddhism and was erected in 1234 by Priest Genchi, a disciple of Ho-nen, who founded the sect. Its gate is regarded as one of the most impressive of all the temple gates in Japan. The great Enshu Kobori designed the garden surrounding the superior's quarters.

KIYOMIZU TEMPLE: On a hill amidst a dense grove of trees, the noted Kiyomizu Temple was founded in 798. The main hall sits on a high cliff overlooking a deep valley. The sprawling complex includes over a dozen buildings and structures, many of which are National Treasures.

HOKO TEMPLE: Built in 1586 by Hideyoshi Toyotomi, who unified the country and set the stage for the foundation of the Tokugawa Shogunate, the Hoko is also called Dai-Butsu-Den, or Great Buddha Hall, because it originally housed a huge image of Buddha.

KYOTO NATIONAL MUSEUM: Erected in 1897 by the Imperial Household Agency, the museum has 17 exhibit rooms in which are displayed over 2,000 of the finest and rarest pieces of art, handicrafts, and religious objects, donated by temples, shrines, and individuals in Kyoto.

NISHI HONGAN TEMPLE: School headquarters of the Jodo-Shinshu sect, this great temple complex contains what is regarded as the finest examples of Buddhist architecture in Japan. The temple is dedicated to Kenshin Daishi (1173–1244), founder of the sect. In 1602, the soon-to-be *shogun* Ieyasu Tokugawa sponsored the founding of a rival to the Jodo-Shinshu sect by Priest Otani (a former abbot of the Nishi Hongan Temple). The temple of this rival sect was known as the Higashi (East) Hongan Temple.

DAIKAKU TEMPLE: Originally a villa built for Emperor Saga, the Daikaku was converted to a temple in 867 by Emperor Junna, who appointed a favorite prince as its founder and abbot. The temple is famous for its paintings by great masters of the past.

KATSURA IMPERIAL VILLA: Adjacent to the Katsura River, this outstanding example of Japanese architecture and garden design was built in the 1620s for Prince Toshihito, brother of Emperor Goyozei (1571–1617). The complex contains a number of magnificient buildings, including a veranda designed especially for moon viewing.

See individual listings of many of the above. Recommended reading: *Introducing Kyoto*, by Herbert Plutschow (Kodansha International).

KYOTO UNIVERSITY / KYOTO DAIGAKU (Die-gah-kuu) Founded in 1897, and thus the second oldest, as well as one of the largest, of Japan's state-run universities, Kyoto Daigaku is located just west of Kyoto's world-famous Silver Pavilion, or Gin Kaku-Ji.

One of the elite universities of Japan, Kyoto is especially noted for its Faculty of Literature museum, which contains many ancient documents relating to history, archaeology, and geography and for the Yukawa Memorial Institute, built in 1952 and primarily financed by Hideki Yukawa, who won the Nobel Prize in physics in 1949.

KYUSHU (Que-shuu)   The southwesternmost of Japan's four main islands and the closest to the Korean Peninsula and China, Kyushu is considered the heartland of Japanese culture. Tradition says that the first emperor, Jimmu Tenno, came from Kyushu, and it is well known that the island acted as the conduit for most of the cultural influences from Korea and China that were to shape and color the civilization of Japan.

The 44,296-square-kilometer island of Kyushu is separated from Shikoku on the east by the Bungo Channel, and from Honshu on the north by the Kammon Straits. It is connected to Honshu by two undersea tunnels and a long suspension bridge.

Like all the other major islands of Japan, Kyushu is extremely mountainous, with numerous peaks soaring to over 1,700 meters above sea level. It is also replete with hundreds of hot springs (many of which have been developed into famous resort spas for centuries), seascapes that are enchanting in their beauty, and thousands of offshore isles and islets that garland the island like jewels.

Kyushu has four of Japan's most beautiful national parks, including Mt. Aso (the world's largest volcano); Unzen-Amakusa, which combines a highland park, a world-renowned hot spring spa, and hundreds of offshore islands; the marine park of Saikai, noted for its seascapes; and Kirishima-Yaku, which encompasses Mt. Takachiho.

In addition to these outstanding areas, Kyushu is also famed for the Hellsprings of Beppu, Yabakei Gorge, the live volcano of Sakurajima in the harbor of Kagoshima, and the Nichinan coast, which is a quasi-national park.

Nagasaki is probably Kyushu's best-known city. After Japan closed its doors to the outside world in 1639, the only crack that was left open was Nagasaki, through which news of the world beyond trickled in ever so slowly over the next 220-odd years.

Nagasaki is also remembered as being the second of Japan's cities to be atom-bombed during World War II (see NAGASAKI).

In earlier times, Kyushu was the landing place of the Mongol invasion fleets in 1274 and 1281. See HISTORY. Kyushu's other major cities are Fukuoka, Kita-Kyushu, and Kumamoto.

LABOR / RODO (Roe-doe)   Japan's labor force is steadily approaching the 60 million mark and consists of approximately 63 percent of the population that is age 15 and older. Men still significantly outnumber women in the labor force by a ratio of about three to two, but the ratio is steadily decreasing.

During the 1950s, '60s, and early '70s, when its economy was one of the fastest growing in the world, Japan experienced a labor shortage. But the oil crisis in 1973 slowed economic growth, and it has never recovered its pre-oil-shock pace.

Because of what amounts to lifetime employment in government, public corporations, and larger commercial enterprises, the unemployment rate in Japan has been held very low by worldwide standards—under 3 percent.

These figures are misleading, however. In Japan the only people who are officially regarded as unemployed are those who are out of work and have registered as seeking employment. The figures do not count people who have been laid off. They are regarded as being on temporary leave.

People who have lost jobs but are working in family businesses are not counted as unemployed. Neither are housewives who are not actively seeking employment.

If Japan used the American system of counting its jobless, its unemployment figures would be much higher. Furthermore, the system of lifetime employment contributes to overemployment in many companies and industries and thus amounts to a social expense that in other countries is more likely to be pushed off on the government.

Because of the Japanese social and economic system, Japanese workers, generally, are exceptionally diligent and loyal. The Japanese management system is very personal. It is more people-oriented than job-slot-oriented.

Young people who go to work for more desirable employers presume that they will be there for life and are therefore very much interested in the success and growth of their employers. Japanese workers know they cannot bounce from one job to another, as so many U.S. workers do, and they are therefore much more concerned about their behavior and productivity.

LABOR UNIONS / RODO KUMIAI (Roe-doe kuu-me-aye)   Japanese labor unions are organized on a company basis—not on a craft or industry basis, as they are in the U.S. In other words, all the members of a particular union belong to the same company and have nothing to do with other unions around the country.

Individual company unions may belong to a national federation, but they remain independent and handle their own affairs as separate entities. Once a year, individual company unions may cooperate with the national federation in public demonstrations to influence employers to give all workers across-the-board pay increases. See SPRING LABOR OFFENSIVE.

At other times, company unions may stage temporary work stoppages in their own firms, but these are normally for short, prearranged durations, designed to impress the employer with their seriousness but not to harm the company seriously.

The leaders of company labor unions remain employees of the company, and once their term of office is over they resume their work as employees. Because negotiations between management and representatives of the company union are ongoing, most disputes are settled before labor and management reach an impasse.

The percentage of unionized workers in Japan's labor force has been falling steadily since the 1950s, when it was around 40 percent. It is now approximately 24 percent. The percentages vary widely with the type of company.

Some 60 percent of the companies involved in transportation and communications are unionized. In finance and insurance, the percentage is about 55, and in mining it is about 47. Only around 9 percent of the companies involved in retailing and wholesaling, and only about 16 percent of the businesses in construction are unionized.

Workers in the manufacturing industries, of which some 35 percent are unionized, account for the majority of Japan's union members.

The three leading national union federations are *Rengo* (the Japanese Trade Union Federation), *Zenroren* (the National Confederation of Trade Unions), and *Zenrokyo* (the National Trade Union Council).

Recommended reading: *Labor Relations in Japan Today*, by Tadashi Hanami (Kodansha International).

LACQUERWARE / SHIKKI (Sheek-key)   Lacquerware has been popular in Japan since it was introduced from China in the seventh century. Because of its versatility, durability, and beauty, it became a handicraft art as well as a utilitarian product. Numerous pieces of lacquerware dating back to the seventh and eighth centuries are on display in the Horyu (Hoe-ree-you) and other temples in Nara.

Several techniques of lacquering and several ways of producing different designs have traditionally been used in Japan. Colors range from vermilion, green, black, and gold to many combinations. Among the most popular lacquerware products are bowls, trays, and jewelry boxes.

The island of Shikoku is famous for its lacquerware industry, and Wajima lacquerware from the district of Wajima is the most famous of all.

LAKES / MIZUUMI (Me-zoo-uu-me)   Because of its mountains, rainfall, and volcanic nature, Japan has numerous lakes. The majority of them are in the mountains, and most are small. The largest and most famous lake in Japan is Lake Biwa (Biwa Ko), near Kyoto in Shiga Prefecture. It is 674 square kilometers, or 260 square miles, in area.

The deepest lake in the country is Lake Tazawa (Tah-zah-wah), which reaches a depth of 423 meters (1,388 feet) and is near Morioka in northeast Honshu.

Other larger lakes include Kasumigaura in Ibaraki Prefecture, Saroma Ko in Hokkaido (a saltwater lake), Inawashiro Ko in Fukushima Prefecture, and Nakaumi in Tottori and Shimane Prefectures (also a saltwater lake).

Among the smaller but most beautiful lakes in Japan are Ashino-Ko (popularly known as Lake Hakone); Chuzenji, which is just above Nikko; and Yamanaka and Kawaguchi, two of the five lakes around the waist of Mt. Fuji.

Since early times, Lake Biwa has been noted for its Eight Beautiful Views, called Omi Hakkei (actually, the Eight Beautiful Views of Omi, where the lake is located). These views are the autumn moon seen from Ishiyama, the evening glow at Seta, dusk and the evening bell at Mii Temple, snow on Mt. Hira at sunset, night rain at Karasaki, boats sailing from Yabase, the sky and the breeze on the lake at Awazu, and wild geese landing on the lake at Katada.

LAND AREA   The Japanese archipelago is made up of over 4,000 islands, all but four of which range from tiny to small. The total land area is approximately 378,000 square kilometers, or 146,000 square miles. This makes Japan only one-twenty-fifth the size of the U.S. (about the size of the state of Montana), one-twenty-sixth the size of China, one twenty-third the size of Brazil, and a little bit larger than Malaysia. Japan is about one and a half times the size of Great Britain and a little larger than Norway and Italy.

LANGUAGE / KOKUGO (Koe-kuu-go)   The Japanese language is unique in a number of ways. Some theories relate it to the Altaic and Korean family of languages, but these theories have not been substantiated. It has its own peculiar sentence structure, and it is very flexible within this structure.

Japanese is based on some 103 syllables made up of only six sounds, and it is therefore phonetically very simple. It has five vowels (a, i, u, e, o) and 14 consonants (k, s, t, n, h, m, y, r, w, g, z, d, b, and p). Consonants never occur alone—only in combination with vowels. The only other sound in the language is the nasal *n*.

Japanese is pronounced very much like Spanish, including trilling of the *r*'s. Japanese may be written with Roman letters in a system called *Roma-ji*, which means Roman letters. Vowels may be pronounced long or short or may be silent. Consonants are pronounced as they are in English.

Care must be taken to distinguish between single and double consonants, which are stressed, as in Italian and French. Doubling a consonant changes the meaning of a word.

Japanese is not a tonal language, like Chinese, but it often requires the accentuation of syllables. Otherwise, the pronunciation is straightforward.

The following charts give an approximate idea of how the language should be pronounced:

PRONUNCIATION CHART I

A	I	U	E	O
(Ah)	(Ee)	(Uu)	(Eh)	(Oh)
Ka	**Ki**	**Ku**	**Ke**	**Ko**
(Kah)	(Kee)	(Kuu)	(Kay)	(Koe)
Sa	**Shi**	**Su**	**Se**	**So**
(Sah)	(She)	(Sue)	(Say)	(Soe)
Ta	**Chi**	**Tsu**	**Te**	**To**
(Tah)	(Che)	(T'sue)	(Tay)	(Toe)
Na	**Ni**	**Nu**	**Ne**	**No**
(Nah)	(Nee)	(Nuu)	(Nay)	(No)
Ha	**Hi**	**Hu**	**He**	**Ho**
(Hah)	(He)	(Who)	(Hay)	(Hoe)
Ma	**Mi**	**Mu**	**Me**	**Mo**
(Mah)	(Me)	(Muu)	(May)	(Moe)
Ya	**I**	**Yu**	**E**	**Yo**
(Yah)	(Ee)	(Yuu)	(Eh)	(Yoe)
Ra	**Ri**	**Ru**	**Re**	**Ro**
(Rah)	(Ree)	(Rue)	(Ray)	(Roe)
		Trill the R's a bit		
Wa	**I**	**U**	**E**	**Wo**
(Wah)	(Ee)	(Uu)	(Eh)	(Oh)

PRONUNCIATION CHART II

Ga	**Gi**	**Gu**	**Ge**	**Go**
(Gah)	(Ghee)	(Goo)	(Gay)	(Go)
Za	**Ji**	**Zu**	**Ze**	**Zo**
(Zah)	(Jee)	(Zoo)	(Zay)	(Zoe)
Da	**Ji**	**Zu**	**De**	**Do**
(Dah)	(Jee)	(Zoo)	(Day)	(Doe)
Ba	**Bi**	**Bu**	**Be**	**Bo**
(Bah)	(Bee)	(Boo)	(Bay)	(Boe)
Pa	**Pi**	**Pu**	**Pe**	**Po**
(Pah)	(Pee)	(Poo)	(Pay)	(Poe)

PRONUNCIATION CHART III

The following 33 syllables are combinations of some of the two sets appearing above.

Rya	Ryu	Ryo
(R'yah)	(R'you)	(Rio)
Mya	**Myu**	**Myo**
(M'yah)	(M'you)	(M'yoe)
Nya	**Nyu**	**Nyo**
(N'yah)	(N'you)	(N'yoe)
Hya	**Hyu**	**Hyo**
(H'yah)	(H'you)	(H'yoe)
Cha	**Chu**	**Cho**
(Chah)	(Chew)	(Choe)
Sha	**Shu**	**Sho**
(Shah)	(Shuu)	(Show)
Kya	**Kyu**	**Kyo**
(K'yah)	(Que)	(Q'yoe)
Pya	**Pyu**	**Pyo**
(P'yah)	(P'you)	(P'yoe)
Bya	**Byu**	**Byo**
(B'yah)	(B'you)	(B'yoe)
Ja	**Ju**	**Jo**
(Jah)	(Juu)	(Joe)
Gya	**Gyu**	**Gyo**
(G'yah)	(G'you)	(G'yoe)

The wild card in the Japanese language and pronunciation system is the nasal sound *n*, which is pronounced something like the n in bond. For example, the word for bread is *pan*, which is made up of two syllables *pa* and *n* and is pronounced pahn. Another example: lawyer is *bengoshi* (be-n-go-shi), pronounced bane-go-she.

There are several good courses in the Japanese language, including a number on cassette tapes. A key point in studying the language is *not* to focus on grammar or vocabulary. Learn it by studying dialogues first and then regular composition.

Also keep in mind that your studying should *all* be out loud in a normal speaking or reading voice. A great part of the challenge of learning a foreign language is the mechanical problem of achieving skill with the tongue and mouth in saying the words properly, smoothly, and at an appropriate speed. The only way this skill can be achieved is repetition—repeating the dialogues and sentences out loud, over and over, until they become automatic.

In the U.S., several different Japanese-language courses and study aids are available from the Kinokuniya bookstore chain, which has shops in Los Angeles, San Francisco, and New York.

One of the most useful Japanese-language books I have found over the years is the *English-Japanese Conversation Dictionary*, by Mr. and Mrs. O. Vaccari, available wherever books on Japan are on sale. See JAPANESE LANGUAGE.

LAWS / HORITSU (Hoe-reet-sue)   During the Tokugawa Shogunate era, it was generally believed by the *bakufu* government that laws should be kept secret—that it would be dangerous if the public knew the laws. When Japan opened its doors to the West, it adopted the German system of laws.

The Japanese still prefer arbitration and compromise to legal recourse, and there is strong pressure from the courts for people and corporations to reach out-of-court settlements.

LAWYERS / BENGOSHI (Bane-go-she)   Japan's first regulation concerning lawyers was passed in 1876, and a lawyer law went into effect in 1895, but the bar association was under the direct supervision of chief prosecutors attached to district courts.

The present Attorney's Law was passed in 1949, and Nichibenren (Nee-chee-bane-rane), the Japan Federation of Bar Associations, was founded on the same day. The law guarantees the independence of the association and sets standards for lawyers.

Persons who have passed the national bar examination or have taught law as a university professor for at least five years, as well as foreign lawyers who have been screened by Nichibenren, are eligible to practice law in Japan.

Nichibenren, headquartered in Kasumigaseki, the government center, has 52 local branch offices, including one in each prefecture. All lawyers are required to register with their local branch office and the main office of Nichibenren. Lawyers are required to have offices and must follow guidelines set by the bar association in charging fees.

Most of Japan's lawyers are in Tokyo and Osaka, and fewer than 500 of them are women.

Japan has fewer than 17,000 lawyers, as opposed to nearly 700,000 in the U.S. But in Japan a variety of other professionals perform functions that are generally handled by American attorneys.

These other professionals include *zeirishi* (zay-e-ree-she) or tax attorneys, *benrishi* (bane-ree-she) or patent attorneys, *shiho shoshi* (she-hoe show-she), or judicial scriveners, and *gyosei shoshi* (g'yoe-say-e show-she), or administrative scriveners. Also, each year hundreds of students who studied law in universities but did not become lawyers go to work in the legal departments of companies and government ministries.

The traditional lawyer in Japan is limited primarily to representing clients in court.

There are no law schools, as such, in Japan. The universities are divided into semi-independent departments, which students enter after completing two years of undergraduate study. The law department is usually the most prestigious of the university departments, and only those with the highest academic credentials (based on the results of their entrance examinations) are accepted into it.

Once in the law department, students study only law, usually concentrating on its theoretical and general aspects.

The national Legal Examination, which lawyers, judges, and public procurators must pass before they are licensed to practice, is extremely difficult. Each year some 20,000 candidates take it, but only about 500 pass.

Under the provisions of Japan's Attorney's Law, passed in 1949 and amended in 1955, foreign attorneys were permitted to practice in Japan as associate members of the bar, which allowed them to practice without having to pass the Legal Examination or know the Japanese language.

Through 1984, there were only some two dozen foreign attorneys in Japan, who were registered to handle matters primarily concerning foreign interests. In June 1984, the Japan Federation of Bar Associations decided to allow accredited foreign lawyers to practice in Japan under the following conditions: Their practice would be limited to out-of-court activities and matters relating to foreign law; they would not be allowed to enter the jurisdiction of Japanese law; they would be officially accredited and administered by the association and given the title of "foreign law consultant"; they would be prohibited from hiring Japanese lawyers.

The Federation said these restrictions were necessary to keep foreign attorneys from encroaching on the established areas of Japanese lawyers. It also said this special accreditation would be granted to lawyers whose past record was sufficiently high to meet Japanese standards and that such accreditation would be limited to two or three years, renewable upon reapplication.

Over the years, only one foreign attorney spoke Japanese well enough to pass the bar examinations in that language. In 1987 the Justice Ministry enacted new regulations permitting foreign attorneys to practice law in Japan without passing the bar exam, but still on a very restricted basis. Despite increasing pressure over the years, as of 1995 these restrictions remain in place.

LIBERAL STAR   This is a monthly tabloid-size newspaper published by the Liberal Democratic Party of Japan for English readers. It is available overseas by subscription from the Liberal Democratic Party, at 1-11-23 Nagata-cho, Chiyoda-ku, Tokyo 100 Japan. It covers domestic and international affairs, the visits of foreign dignitaries, and interviews with authorities in various fields.

LITERARY AGENCIES   Japanese literary agents play a leading role in the translation and publication of foreign books in Japan and, to a considerably lesser extent, in the Japanese books that are published abroad in foreign languages.

The top literary agencies in the country are Japan Uni Agency, Nagai Building, 5th Floor, 1-1 Jimbo-cho, Kanda, Chiyoda-ku, Tokyo 101 Japan; and the Tuttle-Mori Agency, Fuji Building, 8th Floor, 2-15 Jimbo-cho, Kanda, Chiyoda-ku, Tokyo 101 Japan.

The Asano Agency, Inc., Suite 302, Tokuda Building, 4-44-8 Sengoku, Bunkyo-ku, Tokyo 112 Japan, is also an important agency. The founder and president is Kiyoshi Asano (former vice-president of the Tuttle-Mori Agency).

The Japan Uni Agency works closely with a large pool of professional translators and is involved in the translation of many of the books it handles.

LITERATURE / BUNGAKU (Boon-gah-kuu)   Only China and Korea have longer continuous literary histories than Japan. Three of Japan's earliest books were the *Kojiki* (Koe-jee-kee), the *Nihonshoki* (Nee-hone-sho-kee), and the *Manyoshu* (Mahn-yoe-shuu).

The *Kojiki* is an anthology of ancient events, as recited by a court official whose task it was to memorize such matters. It was published in book form in the eighth century. The *Nihonshoki*, also published in the eighth century, is a history of Japan up to that time.

The *Manyoshu*, a poetry anthology, was also a product of this same century. It contains nearly 4,000 poems, most of which are *tanka* (tahn-kah), short poems consisting of 31 syllables in lines of 5-7-5-7-7 syllables, and *choka* (choe-kah), long poems that have any number of pairs of 5-7 syllables and ending with two 7-syllable lines.

The world's first novel of record, the famous *Genji Monogatari* (Gane-jee Moe-no-gah-tah-ree), or *The Tale of Genji*, was written in the early part of the eleventh century by a woman named Murasaki Shikibu, a member of the Imperial Court in Kyoto. It is a long (54 books), insightful, poetic chronicle of the loves, intrigues, failures, and successes of the Court nobles of this fascinating period in Japan's history, with the members of the Genji family as the principal set of characters. The book is available in English in two translations—the first one by Arthur Waley and the second one by Edward Seidensticker.

Another great novel, *Heike Monogatari* (Hay-e-kay Moe-no-gah-tah-ree) or *Tale of Heike*, written in the thirteenth century, was a more popular work than the one written by Lady Murasaki. This book tells the story, in epic fashion, of the splendor and decadence of the last ruling family of the ancient era, their defeat and downfall.

Imbued with the Buddhist concept of the transitory nature of all things and the idea that no matter how high a person or a family may rise, a day of reckoning will come, the story was memorized by storytellers who traveled around the country, relating it to the accompaniment of the *biwa*, a stringed instrument.

During these long centuries, the writing of poetry was more than a national custom. Warriors, fatally wounded in combat, often used their last moment to compose a poem.

With the establishment of the Tokugawa Shogunate in 1603, along with its strict political and social controls, the nature of Japan's literature underwent a significant change. From the epic narratives of wars and the intrigues of the Imperial Court, writers began turning their attention to both the *samurai* and common people in their pursuit of pleasure.

The primary theme in the literature of the 1600s and 1700s was comedy (*warai*) and amusement (*asobi*). Numerous books appeared, detailing the pleasures and peccadilloes of the times, particularly about life in the flourishing entertainment quarters.

By the late 1700s and early 1800s, the Tokugawa Shogunate had lost its dynamism, and the pleasures of the huge red-light districts, the baths, and the bawdy theater had become so commonplace that writers began looking to the past for themes.

Akinari Ueda (1734–1809), the author of two major collections of short stories, *Ugetsu Monogatari* and *Harusame Monogatari*, was a leader in this movement. His writing reflected the classical taste of the past.

The historical novel, called *yomihon* (story book), also came into its own during this period. The two most celebrated authors of this type of book were Kyoden Santo (1761–1816) and Baikin Takizawa (1767–1848). Baikin wrote the long, moralistic novel, *Nanso Satomi Hakkenden*, which covers the period from 1814 to 1841, and was the longest novel written in Japan during the Tokugawa Period.

Novelist Shunsui Tamenaga (1790–1843) is regarded as one of the best of the *ninjo-bon* (real-life romance books) writers who flourished during this period. His most representative work is *Shunshoku Umegoyomi*, an insightful story of the amorous relationships between men and women.

Shortly after the beginning of the 1800s, comical books (*kok-kei-bon*) became the vogue. The three most famous examples of this genre are *Tokaido-Chu Hizakurige*, or *Along the Tokai High Way by Shank's Mare* (on foot), by Ikku Jippensha (1765–1831); and *Ukiyo-Buro* (*The Floating World of the Bath*) and *Ukiyo-Doko* (*A Man of the Floating World*), both by Samba Shiteki (1776–1822).

Hizakurige is the original "road" adventure, chronicling the misadventures of two middle-aged characters from Edo, who get away from quarrelsome wives by taking off on a long walking tour of the famous Tokaido, which connected Edo with Kyoto.

Their adventures along the way, especially in the Post Station inns, where there were always women of pleasure available, gives a humorous but realistic image of what life was like in Japan at that time.

The "floating world" is a euphemism for life in the great red-light districts and massage-baths during the long Tokugawa era, and Samba's two novels provide a penetrating look at this fascinating aspect of life in shogunate Japan.

Ikku's book is available in English: *Shank's Mare—Being a Translation of the Tokaido Volumes of Hizakurige, Japan's Great Comic Novel of Travel & Ribaldry* (Tuttle).

The world of poetry also flourished during the Tokugawa Period. The great Buson Yosa (1716–1783) followed Basho as the foremost haiku poet of his day. He was also one of the leading painters of his time. Next came Issa Kobayashi (1763–1827), who was the first to use colloquialisms in his *haiku*.

Even more dynamic was the development of *senryu* and *kyoka* poetry. *Senryu*, like *haiku*, has 17 syllables but does not require that each poem have a seasonal word. The primary theme of *senryu* was a somewhat cynical or comic view of life. The greatest *senryu* of this period are in a 24-volume anthology called *Yanagidaru* (1765–1791).

While *senryu* were especially popular among the masses, the 31-syllable *kyoka* were more appealing to intellectuals. They were marked by a highly refined wit, with a satirical touch. Shokusanjin Ota (1749–1823) is regarded as the greatest master of the *kyoka* genre of poetry during the Tokugawa Period.

It was during the latter half of the Tokugawa era that *kabuki* reached its zenith. The two great *kabuki* dramatists, Namboku Tsuruya (1755–1829) and Mokuami Kawatake (1816–1893), were among the most popular writers of their day. And this was the period that gave rise to the noted *kabuki* actors Danjuro Ichikawa and Kikugoro Onoe, whose successors adopted their names and thus continued the traditions they established down to the present time.

With the fall of the Tokugawa Shogunate, the restoration of the emperor to power for the first time in many centuries, and the opening of Japan to the outside world for the first time in over 200 years, Japan's literary scene also underwent a series of revolutionary changes.

With both personal and political freedom for the first time in the history of the country and the influence of many English, French, and Russian novels translated into Japanese, Japanese writers began experimenting with new forms of style and expression.

Shoyo Tsubouchi (1859–1935) wrote *Shosetsu Shizui* (*Quintessence of the Novel*), advocating the principle of realism in novels, including the use of familiar speech (as opposed to a highly stylized language that had been adapted from Chinese literature). One of the first Japanese writers to take this new approach was Shimei Futabatei (1864–1909), in his novel *Ukigumo*, which had a marked influence on later Japanese novelists.

Other novelists who helped make the transition from old Japan to new Japan were Koyo Ozaki (1867–1903), Rohan Koda (1867–1947), Roka Tokutomi (1868–1927), and Ichiyo Higuchi (1872–1986).

Tokutomi became known abroad as a result of translations of his work about Japan's feudal family system, which had been carried over into the new age despite its inhuman influence.

The sudden appearance of mass-distributed newspapers and magazines shortly after the turn of the twentieth century saw the rise of literary critics (who became more powerful than the poets and novelists they wrote about) and many other commentators on everything from art to economics.

New-age poets also appeared, expanding on old forms and creating new ones. Shiki Masaoka (1867–1902) was a leader in the *haiku* field, while Akiko Yosano (1878–1942), one of the first female writers to win fame since the great female novelists of the eleventh and twelfth centuries, was the brightest of the *waka* stars.

Kyoshi Takahama (1874–1959) dominated the world of *haiku* for nearly 50 years. Hakushu Kitahara (1885–1942) and Takuboku Ishikawa (1886–1912) were also noted *waka* or *tanka* poets, bringing to this form a more realistic depiction of life.

Several Japanese poets—Toson Shimazaki, Sakutaro Hagiwara, Kyukin Susukida, and Ariake Kambara—whose lives spanned the period from 1872 to 1952, became noted for their Western-style poetry. Hagiwara was especially known for his realistic poetry in colloquial Japanese.

A naturalistic movement began shortly after the turn of the century, when large numbers of Japan's writers began addressing the social and economic problems of the day. Others, however, turned to the personal, sensual side of life. Among this latter group—who are much better known than the former—were Kafu Nagai (1879–1959), Junichiro Tanizaki (1886–1965) and Haruo Sato (1892–1964).

The best known of the traditionalists, who believed that Japan should go back to the ethics and standards of the *samurai*, were Ogai Mori (1862–1922) and Soseki Natsume (1867–1916). Both were important in interpreting various Western philosophies.

The next generation of writers to become famous included Ryunosuke Akutagawa (1892–1927), Kan Kikuchi (1888–1948), and Yuzo Yamamoto (1887–1974). Kikuchi and Yamamoto are known for their realistic plays. Akutagawa is best known for his attempts to interpret human behavior in his short stories, as in *Rashomon* and *Kappa—A Satire*, both of which are available in English from the Charles E. Tuttle Company.

From about 1924, a new generation of Japanese writers took up the cause of social reform and modernism. However, the advocates of social reform were soon suppressed by the government and forbidden to write. They included Takiji Kobayashi (1903–1933), Yuriko Miyamoto (1899–1951), and Shigeharu Nakano (b. 1902).

The second group, known as neo-sensualists, included Riichi Yokomitsu (1898–1947) and Yasunari Kawabata (1899–1972). Kawabata emphasized sensual beauty through lyricism, while Yokomitsu was more of a stylist. Kawabata thus became famous abroad (winning the Nobel Prize for literature in 1968), while few Westerners ever heard of Yokomitsu.

Other writers in this group, all born around the turn of the century, were Masuji Ibuse, Tatsuo Hori, Fumio Niwa, Osamu Daizu, Kazuo Ozaki, Fumiko Hayashi, and Kanoko Okamoto.

All literary freedom was suppressed by the government during the war years, from 1939 to 1945.

Following the return of Japanese sovereignty in 1952 and the sweeping away of the vestiges of the feudal social and political systems, Japanese writers once again began to flourish in all fields. Historical novels, war novels, detective stories, and very commercial popular novels became the vogue.

The most successful of the historical novelists was Eiji Yoshikawa (1892–1962), while Bunroku Shishi (1893–1969), Jiro Osaragi (1897–1973), and Seicho Matsumoto (b. 1909) were among the most successful in the popular fields.

Writers who achieved acclaim for their war books include Rinzo Shiina (1911–1973), Shohei O-oka (b. 1909), and Haruo Umezaki (1915–1965).

One of the most successful and most tragic of Japan's post-1945 writers was Yukio Mishima (1925–1971), whose life reflected so much that was great, as well as tragic in the culture of Japan. See MISHIMA, YUKIO.

Other writers who made their mark after 1945 are: Yasushi Inoue, Shotaro Yasuoka, Junzo Shono, Toshio Shimano, Junnosuke Yoshiyuki, Shusaku Endo, Nobuo Kojima, and Kobe Abe.

These were followed by a younger group born in the 1930s, who knew little or nothing about pre–World War II Japan. Most notable among this group are Shintaro Ishihara (b. 1932) and Kenzaburo Oe (b. 1935).

Ishihara made an extraordinary splash in the late 1950s with the publication of *Taiyo Kisetsu*, or *Season of the Sun*, which was an intimate portrayal of the sensual, nihilistic life of the post-war affluent young. Ishihara later went on to a successful career in the movies and then in politics as a Diet member.

In the late 1980s Ishihara coauthored a book with Akio Morita, cofounder and chair of SONY corporation, *The Japan That Can Say No!*, which was an international bestseller.

Critics described Oe as the most promising writer of this period. His first book appeared in 1957, when he was 22.

The literary world in Japan today is as varied and as dynamic as it is in any other country. Both poetry and the novel continue to flourish. Literary works account for about 20 percent of all the books published in Japan each year, or around 6,000 titles annually.

There are some 100 literary magazines in publication, and nearly all of the newspapers, weeklies, and monthlies in the country serialize novels as part of their regular fare.

There are some 30 major literary prizes awarded each year in such fields as poetry, novels, drama, mystery novels, nonfiction, commentary, and essays. The Akutagawa Prize and the Naoki Prize, both awarded by the prestigious *Bungei Shunju* literary magazine since 1935, are the highest of these awards.

Today, with virtually 100 percent literacy and with formal education and an overpowering thirst for knowledge a primary factor in daily life, the Japanese are among the most avid readers in the world and support one of the largest and most diverse publishing industries. See BOOKS and PUBLISHERS.

Recommended reading: *A History of Japanese Literature—The First Thousand Years*, by Shuichi Kato, translated by David Chibbett (Kodansha International).

LIVING TREASURES   In recognition of the importance of handicrafts in the overall culture of Japan, the Japanese government in 1955 created a system for honoring and rewarding artisans who achieve ultimate mastery of their craft.

Artisans chosen for the honor are officially designated "Important Cultural Properties," but they are popularly called "Living National Treasures."

The purpose of the program is to single out men and women who are uniquely skilled in a particular Japanese art—pottery, textile dyeing, paper making, ceramics, metalwork, *noh*, *kabuki*, etc.—to help ensure that the crafts will not die out.

In addition to the honor, prestige, and a higher price for the artisan's work, the title includes an annual financial grant to help the artisan train others.

LOAN WORDS   Japanese probably has more loan words—adopted from other languages—than any other major language, or at least it seems that way. Almost every Japanese conversation is peppered with loan words, as is a great deal of the writing.

The earliest of the borrowings were, of course, from Korean and Chinese, followed by Portuguese, Dutch, English, Italian, French, and American.

The primary reason for so much borrowing is that there were no Japanese equivalents for so many of the words concerned. In many cases today, however, the foreign words are used simply because they have a special flavor or ambience that the Japanese like—the same way Americans use certain French words.

In adopting a foreign word, the Japanese simply pronounce it in Japanese—that is, convert it into Japanese syllables. For example, blue becomes *bu-ru*. Merit becomes *me-ri-to*. Baseball becomes *be-su bo-ru*, and so on.

Until the foreign student of the Japanese language becomes used to this system, communication can be difficult, because of the number of such words used and because they do not appear in most textbooks on the language.

An interesting aspect of the Japanese propensity to pronounce English words in Japanese is the fact that some people are so familiar with such pronunciation that it is possible to communciate with them entirely in English as long as you pronounce everything as if it were Japanese.

LOCATION / BASHO (Bah-show)   Shaped like a crescent that extends for 3,000 kilometers (1,860 miles) from north to the northwest, Japan lies off the east coast of Asia, parallel to southern Siberia on the north and the southern tip of the Korean Peninsula on the south.

Tokyo is on almost exactly the same latitude as Los Angeles, Athens, and Tehran, and it is five degrees south of the latitude of New York, Beijing, and Ankara.

LOVE & MARRIAGE   More than 70 percent of young, unmarried Japanese women say they prefer to find their own husbands, instead of having a marriage arranged for them by their parents or a matchmaker. Approximately 80 percent of all single girls in Japan date before they are 20, and between 70 percent and 80 percent of those who are between 20 and 24 believe premarital sex is acceptable between partners who love each other.

While the overwhelming majority of young Japanese women prefer a love-based marriage, only about half of them say they would insist on the right to choose their own spouse.

Between 60 percent and 70 percent of the unmarried young women who are employed say they want to continue working after marriage. About the same proportion of Japanese women feel that sexual equality in Japan has a long way to go. The only areas in which true equality exists, they say, is in cultural and recreational activities.

LUCK / UN (Uun)   Like people everywhere, the Japanese have many lucky and unlucky signs, some of them going back to ancient times—and some of them similar to Western superstitions.

Some of the best-known ones:

If your nose itches, someone you know will have a baby. If you sneeze once, someone is speaking well of you. If you sneeze twice, someone is speaking ill of you. If you sneeze three times, someone loves you. If you sneeze four times, you've caught a cold.

If the first person you meet after leaving home in the morning is a woman, it will be a good day. If it is a Buddhist priest, you're in for trouble. If you are out in the open and bird droppings fall on you, it is a good omen.

When the cord on your *zori* or *geta* breaks, you are in for bad news or some misfortune. If a funeral procession overtakes you on the street, it's a bad luck sign. If a snake crosses the road in front of you, money will come to you unexpectedly.

If your ear itches, you will soon hear some good news. If you break a mirror you're in for bad luck, especially if you are a woman. If you stare at someone over your rice bowl (while holding it close to your mouth and eating) you will get uglier as you get older.

MAGAZINES / ZASSHI (Zah-she) Japan's first magazine, *Seiyo Zasshi*, was established in 1867, the year the Tokugawa Shogunate gave up power over the country. This was followed by more than 180 other publications within the next decade, including the well-known *Meiroku Zasshi*, which appeared in 1874.

These first magazines were takeoffs on the journals brought to Japan by Dutch traders during the last years of the shogunate. Most of them were aimed at educating their readers in Western thought, scholarship, and culture.

The next decade saw another boom in the inauguration of new magazines, primarily as a result of the promulgation of the Meiji Constitution. By 1888, there were more than 200 political magazines in the country.

Among the magazine publishers that emerged during this period were Hakubunkan, which quickly developed a large number of low-priced, general-interest publications, and Jitsugyo-no Nippon Sha, which was founded in 1900. The latter company soon passed Hakubunkan as the country's leading magazine publisher, largely because it developed a system of paying sales commissions to retailers and allowing them to return unsold magazines. By 1907, there were over 400 magazines in Japan.

The present-day giant Kodansha was founded in 1910. Its first magazine, *Yuben* (Yuu-bane) became a bestseller, as did its *Kodan Kurabu* (Koe-dahn Kuu-rah-buu), *Shonen Kurabu* (Show-nane), and several other publications. *Kingu* (Keen-guu), one of these new magazines, became the first Japanese magazine to achieve a million circulation, in 1927.

By 1931, Kodansha was selling nearly five and a half million magazines a month, or some 80 percent of the market. Increasing government controls and paper shortages devastated the magazine industry during the late 1930s and war years. In 1944, the government forced the closure of all but 996 magazines, and eventually all of these ceased publication.

Freed of wartime controls in 1945, magazine publishers began trying to make a comeback. By getting a special paper allotment from the Allied Occupation authorities, *Reader's Digest* quickly pushed the circulation of its Japanese edition to 1.4 million copies. *Kingu*, so successful before the war, was unable to make a comeback, and its place was taken by *Heibon* (Hay-e-bone), which emphasized music and films.

There were 4,581 publishers in Japan in 1948, but this fell back to 1,541 by 1953. In 1956, the appearance of *Shukan Shincho* (Shuu-khan Sheen-choe), the first weekly magazine not published by a newspaper company, heralded the beginning of a weekly magazine boom, which resulted in more than 70 weeklies by 1960.

One of the most popular genres of magazines to appear at this time were the *manga* (mahn-gah), or comics. Literally hundreds of them appeared, and four of them now have circulations of over one million a week.

There are currently some 2,000 monthly magazines (235 new monthlies were founded in 1980 and 184 new ones in 1981). Not all of the new ones survive, but the overall number continues to climb upward.

The two categories with the largest number of magazines are popular interest (247) and engineering (204). Other categories and their approximate number of magazines are children's (146), women's (27), general interest (77), literary (64), performing arts (30), fine arts (31), music (49), living (105), hobbies (177), sports (78), economics (163), social problems (25), current topics (43), philosophy (26), textbook aids (33), linguistics (33), education (113), geography/history (17), law (28), science (36), medicine (103), and agriculture/fisheries (26).

The total annual print run of all these monthlies amounts to some 1,846, 700,000, of which 26 percent do not sell (are returned by the retail and wholesale outlets). This means that approximately one and one-third trillion monthly magazines are bought in Japan each year.

Among the best known of the general-interest monthly magazines are *Chuo Koron*, a serious, high-brow publication that treats political, economic, social and cultural subjects in depth and is a leader in the field of opinion journalism; *Bungei Shunju*, the most widely read of Japan's middle-class general-interest magazines, which appeals to the modern tastes but traditional sentiments of the Japanese; *Gendai*, which covers social and economic issues of special interest to the white-collar class; *Shosetsu Shincho*, a literary publication that runs columns on hobbies and stories by leading writers; and *Ohru Yomimono*, a famous fiction publication that awards the prestigious Naoki Literary Prize and the Cartoon Award.

There are some 60 well-established weekly magazines in Japan, with an estimated annual printing of one and one-third trillion. The annual rate of returned (unsold) copies of weekly magazines is about 20.5 percent of all those printed.

Weekly magazines include seven in the children's field, 3 women's magazines, and 16 popular-interest, 14 general-interest, 14 specialized, and 3 sports magazines.

In addition to their regular issues, some monthly and weekly magazines in Japan also publish one or more supplements each year. This adds some 70 million copies to the overall number of magazines printed.

Top names in the weekly magazine field include several published by the giant newspaper companies. *Shukan Asahi*, a mix of light and serious articles, is aimed at students, women, and businesspeople. *Sunday Mainichi* (the oldest weekly in Japan) specializes in documentary-type features of general interest. *Shukan Yomiuri* serializes novels and runs comments on current events, hobbies, and entertainment. The *Shukan Sankei* prints in-depth stories on events and sidelights skimmed by the daily newspapers.

Other major weeklies are *Shukan Gendai* (practical information for a predominantly male readership) and *Asahi Geino* (fiction, news, and gossip about the entertainment world).

Many Japanese publications are affiliated with foreign publications, and some publish Japanese editions of well-known foreign magazines. There has been a Japanese edition of *Playboy*, for example, since the 1960s. The Japanese edition of *Reader's Digest* eventually lost out to more aggressive and practical publications, and closed down in 1985.

Typical of the new breed of magazines in Japan today is one called *Big Tomorrow*. A monthly founded in 1980, the magazine is aimed at young men between the ages of 21 and 25, and it is filled with advice on how young managers can succeed in their business and personal relations. The advice ranges from the crude to the hilarious.

In 1984, *Big Tomorrow* achieved a circulation of 680,000 copies a month and was still growing at the rate of 20,000 a month.

This success naturally bred imitators, two of which are *Big Man* and *Big Success*, which are targeted at men around the age of 30.

MAINICHI NEWSPAPER / MAINICHI SHIMBUN (My-nee-chee Shimboon)   Japan's great *Mainichi Shimbun* originated in Osaka, as did the *Asahi Shimbun*. They were the first of Japan's major newspapers to take a commercial, as opposed to a political, approach in publishing. By 1912, both the *Mainichi* and the *Asahi* had begun to make inroads into the Tokyo area.

It was to be a national disaster—the Great Kanto Earthquake of 1923—that brought the two newspapers to Tokyo in force. The earthquake destroyed the printing plants and office facilities of newspapers in both Tokyo and Yokohama, and the *Mainichi* and *Asahi* jumped in to fill the vacuum. See NEWSPAPERS.

MAJOR JAPANESE COMPANIES   Nearly one-third of the world's 500 largest companies outside the U.S. are Japanese. The largest of the Japanese companies—not necessarily in the order of rank—include Toyota Motor Company, Nissan Motor Company, Nippon Steel Corporation, Hitachi, Matsushita, Mitsubishi Heavy Industries, Idemitsu (Oil) Company, Tokyo Shibaura Electric (Toshiba), Nippon Kokan, and Toa Nenryo Kogyo.

Other large companies are Maruzen Oil, Honda Motor Company, Sumitomo Metal Industries, Mitsubishi Electric, Kawasaki Steel, Toyo Kogyo, Kobe Steel, Taiyo Fishery Company, Mitsubishi Oil, Mitsubishi Chemical Industries, Sanyo Electric, Nippon Mining Company, Showa Oil, Daikyo Oil, Sony, Nippon Electric, Ishikawajima-Harima Heavy Industries, Sumitomo Chemical, Asahi Chemical, Bridgestone Tire, Isuzu Motors, Snow Brand Milk Products, Komatsu, Kawasaki Dockyard, Toyo Rayon, Fujitsu, Mitsui Chemicals, Kubota Iron and Machinery Works, Ube Industries, Nippon Denso,

Showa Denko, Furukawa Electric, Asahi Glass, Matsushita Electric Works, Sharp, Sumitomo Electric Industries, Kanegafuchi Spinning, Dai Nippon Printing, Koa Oil, and Fuji Photo Film Company. See TRADING COMPANIES.

MANAGEMENT / MANEJIMENTO (Mah-nay-jee-mane-to)   There are several key characteristics pertaining to Japan's world-famous management system. Decision making is based on consensus. Larger firms practice lifetime employment, with promotions and wages based on seniority. Unions are company, instead of trade, unions (with the exception of the seaman's union and a few others). The ratio of borrowed capital is high. There is widespread use of subsidiary and affiliated companies for parts manufacturing and dependence on the importation of raw materials and the exportation of finished products.

Takashi Ishihara, president of the immensely successful Nissan Motor Company Ltd. in the 1970s and 1980s, summed up the secret of Japanese management in two words, corporate vitality, which he said was derived from two sources: (1) the separation of ownership and management, whereby managers are able to make decisions based on long-term company interests, free from the narrow self-interest of owners, and (2) the fact that Japanese companies tend to be especially well organized, from top to bottom, into highly motivated groups whose primary concern is the long-term growth of their company.

Ishihara explained that the stock of most major Japanese companies is held by a combination of banks, insurance companies, and other businesses, along with a wide variety of public investors, whose primary goals are long-range capital gains.

Managers are therefore free to manage as they see fit, concentrating on long-term growth. This important management feature is reflected in active long-term investments in plants and equipment, he said.

Ishihara added that Japanese companies are social enterprises first and commercial enterprises second, that perpetuation of the company and winning as much of the market as possible take precedence over short-term profits and dividends, that managers work their way up through the ranks and are part of a human chain that links management with workers.

Also, the personal nature of the relationships among all employees in a company provides for a high degree of empathy that prevents jobs from being regarded as slots and people from being treated like cogs.

Of course, virtual lifetime employment and practically no turnover at all in management personnel is a vital ingredient in the success of Japanese management.

One of the dual concepts that is central to understanding and dealing with the Japanese, in both business and personal matters, is the *tatamae* (tah-tay-my)/*honne* (hone-nay) factor.

Tatemae means something like "framework" or "facade," while *honne* refers to "real interests" or "real intent."

In keeping with their deeply ingrained practice of avoiding conflict, the Japanese first present a general idea of what they are talking about or want—the *tatemae*. Only later—and gradually—does the *honne*, or real aim, emerge.

Noted Japanese psychologist Hiroshi Minami said that in order to understand and deal with the Japanese it is necessary to have a full grasp of the uncertainty that characterizes the Japanese. He says the first of these uncertainties is a combination of weak self-assertion, lack of self-confidence, and a sense of inferiority in interpersonal relations, expressed by such passive traits as reserve, shyness, resignation, and lack of courage. As a result, he explained, the Japanese have a tendency to be very concerned about maintaining harmony in interpersonal relationships by being considerate, gentle, and kind to others.

In an attempt to overcome the sense of uncertainty and their weak selfhood, the Japanese are especially studious and zealous in their work, according to Minami. He said that this sense of uncertainty is a product of the rigid ranking system that developed during the long Tokugawa Period (1600–1868), which was based on hierarchical relationships and the strict maintenance of social differences by the use of honorific language. Although this system no longer officially exists, it is still extremely difficult for the Japanese to establish clear boundaries in relationships—thus the meticulous exchange of name cards, careful introductions, institutionalized gift-giving, and courtesy visits before asking someone for a favor.

Not surprisingly, there is a positive side to the psychological uncertainty of the Japanese. By automatically assuming a passive stance and withdrawing into a group approach in the face of any confrontation, the Japanese are able to ignore or bypass the influence of foreign cultures or pressure from any outside source, whether in business or social relationships.

For a detailed analysis of the unique Japanese management system and the day-to-day practice of business in Japan, see the author's *Japanese Etiquette and Ethics in Business* (Passport Books), first published in 1960; and *How to Do Business in Japan*, first published in 1962. Both have been revised several times.

One of the newest and most fascinating aspects of Japanese management was the appearance in the late 1970s and early '80s of special schools that offer Japanese managers brief but intense training courses.

These courses are not based on anything you might find at Harvard or any of the world's recognized business schools. They are based on concepts and practices you would expect to find in a secret commando or guerrilla training camp, where the emphasis is on physical toughness and rote political orientation.

In addition to rigorous physical training, the enrollees at these management schools are bombarded with the importance of the family, loyalty to the company, and the selfless struggle for the betterment of all. The avowed purpose of some of the schools is to shatter the self-image of the individual totally and to construct a new one based on harmonious cooperation with the group.

The Japanese government and Japanese business leaders in general are concerned about the problems that arise from management differences around the world and have initiated a number of programs to help relieve the situation.

As of July 1983, foreign companies became eligible to join the Japanese Management Association (JMA) as Associate Members and may participate in programs and services conducted in English for their benefit.

The aim of the JMA Associate Member system is to provide foreign managers with information about management and productivity in Japan through forums, newsletters, special reports, and other publications.

For details about the program, contact the Associate Members' Department, Japan Management Association, 3-1-22 Shiba Park, Minato-Ku, Tokyo 105, Japan.

MANYOSHU (Mahn-yoe-shuu) / **COLLECTION OF 10,000 LEAVES**   The outstanding literary work of Japan's Nara Period (710–784) was the *Manyoshu*, an anthology of over 4,500 poems, compiled by the poet Yakamochi Otomo in the eighth century.

The collection contains poems written in many styles, dating from as early as the fourth century and written by people in all classes, from emperors and members of the nobility to the poorest of common people.

Poems in the anthology are classified as seasonal, love poems, allegorical, and occasional. Among the hundreds of poets represented in the work are Akahito and Hitomaro, who are ranked among Japan's Six Great Poets.

The British diplomat F. V. Dickins published an English translation of the *Manyoshu* in 1906. The better-known British diplomat/scholar, W.G. Aston, also translated portions of the work.

Altogether, the *Manyoshu* totals over 120 volumes, with *tanka* poems (31 syllables) predominating, followed by *choka* (long poems). One of the best known of the *Manyoshu* poems is W.G. Aston's translation of one called "In Praise of Yamato" (Yamato is the early name for Japan):

> The land of Yamato
> Has mountains in numbers,
> But peerless among them
> Is high Kaguyama.
> I stand on its summit
> My kingdom to view.
> The smoke from the land-plain
> Rises thick in the air,
> The gulls from the sea-plain
> By fits soar aloft.
> O land of Yamato!
> Fair Akitsu-shima!
> Dear art thou to me.

MARRIAGE / KEKKON (Keck-kone)   Prior to 1945, most marriages in Japan were *omiai* (oh-me-aye), that is, arranged by the parents, a close relative, an employer, or a professional go-between. Today some 70 percent of all marriages in the country are classified as *renai* (rain-aye), or love marriages.

In arranged marriages, the couples are brought together to get acquainted only after both families are satisfied that they would make a suitable match from the viewpoint of social, economic, and educational standing. Then, if the couples approve and like each other, marriage follows.

Most weddings in Japan take place in wedding halls or hotels that have large ballrooms and cater specifically to wedding parties. The more affluent the families, the more elaborate and splendid the wedding parties. Many wedding receptions have 500 or more guests and may cost well over $200 per person.

Weddings may consist of Shinto rites, in which the bride dresses in traditional *kimono* and the groom in traditional male attire. They exchange sips of *O'sake* (Oh-sah-kay) as a symbol of their troth and receive the blessings of a Shinto priest.

Some weddings incorporate Western customs. One that I recently witnessed was held in a famous Chinese restaurant in Harajuku, Tokyo. The bride wore a *kimono*; the groom wore a tuxedo. They marched into the restaurant to the tune of "Here Comes the Bride." After a Shinto ceremony, the couple cut a huge cake with a *samurai* sword.

The *kimono* typically worn by a Japanese bride is the *uchikake* (uu-chee-kah-kay), which has a long train and is embroidered with gold and silver threads in bird or flower designs. It is regarded as the most beautiful of all the *kimono*.

Guests who attend weddings generally bring monetary gifts in special money envelopes. Several members of the party—friends, relatives, employers—make speeches, recounting personal details about the bride and groom, sometimes to their embarrassment. When the wedding is over, the guests are usually presented with a gift from the families of the couple.

At present, the average age of Japanese men at marriage is 27.7. For women, it is 25.2.

One lady entreprenuer in the Kansai (Osaka-Kobe-Kyoto) area has built 32 Wedding Palaces where over 45,000 couples a year take advantage of her wedding package—which includes planning, invitations, the ceremony (Buddhist, Shinto, or Christian), a banquet of any style, gifts for the guests, and honeymoon arrangements.

On a *Taian* (Tie-on), lucky day in the fall, several hundred couples tie the knot at these huge halls.

The computer and video camera have entered the marriage business in Japan in a big way, with numerous dating and mating bureaus offering their services to marriage-hungry men and women. There are also many social clubs designed specifically to bring together young men and women who are looking for marriage prospects.

There is presently an unwritten but strongly felt rule in Japan that the deadline for women seeking marriage is age 25. For men, the deadline is 30. A man who remains unmarried after he is 30 is less likely to get promoted in his job. A woman past 25 has less chance of landing a desirable mate.

MARTIAL ARTS / BUJUTSU (Buu-jute-sue)   The Japanese have apparently always taken an avid interest in sports, and, with the rise of the military class in the twelfth century, several martial arts became an important part of the training of the *bushi* (buu-she), or warriors. These skills included sword-fighting (*kenjutsu*), sword-drawing (*iaijutsu*), unarmed combat (*jujutsu*), archery (*kyujutsu*), spear handling (*sojutsu*), horsemanship (*bajutsu*), and swimming (*suijutsu*).

From the fifteenth century on, these martial arts were gradually standardized into schools, and they were systematized during the long peaceful Tokugawa Shogunate (1600–1867). With the fall of the shogunate in 1867, interest in the martial arts declined. But with the outbreak of war with China in 1894, this interest was revived and promoted by the government, as militaristic nationalism came to the fore.

In 1895, all martial arts came under the centralized control of the Great Japan Martial Arts Association (Dai Nippon Butoku Kai) and became a part of the national education system in 1911.

In 1926, the term *jutsu* (arts) was dropped from the names of several of the disciplines, and *do* (way) was introduced. Thus *kenjutsu* became *kendo*, and *jujutsu* became *judo*.

Martial arts were banned in Japan by the Allied Occupation Forces in 1945, but the ban was lifted in 1950, and thereafter the arts developed rapidly as sports, instead of martial training.

Judo was added to the Tokyo Olympic Games in 1964, and the first World Kendo Tournament was held at the Japan Martial Arts Hall (Nippon

Budokan) in 1970. The World Union of Karate-Do Organizations was also formed and held its first World Championship matches in Tokyo in 1970.

See individual listings for AIKIDO; JUDO; KARATE; KENDO.

Recommended reading: *Modern Bujutsu and Budo*, by Donn Draeger (Weatherhill). Also: *Classical Bujutsu*, by Donn Draeger (Weatherhill).

MARU (Mah-rue)   Most people who have anything to do with Japan have asked about or wondered about the meaning of the word *maru*, which is used as a suffix to the names of passenger liners, merchant ships, fishing boats, and yachts (warships use *kan* / kahn).

Unfortunately, there is no agreement on what the word means or how it came to be applied to ships. One version has that it is a corruption of the word *maro*, which refers to something valuable or is a term of endearment. Another opinion states that it refers to a person bent over in a circle, taking refuge from the dangers of the sea.

Still another version says that merchants centuries ago used the word to denote a family business, and when they went into the shipping business, *maru* was attached to indicate it was a family-owned ship.

Honmaru refers to the central tower of a castle and means "within the circle," which is the innermost and most protected part of the castle. Since a ship at sea is a man's castle, *maru* just might have carried over from this usage.

MARUNOUCHI (Mah-rue-no-uu-chee)   The Marunouchi district of Chiyoda Ward in central Tokyo is usually described as the business center of the city, but there are other business centers, such as Otemachi, adjoining it on the north, that might dispute the description.

In any event, Marunouchi, which encompasses the area directly in front of the Imperial Palace, has enough of the city's major buildings and companies to hold its own.

These include Tokyo Central Post Office, Japanese Railways Building, Japan Travel Bureau Building, the old and new Marunouchi Buildings, Tokyo Chamber of Commerce & Industry Building, NYK Building, Kaijo Building, numerous banks, and Mitsubishi Shoji.

Old-timers will remember that until the 1960s, much of the area was taken up by three- and four-story, British-style, red-brick buildings and was the preserve, so to speak, of the Mitsubishi group of companies. All of the old brick buildings have long since been replaced by modern buildings, and the area has a totally international, cosmopolitan look.

The story of the Marunouchi district is typical of the entrepreneurial spirit of Japanese business leaders. During the long Tokugawa Shogunate (1600–1867), the district was the site for *daimyo* mansions, each of which had a name that ended in *maru*, and the whole area was referred to as Marunouchi, which can be translated rather generally as "the *daimyo* mansions."

When the feudal *daimyo* system ended in 1868, the district became government property. The mansions eventually burned down or were razed, and the area was turned into an army drilling grounds and barracks.

In 1890, the budget of the Imperial Diet was cut so drastically by the Opposition that it resolved to sell the Marunouchi district in order to raise needed funds for various government projects. By this time, the area was a vast, weed-covered field.

The government offered the land to the top *zaibatsu* families (Mitsui, Mitsubishi, Okura, Shibusawa, etc.) on a bid basis. Finally, Yataro Iwasaki, head of the Mitsubishi family, agreed to buy the area for the then princely sum of 1,500,000 yen—as a result of which he was called a fool by less far-sighted people. But he was acting on the wise counsel of the *banto* (manager) of Mitsubishi, Heigoro Soda, who had, during a visit to London, heard how the Lord of Westminister had become immensely wealthy because he owned land in downtown London. Soda urged Iwasaki to buy the land.

Years later, Soda began developing the land, first by putting in a wide, paved boulevard and then constructing brick and stone buildings along the avenue. It was not until the completion of Tokyo Central Station right in the center of Marunouchi in 1914 that the area began to boom.

By 1921, some of the largest and most important buildings in Japan were situated in the Marunouchi district, but it was the great earthquake of 1923 that turned the area into the business center of Tokyo. Fires following the quake destroyed the majority of the wooden office buildings in central Tokyo, leaving the brick and stone buildings in the Marunouchi district untouched.

Hundreds of companies took up temporary quarters in the area, and many of them were to stay when new buildings were put up to accommodate them.

In the 1960s and 1970s, all of the old English style brick buildings that had been the hallmark of Marunouchi were replaced by modern highrise office buildings, making it one of the most profitable and valuable pieces of property in the world.

MASSAGERS / AMMA (Ahm-mah)   The practice of massaging was introduced into Japan from China during the sixth and seventh centuries, and the art is mentioned prominently in the Taiho Law of 701. The popularity of the practice waned in the Middle Ages, but it was revived in the 1600s and remains popular in Japan today.

In the Tokugawa Period (1600–1867), the profession was reserved exclusively for those who were blind, and the training, by apprenticeship to a master, was long and difficult.

Following the Meiji Restoration in 1868, the profession was opened up to anyone, but it was necessary to pass a government examination to obtain a license. In earlier times, *amma* announced their presence in neighborhoods by blowing on a flute. In some rural areas, they may still be heard, but in the cities, *amma* are called in by phone.

Amma are especially popular at the hundreds of hot spring resorts around Japan.

MATSUSHIMA (Mot-sue-she-mah)   On the coast of northeastern Honshu, an hour's ride from the city of Sendai, Matsushima is famed as one of the three most scenic spots in Japan. Matsushima means Pine-Clad Island, but the name refers instead to a bay filled with pine-clad islands—over 260 of them.

Most of the islands of Matsushima Bay are formed of strata of volcanic tuff. Others consist of white sandstone. The range of sizes and shapes of the islands staggers the imagination. Some are mere pinnacles protruding up from the water. Others are large enough to be inhabited.

The winds and water have created archways, caves, and tunnels in the islands and sculpted the pine trees that cover most of them into countless forms. Viewed from any position, in any kind of weather, the bay presents a picture of nature at the height of its glory.

Some people prefer to view Matsuhima following a snowfall, while others prefer dawn on a clear day. The island-dotted bay is equally enchanting in rain or on a moonlit night, when the light glistens on the water, setting the islands off like jewels.

On shore, on a rocky cliff adjoining Matsushima Kaigan Pier, is a pavilion called Kanrantei (Wave-Viewing Pavilion), built in the 1590s by Hideyoshi Toyotomi and presented to Masamune Date, the Lord of Sendai, as a viewpoint for enjoying the beauty of Matsushima. The sliding-door screens in the pavilion were painted by Sanraku Kano, one of the foremost artists of this era.

Next to the Kanrantei is the Matsushima Museum, which contains heirlooms that belonged to the Date family, along with samples of local products.

Besides the Kanrantei pavilion, there are four public viewpoints for enjoying Matsushima Bay that have been celebrated for centuries. Located at the four corners of Matsushima, they are Tomiyama, Otakamori, Tamonzan, and Ogidani. The second of these viewpoints is located on one of the bay islands—Miyato—the largest in the group, which has some 1,500 residents. See DATE, MASAMUNE; SENDAI.

MATSUSHITA ELECTRIC INDUSTRIAL COMPANY   (Mot-sue-ssh-tah) The Matsushita Electric Industrial Company is, of course, one of the largest and most successful companies in the world. The point to be made here is not about the size and success of the company but the philosophy that made the company so successful.

The company was founded in 1918 by Konnosuke Matsushita, who is regarded as the greatest business leader of twentieth-century Japan. Born into dire poverty, Matsushita had to quit school at the age of nine to go to work as an errand boy. His health was so frail that he resigned himself to imminent death several times.

But Matsushita persevered. His philosophy was based on the concept that an enterprise as a whole is as good or as bad as the abilities of the individual employees—not all of the employees as a group. All employees are treated as individuals, and every effort is made to enable them to develop their potential to the fullest. Matsushita holds that a business exists only to contribute to society, not to pursue the goal of profit.

The Matsushita approach to business management epitomizes the Japanese concept of group spirit. It has also been called management by intuition, from Matsushita's lifelong practice of meditating to achieve intellectual and spiritual harmony with the cosmos and to tap into the universal mind.

Recommended reading: *The Matsushita Phenomenon*, by Rowland Gould (Diamond Sha)

MEDICAL CARE   Some 97 percent of all medical services in Japan are administered through National Health Insurance, or Kokumin Kenko Hoken (Koe-kuu-mean Kane-koe Hoe-kane), a government sponsored, tax-supported program that covers from 50 percent to 90 percent of medical care.

This program is available to foreigners living and working in Japan, but the percentage the patient pays is based on a sliding scale pegged to income, and it can be very expensive for someone drawing a high salary. For those who are not in the program, the fact that medical treatment is going to be expensive is a foregone conclusion.

The primary reason for the high expense of private medical care is that less than 3 percent of Japan's doctors are in private practice. The overwhelming majority are involved in the national health insurance program.

The doctors who are in private practice operate their own clinics, some of which are as large as modest hospitals and offer similar services at far higher costs.

Japanese hospitals are spartan by American standards. The families of patients provide them with many of the things they need—sometimes even linen and eating utensils. Families also spend more time visiting patients and helping to take care of them.

Most Japanese hospitals are closed to outside (nonstaff) doctors, and, with few exceptions, private doctors or consultants are not permitted to treat patients admitted to hospitals. Individuals may admit themselves into hospitals without going through a doctor. A doctor without special connections with a specific hospital cannot refer patients to it.

If a patient is referred to a hospital by a doctor on the staff, the chances of faster and possibly better treatment are vastly improved.

Hospital doctors work on rotating shifts, as do hospitals. Emergency rooms are often not open after 5:00 P.M. There are often long lines of people waiting in the reception areas of hospitals, and beds are often lacking. Patients may ask for a specific doctor, but this usually entails a much longer waiting period.

The medical profession in Japan centers on the universities from which the doctors graduate and the affiliated university hospitals. Six years of schooling are usually followed by about five years of internship at one of the university's hospitals.

Interns often develop unofficial side practices in order to earn enough money to sustain themselves. And doctors employed by hospitals may also operate their own clinics as a means of increasing their income.

In all of Japan's major cities, there are doctors in private practice, clinics, and hospitals—often affiliated with religious organizations—who cater especially to foreign residents and visitors. They advertise in local English-language media and are easy to find.

MEETINGS / UCHIAWASE (Uu-chee-ah-wah-say)   In Japan, company executives spend as much as 30 percent to 40 percent of their time in meetings and conferences. Many of these meetings are not in formal office or conference room situations, however. A majority of them take place outside of the office, most often in coffee shops.

Many companies maintain their own coffee shops for the use of lower- and middle-level managers. Top-level executives more often meet in expensive Japanese-style restaurants (*ryotei*), where there are private rooms for small groups.

Uchiawase means "preliminary meeting" or "consultation," and it is at such meetings that Japanese managers come to a general consensus about plans and projects they are working on. Formal decisions are made later in an official setting.

Foreigners with whom the Japanese do business or engage in negotiations are normally excluded from these *uchiawase* discussions. The accepted way for foreigners to conduct their own *uchiawase* is to invite their Japanese counterparts out to coffee shops, restaurants, and nightclubs. Recommended reading: *Japanese Etiquette and Ethics in Business*, by Boye Lafayette De Mente (Passport Books).

MEIJI (May-e-jee)   Meiji (Great Period) is the name given to the reign of Emperor Mutsuhito, who became emperor in 1868, when he was 16, and reigned until his death in 1912, at which time Meiji became his posthumous name. Meiji proved to be an enlightened and able leader and is ranked among the greatest heroes of Japan.

The transfer of power from the Tokugawa Shogunate to the Imperial Court in 1868 is known as the Meiji Restoration. See MEIJI MEMORIAL PICTURE GALLERY; MEIJI PARK; MEIJI SHRINE.

MEIJI MEMORIAL PICTURE GALLERY   Built in memory of Emperor Meiji, who died in 1912, the Meiji Memorial Picture Gallery is a large, impressive building that is the centerpiece of Meiji Park (which was originally a huge garden estate).

The gallery was built to house 115 great paintings that show memorable scenes during the life and reign of the famous emperor, beginning with his birth in Kyoto, his death in Tokyo, and his internment at the Grand Shrine of Ise.

Half of the paintings, all done by Japanese masters, are in Japanese style. The others are in Western style. The paintings are so arranged in the gallery that visitors may walk through the history of the Meiji period from beginning to end.

In front of each painting is an inscribed plaque that describes the scene depicted, in both Japanese and English. The plaques were redone in 1982, at which time the author of this book had the extraordinary pleasure of writing the English inscriptions.

MEIJI PARK   Officially known as Meiji Shrine Outer Garden and more recently as Meiji Olympic Park, this large landscaped area within central Tokyo was once the private garden and estate of a *daimyo* feudal lord.

Beginning in 1912, the grounds were turned into a huge public park and recreational area, and have since been one of the most popular spots in Tokyo. Among the important facilities in the park is the National Stadium, which has a seating capacity of 85,000.

Also in the park are the Jingu Baseball Stadiums (No. 1 and No. 2), the Prince Chichibu Rugby Football Stadium, the Tokyo Gymnasium, the Metropolitan Indoor Swimming Pool, the Meiji Memorial Picture Gallery, and Meiji Memorial Hall.

MEIJI SHRINE / MEIJI JINJA (May-e-jee Jeen-jah)   Near Harajuku Station in western Tokyo, Meiji Shrine is one of the largest, most beautiful and most popular in Japan. Dedicated to Emperor Meiji, who reigned from 1868 to 1912, it was completed in 1920, following a national outpouring of support that was unprecedented.

The grounds of the shrine cover an area of 72.4 hectares and are known as the Inner Garden. There are several entrances to the shrine. The main one, adjoining Jingu Bridge, next to Harajuku Station, requires a walk of close to half a mile to reach the principal shrine.

Each of the entrances is marked by a huge *torii* made of cypress wood that is over 1,700 years old. Behind the main shrine is a Treasure House, where many of the things owned and used by the emperor and empress are on display.

Set amidst a forest of trees and shrubs donated by people from all over the country, including a large iris garden, and constructed in the traditional Shinto style, the shrine is one of the most impressive structures in Japan.

Many festivals are held each year at the shrine, the most important being on November 1, November 3, and May 3.

On New Year's eve, several hundred thousand people begin converging on Harajuku just before midnight, marching en masse up the major thoroughfares, to worship at the shrine just after midnight—a traditional pilgrimage known as Hatsu-Mairi, or the First Visit (to a shrine or temple) of the new year.

MEIJI VILLAGE / MEIJI MURA (May-e-jee Muu-rah)   Adjoining a lake in the foothills, about an hour from Nagoya, Meiji Mura is an open-air museum that contains some 70 buildings of the Meiji era (1868–1912) on a 250-acre wooded and landscaped site.

The village, which is visited by more than a million people a year, was created by architect/engineer Yoshiro Taniguchi, and Motomo Tsuchikawa, a high school friend who rose to become vice-president of the Nagoya Railroad Company.

Concerned that the distinctive architecture of the Meiji period would be totally lost, Taniguchi persuaded Tsuchikawa to raise the money needed to buy the land and buildings and move them to the site.

The village has homes, business structures, churches, a railroad, a prison, a lighthouse, shops, etc. It also has the front and lobby of the famous old Imperial Hotel, which was designed by Frank Lloyd Wright. (See IMPERIAL HOTEL.)

The museum is open to sightseers daily, for a modest fee.

MIKOSHI (Me-koe-she)   *Mikoshi* are the portable shrines, some huge in size, that celebrants carry on their shoulders during festivals.

The *mikoshi* symbolizes the shrine sponsoring the festival and is the temporary abode of the shrine god or goddess during the event. Some of the *mikoshi* seen throughout Japan each year have not changed in more than a thousand years.

It is customary for the men and women who carry the *mikoshi* to dress in traditional attire, to swing and sway as they march through the streets to simulate revelry, and to shout Yoisa! Yoisa! to attract the spirit of the shrine.

MINAMOTO, YORITOMO (Me-nah-moe-toe, Yoe-ree-toe-moe)   One of the best-known names in Japanese history, Yoritomo Minamoto was the leader of one of the greatest warrior families and the man who founded the shogunate form of government that was to last from 1192 until 1868.

The Minamoto clan, also known as the Genji, was one of many warrior clans that became very powerful in the eleventh and twelfth centuries and began to struggle against each other and against the now weakened noble families that had controlled Japan since 660 A.D.

Born in 1147, Yoritomo and his half-brother Yoshitsune waged a 35-year war against the Taira clan (Heike), finally annihilating the clan, the young emperor, and several members of the Imperial Court at the sea battle of Danno-Ura in 1185. (The infant emperor's grandmother took him in her arms and leaped into the sea, followed by his mother and their ladies-in-waiting.)

Having achieved military supremacy throughout Japan and exercising control over the enthronement of a new emperor who became just a figurehead, Yoritomo set up his military headquarters at Kamakura, far away from Kyoto.

Following the Battle of Danno-Ura, Yoshitsune married a Taira, earning the wrath of Yoritomo, who set out to destroy him. See MINAMOTO, YOSHITSUNE.

In 1192, Yoritomo had himself appointed *shogun* by the emperor—an old title that had been used several hundred years before to designate generals sent against the Ainu, the Caucasians who inhabited central and northern Japan when the Japanese arrived. It translates very well as generalissimo.

Yoritomo died in 1199 and was succeeded, in turn, by his two sons, Yoriie and Sanetomo. But Sanetomo was assassinated by his nephew (a member of the Hojo family) in 1219, bringing an end to the Minamoto House. The Hojo family, the leading advisors to the shogunate, invited the noble Yoritsune Fujiwara from Kyoto to become *shogun*, but the actual power of the government was usurped by Yoshitoko Hojo, whose family was to continue as regents for the military government until 1333.

MINAMOTO, YOSHITUNE (Me-nah-moe-toe, Yoe-sheet-sue-nay)   One of the most romanticized figures in Japan's history, Yoshitsune Minamoto, the younger half-brother of Yoritomo, the man who established Japan's first shogunate, was born in 1159, the ninth son of Yoshitomo Minamoto.

When his father was defeated by Kiyomori Taira, Yoshitsune's life was spared, and he was sent to Kuramayama Temple in Kyoto. With the help of a metal dealer named Kichiji, he escaped and fled to northern Japan, where he lived with the family of Hidehira Fujiwara, a branch of the famous noble house that had ruled Japan since 660.

In Mutsu, he spent his early years learning the skills of war and other martial arts, and in 1180, when he was 21, he joined his half-brother Yoritomo, who was gathering an army in Izu to go against the Taira clan.

Yoshitsune's skill, daring, and courage made him a very successful general —so much so that his brother became suspicious of his ambitions. After the great Battle of Danno-Ura, at which the Taira were eliminated, Yoshitsune married the daughter of Lord Taira. This made Yoritomo believe Yoshitsune had turned against him.

Yoritomo sent a troop of warriors to kill Yoshitsune, but one of the younger man's faithful friends, Benkei, whom he had met in Mutsu, saved his life. The two of them, along with a small band of trusted retainers, then fled into the mountains of Yoshino.

There the small group was accosted by a band of dangerous *yamabushi* (yah-mah-buu-she), or itinerant priests, who infested the area and were on Yoritomo's side. This time, Yoshitsune was saved by his retainer Tadanobu.

Thereafter, there are conflicting stories about what happened to the popular young warrior, including several more close calls in which his large friend Benkei played a prominent role. But it is known that Yoshitsune was able to reach the castle of Koromogawa, where he expected to find his old protector, Hidehira Fujiwara.

Hidehira had died, however, and had been succeeded by his cowardly son, Yasuhira, who quickly betrayed Yoshitsune, his wife, and friends to Yoritomo's agents. The small band of refugees were either killed or committed *harakiri*.

MINING / KOGYO (Koag-yoe)   Mining is an old and well-established industry in Japan, but the industry is in trouble. Discovering and developing ore deposits is difficult because of convoluted, mountainous terrain. The productivity of existing mines is declining, while the age of the miners and the cost of mining is going up. The ores that are found in Japan contain a relatively large percentage of impurities, and pollution problems are becoming increasingly serious.

Among the ores mined in Japan are copper, lead, zinc, bauxite, iron, manganese, dolomite, and limestone. Except for limestone and sulfide ore, Japan imports most of the minerals it needs, including iron ore, tin, bauxite, copper, and coal.

MINSHUKU (Meen-shuu-kuu)   Japan's not-so-well-known *minshuku* deserve to be better known. They are people's lodges, or inns that are more modest than the popular *ryokan* and a lot less expensive.

Altogether, there are some 24,000 *minshuku* in Japan, of which approximately 200 have been designated as International Minshuku, meaning their facilities and services are adequate to fit the needs and expectations of most foreign visitors.

Minshuku are run by their family owners and are traditional Japanese style, with breakfast, supper, and usually a Japanese bath (some have showers). Besides the savings, *minshuku* offer the foreign visitor to Japan an opportunity to experience Japanese life as it has been lived for centuries.

Guests are expected to bring their own personal articles, and it doesn't hurt to have a towel or two of your own, along with a small supply of toilet paper if you are going into a distant rural area.

Most *minshuku* are located on farms, in fishing villages, at resorts, and near temples.

For detailed information about *minshuku*, contact the Japan Minshuku Association, Kotsu Kaikan Bldg., 2-10-1 Yurakucho, Chiyoda-ku, Tokyo, Japan, or any of the offices of the Japan National Tourist Organization.

MISHIMA, YUKIO (Me-she-mah, Yuu-kee-oh)   One of Japan's most brilliant and controversial twentieth-century writers, Yukio Mishima was born in 1925 and committed ritual suicide in the way of a *samurai* in 1971, at the age of 46.

Mishima wrote novels and plays of extraordinary power and beauty. More of his works have been translated into English than those of any other Asian writer, and during his lifetime he was often mentioned as a candidate for the Nobel Prize in literature.

Besides his writing, which he did at night, Mishima was a devotee of the way of *bushido*, the ethics of the *samurai* of feudal Japan, and a champion body builder.

He was a strong nationalist and trained and equipped his own small elite military force. In 1971, he and his men broke into the Tokyo headquarters of the national self-defense force and attempted to persuade the commanding general to participate in a coup.

Rebuffed by the military and under siege in the office he had seized, Mishima disemboweled himself in the honored tradition of the *samurai*, after which his chief aide cut his head off with a sword.

Among Mishima's best-known books are *The Temple of the Golden Pavilion*, *The Sound of Waves*, *Five Modern Noh Plays*, and *Sun and Steel*.

I met Mishima in the 1960s, when he was at the height of his fame, and admired him for his dedication to writing, to the development of his body and mind, and to the pursuit of his ideals—but I had no thought of where his zeal would lead him.

MISSIONARIES / DENDOSHI (Dane-doe-she)   The very first foreign missionaries in Japan were from Korea and China, probably sometime between 300 and 500 A.D. The first Western missionary of record was Francis Xavier, a Spanish Jesuit who arrived in Kagoshima from Malacca in 1549.

The country was involved in clan warfare at that time, as leading feudal lords (*daimyo*) fought to claim power from the weakened and ineffective Ashikaga Shogunate.

The Lord of Satsuma (in Kagoshima), impressed with Xavier and the gifts he brought, gave him permission to teach Christianity in the Satsuma fief. Xavier stayed in Japan for 10 months, during which time he made arrangements for other Jesuits to follow him.

Because of the turmoil of the times, several other feudal lords cooperated with the Jesuits (mostly Portuguese) who followed Xavier—primarily because of the guns, ammunition, and other Western products the Jesuits used in bartering for religious privileges and converts.

The common Japanese, at the complete mercy of their feudal lords, who treated them as chattel, were less cynical in their reaction to Christianity, which stressed individual freedom and human rights. Many thousands of the conversions that followed were as sincere as the product of genuine religious fervor can be.

These early missionaries were not content to confine themselves to religious work, however. Their political intrigues and the military threat that they posed eventually turned the new shogunate government against them.

From the late 1500s, both Japanese converts and foreign missionaries came under increasing persecution, first from Hideyoshi Toyotomi and then from the Tokugawa Shogunate, which began in 1603.

Finally, in the 1630s, the shogunate decided to eliminate the missionary and Christian presence in Japan. All missionaries were deported. In the winter of 1637, the largest group of Japanese converts in the country took refuge in a castle on Shimabara Peninsula.

They were besieged by a shogunate army and then systematically slaughtered.

Among the very first Westerners to arrive in Japan after the country reopened its doors to the outside world in 1854 were missionaries. But their expectations of soon converting Japan's millions to Christianity were doomed to failure.

With the downfall of the Tokugawa Shogunate in 1867, the lives of the Japanese were revolutionized in a matter of days and weeks. No longer were they owned by feudal lords. For the first time in the history of the country, they had some rights of their own. Western thought and ways began to flood into the islands.

In this new heady atmosphere, taking on a new religion that was intellectually simple-minded, very poorly explained by missionaries who could not speak Japanese, and that basically forbade its adherents from doing things that had been traditional for thousands of years made no sense at all to most Japanese.

Among the first things the missionaries did to the few followers they were able to attract was to forbid them from taking a bath more than once a week. Daily mixed bathing had been the custom in Japan for hundreds of generations, but to the sexually obsessed missionaries such behavior was a serious sin.

In subsequent years, Christian missionaries in Japan have continued their efforts to turn Japanese into Christians, but with very limited success. The effort is institutionalized and goes on because it has gone on before, not because there are any real hopes that the situation will change significantly.

Christian missionaries in Japan have, however, made substantial contributions to the country (see HEPBURN, DR. CHARLES), but generally only in an educational sense. Most of them have ended up being little more than English-language teachers.

Japanese who do profess to be Christians also remain Buddhists and Shintoists to some degree, since it is virtually impossible to be Japanese and not be influenced by these two cultural forces.

MISTRESSES / NIGO SAN (Nee-go Sahn)   Until recent times, mistresses were a common and accepted part of Japanese society—just as they were, and still are, in many other parts of the world.

The practice of mistress keeping in Japan was limited to upper-class men in earlier periods, but eventually became common among the merchant class, as well.

Again, just as in England, France, Russia, and many other nations in earlier ages, there are several reasons why mistress-keeping flourished. There were no religious sanctions against it. There was no element of love in most marriages, and it was vitally important to upper-class men that they produce male offspring.

The history of Japan—with its sophisticated Imperial Court and large group of nobles, the long shogunate dynasties that also maintained a court with numerous retainers, and its 200-plus feudal lords who were like kings in their own domains—is replete with tales of mistresses. Some of them played vital roles in the affairs of the country.

During the long, peaceful, and relatively prosperous Tokugawa Shogunate (1603–1868), mistress-keeping came to be a high art, with detailed customs and rules. There were different categories of mistresses and mistress keepers.

The practice of mistress-keeping in Japan has changed with the times. It is no longer totally sanctioned by society or the law, but exists in the same fashion that one finds in most Catholic countries.

As in the past, most mistress-keeping is closely related to the *mizu shobai,* or "water business," i.e., the entertainment trades.

MITI (MINISTRY OF INTERNATIONAL TRADE & INDUSTRY) / TSUSANSHO (T'sue-sahn-show)   Japan's Ministry of International Trade and Industry, known by its initials, MITI, is one of the most important and best known of Japan's government agencies.

MITI owes its prominence and power to its role in helping transform Japan from an agricultural/ handicraft economy in 1868 to a major industrial economy by 1895 and in helping Japan recover after the disaster of World War II.

Following the downfall of the Tokugawa Shogunate in 1867, the government, primarily through MITI, became directly involved in investing in heavy industries and in providing support and guidance to industry across the board.

In the decades that followed, the companies financed by the government were turned over to private interests, but MITI and other government agencies have continued to act in the capacity of planner, organizer, and coordinator of Japan's industry and trade and to exercise direct control in the case of energy and power resources.

Unlike in the U.S., where government and industry have traditionally been cast in the role of antagonists, the relationship between government and industry in Japan has been one of cooperation and support.

MITI's influence on industry in Japan is generally exercised through a system known as *gyosei shido* (G'yoe-say-ee She-doe), or "administrative guidance." Until the late 1980s this guidance was usually accepted voluntarily and in good spirit because there was both trust and confidence in MITI's methods and goals.

Since the collapse of Japan's so-called "bubble economy" in 1990, the government has been under increasing pressure to deregulate the economy, and business has become more and more critical of the *gyosei* system.

MITO (Me-toe)   In a country filled with places of extraordinary historical interest, it is difficult to pick out one that is more outstanding than another, but an area of special interest is the city of Mito, capital of Ibaraki Prefecture, 117.5 kilometers northeast of Tokyo.

Mito was the headquarters of the fief Ieyasu Tokugawa gave to his eleventh son, Yorifusa, who established one of the three main branches of the Tokugawa family. The Mito Tokugawas were especially noted in Japan for maintaining at the highest level the way of life prescribed for the *samurai* by the concepts of *bushido* (The Way of the Warrior).

The head of the House of Mito was automatically the *vice-shogun*, but in consideration for this hereditary right, was disbarred by law from becoming *shogun*. The second head of the Mito branch of the family, Mitsukuni (1628–1700), is regarded as the most outstanding of this line.

Mitsukuni is perhaps best known for having started to compile the *History of Great Japan*, which was not completed until 1906 and was comprised of 397 volumes. This work is credited with having had a significant influence on the decision of the last *shogun* to step down in favor of the Emperor in 1867–68.

Among the attractions of this picturesque city are the grounds of the Mito lord's castle and the Kodokan (Koe-doe-khan), a school founded by Nariaki Tokugawa, the ninth lord of Mito, who lived from 1800 to 1860, and Tokiwa Park, also known as Kairaku-En, one of the three most noted landscaped gardens in Japan (the other two are Kenroku-En in Kanazawa City and Koraku-En in Okayama City).

Nariaki designed the garden as a retreat for himself, and it was completed in 1843. It was turned into a public park in 1873, five years after the end of Japan's shogunate form of government. When first completed, the garden contained 10,000 *ume* (plum) trees—of which some 3,000 remain today and are a major attraction when they begin blooming in late February.

There are literally hundreds of other places in Ibaraki Prefecture that are of special interest (shrines, hot spring spas, etc.), two of which are the Joban Hawaiian Center and Iwaki.

The Joban Hawaiian Center is a seven kilometer-square domed recreational site near Yumoto, where hot sulfide spring water is pumped into the center to keep it at summer temperatures all year around. The huge dome contains several swimming pools and water chutes, a number of stages for various kinds of performances, and a garden of tropical plants.

Iwaki is the largest city in Japan in area—almost equal to the total area of Kagawa Prefecture—as the result of combining the towns of Nokoso, Izumi, Yumoto, and Taira into one municipal area in 1966. Taira was the castle town of the Ando clan, and Nakoso is celebrated in Japanese history as the site of a huge fortress barrier that was built there in ancient times as protection against raids by Ainu tribesmen. (See AINU.)

MITSUBISHI CORPORATION / MITSUBISHI SHOJI (Sho-jee)   The Mitsubishi Corporation, the trading arm and leader of the huge Mitsubishi group of companies, was Japan's largest general trading house until the late 1980s, when it was finally passed by Ito-Chu.

Historically speaking, Mitsubishi dates from the days of the Tokugawa Shogunate, but in its present form it was established in 1950, following the breakup of the the huge *zaibatsu* combines (of which Mitsubishi was one) by the Allied forces occupying Japan following the end of World War II.

There are over a 100 companies in the Mitsubishi Group, with a nucleus of 26 key companies and 18 others. Mitsubishi Trading is noted for the degree of control it exercises over the group. This control and coordination is applied through a so-called Friday Club, made up of the presidents of the 26 key companies. The club meets on the second Friday of each month.

There is a Mitsubishi company in almost every category of business in Japan, and in virtually all cases they are either the industry leader or among the top two or three companies.

MITSUI & COMPANY, LTD.   The story of the present-day Mitsui companies is one of the great commercial and personal sagas of Japan, going back to the Fujiwara family, which in the seventh century A.D. usurped the power of the emperor and, through continuous intermarriage with the Imperial family, dominated the government for the next 400 years.

In 1100 A.D., one of the Fujiwara descendants left the Court at Kyoto to seek his fortune in Omi Province, near Lake Biwa. There he discovered three wells, in one of which was a treasure of hidden gold.

As was common on momentous occasions, the lucky man changed his name to Mitsui, meaning Three Wells. Despite the fact that those of noble rank and the *samurai* class of hereditary warriors that developed during these decades generally did not engage in business, the Mitsui family gradually became merchants, while retaining their *samurai* status.

For the next several hundred years, the fortunes of the Mitsui family waxed and waned with the political stablity of the country. Finally, in the early 1600s, after the establishment of the Tokugawa Shogunate and the closing of Japan's doors to the outside world (see TOKUGAWA, IEYASU; HISTORY; SHOGUNS; etc.), Sokubei (or Takatoshi) Mitsui, the head of the family at that time, officially gave up his exalted *samurai* rank and announced that thereafter the family would be commoners and engage in commerce exclusively.

Sokubei opened a *sake* and *shoyu* brewing business called Echigo-Ya, after his father, who had been the hereditary Lord of Echigo. Later, Sokubei's wife opened a pawnshop to help the struggling business survive.

Sokubei died in 1633, but his wife and their eight sons continued operating the business. She sent their oldest son, Saburozaemon, to Edo (Tokyo), the shogunate capital, to start up a dry goods store. As the years went by, it became apparent that the youngest son, Hachirobei, had the most business talent, and he was sent to Edo to work with Saburozaemon.

Hachirobei was a farsighted man who learned early that dealing with the *daimyo* and *samurai* was a dangerous business because they could not be forced to pay their bills. He first went into the moneylending business, confining his loans to other merchants and commoners, and in 1673 he opened a dry goods store in Kyoto, the Imperial capital.

There, he introduced a startling innovation. Instead of selling his merchandise on long-term credit at inflated prices, as had been done traditionally, he began selling at low fixed prices for cash. He also began selling cloth in any lengths desired, instead of prescribed lengths.

Both innovations were very popular, leading Hachirobei to open a large store in Edo (Tokyo). He became a pioneer in advertising his stores and soon was the most successful merchant in the country. He became a patron of the most famous woodblock print artists of the time, developed a prototype of double-entry bookkeeping, and established the system of settling accounts by money orders.

Hachirobei established exchange houses to provide banking operations for the business. One of these exchanges, set up to handle tax money for the shogunate government, was the predecessor of Mitsui Bank.

By the time he died in 1694, at the age of 73, Hachirobei had set up his six sons as the heads of collateral families in charge of different phases of the family business—a business that was not only to outlast the Tokugawa Shogunate, but to play a leading role in the transformation of fedual Japan into a modern industrial nation in the late 1800s and in the rebuilding of Japan following the debacle of World War II.

Before the family holdings were broken up by the Allied Occupation forces after the end of World War II, the Mitsui family owned and operated the largest commercial conglomerate the world has ever seen, with some 3,000,000 employees. See ZAIBATSU.

The survival and extraordinary growth of the House of Mitsui is attributed to the Family Constitution drawn up by Sochiku Mitsui, the oldest son of Hachirobei and based on principles laid down in his father's will.

Each male member of the family was required to take the following oath upon coming of age:

"In obedience to the precepts of our forefathers and in order to strengthen the everlasting foundation of the families of our House and to expand the enterprise bequeathed by our forefathers, I solemnly vow that I will observe and follow the regulations handed down in the Constitution of our House, and that I will not wantonly seek to alter them. In witness thereof, I take the oath and affix my signature thereto in the presence of the august spirits of our ancestors."

Today, the Mitsui Group is one of Japan's largest industrial/commercial conglomerates. Each of the companies in the group operates independently, but all cooperate in areas of mutual interest.

Altogether, there are several hundred companies and subsidiaries in the group, including four in cement, six in chemicals, six in commerce and trade, six in construction, three in energy, four in engineering, five in finance and insurance, four in food processing, six in machinery, one in mining, six in nonferrous metals, one in paper, two in real estate, one in steel, one in synthetic fibers and plastics, two in transportation, two in warehousing, two in travel, and one in the information industry.

Liaison among the group companies is provided by the Nimoku-Kai (Nee-moe-kuu Kie), or Second Thursday Conference, which is made up of the presidents of the 24 leading group companies, and through the Getsuyo Kai (Gates-yoe Kie), or Monday Conference, which is made up of the managing directors of 62 companies in the Mitsui Group.

These two bodies provide a forum for discussions and for the exchange of views. In addition, members of the Group have a number of ongoing committees engaged in public relations and research and acting as advisors to the Nimoku Kai.

Mitsui & Company, the Group's major trading enterprise, has some 50 offices in Japan and over 130 offices in 77 countries—all linked by privately leased telex and telephone networks.

In fact, the communications system maintained by Mitsui gives an impressive indication of its size and the scope of its operation. It has four large computerized communication centers: one in Tokyo that covers all of Asia; one in New York covering North, Central, and South America; one in London covering Europe and Africa; and one in Sydney, Australia, covering Oceania. A subcenter in Bahrain covers the Middle East.

These centers are linked to each other by satellites and operate 24 hours a day. In addition to these telex and telephone networks, Mitsui operates a mail service, equivalent to that of a city with a population in excess of 125,000.

Mitsui's communication centers monitor currencies, political matters, economic activity, social changes—and even the weather. They are regarded as being part of one of the largest and most efficient intelligence systems in the world.

Offshore trading by Mitsui, of special importance to the U.S. and several other countries around the world, involves foodstuffs, gas and petroleum, bulk chemical products, metals, textiles, paper, etc.

In addition to belonging to one of Japan's three largest trading companies, the American branch of Mitsui & Co., Ltd. is the U.S.'s fourth largest trading company.

Recommended reading: *The Mitsui Story: Three Centuries of Japanese Business* (Mitsui & Co., Ltd); and *The 100-Year History of Mitsui & Co., Ltd*. (Mitsui & Co., Ltd).

MIURA PENINSULA (Me-uu-rah)   One of the most beautiful and important geographical features of the island of Honshu, the Miura Peninsula projects into the Pacific Ocean in a southeasterly direction, between Tokyo Bay on the northeast and Sagami Bay on the southwest.

On the Tokyo Bay side of the peninsula, the major city is the great naval port of Yokosuka. Further on down, where a spit reaches out into Tokyo Bay, is Uraga, which is famous in history as the shogunate checkpoint for all shipping entering the bay.

On the west, or Sagami Bay, side of the peninsula are the famous resort/residential cities of Zushi and Hayama and numerous other smaller cities, towns, and villages.

Kamakura, the shogunate capital of Japan from 1192 until 1333, is located at the base of the peninsula, facing Sagami Bay. Just west of Kamakura, at the head of Sagami Bay, is the famous beach and resort area of Enoshima.

A treasure house of historical sites and scenic wonderlands, the peninsula is a favorite residential area, as well as a playground for people from the Tokyo/Kawasaki/Yokohama areas. See KAMAKURA; YOKOSUKA; ADAMS, WILLIAM; HISTORY; SHOGUN.

MIYAKO HOTEL (Me-yah-koe)   One of Kyoto's premier hotels, the Miyako is situated in 16 acres of landscaped gardens on a wooded hillside overlooking the downtown area of the city.

The hotel is distinctive and popular because it combines some of the best of Western comfort with Japanese beauty to achieve one of the most attractive and comfortable hotels in the country. Besides the usual Japanese amenities—which include a steambath and masseurs—the hotel has four swimming pools.

MIYAMOTO, MUSASHI (Me-yah-moe-toe, Muu-sah-she)   Musashi Miyamoto was one of Japan's most famous feudal-age *samurai* swordsmen. After practicing with the sword for several hours a day for more than 30 years and taking on dozens of opponents in battles to the death, Miyamoto arrived at the point where he could not be defeated in fair combat.

Miyamoto's skill with the deadly *samurai* sword made him a legend in his time, and his immortality was assured when Japanese novelist Eiji Yoshikawa fictionalized his life story in a book by the same name in the mid-1940s.

An English edition of the book, translated by Charles S. Terry, was brought out by the huge Japanese publishing house Kodansha in the early 1980s and became something of a best-seller in the U.S.

Near the end of his remarkable life, Miyamoto wrote his own biography, explaining his philosophy and telling how he had achieved such mastery with the sword. He called his book the *Book of Five Rings*. In the early 1980s, an American edition of the book was published, and it received some notoriety in the U.S. as a guide to understanding the Japanese business mentality—a phenomenon the Japanese viewed with considerable amusement, if not a little sadness.

MIYANOSHITA (Me-yah-no-shh-tah)   One of the most famous of the hot spring spas in the Hakone district, southwest of Tokyo, Miyanoshita is also a primary gateway to the resort/recreational area. Roads radiating out from Miyanoshita lead to numerous other resorts and scenic places in and on the great volcanic caldera that makes up Hakone.

The oldest Western-styled hotel in the Hakone district, the world-famous Fujiya, which opened in 1878, is also in Miyanoshita. The Miyanoshita hot springs, with temperatures ranging from 62 to 78 degrees centigrade, have been documented as bringing relief to rheumatism, gout, nervous disorders, and female ailments.

MIZU SHOBAI / WATER BUSINESS *Mizu shobai* (Mee-zoo sho-bye)   is an old term, now slightly dated, used in reference to the world of entertainment, particularly that having to do with bars, cabarets, nightclubs, massage baths, *geisha* houses, and women.

The term literally means "water business" and no doubt owes its origin to the fact that much of the entertainment of early Japan revolved around hot spring spas and bathhouses, including ones that functioned as houses of prostitution.

The other possibility is that the term refers to the ephemeral nature of pleasure—which, like water, is bright and sparkling but soon evaporates. See WATER BUSINESS. Recommended reading: *Bachelor's Japan*, by Boye Lafayette De Mente (Tuttle); *Japan at Night*, by Boye Lafayette De Mente (Passport Books).

MOCHI (Moe-chee)   *Mochi*, often described as rice cake, would better be described as a type of rice bread. It is made of an especially glutinous kind of rice that is thoroughly steamed and pounded with a heavy wooden mallet until it is a thick, heavy paste.

This paste, which is cut into small, manageable pieces, hardens. It is used as an ingredient in several dishes and is also eaten baked and broiled, with soy sauce (or, in recent times, with a sugar coating).

Mochi has been a popular food in Japan since ancient times, and it is a traditional New Year's item, when it is eaten in a thick broth called *zoni*. It is also eaten broiled at this time. Most people now buy their *mochi* ready-made, but until around the 1960s the majority made it at home in a traditional New Year's ceremony that involved the whole family taking turns with the pounding.

Mochi is a popular gift item, being regarded as a good luck omen, especially for safe childbirth.

MODELING   Fashion and other product modeling has been big business in Japan since the 1960s. Foreign models, including internationally known movie stars, appear regularly in Japanese print and television commercials.

At any one time, there are several hundred foreign models, men and women, listed with the various modeling agencies. These models come from all over the world, on two-month visas. Their earnings range from two or three thousand dollars a month to ten thousand dollars or more. Internationally established movie stars command huge fees.

At present, foreign female models that are most in demand are in the 15–20 age bracket. Male models in the 20–30 age range are preferred.

One of the largest and most successful of the agencies in Tokyo is Folio, Inc., which was founded in 1979 and has some 800 clients.

The business may be glamorous on the surface, but it is a hard and demanding profession, says a spokesperson for Folio. Being young, beautiful, and often vulnerable, foreign models in particular need special care and guidance, the spokesperson said.

A significant percentage of the girls, away from home and in a strange country, where they cannot speak the language and are not familiar with the customs, fall prey to the enticements of the jet-set life in the Roppongi entertainment district of Tokyo. See FASHION MODELS.

MOHAMMEDAN MOSQUE   Japan has two Islamic mosques, one in Tokyo and the other in Kobe. The mosque in Tokyo is a short distance from Higashi Kitazawa Station on the Odakyu Electric Railway. It is one of the more exotic landmarks in Shibuya Ward.

MONEY / OKANE (Oh-kah-nay)   Until 1868, the wealth of Japan's feudal clans was figured in terms of rice production, but rice was far too cumbersome and complicated to be used as a medium of exchange, so coins and small bars of metal—in units called *ryo* (rio)—had been in use as currency for a long time.

The first paper money appeared in Japan in about 1615—in the form of notes issued by merchants in Ise and Yamada. The practice was soon picked up by the larger merchant houses of Osaka and Sakai. See MITSUI & CO.

Then the *daimyo* feudal lords began to issue clan notes. The Tokugawa Shogunate realized it should do something to stabilize the situation, but its orders to the clans to stop issuing paper money were ignored. Not being able to control the currency was one of the major problems of the shogunate and contributed to its demise in 1868.

The new Meiji Government that took over in 1868 issued four kinds of paper money—all printed on copper plates that could be easily duplicated.

Counterfeiting became rife, so the government began having its currency printed in Germany, where printing technology was further advanced.

In 1871, the monetary unit was changed from *ryo* to *yen* (pronounced like "inn" in Japanese). Modern banks appeared in Japan in 1872, and all of them issued their own notes, first printed in the U.S. See BANKS.

Yen presently comes in both coins and bills. There are 10-, 50-, 100-, and 500-yen coins, and 500-, 1,000-, 5,000-, and 10,000-yen bills. The yen floats on the foreign exchange markets.

MONGOL INVASIONS   Twice in the thirteenth century, Kublai Khan, the first Mongol emperor of China, sent invasion fleets to Japan—the first one in 1274 and the second one in 1281.

The Khan first demanded that Japan become a tributary to China in 1268, but the shogunate authorities in Kamakura ignored the ultimatum. In the next few years, several other Chinese envoys arrived, with their demands growing more belligerent.

The shogunate ordered the feudal lords in northern Kyushu to fortify the coastline.

In 1273, the shogunate rebuffed still another Chinese envoy. In November of the following year, a Chinese armada of some 900 ships and over 30,000 troops, including Mongols, Chinese, Tartars, and Koreans, devastated the Japanese islands of Tsushima and Kii in the straits between Kyushu and Korea and then attacked the port city of Hakata in northern Kyushu.

Used to fighting hand-to-hand combat with swords and spears, the Japanese *samurai* were no match for the cavalry tactics and weapons of the Mongols and were forced to retreat. When night fell, the Mongols withdrew to their ships instead of pressing their advantage—apparently because of an approaching typhoon.

During the night, the typhoon sank well over half the Mongol fleet and caused the drowning of close to half of all the troops that were aboard the ships. The surviving ships broke off the attack and returned to China.

Kublai Khan was not to be so easily denied, however. In 1275, he sent another envoy to the court of the *shogun* in Kamakura. The envoy was summarily beheaded on Katase Beach near Enoshima. Not content with just this act of revenge, the shogunate decided it would take the fight to the enemy and invade the Khan's vassal state of Korea.

While preparing for the invasion of Korea, the shogunate ordered the lords of Kyushu to build stone walls along the coast.

In 1279, the Khan dispatched another envoy to Japan. He, too, was executed by the shogunate, which by this time knew another invasion was imminent.

The second invasion, this time by a fleet said to have been even larger than the Spanish Armada that attacked England, arrived off the coast of northern Kyushu in late 1281. Once again, the Japanese defenders were getting the worst of it when, just as before, a typhoon smashed into the Mongol fleet, destroying it—giving rise to the belief that Japan was defended by *Kami Kaze* (Kah-me Kah-zay), or Divine Winds.

Undaunted, the Mongols planned a third invasion of Japan in 1283 but delayed it because of other affairs. The following year, they sent another envoy—who, being aware of the fate that befell his two predecessors, went only as far as the island of Tsushima.

In 1284, the Mongols invaded Vietnam, giving the shogunate more time to construct defenses. The Mongols were defeated by the Vietnamese, further delaying their designs against Japan. The Mongols then turned their attention to Java, which they invaded in 1292—only to withdraw in 1293.

In 1293, the still ambitious Kublai Khan began laying plans for a third invasion of Japan and ordered Korea to mobilize. He died the following year, however, and the plans for the invasion were canceled. Five years later, his successor sent an envoy to Japan, calling for a trade and friendship treaty between the two countries.

Thus ended the first outside threat the Japanese had faced in their long history. See HISTORY; SHOGUN.

MOON VIEWING / TSUKI-MI (T'sue-kee-me)   The practice of moon viewing has been an established aesthetic and artistic custom in Japan since ancient times, though it is now considerably diminished by the fast pace of modern life.

In mid-autumn, when the moon was full, people would gather in parks and on high places, verandas, and specially built platforms to enjoy the beauty of the moon, eat specially prepared foods, drink *sake*, and compose *haiku* poetry celebrating the moon.

Ages ago, places that were especially outstanding moon viewing spots came into use, and moon viewing platforms or pavilions were built on the sites. Some of these platforms and pavilions still exist, and many of the country's noted moon-viewing locations are still used today. See MATSUSHIMA.

MORIOKA (Moe-ree-oh-kah)   In the north-central area of Honshu, Morioka is the capital of Iwate Prefecture and the ironware capital of Japan. During the days of the *shogun*, Morioka was called Nambu, and it was the castle town of the Nambu clan (the whole province was called Nambu at that time).

The area has been known for centuries for its Nambu *tetsu bin* or iron kettles. It is also known today for its Chagu-Chagu Umakko festival, held on June 15 to celebrate horse raising, and a cherry tree that is listed as a National Monument—the famous Ishiware Zakura, or Stone-Breaking Cherry Tree, which has grown up through a fissure in a huge block of granite.

The ruins and grounds of the Nambu clan castle are now a city park. Kei Hara, one of the most famous political leaders of the Taisho era (1912–1926), was born in Morioka. There is a memorial hall in the city dedicated to him.

MOUNTAINS / YAMA (Yah-mah)   Japan is one of the most mountainous island chains in the world. Plains and basins account for only about 29 percent of the total land mass—the remainder is made up of hills and mountains.

The whole archipelago is basically a chain of peaks and ranges, with slopes and basins on either side. These high mountain ranges, forming a backbone that traverses the center of the four main islands, have historically divided Japan into two parts—one facing the Pacific and the other facing the Asian mainland. There are 11 peaks that are over 3,000 meters in height and 13 that are over 2,500 meters—all of them on the main island of Honshu. Of these 24 high peaks, eight are dormant volcanoes, including three of the highest ones in the country.

The top 10 peaks are Mt. Fuji (3,776 meters), Mt. Shirane (3,192), Mt. Hodaka (3,190), Mt. Yariga (3,180), Mt. Arakawa (3,141), Mt. Akaishi (3,120), Mt. On-Take (3,063), Mt. Shiomi (3,047), Mt. Senjoga (3,033), and Mt. Norikura (3,026).

There are literally hundreds of other peaks on Honshu and the other islands that range from 1,000 to 2,500 meters. See MT. FUJI; MT. ASO; MT. KOYA. Many peaks in the Japan Alps (see JAPAN ALPS) are over 3,000 meters high, including a number that are also volcanic.

Among them are Shirane-san (She-rah-nay-sahn), 3,192m, in Yamanashi and Shizuoka prefectures; Hodaka-dake, 3,190m, in Nagano and Gifu prefectures; and Yariga-take, 3,180m, also in Nagano and Gifu prefectures.

Mt. Fuji, an extinct volcano cone that rises to a majestic 3,776 meters (12,388 feet) and towers over the islands like a sentinel, is the highest mountain in Japan. See MT. FUJI.

MOVIES / EIGA (A-e-gah) Japan's first small film studio was established in Tokyo in 1904, but it was not until 1912, when Nikkatsu was founded, that the industry really got started. The industry did not come of age internationally until 1950, however, when Akira Kurosawa's masterpiece, *Rashomon* (Rah-sho-moan), appeared.

Other directors and Japanese-made films that have received international honors were Kenji Mizoguchi and his celebrated *Ugetsu Monogatari*, Yasujiro Ozu and *The Tale of Tokyo*, and Keisuke Kinoshita, Tadashi Imai, Kon Ichikawa, Hiroshi Inagaki, Teinosuke Kinugasa, and Kaneto Shindo.

From the 1950s to the 1980s Japan's film industry was dominated by the Big Four—Nikkatsu, Toho, Shochiku, and Toei. These studios produced several hundred films a year and became known worldwide for the many innovations they introduced into the world of films.

Among the best known of Japan's actors and actresses from the 1960s into the 1980s were Toshiro Mifune and Machiko Kyo.

By the early 1980s Japan's film industry had gone into decline, primarily producing pornographic films and distributing foreign films.

MT. ASO (Ah-soe) Mt. Aso is actually five quite separate volcanic peaks in the Aso National Park in Kumamoto and Oita prefectures, making up portions of central and northeastern Kyushu. The largest of the peaks—Nakadake—is also the most active. Its crater is about 600 meters across and 160 meters deep. The highest of the peaks, Takadake, rises 1,592 meters above sea level.

There are three villages and three towns on the plains adjoining the five peaks—plains which were originally the crater of an even larger volcano, measuring 25 square kilometers in area.

The very least that can be said of the Mt. Aso area is that it is one of the most scenic spots on the face of the earth.

MT. FUJI / FUJI-SAN (Fuu-jee Sahn)   Towering up from the prefectures of Shizuoka and Yamanashi, southwest of Toyko, and visable for hundreds of miles, Mt. Fuji is considered one of the two most beautiful conical volcanoes in the world.

The traditional symbol for Japan and the inspiration for poets and artists from time immemorial, Mt. Fuji, at 3,776 meters, is Japan's highest and best-known mountain. Its name is believed to be derived from an Ainu word meaning Fire Mountain. (The Ainu were the original Caucasian inhabitants of central and northern Japan.)

Mt. Fuji's last eruption was in 1707, when it blanketed Edo (Tokyo), 100 kilometers away, with a thick layer of ash. Prior to that, it erupted fairly often —there are 18 eruptions on record—and apparently smoked continuously. Now only wisps of steam, measured at 80 degrees centigrade, waft up from one isolated section of the summit.

Mt. Fuji was considered sacred until the Meiji Restoration in 1868. The practice of climbing the mountain as a sign of religious piety developed very early. Documents written in June 1500 refer to endless streams of people hiking up the graceful peak. Later, the mountain became an object of worship, and an organization called Fuji-Ko, or Fuji Worshippers, was formed. Women, however, were not allowed to climb the mountain.

Now somewhere around half a million people, including children and elderly people, climb the mountain every summer. The first foreigner to climb Mt. Fuji was Sir Rutherford Alcock, the first British minister, who made the ascent on July 26, 1860. Lady Parkes, the wife of the British minister to the court of Edo, was the first foreign woman to reach the summit—in 1867.

There is a popular saying in Japan that everyone should climb Mt. Fuji once but that anyone who does it twice is a fool. (I have climbed it three times!) The climbing season lasts only from the first of July to the end of August, because of the cold weather and the danger from high winds.

The crater of Mt. Fuji, circular in shape, is approximately 300 meters wide and is relatively level, lying only 220 meters lower than the rim's highest peak. Authorities believe there was once a lake in the crater. Now it is filled with snow about 10 months out of the year—and mountain climbers, the rest of the time.

There are six popular climbing routes up the mountain—Yoshida, Kawaguchiko, Shoji, Gotemba, Subashiri and Fujinomiya—each starting from a different point around the base.

Each of the trails is divided into 10 sections called *go* (go). The distance between the *go* (or stations, as they are called in English) is based on the difficulty of the climb between them.

The beginning of each trail is *Ichi* Go (first station). Next is *Ni Go* (second station), etc. There are rest stations at the end of most of the *go*, with toilet facilities and rough, stone-covered shelters. There are substops in between many of the stations—and they can be confusing to tired climbers who measure their progress by counting stations.

The tree line extends to between the fifth and sixth stations, and it is mostly bare from there on to the top.

Many climbers start in the late morning or early afternoon, reach the seventh or eighth station by dark, stay overnight in one of the stone huts, get up to watch the sunrise the next morning, and then finish the climb.

The stations serve various Japanese noodle and rice dishes (and beer, which porters tote up the mountain on their backs), but it is always a good idea to take along various kinds of snacks and a canteen of water—along with toilet paper. Foreigners who do not speak Japanese enjoy the adventure more if they go with Japanese friends.

There is a weather observation radar station on top of Mt. Fuji, able to spot approaching typhoons as much as 800 kilometers away. (Flying into Tokyo from Hawaii, I have seen Mt. Fuji from over 200 miles out—a magnificent sight.)

The first portion of the climb up Mt. Fuji is easy, as the ascent is gradual and the footing solid. The last 1,000 or so feet are rather difficult, however, and require both caution and perseverance.

Many climbers buy walking sticks at the beginning of their climb and get the number of the stations burned onto them as they progress up the mountain. Descending the mountain, many climbers leave the established trails and come down the ash slides, but the practice is dangerous and discouraged.

Most climbers today ride buses part-way up the mountain and begin their hike at the third, fourth, or—most often—fifth station.

Although the climbing season on Mt. Fuji is limited to July and August, the waist of the mountain, with its five beautiful lakes and extensive forests, is a favorite year-round recreational area.

There are four main gateways to Mt. Fuji and the five Fuji lakes—Gotemba, Fuji-Yoshida, Kawaguchiko, and Fujinomiya—and a number of popular tours to the various districts.

The Mt. Fuji lake area is extensively developed as winter and summer resorts. The Lake Yamanaka area is especially popular as a summer resort, with hotels, villas, and clubhouses—most of them belonging to colleges and other organizations—lining its shores.

On August 26 each year, the city of Fuji-Yoshida (the main gateway for people from Tokyo) and the Sengen Shrine stage a Fire Festival that marks the approaching end of the climbing season (August 31).

Dozens of huge bonfires are lighted at different places around the city, and operators of huts on Mt. Fuji's Yoshida Trail follow suit, making a spectacular nighttime display that literally spirals up into the sky. Young men carry a heavy, vermilion-lacquered portable shrine shaped like Mt. Fuji through the streets—a custom that began centuries ago, when Mt. Fuji was active and the festival was intended to keep the god of the mountain quiet.

MT. KOYA / KOYA SAN (Koe-yah Sahn)   An hour and 40 minutes from Osaka, Mt. Koya is famed for the monastery on its summit, founded in 816 by Kobo Daishi, the great exponent of the Shingon sect of Buddhism.

The huge monastery covers over 99 hectares, and includes over 120 temple buildings (many others have been lost to fires over the centuries). The precincts of the monastery are surrounded by huge, old trees that are as magnificent as the main temple buildings.

In earlier times, women were not allowed to enter the Koyo-san monastery, but today it is visited by more than a million people every year. There are no inns in the little town of Koya, but 51 temples in the vicinity provide lodging and vegetarian food for visitors. The complex is very large, and it takes many hours for just a casual introduction to it.

MUSIC / ONGAKU (Own-gah-kuu)   There are several categories and subcategories of traditional Japanese music, classified by period of origin. These include *gagaku* (gah-gah-kuu), ancient; *nogaku* (no-gah-kuu), medieval; and the music of the still popular *shamisen* (shah-me-sen) and *koto* (koe-toe), recent.

Among the popular subclasses of traditional Japanese music are *sokyoku* (soe-k'yoe-kuu), *nagauta* (nah-gah-uu-tah), *kouta* (koe-uu-tah), and *yokyoku* (yoe-k'yoe-kuu).

Sokyoku, developed in the second half of the sixteenth century, is music played on the *koto*, a kind of harp, often in concert with the *shamisen* and *shakuhachi* (shah-kuu-hah-chee), a five-holed bamboo flute.

Nagauta, which means long song, is a kind of epic song that was first identified with the *shamisen* and, later, with *kabuki*. It then absorbed elements from regional music (*ji-uta*), puppet ballads (*jouri*), and folk songs (*minyo*), becoming very lively in accompaniment with flutes and hand-drums.

Kouta dates from the early nineteenth century but is based on popular songs of the fifteenth and sixteenth centuries. Short, dittylike songs sung in quick tempo in a suppressed voice, *kouta* are accompanied by a *shamisen* plucked with the bare fingers.

Yokyoku, associated with the *noh* drama since the fifteenth and sixteenth centuries, are rhymes based on seven–five syllables or five–seven syllables.

The usual subject is tales from the famous *Kojiki* and *Nihonshoki* historical records, or the great *Genji Monogatari* and *Heike Monogatari* epic novels of the eleventh and thirteenth centuries. (See individual listings for these books.) Ordinarily sung to the accompaniment of flutes and drums, *yokyoku* is also performed independently of *noh*.

The history of music in Japan has been closely associated with the importation of musical instruments that have come to be regarded as traditionally Japanese—the *koto*, the *shakuhachi*, and the *shamisen*, in particular.

The *koto*—a 13-stringed, harp-like instrument—was brought to Japan from China in the sixth century. A primitive form of the *shakuhachi*, or flute, arrived from China in the eighth century, and the more modern form was imported from China in the mid-thirteenth century. The popular *shamisen* came to Japan from China in the mid-sixteenth century via Okinawa.

The *koto* was thoroughly Japanized, the *shakuhachi* disappeared entirely from China, and the *shamisen* was developed far beyond the early Chinese version. A large plectrum was developed as a pick held in the palm of the hand, and *shamisen* of different sizes and thicknesses were developed to play different kinds of music.

An indication of the importance attached to music in early Japan was the creation of an Office of Music in the Imperial Court in 701. Sponsored by this office, the music of court ritual (*gagaku*) became firmly entrenched and is still practiced today under the auspices of the Imperial Household Agency.

From the ninth century on, the various forms of foreign music imported into Japan were blended with native folk music, resulting in the development of *dengaku* (dane-gah-kuu), a kind of classical dance that grew out of Shinto rituals connected with planting and harvesting, and *sarugaku* (sah-rue-gah-kuu), a comic dance that is considered a forerunner of *noh*.

From the thirteenth century on, tales from the great epic novel *Heike Monogatari* (about the rise and fall of the powerful Heike clan in the twelfth century), recited to the musical accompaniment of the *biwa*, became popular among the warrior class.

Noh music emerged in the latter part of the fourteenth century, and the adoption of the *shakuhachi* by a popular Buddhist sect resulted in a revival of this instrument.

From about 1550, a nationwide renaissance of the performing arts by and for the common people led to a national craze for *noh*, *kabuki*, and *bunraku* plays.

The study and performance of *koto* and *shakuhachi* music came under the control of *emoto* (ee-eh-moe-toe), a school system based on long years of apprenticeship to authorized teachers. Thus, both the teaching and playing of these two instruments became the exclusive monopoly of a few people licensed by the masters of these schools. See GRAND MASTERS.

Between 1868 and 1912, Western music spread throughout the Japanese educational system and thrived alongside traditional Japanese music.

Western church music first appeared in Japan as far back as 1549—brought in by Christian missionaries. But when Christianity was banned in the early part of the seventeenth century, Western music totally disappeared.

After the downfall of the Tokugawa Shogunate in 1867–68, interest in Western music resurfaced, and in 1879 the new government invited musical education experts from the U.S. to come to Japan and help incorporate Western music into the national school system.

By 1910, there were a number of well-known Japanese composers of Western music and songs. This phase ended with the militaristic xenophobia of the 1930s, however, and did not reappear until after the end of World War II.

Today both Japanese and Western music flourish in Japan and constitute a major industry. There are 12 major symphony orchestras in Japan—seven in Tokyo, and one each in Sapporo, Gunma, Nagoya, Kyoto, and Osaka. Their regular concerts and overseas tours draw enthusiastic responses.

The annual Osaka International Festival, originated in 1958, provides Japanese and foreign musicians with the opportunity for cultural exchanges.

Individual Japanese artists have won numerous music contests around the world, and several, including Seiji Ozawa and Hiroko Nakamura, became well known on the international music scene.

("Dragon Festival," Nagasaki)

NAGASAKI (Nah-gah-sah-kee)   Now the fourth largest city in Kyushu and the capital of Nagasaki Prefecture, Nagasaki is one of the world's most beautiful port cities and has played a key role in Japan's remarkable history.

The port was known as Fukaenoura or Tamanoura until the latter part of the twelfth century, when Yoritomo Minamoto, founder of the Kamakura Shogunate, gave it as a fief to Kotaro Nagasaki.

It was not to become important until 1571, however, when it was opened up to foreign trade with China, Southeast Asia, and ships from Portugal, Spain, and Holland. In 1587, Hideyoshi Toyotomi, the immediate predecessor of *Shogun* Ieyasu Tokugawa, made it his headquarters in his fight against the Lord of Satsuma, and thereafter it was governed by prefects appointed by the *shogun* in Edo.

In 1639, the Tokugawa Shogunate expelled all Spanish and Portugese citizens from the country and banned all trade with outsiders, with the exception of the Chinese and Dutch. One small Dutch trading post was allowed to continue operating on a tiny, man-made island called Dejima (Exit Island), in Nagasaki Bay.

For the next 213 or so years, this tiny enclave was Japan's only source of information from the outside world. Foreigners were not allowed into the country, and the thousands of Japanese who happened to be abroad when the exclusion order was given were not allowed to return home. The exclusion policy was total.

During this long period of isolation, some Western learning, particularly medicine, botany, and military arts, seeped into Japan through Dutch and Chinese publications—and from the more learned members of the Dutch traders who manned the outpost at Dejima for over two centuries.

When Japan began opening its doors to the West in the 1850s, hundreds of Japanese flocked to Nagasaki to acquire Western learning. But, as other Japanese ports opened, and educational centers were founded in Tokyo and other more accessible areas, Nagasaki faded from the limelight.

Following the fall of the Tokugawa Shogunate in 1867, Nagasaki participated in the rapid modernization program, becoming a major industrial center. It was particularly important in shipbuilding.

This industry was to make Nagasaki the second target for atom-bombing at the close of World War II. At exactly 11:02 A.M. on August 9, 1945, the city was to suffer the same fate as Hiroshima had a few days earlier. But in the case of Nagasaki, the destruction was not so utterly complete as it was in Hiroshima because of the hilly terrain of the city.

Today, Nagasaki is a thriving commercial and industrial center, with shipbuilding, electrical machinery, and steel the leading products. The Nagasaki Shipyard, managed by Mitsubishi Heavy Industries, is said to be the world's largest.

Nagasaki, with its mild winter climate and sea breeze–tempered summers, superb scenery, and uncountable historic sights, is also one of Japan's most important tourist destinations. There are the usual temples, shrines, and parks, along with many places associated with the international community —Catholic churches, Glover Mansion (the old British mansion that was the setting for the opera *Madame Butterfly*), Dejima (the man-made island on which the Dutch were secluded for 213 years), and the Peace Park, which marks the place the atom bomb exploded.

NAGASAKI HOLLAND VILLAGE   In 1983, the Japanese government and private industry, with technical and historical advice from Dutch experts, opened the first portion of a huge "Dutch Village" situated in a spectacularly scenic cove a short distance from Nagasaki. The village, completed in 1985, is a condensed version of seventeenth-century Holland.

The Nagasaki Holland Village commemorates Nagasaki's long ties with the Dutch, beginning in 1609, when a Dutch delegation received authorization from the Tokugawa Shogunate to open a trading post in Hirado in Nagasaki Province. When the *shogunate* began its exclusion policy in 1639, the Dutch were the only Europeans allowed to continue their trading activities with Japan. The trading post was moved to a small man-made island called

Dejima, in Nagasaki Harbor, in 1641, where it was staffed by rotating teams of Dutch traders until 1854.

The village attracts over two million visitors a year.

NAGOYA (Nah-go-yah)   The capital of Aichi Prefecture and Japan's fourth largest city, Nagoya grew up around a castle first built there in the 1500s by the Imagawa clan and later replaced by a larger castle built by the Oda clan. The area really began to grow after Ieyasu Tokugawa, the founder of Japan's last shogunate government, built a magnificient fortified castle there in 1612 for his son Yoshinao.

Situated on Nobi Plain in a commanding position between Tokyo and the Kyoto-Osaka area, Nagoya is sometimes called Chukyo, or the Middle Capital, and serves as the central hub for a large portion of the Chubu (Central) District of Honshu, which comprises nine prefectures.

Nagoya, made up of 14 wards (*ku*), is famous for having the widest and straightest major thoroughfares—a legacy of a fast and effective city-planning job immediately following the end of the Pacific War in 1945. The city was wisely divided into four districts—the central area for commerce, the east and west districts for residential areas, and the north and south sectors for industry.

Nagoya is two hours from Tokyo via the superexpress Hikari (He-kah-ree), or Bullet Trains, and two hours and 45 minutes via the slower Kodama trains.

Famous for its pottery since ancient times, the Nogaya area is now a center for numerous other industries, including cloisonné, lacquerware, clocks, toys, wooden articles, musical instruments, paper products, sewing and weaving machines, and chinaware, along with automobiles, ships, and woolen goods.

Nagoya has its share of places of special interest. Among them are Nagoya Castle (visitors may enter the Lord's Room, Hanshu-no Ma, on the top floor and see dozens of Important Cultural Properties), the Toshogu Shrine (dedicated to Ieyasu Tokugawa, who came from this area), a dozen or more other impressive shrines and temples, and several outstanding parks (including one in which the great Nobunaga Oda is buried).

There are also dozens of other places of extraordinary interest in the vicinity of Nagoya: the Inuyama Castle on Kiso River, built in 1440 and thus Japan's oldest existing fortified castle; the Kiso Rapids (famous for its boat runs); and Gifu (where the Nobunaga Oda clan had its family castle).

Within an hour or so of Nagoya are numerous famous shrines, temples, parks, and hot spring resort spas (Gamagori being one of the most noted).

NAKAHAMA, MANJIRO (Nah-kah-hah-mah, Mahn-jee-roe) Born in 1826 in the fishing village of Nakanohama on Shikoku, Manjiro Nakahama was to live one of the most extraordinary lives of adventure ever to befall any man and to play a leading role in the history of his country.

Manjiro's father died when he was very young, forcing him to take up fishing to help earn a livelihood. At the age of 15, he and another youth of 16 and three men set out from the port of Usaura to fish for sea bream in the coastal waters. A violent storm came up, swept them out to sea, and finally cast them up on one of the most distant islands in the Izu group.

In late June of 1841, the five castaways were picked up by an American whaling vessel, under the command of Captain Whitfield, and taken to Honolulu. The Americans were well aware of Japan's strict policy of not allowing anyone, even Japanese castaways, to enter the country, so Captain Whitfield offered to take Manjiro to sea with him, while his companions were given jobs in Hawaii.

Two years later, when Captain Whitfield returned to his home in Fairhaven, Massachusetts, he took Manjiro—now called John Muny—with him. Under the watchful eye of Mrs. Whitfield, Manjiro lived with an American family in Fairhaven and went to school for three years.

In 1846, Manjiro, then 24, returned to Honolulu on the whaler *Franklin*. One of the three men he had been shipwrecked with had died. The two others had left on a ship headed toward Japan in an attempt to return home. Only his young friend Toraemon, apprenticed as a carpenter, was still in Hawaii.

Just a few days later, however, his two older companions returned to Honolulu and, having failed in their efforts to return home, discouraged Manjiro from making the attempt. Manjiro remained aboard the whaler *Franklin* and rose to become second mate before leaving the sea and joining the California Gold Rush.

Still anxious to return to Japan, Manjiro went back to Honolulu and there boarded the vessel *Sarah Boyd*, whose captain agreed to drop him off in Japan. Going ashore in Kagoshima, one of the more liberal and international-minded feudal fiefs, Manjiro managed to talk the authorities into letting him return to his home village.

The news of Manjiro's return from abroad was reported to the shogunate in Edo, however, and, when Commodore Perry and his Black Ships arrived in

Edo Bay in 1853, he was called to Edo to act as a translator. He was kept under close guard and not allowed to meet any members of the American mission.

The shogunate authorities recognized the value of Manjiro's knowledge, however, and appointed him secretary to the Department of Shipbuilding and Navigation. He subsequently taught English and whaling methods and served as the captain of a whaler that was wrecked in the Bonin Islands.

Then, in 1860, Manjiro was appointed the official interpreter for Japan's first diplomatic mission abroad, during which time he met the president of the U.S. and the heads of state of several European countries.

Back in Japan after the long mission, Manjiro was dismissed from his post with the Navy because of his close friendships with many Americans. He was then invited to teach whaling to the Satsuma clan in Kyushu. He did not return to Edo until 1867, the year the last Tokugawa *shogun* resigned, ending the government of the shogunate and returning the Emperor to power (the transfer of power actually did not take place until the following year).

Three years later, Manjiro was selected to accompany Iwao Oyama (who was later to become Field Marshal Oyama and a major architect of the new Japan) on a mission to the U.S.. While there, he visited his old friends in Fairhaven but became ill and returned to Japan.

Recovering his health, Manjiro taught English and navigation during the last years of his life, dying in 1898 at his son's home near Tokyo's famous Ginza district, a poor fisherboy who had grown up to become a legend in his own time.

NAME CARDS / MEISHI (May-e-she)   Business cards or calling cards are a very important part of personal and business etiquette in Japan. Given the nature of interpersonal relationships that have been traditional in Japan for centuries, it is vital that people know the name, rank, position, and relative standing of anyone they meet in order to use the right level of language and appropriate behavior toward them.

Normally, the younger or lower-ranking person offers his or her name card first—turned so the other person can read it immediately. It is impolite to hand out cards that have been written on or damaged.

Foreign visitors going to Japan on business or for pleasure are advised to take an ample supply of *meishi*. For executives, it is also a considerable advantage to have their names, companies, and addresses printed in Japanese, as well as English, on the reverse side of their cards. (This special service is provided by Japan Air Lines for its passengers.)

The word *meishi* literally means "name-thorn" and apparently derives from the ancient Chinese practice of signing names with splinters of bamboo or some other wood.

NAMES / NAMAE (Nah-my)   Prior to 1868, common people in Japan generally did not have family names. They were known by their first name and their district, the place where they worked, or their craft or trade—Taro the Tofu Seller, Taro from Owaricho, and so on.

In 1870, two years after the fall of the Tokugawa Shogunate and abolition of the feudal system, ordinary people were given the legal right to adopt last names. People without surnames chose names that referred to their environments and to sentiments that appealed to them. Some adopted the names of their former feudal lords.

Tokugawa, for example, means Virtuous River. Suzuki means Bell Tree. Ogawa means Large River. Hana means Flower.

Feminine given names are generally those of flowers, seasons, and esoteric sentiments—Haruko (Spring Child), Yukiko (Snow Child), Natsuko (Summer Child), Yoshiko (Good Child), Kiyoko (Pure Child).

Masculine names often refer to the individual's position in the family—Jiro (Younger Fellow), Saburo (Third Fellow), Goro (Fifth Son). Some consist of numbers: Ichizo (13), Isoroku (56).

At the time that commoners adopted family names, most people also chose family crests for themselves—a privilege that had previously been granted only to the *samurai* and nobility. But the use of crests diminished rapidly over the next several decades; so their selection was more of a gesture toward the past than anything else.

NARA (Nah-rah)   The first permanent capital of Japan, from 710 until 784, Nara is the center of an area that is regarded as the cradle of Japanese arts, crafts, literature, and industries. Now a major city, with a population of nearly a quarter of a million and the capital of Nara Prefecture, Nara continued to be a major religious and cultural center long after the capital was moved to what is now Kyoto in 794. (It was located in Nagaokakyo from 784 to 794.)

The biggest attraction of the area now is Old Nara, which includes buildings, parks, and ponds that date back to the heyday of the city in the eighth century—all in an area of special scenic beauty.

Among the special places of interest in Old Nara are Nara Park, a 525-hectare, tree-covered site that boasts a large herd of tame deer; Kofuku Temple, founded in 669 by the consort of Kamatari Fujiwara, the founder of one of Japan's first great dynastic families, headquarters of the Hosso sect of Buddhism and one of the Seven Great Temples of Nara; the much-photographed Five Story Pagoda, the second highest in Japan and first built in 730.

Also worth seeing are the Treasure House, built on the premises of Kofuku Temple to store national treasures; the Kasuga Shrine, founded in 768; and the great Todai Temple, grand headquarters of the Kegon sect of Buddhism, built between 745 and 752. It is said to be the largest wooden structure in the world and houses one of the largest bronze statues in the world.

There are over a dozen other major temples and ancient buildings of importance in Nara, each with its own amazing history. Nara is about an hour's train ride from Kyoto and Osaka.

NARITA (Nah-ree-tah)   Narita, in Chiba Prefecture, some 68 kilometers from downtown Tokyo, was famous long before it became the home of the New Tokyo International Airport. The city's major claim to historical fame is the Shinsho Temple, founded there in 939 in connection with a rebellion led by Masakado Taira.

The temple belongs to the Shingon sect of Buddhism and is dedicated to Fudo, the God of Fire. The grounds today cover nearly 20 hectares, and the huge shrine complex includes a great gate, Main Hall, Main Quarters, Three Saints' Hall, Buddha's Hall, a former Main Hall, a belfry, and a three-storied pagoda, along with a library, museum, and school.

The temple attracts more than seven million visitors each year (the largest number on New Year's Day). Another major occasion is the Setsubun, or Bean-Throwing, Festival on February 3 or 4, along with other events that take place in January, May, and September.

In the middle of winter, many men go to the temple to fast and practice asceticism (by pouring ice-cold water over themselves and walking around the Main Hall 100 times while reciting prayers). There is a large, attractive park behind Shinsho Temple.

NASU SPAS (Nah-sue)   Some two train hours northwest of Tokyo along the base of Mt. Nasu, the Seven Spas of Nasu have been famous since ancient times for the beauty of the surrounding area and the efficacy of the mineral baths.

The seven spas include Nasu-Yumoto, Kita, Benten, Omaru, San-dogoya, Takao, and Itamuro. Legend has it that the first and largest of the hot springs, Nasu-Yumoto, was discovered by a warrior who chased a wounded deer into the bushes in the seventh century.

The area is celebrated for its azalea flowers in the spring and golden tree leaves in the fall.

NATIONAL ANTHEM   Japan's national anthem, "Kimigayo" (Key-me-gah-yoe), was taken from a *waka* poem found in an anthology compiled some time before the tenth century.

The words of the song mean "May the reign of the emperor continue for a thousand, nay, eight thousand generations and for the eternity it takes for small pebbles to grow into a great rock and become covered with moss."

The melody for the anthem was written by Hiromori Hayashi, an Imperial Court musician in the Meiji Period (1868–1912). The song was officially designated as the national anthem in 1893.

NATIONAL BIRD   Japan's national bird is the *kiji* (kee-jee), or Japanese pheasant. While famed in myths and folklore, the *kiji* was not designated the national bird until 1947.

Found only in Japan, the *kiji* is noted for the marked difference in the males and females. The male of the species, much larger than the female, has a red face and dark green neck, breast, and stomach. Its back is purplish, and it has a spectacularly long tail with numerous black stripes. The female, light brown with black spots, has a short tail.

The Japanese pheasant appears as a design motif and is often used as an example of beauty unique to Japan.

NATIONAL DIET LIBRARY / KOKURITSU TOSHOKAN (Koe-kuu-ree-tsue Toe-sho-khan)   Japan's National Diet Library, adjacent to the National Diet Building on the north side, was completed in 1961. It is a contemporary-styled, six-story building with two basement levels and a total of 26,400 square meters of floor space.

The library contains over 2,500,000 books, 25,000 different periodicals, 37,000 maps, 51,000 phonograph records, and over 31,000 reels of microfilm.

The National Diet Library has 30 branches, including ones in Ueno Park, the Tokyo Bunko, and the Seikado Bunko. The library is open from 9:00 A.M. to 4:30 P.M., daily except Sundays, national holidays, and the last day of the month.

The library has a substantial collection of books in English and welcomes foreign visitors.

NATIONAL FLAG   Japan's national flag is called *Nisshoki* (Nees-show-kee), or The Flag of the Rising Sun. It consists of a bright red sun in the center of a white banner.

The Rising Sun flag was in use as early as the sixteenth century to identify ships as Japanese. Prior to that, it was used on banners and shrine flags. It was formally named the national flag in 1870.

NATIONAL FLOWER   While never officially designated as such, the Japanese generally consider the *sakura* (sah-kuu-rah), or cherry, as their national flower. The cherry blossom—beautiful, fragile, and transitory—has long appealed to the sensibilities of Japanese and was particularly favored by the *samurai* warrior class who saw in it a reflection of their own lives—full of grace and beauty and resigned to an early death.

So taken were the Japanese by the ethereal beauty and fragility of cherry blossoms that well before the turn of the tenth century, cherry blossom viewing was an organized spring ritual. Every district had its favorite cherry blossom viewing spots, and the well-to-do had special buildings or grandstands constructed as vantage points from which to view the blossoms while drinking *O'sake* and, often, writing poetry to celebrate them.

A number of these stands, built nearly a thousand years ago, are still in existence.

Present-day locations that are famous as cherry blossom viewing spots include Ueno Park in Tokyo and Yoshino, near Nara. There are hundreds of other noted places.

The *kiku* (kee-kuu), or chrysanthemum, traditionally used as the Imperial Crest, has also been used at different times and in different ways as symbolic of Japan.

NATIONAL HOLIDAYS   Japan has a large number of national holidays, some of which last for more than one day. They are a vital part of national life.

JANUARY 1–3—New Year's/*Oshogatsu* (Oh-show-got-sue): This is Japan's premiere national holiday (which used to last for five days or more). It is marked by visits to families, friends, shrines, and temples; special foods and drinks; and numerous other festivities, including the exchanging of gifts.

On New Year's eve millions of people gather at their guardian shrines or famous temples to witness the ringing out of the old year and ringing in the new year.

The first day of work after New Year's is usually marked by a party atmosphere, during which people exchange congratulations on the opening of the new year and express their wishes for a happy and successful new season. The customary greeting on meeting someone for the first time after the turn of the year is "Shinnen Akemashite Omedeto Gozaimasu," or "Congratulations on the opening of the New Year." See FESTIVALS.

JANUARY 15—Adults' Day/*Seijin-no Hi* (Say-e-jeen-no He): This day is dedicated to the young people who have attained their 20th birthday during the year. The new adults are encouraged to persevere in their educational and work goals and thereafter conduct themselves with all the responsibility expected of adulthood.

FEBRUARY 11—National Foundation Day/*Kenkoku Kinen-no Hi* (Kane-koe-kuu Kee-nane-no He): This is Japan's 4th of July, when the founding of the country is celebrated. The date corresponds to the legendary ascension to the throne of Japan's first emperor, Jimmu, in 660 B.C.

MARCH 20 or 21—Vernal Equinox Day/*Shumbun-no Hi* (Shume-boon-no He): This day is set aside for the people to commune with nature and reaffirm their relationship with all things in nature.

MAY 3—Constitution Memorial Day/*Kempo Kinen Bi* (Kim-poe Kee-nane Bee): This day marks the date when Japan's constitution went into effect.

MAY 5—Children's Day/*Kodomo-no Hi* (Koe-doe-moe-no He): May 5 was traditionally celebrated as Boys' Day, but after 1945 it was changed to include all children. Adults are reminded of the need to understand and guide children, and children are reminded of their obligation to respect and obey their parents.

May 3 and May 5 together are popularly known as Golden Week and offer many people an opportunity to take off from work for five or more days

SEPTEMBER 15—Senior Citizens' Day/*Keiro-no Hi* (Kay-e-roe-no He): In Japan respect for the elderly has a long and honorable tradition, and it is continued in this special day set aside for them.

SEPTEMBER 23—Autumn Equinox Day/*Shubun-no Hi* (Shuu-boon-no He): This is the day for paying respects to and honoring one's ancestors.

OCTOBER 10—Sports Day/*Taiiku-no Hi* (Tie-e-kuu-no He): The mental and physical benefits of sports are celebrated on this day with numerous sports activities around the country.

NOVEMBER 3—Culture Day/*Bunka-no Hi* (Boon-kah-no He): Numerous activities are held to mark the importance of culture and the love of peace and freedom. This is the day the government makes special awards to people who have made significant contributions to the nation's culture. See NATIONAL LIVING TREASURES.

NOVEMBER 23—Labor Thanksgiving Day/*Kinro Kansha-no Hi* (Keen-roe Khan-shah-no He): This is the day for honoring workers and for promoting respect for labor and the contributions it makes to the country.

DECEMBER 23—Emperor's Birthday/*Tenno Tanjobi* (Tane-no Tahn-joe-bee): On this day, the Imperial family appears on the balcony of the Imperial Palace to accept the good wishes of the people and exchange greetings with them.

NATIONAL PARKS   Japan is one of the most picturesque countries in the world, with a range and variety of scenic beauty that has deeply influenced the philosophy, religions, and daily lives of the Japanese.

The combinations of coastlines, coves, inlets, hills, mountains, rivers, gorges, valleys, volcanoes, trees, and other foliage, coupled with four distinct

(Bandai Asahi National Park)

seasons that color the country in a kaleidoscope of hues, have resulted in a land that is blessed with beauty.

Very early in their history as a people, the Japanese recognized the extraordinary beauty of the land and incorporated a deep appreciation for it in their way of life. Their homes, shrines, and temples were built in settings of special beauty so they would be able to enjoy it on a daily basis. The Japanese did not attempt to change nature, but to blend in with it.

In more recent times, great areas of special beauty were set aside as parks, national, quasi-national and prefectural. There are 27 national parks in the country, encompassing nearly five and a half percent of the nation's total land area.

Five of these national parks, including Daisetsuzan, the largest, are in Hokkaido. They are characterized by volcanoes, mountain lakes, hundreds of hot springs, virgin forests, and swamps.

The Towada-Hachimantai National Park in northern Honshu is noted for its superb seascapes. The Nikko National Park is noted for its beautiful forest-covered mountains, Lake Chuzenji, Kegon Falls and Toshogu Shrine, where *Shogun* Ieyasu Tokugawa is buried. The Fuji-Hakone-Izu National Park encompasses Mt. Fuji, the five lakes around it, the fabulous Hakone hot spring resorts, part of the Izu Peninsula, and the Seven Isles of Izu.

Besides these huge national parks, there are a total of 47 quasi-national parks that are smaller, but no less beautiful in their own way—their size often deliberately limited in the interest of space. Suffice to say that it is impossible to travel very far in any direction in Japan without encountering areas of incredible natural beauty.

Recommended reading: *National Parks of Japan*, by Mary Sutherland and Dorothy Britton (Kodansha International).

NATIONAL STADIUM   Japan's National Stadium, one of the largest arenas in the world, with a seating capacity of 85,000, is located in Tokyo's Meiji Park (Meiji Shrine Outer Garden), midway between Shinanomachi and Sendagaya stations on the Chuo Line.

The stadium was used during the 1964 Olympics. That same year a bronze bust relief of Jigoro Kano, the originator of Kodokan *judo* and a long-time member of the International Olympic Committee, was erected at the main entrance of the stadium.

NATIONAL THEATER / KOKURITSU GEKIJO (Koe-kuu-reet-sue gay-kee-joe)   Japan's first state-owned theater, the Kokuritsu Gekijo is one of the most spectacular buildings in the country. Built in traditional-contemporary style (in 1960), it faces the Imperial Palace Grounds and is a short walk from the National Diet Building.

The building contains two theaters—one that seats 1,764, and one with 630 seats. The larger hall is used for *kabuki* and musical performances, including traditional court music and other traditional music and dances. The smaller theater is used for puppet shows (*bunraku*), traditional comedy shows (*kyogen*), and Japanese music and dance.

NATIONAL VACATION VILLAGES / KOKUMIN KYUKA MURA (Koe-kuu-meen que-kah muu-rah)   Begun in 1961 by the nonprofit National Vacation Village Association, the Kokumin Kyuka Mura are vacation village health resorts located in national parks or quasi-national parks that are noted for their hot springs and outdoor recreational attractions.

There are some two dozen such villages around the country, and they attract more than a million visitors a year. Accommodations, all Japanese style, are inexpensively priced. The villages are open to foreign visitors. For locations and other details, check with the Japan National Tourist Organization. (See addresses in this book.)

NETSUKE (Nate-sue-kay)   Traditional Japanese apparel does not have pockets; thus, both men and women carry purses or pouches, suspended from their *obi*, or waist bands, when they are dressed in traditional garments. *Netsuke* are the small, ornamental toggles that are used to attach these accessories.

Netsuke came into common use in the sixteenth century, but they became a really important part of the costumes of the merchant class during the seventeenth century, when well-to-do merchants wanted something to compete with the fancy sword guards of *samurai* and *daimyo*.

The carving of *netsuke* thus became a highly paid profession and developed into a special art that flourished throughout the long Tokugawa Shogunate (1603–1867).

Netsuke carved during the Tokugawa Period are now collectors' items and are much in demand in Japan, the U.S., and Europe. *Netsuke* are carved out of such materials as ivory, shell, coral, wood, and precious metals.

Measuring about four centimeters (1.2 inches) across, *netsuke* are intricately carved in the form of people, animals, and other familiar objects.

Dealing in *netsuke* is a popular profession, and those made by well-known carvers command substantial prices.

Recommended reading: *Collectors' Netsuke*, by Raymond Bushell (Weatherhill); and *Masterpieces of Netsuke Art*, by Bernard Hurtia (Weatherhill)

NEW OTANI HOTEL (Oh-tah-nee)   Tokyo's New Otani, adjoining the famous Akasaka entertainment and restaurant district, is one of the city's more spectacular hotels. Consisting of two high-rise towers connected by a mall, it has the usual shopping arcade, several restaurants, bars, and clubs. But what makes it especially distinctive is its 10-acre, 400-year-old landscaped garden.

The hotel was built on the site of a *daimyo* mansion whose garden was kept and improved on. While not historically famous, the garden now is one of the largest and most beautiful in the city—an oasis in the heart of teeming, tumultuous Tokyo.

NEWSPAPERS / SHIMBUN (Sheem-boon)   During the early decades of the Tokugawa Period (1600–1867), the news was brought to the people of Japan via prints made from tile blocks, which were known as *kawara ban* (kah-wah-rah bahn), or "roof-tile prints." The first *kawara ban* are believed to have appeared in 1615 to announce the fall of Osaka Castle to the troops of Ieyasu Tokugawa, the retired *shogun*. Young boys and men sold the prints in the streets.

The ritual suicide of the 47 *ronin* of Ako in the early 1700s was reported the same day by *kawara ban*, whose dealers are said to have made a small fortune because of the number of the prints sold following this celebrated incident. See FORTY-SEVEN RONIN.

The first Japanese language newspaper in Japan, the *Batabia Shimbun*, founded in 1862 by the Tokugawa Shogunate, was made up of translations from a paper published in Batavia. It was printed in magazine format, from woodblocks.

The first English language newspaper in Japan was the biweekly *Nagasaki Shipping List and Advertiser*, founded in 1861 by A. W. Hansard, an Englishman who lived in Nagasaki.

Japan's first daily newspaper was the *Yokohama Mainichi Shimbun*, which printed its first issue on January 28, 1871, and survived until 1940. The following year, the *Tokyo Nichi-Nichi Shimbun*, forerunner of today's *Mainichi Shimbun*, made its debut, along with the *Yubin Hochi Shimbun* (today's *Hochi Shimbun*) and the *Kochu Shimbun*, forerunner of the *Yamanashi Nichi-Nichi Shimbun* in Kofu City, Yamanashi Prefecture.

For the most part, these first newspapers carried government announcements and proclamations and were written in classical Chinese *kanbun*. Readership was primarily limited to the well-educated upper classes.

These newspapers were followed soon thereafter by papers catering to the general public. The great *Yomiuri Shimbun* began in Tokyo in 1874, and both the *Asahi Shimbun* and *Mainichi Shimbun* began in Osaka in the same decade.

Despite a revised version (in 1883) of the Press Law of 1875, which gave the government extraordinary powers over opposition-oriented newspapers, the press continued to expand. In 1882, Yukichi Fukuzawa, regarded as the most enlightened thinker of the time, founded the *Jiji Shimbun*, which lasted until 1936.

Japan's first true news agency, Jiji Tsushin Sha, was founded in 1888, but lasted for only two years.

The Great Kanto Earthquake of 1923 helped the *Mainichi Shimbun* and *Asahi Shimbun*, both founded in Osaka, gain a foothold in Tokyo, and thereafter, along with the *Yomiuri*, dominate Japan's newspaper world. The quake destroyed the printing plants of the Tokyo newspapers, giving the two Osaka-based papers the opportunity to extend their influence nationwide.

On January 1, 1924, the *Asahi* and *Mainichi* newspapers printed a record one million copies each.

With the rise of militarism in Japan in the 1930s, the government consolidated all the news services under the Domei Tsushin Sha (1936) and created an Information Committee to standardize news dissemination. When war broke out with China in 1937, all news became subject to the approval of the army and navy ministers.

By 1944, newsprint shortages had resulted in a drastic reduction in the number of newspapers, and all were limited to no more than two pages. From a high point of 1,200 dailies, the number dwindled down to 55, with only one paper allowed in each prefecture.

Today there are three kinds of newspapers in Japan—national papers, regional papers, and prefectural/local papers. Among the main regional papers are the *Hokkaido Shimbun, Tokyo Shimbun, Chunichi Shimbun*, and the *Nishi Nippon Shimbun*.

The average number of pages for the national, regional, and prefectural dailies is 20–24 for morning editions and 8–12 for afternoon editions. They produce some 5–6 morning editions and 3–4 evening editions. No evening editions are printed on Sundays. The ratio of news to advertising is about 57 percent news to 43 percent advertising.

Japanese newspapers usually do not give their reporters by-line credit for their stories. Because they also tend to write most of their own stories, as opposed to using material from wire services, they have very large staffs by international standards.

The *Asahi, Mainichi* and *Yomiuri* employ well over 1,000 reporters each, and, as in other major industries, employment is expected to be for life. It would be unthinkable, for example, for an *Asahi* man to move to the *Mainichi* or to any other newspaper.

One of the most controversial characteristics of Japanese journalism is the existence of so-called press clubs, of which there are about 400. Virtually every important news source in the country—government ministries, political parties, key economic organizations, private bodies, local government offices, court houses, police headquarters, etc.—is covered by one specific press or reporter's club.

The individual clubs totally control the dissemination of news from these sources, as far as Japanese newspapers are concerned. The only clubs open to foreign correspondents are the club that covers the prime minister's office, and the one covering the Foreign Ministry.

Foreign correspondents and other reporters who are not members of these clubs can approach news sources independently, but they are prevented from taking advantage of the official press conferences arranged by sources or by the clubs themselves (and the latter are extremely powerful, since they control access to Japan's leading news media).

There is continuing pressure from the foreign correspondents fraternity in Japan for these exclusive clubs to open their doors to non-Japanese press members, but there is little chance of this happening on any broad scale.

Japan's major newspapers maintain large overseas networks (as do news agencies and radio and televisions stations), with some 400 correspondents stationed in 34 different countries. The tendency here again is for Japanese newspapers to depend more on their overseas correspondents than on news agencies.

General interest newspapers in Japan devote an average of 16 percent of their space to international news.

Japanese newspapers are leaders in the use of sophisticated electronic technology in typesetting and printing newspapers. Some have totally automated their production system, including the preparation and loading of bundles going out to delivery agents.

Five of Japan's 177 daily newspapers are national and have the world's largest daily circulation. These five are the *Asahi Shimbun* (Ah-sah-he Shim-boon), the *Yomiuri Shimbun* (Yoe-me-uu-ree Shim-boon), the *Mainichi Shimbun* (My-nee-chee Shim-boon), the *Sankei Shimbun* (Sahn-kay-e Shim-boon), and the *Nihon Keizai Shimbun* (Nee-hone Kay-e-zie Shimboon). See individual listings.

Yomiuri, the largest, has a morning circulation of approximately nine million. The *Asahi* has nearly eight million, and the *Mainichi* nearly five million in circulation. All of these five major dailies are affiliated with one of Tokyo's commercial TV networks—namely, ANB, NTV, TBS, Fuji, and Television Tokyo, respectively.

Some 92 percent of Japan's newspaper sales are to regular subscribers through district and neighborhood delivery agents.

NEWSPAPERS IN ENGLISH   There are four daily English language newspapers in Japan and a number of weekly specialized tabloids. The dailies are the *Asahi Evening News*, *The Daily Yomiuri*, *The Japan Times* (which also has a daily airmail edition and a weekly edition—*The Japan Times Weekly*), and the *Mainichi Daily News*.

The Asahi Evening News, owned by the huge Japanese-language *Asahi Shimbun*, is Japan's only English-language evening newspaper and is noted for reflecting the editorial viewpoints of its parent company. William Lederer, who wrote the books *The Ugly American* and *A Nation of Sheep* and once worked on the *Asahi Evening News*, described the AEN is the best newspaper in the world.

The Daily Yomiuri, owned by the nationally circulated *Yomiuri Shimbun*, carries both international and local news and is particularly known for its coverage of the political scene in Japan.

The Japan Times, the only major English language daily newspaper in Japan not owned by one of the vernacular papers, has the largest circulation of any of the English language newspapers and is the oldest (founded in 1897).

The Japan Times is the most internationally oriented of the English-language dailies in Japan and covers political, social, business, financial, sports, and entertainment news. One of the most important of its features is a large Classified Ads section.

Over the decades, many of the foreign writers who have specialized in Japan (including myself) were either contributors to or staff members on *The Japan Times*. Thousands of former foreign residents of Tokyo and other parts of Japan continue to subscribe to *The Japan Times* after returning to their home countries.

The *Mainichi Daily News*, a subsidiary of the huge, nationally circulated *Mainichi Shimbun*, has its own personality in that it appears to be less for-eignized than the other subsidiary newspapers, with one page devoted entirely to Japanese news.

The *Nikkei Weekly* is the international edition of the *Nihon Kezai Shimbun* (*Japan Economic Journal*), which is the Japanese equivalent of the *Wall Street Journal*. It is printed in Tokyo, Los Angeles, and Heerlen (The Netherlands) and covers the economy, trade, finance, the stock market, and politics in Japan.

NEWS SERVICES   Japan's first news service, Jiji Tsushin Sha (Jee-jee T'sue-sheen Shah), lasted only from 1888 to 1890, but it was followed by the Teikoku News Agency in 1892 and the Nippon Denpo News Agency (which was to become Dentsu Inc.) in 1901. The first international news agency in Japan appeared in 1914 as a result of an affiliation, arranged by several influential businesspeople and diplomats, with the Associated Press of the U.S.

In 1918, government sources sponsored the inauguration of the Toho News Agency to help publicize Japan's side of its activities in regard to China. In 1926, Kokusai and Toho merged to form the Nihon Rengo News Agency.

For the next decade and a half, Rengo, a nonprofit company backed by the U.S.'s Associated Press, and Dentsu, a commercial operation backed by United Press of the U.S., competed fiercely against each other.

In 1936, the government ended the competition by forcing the two agencies to merge and become the Domei News Agency. Following the end of World War II, Domei was declared a monopoly by the U.S. Occupation Forces, and the agency was split into Kyodo News Service and Jiji Press.

Kyodo News Service is a cooperative owned by 63 Japanese newspapers, including the giant *Asahi*, *Yomiuri*, and *Mainichi*. Kyodo also supplies news on a contract basis to other newspapers and 60 commercial broadcasting companies. It has working arrangements with AP and UPI of the U.S., Reuters of Britain, Tass of the Soviet Union, and Xinhua of China. It also maintains correspondents and stringers in some 40 major cities around the world.

Jiji Press is now a stock company owned by its employees. It distributes to some 150 newspapers and broadcasting stations throughout Japan by facsimile and leased wire. It has exclusive rights to distribute in Japan stories of Agence France-Press, Reuters Economic Service, and Deutsche Press-Agentur. In 1975, Jiji became the first Japanese news agency to inaugurate an overseas facsimile transmission system, which now transmits daily Japanese news to its 13 overseas offices for distribution to Japanse diplomatic missions and Japanese companies.

NEW YEAR'S CALL   It is customary in Japan to pay a courtesy call on customers, superiors, and others with whom you have a special relationship, some time after January 3 to wish them a happy new year and to ask for their continued friendship, goodwill, help, or support during the new year.

This is an institutionalized practice that is very meaningful and important in maintaining good relations with clients and others, especially if some or all of one's business depends on them. It is also customary to present a gift of some kind on this occasion.

NEW YEAR'S PARTY / SHIN NEN KAI (Sheen nane kie)   In the old days in Japan, it was customary to hold New Year's parties sometime from around the 3rd to the 10th, depending on when people went back to their normal routines.

Such parties are still common, but the majority of them are held at the workplace or in restaurants and involve fellow employees. The parties are actually official New Year greeting occasions, when people congratulate each other on the opening of the new year, and ask for the understanding, goodwill, and support of their colleagues and customers for the coming year.

NHK / JAPAN BROADCASTING CORPORATION NHK,   which is short for Nippon Hoso Kyokai (Neep-pone Hoe-so K'yoe-kie), literally the Japan Broadcasting Association, is probably the best-known and most popular radio and television network in the country.

NHK originated radio broadcasting in Japan in 1925 and television broadcasting in 1953. It remains today the only noncommercial public corporation in the broadcasting field—but it is not controlled or operated by the government.

Under the provisions of a Broadcast Law passed in 1950, NHK levies a monthly fee on all households in the country that receive its broadcasts—

with those having color TV sets paying a slightly higher fee. The same law prohibits NHK from engaging in commercial advertising.

NHK broadcasts close to 1,000 hours a day over its five domestic networks (on national and local levels)—two television, two radio, and one FM—with virtually 100 percent national coverage.

The various daily programs are divided into news, culture, entertainment, and education, with the amount of time devoted to each category varying according to the network.

The First Radio Network devotes 42.7 percent of its time to news, 31.9 percent to cultural subjects, 24 percent to entertainment, and 1.4 percent to education.

The Second Radio Network devotes 81 percent of its broadcast hours to education, 13.7 percent to culture, and 5.3 percent to news. The FM Network spends 48.8 percent of its time on culture, 30.7 percent on entertainment, 12.6 percent on news, and 7.9 percent on education.

The General TV Network of NHK devotes 36.4 percent of its time to culture, 31.8 percent to news, 22.3 percent to entertainment, and 9.6 percent to education. The Educational TV Network is devoted solely to education (84.5 percent) and culture (15.5 percent).

Presenting this kind of programming and being strictly noncommercial, NHK commands a high percentage of Japan's television viewers and radio listeners. It is noted for the superior quality and variety of its programs, regularly dispatching teams of directors and crews all over Japan and the world to produce documentaries on every conceivable subject.

NHK also operates a very large Overseas Broadcasting Service, with a daily total of some 38 hours in 23 languages. This service is divided into General and Regional Service.

The General Service division broadcasts for 30 minutes every hour in English and Japanese. The Regional Service is broadcast to specific linguistic areas—in languages ranging from English, French, German, Italian, Arabic, Chinese, Korean, Vietnamese, Malay, and Russian to Burmese, Thai, Bengali, Hindi, Urdu, and Swahili.

NHK's overseas broadcasts consist of news, entertainment, sports, and music.

NICHIREN (Nee-chee-rane)   One of Japan's most famous religious leaders, Nichiren was born in 1222 in the little village of Awa-Kominato, in what is now Chiba Prefecture on Boso Peninsula, southeast of Tokyo. He became a Buddhist priest at the age of 15, studied for three years at a Buddhist monastery on Mt. Hiei, near Kyoto, and then returned to his native village.

Nichiren was a fiery preacher who began espousing a new doctrine that quickly got him expelled from Kominato. Going to Matsubagayatsu in Kamakura, south of present-day Tokyo, in the Miura Peninsula, he built a hermitage and spent the next three years studying, writing, and preaching on the streets of Kamakura (which at that time was the shogunate capital of Japan).

The two most important tracts that Nichiren wrote during these years were *The Defense of the State* and *On Public Peace*. The Kamakura Shogunate did not take criticism lightly and exiled the outspoken priest to Ito, on Izu Peninsula (now a noted hot springs resort).

On his release from exile, Nichiren returned to Kamakura and began preaching in the streets again—more vehemently than ever. He was again arrested and taken to Katase Beach, the official execution grounds, to be beheaded. But the executioner's sword broke when he tested it, and the officials decided to let the priest go.

Nichiren did not choose to stay out of trouble with the shogunate, and some time later he was exiled to the cold island of Sado, off the coast of Niigata, in the Japan Sea.

Finally, after a stormy career of over 40 years, Nichiren died in 1282 at the age of 60, in Ikegami, now part of Tokyo. He was buried at Kuon Temple in Minobu, west of Mt. Fuji.

Nichiren's disciples built a temple in Kominato in 1276 to commemorate his birth. The Temple, called Tanjo (Birthday) Temple, was destroyed by a tidal wave and fire, and the present building was completed during the Tempo era of the Tokugawa Period (1830–1843).

In February every year, when Nichiren's birthday is celebrated, the temple is filled with visitors. There are several Nichiren sect temples in Kamakura, including the Anokokuron, founded in 1274 by Nichro, one of Nichiren's chief disciples. The primary treasure in the temple is a copy of Nichiren's *On Public Peace* tract (Ankokuron), transcribed by Nichiro.

NIEMON JIMA (Nee-eh-moan Jee-mah)   If you are ever on the southern tip of Boso Peninsula (Chiba Prefecture)—maybe to see the 1,500 women divers of Shirahama gather seaweed, ear shells, and top shells off the picturesque coast—you are close to a place famous in Japanese history: the tiny islet of Niemon.

Niemon Island is where Yoritomo Minamoto, the founder of Japan's first shogunate dynasty (in 1192), was hidden from his enemies by the Niemon family prior to becoming the supreme military power in the country.

After becoming *shogun*, Yoritomo gave the island to the Niemons as their own private fief.

Today there is a famous Flower Zone adjoining the Niemon pier in the port town of Futomi, where flowers of many kinds are raised in hothouses.

NIGHTCLUBS / NAITO KURABU (Nie-toe kuu-rah-buu)   Japan has the largest variety of nighttime entertainment facilities of any nation in the world, ranging from a dozen or more different kinds of bars and at least as many different types of lounges, plus beer halls, dinner show clubs, *geisha* inns, cabarets, and so on.

Legally speaking, there is no such thing as a nightclub in Japan, since all entertainment establishments that employ hostesses are classified as cabarets —and all of Japan's so-called nightclubs have hostesses.

But there are basic differences between a regular cabaret and a so-called nightclub. A cabaret that calls itself a nightclub caters specifically to foreign, as well as Japanese, clientele. Nightclub patrons have a choice of whether or not they want the company of a hostess.

Entertainment in a nightclub is more likely to be Western style or a combination of both Japanese and Western. Nightclubs are more likely to have full kitchen facilities and serve full meals.

Nightclubs cater to couples, as well as single men—and one of the favorite after-hours activities of cabaret hostesses is to get their customers to take them to a nightclub after their cabaret closes. Cabarets generally close at 11:00 P.M.—with 30 minutes for everybody to clear out, while nightclubs that serve food (and qualify as restaurants) stay open to the wee hours.

Finally, the clientele of most cabarets are executives on expense accounts, who usually charge their bills to their firms. Nightclubs, especially where foreign customers are concerned, are more likely to be run on a strict cash basis. Nightclubs also have table or cover charges that are separate from any other consideration, while in cabarets the table charge usually comes in the form of a tray or basket of *o'tsumami* (*oh-t'sue-mah-me*), which consists of peanuts, *osembe* (oh-sem-bay) rice cracker nuggets, etc.).

There is some crossing over of the distinctions between cabarets and nightclubs, depending on the individual place.

NIIGATA (Nee-gah-tah)   The capital city of Niigata Prefecture, Niigata is Japan's chief port on the Japan Sea side of the main island of Honshu. The city sits on an estuary of the Shinano River and is separated from the sea by a row of low sand hills. It is crisscrossed by many canals that once were important transportation arteries.

Niigata was one of the first ports in Japan to be opened to foreign trade after the fall of the Tokugawa Shogunate in 1867. It is now known for its chemical industry, based on oil and natural gas in the area, and as the gateway to Sado Island. The Niigata Festival, which is held from August 21 to 23 each year, is one of the most popular annual events in the city.

The Bullet Train from Tokyo to Niigata (170 miles/two hours) passes through 23 tunnels, including the 13.8-mile-long Shimizu Tunnel.

NIKKO (Neek-koe)   Nikko is both a national park and the mountain town in which the spirits of three of Japan's greatest heroes are interred—Yoritomo Minamoto, Hideyoshi Toyotomi, and Ieyasu Tokugawa.

Encompassing an area of 140,698 hectares and sprawling over parts of Tochigi, Gunma, Fukushima, and Niigata prefectures, northwest of Tokyo, Nikko National Park has two great things going for it—it is one of the most scenic spots on earth, and it is the location of the Toshogu (Toe-show-guu), the mausoleum of Ieyasu (and his grandson Iemitsu), and the shrine complex that commemorates Ieyasu and the two other heroes named above.

The park is comprised of mountains, rivers, waterfalls, cascades, lakes, and huge, old trees in a combination so extraordinary that the word "magnificent" cannot do justice to it. Then there are the mausolea and shrines of Nikko, as impressive in their own way as the pyramids of Egypt.

In an attempt to suggest the unusual variety and depth of the beauty of Nikko, the Japanese have a saying: "Never say *kekko* ("wonderful") until you've seen Nikko!" The region has such a wide variety of topographical characteristics and plant life, as well as a large network of streams, that it is often described as one vast natural museum.

Besides the attractions of the Toshogu in Nikko town, the park includes the Kegon Waterfalls and Lake Chuzenji, just above Nikko; summer and winter (ski) resorts in Oku-Nikko; and two major spas, Shiobara and Nasu, and numerous lesser ones.

There are three ways of reaching Nikko proper from Tokyo—by the Japanese Railways (JR) from either Tokyo or Ueno Stations, Tobu Railway's Nikko Line from Asakusa Station in northeast Tokyo, and by bus or private vehicle via the historically famous Nikko Highway.

The trip from Tokyo to Nikko by train takes a little over two hours.

NIKKO MAUSOLEA When *Shogun* Ieyasu Tokugawa, the founder of Japan's last great feudal dynasty and the benefactor of Pilot Will Adams, died in 1616 he was buried temporarily at Kunozan in Shizuoka. But Ieyasu left instructions that he was to be buried in the mountain religious center of Nikko, now some two train hours north of Tokyo, and this was done the following year.

In 1634, Iemitsu, Ieyasu's grandson and the *shogun* at that time, initiated the construction of a mausoleum and shrine to honor his famous grandfather. Thousands of carpenters and artisans were brought from Kyoto and Nara to work on the project. They were organized into teams and set to competing against each other, often working around the clock.

The buildings, completed in 1636, were among the most elaborate and probably the most expensive structures built in Japan up to that time.

Altogether, 15,000 men were employed in the construction of the mausoleum and shrine. Over 2,489,000 gold leaf sheets were used in the gilding of the mausoleum.

Iemitsu's successor, Ietsuna, granted the memorial a fief to provide for its maintenance, and the emperor appointed an Imperial Prince to preside over the shrine—a system that was to be continued until 1868, when the last *shogun* stepped down.

Some 17 years after the completion of Ieyasu's memorial shrine, a second mausoleum was built for Iemitsu.

During the remainder of the long Tokugawa Shogunate, the buildings were completely renovated every 20 years. It took 10 years to collect duplicates of the timber and other materials used in the construction of the mausoleum and shrine and another 10 years to complete each renovation, so work of one kind or another was in progress at all times.

All of the feudal lords of Japan were ordered to contribute to the building of the memorial to Ieyasu. Masatsuna Matsudaira could not afford to match the offerings made by some of the richer fiefs, but he came up with a plan that was to make his gift the best of all. He had his men plant Japanese cedars along the roads leading to the shrine—a project that took 20 years. Today, some 13,000 of those trees are still standing.

In 1867, when the last *shogun* decided to turn power over to the emperor, a group of Tokugawa *samurai* took possession of the shrine and mausolea and vowed to hold them against the Imperial forces to the death. Fearing that the treasured buildings would be destroyed in any conflict, Count Taisuke Itagaki, a leading statesman of the era, persuaded the shogunate loyalists to leave the buildings, thus saving them for posterity.

Today the Mausolea of Nikko are one of Japan's most famous sights, attracting hundreds of thousands of Japanese and foreign visitors every year.

The shrine complex, popularly known as the Toshogu (Toe-show-goo), consists of 15 major structures, including a huge granite *torii*, a five-story pagoda, two huge gates, a main hall, the tomb of Ieyasu, a storehouse, and stables. One of the gates, *Yomeimon*, is regarded as the most luxurious gate in Japan and itself is a registered National Treasure.

To see all of the wonders of the Toshogu takes several hours at least—it is often said more than in jest that it would take 24 hours just to appreciate all of the features of Yomei Gate.

The big event in Nikko is the Spring Festival of Toshogu Shrine, held each year on May 17 and 18 and featuring a procession of 1,000 people attired in the costumes of *samurai*, priests, and officials of the Tokugawa era.

On the morning of May 18, the spirits of Yoritomo Minamoto, Hideyoshi Toyotomi and Ieyasu Tokugawa, Japan's greatest military leaders, are transferred to portable shrines (*mikoshi*), taken in procession to the Sojourning Hall, where sacred music is played, offerings are made, and sacred dances are performed. Afterward, the spirits are returned to their resting place.

Another event on this day is a demonstration of *yabusame*, or horseback archery, by horsemen dressed in hunting attire of the feudal age. See YABUSAME.

A smaller Autumn Festival is held on October 17, but it is often attended by a larger number of people than the spring celebration because Nikko is one of the prime beauty spots of Japan during the fall season.

There are other events held in Nikko during different times of the year, and it is one of the nation's major sightseeing destinations throughout the spring, summer, and fall.

NIKKO-YUMOTO SPA / NIKKO-YUMOTO ONSEN (Neek-koe Yuu-moe-toe Own-sin)   About 30 kilometers from Nikko Station (and 13 kilometers from Lake Chuzenji, above Nikko), the Nikko-Yumoto Spa is famous all year-round for its hot springs and in winter for its ski slopes and ice-skating rinks.

The resort, surrounded on three sides by mountains, is noted for its easy accessibility, the abundance of its hot mineral waters, and other recreational facilities in the area.

NINJA (Neen-jah)   Now a fairly well-known word around the world, a *ninja* is a practitioner of *ninjutsu* (neen-jute-sue), or "the art of stealing in," a very special category of secret agent that developed in feudal Japan and played a vital role in the lives and fortunes of the *shogun* and the provincial *daimyo* lords.

The *ninja* belonged to specific *ninja* families, who usually lived in remote mountain areas. They kept their identities secret and trained in secret, beginning virtually as soon as they were able to walk.

They were trained in running (forward, backward, and sideways), climbing, jumping, crawling, and hiding; hanging from rafters and trees; swimming (especially under water); fighting with an amazing variety of weapons, including many that they developed themselves; and using poisons, medicines, and other chemicals.

So incredible were their feats of strength, speed, and skill, along with their ability to penetrate the most closely guarded areas and never be seen, that common people believed they could make themselves invisible and perform other magical feats.

When at work, the *ninja* wore especially designed black costumes in which their weapons and other aides were artfully concealed—and they almost always worked at night.

The *ninja* were hired by the different *daimyo* and *samurai* families as spies, terrorists, and assassins, especially during periods of internal strife, and they were the most feared of all the enemies a person could face.

There are voluminous records of the exploits of *ninja*, attesting to their total dedication and extraordinary ability to perform feats that would put even James Bond to shame—and their feats were for real.

Not all of the incredible skills of the *ninja* have been totally forgotten. There are several *ninja* devotees in Japan today who are able to duplicate many of the feats of these feudal masters of death.

Recommended reading: *Ninjutsu—The Art of Invisibility*, by Donn Draeger (Charles E. Tuttle Company); *The Ninja and Their Secret Fighting Art*, by Stephen K. Hayes (Tuttle); *Ninja: The Invisible Assassins*, by Andrew Adams (Ohara Publications); and *Ninja: Warrior Path to Togakure*, by Stephen K. Hayes (Ohara).

NISHIJIN (Nee-she-jeen)   Nishijin is a district in Kyoto that over the centuries has become famous for its silk brocades and other elaborately woven fabrics. The area got its name during the Onin War (1467–1477) when a West Camp (Nishi Jin) was set up on the northwestern outskirts of the city.

Because much of Kyoto was destroyed during the war, most of the weavers in the city moved to Nishi Jin and set up operation there. The area eventually became synonymous with woven fabrics, especially silk brocades.

The district got its biggest boost when the Tokugawa Shogunate ordered that all the nobles and members of the Imperial Court in Kyoto were to wear costumes made of fabrics woven at Nishijin.

Nishijin still makes the finest brocades in Japan, and its fabrics are much in demand by *noh* and *kabuki* actors and the TV and film industry and for making ornamental *obi* for *kimono*.

NITOBE, DR. INAZO (Nee-toe-bay, E-nah-zoe)   Born in 1862 in Morioka on northern Honshu to a well-known *samurai* family, Inazo Nitobe attended Sapporo Agricultural College and then served briefly in the Hokkaido Colonial Government before leaving to study economics, history, and literature at Johns Hopkins University in the U.S. for three years.

Returning to Japan in 1888, he was appointed an assistant professor at his alma mater, but chose to go to Germany the same year to study at Bonn and Halle universities.

Back in Japan in 1891, Nitobe again joined Sapporo Agricultural University, became an engineer for the Hokkaido government and then served as engineer to the government of Taiwan. In 1909, he became a professor at the Tokyo Imperial University and, in 1914, president of Tokyo Women's University.

In 1919, Dr. Nitobe became the Under-Secretary of the League of Nations, a post he held until becoming chairman of the board of directors of the Institute of Pacific Relations in 1926.

A prolific writer, Dr. Nitobe published several books, including the best-selling *Bushido—The Way of the Warrior*, which delved into the moral and philosophical underpinnings of the code of the *samurai*. He also achieved an international reputation as an educator and expert in international affairs and was one of the best known of Japan's Meiji era figures.

He died in Victoria, British Columbia, in 1933, while attending a conference of the Institute of Pacific Relations.

NOBEL PRIZE WINNERS   As of this date, there have been eight Japanese Nobel Prize winners, primarily in science. The first three winners were Hideki Yukawa, who won his prize for showing that the meson provides the nuclear force between the proton and neutron (1949); Shinichiro Tomonaga, for work in the field of quantum electromagnetics (1965); and Yasunari Kawabata, for his novels *Snow Country, Dancing Girl of Izu, The Thousand Cranes, The Sound of the Mountain*, and other works (1968).

More recent winners were Leona Esaki, for research on the tunnel effect in semiconductors, and development of the Esaki Diode (1973); Eisaku Sato, for his efforts on behalf of peace (1974); and Kenichi Fukui, for developing the frontier orbital theory in chemical reaction processes (1981).

The newest Nobel Prize winners are Susumu Tonegawa, who won the medical science and physiology prize in 1987, and Kerryaburs Oe, who won the 1994 Nobel Prize for literature.

NOBORIBETSU SPA (No-boe-ree-bate-sue)   In between Muroran and Sapporo, on Hokkaido, the Noboribetsu Spa is one of the most extraordinary and famous hot spring resorts in Japan. Located in a large ravine formed by the Kusurisambetsu River and walled in by heavily timbered mountains, the spa consists of 11 hot springs with varying mineral content and temperatures.

The springs have been in use since the 1600s, because it is known that the famous Zen priest Enku visited them before the beginning of the Tokugawa Period in 1603. But they really became popular only after 1858, when a man named Kinzo Takimoto went there to get help for a skin disease and was so impressed with the place that he and his wife opened an inn there and began promoting the medicinal value of the hot springs.

The best known of the dozens of hot spring inns in the ravine is still the Daiichi Takimoto. There are 40 baths in its bathing room, with 10 different kinds of mineral water.

Only 400 meters from Noboribetsu is a place called Jigoku Dani, or Valley of Hell, which is the source of the hot waters that supply the inns of Noboribetsu. An immense depression (1.6 kilometers in circumference and about 100 meters deep) that is filled with cones and sinter hills, Jigoku Dani is an awesome sight.

A short distance away, up a hill and through the woods, one comes to the rim of an immense chasm that is apparently the remains of a crater. At the bottom of the crater is a lake of hot mud and boiling water. Sulfurous steam pours out of a peak on the far side of the lake.

There are a number of other hot spring spas in the vicinity, including New Noboribetsu Spa and Karurusu. The latter is distinctive in that the baths are carved out of bed-rock along the sides of a ravine, instead of being inside the *ryokan*.

The baths are especially popular, even during the winter months when it is very, very cold. The spa is named after the famous Karlsbad Springs in Czechoslovakia because its waters are similar in mineral content and are known to be beneficial in relieving the same kind of ailments (nervous disorders, rheumatism, spinal problems, etc.).

There is also an Ainu Museum in the Noboribetsu Spa complex.

NOGI, GENERAL MARESUKE (No-ghee, Mah-ray-sue-kay)   One of Japan's most famous post-shogunate generals, Maresuke Nogi was born in 1849 and took part in the fighting surrounding the fall of the shogunate in 1868, the war with China in 1895, and the war with Russia in 1905.

As a result of his brilliant performances in the wars against China and Russia, he became a national hero and was greatly prized by Emperor Meiji, to whom he gave total loyalty in the highest *samurai* tradition.

When Emperor Meiji died in 1912, General Nogi and his wife committed suicide just as the emperor's funeral cortege was leaving the palace.

In 1916, a shrine (Nogi Jinja) dedicated to the famous general was built on Momoyama (Peach Hill) on the outskirts of Kyoto, near the mausoleum of Emperor and Empress Meiji.

There is also a shrine dedicated to Nogi in Tokyo's Minato Ward, at Nogizaka (Nogi Slope), now a stop on the Chiyoda Subway Line.

NOGUCHI, DR. HIDEYO (No-guu-chee, He-day-yoe)   One of the most brilliant scientists of the Meiji and Taisho eras (1868–1928), Dr. Hideyo Noguchi was born to peasant parents in Fukushima Prefecture in 1876 and took up the study of medicine while he was still in his teens.

In 1899, Noguchi entered the University of Pennsylvania, where he studied bacteriology. After graduating, he went to work for the Carnegie Science Laboratory, which sent him to Europe to study serum therapy.

Already recognized as a brilliant research scientist by this time, Dr. Noguchi was invited to join the staff of the Rockefeller Institute and in 1925 went to the African Gold Coast to study the cause of yellow fever.

Noguchi contracted the disease he was studying and died from it in 1928.

NOH (Noh)—**AND OTHER DRAMA FORMS**   The oldest form of theater in Japan, *noh* began as a rustic, mimetic art form called *sarugaku* in ancient times, but did not really begin to flourish until the fourteenth century, when it came under the special patronage of the *samurai*, or ruling class.

The reknowned Kan'ami and his more famous son Zeami refined the drama form, and gained the official support of *Shogun* Yoshimitsu Ashikaga (1368–1394).

Noh is a highly stylized dance drama performed to the accompaniment of music and singing. Principal *noh* actors wear masks to enhance the sublimation of reality and symbolic movements, adding to the depth and impact of the form.

Elaborate costumes, along with the masks, are the main elements setting the unique mood and form of *noh*.

Altogether there are some 250 *noh* plays, generally grouped into five main classifications according to subject matter. These five categories are *shin* (god), *nan* (man), *nyo* (woman), *kyo* (madness), and *ki* (demons).

The stylized singing that is part of the *noh* drama is called *yokyoku* (yoe-k'yoe-kuu), and it is also practiced as an independent art.

Early in the Tokugawa Period (1603–1867), the Tokugawa Shogunate licensed five schools of *noh* for the entertainment of the ruling *samurai* class, and it has flourished ever since.

Recommended reading: *Noh—The Classical Theater of Japan*, by Donald Keene (Kodansha International).

Other traditional drama forms that are popular in Japan include:

KYOGEN: Short comic plays that were developed about the same time as *noh*, usually on the same bill, *kyogen* are characterized by their realism and ribald humor.

SHINPA: Developed in the Meiji era (1868–1912) to depict the manners and customs of contemporary Japan, *shinpa* (sheen-pah), or "new school drama," features a more naturalistic style of acting than does the traditional *kabuki*, and includes actresses, as well as *oyama*—male actors who portray female characters.

SHINKOKUGEKI: A form of popular theater that mainly presents realistic period dramas, *shinkokugeki* (new national theater) dates from the same period as the *shinpa*.

Japan is also famous for its musical revues, particularly the Takarazuka revues, which feature all-female casts. Organized along the lines of French revues, the large-scale Takarazuka musicals attract large audiences, mostly of young women, and their stars are national figures.

Japan's *shingeki* (sheen-gay-kee), or "new theater," grew from the desire to reflect modern social conditions in contemporary terms. First came translations of Western dramas and then, in the 1920s, the proletarian drama movement. In the late 1960s, small avant garde groups called *angura* (ahn-guu-rah), short for "underground," appeared and won praise for their innovative techniques.

There are 550 privately owned playhouses and 500 cultural halls in Japan. Most large playhouses are owned by Japan's Big Two entertainment conglomerates, Toho and Shochiku, and present *kabuki*, *shinpa*, revues, comedies, and other types of stage entertainment. Plays usually run for around a month.

Most *shingeki* troupes rent theaters as they are needed. Several of the troupes have organized clubs to help them meet their financial needs.

Japan's spectacular Kokuritsu Gekijo (Koe-kuu-reet-sue Gay-kee-joe), or National Theater, constructed in 1960, presents such traditional performing arts as *noh* and *kyogen*.

NOREN (No-rane)   Noren are the short, split curtains that one still sees hung in front of many eating and drinking establishments, as well as some shops selling traditional Japanese goods.

Originally designed to help keep out dust and block the sun, *noren* were already in common use during the Heian era (794–1185). They became even more popular in the Muromachi Period (1333–1568), with the development of larger stores, because they made it easier for large numbers of customers to come and go.

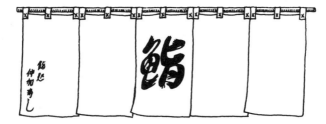

It was during this period that it became customary to dye the *noren* navy blue and for the name or crest of the shop to appear on them in white. As time went by, the *noren*/crest of individual shops came to be widely recognized and identified with the image and reputation of the shop.

It also became customary that when favored apprentices left a shop to set up their own business they were allowed to use the *noren*/crest of their master, not only to help them get off to a good start, but also as a sign of their obligation to their former master.

Besides their traditional use, *noren* are now sometimes used for decorative purposes and as room dividers. They are generally made of cotton cloth but also come in hemp and wood or plastic beads.

NO-SHOP SALES   By the mid-1980s, a revolution in consumer buying was well underway in Japan. This revolution was described by the Japanese retail industry as "No-Shop Sales," meaning mail-order and door-to-door sales.

By 1985, marketing via mail, catalogues, radio, television, newspapers, and magazines was growing at an annual rate of 15.4 percent, causing the major trading companies, manufacturers, and retailers to revise their marketing approach.

Among the developments was a rapidly expanding network of home delivery services by express courier companies.

Since the tightly controlled distribution system in Japan had long been a barrier to foreign companies trying to enter the market, this new trend was of special interest to them.

NURSERY SONGS   More than perhaps any other people, Japanese mothers, grandmothers, and others sing nursery songs to babies and small children. Many of the songs sung are traditional, having been passed down for generations. Among the most popular titles are "First Star," "Bird in the Cage," "How Old Are You, Moon?" "Through the Bridge," and "Zuizuizukkorobashi."

Over a dozen songs of contemporary origin, such as "Baby Raven," "Dragonfly," "Canary," "Red Shoes," and "Desert in the Moonlight," are also known by virtually every child in Japan.

The age-old custom of singing to babies is one of the reasons why most Japanese grow up able to sing fairly well and are willing to sing at parties and other gatherings without the kind of embarrassment that afflicts the typical Westerner under similar circumstances.

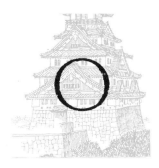

O'BON (Oh-bone)   This is the Buddhist Feast of All Souls, one of Japan's most important festivals. It originated in India as a ceremony to provide some respite for the unhappy souls of the departed who did not enter into Nirvana. They were invited to return to the land of the living during this period when the gates to Hades are temporarily open.

The practice is believed to have started in Japan during the reign of Empress Saimei in the seventh century, although there were Shinto rituals on behalf of the dead prior to that time.

Depending on the area, O'bon is celebrated from July 13 to 16, or from August 13 to 16, if the lunar calendar is followed. On the 13th, people visit the graves of their ancestors, burn incense, and in the evening hang lanterns over the graves. The spirits are then invited to the homes. On the 15th, special foods are prepared and served, with some families setting places for their departed relatives.

In the old days, it was customary for people to carry lighted lanterns from the graves to their homes, showing the way for the spirits, and to light bonfires in the front of their homes to help guide the spirits.

It was also common for the food and other special things prepared for the spirits to be put into small straw boats, lighted with candles, and set adrift in rivers or in the ocean to comfort those who died at sea.

Far from being a sad time, O'bon has traditionally been a joyous and welcome occasion, especially in the countryside, with the rice planting over, homes cleaned up, and special foods prepared, both for the spirits of the dead, as well as for the return of children and relatives from the cities.

Since ancient times, the occasion has been marked all over the country by dancing that was first ritualistic but eventually came to be done for the joy of it—the famous *Bon Odori* (Bone oh-doe-ree), or O'bon dances.

These dances usually begin in the early evening around dusk and continue on into the night, either at shrines or temples, or, in some places, like Tokushima, in the streets. Dancers dress in the light cotton *yukata* (you-kah-tah) *kimono* robes and sandals and dance to the music of flutes, drums, and the *shamisen*, played by musicians on a raised, high platform.

The dances have different names in different regions. The one in Tokushima is the famous *Awa Odori* (Ah-wah Oh-dore-ree), featured in many movies and television specials and usually seen each year on TV news during O'bon.

Folk songs are also an integral part of the O'bon festival, one of the most popular being "Tanko Bushi" (Tahn-koe Buu-shee) or "Coal Miners' Song," which is also a popular party song throughout the year.

The traditional Bon Odori song of Mito declares

> *Ha! Bon ga kitano ni*
> *Odoranu yatsu wa,*
> *Kibutsu, kanabutsu,*
> *Are sa, ishi botoke!*

> Now O'Bon has come,
> He who does not dance
> Is like a wooden or metal Buddha,
> Or one of stone!

ODA, NOBUNAGA (Oh-dah, No-buu-nah-gah)   A descendant of the famous Taira clan and a hereditary *daimyo* (provincial lord), Nobunaga Oda was born in 1534. Like his *samurai* ancestors, Nobunaga's passion was martial arts and the strategy of war, at which he became an expert.

In fact, Nobunaga spent so much time engaged in military exercises that he neglected his domain until one of his retainers sent him a letter, urging him to change his ways before he brought on the downfall of the House of Oda. The retainer then committed suicide for having exceeded his authority in admonishing his own lord.

The letter and his retainer's death sobered Nobunaga, however, and he began to take his reponsibilities seriously. At the age of 20, he married the daughter of Hidetatsu Saito, another well-known *daimyo*.

Japan was in turmoil at this time, as the Ashikaga *shoguns* had become weak and ineffective, and competing *daimyo* fought each other for military supremacy. As a ranking lord and a known military expert, Nobunaga was ordered by the emperor (Ogimachi) to restore peace to the land.

In 1564, Nobunaga conquered the province of Mino. He then set up his military headquarters at Gifu, southwest of present-day Nagoya, and attacked the powerful Lord of Omi. Nobunaga's forces met especially stiff resistance, however; so he enlisted the aid of several other *daimyo* in the area, including Shingen Takeda, Nagamasa Asai, and Ieyasu Tokugawa.

With these combined forces, Nobunaga soon defeated the Lord of Omi, making himself the leading power in central Japan. In 1569, Nobunaga went to the rescue of the Ashikaga *Shogun* Yoshiaki in Kyoto, who came under attack by two local *daimyo*.

After defeating the *shogun's* attackers, Nobunaga became the patron of both the emperor and the *shogun*. He had new palaces built for both of them and put the latter under the protection of his most able general, Hideyoshi Toyotomi.

During the previous decades of turmoil, the Buddhist monks of Mt. Hiei, adjoining Kyoto, had taken up the arts of war to protect themselves and their monasteries. But as their skills in the martial arts grew, they became aggressive and began demanding tribute and other concessions from the Imperial Court in Kyoto.

Nobunaga resolved in 1570 to end the power of the armed, fighting priests, but because they were supported by several *daimyo* in the area, he devised the strategem of supporting the growing number of Christian converts and using them as tools to weaken the influence of the Mt. Hiei monks.

He began by having a temple built for the Christians in Kyoto, but this turned his former ally Lord Shingen Takeda against him. Takeda convinced *Shogun* Yoshiaki that Nobunaga was out to destroy him, and the *shogun* agreed to support Takeda in a move against Nobunaga.

Learning of the plan through his spies, Nobunaga attacked the *shogun's* palace, captured him and sent him into exile, thus ending the Ashikaga Shogunate that had begun in 1333.

This action precipitated all-out war between the contending clans. With one success after another, and in particular with the help of his peasant-general Hideyoshi Toyotomi, Nobunaga became the de facto ruler of Japan.

Nobunaga used his power to rebuild the portions of Kyoto that had been destroyed in the fighting and to construct the great castle of Azuchi in Omi, near Lake Biwa—a castle that owed some of its styling to pictures he had been shown by Jesuit priests.

But Nobunaga's imperious and arrogant ways made him many enemies, who referred to him as Baka Dono, or Lord Fool. In 1582, while resting at the Honno Temple in Kyoto, he was assassinated by one of his own retainers. Thus ended the life of another of Japan's famous warlords. See TOYOTOMI, HIDEYOSHI.

OFUDA (Oh-fuu-dah)   Foreign visitors to temples in Japan are often intrigued by the strips of white paper hanging from the walls, ceilings, and pillars. These paper strips, called *ofuda*, bear the names of people who have visited that particular temple.

The practice is said to have originated in the tenth century, when Emperor Kazan resigned, became a Buddhist priest, and went on a pilgrimage to 33 noted temples in the western part of Honshu.

When he reached the last temple, the Kegon in Mino Province, he inscribed the details of his Journey on a board and hung it up at the temple.

The custom grew and was especially popular during the peaceful days of the Tokugawa era (1600–1867). The *ofuda* came to be made in elaborate colors and fancy designs and were much sought after by collectors.

At first, it was only commoners who made such pilgrimages (one of whom vowed to visit 1,000 temples and put his *ofuda* on all of them), but later many feudal lords took up the practice—but their *ofuda* were made of wood, instead of paper.

On April 5, 1807, there was a large gathering of *ofuda* pilgrims in Edo, where *ofuda* were exchanged. The custom had greatly declined by World War II and the years immediately thereafter, but by the 1970s it was once again popular.

OGASAWARA ISLANDS (Oh-gah-sah-wah-rah)   This group of 30 islands, lying from 1,000 to 1,200 kilometers southeast of Tokyo, in the Pacific, includes Iwojima of World War II fame, when it was the site of a desperate battle between U.S. and Japanese forces.

The islands were settled by the Japanese following their discovery in 1593 by Sadayori Ogasawara, the lord of Nagano. The two largest and best known of the islands are Chichi Jima (Father Island), and Haha Jima (Mother Island).

Residents of the islands are farmers and fishermen or engage in a thriving tourist business, the subtropical climate and quiet beaches attracting many visitors from Tokyo and other areas of the main islands.

The islands are under the administrative jurisdiction of Metropolitan Tokyo.

OKA, TADASUKE (Ohh-kah, Tah-dahs-kay)   More popularly known as Echizen-no Kami, Oka (1677–1751), was the civil governor of Edo during the rule of *Shogun* Yoshimune and the most famous judge of his time.

Oka's wise judgments were so popular that a book was written about them. Reading the book, one is struck by the similarity of his wisdom and judgments to those of Solomon. Like Solomon, he depended primarily on common sense and a shrewd knowledge of people.

OKAYAMA (Oh-kah-yah-mah)   Another old castle town founded in the sixteenth century, Okayama faces the Inland Sea, an hour's train ride southwest of Kobe. The capital of Okayama Prefecture, and known for its Bizen-yaki stoneware, cotton textiles, matting, peaches, and other products, the city is best known as the location of one of the three most celebrated gardens in Japan.

The garden in Okayama, now called Korakuen Park, was laid out in 1700 by Tsunamasa Ikeda, *daimyo* of the province, as a place for strolling. The garden grounds, landscaped according to the Enshu school, cover 11.5 hectares and include teahouses, several ponds, cascades, mounds, and groves of pine, maple, cherry, and plum trees.

The garden is across the Asahi River from the ruins of the Okayama Castle and is accessible via two long footbridges.

Okayama also has other claims to fame, including the Ikeda Industrial Zoo, established by Takamasa Ikeda, who married one of Emperor Hirohito's daughters.

OKAZAKI (Oh-kah-zah-kee)   A city of some quarter of a million people, Okazaki is 40.1 kilometers southwest of Nagoya on the famed Tokai-Do train line and is historically famous as the birthplace of Ieyasu Tokugawa, considered by some as the greatest military and political leader Japan has produced.

The grounds of the Tokugawa family castle have been converted to a park (the Okazaki Park), and in 1959 a three-storied castle tower was built on the site of the old castle.

A bridge that spans the Yahagi River near the park is said to be the place where Hideyoshi Toyotomi, later to become the military ruler of Japan and the patron lord of Ieyasu (but then a runaway vagrant), met the famous robber chief Koroku Hachisuka and became a member of his band.

After Hideyoshi became the supreme power in Japan, with the help of Hachisuka, he made the former robber a *daimyo* and gave him a fief.

A well on the grounds of the Tokugawa castle provided the water that was used to wash Ieyasu following his birth.

Today Okazaki is also noted for producing over 70 percent of Japan's fireworks and for its 500 spinning and weaving factories.

OKINAWA (Oh-kee-nah-wah)   The prefecture of Okinawa is made up of 60 islands, in four major groups, 685 kilometers south of Kyushu. The largest and best known of these islands is Okinawa, which has a land area of 1,220 square kilometers.

During World War II, Okinawa was the scene of a great battle between U.S. and Japanese forces, after which the island chain was occupied by American troops and other personnel until 1972. That year, the islands were returned to Japan and became Okinawa Prefecture.

Being closer to Southeast Asia and the recipient of migrations and cultural influences from that region since long before recorded history—and also being isolated from the mainstream of Japanese life by hundreds of miles of ocean—the Okinawans developed their own distinctive culture that set them apart.

With the coming of the modern era, however, and having the close-knit ties that come with being a full prefecture, the differences between Okinawa and the rest of Japan are rapidly diminishing.

Agriculture, stock farming, and fishing are still major industries on the islands. But tourism from the main islands of Japan is becoming more and more important, with the development of hotels, entertainment, and recreational facilities. At the same time, traditional industries continue to flourish—ceramics, abaca cloth, lacquerware, glassware, leatherware, woven cloth, and cotton, plus linen and silk goods dyed in a style known as *bingata*, which results in bright colors and attractive designs featuring landscapes, plants, animals, and geometric patterns.

Okinawa also has its shrines and annual festivals (which are still distinctively Okinawan). The most colorful of these events, called Juriuma and held on January 20, includes 100 dancing girls in bright folk costumes parading through the streets to the accompaniment of drums, gongs, flutes, and the *shamisen*.

The main island also has its castle and castle ruins, where feudal lords once lived and reigned, along with numerous other historical places and things.

On the southern part of Okinawa is the Okinawa Old Battlefield Quasi-National Park, a 30.8-square-kilometer area in which there are 67 monuments to the 244,136 soldiers and civilians who were killed during World War II.

Naha (Nah-hah) is the largest city, the capital, and the political, economic, and cultural center of the prefecture. Its population is rapidly approaching half a million.

The second largest city in Okinawa is Okinawa City, located in the central part of the island, 24 kilometers northeast of Naha. The U.S.'s huge Kadena Air Force Base is a short distance west of Okinawa City, which is where most of the GIs go for shopping and recreation.

Besides its semitropical climate, beaches, fishing, and growing recreational facilities that are attracting more and more tourists from the main islands of Japan, Okinawa is also famous for its bullfights, which have been taking place since very early times.

The bullfights are staged at Gushikawa, eight kilometers northeast of Okinawa City, every Sunday afternoon. The bulls meet in a 15-meter ring, butt each other, lock horns, and try to push each other out of the ring.

Okinawa is most proud of the Okinawa International Ocean Exposition, which was held for six months in 1975, with the theme "The Sea We Would Like to See," and was concerned with both developing and preserving the world's oceans. The Expo included a number of Fish Pavilions; a large Marine Life Zoo; an artificial island city of the future covering 10,000 square meters; a Seaside Bazaar; clusters of pavilions dedicated to science and technology, ethnic studies and history; and a Shore Park planted with subtropical sago palm and adan trees.

The site of the Expo is now a major recreational area and tourist attraction.

OKURA HOTEL (Oh-kuu-rah)   Tokyo's Okura Hotel, consistently recognized as one of the top hotels in the world, is another Japanese hotel with a fascinating story behind it.

When the Tokugawa Shogunate fell in 1868, Baron Kihachiro Okura was one of a handful of extraordinary men who proceeded—with the government's help—to develop several huge commercial and business combines that came to be known as *zaibatsu*.

A farsighted man, Baron Okura was one of the founders of the famous Imperial Hotel (see individual listing), which was originally managed by his son, Kishichiro (later to inherit his father's extensive business holdings and title).

Between World Wars I and II, Baron Okura, the son, made a special study of the top hotels in Europe and opened Japan's first resort hotel, the Kawana, in 1928. In 1937, he opened a second resort hotel, the noted Akakura Kanko.

Purged by the Allied Occupation authorities in 1945 (because of his involvement with a major *zaibatsu* firm), Baron Okura enlisted the aid of Iwajiro Noda to help him realize a lifelong dream—the building of a major world-class hotel in Tokyo that would combine the Japanese traditions of art and hospitality with the European tradition of cordiality he had experienced in Europe.

In 1945, Noda, who had been stationed abroad for many years before World War II and had married an American wife, was selected by the staff of General Douglas MacArthur, the Supreme Commander of the Allied Powers, and the Japanese government to coordinate the democratization of the Japanese economy.

In the process of breaking up the great *zaibatsu* combines, Noda met and impressed Baron Okura. When the Occupation ended, the two began making plans for what was to become the Okura Hotel, which opened in May 1962. The hotel, situated on the slope of a low hill overlooking the Imperial Palace and downtown Tokyo, was built on a site that was originally the garden grounds of a museum his father had founded.

The original Okura Hotel is now the flagship of a chain of 10 hotels and resorts in Japan and other countries.

The Okura has an Executive Service Salon designed for visiting businesspeople. Its services include data, economic news, secretaries, interpreters, translators, typing, copying, couriers, business-card printing, a library, and pamphlet display space.

The hotel is across the street from the American Embassy and JETRO and within a block of the American Chamber of Commerce in Japan. The colorful and exciting Akasaka entertainment district is a short walk from the Okura.

ORIGAMI (Oh-ree-gah-me)   This is the traditional Japanese art of making decorative/ornamental designs out of paper by folding and cutting. It is also referred to as *kirigami*, or paper-cutting.

OSAKA (Oh-sah-kah)   Situated on deltas formed by the Yodo River and the former Yamato River, Osaka is Japan's second largest city, a major port, and the primary commercial, industrial, and administrative center in the southwestern half of Honshu.

The area had been settled in ancient times, but it was in the fourth century A.D., after the Emperors Ojin and Nintoku both built palaces there (on the hill now occupied by Osaka Castle), that it began to grow into an important community—and was called Naniwa, or Rapid Waves.

It was not until the time of Hideyoshi Toyotomi (1536–1598) that Osaka was to grow into a major commercial city. He built the largest castle in Japan there and persuaded merchants from the surrounding areas of Sakai and Fushimi to move their businesses there.

All during the long Tokugawa Shogunate from 1600 to 1867, Osaka continued to grow. When it was organized into a municipality in 1889, it had a population of nearly half a million.

Present-day Osaka, often referred to as the Venice of Japan because of the numerous canals that traverse the city, is divided into 26 wards and is noted for its commerce and industry, its huge entertainment and shopping districts, and its art.

The most popular shopping district in the city is Shinsaibashi (Shee-sie-bah-she), with its long covered-street arcade lined with hundreds of shops and restaurants. The liveliest entertainment area is Dotombori (Doe-tome-boe-ree), with its bars, clubs, cabarets, and restaurants.

The city is especially famous for its wholesale industries, which have their own distinctive areas that date back for centuries, and for the greeting used by the merchant class in the old days: "Are you making money?" instead of "How are you?" Some 40 percent of Japan's exports pass through the city.

Osaka is three hours and 10 minutes from Tokyo via the Hikari Bullet Train, one hour and seven minutes from Nagoya, and 17 minutes from Kyoto.

In a city as old and as large as Osaka, it is not surprising to find that it has dozens of important annual events. Among them are the Ebisu Shrine Festival from January 9 to 11, during which women in colorful *kimono* carry palanquins through the streets, and people pray to Ebisu (the patron deity of business and good fortune) for a good year. The Shiten-no Temple's Doyadoya festival on January 14, during which young men in loincloths jostle each other around the temple, is a ritual designed to attract and please the harvest deity.

Other events during the year include the Osaka International Festival, the Osaka Port Festival, a huge boat festival, a summer or palanquin festival, and a *noh* festival.

Places of special interest in Osaka would fill a book by themselves. Besides such places as the Umeda Underground (shopping) Center, the Kita (North) and Minami (South) amusement centers, giant-sized cabarets and Turkish baths, there are the Osaka Merchandise Mart, several museums, several major shrines, a number of parks and gardens, and the great Osaka Castle overlooking the city.

The most important of the temples in the city is the Shiten-no—Tenno-Ji, for short—founded by Prince Shotoku in 593. The precincts, which cover 9.6 hectares, contain some of the oldest buildings and artifacts in Japan, along with other treasures, such as the swords of Prince Shotoku.

Within an hour or so of Osaka are literally hundreds of other places of special interest, including the Mausoleum of Emperor Nintoku (one of the founders, you might say, of Osaka), near Mikunigaoka. Called the Daisenryo, it covers 48 hectares, is 35 meters high at its highest point, is surrounded by three moats, and is the largest of its kind in the world.

For gourmets who like Japanese food, Osaka is a mecca. Over the centuries, its well-to-do businesspeople have been fanciers of specialty dishes developed for their highly discerning palates. Some of these dishes include *Osaka-zushi*, *fugu* (globe fish—which is deadly if not prepared right), and *tako-yaki* (tah-koe-yah-kee), or wheat dumplings with bits of octopus.

Osaka's special breed of gourmets are known as *kuidoraku* (Kuu-e-doe-rah-kuu), or "extravagant gourmets."

OSAKA CASTLE / OSAKA JO (Oh-sah-kah Joe)   Built in 1586 by Hideyoshi Toyotomi, then the military ruler of Japan, the Osaka Castle was the largest and most impressive castle in Japan, especially noted for the size of the great granite stones that formed its base. (Hideyoshi requisitioned the stones from his generals.)

In 1615, the castle was attacked by the forces of the Tokugawa Shogunate. Hideyoshi's heirs, including his son, were killed, and the castle was almost completely destroyed. It was later rebuilt by the Tokugawa *shoguns* as a symbol of their power.

In 1867, when the last Tokugawa *shogun* agreed to turn power over to the emperor, *samurai* who did not want the shogunate to end set fire to the castle and destroyed much of its interior. It was not until 1931 that the castle was once again renovated, this time with the main tower made of ferro-concrete.

The large gardens around the castle are now a park, which encompasses the Municipal Museum and the Hokoku Shrine, dedicated to the Toyotomi family.

OZAKI, YUKIO (Oh-zah-kee, Yuu-kee-oh)   Born in Kanagawa Prefecture in 1859 and educated at Keio University and Tokyo Imperial University, Yukio Ozaki was to become one of Japan's leading statesmen and a renowned orator.

Ozaki began his career as a journalist, then joined the government as the Secretary of the Board of Statistics in 1881. The following year, he joined Marquis Okuma to form the Progressive Party, one of Japan's first political parties.

But his outspoken attacks against the government of Emperor Meiji resulted in his being exiled. He was ordered to leave Tokyo in 1887 under the provisions of the Peace Preservation Act.

Choosing to travel abroad, Ozaki spent the next two years traveling and studying in the U.S. and Europe. He returned home in 1889, was elected to the Diet in 1890, and became Councilor to the Foreign Office in 1897 and Minister of Education in 1898.

In 1900, Ozaki joined the new Seiyukai Party that had just been founded by Prince Hirobumi Ito. He served as the mayor of Tokyo from 1903 to 1912 and then was the Minister of Justice for two years.

After retiring from politics, Ozaki remained a potent behind-the-scenes power for several decades. He wrote several books, including one in English, *Japan at the Crossroads*, which was published in London in 1932 and widely read in government and diplomatic circles.

Ozaki died in 1954 at the age of 95. His career had spanned the most remarkable period in Japan's extraordinary history. He both saw and helped Japan change from a feudal kingdom of warlords and warriors to a modern nation.

PACHINKO (Pah-cheen-koe)   This is a pinball game that uses small steel balls in a vertical machine, on which there are numerous holes blocked by obstacles. The object is to get as many balls into the holes as possible. The more difficult the hole, the more it pays off—in more steel balls.

If you have any balls left when you stop playing, you can exchange them for such prizes as candy and cigarettes. *Pachinko* became very popular shortly after the end of World War II as a form of inexpensive entertainment.

The game is enormously popular—some 29 million people play it regularly, spending in excess of $150 billion a year (which is three times Japan's annual defense budget and approximately one-fourth of what the Japanese spend for leisure and recreation. There are presently some 17,000 *pachinko* parlors in the country—most of which are owned by Korean residents of Japan. Some players become very skilled at the game, and there are fairly large numbers who play it for profit, selling their prizes back to the parlors or elsewhere for money.

The name *pachinko* comes from the sound the balls make when they strike the various obstacles in the machine.

PAINTINGS / E (Eh)   There are two styles of painting in Japan—traditional Japanese style and Western style. Japanese-style painting was imported along with Buddhism from China in the fifth and sixth centuries. These early paintings, called *suiboku* (sooey-boe-kuu), were black and white drawings of wash and line, stylized and allusive.

As time passed, elaborate paintings on Japanese paper, in *sumi* (sue-me), or soot ink, and on silk, using mineral colors, became popular. During the Edo Period (1600–1867), a form of painting called *ukiyoe* (uu-kee-hoe-eh), or "floating world," came into vogue.

Some *ukiyoe* were painted by hand, but it was as prints that they became widely known. The first *ukiyoe* subjects emphasized the beautiful women of the entertainment districts but went on to include the theater, *sumo* wrestlers, historical themes, birds, flowers, and landscapes.

In the mid-1800s, Harunobu Suzuki developed a method of multicolor printing, heralding a golden age of color prints. Among the most popular of these prints—especially in the West—was a pornographic genre called *shunga* (shune-gah).

The arrival of *ukiyoe* prints in Europe created a stir among artists and collectors and is said to have had a significant influence on French impressionist painters.

Most contemporary Japanese painters paint in the Western style, but there is still an important market for traditional Japanese art in traditional settings.

PAPER DOORS / FUSUMA (Fuu-sue-mah) or **SHOJI** (Sho-jee)   There are two kinds of sliding paper doors or screens in traditional Japanese homes, inns, and buildings. One is called *fusuma* and consists of thick paper pasted on both sides of a wooden frame and decorated with paintings. The other type is called *shoji*, and is made of very thin, white rice paper pasted over wooden laths.

The heavier, totally opaque *fusuma* are used both as doors and as wall panels. The translucent *shoji* are used as partitions between rooms and as substitutes for windows, since they admit a soft, diffused light.

The simplicity of the *shoji* panels, as well as the more decorative *fusuma*, are an integral part of the special charm of a Japanese room. The *shoji* in particular suggest an openness and intimacy that adds to their appeal.

PATENTS / TOKKYO (Toke-yoe)   A very important sign of the technological progress Japan has made since 1971 is the ratio of foreign to Japanese patent applications. In 1971, foreign individuals and companies made 25.9 percent of all the patent applications in Japan. By 1980, this foreign percentage had fallen to 13.2, and it is still dropping.

The U.S. presently accounts for some 40 percent of the foreign patent applications made in Japan each year, followed by West Germany, France, Britain, Switzerland, the Netherlands, and others.

The largest number of foreign patent applications are in chemistry. Next is machinery, and third is daily consumer products.

In 1980, a total of 191,020 patent applications were filed in Japan—165,730 of them by Japanese nationals.

By the end of the 1980s, the Japanese were filling as many patents *in the U.S.* as Americans did, but Americans have since regained the lead.

PEARL ISLAND A small island in the harbor of Toba City (just 16 kilometers from the Grand Shrines of Ise), the Mikimoto Pearl Island is where the famous Kokichi Mikimoto, the son of a poor noodle maker, first succeeded in producing a cultured pearl in 1893.

Toba City faces the Bay of Ise on the Pacific Coast side of Shima Peninsula, in Mie Prefecture, and is 131.5 kilometers from Nagoya. Besides Pearl Island and its pearl farms, Toba City also boasts a seven-story air-conditioned Tourist Center and the Mikimoto Pearl Museum.

PEARLS / SHINJU (Sheen-juu) Until just after the turn of the twentieth century, pearls were a relatively rare accident of nature. An irritant of some kind would find its way inside the shell of a oyster or other mollusk, and the mollusk would protect itself from the irritant by covering it with successive layers of nacre, ranging in color from pale white to a lustrous pink.

All of this was to be changed by Kokichi Mikimoto, born in 1858 to a poor noodle maker in Toba City. While in Yokohama in 1891, he saw tiny, imperfect natural pearls being sold at high prices and resolved that he would figure out a way to make better pearls faster. He returned to Ago Bay, on the south side of Shima Peninsula, and, after two years of repeated failures, found that a tiny bead of mother-of-pearl inserted into the gonad of an oyster would result in the growth of a pearl that was totally authentic—only the chance factor in its birth was removed.

It was to take 12 more years of heartbreaking endeavor before Mikimoto was to succeed in growing a perfectly spherical pearl and making his method of pearl culturing commercially feasible.

With this breakthrough, pearl farming eventually developed into a major industry in Japan. For the first several decades, pearl oysters were collected from natural seabeds for artificial seeding, but now most of them are raised for that purpose.

Young oysters are placed in baskets and suspended into the sea from rafts for two or three years. They are seeded during the summer months (May–October) after they reach six to seven centimeters in size. The mother pearl oyster is wedged open while it is breathing, and a pearl nucleus—a tiny piece of mother-of-pearl—is inserted into the gonad.

The mother pearl oysters are then suspended from rafts in metal-mesh bags at depths of 0.5 to 1.0 meters. During the growing process, the shells are periodically cleaned and are moved to warmer areas if the water temperature falls below 15 degrees centigrade (59 degrees F.).

It takes about six months to produce a small pearl (up to seven millimeters) and one to two years to produce pearls over seven millimeters in size. November is considered the best time to harvest pearls, but the process goes on all year, and it is very popular with tourists who visit the pearl farms.

Japan's best-known pearl farms are in Mie Prefecture, near Nagoya, and the most popular tourist spot is Pearl Island, where Mikimoto first succeeded in producing pearls. Pearl culture demonstrations are held daily on the island, which is attached to the mainland by a 63-meter bridge.

The Mikimoto Pearl Museum in Toba City is also worth a visit.

Kokichi Mikimoto lived to see cultured pearls become accepted worldwide and grow into a multimillion dollar a year industry. He died in 1954 at the age of 96.

PEERAGE   When Japan's last great shogunate dynasty fell in 1867, a peerage system was established to cover members of the Imperial family, the former clan lords (*daimyo*), and leading businesspeople of the day.

At this time, there were 1,016 aristocratic families in Japan — 136 of them with pedigrees as long as the emperor's and 248 of them belonging to the Tokugawa Shogunate lineage.

Altogether, the new Imperial government designated 10 Imperial princes not of the main line, 11 non-Imperial princes who were called dukes, 35 marquises, 90 counts, 360 viscounts, and 510 barons.

Japan's present constitution, which was partially drafted by the U.S. Occupation Forces and went into effect soon after the end of World War II, ended the peerage system with seven words: "Peers and peerage shall not be recognized."

PEOPLE'S LODGES / KOKUMIN SHUKUSHA (Koe-kuu-meen shuu-kuu-shah)   As part of their efforts to encourage outdoor recreation and tourism, many of Japan's prefectures and the central government have helped finance the building of some 500 People's Lodges throughout the country.

The lodges, primarily located in natural parks, are designed to provide basic accommodations for people who cannot afford regular commercial inns and hotels. Several million people use the lodges each year. Foreign visitors may also take advantage of the Kokumin Shukusha by making reservations well in advance through travel agents or directly with the lodges.

For a list of the lodges, contact the Japan National Tourist Organization.

PERMANENT RESIDENCY   It is possible for foreigners who meet specific requirements to become permanent residents of Japan. These requirements include being 20 years of age or older, with sufficient assets or income to support one's self and dependents, having good character and good health, and having lived in Japan for 10 years or more.

This latter requirement is waived in the case of individuals who have made significant contributions to Japan, who are wives of Japanese men, who have Japanese wives, or who are former citizens.

PERRY, COMMODORE MATTHEW C.   Born in 1794 (and the brother of the famous Oliver Hazard Perry), Commodore Perry of the U.S. Navy, more by luck than anything else, was the first major power representative to deliver what amounted to an ultimatum to Japan to open its ports to Western ships and trade, in July 1853.

Commodore Perry and his squadron of 12 black warships (later to become famous in Japan as the Black Ships), dropped anchor off the barge port of Uraga on Miura Peninsula at the mouth of Tokyo Bay (see URAGA) and delivered a letter—addressed to the emperor—with the notice that he would return in six months for an answer.

The Tokugawa Shogunate had been told by the Dutch traders on Dejima in Nagasaki Bay that Perry was coming, but they had not been informed that he was bringing a whole fleet of steam-powered warships, something the Japanese had not seen before.

The Japanese had expected Perry to stop at Nagasaki, but when he steamed into Tokyo Bay, near the *shogun's* castle headquarters in Edo, in large ships that belched smoke and fire, they were both impressed and frightened by the implied threat.

That same year, a Russian envoy named Poutiantine sailed into the port of Nagasaki with a similar demand.

The Tokugawa Shogunate, virtually impotent at this time in Japan's history, had taken the matter up with Emperor Komei and his Court of advisors in Kyoto.

But when Perry and his ships returned in the fall, the Japanese had still not been able to reach a decision.

This time, Perry anchored his ships just offshore of what is now the port of Yokohama, very near the *shogun's* capital in Edo. He informed the officials there that if the Emperor's representative did not soon agree to meet him at a suitable location, he would sail right up to Edo.

Finally, the representatives of the *shogun* agreed to meet Perry and his aides on Yokohama beach, then called Kanagawa, and began feverish preparations to build a special Treaty House to receive them. The meeting occurred on March 8, 1854.

Perry and his chief officers went ashore with 300 armed marines. They were received with great formality and courtesy. Following several days of negotiating, the Treaty of Kanagawa was signed, giving the U.S. access to two Japanese ports and the right to establish consulates in the country.

Shimoda, at the end of Miura Peninsula, then no more than a tiny fishing village, was designated as the first port. Selection of the second port was put off until some time later.

Thus, America became the first nation to establish official diplomatic relations with Japan in the history of the country. The first American Consul in Japan was to be Townsend Harris. See HARRIS, TOWNSEND; HISTORY.

PERSONNEL MANAGEMENT   One of the key characteristics of personnel administration in larger Japanese companies is the custom of regularly and systematically transferring personnel from one job to another and from one department to another.

This practice, which shocks most American managers, is regarded by Japanese management as one of its strongest points.

The positive aspects of this system are seen as reducing poor morale, idleness, and corruption; giving all employees the opportunity to learn many jobs and to learn and appreciate the relationship between departments; and helping to train managers who will have a well-rounded view of the company's overall operation.

In larger Japanese companies, virtually everyone starts at the bottom. In some cases, those with technical backgrounds start out as clerks at the head office, and those with liberal arts backgrounds are assigned to factories, to give everyone the widest possible variety of experiences.

This job-rotation system continues as the employees advance up the escalator of seniority. Individuals with exceptional talent thus become known to the managers of many departments and are gradually advanced into the more important management positions.

In many companies, job rotation never ends, unless an individual reaches the very top. It is seen as a process of continuous on-the-job training.

PHP INSTITUTE (PEACE, HAPPINESS AND PROSPERITY)   PHP Institute, a nonprofit corporation established by Konnosuke Matsushita, founder of the great Matsushita Electric Co. and prototype of the Japanese executive-philosopher, is primarily known for the monthly magazine it publishes, called *PHP Intersect* ("Where Japan Meets Asia and the World"). *PHP Intersect* covers a variety of topics, including business management, conservation, culture, and life-styles, and it is distributed around the world.

Articles in *PHP Intersect* are written by professionals and expert laypeople who have distinguished themselves by innovative thinking and exemplary achievement. See OTHER SOURCES.

POETRY-READING PARTY / UTA KAI HAJIME (Uu-tah Kie Hah-jee-may)   For centuries, one of the most popular New Year's events in Japan has been poetry-reading parties. The most famous is the party held by the emperor and empress at the Imperial Palace to celebrate New Year's and known as Uta Kal Hajimae, or First Poetry Reading.

Each year, some 30,000 to 40,000 poems are submitted to the contest, which has a different theme every year. A "green theme" poem submitted by Empress Michiko (when she was still Princess Michiko and had just come back from Africa) read:

> Vast African Sky
> Over the green of the coconut palms,
> A new day flares forth.

POLICE / KEISATSU (Kay-e-sot-sue)   Japan's National Police Agency, under the supervision of the National Public Safety Commission, supervises prefectural police departments, which are directly under prefectural public safety commissions and the governors.

The prefectural police organizations and the Tokyo Metropolitan Police Department (which is a separate organization) have precincts under the local jurisdiction of a police station. Each station in turn has a number of the famous *koban* (koe-bahn), or so-called police boxes—street-corner police posts—in its precinct. See POLICE BOXES.

Altogether, there are 1,215 police stations in Japan, approximately 6,000 dispatch police boxes, and some 9,600 resident police boxes. The total number of policemen in Japan is approximately 28,500—or about one for every 552 people, as compared to one for every 363 people in the U.S. and one for every 401 persons in Great Britain.

In recent years, the number of policewomen in Japan has increased significantly, currently numbering in excess of 7,000—not counting 11,000 female general employees.

Japan's police agency owns a fairly large fleet of fixed-wing airplanes and helicopters and has police airfields in 20 of its 47 prefectures.

POLICE BOXES / KOBAN (Koe-bahn)   The system of establishing small police outposts on important street corners was started in Edo (Tokyo) in 1628 by the Tokugawa Shogunate to help protect the townspeople from being killed by roughneck *samurai* (who no longer had any wars to fight and whose code of *bushido* ethics had weakened).

These *samurai* would waylay passersby and cut them down to demonstrate their fighting skills and to try out new swords—taking advantage of a law that made it legal for a *samurai* to immediately kill a commoner who behaved in an unacceptable manner—a practice that came to be known as *tsuji giri* (t'sue-gee ghee-ree) or "street-corner killing."

These police boxes were under the supervision of the town *bugyo* (magistrate) and were called *tsuji ban*, or "corner guards." There were eventually three kinds of *tsuji ban*—one kind operated by the shogunate, one by the *daimyo*, and one by Tokugawa retainers. At one time, there were 898 *koban* in Edo (Tokyo).

When modern police methods were adopted in the Meiji Period (1868–1912), the old *koban* system was continued. (When the American Armed Forces took over Japan in 1945, they closed most of the *koban* in favor of the American system of patrolling.)

Today there are police boxes in every city and town in Japan, and they are a major factor in the world-renowned safety of Japan's streets.

Besides watching over what is going on in their neighborhoods, the police officers stationed in the *koban* also serve as sources of information for people looking for addresses in the area. See ADDRESSES.

There are two types of *koban*—*hashutsujo* (hah-shute-sue-joe) and *chuzaisho* (chuu-zie-show). The former, dispatch-type *koban*, are the larger of the two and are located in denser, business sections of towns and cities. The latter, smaller *koban* are located in residential areas.

POLITICAL PARTIES   Japan's first political party, the Aikoku Koto (Aye-koe-kuu Koe-toe) was formed in 1874 under the leadership of Taisuke Itagaki. One of its first actions was to present a petition to the emperor requesting the establishment of a parliamentary form of government.

In the years that followed, many parties appeared and disappeared as a result of interparty struggles or suppression by the government.

The first cabinet to be formed by the leader of a party occurred in 1914, but the famous *genro* (gane-roe), or "elder statesmen," who had led Japan during the exciting years of industrialization following the Meiji Restoration, continued to exercise real power. (See GENRO.)

It was not until after the end of World War II and the promulgation of the new constitution in 1946 that true party cabinets were formed.

The Liberal Democratic Party, formed in 1955 through a merger of two conservative parties, held power until 1993, when it was replaced by the new Japan New Party, under the leadership of Morihiro Hosokawa, who became the prime minister in August 1993 and resigned in April 1994 after being charged by his opponents with unethical financial transactions.

The Japan Socialist Party, formed in 1945 as the result of a merger of several prewar workers' parties, has had one brief stint in power—from May 1947 to March 1948. The JSP traditionally opposed the Japan-U.S. security treaty and advocated unarmed neutrality.

The Komeito, formed in 1964 as the political arm of the Soka Gakkai (Soe-kah Gock-kie), a religious organization affiliated with the Nichiren Shoshu sect of Buddhism, advocates a welfare society based on what it calls Humanitarian Socialism. In 1970, the party was split off from the Soka Gakkai and is now independent.

The Democratic Socialist Party was formed in 1960 by a splinter group that bolted the Japan Socialist Party. It is a middle-of-the-road party dedicated to the creation of a socialist society through democratic processes.

The Japan Communist Party dates from July 1922, when it was founded as an underground political association. The party became legal after the end of the Pacific War in 1945. The JCP works for fewer ties with the U.S. and better conditions for workers.

The New Liberal Club was formed in June 1976 by six Diet members who broke away from the Liberal Democratic Party. Its policies are primarily conservative.

The United Social Democratic Party, founded in March 1978 through a merger of three Socialist Party Diet members and three Socialist Citizens' League members, advocates the creation of a new and liberal socialism.

In 1993 a new opposition party, called Shinseito, was formed, and in the spring of 1994, in coalition with the Japan Socialist Party (JSP), ended the 39-year reign of the Liberal Democratic Party. Tomiichi Murayama, leader of the JSP, was elected prime minister. The JSP subsequently changed its official position on the U.S.-Japan Security Treaty and Japan's self-defense forces.

In December of 1994 Shinseito was disbanded and replaced by yet another coalition party named Shinshinto or New Frontier Party.

Shinshinto was made up of nine political groups, including Shinseito, Komeito, the Japan New Party, the Democratic Socialist Party, and five smaller parties.

Political analysts described Shinshinto as a stop-gap maneuver by former LDP prime ministers and leaders to return to power, and predicted that it would not survive for more than a few months.

Most of Japan's so-called political parties are, in fact, political factions made up of professional politicians rather than national parties.

POLLUTION / KOGAI (Koe-guy)   Japan was a leader in attempts to control automobile exhaust pollution. As a result of laws passed in the early 1970s, the emission of hydrocarbons, nitrogen oxides, and carbon monoxide dropped dramatically from 1975.

When compared with the U.S., Japan is a little ahead in the control of hydrocarbons and substantially ahead in nitrogen oxides and carbon monoxide controls. In permissible automobile noise levels, Japan ranks even with the U.S.

POPULATION / JINKO (Jene-koe)   In terms of population, Japan is the seventh largest nation in the world, behind China, India, Russia, the United States, Indonesia, and Brazil.

The population is approximately 125 million and is creeping upward at the rate of about half a million per year. Most Japanese—some 70 percent— are concentrated along the Pacific seaboard, on the coastal plains between Tokyo and the northern part of Kyushu.

Because 70 percent of Japan's total land area is mountainous and virtually uninhabitable, the bulk of the population actually lives on less than 10 percent of the land space—or an area about the size of one large county in the U.S.

PORNOGRAPHY   Pornography, in the form of woodblock prints, erotic drawings, and writings, has a long and sanctified history in Japan. And the industry still flourishes in all of its more modern forms.

In pre-1945 Japan, it was common for newlyweds to be presented with a colorful sexual-position chart, and such charts were therefore common in homes.

Today the most conspicuous form of pornography is monthly magazines, particularly the very popular cartoon magazines, of which some 80 to 100 are explicitly erotic in nature.

A number of well-known daily newspapers feature erotic photographs, illustrations, and copy, and it is common to see them being read on trains, subways, and other forms of public transportation.

Japan's laws about the importation of pornographic material are very strict, however. Censors go through every copy of such imported publications as *Playboy*, inking out genitalia and pubic hair.

PORTUGUESE IN JAPAN   The first Westerners of record to set foot in Japan were Portuguese traders who were sailing to Macau in a Chinese junk when they were blown off course by a typhoon and accidently landed on the tiny island of Tanegashima, 200 miles south of the coast of Kyushu, on August 25, 1543. The residents of Tanegashima were both fascinated and repelled by the Caucasians, but what most interested the Lord of Tanegashima was the muskets the Portuguese had in their possession. He lost no time in getting one of the guns and ordering his retainers to set up shop and begin manufacturing them.

Among the other things the Portuguese introduced to the islanders were tobacco and venereal disease.

Soon after this, the enterprising lord was selling muskets to *daimyo* on the main islands, and, for many decades, muskets were called Tanegashima.

(In less than a decade, every clan lord in the country had his own company of musketeers, and, only 32 years later, in 1575, an army of 3,000 men armed with muskets turned the tide of a major battle in favor of Nobunaga Oda, who went on to gain military hegemony over the other clan lords. And yet, unlike any other culture on record, the Japanese then turned their backs on this new weapon technology and went back to the sword for nearly 250 more years. Ironically, the last time guns were used in Japan before they were outlawed in 1637, was to crush the rebellion of Christians in Shimebara.)

The Portuguese repaired their ship and continued on to Macau, spreading the news of their discovery of a new land. Within months, Portuguese expeditions set sail for Japan from their settlements in China, India, and other areas of Southeast Asia. By 1549, they had established several trading companies in Kyushu and had been followed to Japan by Jesuit priests from the Portuguese colonies of Goa and Macau.

The best known of these priests was the Jesuit missionary Francisco Xavier, who arrived in Kagoshima in 1549, and during a 10-month stay, received permission from the Lord of Satsuma to preach Christianity in Satsuma. He visited Hirado, Yamaguchi, Kyoto, and Oita before leaving Japan.

The first Portuguese trading vessel arrived at Hirado on Kyushu in 1550, and, within five years, both Hirado and Sakai were prospering as trading ports. In 1570, Nagasaki was also opened to foreign trade.

This was a period of almost continuous clan warfare in Japan, and the *daimyo* were more interested in the firearms and science of the traders and missionaries than in their new religion. The number of converts the Jesuit missionaries made among the *daimyo* and *samurai* depended almost entirely on how many guns they were able to deliver.

Lord Nobunaga Oda, who was to become the de facto *shogun* of Japan in the 1560s, was impressed with both the learning and the bravery of the Jesuit priests and acted as their patron during his lifetime.

The religious and financial ambitions of the Portuguese missionaries were to be their undoing, however, as they became more and more involved in trying to keep other traders out of Japan. Hideyoshi Toyotomi, Nobunaga's successor, finally banished Jesuit missionaries from the country, but allowed Portuguese traders to continue their activities.

Finally, in 1639, the third Tokugawa *shogun* expelled all foreigners from Japan, except for one small Dutch trading post established on an islet called Dejima in Nagasaki Bay.

One of the most remarkable—and important—of the Portuguese Jesuits in Japan during the so-called Christian Century was Joao Rodrigues, one of few early foreigners to become fluent in Japanese. Because of his ability as an interpreter, he was involved in many of the most extraordinary events of his time. His name was used by Robert Clavell in his book *Shogun*.

Rodrigues arrived in Japan in 1577, when he was 16 years old, and entered a seminary. In addition to his activity as a liaison between the Portuguese traders and the *daimyo* of the different fiefs, Rodrigues became a scholar, writing the first Western book on Japanese grammar, customs, and history. He was also a successful businessman.

When Ieyasu Tokugawa became *shogun* in 1603, Rodrigues was appointed the official agent for arranging the allotments of silk that went to different merchants and played a key role in setting the price of bulk shipments—a role that won him many enemies among the Portuguese, as well as the Japanese.

When the Portuguese were driven out of Japan, Rodrigues settled in Macau, studied Chinese, wrote several other books, served as chaplain for the China traders who lived in the Portuguese colony, and later had a hand in organizing troops to help the Ming armies fight the Manchu.

Trapped in the seige of Tengchow in 1632, Rodrigues escaped by leaping out of a window. He made his way back to Macau, dying there the following year at the age of 72 from a neglected hernia.

Recommended reading: *This Island of Japan*, by Joao Rodrigues, translated by Michael Cooper, S.J. (Kodansha International).

POSTAL SERVICE / YUBIN (Yuu-bean)   Despite the fact that most streets in Japan are not named and house and building numbers have nothing to do with streets (see ADDRESSES IN JAPAN), the country has one of the world's most efficient postal systems.

Altogether, there are over 23,100 post offices in Japan and several hundred thousand street mail boxes throughout the country.

Besides handling letters and parcel post, the Japanese postal system offers a variety of financial services, including acting as a repository for savings accounts, paying approximately the same interest rates as banks.

Foreigners may utilize this service, and, when they leave Japan, they may have their savings transferred to an account abroad (this is important because withdrawals from a Japanese post office account—or a Japanese bank account —cannot be made from abroad).

POTTERY / SETOMONO (Say-toe-moe-no)   Pottery was being made in Japan during the Stone Age, and two of its earliest periods are named after the types of pottery produced during those periods—Jomon-type and the later Yayoi-type.

It was not until the thirteenth century, however, that what is now referred to as ceramic art developed in Japan. Credit for this is given to one Shirozaemon Kato (1169–1249), who established a kiln in a place called Seto in Owari Province (now Aichi Prefecture) after studying the art of ceramic making in China.

Kato is said to have traveled all over Japan looking for a place that had the best clay, before settling on Seto. From this period on, pottery making flourished and came to be known as Setomono or Seto Things, from the place where it was made.

Other kilns were gradually established in other parts of the country, and many of them were also to become famous. Eventually, virtually all the provinces had their own kilns and particular styles.

One of the most famous of the kilns outside of Seto was one in Arita (Saga Prefecture), founded in 1598 by a Korean potter named Li-San Ping.

During the following Tokugawa Period (1603–1867), the art of pottery making achieved very high levels. A number of the kilns and styles founded during the early Tokugawa years are still flourishing, particularly Kutani of Ishikawa Prefecture and Kyo ware of Kyoto.

Masters of the art of pottery making have been recognized and honored in Japan since it first began, and their names are an important part of its history. Among contemporary masters were Munemaro Ishiguro (1893–1968), Toyo Kanashige (1896–1967), Hijime Kato (1900–1967), Hazan Itaya (1872–1963), Kenkichi Tomi-moto (1886-1963), and Shoji Hamada (b.1894), whom I have had the pleasure of watching work on a number of occasions.

In recent decades, many Westerners have gone to Japan to study the art of pottery making.

Recommended reading: *The World of Japanese Ceramics*, by Herbert H. Sanders, with Kenkichi Tomimoto (Kodansha International); *Tamba Pottery: The Timeless Art of a Japanese Village*, by Daniel Rhodes (Kodansha International); and *The Japanese Pottery Handbook*, by Penny Simpson and Kanji Sodeoka (Kodansha International).

PREFECTURES / KEN (Ken)   Japan is divided into 47 prefectures that are grouped into eight regions. From north to southwest, these regions and the prefectures within them are Hokkaido (Hoke-kie-doe)—the only region that is made up entirely of one prefecture, by the same name; Tohoku (Toe-hoe-kuu)—which includes the prefectures of Aomori, Akita, Iwate, Yamagata, Miyagi, and Fukushima; Kanto (Khan-toe)—Ibaraki, Tochigi, Gunma, Saitama, Chiba, Tokyo, and Kanagawa; Chuba—Shizuoka, Yamanashi, Nagano, Niigata, Toyama, Ishikawa, Fukui, Gifu, and Aichi; Kinki (Keen-kee)—Mie, Shiga, Kyoto, Nara, Osaka, Wakayama, and Hyogo; Chugoku (Chu-go-kuu)—Tottori, Okayama, Hiroshima, Shimane, and Yamaguchi; Shikoku (She-koe-kuu)—Kagawa, Tokushima, Kochi, and Ehime; and Kyushu (Que-shuu)—Fukuoka, Saga, Nagasaki, Kumamoto, Oita, Miyazaki, Kagoshima, and Okinawa. See JAPAN.

PREPARATORY SCHOOLS / YOBIKO (Yoe-bee-koe)   Talk about prep schools! Japan has more prep schools than any other country by far, and they play a far greater role in the lives of hundreds of thousands of Japanese each year.

Because of the extraordinary competition to get into Japan's most prestigious universities, which is by examination, huge numbers of high school students fail the university entrance exams each year. Large numbers of those who fail these examinations enroll in *yobiko* to cram for retaking the exams the following year.

Students who fail to pass university examinations the first time are popularly referred to as *ronin*, meaning "wave men," in reference to feudal age *samurai* who, after losing their lord for some reason, would roam the country, oftentimes using their sword-fighting ability to cause trouble of some kind.

Over the years, various of the *yobiko* have developed national reputations for helping large numbers of their students succeed in passing the entrance exams of the most desirable universities. And they have become difficult—and costly—to get into because of their success.

Such prep schools often advertise the percentage of their graduates who pass the Joint University Entrance Examination Achievement Test as a way of attracting new students.

Just before examination time each year, usually in January, hundreds of thousands of young Japanese visit shrines and temples to pray for success. One of the most popular of these shrines is Yushima in Tokyo. The shrine is dedicated to Tenjin Sama, the spirit of Michizane Sugawara, a famous ninth-century scholar.

PRESS CLUBS / PURESU KURABU (Puu-ray-sue kuu-rah-buu)   Press clubs in Japan are quite different from press clubs in the U.S. and other countries. In Japan, reporters from the major news media belong to individual clubs that are concerned with designated news sources—government ministries and agencies, industries, etc., just as in the U.S. individual correspondents are assigned to the White House, the State Department, and so on.

The key difference is that in Japan the individual clubs have exclusive rights to the specific news conferences. Reporters who are not members of the Steel Industry Press Club, for example, are not allowed to attend steel industry press briefings.

The control of the various important news sources by these press clubs is virtually absolute and influences the way news is reported in Japan. Among other things, these clubs assume the right to be selective in what they report. If they believe that a certain piece of news would be detrimental to the interests of Japan, they suppress it.

It was not until the late 1970s that foreign correspondents in Japan won the right to attend press briefings by the Prime Minister's Office. See FOREIGN CORRESPONDENTS.

The press clubs, in effect, act as a filter for the news that gets printed and broadcast by Japan's leading communications media. Reporters from smaller, less powerful Japanese media are not allowed to become members of these press clubs.

Some news sources hold special briefings for reporters not eligible to join the press clubs.

In the early 1990s, the Foreign Correspondent's Club of Japan mounted a determined effort to break the news monopoly held by the Japanese press clubs, with significant success. Several of the clubs opened their doors to carefully selected foreign journalists, but the battle for equal access to Japanese news sources is far from being over. See NEWSPAPERS.

PRISONS / KEIMUSHO (Kay-e-muu-show)   There are presently 74 major prison facilities in Japan—58 prisons, 9 juvenile reformatories, and 7 detention facilities, along with 115 branch facilities made up of 9 prisons and 106 detention jails.

A number of these prison facilities are Open Prisons—that is, the inmates' activities within the compounds are not supervised, factories and mess halls remained unlocked, and inmates may have private meetings with relatives and other visitors.

The Justice Ministry has licensed 100 rehabilitation-assistance societies to help parolees, in addition to the publicly employed probation officers and volunteers who watch over and help parolees.

PROCESSIONS OF THE LORDS / DAIMYO GYORETSU (Dime-yoe g'yoe-rate-sue)   In 1635, 32 years after the beginning of the Tokugawa Shogunate, Japan's last great *samurai* dynasty, the third Tokugawa *shogun*, Iemitsu, established a political control system known as *Sankin Kotai* (Sahn-keen Koe-tie), or Alternate Attendance.

Under this system, the Shogunate government divided the country's 270 feudal lords, known as *daimyo*, or "great names," into two groups and legally required all except the smallest and weakest of them to build mansions in Edo (Tokyo), keep their families there at all times, and spend every other year in Edo in attendance at the *shogun's* Court.

This meant that the *daimyo* had to travel once a year either to or from their fiefs and Edo. But the law did not stop there. The *daimyo* had to bring a specific number of retainers with them on each trip, depending on the size and wealth of their fiefs. The attire and equipment of each retainer was prescribed, as was the route the procession was to follow.

Daimyo of the richer provinces were required to bring with them 1,000 or more retainers. The largest of the fief lords, Maeda, maintained four mansions in Edo, with a total permanent staff of 10,000 persons. When he came to Edo for his turn at Court, he brought several thousand additional retainers with him.

Since there were over 250 major *daimyo* in the country to which the Sankin Kotai law applied, this meant that at any one time there were dozens of great, colorful processions moving along the national roads in all seasons.

The *daimyo* whose fiefs were in distant parts of Japan were thus required to be on the road for several weeks at a time, each way.

These great, elaborately costumed corteges, known as *daimyo gyoretsu*, moved at a stately pace along the principal roads of Japan, stopping over each night at Post Stations established for that purpose. Providing nightly accommodations for such large masses of regular travelers required a vast network of inn/hotels, the likes of which existed in no other country.

But not just any ordinary inn would suffice for the comfort and convenience of a powerful *daimyo* feudal lord, his personal attendants, and the other persons of high rank who traveled these busy thoroughfares.

It thus came about that three categories of Japanese-styled inn/hotels were established at each of the Post Stations on all of the national highways leading to Edo.

First in order of rank and quality were the *honjin* (hohn-jeen), literally "headquarters hotels," which were reserved for the *daimyo*, their highest retainers, members of the Imperial family, high government officials, and ranking priests. These *honjin* inns were built in the same style—and with the same dedication to quality—as were royal mansions in Kyoto and *daimyo* mansions in Edo.

The second-ranked category of accommodations at these bustling Post Stations were known as *waki-honjin*, or "annex honjin." They were reserved for the exclusive patronage of very important people who were of lesser rank or couldn't get reservations at the main *honjin* because they were full.

The *honjin* hotels were relatively large and imposing, built of the finest materials available in Japan, and representative of classic Japanese architecture. Their standards for service and exclusivity were so exacting that guests were limited to a maximum of nine or ten at a time.

The lower-ranking members of these huge feudal lord corteges, along with ordinary travelers, stayed in a third category of lodging known as *hatago* (hah-tah-go).

One can begin to appreciate the number of travelers constantly moving to and fro in Japan from the number of these special inns on just the five most famous of these Processional Roads. On the Tokai-Do, which ran between Kyoto and Edo, there were 111 *honjin*, 68 *waki-honjin* and 2,905 *hatago* inns.

The Nakasen-Do had 93 *honjin*, 102 *waki-honjin* and 1,812 *hatago* inns. The Nikko-kai-Do had 23 *honjin*, 20 *waki-honjin* and 820 *hatago*. The Oshu-kai-Do had 11 *honjin*, 11 *waki-honjin* and 267 *atago*. On the Koshu-kai-Do, there were 45 *honjin*, 44 *waki-hon-jin* and 505 ordinary inn-hotels.

It is estimated that up to 10 percent of the annual income of the feudal fiefdoms was spent on these annual journeys—which continued for over 200 years and were undoubtedly the most spectacular feature of Japanese life for these many generations.

Not only did these great *daimyo gyoretsu* result in the development of a highly sophisticated network of inns throughout the country (in which the traditions of service that are still characteristic of Japanese inns and hotels were firmly established), they also contributed to the spread of culture and to the economic well-being of the rural areas through which they passed.

There were, in fact, few areas of Japanese life that were not touched and colored by the Processions of the Lords.

(The inn featured in the novel *The Japanese Inn*, by Oliver Statler, was one of these Post Station inns on the Tokai-Do.)

PROSTITUTION / BAISHUN (By-shune)   Prostitution was legal in Japan until April 1, 1956. On that date, prostitution houses and the women who worked in them were given a one-year grace period to get out of the business. It had long been an honorable profession in Japan, just as it was and is in many other Eastern, as well as Western, countries.

The Japanese had some advantages, however, because sex and sin were not related. Engaging in premarital or extramarital sex was not a moral issue in Japan. For much of Japan's history, there were strict sanctions against promiscuous sexual behavior by the common people, but among nobles and the privileged *samurai* class, such affairs were commonplace.

In later centuries, however, particularly during the long and peaceful Tokugawa Shogunate (1600–1867), entertainment quarters and other areas of assignation for all classes abounded. Each city had one to a dozen or more licensed red-light districts and often a similar number of unlicensed, or blue-light, districts.

In addition, inns within the towns and cities and along the great walking highways commonly served as houses of assignation.

Tokyo's famous Yoshiwara and entertainment quarters of Kyoto in particular were colorful, exciting places that inspired many of the arts that flourished during the Tokugawa Period.

As in other countries, prostitution in Japan was closely related to economics. In bad times, young girls were regularly sold to prostitution houses, and others chose the trade as the only occupation open to them.

The movement to prohibit legal prostitution in Japan was primarily the work of a number of women who were elected to the Diet (Japan's Parliament) just after the end of World War II. Enough male members went along with the women because they were concerned about the bad press Japan was getting around the world.

Naturally enough, prostitution did not disappear from Japan, but there is no doubt that it was considerably diminished by the new law. As in the U.S. and elsewhere, it is now practiced by call girls, attendants in massage parlors, and by thousands of women involved in the entertainment trades. See MIZU SHOBAI.

PROVERBS / KOTOWAZA (Koe-toe-wah-zah)   Like people everywhere, the Japanese have their favorite proverbs, and, because of their very long history, traditions of oral literature, and the cultural infusions from China—which is even older—they seem to have more than the average.

Some of their favorites:

Akujo no fuka-nasake.
Ugly women are more passionate.

Akusai wa hyakunen no fusaku.
A bad wife is 100 years of bad harvests.

Atama hagetemo uwaki wa yamanu.
Philandering is not stopped by a balding head.

Au wa wakare no hajime
Meeting is the beginning of parting.

Bijin ni toshi nashi.
Beautiful women have no age.

Binbonin no ko takusan.
Poor people have many children.

Deru kui wa utareru.
A protruding nail gets hammered down.

Edo no kataki wo Nagasaki de utsu.
Take revenge at an unexpected place.

Go ni irite wa go ni shitagae.
When in a village, do as the villagers do.

Hanzai no kage ni onna ari.
There is a woman in the shadow of every crime.

Hito wa mikake ni yoranu mono.
People are not what they appear to be.

Horeta youkume ni abata mo ekubo.
To a lover, pockmarks are dimples.

Hyakubun ikken ni shikazu.
Hearing 100 times is not as good as seeing once.

I no naka no kawazu, takai o shirazu.
A frog in the well does not know the ocean.

Jigoku no sata mo kane shidai.
Even the judgment of hell depends on money.

Ju yoku go o seisu.
Win by yielding.

Kane areba baka mo danna.
With money a fool can be a lord.

Kanemochi kenka sezu.
Rich people do not fight.

Kunshi hyohen.
A wise man changes his mind.

Makeru ga kachi.
He who is defeated wins.

Musume o miru yori, haha o miyo.
Look at the mother instead of the daughter.

Nyobo to tatami wa atarashi ho ga yoi.
Wives and *tatami* are better when new.

Sake wa honshin o arawasu.
People reveal their true selves when drunk.

Shojiki mo baka no uchi.
Being too honest can be foolish.

Suezen kuwanu wa, otoko no haji.
It is shameful for a man to refuse a woman when
she offers herself to him.

Tabi no haji wa kakisute.
Travelers are shameless.

Wa-kon Yo-sai.
Western knowledge with Japanese spirit.

PUBLIC OPINION   The Japanese government, as well as private research organizations, regularly take public opinion polls to see what the Japanese think about themselves, Japan, and numerous other subjects.

A recent poll concerning their attitudes about Japan showed that the average Japanese took special pride in the long history and traditions of the country, the hard-work ethic and talent of the people, the beauty of the land, the high level of culture and the arts, the high educational standards, the inherent kindness of the people, economic prosperity, the high level of science and technology, social stability, the people's sense of duty, and national unity—in that order.

Reactions to a survey about prevailing moods were more mixed but indicative of the times. Asked to list their positive moods, the people named feelings of peacefulness, stability, vigor, comfort, cheerfulness, a sense of responsibility, solidarity, and compassion—in that order.

On the negative side, the things that most bothered people were irresponsibility (of others), egocentrism, too rapid changes, restlessness, unease and irritability, feelings of discontinuity, languor, and gloominess—in that order.

Nearly 45 percent of all Japanese consider themselves in the upper middle class, and 35 percent consider themselves in the lower middle class. Over four percent say they are in the lower upper class, and one percent rank themselves as upper class. Eight percent say they are in the upper portion of the lower class, and about three percent say they are in the lower portion of the lower class.

PUBLICATIONS IN ENGLISH ON JAPAN   One of the best sources for information about books, magazines, and other informational materials on Japan is International Marketing Corporation (IMC), IPO Box 5056, Tokyo 100-31, Japan, or, Pacific Subscription Service, P.O. Box 811, FDR Station, New York, NY 10150.

IMC handles many books and magazines directly as a subscription and export agent and also publishes two annual catalogues on the books and magazines published in Japan in English by over 1,000 publishers. See OTHER SOURCES.

PUBLISHING / SHUPPAN (Shupe-pahn)   Japan has one of the world's largest and most varied publishing industries. Each year some 30,000 different books and thousands of magazines are published, with the total number of copies well in excess of one billion.

In recent years, books in the social sciences have led the industry, with some 7,000 titles, or about 22 percent of the total published. Literature was next, with around 6,000 titles, or 20 percent of the total, followed by art, technology, natural sciences, juveniles, history, philosophy, industry, language, general, and academic reference books.

Altogether, Japan has 4,300 book publishing companies (and there are approximately 12,200 book stores in the country). There is a Books-on-Japan-in-English Club, which involves 45 leading publishers that produce books in English, along with five printing companies and three book exporting companies.

Japanese book publishers participate in international exhibits around the world each year.

Some 3,000 magazines and other periodicals are published in Japan, with the largest number in engineering (approximately 5,000), followed by economics and statistics (some 250), medicine and hygiene (170), education (160), literature (185, including 15 on *tanka* poetry and 30 on *haiku*), and children's magazines (110).

Other leading categories include foreign affairs, household affairs, agriculture/stock raising/forestry and fisheries, fine arts, sports, general literature, general interest, social sciences, business, and traffic and communications.

The total number of magazine copies printed in Japan each year is well over three billion.

The four biggest women's magazines in the country are *Fujin Kurabu* (*Ladies' Club*), *Shufu no Tomo* (*Housewives' Friend*), *Fujin Seikatsu* (*Ladies and Living*), and *Shufu to Seikatsu* (*Housewives and Living*).

The leading general readership monthly magazines include *Bungei Shunju* (literally *Literary-Art Spring-Fall*), *Chuo Koron* (*Central Review*), and *Sekai* (*World*).

There are some 50 magazines published in English in Japan, ranging from professional journals and business publications to cultural and religious magazines. See BOOK PUBLISHING; OTHER ENGLISH LANGUAGE SOURCES; MAGAZINES.

QUALITY / HINSHITSU (Heen-sheet-sue)   Japan's reputation for the quality of its products has swung from one extreme to the other.

In the sixteenth century, most Japanese exports were folkcrafts and handicrafts of such high quality that they often qualified as masterpieces.

When Japan began industrializing in the 1870s, all the Western-type products it made were imitations—and usually cheap imitations, at that. Western importers who flocked to Japan from this period until the beginning of World War II—and again soon after the war ended—had one primary interest in mind: price.

Import houses and especially major American retail chains like Sears and Wards bought huge quantities of consumer merchandise from Japan strictly on the basis of price. Their buyers controlled the quality of the goods they bought by setting the price they would pay.

As the first editor of a pioneer English-language trade journal covering Japanese-made consumer merchandise for export, first called *Oriental America* and then *The Importer*, I was to witness this interplay between Japanese manufacturers and Western importers thousands of times from the mid-1950s until 1962.

To the Japanese, who had been imbued with traditions of quality for generations, much of the merchandise they turned out for American and European markets—at the behest of foreign buyers—was not fit for sale in Japan.

By the late 1950s, the Japanese had begun to turn this situation around. They began upgrading the quality of their products despite pressure from foreign importers to keep both the quality and price down.

Within a decade, Japan was world-famous for the quality of almost everything it exported and was recognized as the leader in a number of product categories. One of the reasons Japanese manufacturers were able to achieve this remarkable position so rapidly was that they began doing their own selling abroad, bypassing importers who were mostly interested in making big money fast.

QUALITY CONTROL (QC)   Much to their surprise, the Japanese suddenly became famous for their quality control in the 1970s—surprised because they imported the concept of quality control from the U.S. between 1945 and 1950.

During the early years of the U.S. Military Occupation of Japan, the U.S. Army introduced the principles of statistical quality control to Japanese industry. Dr. W.E. Deming, an American quality control authority who had written extensively on the subject, was invited to Japan to help spread the idea.

In 1949, the Union of Japanese Scientists and Engineers (JUSE) established a Quality Control Research Group and began holding seminars on the subject. That same year, an Industrial Standardization Law was passed, and the use of the Japan Industrial Standards (JIS) mark on certain products became law.

The Japanese Standards Association (JSA) was founded and began research in QC methods. In 1950, JUSE began publishing a magazine called *Standard Quality Control*, and JSA began publishing *Standardization and Quality Control*.

In 1951, the Deming Prize for Application was established, followed in 1953 by the Ministry of International Trade and Industry Prize and the QC Literature Prize in 1954.

But there were problems. First, QC tended to rely on excessive statistical methods and formality in standardization. Second, QC primarily involved only top management.

In 1954, Dr. J.M. Juran, another American QC expert, was invited to Japan to help rationalize the Japanese approach. He emphasized that quality control had to be applied on all levels of management to be successful.

For the next five years, Japanese industry adapted the Deming and Juran approaches to fit their own environment, involving top managers, as well as supervisors and workers. In 1960, National Quality Month was started, and the Q Flag and Q Mark were established.

In 1962, the first QC Circles were organized, and publication of a magazine called *Genbato-QC* (*QC for the Foreman*) was inaugurated. Next came CWQC, or Company-Wide Quality Control, and the Japanese were on their way to creating a revolution in both the concept and practice of quality control that would impact on the rest of the world in the 1970s and '80s.

A Quality Circle is a group of five to ten people—made up of a leader, who may be a manager, foreman or worker—that acts independently of management to improve product quality, productivity, human relations, and the talents and skills of the individuals involved. There are presently over one million QC in Japan, and there are numerous annual activities to promote their growth and effectiveness.

QC Circle Conferences are held over 100 times a year throughout the country. October and November are quality control promotion months. A QC Control Headquarters with eight regional branches, established by JUSE, coordinates quality control activities throughout the country. One of the secrets of the success of quality control in Japan is the fundamental Japanese business philosophy that learning and training are an unending process that continues from the first day an employee enters the company to the day of retirement. Some companies retrain their top management every three years and their middle management every five years.

From the early 1960s until the beginning of the 1990s, the Union of Japanese Scientists and Engineers was looked upon as the world leader in Total Quality Control technology and processes, and set the standards for manufacturers worldwide.

During the 1980s thousands of American and European companies took the Japanese lesson to heart and began emulating their Japanese counterparts. They then went on to create their own system of quality control under the banner of the International Standards Organization (ISO), founded in 1987.

By the early 1990s the ISO's 9000 product quality approval certificate had become so important in the U.S. and European markets that Japanese manufacturers began seeking ISO certification and downplaying the role of the JUSE. The standards were translated into Japanese and published as the Japan International Standards Z 9000 (JIS Z 9000) in 1991.

In 1993 the Japan Accreditation Board for Quality System Registration (JAB) was established under the sponsorship of thirty-nine Japanese business organizations. By the end of that year JAB had certified 367 Japanese companies as complying with ISO 9000 requirements. Another 233 Japanese companies had already received certification abroad.

Shortly thereafter some Japanese companies and industrial organizations began withdrawing from the JUSE in favor of the ISO system, which emphasizes documentation and top-down responsibility, instead of the Japanese way of unwritten rules and worker responsibility.

Since the founding of the Japan Accreditation Board, the number of Japanese companies being certified has been running in excess of 200 companies each year. Trade media reports suggest that the ISO system will eventually replace the TQC system as Japan's primary method for controlling product quality.

RACE / JINSHU (Jeen-shuu)   Since most Japanese babies are born with a blue mark known as the Mongolian spot at the base of the spine, it is apparent that the Japanese are primarily an Asian Mongoloid race.

Paleolithic stone implements and human bones found in Japan show that the islands have been inhabited for over 10,000 years—probably for a much longer period—by a Mongolian people as well as by a Caucasian people known as Ainu (See AINU).

Recent research indicates that these early Mongolian people were the true ancestors of the present Japanese and that later migrations of Koreans, Chinese, and people from Southeast Asia were absorbed by these first settlers.

Except for mixtures between Japanese and the Ainu (who originally inhabited Hokkaido and the main island of Honshu, if not the other islands, as well), along with intermarriages with other non-Asian races, all Japanese have Mongoloid features, from the color of the hair and the epicanthic fold of the eye to skin coloration.

Within these boundaries, the Japanese vary widely in appearance. See JAPANESE.

RACE RELATIONS / JINSHU KANKEI (Jeen-shuu khan-kay-e)   Japan is an island nation that has been isolated from the rest of the world for most of its history. With the exception of the Ainu, the Caucasian aboriginal race that apparently first settled in the islands, the Japanese are also one of the most homogenous of any national groups.

The Japanese, over their centuries of virtual isolation, also developed a singular culture and ethnic viewpoint that resulted in them compulsively distingushing between themselves, other people, and non-Japanese.

These factors conditioned the Japanese to be even more conscious of race than are most Westerners. This consciousness, along with cultural traditions that proclaimed their superiority, has resulted in numerous incidents of racial discrimination in the past.

At the same time, a very limited exposure to other races and a philosophy of tolerance and acceptance serves to reduce the impact of racial bias in Japan. However, the non-Japanese in Japan, including Chinese and Koreans, are always made to feel foreign, to feel out of place—even when the reception is positive.

This attitude persists among the Japanese even when the foreigner is totally bilingual, was born and raised in Japan, and is familiar with the Japanese way of doing things. Fortunately, this attitude is generally benign.

RADIO BROADCASTING / HOSO (Hoe-so)   A public demonstration of radio broadcasting was staged in Nagoya in 1919 by the *Shin Aichi Shimbun*, but the first officially founded broadcasting company was the Tokyo Broadcasting Station, which began operating on March 22, 1925, as a semi-government corporation. This is the date now celebrated as Broadcasting Day.

This company was followed in 1926 by the Osaka Broadcasting Station and the Nagoya Broadcasting Station, all three of which were to merge into Nippon Hoso Kyokai, the predecessor of today's NHK.

Japan began overseas shortwave broadcasting in 1935, and thereafter radio was to play a key role in the country's history.

New postwar laws opened the way for the rapid growth of Japan's broadcasting industry from 1951 on.

Today broadcasting is a major industry in Japan. There are 1,018 radio broadcasting stations, including 504 medium-wave stations, 491 FM stations and 23 short-wave stations. Among the medium-wave stations, 315 are owned by the Japan Broadcasting Corporation (NHK), a public broadcasting network financed by the government and monthly fees paid by TV owners directly to NHK.

There are 48 commercial broadcasting companies in the country, with a total of 189 stations. NHK also owns 484 of the country's FM stations. The other seven are owned by commercial companies. And, finally, NHK's Radio Japan arm owns 21 of the 23 short-wave radio broadcasting stations.

NHK's major broadcast facilities are in Tokyo, Nagoya, and Osaka, with local stations spread throughout the country. Most of its programs are planned and produced in Tokyo at the corporate headquarters, but some are done by local stations.

NHK is known worldwide for the quantity and quality of its documentary programs. It hires top directors, writers, and photographers and sends them all over the world to do films on every imaginable topic. Its short-wave broadcasts in foreign languages, covering cultural, economic, and social subjects, are also highly regarded.

NHK devotes approximately 39 percent of its broadcast time to news, 25 percent to cultural topics, 25 percent to entertainment, and 2 percent to education.

The corporation is able to get virtually all of Japan's top entertainers to appear at least once and often several times a year on special shows, without charge or for just token fees.

RAILROADS / TETSUDO (Tate-sue-doe)   The first railway in Japan was opened in 1872 between Shimbashi (Tokyo) and Yokohama, under the supervision of British engineers. Today there are some 30,000 kilometers (18,000 miles) of railways.

A major change was made in 1987 when the government privatized the huge, money-losing Japan National Railways, breaking it up into 11 regional companies, and charging them with the responsibility of both improving their service and making a profit. These 11 companies, known collectively as the Japan Railways (JR) Group, provide long-distance as well as local commuter service, while dozens of other pre-existing private lines provide short-distance and commuter service.

For statistics buffs, the combined JR Group has some 5,300 stations throughout the country, and carries over seven billion passengers a year.

Japan is famous for its so-called Bullet Trains, which were first inaugurated in 1964 and were the fastest (127 mph) and most efficient trains in the world. Some of the newer Bullet Trains cruise at 136 mph. In Japanese, the Bullet Trains are referred to as the *Shinkansen* (Sheen-khan-sen), or New Trunk Lines.

All of Japan's railways are often crowded well beyond their rated capacity. Some coaches carry more than twice the number of passengers they are designed for, during morning and evening rush hours. In winter, when people wear heavy overcoats, the crowding on local commuter trains especially is so intense that station platform attendants are employed to push protruding passengers far enough inside to get the doors closed. On frequent occasions, the pressure of densely packed commuters pushes windows out.

Despite the overcrowding, Japan's railroads are probably the most efficiently run in the world and are famous for their incredible punctuality. They normally leave from and arrive at stations within one to 10 seconds of their schedule.

RAIN / AME (Ah-may)   All areas of Japan, except for Hokkaido, the northernmost island, have a hot, humid rainy season, called *baiu* (by-uu) or *tsuyu* (t'sue-yuu), which begins in early June and ends around mid-July.

There is a well-defined typhoon season from August through October during which the southwestern half of the islands—including the Tokyo area—are regularly hit by storms that include a considerable amount of rain.

It rains frequently in between the rainy season and typhoons, but most of these periods are brief, and in the summer, fall, and winter there are frequent dry spells that last for several weeks.

Generally speaking, winters on the Pacific side of Japan are relatively dry, with many clear (but often windy) days. In the central mountainous areas and on the Japan Sea side, winters are marked by heavy snowfalls.

The average rainfall in Tokyo is 1,503 millimeters. The wettest month, October, has an average of 320 mm. The driest month, December, averages 43 mm of rain. Rainfall in Tokyo during the June-July rainy season is regular but relatively light.

Experienced visitors to Japan often take a raincoat regardless of the season, but they will normally buy umbrellas there only if they need them (they are plentiful and readily available around transportation terminals).

RANKING   Japan has been described as having a vertical society, meaning that people—and things—are ranked according to seniority (which may be determined by a number of factors).

Generally speaking, most ranking in Japan today is based on length of time in school, in a company or organization, and in position. Age is also an important factor, both personally and professionally.

Also generally speaking, all promotions in Japan—business and professional —are based on a time factor rather than ability or performance until one reaches the higher echelons of management. Then, and only then, in most cases, are individuals selected on the basis of personal ability and accomplishments.

This fundamental attitude permeates the Japanese system and contributes enormously to the cooperative spirit of Japanese employees and the low turnover rate in companies. To advance their economic and social level, they must generally stay with the same employer.

The promotion system in most Japanese companies is very much like that in the military. Everybody enters the company on the lowest level and must spend a specific number of years in a grade before being advanced to the next higher position.

It is also customary in Japan to rank companies according to their annual sales, paid in capital and/or market share, and number of employees. This ranking tendency carries over into other areas of Japan's economic and social life, including the height of buildings, towers, and so on.

When the Tokugawa Shogunate fell in 1867, the new government set up a system of noble ranks for the various members of the Imperial family and hereditary Court nobles and *daimyo*. There were 16 grades or ranks in the court peerage, originally based on the steps of the staircase at the Imperial Palace on which the nobles took positions on formal occasions.

The peerage system was abolished at the end of World War II in 1945.

RAW FISH / NAMA ZAKANA (Nah-mah zah-kah nah)   Certain types of raw fish are considered a delicacy among the majority of Japanese and have long been an important part of the national diet.

Raw fish is generally eaten as *sashimi* (sah-she-me), sliced fish, or as sushi (sue-she), slices of raw fish on vinegered buns of rice, after it is dipped in *shoyu*, a soy sauce.

People who literally turn up their noses at *sashimi* or *sushi* do so because they presume it will both smell and taste bad. Many of those who have the courage to try raw fish Japanese style find that it does not have a dead-fish smell and does not taste bad. Both the smell and taste are new, but once many people get beyond their hangups about raw fish they become aficionados.

If you want to extend the pleasures of your palate with *sushi* or *sashimi*, try *maguro* (mah-guu-roe) tuna first. It has a mild, almost sweet taste that is refreshing.

RECEPTIONISTS / UKETSUKE (Uu-kate-sue-kay)   Many large office buildings in Japan, as well as department stores, have receptionists or information clerks stationed in the main lobby or near their main entrances.

This is especially important because almost no Japanese company office has an in-office receptionist. When you walk into the door of a company you are more often than not right in the middle of a bunch of desks, and no one in the office is specifically responsible for taking care of visitors.

In smaller buildings that do not have lobby receptionists, you have no choice but to go right into the middle of things and, once in, signal your presence (by bowing) to who ever looks up and notices you. See *How to Do Business in Japan*, by Boye Lafayette De Mente (NTC Business Books).

Where there are *uketsuke*, proper etiquette requires you to identify yourself and give the name of the person or department that you have business with to the receptionist. He or she will call the individual concerned and announce your presence.

REISCHAUER, EDWIN O.   The only American ambassador to Japan who spoke Japanese, internationally known educator and author Edwin O. Reischauer was born in Tokyo on October 15, 1910, to American missionary parents. He was graduated from the American School in Japan in 1927 and then went on to take degrees from Oberlin College and Harvard University. He then spent a year each at Tokyo University, Kyoto University, and in Peking, China.

Reischauer then taught Japanese history at Harvard. When World War II broke out, he joined the State Department and later the U.S. Army. He was discharged from the army in 1945 as a Lt. Colonel and rejoined the faculty of Harvard.

In 1961, Reischauer was appointed American ambassador to Japan, a post he was to hold until August 1966. Reischauer and his Japanese-American wife were one of the most popular American diplomatic couples ever to serve in Japan.

Reischauer's books include *Japan Past and Present; The United States and Japan; Translations from Early Japanese Literature; Wanted: An Asian Policy; East Asia: The Great Tradition; Japan: The Story of a Nation;* and *The Japanese.*

RELIGIONS / SHUKYO (Shuu-k'yoe)   The Japanese are frequently referred to as being Shintoists, Buddhists, Christians, and so on, but they are also often described as being nonreligious. The truth of the matter is that the Japanese are poly-religious. They practice some tenets of several religions

(The Great Todai Temple, Nara)

as part of their everyday lives, without thinking of the practices as being religious or belonging to any particular religion.

This approach to religion appears to derive from the influence of Shintoism, the native religion, which grew out of a naturalistic reverence for all things, with cleanliness, fertility, and paying proper respect to the spirits of all things as its foundation.

Shintoism was not an exclusive or predatory religion. There was no written liturgy, and it did not seek converts. It was simply a way of life—one that included the concept of selfless love for everybody and everything. See SHINTOISM; BUDDHISM; CHRISTIANITY; CONFUCIANISM.

Japan's shrines, temples, and churches are listed according to classifications set by the Religious Judicial Persons Law, which gives religious organizations legal standing.

Shinto shrines, Buddhist temples, Christian churches, monasteries, and similar organizations that have facilities for worship fall under a category called *tan'i hojin*, or "unit corporations." Sects, denominations, churches, orders, dioceses, and similar organizations that have jurisdiction over the units listed in this category are called *hokatsu hojin*, or "comprehensive corporations."

There are presently 85,000 Shinto shrines and organizations in the country, approximately 77,000 Buddhist temples and related organizations, over 3,000 Christian churches and their affiliates, and 15,500 others.

Some 98 million Japanese are followers of Shinto, 88 million are counted as Buddhists, about one million are described as Christian, and nearly 14 million are listed as "Other." This adds up to more than the population of Japan because many people are listed in more than one category.

The history of Buddhism in Japan is so intimately integrated with the culture, politics, and society in general that they cannot be separated. Shintoist rites constituted the nucleus of government functions until the eighth century, when it was supplemented by Buddhist rites, and again from 1868 until 1945, when it was the state religion of Japan.

Between 710 and 794, six different Buddhist schools of thought were introduced into Japan. During the Heian Period from 794 to 1185, two famous Japanese monks, Dengyo Daishi and Kobo Daishi, laid the foundations for what was to become true Japanese Buddhism.

Dengyo Daishi established the Tendai sect at the Enryaku Temple on Mt. Hiei, north of Kyoto, and Kobo Daishi established the Shingon sect on Mt. Koya, south of Nara. These two places are now regarded as the birth-places of Japanese Buddhism.

There were to be numerous other sects of Buddhism formed in sub-sequent centuries, including Jodo, Rinzai, Soto, and Nichiren in early times and Reiyukai, Rissho Kose-kai, Tenrikyo, Seicho no Ie, Sekai Kyuseikyo, and PL Kyodan in more recent years. Among the most important of these earlier sects was Zen Buddhism, introduced from China by the noted monks, Eisai and Dogen. Eisai founded the Rinzai sect, Dogen the Soto sect.

Zen was to have a profound, seminal effect on Japan's history from the thirteenth century on, helping shape the core of *samurai* ethics and philoso-phy and influencing both the nature and quality of the feudal government, along with the total culture of the country.

RESTAURANTS / SHOKUDO (Show-kuu-doe)   There are nearly 1,200,000 places in Japan in which one may eat out, making Japan one of the restaurant capitals of the world and providing a special ambience that is a major part of the attraction of visiting and living in the country.

These eating establishments include restaurants, noodle shops, *sushi* shops, *ryotei* (Japanese-style restaurants), cabarets, nightclubs, bars, beer halls, coffee shops, and other places that are not easily classified.

There are over 840,000 places classified as restaurants, including over 26,000 noodle shops, 50,000 *sushi* shops, approximately 13,000 *ryotei*, 162,000 coffee shops, and over 30,000 others.

These places range in size from tiny closetlike shops offering one spe-cialty to department-store-size buildings with dozens of specialties and styles offered on the different floors.

Japan has some of the best Chinese restaurants, some of the best steak houses, and some of the best French restaurants to be found anywhere. Within the range of traditional Japanese food restaurants are hundreds that have a nationwide reputation for the quality of their food. See DINING OUT and FOOD.

There are some eight or nine categories of Japanese restaurants, depend-ing on your definitions, and at least a dozen other specialty-type restaurants. The main restaurant categories include: *osoba-ya* (*ya* means shops), *koryori-ya*, *shokuji dokoro*, *sushi-ya*, *chuka ryori-ya*, *shokudo*, *kissaten* (coffee shops), *nomi-ya* (drinking places), and the specialty restaurants.

Osoba shops are usually modest in size and price and are one of the most common type of restaurants in Japan. They usually feature several Japanese noodle dishes and several Chinese noodle dishes. There are five types of Japanese noodles.

Soba noodles, which originated in Japan, are long, brownish-gray noodles made of buckwheat flour and are square shaped, instead of round. They are served in a hot soup stock garnished with bits of meat and vegetables—or cold, with a soy sauce.

Udon noodles, long and white and made from flour, are fat and round. *Hiya mugi* noodles are long, thin, white noodles made from wheat flour and served chilled in the summer. *Somen* are also long, thin, white wheat flour noodles, generally served in a bowl of chilled water in summer. In the Osaka area, *somen* is called *kishimen*.

Chinese noodles, long, thin, and light yellow, are made of flour, eggs, and a mineral water called *kansui*. They are served boiled or fried in many different dishes, each with its own distinctive appearance and additional ingredients.

The more popular dishes include *chashu men* (noodles in pork bouillon, with slices of pork and a few pieces of spinach or other green vegetable); *gomoku soba* (noodles in a pork broth with a few pieces of meat, fish cake, bits of vegetables, half a boiled egg, and a few other odds and ends).

Sushi shops are regarded as the most distinctively Japanese of all the different types of restaurants in the country. They serve the famous raw fish and other types of seafood on top of buns of rice that have been delicately flavored with vinegar, sugar, and salt. See SUSHI.

Koryori-ya restaurants are usually small and often have a folkcraft decor, along with private or semiprivate *tatami*-mat rooms for individual parties. They serve a variety of fish and vegetable dishes prepared in the traditional way. Some of these restaurants are exclusive and expensive.

Shokuji dokoro are small, less expensive versions of the *koryori-ya*, and are sometimes called *meshi-ya* (places to eat). They usually have a counter and a few tables, with a limited menu of more popular dishes.

The *chuka ryori-ya* are modestly decorated, inexpensive, neighborhood, Japanized Chinese-style restaurants that mostly serve rice and noodle dishes (not Peking Duck and all the other specialties). They are found in virtually every commuter station and neighborhood shopping district.

The popular *shokudo* restaurants are sometimes described as cafes or mixed restaurants because they offer a variety of Japanese, Chinese, and Western dishes in an inexpensive setting. Like most nonexclusive restaurants in Japan, they have wax models of their dishes on display.

Japan's speciality restaurants come in all sizes and price ranges and are named after the food they serve. The smaller, less expensive ones include *odenya, okonomiyaki-ya, onigiri-ya*, and *yakitori-ya*.

Restaurants specializing in *kamameshi* (rice mixed with meats and vegetables cooked in a pot), *tempura, tonkatsu* (pork cutlets), and *unagi* (eel) are likely to be larger in size and higher priced.

Next come *sukiyaki, kani* (crab), *teppan yaki* (beef and vegetables cooked on an open grill), and *kyodo ryori*, or restaurants that specialize in regional dishes.

Both *nomi-ya* (drinking places) and *kissaten* (coffee shops) offer a variety of snack-type foods, with the latter generally being Western-style.

The most elaborate and generally most expensive traditional Japanese meals are served in the exclusive *ryotei* (rio-tay-e) restaurants, which look more like inns than restaurants. All meals are served by appointment in private Japanese-style rooms. It is necessary to have an introduction to make a reservation at some of these places.

This summary just begins to touch on the variety of restaurants and foods in Japan.

In addition to traditional and contemporary Japanese-style restaurants, Japan also boasts some of the best Western-style restaurants in the world, including French, Greek, Chinese, Indian, German, and American styles.

Tokyo, Yokohama, Kobe, and Osaka are world-renowned for their steak houses, which serve the famous Kobe or Matsutaka beef.

For a fine introduction to traditional Japanese foods, see *Eating Cheap in Japan—The Gaijin Gourmet's Guide to Ordering in Non-Tourist Restaurants,* by Kimiko Nagasawa and Camy Condon (Shufunotomo Co. Ltd.).

RETAIL CHAIN STORES   Retail chain stores are one of the mainstays of Japan's mass consumer market. The top 10 chains, which together have nearly 900 branches, do a significant amount of Japan's total retail business.

The top 10 chains are Daiei (Die-eh), a supermarket chain that is by far the largest retail operation in the country (well over one billion yen in annual sales); Ito Yokado (E-toe Yoe-kah-doe), Seiyu (Say-e-yuu), and Jusco, all supermarket chains; Mitsukoshi (Meet-sue-koe-shie), Japan's leading department store chain; Nichii (Nee-cheee), a supermarket chain; Daimaru (Die-mah-rue), a department store chain; Takashimaya (Tah-kah-she-mah-yah) and Seibu (Say-e-buu), both department store chains; and Yuni (Yuu-nee), the smallest of the supermarket chains.

RETIREMENT / INTAI (Een-inn-tie)   Soon after 1945, the retirement age in Japan was more or less officially set at the age of 55. At that time, the average life span of the Japanese was a little over 60.

As the standard of living went up and the life span increased, pressure to extend the age of retirement beyond 55 also grew. By the early 1980s, 40 percent of Japan's larger firms had advanced their retirement age to 60. Others have set their retirement age at 58, and the overall tendency is for other companies to push theirs upward.

Since the wages paid by Japanese companies rise, almost automatically, with seniority, the aging of the work force beyond 55 is a serious problem. Retirement benefits also increase dramatically with seniority; so the longer an employee has been with a company, the heavier the financial burden the company must bear.

In a company that is capitalized at 500 million yen or above and has 1,000 or more employees, a retiring employee may receive a lump-sum payment amounting to 40 times the monthly salary at the time of retirement—or nearly three and a half years of pay. Of course, the smaller the company, the smaller the retirement allowance is likely to be.

Most Japanese companies that have more than 30 employees have mandatory retirement systems. In the large, major firms, 99.5 to 99.9 percent of the companies have mandatory retirement. In medium-size companies (100–999 employees), from 93.7 to 98.3 percent require their employees to retire at specific ages.

The smaller the company, however, the higher the mandatory retirement age is likely to be. Some 40 percent of companies with 30–99 employees have 60 as their retirement age. Over 30 percent of those with 100–299 employees also keep employees until they are 60. Only 25 percent of those with 300–999 employees, 23 percent of those with 1,000–4,999 employees and 28 percent of those with 5,000 employees or more have 60 as their retirement age.

In order to relieve the cost of retirement, some companies require employees to retire at 55 and then hire them back as temporary employees at reduced salaries. Other companies, especially larger ones, also make arrangements for retired employees on the managerial level to go to work for subsidiary firms at lower wages.

Another effect of an older retirement age is that it blocks the promotion of younger people, who have to wait longer for positions to open up.

The combination of the seniority and retirement system in Japan is of course another factor that discourages job changing and works to perpetuate the lifetime employment system.

There is another form of retirement in Japan that is unusual, if not unique, called *inkyo* (een-k'yoe), which originated in old Japan, when retirement was sometimes preferred to the responsibilities of life or office.

In this type of retirement, the head of a family (or company or country) yielded his position to a successor in order to be free to take up other pursuits or just enjoy life. In the case of a number of emperors, *shogun*, *daimyo*, and even common people, the aim was to continue to exercise control from the background without any of the day-to-day responsibilities.

This form of retirement from public life is still common in Japan, especially among politicians and successful businesspeople.

RICE / KOME (Koe-may)   Rice farming with irrigated paddies was introduced into Japan from Korea and China some time during the first centuries A.D., first taking root in Northern Kyushu and then spreading to the Nara plain, where the first Imperial Court emerged. Thereafter, it was to become the primary occupation of the bulk of the population and played a seminal role in the development of Japan's economic, social, and political systems.

The cooperative approach to farming required by the massive irrigation of rice fields is credited with being a primary factor in molding the distinctive character of the Japanese.

Until 1868, rice was the basic economic unit in Japan, very much like the role that gold played in Europe in earlier days. The size (tax obligations, political clout, and social standing) of Japan's feudal fiefs was expressed in terms of how many *koku* (koe-kuu) of rice the land produced. (One *koku* = approximately five bushels.)

Rice, historically the centerpiece of Japan's economy, is still the staple food and of vital importance to the well-being of the country. As technology has advanced, however, the number of Japanese farm families engaged in the production of rice has dropped dramatically since 1945.

The per capita consumption of rice peaked at 118.3 kilograms in 1962, and domestic production could not meet the demand. But advances in rice-growing technology during the 1960s resulted in over-production and government controls, established in 1971.

In addition to limiting the acreage for rice planting, the government began buying all of the rice legally produced in the country at a greatly subsidized price and then selling it to wholesalers. This system resulted in the price of rice in Japan ballooning to around five times that of the world price.

By 1990 the annual per capita consumption of rice had dropped to 70 kilograms. In 1993 bad weather wiped out over half of Japan's annual rice crop, which resulted in a severe shortage and a decision by the government, vehemently opposed by the country's rice farmers, to import rice to make up for the shortfall.

This action heated up the debate about Japan's controversial policy of limiting rice production, subsidizing its price, and prohibiting rice imports. By the mid-1990s, annual consumption per person was down to around 60 kilograms, the overall rice paddy area was below 700,000 hectares, and there were increasing calls for the government to deregulate the industry.

At present, some 5 percent of the population is engaged in farming, which is characterized by the small size of individual farms. Japan's rice-producing potential is given as around 13.6 million tons, but until the early 1990s, annual production was around 10 million tons, which was two million tons more than the market could absorb each year.

In the meantime, the per capital consumption of rice in Japan continues to fall, as the younger generations find bread more to their liking.

RIKUGI GARDEN / RIKUGIEN (Ree-kuu-ghee-in)   One of the most famous landscaped gardens in Tokyo, the Rikugien was designed by feudal lord Yoshiyasu Yanagisawa (1658–1714) in the early 1700s. The garden includes a large pond with an island and a hill covered with a dense grove of trees.

A teahouse on the hill is said to have been a favorite resting place of the fifth Tokugawa *shogun*, Tsunayoshi, as well as other high officials of the early eighteenth century.

The garden was given to the city of Tokyo by Baron Kyuya Iwasaki, the head of the great house of Mitsui, in 1934. It is located a short distance from Komagome Station on the Yamanote Line.

Only a short walk from Rikugien is the Oriental Library (Toyo Bunka), a branch of the National Diet Library, which has nearly half a million titles, primarily dealing with Asia.

RIVERS / KAWA (Kah-wah)   Rivers in Japan, of which there are many, are mostly short and fast-flowing because of the mountainous terrain and limited size of the country's plains. The longest river in the country, the *Shinano* (She-nah-no), is only 367 kilometers (228 miles) long. It begins in the mountains northwest of Tokyo and flows into the Japan Sea at Niigata, on the west side of Honshu.

The four other longer rivers in Japan are the Tone Gawa, which flows through Gunma and Chiba prefectures and is 322 km long; the Ishikari Gawa in Hokkaido, which is 268 km in length; the Kitakami Gawa in Iwate and Miyagi prefectures, 249 km; and the Kiso Gawa in Nagano and Aichi prefectures, 227 km.

Because the majority of Japan's rivers drop from great heights very quickly, they provide considerable hydroelectrical power, and have carved out canyons and gorges that are unsurpassed anywhere in the world for their scenic beauty. But only a few of Japan's rivers can be used, for short distances, as waterways.

There are a number of other rivers in Japan that are far more famous than those mentioned above—in particular, the ones that flow through major cities, such as the Sumida (Sue-me-dah) in Tokyo, and the ones flowing between the Tokyo area and the Kyoto area that travelers had to cross in order to reach these cities and all those in between.

During the long Tokugawa Period (1600–1867), the shogunate prohibited the construction of bridges as a means of military control, thus making it necessary to cross rivers by boat or on foot.

Because of heavy rainfall during the annual rainy season and also during the typhoon season, all these rivers were subject to frequent flooding, making passage dangerous or impossible. Ferry boat and palanquin stations developed on the banks of all of the larger of these rivers, offering their services to travelers who chose not to ford the streams on foot—or to swim them during flooding.

Among the most famous of these rivers were the Shinagawa and the Tamagawa, which separated Edo (Tokyo) from all the main cities of the southwest.

ROADS / DORO (Doe-roe) Japan has a total of 1,105,000 kilometers of roadways, of which only about 45 percent are paved. Over 95 percent of the country's national highways are paved, however, as are 83 percent of the prefectural roads.

Japan's first expressway (freeway), the Meishin Expressway, was completed in 1965. This was quickly followed by the Tomei Expressway, the Chuo Expressway, and others. The country's expressways currently total over 3,000 kilometers and are steadily being expanded.

The story of Japan's roads is the story of the country to a degree far beyond the usual expectations.

In the seventh century, Japan was divided into eight administrative regions —one in the vicinity of Kyoto, the capital, called *Kinai* (kee-nie), or Within the District, and seven in the country at large, called *Do* (Doe), or Circuits, each of which was made up of six to fifteen provinces.

Main highways were built radiating out from the capital to the regional headquarters of each of these eight regions to facilitate travel and the transportation of rice and other produce. Government officials in charge of transportation were stationed on each of these roads.

The roads to the seven Circuits were given names based on the areas they passed through—names that were to become famous in Japanese history thereafter.

They were the Tokai Do (Toe-kie Doe), or Eastern Seaboard Highway; the San-in Do (Sahn-inn Doe), or Japan Seaboard Highway; the Sanyo Do (Sahn-yoe Doe), or the Inland Sea Highway; the Saikai Do (Sie-kie Doe) in Kyushu; the Nankai Do (Nahn-kie Doe) in Shikoku; the Hokuriku Do (Hoe-kuu-ree-kuu Doe), on the Japan Seacoast side of central Honshu; and the Tosan Do (Toe-sahn Doe) in northern Honshu.

By the 900s, these roads were divided into three classifications—Great Roads, Medium Roads, and Minor Roads. One of the Great Roads, called Sanyo Do, went from Kyoto to Kyushu and was the most important road in the country at that time. There were post stations along these roads, with a post station master and staff, every 30 *ri* (about 72 miles), which maintained horses for use by officials (common people were not allowed to ride horses as transportation). Stations on the Great Roads kept 20 horses; those on Medium Roads, 10; and those on Minor Roads, 5.

As early as 710, the government ordered local lords to plant trees along the roads in their domains, and Buddhist priests made a practice of building rest-houses along the roads.

When Kamakura became the military capital of Japan in 1192, the Tokai Do, or Eastern Sea Road from Kamakura to Kyoto, replaced the Sanyo Do as the most important highway in the country.

In 1557, Nobunaga Oda set up national standards for the roads, requiring that main roads be three *ken*, two *shaku* (five and a half meters) wide. Secondary roads were to be two *ken*, two *shaku* wide; and minor roads, one *ken* wide. Oda also ordered local *daimyo* to plant pine or willow trees along the roads and instituted a system of distance markers along the highways.

When Ieyasu Tokugawa became *shogun* in 1603 and made Edo (Tokyo) the new seat of government, he ordered that all distances in the country were to be measured from Nihon Bashi (Nee-hone Bah-she), or Japan Bridge, in the center of the city, and the Tokai Do, Nakasen Do, Oshukai Do, Koshuikai Do, and Nikkokai Do quickly became the most important highways in the country.

The Tokugawa Shogunate then ordered that major roads be widened to 10.8 meters, secondary roads to 5.4 meters, lanes and horse paths to 3.6 meters, walkways to 1.8 meters, and field paths to 0.9 meters. The *shogun* had milestones placed every *ri* (about 2.3 miles) along the roads.

Tokugawa also ordered the planting of more trees, and on the heavily traveled Tokai-Do he stipulated that 100 horses and 100 men be maintained at post stations. The Nakasen-Do stations were to have 50 horses and 50 men; the Nikko-Do and other roads, 25 horses and 25 men.

Because of the importance of these great roads to the provincial lords who had to travel to Edo every other year by law (See PROCESSIONS OF THE LORDS), the shogunate assigned a special magistrate to administer the affairs of each one. There were toll barriers at different places along the roads, and the fees charged to travel them were high. To avoid these tolls, common people and merchants often used the unofficial minor roads that ran through the mountains.

There were 53 posting stations on the Tokai-Do, the most traveled of all the highways. These stations were immortalized by the famous Ukiyoe artist Hiroshige Ando, after he made a trip in 1832 from Edo to Kyoto as a member of an official party to present a horse to the emperor. Hiroshige called his series of prints *Gojusan Tsugi*, or *Fifty-three Posting Stations*.

Most of these famous stations are now cities or towns. Among those that are still prominent are Shinagawa, Kawasaki, Kanagawa, Hodogaya, Totsuka, Fujisawa, Hiratsuka, Oiso, Odawara, Hakone, Mishima, Numazu, Yoshiwara, Okitsu, Kuwana, Yokkaichi, Seki, Sakanoshita, Ishibe, Kusatsu and Otsu.

Japan entered the era of modern, high speed, toll expressways in 1959 with the formation of the Tokyo Expressway Corporation and by 1973 had 10 major freeways in operation. Many more have since been added.

ROBOTS / ROBATO (Roe-bah-toe)   Japan's robot population at the beginning of 1985 was over 100,000—the largest in the world. It has been growing by robotic leaps and bounds since. The first industrial robot in Japan was not made there, however. It was imported from AMF of the U.S. in 1967.

The progress of Japan's robots and their impact on industry is covered by a company called Survey Japan, which publishes *The Japan Robot News*, a quarterly newsletter. Survey Japan is located at 61 No. 6 Building, 4-5 Kojimachi, Chiyoda-ku, Tokyo, 102, Japan.

There is also a growing volume of robot literature by Japanese authorities, available from Survey Japan and from other publishers. Some of the Titles: *Robot Revolution* (Nihon Keizai Shimbun), *Robots* in the Japanese Economy (Survey Japan), *Industrial Robot* (Nihon Keizai Shimbun), *The Practical Manual of Industrial Robots* (Shin Gijutsu Kaihatsu Center).

In early 1983, scientists at Nippon Telegraph and Telephone Public Corporation announced that they had developed a robot that could read the news with 99.5 percent accuracy.

Described as half computer-half humanoid, the scientists said the robot was able to deliver sentences with the proper inflections.

In 1984, RRM Corporation of Osaka produced what will likely become the forerunner of home servant robots. Their four-foot, seven-inch "maid," is appropriately trademarked "Family Robot." Besides sweeping, cleaning, and performing other chores, the robot also acts as a security guard.

Major robot manufacturers in Japan include Matsushita Electric Industry Co., Kawasaki Heavy Industries Co., Yasakawa Electric Manufacturing Co., Dainichi Kiko Co., and Star Seiki Co. Others that are rapidly expanding their production include Hitachi Ltd., Mitsubishi Electric, Nippon Electric, and Fanuc Ltd.

Altogether, there are over 120 companies manufacturing robots in Japan, and the country produces an estimated 60 percent of the world's robots.

RONIN (Roe-neen)   Literally "wave men," *ronin* refers to *samurai* who became masterless during Japan's feudal age and to high school graduates in present-day Japan who fail to pass entrance examinations to universities.

In feudal Japan, when *samurai* lost their masters because of war or politics or because they were discharged for some offense, they were in a serious predicament. They could not go into commercial business, and other *Daimyo* in the country were unlikely to take them on because their loyalty would always be questionable.

Many of these men roamed the country, looking for odd jobs—hiring their deadly swords out to unscrupulous lords, merchants, and others—or becoming highway robbers.

The more turbulent the times, the larger the number of *ronin* there were likely to be and the more mischief they were likely to get into.

There are many stories of *ronin* whose high values prevented them from resorting to unethical or illegal ways of making a living. For such men, suicide was often the only way out. There were also some who practiced a kind of extortion on the more kind-hearted *daimyo*.

These *ronin* would present themselves at the mansions of these lords, and ask permission to use a corner of their garden in which to commit *harakiri*. The *ronin* expected the lords to take pity on them and give them a sum of money.

A favorite theme of *chambara* movies is the good-hearted, but desperate, *samurai* who unknowingly goes to the villa of a mean-hearted lord. The lord readily gives the *ronin* permission to kill himself and then orders his retainers to make sure he does—even though he has pawned his real sword and must use one made of wood to saw open his stomach.

The most famous historical event involving *ronin* is one of the great dramas of Japan. See FORTY-SEVEN RONIN.

Applying the word *ronin* to high school graduates who fail to get into the university of their choice is both poetic—in a sad way—and satirical. Some students are lucky and remain *ronin* for only a year. Others fail the university examinations year after year and remain in limbo like the less fortunate *ronin* of an earlier age.

ROPPONGI (Rope-pong-ghee)   The Roppongi area of Minato Ward in Tokyo, on a low hill a short distance from downtown, is one of the city's several dozen famous entertainment areas. What makes this one different is that it is especially popular among foreign residents and is a gathering place for well-known Japanese movie and television stars.

Roppongi has more restaurants, bars, nightclubs, cabarets, teahouses, snack shops, and discos than many countries have. At night, it literally throbs with the sound of people enjoying themselves—and with other people who go there to watch people enjoying themselves.

There are several dozen foreign-style restaurants in Roppongi, including a number owned and operated by foreigners.

SADO ISLAND (Sah-doe)   The fifth largest of Japan's major islands, Sado lies in the Japan Sea off the coast of Niigata and is part of Niigata Prefecture. Only 857 square kilometers in land area, Sado has a population of around 100,000. Two parallel mountain chains divide it but provide a fertile plain in between where rice is grown.

Isolated in the cold waters of the northern Japan Sea until recent times, Sado is famous in Japanese history because it was used as a place of exile for political figures, including one emperor, Juntoku (1197–1242), whose forces were defeated by the Regent Yoshitoki Hojo when the emperor tried to overthrow the Kamakura Shogunate and regain real power for the throne.

The island is also noted for its *okesa* (oh-kay-sah), or ballad songs, the Japanese crested ibis (found only on Sado), and its gold mines—which have been worked since the discovery of gold there in 1601. During the Edo (Tokugawa) Period, the mines were worked by prison labor. They became Imperial property when the shogunate ended in 1867.

Sado is now a popular tourist destination in the summer.

SAGA (Sah-gah)   Saga, the capital of the prefecture by the same name, is now known as a distribution center for rice and other agricultural products. Historically, it is noted as the castle town of the famous Nabeshima clan and for the man who was *daimyo* of the clan when the Tokugawa Shogunate fell in 1868 and the *daimyo*/clan system was abolished.

This memorable figure was Naomasa Nabeshima (1814–1871), better known as Kanso, who played a leading role in the movement to restore Imperial authority to Japan, primarily by selecting and championing exceptionally able young men for the new government.

The two best known of Nabeshima's proteges were Count Taneomi Soejima (1828–1905) and Marquis Shigenobu Okuma (1838–1922), who became leading statesmen of their time.

Saga is also known for its annual mid-October Menfuryu festival, which has been sponsored by the Saga and Matsubara shrines since around 1475. Youths wear goblin masks and dance in the streets to the music of gongs and drums.

SAIGO, TAKAMORI (Sie-go, Tah-kah-moe-ree)   One of the most important leaders in the movement that brought about the downfall of the Tokugawa Shogunate and the restoration of Imperial power in Japan in the 1860s, Takamori Saigo, from the powerful Satsuma clan in Kyushu, was made a Marshal of the Imperial army in 1872.

But Saigo soon broke with the government over its policy of intervention in the affairs of Korea and retired to Kagoshima.

There he founded a school to train young men in political and military science. The Meiji government, sure that Saigo was preparing for a rebellion, tried unsuccessfully to lure him to Tokyo.

Finally, in February 1877, Saigo took command of Kagoshima and then marched toward Kumamoto. He and his army of 15,000 men were met on the road by an army sent out from Kumamoto. His forces were victorious and laid seige to the city. But after several battles, reinforcements sent in by the Meiji government from all over Japan forced him to retreat to Kagoshima.

Imperial forces surrounded Kagoshima, and the final battle took place on September 24, 1877, at Shiroyama. Saigo was wounded and his army was routed. He had one of his retainers, Shinsuke Beppu, behead him.

Despite the fact that he had revolted against the Imperial government, Saigo was regarded as a hero for his role in ending the Tokugawa Shogunate and was much admired for his courage and loyalty to his ideals. A huge statue was erected in his honor in Ueno Park in Tokyo, and in 1922 his son received the title of Marquis.

SAKE (Sah-kay)   *Sake*, or rice wine, has been brewed in Japan since the beginning of Japanese civilization, and it was the only alcoholic drink known in the country until the introduction of wines and whiskeys by foreign traders in the sixteenth century.

In early Japan, the brewing and drinking of *sake* was closely related to Shintoism. Every community shrine had its own rice paddies, and it was the rice from these fields that was made into *sake*—which in its earliest days was a gruel that was eaten.

After *sake* had been further refined into a clear liquid, it was still considered a special offering to the gods, but as time passed it became common to drink it at parties and banquets not associated with shrine rituals.

To make *sake*, the rice is washed, soaked, and then steamed until well done. Then yeast and fresh spring water are added to induce fermentation. After fermentation, the wine is separated from the rice residue by running it though a press. The wine is then filtered and placed in large vats, where it settles and becomes clear.

The alcoholic content of *sake* taken from the upper portion of the vat is from 12 percent to 14 percent. That taken from the lower, turbid portion has up to 17 percent or 18 percent alcohol, while that distilled from the dregs, called *shochu* (sho-chuu), ranges from 50 percent to 60 percent alcohol.

A sweetened variety of *sake*, called *mirin* (me-reen), has from 9 percent to 21 percent alcohol.

Sake, graded on the basis of taste, color, and aroma, comes in three grades —*tokkyu* (first grade), *ikkyu* (second grade), and *nikkyu* (third grade)—which are also used for taxing purposes. The first two grades must pass a sensory test by government inspectors and are taxed at 150 percent ad valorem.

Sake is also categorized as sweet (*amakuchi*) or dry (*karakuchi*)—both of which are derived from a combination of five tastes: sweet, sour, astringent, pungent, and bitter.

There are several standard sizes for *sake* bottles, but one of the most popular holds 1.8 liters or almost half a gallon, of the potent brew. It is normally served in small, rounded pitchers called *tokkuri* and drunk from tiny, thimble-sized cups called *sakazuki*.

In *sake*-drinking etiquette, those who pour their own or allow their drinking companions to pour their own are considered unlettered or impolite. You fill the other persons's cup, and they fill yours. Your cup should always be picked up and held in your hand when the other person is pouring.

If someone offers you more *sake* and your *sakazuki* is still full, etiquette requires you to at least take a sip from it and then hold it out for refilling. (The same goes for beer drinking).

It is common practice for women to place an honorific "O" in front of *sake*, i.e., *O'sake*. More polite men may do the same. Several districts in Japan have been noted for the quality of their *sake* since ancient times, including Nada (in Kobe), Akita, Nagano, and Hiroshima.

During the fermentation process, the mixture—bubbling and making sounds—seems to be almost alive. A visit to a *sake* brewery is quite an experience (the aroma permeates the area for many blocks in all directions).

Popular *sake* brands include Hakutsuru (White Crane), Ozeki, and Gekkeikan.

The Gekkeikan brand of *sake*, brewed by Okura Shuzo Company of Kyoto, was originated in 1637 under the auspices of a *samurai* family. During the long reign of the Tokugawa Shogunate, it became a favorite of the *samurai* class and still today is one of the most prestigious brands in the country.

Altogether, there are some 2,600 *sake* brewers in Japan and around 4,000 brands.

Besides its popularity as a social drink, *sake* has traditionally been used for medicinal benefits, as well. It is also used in cooking, as a polish for pine furniture and fingernails, and as a skin conditioner.

SAMURAI (sah-muu-rie)   From the latter part of the Heian era (794–1185), warriors were called *bushi* (buu-she), a term that had been introduced from China. In earlier times, court officals who waited upon the emperor were known as *saburo-bito*, from the word *saburo*, which means "to serve" or "wait upon." *Bushi* assigned to guard the emperor came to be known as *saburai*.

By the thirteenth century, hereditary warriors, as well as officials serving princes, court ministers, and other persons of high rank, were called *saburai*.

Originally, this word referred only to higher class warriors and court officials. Eventually it was changed to *samurai* just to make it easier to pronounce.

Japan's famous class of *samurai* warriors was further strengthened by an institution established in 1185 by Yoritomo Minamoto, a few years before he set up the country's first shogunate government.

Achieving military success in the country, Yoritomo obtained permission from the emperor to establish a system of *shugo* (shuu-go), or "guards," for all of the districts and provinces as a means of keeping order.

The position of *shugo* gradually became hereditary and consolidated the development of an elite class of professional warriors. As the generations passed, these warrior families became clans and grew to be more powerful than the hereditary lords they served (most of whom were descendants of noble families from Kyoto). These *shugo* gradually came to be known as *samurai* (which is another reading for "guards"). They developed a code, based on Confucian and Zen Buddhist principles, that came to be known as *bushido*, or the Way of the Warrior. This code was to dictate virtually every aspect of their lives and influence the total culture of the country until modern times.

The essence of the *samurai* code was total loyalty to their feudal lord; a willingness to give their lives in the defense of their lord, his honor, and their own; a strict regimen of martial training; and a sternly refined etiquette that governed their actions and behavior in all things.

Part of the code of the *samurai* was to commit suicide rather than be captured in war or dishonored by failure. The code of the *samurai* applied to the women, as well as the men, in this elite class.

One special category of *samurai* were the *hatamoto* (hah-tah-moe-toe), the higher ranking warriors who were the *shogun's* personal guard. During the Tokugawa Shogunate (1600–1867), the *hatamoto* were direct vassals of the *shogun*, and their annual revenue was fixed at a minimum of 10,000 bales of rice.

After the privileged class of *samurai* was abolished in 1868, the word *shizoku*, which is the Chinese pronunciation of the same word, was substituted and extensively used until 1945, so that former *samurai* families were still distinguished from the common people.

Even today, in some rural areas of Japan, the descendants of *samurai* feudal lords are treated with special respect reminiscent of the Tokugawa Period, which officially ended in 1867.

Recommended reading: *Hagakure: The Book of the Samurai*, by Tsunetomo Yamamoto, translated by William Scott Wilson (Kodansha International).

SAN BONAVENTURA The *San Bonaventura* was apparently the first Japanese ship to cross the Pacific Ocean. Reportedly built under the supervision of Will Adams, the English pilot who had become an adviser to *Shogun*

Ieyasu Tokugawa, the ship was dispatched in 1613 by Masamune Date, the Lord of Sendai, under the command of one Rokuemon Hasekura (with a Franciscan priest aboard as interpreter and guide).

Lord Date's purpose in sending the ship eastward is not known, but it is presumed that he was interested in the wealth and power that had come into the hands of the lords on the southern island of Kyushu and wanted his own foreign contacts.

The ship, with a crew of 68 Japanese and Portuguese, left Tsukinoura in what is now Miyagi Prefecture on September 15, 1613, took the Great Circle route along the Aleutian Islands (where they must have frozen), skirted the California coast, and four months later arrived in Acapulco.

From Acapulco, the ship made its way to Seville, Spain, arriving in November 1614, where Hasekura and his mission were given an audience by the King of Spain. (He was later baptized as a Catholic.) After three months in Seville, the *San Bonaventura* called on numerous ports in the Mediterranean, arriving at Naples, Italy, in November 1615.

In Italy, the Japanese were greeted by Pope Paul V, and Hasekura's portrait was painted for the Vatican archives. What happened from this point on is unknown, until Hasekura arrived back in Sendai near the end of 1620, presumably having circumvented the globe.

Japan had changed a great deal while Hasekura was gone, and, despite the rich gifts and books he brought back to his master, he was ordered to renounce the Christian faith. He refused, was forced to retire, and remained under house arrest until he died of natural causes two years later. Twenty years later, his son Tsuneyori, who had also become a Christian, was put to death by Tadamune Date, the son of Hasekura's master, Masamune. See DATE, MASAMUNE, PORTUGUESE IN JAPAN, ADAMS.

SAN MON (Sahn Moan)   Entrances to the grounds of Buddhist temples are marked by gates (*san mon*), some of which are very large and elaborate —so large and elaborate that visitors to Japan sometimes think the gate is the temple. The gates to Buddhist temples are quite different from Shinto shrine gates. See TORII.

SCENIC TRIO   Japan has three areas that are so beautiful that they have been known and celebrated since ancient times—Amanohashidate on the Japan Sea side of Honshu, west of Kyoto; Matsushima, near Sendai in northeastern Honshu; and Miyajima, near Hiroshima. See individual listings.

SCIENCE CITY   Until the 1960s, Tsukuba was a cluster of small rural towns set amidst farms and pine groves 37 miles from Tokyo. It has since been transformed into a bustling Science City, with a population of thousands of scientists, engineers, technicians, and their families.

Tsukuba is now the home for 43 governmental and four private research institutes, along with two universities, representing 40 percent of Japan's research effort.

Research projects at Tsukuba include such fields as lasers, robotics, bionics, and sophisticated electronics.

Several hundred foreign scholars and technicians are conducting research at Tsukuba, and the city is visited each year by thousands of scientists, government officials, and the curious from around the world.

Manufacturing plants are banned in the Tsukuba area, as are such distractions as *pachinko* parlors, but the city has 94 parks and plazas and numerous pools and pedestrian walkways for the benefit of its residents.

SEASCAPES / KAIHIN (Kie-heen)　Altogether, Japan has 16,120 miles of seacoast that alternates among white-sand beaches bordered by groves of gnarled pines, precipitous cliffs also clad in pines, lagoonlike bays dotted with emerald islets, secluded coves and inlets bounded by jagged walls of stone, caves, natural bridges and gates sculpted from fantastic rock formations.

Offshore, Japan is ringed by a necklace of islands sitting in blue water, adding to seemingly unending stretches of coastline so beautiful that many visitors find themselves intoxicated by the sight.

SEASONS / KISETSU (Kee-sate-sue)　The spring, summer, fall, and winter seasons are very pronounced in Japan, particularly as you go northward. In the Kanto and Kinki districts of central Honshu, where the bulk of the population lives, the spring months are March, April, and May—sometimes lapping over into June. Summer begins in June, when the rainy season ends, and officially goes through August. As far as temperatures are concerned, it is still summer until the latter part of September, especially in the lowland areas.

Fall really begins in late September and usually ends in mid-November. Naturally, the further north you are, the earlier winter begins and the longer it lasts. In Hokkaido, it generally begins snowing in October, while southern Kyushu is still enjoying warm days.

SEATING ETIQUETTE   There is a specific place of honor in a Japanese-style room that determines the order of seating of guests. This seat of honor, called *kami-za* (kah-me-zah), is the one in front of and nearest to the *tokonoma* (toe-koe-no-mah), or beauty alcove.

The chief guest sits with his or her back to the *tokonoma*, with the second-ranking guest on his or her left, and the third-ranking guest on the other side of the room, facing the first guest. The host sits at the lower end of the room —usually nearest the door.

In any situation where two people are sitting side by side, the ranking person is on the left. The wife is always expected to sit on her husband's right.

SEED GENE BANK   In the early 1980s, Japan's Ministry of Agriculture, Forestry and Fisheries founded a seed gene bank called the National Institute for Agro-Biological Resources. The seed gene bank has five subbanks— edible plants, microorganisms, animals, marine plants, and forest plants. The program is designed to make Japan competitive with other nations that have stocks of seed and animal genes as part of their agricultural strategies. Teams are being sent to South America and Southeast Asia to obtain sample genes of plants and animals that are likely to become extinct as a result of enviornmental change.

SEKIGAHARA (Say-kee-gah-hah-rah)   This is the site of the Battle of Sekigahara in Mino Province (now Gifu Prefecture), where, on October 21, 1600, Ieyasu Tokugawa's army of 80,000 men met and defeated Hideyori Toyotomi's army of 130,000 men, thus setting the stage for Ieyasu to become *shogun* three years later.

Hideyori, the son and heir of Hideyoshi Toyotomi, with whom Ieyasu had been allied until Hideyoshi died in 1598, was only seven years old at that time, and the army that fought at Sekigahara was commanded by Mitsunari Ishida, the leading general of the Toyotomi clan.

SELF-DEFENSE FORCES   Japan's military organization, known as Self-Defense Forces (SDF), was formally established in 1954 and consists of a Ground Self-Defense Force (army), Maritime Self-Defense Force (navy), and Air Self-Defense Force (air force).

There are approximately 250,000 uniformed personnel in the three branches of the military (over 60 percent of whom are in the Ground SDF, or army), all of whom are volunteers. Japan has no conscription system.

Japan's constitution forbids the use of its military forces for any purpose other than self-defense against an attack by an outside enemy and the preservation of public order. So far, the SDF has never been mobilized for either purpose.

Besides defense patrols and training maneuvers, the SDF has primarily been used to aid disaster-stricken areas and in construction projects. It is also occasionally used to help in crowd control during athletic events.

The most significant happening in the history of the SDF was the passage in 1992 of the PKO Bill which gave the government authority to send Japanese troops abroad on peace-keeping missions.

The first such mission, to Cambodia in 1993, continued the controversy that marked the "forced" passage of the PKO bill by the Liberal Democratic Party.

A member of a small contingent sent to Cambodia—to help build a road—was killed by an unidentified sniper, creating a national furor in Japan.

SENDAI (Sen-die)   Three train hours north of Tokyo, Sendai is the capital of Miyagi Prefecture and the economic, political, and cultural center of the Tohoku District of northeastern Honshu—an area that was once referred to as Michinoku or The Black Country, because of its severe winters, mountainous terrain, and the difficulties involved in developing it.

These same snowy winters and picturesque mountains, along with distinctive life-styles and characteristics that set its inhabitants apart, now make the Sendai area a popular tourist destination.

During the long Tokugawa Period, Sendai was the headquarters of the famous Date clan. In 1602, Lord Masamune Date built his castle on a hill overlooking the town from the west, following which the town gradually grew into a city.

Masamune was the most powerful *daimyo* in northeastern Honshu prior to and during the Tokugawa era. He was a close ally of Hideyoshi Toyotomi, Ieyasu Tokugawa's predecessor, and when Ieyasu became *shogun* in 1603 he continued this key role with the shogunate.

Masamune was interested in Christianity, and when Ieyasu's successor began to jail Christians in Edo, he obtained the release of the Franciscan priest Luis Sotelo and brought him to Sendai. He also sent his own emissary to Spain and Rome, with Sotelo going along as interpreter and guide.

When he died in 1636, Masamune had the largest fief north of Edo, and Sendai was the leading city in northern Japan.

Although primarily known for its handicraft industries, Sendai was nearly destroyed by bombing raids during World War II. When the war ended, the city took advantage of the opportunity to plan its streets and roads, and it is now one of the most rationally designed cities in the country.

Sendai is surrounded by heavily forested hills, and there are so many wooded areas within the city limits that it is known as the Metropolis of Woods. Its primary industries today are metal, iron and steel products, electrical appliances, rubber, woodenware, foodstuffs, lacquerware, beer, and

O'sake. Products made of a dark brown or black ignite rock called *umoregi*, found in the nearby hills, are a specialty of the city.

Places of special interest in Sendai include the ruins of the Date castle, called Aobajo, or Green-leaf Castle, the Osaki Hachiman Shrine, and a wild-flower botanical garden. Within a short distance of the city are several noted hot spring spas (Akiu, Jogi, Sakunami), the Zuigan Temple, and a pavilion especially designed on a rocky cliff near the Matsushima-Kaigan Pier to view the beauty of the bay (Kanrantei).

The centerpiece of scenic Tohoku is Matsushima, known since ancient times as one of the three most beautiful places in Japan. Matsushima means Pine-Clad Island, but this is a whole bay of islands—260 of them. See MATSUSHIMA.

Before the coming of the Japanese, the Tohoku district was inhabited by a Caucasian race known as Ainu. White of skin, with very large, round eyes and heavy body-hair, the Ainu were gradually driven northward by the Japanese, but intermingling over the centuries produced a mixed race of Ainu-Japanese that is much in evidence in the Sendai area, especially in small towns and villages on the way to Sendai. See AINU.

SEN-NO RIKYU (Sin-no Ree-que)   Probably the best known of Japan's tea masters, Sen-no Rikyu was born in 1521 and lived until 1591, at which time he was forced to commit suicide by Hideyoshi Toyotomi, who had previously been his patron.

Also a noted poet and master of the art of flower arranging, Rikyu was appointed official tea master by Nobunaga Oda, the most powerful *daimyo* of his day and the de facto ruler of Japan, in the 1560s.

When Nobunaga died in 1582, Hideyoshi became his successor and made Rikyu his chief tea master. The roving eye of the Taiko (Great Person), as Hideyoshi was called, also fell upon Rikyu's beautiful daughter. But Rikyu refused to send her to his master, thus incurring his wrath.

Apparently reluctant to attack the famous tea master directly, Hideyoshi bided his time. Sometime later, Rikyu was accused of putting a statue of himself in the temple of Murasakino. Hideyoshi accused him of gross arrogance unbefitting the grand master of tea and invited him to commit *harakiri*.

A request from the Taiko was a command. Rikyu, then in his seventieth year, asked to be allowed to conduct one more tea ceremony before taking his own life. His request was granted—and the ceremony is said to have been one of the best the old master ever conducted.

The essence of the tea ceremony promoted by Rikyu was simplicity and rusticity within very strict standards of beauty and naturalness—a style that is referred to as *wabi-cha* or "rustic tea."

The particular style of tea ceremony originated by Rikyu was split into three schools by his grandsons—and called the Three Houses of Sen. These three schools—Omote Senke, Ura Senke, and Mushanokoji Senke—are still among the most popular tea ceremony schools in Japan today.

The terms *omote* (front) and *ura* (rear) came into use because the older and younger brothers of Rikyu's great-grandsons were teaching the tea ceremony on the same premises in Kyoto, the older brother in the front of the house and the younger brother in the rear. As time went by, the separate locations diverged into separate schools.

In addition to having helped establish the tea ceremony as an important cultural activity, Sen-no Rikyu was also a celebrated master of the art of landscape gardening. See GARDENS.

SETO (Seh-toe)   Forty-five minutes from Nagoya by the Seto train line, Seto City is one of Japan's main porcelain centers.

The first kiln was established there by Toshiro Kato around 1200—after which he reportedly traveled to China to study the art of porcelain making and then went all over Japan seeking a place that had better clay than that of Seto.

Failing to find anything better, Kato returned to Seto and gave birth to an industry that now includes nearly 1,000 factories and well over 1,000 kilns. Visitors to Seto are welcomed in many of the kilns.

SETSUBUN (Sate-sue-bune)   This is the popular Throwing of the Beans ceremony to mark the end of the coldest period of the year on February 4. Going back to ancient times when it was a ritual to ward off evil and ensure good luck, *setsubun* is now practiced at homes, as well as at shrines and temples, which often invite famous movie stars or other personalities to participate in ceremonies that are frequently televised.

Large crowds gather at these places to watch the *Mame-maki* (Mah-may-mah-kee), or Throwing of the Beans, and hopefully catch a few for good luck. When throwing the beans, the thrower calls out loudly: *"Fuku wa uchi! Fuku wa uchi! Oni wa soto!"*—"Good fortune come in! Good fortune come in! Devils get out!"

SEVEN GODS OF GOOD LUCK   In Japanese religious mythology, there are seven gods of good luck who have played an important role in the cultural history of the country. These seven gods are:

BENTEN (Bane-tane), a female deity, usually shown seated on a dragon or serpent and playing a lute, is the goddess of eloquence and the arts.

BISHAMON (Be-shah-moan), the god of war, a wild looking fellow in armor, holding a spear in one hand and a pagoda in the other, does in evil-doers.

DAIKOKU (Die-koe-kuu), the god of wealth, is a smiling old man wearing a hood, sitting on bales of rice, carrying a bag full of treasures over his shoulder, and holding a small mallet.

EBISU (Eh-be-sue), the god of fishermen (and merchants), is a smiling, portly figure in court robes, holding a large red snapper in one hand, with a fishing rod over his shoulder.

FUKUROKUJU (Fuu-kuu-roe-kuu-juu), the god of wealth and longevity, has a short body but long head and beard and is usually depicted holding a stick with a *sutra* scroll tied to it. He is usually attended by a crane or a tortoise, both symbols of longevity.

HOTEI (Hoe-tay-e), the god of contentment and happiness, is a fat fellow with a large, protruding stomach and a happy face. He carries a bag on his back and holds a fan.

JUROJIN (Juu-roe-jeen), the god of longevity, an old man with a long white beard, carries a holy staff bearing a sacred scroll and holds a fan. He is usually accompanied by a stag or a crane.

SEVEN ISLES OF IZU / IZU SHICHI TO (E-zoo she-chee toe)   These seven islands lie off the coast of Izu Peninsula and extend in a chain from the lower reaches of Tokyo Bay southward for some 290 kilometers. The most famous of the islands, all of which are volcanic and are an extension of the chain that includes Mt. Fuji, are Oshima and Hachiojijima. The others are Toshima, Niijima, Kozushima, Miyakejima, and Mikurajima.

Oshima, the largest of the seven islands, boasts a live volcano, a picturesque way of life that goes back for centuries, a mild climate, huge fields of camellia flowers, and a thriving dairy industry. Passenger ferries leave Tokyo for Oshima daily and are almost always crowded with tourists and locals returning home after a visit to the big city.

In ancient times, all the of Isles of Izu were used as places of exile for out-of-favor notables. Two of the most famous of these exiles were Tametomo Minamoto (1139–1170), a famous archer who was banished to Oshima when he was 17, and Hideie Ukita, a feudal lord (*daimyo*) under Hideyoshi Toyotomi, whom Ieyasu Tokugawa defeated at Sekigahara in 1600 and sent to Hachiojima in 1611, where he survived for another 44 years.

SEVERANCE PAYMENTS   It is established practice for Japanese companies to make severance payments to workers who are let go for whatever reason (other than some serious criminal offense). These payments are based on the length of time the employee worked, the basic monthly wage, and the employee's reason for leaving.

Such payments are made when an employee is fired, when a company goes out of business, and when the employee retires. See RETIREMENT.

SEX / SEI (Say-e)   Unlike Christianized countries, Japan has never associated sex with religion or any sense of sin. The Japanese have always recognized sex as a physical action necessary for both procreation and mental and physical well-being—at least for men.

There was, traditionally, a double standard in sexual matters. Premarital and extramarital sex for men was regarded as a natural part of life, but their partners in such liaisons were generally public women who worked in the entertainment trades.

At the same time, romantic liaisons were also common among the upper classes, particularly the nobles. The *shogun, daimyo,* and upperclass *samurai* typically had one or more mistresses.

Until 1956, legal red-light districts flourished in Japan, and most of the thousands of inns around the country functioned as houses of assignation. Today, there are thousands of so-called love-hotels in major cities catering to couples by the hour or by the night.

The Japan Sexual Education Association (JSEA) reports that young Japanese women are becoming more sexually liberated—and attributes this to the emergence of the philosophy of equal rights and the decline of family traditions.

The JSEA said a recent survey showed that 13.4 percent of the females from age 13 to 21 had engaged in sex, while 18.7 of the males in the same age group reported having had sex.

Girls now think and act more freely in sexual matters, the report said.

Sex is one business in Japan that seems to be immune to economic ups and downs. A recent review by Kyodo News Agency of sex-related businesses in Tokyo showed that love-hotels, massage bathhouses, and similar establishments were doing better than ever.

Kyodo said there were about 35,000 so-called love-hotels in Tokyo, which have an average of 20 rooms each and are used by an average of 2.3 couples per day. The total earnings of the Tokyo love-hotels was estimated at three trillion yen the previous year.

SHIKOKU (She-koe-kuu)   The smallest of Japan's four main islands, Shikoku has a total land area of 18,787 square kilometers and is divided into four prefectures—Tokushima, Kagawa, Ehime, and Kochi. The island is traversed by several mountain ranges and has a number of rivers, including the Yoshino (194 km) and the Shimano (145 km).

While not in the mainstream of Japanese life, Shikoku has been populated since the earliest times. The famous Buddhist priest Kukai, known posthumously as Kobo Daishi, was born on the island in 774. He was the founder of or is related to 88 Buddhist temples scattered around the island and famous since the early 1600s as a sacred pilgrimage.

Still today, over 100,000 people a year complete the circuit of the temples —many of them on foot, as it was always done in the old days.

Suffice it to say, Shikoku abounds in historic and scenic places that make it a popular destination for travelers. The island is especially noted for the

(Ritsurin Koen in Takamatsu)

beautiful Awa Odori folk dance, Ritsurin Park in Takamatsu, dogfighting in Kochi, bullfighting in Uwajima, and the hot springs in Matsuyama.

Shikoku is also known for its agriculture, lacquerware, and pottery. See JAPAN.

Recommended reading: *Japanese Pilgrimage*, by Oliver Statler (Morrow).

SHIMABARA (She-mah-bah-rah)   On a gourd-shaped peninsula east of Nagasaki, Shimabara is famous as the place where some 38,000 Christian converts took refuge from a Tokugawa Shogunate army of 120,000 in the early 1600s and, after a siege that lasted for three months, were annihilated.

The peninsula, part of the Unzen Amakusa National Park, is one of the most scenic spots in Japan.

SHIMODA (She-moe-dah)   Near the tip-end of Izu Peninsula on the southeast side, Shimoda is now an important port and fishing base, as well as a gateway for sightseeing and recreational facilities in the area. It is best known in history, however, as the place where Townsend Harris, America's first diplomatic envoy to Japan, lived for more than a year, beginning on September 3, 1856.

Shimoda was also the first port opened to trade with the U.S. by the Tokugawa Shogunate, following the Treaty of Kanagawa, which was signed in 1854.

As it happened, however, designating Shimoda as a trading port was a subterfuge by the shogunate to delay the opening of the country as long as possible. The port was far removed from the population centers and principal roads.

Harris soon found out that Shimoda was useless as a foreign trade port. After he received permission to move the consulate to Edo (Tokyo), in

November 1857, Shimoda was out of the limelight until 1934, when Japanese and American diplomats helped launch an annual festival called Kuro Fune Matsuri, or Black Ship Festival, to mark the arrival of Commodore Perry and his fleet of black warships in 1853.

The festival, held in mid-May each year, is one of the major events on the Izu Peninsula, and attracts members of the diplomatic corps in Tokyo, as well as tourists and Japanese. See HARRIS, TOWNSEND; PERRY, COMMODORE MATTHEW C.

SHIMONOSEKI (She-moe-no-say-kee)   On the southernmost tip of Honshu, across from Kyushu's port city of Moji, Shimonoseki has been a gateway to Honshu, the largest island, since Japan's earliest days. But it owes its fame to two major historical events.

The first of these events was the Battle of Danno-ura offshore and on the beach of the city in 1185, when the Taira (Heike) clan was wiped out by the Minamoto (Genji) clan—a great battle recounted in *Genji Monogatari*, regarded as the world's first novel.

In 1863, the Choshu clan, joining those who wanted to expel the barbarians and keep Japan closed to the outside, fired on ships passing through the straits, and sealed the city off. The following year, a fleet of American, French, British, and Dutch ships retaliated by bombarding Shimonoseki for three days, inflicting heavy damage.

This demonstration of naval power convinced the Choshu leaders that the shogunate should go and that Japan should modernize. They joined the Satsuma clan of Kyushu in opposing the *shogun* and demanding that the emperor be returned to power.

SHINAGAWA (She-nah-gah-wah)   Now an important residential and hotel area, as well as a major commuter train terminal, Shinagawa was known in Tokugawa times as one of the Post Stations on the great Tokai-Do walkway, just outside of Edo (Tokyo). It was the first stop for travelers leaving Edo and the last stop before travelers entered Edo—and was therefore of special importance.

The Kaian Temple in the area was founded by Tokiyori Hojo, the fifth regent of the Kamakura Shogunate, in the thirteenth century. Two of Japan's most famous statesmen, Prince Tomomi Iwakura (1825–1883) and Lord Yoshinaga Matsudaira (1828–1890), are buried on the grounds of the Temple.

A short distance away, near Oimachi Station on the Yamanote Line that encircles central Tokyo, is the tomb of Hirobumi Ito, who played a key role in the drafting of Japan's first constitution (which went into effect in 1889) and was the country's first prime minister. See GEISHA.

The Pacific Hotel, the Takanawa Prince Hotel, and the New Takanawa Prince Hotel are located within walking distance of Shinagawa Station.

SHINJUKU (Sheen-juu-kuu)   Adjoining Chiyoda Ward, which encompasses the Imperial Palace and much of Tokyo's financial and government districts, Shinjuku was originally the site of several huge, feudal lord estates and then developed into a popular residential area because of its higher elevation and proximity to downtown Tokyo.

It is still a popular residential district, but the area around Shinjuku Station, which is one of the largest and busiest commuter terminals in the country, has become a major business, hotel, and entertainment center and is a city within its own right.

Four of Japan's leading department stores—Isetan, Mitsukoshi, Odakyu, and Keio—have stores there, and there are hundreds of restaurants, bars, and cabarets, along with half a dozen movie theaters and other entertainment establishments.

In the 1970s, several huge high-rise buildings were erected on the west side of the station area, including the 225-meter-high Mitsui Building, the highest building in Japan.

Leading hotels in the area include the Keio Plaza, the Century Hyatt, and the Tokyo Hilton.

Shinjuku Station by itself is like a small city, with dozens of shops, restaurants and other facilities within its premises. Well over a million people pass through the eight-story, three-basement station each day.

SHINJUKU NATIONAL GARDEN / SHINJUKU GYO-EN (Sheen-juu-kuu G'yoe-inn)   Formerly the villa grounds of the Naito *daimyo* family, the Shinjuku National Garden is near Sendagaya Station on Tokyo's Chuo Line, close to the city's famous Meiji Shrine Outer Garden.

When the system of feudal *daimyo* lords was abolished in 1868, the grounds became the property of the Imperial Household. After World War II, they were transferred to the state, which opened the garden portion to the public.

The garden is filled with cherry trees and a huge greenhouse that contains orchids and other kinds of subtropical and tropical plants.

In November of each year, chrysanthemum shows are held in the garden and are traditionally attended by the emperor and empress.

SHIN KAMMON TUNNEL (Sheen Kahm-moan Toe-nay-rue)   Completed in 1974, this undersea train tunnel passes beneath the Kammon Straits, connecting the islands of Honshu and Kyushu. The tunnel is 18,675 meters long, making it one of the world's longest undersea tunnels, but only 880 meters of this distance is under the sea floor.

Used exclusively by the famous Shinkansen Bullet Trains, it is 9.6 meters wide and 8.1 meters high.

(Izumo Taisha Shrine)

SHINTO / THE WAY OF THE GODS (Sheen-toe)   The indigenous religion of Japan, Shinto is basically a worship of or paying reverence to all things in nature, including one's ancestors. Shinto teaches that all things, animate and inanimate, have their own *kami* (kah-me)—spirits or gods.

The greater of these *kami* are to be worshipped at *jinja* (jeen-jah), or "shrines." Since there were many gods in the Shinto pantheon, shrines abound in Japan. If one included all the tiny roadside and hillside *jinja*, the number, in earlier years, would probably have been in the millions. Today there are well over 100,000 shrines of all sizes and hundreds of major ones.

From earliest times, Shinto emphasized bodily cleanliness and fertility. One result of this was that the Japanese were among the first, if not *the* first, to invent the hot bath and make it a daily ritual. Another result was the development of religious festivals that were intended both to celebrate and increase human fertility.

Early Shintoism indicated to the Japanese that they were descendants of divine beings and were therefore very special. The emperor was the high priest and governed in the name of the leading deities. In the 1870s, Shintoism was reinstated as the national religion of Japan and its teaching and activities came under the control of the government. The emperor was deified, and people were taught that he was a living god.

At the end of World War II, the state religion was abolished, and Shinto observances became a matter of personal choice. Today the Japanese do not necessarily practice Shintoism as a religion, but many typical and traditional customs are Shintoist—taking newborn children to shrines, performing wedding ceremonies, dedicating buildings, etc.

It is also a popular custom for people to visit famous shrines around the country, especially during the New Year period. All local shrines have their own festivals, which are well attended by people living in the neighborhood —and, if the shrines are famous, by people from all over the country.

One of the dance and music forms that accompanies Shinto ceremonies is called *kagura* (kah-guu-rah), which is performed by young shrine maidens praying for a good harvest.

The best way to tell a Shinto shrine from a Buddhist temple is the *torii* (toe-reee) gate—two upright pillars with a crosspiece on top.

Thus, while few Japanese (only around two million) list themselves as being Shintoists, all Japanese are influenced by and at one time or another follow Shinto precepts.

Some 90 percent of the Shinto shrines in the country belong to the Jinja Honcho, or Association of Shinto Shrines. The association recognizes the Grand Shrines of Ise as the chief shrine in the country. Amaterasu Omikami, the ancestral deity of the Imperial family, is enshrined at Ise. Each prefecture has a shrine board that administers matters concerning the members.

Shinto has no specific founder and has never had an explicit dogma. Because different shrines have different *kami* (gods) and somewhat different teachings, the Association of Shinto Shrines has drawn up and published a set of principles to define Shinto (The Way of the Gods).

The manifesto, called *General Principles of a Pious Life*, states:

"Shinto is the great way of eternal heaven and earth. It fosters a noble spirit and lays the foundation of great peace. Its mission is achieved through revering the merciful consideration of the *kami*, transmitting our ancestors' teachings, manifesting the essence of the way of the *kami*, and promoting the welfare of humanity.

Here are set forth the general principles of the Correct Way, which we will endeavor to practice. We hereby pledge our efforts to enhance the way of the *kami*:

1. By being grateful for the blessings of *kami* and the favor of ancestors, and by devoting ourselves to ritual activities with a pure and sincere heart.

2. By serving the world and other people, and by building and reinforcing the world in the service of *kami*.

3. By embracing the merciful mind of *kami*, by leading a harmonious life, and by praying for the prosperity of the nation as well as the peaceful co-existence and prosperity of the entire world.

Japan has always been a fertile land for the propagation of religous thought, with the exception of Christianity. Despite an enormous amount of effort since the late 1850s, Christian missionaries in Japan have not done well. The humane precepts of Christianity are nothing new to the Japanese, and now that they are free to believe and practice whatever they wish, the other aspects of Christianity appear to hold very little appeal for them.

Total acceptance of Christian dogma virtually requires that one be raised in the religion from young childhood. By the time the missionaries get to most Japanese, it is too late.

Recommended reading: *Shinto: Japan's Spiritual Roots*, by Stuart Picken (Kodansha International). *The Looking Glass God*, by M. Nahum Stiskin (Weatherhill). Stiskin's book delves into the deepest meanings of Shintoism by analyzing the root *kanji* characters originally used to describe it, showing that it is a far more profound and comprehensive body of thought than believed by most Western scholars.

SHIOBARA SPAS (She-oh-bah-rah)   The famed Shiobara spas—there are 11 of them—are located in a V-shaped valley formed by two immense mountains, Mt. Takahara and Mt. Nasu, approximately two-and-a-half hours northwest of Tokyo, in the grand Nikko National Park.

The swift-flowing Hoki River rushes down the valley in a series of cascades that rival those on the Hayakawa River of Hakone. Numerous tributary streams from the two mountain peaks career down deep ravines to join the Hoki River, adding to the indescribable beauty of the area.

These spas were discovered in the ninth century and have been in use ever since, but it was not until the 1870s—after the noted Viscount Michitsune Mishima, then governor of Tochigi Prefecture, had roads built to them— that they began to attract visitors from outside the district.

Among the best known of the Shiobara spas are Oami, Fukuwata, Shinoyu, Shiogama, Monzen, Furumachi, and Oku-Shibara. The inns of Shionoyu Spa are situated along a ridge above the springs; so guests must descend some 100 steps to enter the outdoor baths, many of which are hewn out of natural rocks.

Each of the Shiobara spas is noted for the natural beauty of its setting, and several have their own unique attractions. Among the sights near Oami is a pool of boiling water so deep the bottom has not been found.

SHIPS / FUNE (Fuu-nay)   The Japanese were not known as shipbuilders during the early history of the country, but by the first centuries A.D. they were regularly sailing to Korea and China and, in later centuries, to Southeast Asia.

Encouraged by the shipbuilding knowledge of the pilot Will Adams, *Shogun* Ieyasu Tokugawa had a number of seagoing vessels built in the early 1600s and carried on a thriving trade with the Asian mainland and the islands of Southeast Asia. During the heyday of this trade, from 1604 to 1635, Japanese ships swarmed all over Southeast Asia, going as far as Thailand and Borneo, carrying such goods as rice, pottery, lacquerware, silver, and copper and returning with silk, sugar, sandalwood, leather products, and other items.

Japanese pirate ships also flourished during this period and were feared throughout Southeast Asia.

One of the Japanese sailors who went to Taiwan in 1615—formerly a palanquin bearer for the Lord of Numazu—wound up in Thailand, where he became the leader of the large Japanese community, a trusted adviser and general for the king and married a Thai princess, only later to be poisoned by a jealous opponent.

The life story of this remarkable merchant-adventurer-soldier was made into a movie by Daiei Motion Picture Co. in 1959.

Even after the country closed its doors to the outside world in 1639, coastal shipping was an important part of the Japanese economy throughout the 200-plus years of the Tokugawa era.

Some of the ships plying the coasts of Japan were especially designed to carry specific cargoes—*sake*, rice, and other products.

SHIZUOKA (She-zoo-oh-kah)   On the famous Bullet Train line, midway between Tokyo and Nagoya, Shizuoka City is now noted as the tea-trading center of Japan and the capital of Shizuoka Prefecture, which is also first or second in the production of mandarin oranges in Japan.

In the olden days, Shizuoka was famous not only for its tea and mandarin oranges, but because it was the twentieth Post Station on the fabulous Tokai Do Highway that connected Edo (Tokyo) with Kyoto (see PROCESSIONS OF THE LORDS) and was also the home for 25 years of the great Ieyasu Tokugawa, who founded the Tokugawa Shogunate, and befriended Will Adams, the English ship's *anjin* (ahn-jeen), or "pilot."

During his many years in Shizuoka, Ieyasu lived in the Castle of the Floating Isle, the ruins of which can still be seen. The castle site, surrounded by moats and a stone wall, is now part of a park in the northern part of the city.

Contemplating the scene today, one is able to imagine the splendor and glory of the place when Japan's most powerful man lived there—a place he chose in part because of its outstanding scenic beauty and its healthy climate.

During the days of the Tokugawa Shogunate, Shizuoka—then called Sumpu (Sume-puu)—was strategically important because it served as a western outpost of Edo.

SHOCHU (Show-chuu)   *Shochu*, the "white lightning" of Japan, is distilled from the dregs of *sake*, Japan's national drink. It is the fourth most consumed alcoholic beverage in the country—following beer, *sake*, and various whiskeys and brandies.

Considerably stronger than *sake*, *shochu* was consumed almost entirely by the laboring class until the early 1980s, when it began to catch on as a popular cocktail drink among white-collar workers. It was and still is a special favorite of construction workers.

Another drink popular with some laborers is one called *awamori* (ah-wah-moe-ree), which is now distilled from rice but was originally made from millet (*awa*). It is even stronger than *shochu*.

SHOGUN (Show-goon)   The title *shogun* is a derivative of *Sei-i-tai-shogun*, which translates, more or less, as "Great-Barbarian Subduing General" and was first used around the sixth century to designate generals sent to subdue Caucasian Ainu tribes inhabiting the eastern and northern portions of Honshu.

In 1192, when Minamoto clan leader Yoritomo established himself as the supreme military power in the country, he was given the title *Sei-i-tai-shogun* by the emperor, apparently because it was the highest military title in the land.

The closest English approximation would probably be generalissimo, but in effect it meant that Yoritomo was the military dictator of Japan.

Yoritomo thus became Japan's first *shogun*. Rather then remain in Kyoto, which he saw as an effete society of weaklings, Yoritomo chose Kamakura in distant eastern Honshu for the site of his administrative government, which was called *bakufu* or "camp office." He retired in 1199 in favor of his son, Yoriie, in order to ensure that the position would be passed on to his descendants. Yoriie was succeeded by his younger brother Senetomo, but the latter was assassinated in 1219.

Sanetomo was the last of Yoritomo's family, so the Hojos, the most powerful members of the *bakufu* government in Kamakura, invited Yoritsune Fujiwara, whose family had virtually ruled Japan for the previous 300-plus years, to fill the post of *shogun*.

Yoritsune accepted the invitation, but actual power was in the hands of Yoshitoki Hojo. His descendants were to continue acting as regents for the *shogun* until 1333, when the Kamakura Shogunate fell.

The fifth Kamakura *shogun* was also a Fujiwara (Yoritsugu), but from 1252 on, the Hojos invited Imperial princes to assume the role, while they maintained power. The Imperial prince-*shoguns* were Munetaka (1252–1266), Koreyasu (1266–1289), Hisaakira (1289–1308), and Morikuni (1308–1333).

In 1333, Takauji Ashikaga rose in rebellion and defeated the Kamakura Shogunate, which had been weakened by its defense against the Mongol invasions of 1274 and 1281. He was appointed *shogun* in 1338. His descendants were to rule as *shogun* for the next 235 years—or until 1573.

By the 1500s, the Ashikaga *shoguns*, who set up their government in Kyoto, had lost control of the country, bringing on an age of wars between clan leaders fighting for supremacy.

First, there was Nobunaga Oda (1534–1582), a descendant of the famous Taira clan. In a series of battles, he emerged as the paramount leader but was assassinated by one of his own retainers when he was 49 years old.

Nobunaga was succeeded by Hideyoshi Toyotomi, his ablest general, who went on to consolidate his power over all of Japan. Hideyoshi chose not to assume the title of *shogun*, and when he died in 1598 his son Hideyori was still a young boy.

In the battles that followed Hideyoshi's death, one of his chief allies, Ieyasu Tokugawa, emerged the victor and in 1603 established the Tokugawa Shogunate in Edo (Tokyo).

Fourteen of Ieyasu's direct descendants were to reign as *shogun*—until the year 1867, when the last one, Yoshinobu, abdicated in favor of restoring the emperor to power.

Western contact with Japan began in earnest in the last half of the 1500s, but was to end abruptly in the 1630s when Tokugawa Iemitsu, Ieyasu's grandson, closed the country to outsiders.

Finally, it was the inability of the last four Tokugawa *shoguns* to deal with internal problems and the Western powers that brought the downfall of Japan's last great feudal dynasty. See HISTORY; ODA, NOBUNAGA; TOYOTOMI, HIDEYOSHI; TOKUGAWA, IEYASU; ADAMS, WILL.

SHOTOKU TAISHI (Show-toe-kuu Tie-she)   Revered in Japan as one of its great scholars and most influential cultural figures, Shotoku Taishi was the son of Emperor Yomei, who reigned in the sixth century. Taishi convinced his father that Buddhism did not conflict with Shintoism, the native religion, and thereafter did all he could to propagate the faith, including having the famous Shitenno Temple built in Osaka.

Prince Shotoku became the regent to his aunt, Empress Suiko, during which time he composed the country's first written laws. The prince died in 621. In his later years, he was known as the Prince With Many Wise Ears, because he could reputedly give wise answers to as many as 10 people talking to him at the same time.

Prince Shotoku encouraged the spread of literature and painting, and he was responsible for the construction of so many temples that he is still honored as the patron saint of carpenters. See HISTORY; BUDDHISM.

SHRINES / JINJA (Jeen-jah)   Shinto edifices are called shrines (while Buddhist buildings are called temples). In earliest times, the only Shinto shrine in Japan was the Imperial Palace, where the emperor, reportedly a direct descendant of the Shinto gods who created the islands, lived and where the Three Sacred Treasures (Imperial Regalia)—a Mirror, a Sword, and a Jewel —were kept.

According to Japanese mythology, the Mirror was given by the Sun Goddess, Amaterasu Omikami, to her grandson, Ninigi-no Mikoto, when he came down to earth to reign, with instructions to keep it in the Imperial Palace.

At this time, the emperor himself was the chief high priest, and there was little if any distinction between his secular and religious duties.

In 92 B.C., it was decided that the Mirror might become desecrated by being so close to so many people in the Palace, and it was moved outside of the Palace. Then around the third century A.D., it was decided to move it still further away, and a shrine was built for it at Kasanui, near Nara (which was to become the Imperial Capital in 710).

Eighty-eight years later, the decision was made to build a new, much more elaborate shrine for the Sacred Mirror at a place called Ise on the southeastern tip of the Kii Peninsula—a place that was isolated at that time and known for its extraordinary beauty.

Thus, the shrine built at Ise, called Jingu, which may be translated as Abode of the Gods, became the national shrine of Shinto, where the spirits of emperors went to dwell upon death. See GRAND SHRINES OF ISE.

Then, as the population grew and the Imperial kingdom expanded, it became customary to build branch shrines in other areas. Finally, there was hardly a community in the country that did not have its local Shinto shrine, and there were hundreds of others in distant, often isolated mountain regions —places deliberately sought out for their beauty and isolation, both of which were deemed pleasing to the Shinto gods.

It also became the practice to erect miniature Shinto shrines along roads, at crossroads, wherever auspicious events occurred, and on hilltops or rises, since it was believed that the spirits of things were to be found in high places.

Still today, it is customary for the emperor and other high officials to visit the Grand Shrines of Ise and for events of national importance to be reported to the shrines.

Shinto shrines generally face toward the south and sometimes to the east —never to the west or north, which are considered unlucky. Shrines are almost always accompanied by groves of *sakaki* trees, which are considered sacred, and they are built of lumber from *hinoki*, or Japanese cypress, a tree with an especially beautiful grain that is easy to work with but very durable.

There are now several architectural types of Shinto shrines, but they are always simple and austere when compared to Buddhist temples.

The entrance way to Shinto shrines is marked by a distinctive gateway called *torii* (toe-ree-ee), which consists of two upright posts and two horizontal crosspieces at the top. The materials of the *torii* vary from wood to stone, but the design is always the same—four intersecting lines, three of which are always straight, with the top one sometimes curved in a graceful arc.

In some cases, the *torii* are quite some distance from the shrines themselves —reputedly to give adherents time to compose themselves before they arrive on the sacred precincts of the shrine.

The *torii* were originally bird perches on which live cocks, brought as offerings to the Sun Goddess, Amatersu Omikami, were placed by worshippers. In the beginning, the *torii* were placed on all sides of the shrines. Eventually, when the perches came to be symbolic of shrines, they were made larger and placed only at the front.

At first, the *torii* were made of unpainted wood, but later many of them were painted. Now some of them are made of metal or concrete, and there are some half a dozen different designs.

Another interesting note: Drums have traditionally been associated with Shinto festivals (while bells are associated with Buddhist celebrations).

SHURI-KEN JUTSU (Shuu-ree-ken jute-sue)   During the interclan intrigues and fighting in the sixteenth century, a new weapon that came into use was a small, star-shaped metal disk with very sharp points, called *shuri-ken*, which was used for throwing.

Prior to this, the most important throwing weapons were small swords or daggers. The advantage of the *shuri-ken* was that it required far less skill to throw it effectively, since there were deadly points all around the disc. It was also small, and several of them could easily be carried in one's clothing. The *shuri-ken* became one of the favorite weapons of the *ninja*—the professional agent/assassin families that flourished in feudal Japan.

Special schools were established to teach the art of throwing *shuri-ken* (called *shuri-ken jutsu*). Among the most famous of these were the Yagyu, Negishi, and Shrai schools.

Many of the *ninja, samurai,* and others of this era developed incredible skill with the *shuri-ken.* They were able to throw them from any position or angle with devastating accuracy. They are often seen in present-day *samurai* movies.

SIGNS / KAMBAN (Kham-bahn)   I believe there are more signs in Japan, of one kind or another, than in any other country. The problem for the visitor or tourist is that most of them are written in Japanese *kana* or *kanji* characters. Thus, if you cannot read the language, the signs will not be of much help.

There are, however, many signs that are international in nature and can be readily understood by most people. The following commonly seen signs are provided courtesy of the Japan National Tourist Organization:

Rest Room

Men's Room

Ladies' Room

Information

Ticket Window

Temporary
Luggage Storage

Shopping

Restaurant

Bus

Public Telephone

Taxi

Hand Rail

End Moving
Walkway, 10m

Money Exchange

Coin Locker

Arrival   Departure   Meeting Service   Hand Baggage   Temporary Parcel Storage

Stairway (Down)   Stairway (Up)   No Smoking   Super Express Train Platform   Post Office

Subways (Eidan)   Subways (Toei)   Taxi Stand

SILENT LANGUAGE   Perhaps more than any other people, the Japanese have developed the ability to communicate nonverbally. Indeed, such communication became a high art during Japan's long feudal age. The Japanese acquired this skill primarily because of the extraordinarily refined and restricting etiquette that became the hallmark of behavior in formal situations and in public.

In numerous official and semioffical gatherings, as well as in some public meetings, speech was either prohibited or was severely limited. Even one's facial expression was prescribed, making it difficult or impossible to convey messages or emotions in this manner.

A totally bland, impassive expression was often a major part of the pursuit of social harmony that was so important in Japanese society. Looking directly into someone's eyes, especially a superior, was traditionally considered disrespectful and challenging and could be a very dangerous thing to do.

Among the techniques for communicating silently were using a small folding fan to give different signals, nodding, inclining the head, and moving the eyes. Even clothing can be used to communicate.

So adept are the Japanese at understanding the most inconspicuous movement—or just the hint of something in someone's speech—that many conversations are so abbreviated that they are incomprehensible to outsiders. The homogeneity of their culture gives the Japanese something akin to a herd instinct, which often makes it possible for them to know what other Japanese are thinking—without any exchange of words.

SILK / KINU (Kee-nuu)   Silk has been produced in Japan since the second century B.C., and for a long time the Japanese were the world's largest producers of raw silk.

The two major centers of silk production in Japan today are Nagano and Aichi prefectures, and there is a Silk Center and a Silk Museum in Yokohama.

Until modern times (which began in Japan in 1868), the *kimono* of the *samurai* and nobility of Japan were made of silk. Today most of the silk produced in Japan is exported.

SINGING / UTA UTAU (Uu-tah uu-tao)   Singing folk and popular songs has been an integral part of Japanese culture since the earliest times. Associated with different types of work, festivals, and entertainment, singing is something that everyone is expected to be able to do. Still a major social and recreational activity in Japan, it is taught in the public schools. See FOLKSONGS; KARA-OKE.

SISTER CITIES   Some 150 of Japan's cities have Sister City ties with cities abroad. Usually these ties involve cities that have a number of things in common—size, principal economic activity, etc., and one city may have several such relationships.

Yokohama, for example, has Sister City ties with Bombay, Lyon, Manila, Odessa, San Diego, Shanghai, and Vancouver. Hiroshima's Sister Cities are Honolulu and Volgograd. Nikko's Sister City is Palm Springs. Himeji's Sister City is Phoenix, Arizona.

Others Sister Cities are Okayama-San Jose, Osaka-San Francisco-Sao Paulo-Shanghai, Sapporo-Munich-Portland, Sesebo-Albuquerque, Sendai-Acapulco-Minsk-Rennes-Riverside, Shimoda-Newport (RI), Takamatsu-St. Petersburg, Takayama-Denver, Tokyo-New York, Toyota-Detroit, and Wakayama-Bakersfield.

Sister Cities sponsor cultural and educational exchange programs and otherwise work to develop close, cooperative, and beneficial relations.

SIZE (HEIGHT) SEI (Say-e)   One of the more remarkable changes in Japan since 1945 has been in the average height of the people. In the two decades between 1961 and 1981, the average height of boys at the age of six went from 112 centimeters to 115.9cm. Twelve-year-olds went from 142.3cm to 149.8cm. Fifteen-year-olds went from 161.8cm to 167.3cm, and 17-year olds went from 165.2cm to 169.7cm.

Girls have undergone a similar spurt in average height, with corresponding increases in the average weight of both sexes.

The dramatic change is attributed to better diets, including the consumption of grains other than rice, along with more meat and dairy products. It is predicted by some that the average height of the Japanese will continue to increase until it is comparable to that of other people who eat similar diets.

Today, a very conspicuous percentage of Japanese teenagers, both girls and boys, are approaching the heights found in traditional meat, dairy and non-rice grain-eating societies. The change in the size of younger Japanese is so dramatic that architects and builders of buses, trains, and various personal use items have had to enlarge their standard production measurements.

SKIING / SUKIINGU (Suu-kee-ing-guu)   With its great mountain ranges and wintertime snowfalls, plus the ubiquitous hot springs, Japan is a skier's paradise. There are, in fact, 47 noted ski resorts in the country—three of them in Hokkaido, six in northeastern Honshu, 34 in east-central Honshu, and four in west central Honshu.

In Hokkaido, the ski season starts as early as October at the Mt. Daisetsu ski resort, in November at the Teine Olympia Ski Resort near Sapporo, and in December at the Niseko resort near Kutchan.

On the main island of Honshu, the start of the ski season depends on the altitude and location of the resort, some of them opening in November, but most of them in December.

Among the best-known resorts on Honshu are Akakura, Bandai, Iwappara, Kusatsu, Nikko, Nozawa, Shiga Heights, Yuzawa, Tateyama, Zao, and Mt. Daisen.

Many of the ski resorts are combination hot spring spas, providing patrons with the opportunity to enjoy the best of both worlds. During the ski season, Ueno Station in Tokyo becomes a forest of skis and poles, with as many as 100,000 skiers passing through the station in a 24-hour period.

A complete list of the ski resorts in Japan is available from the Japan National Tourist Organization. See JNTO listing.

SLEEPING MATS / FUTON (Fuu-tone)   Traditional Japanese bedding consists of floor mattresses and quilts called *futon*, sized for the individual, which are placed on the floor at night and stowed in closets during the day.

The *futon* are placed directly on the clean, aromatic reed-mat (*tatami*) floors when needed and folded up each morning—or hung outside in the sun to air out.

Futon are not only comfortable, they are eminently practical, since it is possible to provide sleeping space for additional people just by spreading other *futon* and to make other use of the same room during the day. They are also less expensive than Western-style beds.

Futon are sold in children and adult lengths.

The word *futon* comes from the Japanese pronunciation of the Chinese word for cushions Zen priests sat on. It was brought to Japan by Japanese priests who went to China during the Sung Dynasty (tenth and eleventh centuries) to study Buddhism.

Until that time, Japanese bedding appears to have been straw mats, with coverings made of the same material. The oldest Japanese word for bedding is *yobusuma* (yoe-buu-suu-mah), which means "night dress." As these straw mattresses and quilts were improved, they gradually came to be called *futon*, from the more attractive and comfortable floor cushions imported from China.

SMOKING / TOBAKO WO SUIMASU (Toe-bah-koe oh sooey-mahs)
The pattern of smoking tobacco in Japan is similar to that of the U.S.—the

percentage of men smoking has begun to decline, while more and more women are taking up the habit.

At present, 28 million Japanese males and seven-and-a-half million females smoke. Among adult males, this is one the highest percentages in the world (over 70 percent).

There is a movement in Japan to encourage smokers to give up the habit and to prevent young people from taking up the habit. But the program is far behind that of other countries.

The three most popular Japanese cigarette brands are Mild Seven, Seven Star, and Hi-Lite. Each year, well over 300 billion cigarettes are consumed in Japan. The industry is operated and controlled by the Japan Tobacco and Salt Public Corporation, which was a government monopoly until 1984–85 and is now quasi-private.

Tobacco smoking was introduced into Japan by Portuguese traders who were shipwrecked on the island of Tanegashima south of Kyushu in the early 1540s. See PORTUGUESE IN JAPAN.

SNOW FESTIVAL / YUKI MATSURI (Yuu-kee mot-sue-ree)   One of the biggest and most spectacular winter events in Japan is the Snow Festival of Sapporo, Hokkaido, held each year from February 1 through 5 in Odori Park and at Makomanai.

Hundreds of people spend days carving huge and elaborate snow sculptures, depicting mythological creatures, castles and so on, out of tons of snow. Participants compete for prizes and awards, and the festival attracts visitors from all over the country, as well as from overseas.

SOAPLANDS / TURKISH BATHHOUSES   Bathhouses offering massage services have been popular in Japan from early times. When the great entertainment quarters of Edo fell into disfavor with the shogunate during the early years of the Tokugawa Period (1600–1867), this kind of bathhouse quickly developed into a special category of its own.

The massage baths grew both in size and number and became sex palaces patronized by all the classes that could afford them.

Massage baths, now called Soaplands, still abound in Japan. They are no longer what they used to be, but some of them are larger and quite luxurious by present-day standards, and scantily clad girls are still the featured attraction.

Most of the massage parlor baths (there are over 200 in Tokyo), are in or near well-known entertainment districts. Most of them cater to men, but there are several that welcome both men and women.

In all of them, the routine is similar. The patron is given a steambath, a hot water bath, and then a lengthy massage by a girl dressed in halter-bra and shorts.

Most Soaplands have beer and soft drinks available. Some adjoin restaurants and offer their patrons hotel-type room service. Many of them also launder the patron's underwear while he or she is being administered to.

One of Osaka's largest baths consists of eight stories above ground and two below and includes one floor reserved for women, a huge public bath on the fifth floor, and a garden bath on the seventh floor.

Some of the baths cater to Western clientele and stock their waiting lounges with English-language business publications, such as the *Wall Street Journal* and *Fortune*.

Many of Japan's leading hotels have in-house Soaplands for the convenience of their clients—although these are more likely to be conservative in the special services they offer.

In 1984, the Japanese government received several letters of complaint from Turkish citizens about the custom of calling the "hot-pillow" massage baths "Turkish," regarding it as a slight on their nation. The government and the bathhouse association finally agreed to rename the bathhouses "Soaplands" in 1985.

SOCIAL SECURITY / SHAKAI FUKUSHI (Shah-kie Fuu-kuu-she)   In Japan, Social Security—for those in need who have not reached retirement age or do not receive adequate pensions—is referred to as Livelihood Assistance. At present, one and a half million people are receiving varying amounts of financial support from the government.

People may receive such support if they have suffered an injury or illness, experienced a drastic fall in earned income, attained a certain age, or if they are members of fatherless households.

There are several pension systems in Japan, all under government regulations. They include the plans of private corporations, a national plan covering employees of firms with fewer than five employees (most of which are unincorporated) and self-employed individuals, and the plans of mutual aid societies.

Foreigners resident in Japan can participate in national pension plans.

A study that has been underway for some time has concluded that all the present public pension programs should be integrated into one. This new program would cover everyone, and those over the age of 65 would receive fixed amounts.

Japanese law stipulates that every citizen must have some kind of health insurance, and all come under a national medical care program. Individuals making use of this program pay only a nominal amount when they go to doctors, clinics, and hospitals that cooperate in the program.

SOGORO'S SACRIFICE (Soe-go-roe)   In the mid-1600s, the *daimyo* of the province that is now Chiba Prefecture, Masanobu Hotta, was inexperienced and incapable, and his retainers took advantage of the situation to impose heavier and heavier taxes on the 4,000 or so farmers in the Kozu district.

Sogoro Kiuchi, head man of the village of Kozu, agreed to act as spokesman for the farmers and presented a petition to the *daimyo*, asking that the taxes be reduced. The request was denied. Finally, Sogoro decided that the only way out of the dilemma was to present a petition to the *shogun* himself—an act that was punishable by death.

After saying good-bye to his family, Sogoro went to Edo and waited for an opportunity. In the winter of 1650, the *shogun* went to Ueno to visit the temples there. Sogoro evaded the *shogun's samurai* guards, rushed up to his palanquin and thrust the petition into the hands of the surprised *shogun*.

After reading the petition, the *shogun* ordered *Daimyo* Hotta to investigate the charges and remedy the situation if they were justified. This was done, but Hotta was so angered by the incident that he had Sogoro, his wife, and their two sons—one three and the other eleven—beheaded.

Sogo and his family were buried in the garden of the Tosho Temple in the village by that name, and a sanctuary called the Sogo Reido was built in their memory. In 1753, on the 100th anniversary of their execution, the descendants of the *daimyo* who had brought about their deaths, erected tombstones over their graves. The old sanctuary was replaced in 1921.

The story of Sogoro has been told many times and is the subject of a famous *kabuki* play.

SOKAIYA (So-kie-yah)   The *sokaiya* are minority stockholders in major companies, closely linked with organized crime, who for decades made a profitable business of controlling stockholders meetings by intimidating other stockholders and preventing them from raising questions about the company or its board of directors. They would then charge the companies substantial sums of money for this so-called service.

A revision of the country's commercial codes in 1982—the first since 1950 —went a long way toward eliminating the power of the *sokaiya*, but they were not expected to give up so easily, and predictions were that they would find some other way to stay in business.

These predictions were accurate. By 1984, there was ample evidence that most of the corporations listed on the Tokyo Stock Exchange were once again paying the *sokaiya* off in under-the-table arrangements.

In the early 1990s new, more stringent regulations were passed in an effort to control the activities of the *sokaiya*, and there are indications now that more and more companies are refusing to deal with stockholders connected to crime syndicates. There are an estimated 5,000 *sokaiya* groups in the country.

SONY   One of the most impressive of Japan's postwar industrial miracles, the company that is now known worldwide as Sony was founded in 1946 by two young ex-navy men, Masaharu Ibuka and Akio Morita.

The fledgling Sony empire began in a bombed-out store in a suburb of Tokyo, with 500 dollars Morita borrowed from his *sake*-brewing father. The new company was named Tokyo Tsushin Kogyo Kabushiki Kaisha, or Tokyo Communications Industrial Co. Ltd.

In 1956, the company was still struggling, but it was on the verge of a major breakthrough. Using new, American-invented transistors, the company had produced a tiny radio that was given the brand name Sony.

TTKK begin looking for foreign agents for their new product. Among other things, the company placed a one-sixth page advertisement in a brand new trade publication called *Oriental America*, which had been founded in Tokyo a few months earlier by American Ray Woodside and was being mailed to selected importers in the U.S., Canada, and Europe.

Shortly thereafter, TTKK made contact with General Distributors in Canada and Delmonico in the U.S. These two firms immediately saw the potential of the new Sony radio and became agents for the innovative new product. The following year, TTKK changed its name to Sony.

There are many reasons why Sony became such a huge success so quickly —including many of the factors that also applied to other Japanese companies that grew up during this period. But Sony had something special, as well. Its two founders were extraordinary men, even in a country filled with extraordinary men.

One of the early policies of TTKK had been to employ only engineers, and if memory serves me correctly, there was one year in the late 1950s when every employee (400, I believe) was in fact an engineer.

Perhaps more important, however, was Akio Morita, the senior partner in the firm, and the company's front man. Exceptionally intelligent, quick-witted, filled with ambition and energy, Morita was similar in many ways to the young *samurai* of the 1860s, '70s, and '80s who helped transform a feudal, agricultural society into a major industrial power in under three decades.

In typical Japanese fashion, the more successful Sony became, the more of a philosopher Morita became. With his ability to speak English (an ability he worked prodigiously to develop) and his outgoing personality, Morita also became a leading spokesperson for Japan on the international scene.

SOPHIA UNIVERSITY / JOCHI DAIGAKU (Joe-chee Die-gah-kuu) Sophia University has long been well known in Japan and abroad because of the large number of foreign students who attend its International Department and the quality of the English-language ability of its Japanese graduates.

In the 1960s and '70s, Sophia also became known for its economic research activities headed by Fr. Robert Ballon, who authored several books on Japanese business, labor, and management.

Operated by a Jesuit order of the Catholic Church, Jochi is located in the Yotsuya district of Tokyo's Chiyoda Ward, just west of the Imperial Palace grounds. The university has grown enormously in both size and reputation since 1953–55, when I was a student there.

SPACE EXPLORATION   Japan's space industry made its first launching —of a pencil-type rocket—in 1960. Ten years later, Japan became the fourth nation in the world to orbit an artificial satellite. This was followed by a series of launchings of weather satellites and small stations designed for experiments in communications, broadcasting, and X-ray astronomy.

The industry is steadily advancing the use of interplanetary space probes and broadcasting service satellites. Japan's space ports are located at Uchinoura and on Tanega Shima. See TANEGASHIMA for the role this tiny island played in Japan's first encounter with Westerners.

SPLIT-LEVEL ECONOMY   People around the world have heard about the giants of Japanese industry—Toyota, Nissan, Sony, Matsushita, Mitsui, Mitsubishi, and so on—and they have the impression that all or most Japanese companies are very large and powerful.

In fact, only 0.6 percent of all Japanese enterprises are large-scale. The overwhelming majority—99.4 percent—are very small (three employees or fewer) to medium-size (300–999 employees).

Small enterprises in Japan account for 53 percent of manufacturing, 61 percent of wholesaling, 79 percent of retail business, and 15 percent of all exports of industrial products.

It is characteristic of the Japanese economy that the relatively small number of very large companies subcontract a significant percentage of their production and assembly work to smaller, wholly owned subsidiaries or affiliated companies.

For a detailed discussion of this aspect of the Japanese economy, see *How to Do Business with the Japanese*, by Boye Lafayette De Mente (NTC Business Books).

SPRING LABOR OFFENSIVE / SHUNTO (Shune-toe)   Japanese labor union federations—and individual unions, as well—have developed the custom of negotiating for wage increases once a year, from April through May, in a process that is known by the abbreviation *Shunto* or Spring Labor Offensive.

During this period, the federations meet with their counterparts in management in ongoing negotiations and also hold large labor rallies in the streets, marching along prescribed routes.

The marchers carry colorful banners and flags and wear headbands to signify their unity. See HACHIMAKI. Since many of the labor banners are red or have red lettering on white, foreign visitors in Japan sometimes mistakenly believe the marches are Communist inspired.

The independent unions of some companies may hold strikes during these negotiations, but they are mostly symbolic, and care is generally taken to ensure that work stoppages are minor and do not harm the company. The unions of public service companies, however, are more militant and have caused work delays of several days in past years.

STAGECOACHES / BASHA (Bah-shah)　Before the ending of the Tokugawa Shogunate in 1868, Japan had no wheeled passenger transportation of any kind. Only the elite *samurai* upper class and members of the nobility were allowed to ride horses or be carried in palanquins. Everybody else walked.

But, in the 1870s, two enterprising New Zealand brothers named Hoyt established a stagecoach line between Tokyo and Yokohama, and another company operated between Odawara and Oiso. Japanese entrepreneurs got into the business, and in some remote areas of Japan stagecoaches were in use until the introduction of buses.

Two of the Hoyt brothers' stagecoach drivers, Tom Sayers and Frank Rutherford, were Americans. Rutherford died of smallpox in 1871 and was buried in the now famous foreign cemetery in Yokohama.

STANDARDS INFORMATION CENTER (SIC)　The Standards Information Center, founded in Tokyo by the Ministry of International Trade and Industry (MITI) in 1983, is designed to provide foreign exporters with information about Japan's test standards drafting procedures.

Specifically, the SIC is charged with collecting and publicizing MITI's production standards, responding to queries about these procedures, helping manufacturers and exporters abroad get information about new standards to be introduced, and serving as a go-between for foreign companies seeking information about standards set by private organizations in Japan.

Contact: Officer in Charge, Standards Information Center, Export and Design Division, Trade Administration Bureau, MITI, 1-3 Kasumigaseki, Chiyoda-Ku, Tokyo, Japan.

STATION BOX-LUNCHES / EKI-BEN (Eh-kee-bane)　One of the special pleasures of long-distance train riding in Japan is taking advantage of the special box-lunches that are sold in and near stations and on the boarding platforms. At many stations, *eki-ben* sellers go up and down the platforms during stops, and passengers buy through their coach windows. Some long-distance trains have *eki-ben* vendors on board, going to and fro through the aisles, pushing small carts or carrying trays.

The first *eki-ben* dealer is said to have appeared at Utsunomiya Station around 1887, selling rice balls and pickles wrapped in bamboo leaves. Today dozens of stations around the country are noted for certain kinds of *eki-ben*. The specialty of Yokohama, for example, is *shumai*, a flour bun filled with bits of meat and vegetables, a favorite Chinese snack.

At Tokyo Station, one can buy several different varieties of *eki-ben*, including chicken, *sushi*, rice, an assortment of vegetables and seafood, and sandwiches on white bread. Station vendors also sell tea, beer, and *sake*; so it is possible to have a full meal on trains without dining facilities. Many kinds of box-lunches are presented in convenient wooden boxes and are generally referred to as *bento*.

Some station vendors sell their tea in attractive ceramic pots made locally —and the traveler ends up with a very practical souvenir.

STONE LANTERNS / ISHI DORO (Ee-she doe-roe)   Seen in yards, gardens, and temple and shrine grounds all over Japan, *ishi doro* developed from torches and bonfires lit at shrines and temples in ancient times to provide light for services and rituals. Gradually, they came to be placed around homes and on roadsides to guide people at night.

The Toma Temple in Yamato, near Nara, has a stone lantern that dates from 682.

As the centuries passed, the lanterns became more varied and artistic in their shapes and sizes. Tea masters in the sixteenth and seventeenth centuries adapted small versions of the lanterns for use in private gardens and the gardens of teahouses.

Most stone lanterns are made of granite, but there are many made of metal, as well. Temples and shrines often have *ishi doro* made of bronze. Tokyo's popular Oriental Bazaar in the Harajuku district sells stone lanterns to many foreign visitors.

One famous stone-lantern maker in Tokyo has been in business for several hundred years.

STORY TELLING / RAKUGO (Rah-kuu-go)   One of the most popular forms of traditional Japanese entertainment is the telling of long humorous stories, mainly in the form of monologues, called *rakugo* (rah-kuu-go).

Dating from the early years of the sixteenth century, *rakugo* was well-entrenched by the middle of the seventeenth century and by this time included the use of gestures and facial expressions, along with a punchline at the end of the story.

Rakugo entertainers are ranked according to skill and experience, with beginners known as *zenza* (zen-zah), or "curtain raisers," referring to the fact that they go on first or while the audience is being seated, to warm up the crowd.

One who has earned the reputation of being a master of *rakugo* is called a *shin'uchi* (sheen uu-chee)—one who strikes the heart or one of true value, because of his or her ability to attract large audiences. The *shin'uchi*, like all stars, is the last to perform.

There are three other kinds of storytelling in Japan: *manzai* (mahn-zie), *naniwabushi* (nah-nee-wah-buu-she), and *kodan* (koe-dahn).

Manzai features two performers who specialize in slapstick, wisecracks, and comic skits. It is a modernized version of a dramatic form that originated in the thirteenth century (and had to do with driving away demons and bringing in good luck). *Manzai* performers usually write their own material. In recent years, three-member *manzai* teams have appeared on the scene, and some have introduced musical instruments as part of their act.

Naniwabushi, favored by older people, consists of a solo recitation that is partly sung in a very stylized, sober voice and partly narrated as dialogue. The most popular *naniwabushi* theme is love versus duty or good versus evil.

Kodan storytelling, less popular than the other forms, is the recitation of a famous historical event that is of specieal human interest. The stories are told in a flat, monotonous chant. *Kodan* dates from the seventeenth century.

The most famous *kodanshi* (*kodan* storyteller) of the Tokugawa era was a man named Shidoken, who arrived in Edo in 1692 at the age of 20, after having run away from a temple. Without any money to feed himself, he happened upon a storyteller nicknamed Ginnan Osho (Ginko Tree Priest) who sat under a ginko tree at the Kannon Temple in Asakusa and told stories, after which people tossed him money.

Shidoken thought this was an ideal way to make a living; so he picked out a nearby spot for himself, sat down, and began telling stories, adding a special touch that quickly attracted the crowds. He became so popular that Ginnan Osho had to leave and find a new place.

Shidoken's audiences became so large he had to build a platform to sit on so his audiences could see and hear him. He was soon a famous figure in Edo and continued in the profession of *kodan* for the next 63 years, dying at the age of 83 in 1765.

STUDENTS / GAKUSEI (Gock-say-e)   Japan often seems to be a land of students, and with nearly 30 million attending school in a small country where the population is concentrated in a tiny percentage of the landmass, this impression is valid.

Attendance by children of school age in Japan was already high in 1980, when it went up a little as a result of a law passed in April 1979 making it mandatory that all mentally and physically handicapped children, as well as children who are chronically ill, be educated.

Approximately 95 percent of all students in Japan go to upper secondary schools after completing the nine compulsory grades (six years of elementary and three years of lower secondary school).

Some 65 percent of Japan's children attend kindergarten, and another 26 percent attend child-care centers. Around 38 percent of Japan's high school graduates go on to colleges and universities.

On the average, Japanese youth are more studious than their Western counterparts, at least until they finish high school. A primary reason for this is that entry into the more desirable schools is by examination, and graduating from a highly reputable school is a vital factor in later employment opportunities.

Parents exert extraordinary pressure on their children to do well in school, knowing that their success in school will determine the quality of their adult lives.

During the late 1950s and 1960s, hundreds of thousands of university students in Japan were very active politically. A number of student organizations, especially the Zengakuren (All-Japan Students Federation), achieved considerable prominence and power.

These students played a vital role in the downfall of the Kishi government in the early 1960s and later delayed the opening of the New Tokyo International Airport in Narita for several years.

By the early 1990s social conditions had changed to the point that truancy among high school students had become a problem for the first time. There was also growing pressure for Japan to change its rigid, learn-by-role-memory method of education.

SUBWAYS / CHIKATETSU (Chee-kah-tate-sue)   Japan's subways, particularly those in Tokyo, are world-famous for their efficiency and for being crowded during morning and evening rush hours. There are subway lines in Tokyo, Osaka, Kyoto, Nagoya, Kobe, Yokohama, Sapporo, and Fukuoka.

There are more than a dozen subway lines in Tokyo, most of them intersecting at various points around the city, making it possible to transfer from one line to another. Seven of the lines come together or are within walking distance of each other in the Hibiya/Tsukiyabashi/Ginza areas of downtown Tokyo.

Station names in the Japanese subway systems appear in Roman letters (*Roma-ji*), *hiragana*, and *kanji*, so that children who have not yet learned *kanji*, as well as foreign visitors, can read the names.

SUICIDE (Ritual) / **HARAKIRI** (Hah-rah-kee-ree)   Ritual suicide, or *harakiri* in common language and *seppuku* (sape-puu-kuu) in formal language, was an important aspect of feudal Japan (1192–1868). It developed as an integral part of the code and discipline of the *samurai* warrior class.

Harakiri, which literally means "stomach cutting," is a particularly painful method of self-destruction, and, prior to the emergence of the *samurai* as a professional warrior class, it was totally alien to the Japanese.

The early history of Japan reveals quite clearly that the Japanese were far more interested in living the good life than in dying a painful death. It was not until well after the introduction of Buddhism, with its theme of the transitory nature of life and the glory of death, that such a development became possible.

To the *samurai*, *seppuku*—whether meted out as punishment or chosen in preference to a dishonorable death at the hands of an enemy—was an unquestionable demonstration of their honor, courage, and moral character.

When *samurai* were on the battlefield, they often carried out acts of *harakiri* rapidly and with very little formal preparation. But on the other occasions, particularly when it was ordered by a feudal lord or the *shogun*, *harakiri* was a very formal ceremony, requiring witnesses and considerable preparation.

In 1868, Lord Redesdale, a British diplomat stationed in Japan, along with six other foreigners, was asked to serve as a witness at the *seppuku* of a *samurai* of the Bizen clan who had ordered Japanese soldiers to fire on the foreign settlement in Kobe (then called Hyogo).

The detailed description of the ceremony that Lord Redesdale published in his book, *Tales of Old Japan*, was the first account by a foreigner of this remarkable custom. In this ritual suicide, the victim was a handsome, 32-year-old man who carried out the ceremony to perfection, both fascinating and shocking the Englishman.

Not all Japanese *samurai* or lords believed in *harakiri*, even though many of them followed the custom. The great Ieyasu Tokugawa, who founded Japan's last Shogunate dynasty in 1603, eventually issued an edict forbidding *harakiri* to both secondary and primary retainers.

The custom was so deeply entrenched, however, that it continued, and in 1663, at the urging of Lord Nobutsuna Matsudaira of Izu, the *shogun*ate government issued another, stronger edict, prohibiting ritual suicide. This was followed up by very stern punishments for any lord who allowed any of his followers to commit *harakiri*.

Still, the practice continued throughout the long Tokugawa reign, but it declined considerably as time went by.

There were many forms of *harakiri*, including a form to show contempt for an enemy, one to protest against injustice, and one to save others.

The location of an officially ordered *seppuku* ceremony was important. Often, the ritual was performed at temples (but not Shinto shrines), in the gardens of villas, and inside homes. The size of the area available was also important, and it was prescribed precisely for people of high rank.

All other matters relating to the act were carefully prescribed and carried out in the most meticulous manner. The most conspicuous participant in *seppuku*, other than the victim, was the *kaishaku* (kie-shah-kuu), or assistant, who was responsible for cutting off the victim's head after he had sliced his abdomen open.

The *kaishaku* was generally a close friend or associate of the condemned.

Recommended reading: *Hara-Kiri—Japanese Ritual Suicide*, by Jack Seward (Tuttle).

Ordinary suicide, called *jisatsu* (jee-sot-sue), is common in Japan today, but the Japanese do not lead the world in suicides. Japan's suicide rate is only slightly higher than the official U.S. rate and well below that of Switzerland and other Northern European and Eastern Bloc countries.

Japan's reputation for suicides is a holdover from the days of the *samurai* and more recent war years, when Japanese soldiers committed suicide rather than be captured, and *kami-kaze* ("divine wind") pilots were used in suicidal missions against the U.S. armed forces advancing on Japan.

In present-day Japan, people kill themselves for reasons that are familiar —failed businesses, too much business pressure, and involvement in scandals. Other somewhat less common reasons are failure in competitive school examinations, involvement in love triangles, and inability of lovers to be together.

While suicide is deplored in Japan, it does not have the sinful overtones that are common in the West.

SUICIDE FOREST   The United States has its Golden Gate Bridge and other favorite suicide spots. Japan has the Forest of Aokigahara, at the foot of famed Mt. Fuji.

For apparently the same reason that the Golden Gate Bridge acts as a magnet for people contemplating suicide, the dense forest of Aokigahara attracts suicidal people from all over Japan.

Police estimate that from 20 to 50 people kill themselves each year in the dense forest, which is known in Japanese as Jukai, or Sea of Trees. The number of people who die in the woods each year is uncertain because it is presumed that all the bodies are not found.

The television dramatization in the early 1970s of a popular book, *Nami No To* (*Tower of Waves*), by Seicho Matsumoto, turned Aokigaha into a mecca of suicides. In the book, a woman vanishes into the forest, leaving the implication that she went there to die.

SUMO (Sue-moe)   Dating back to mythical times, when it was said to be popular among the gods, *sumo* is a unique form of wrestling that was widely practiced before the sixth century as a sport, as well as a form of divination to predict the outcome of harvests and invoke the goodwill of the gods.

Sometime around the sixth century, *sumo* wrestling left the precincts of Shinto shrines and became an immensely popular spectator sport, patronized by both emperors and *shogun* as the centuries went by.

The practices and traditions of *sumo* have continued down to the present time, and *sumo* remains one of the most distinctive and popular sports in the country.

Sumo is distinctive in many ways. The wrestlers begin training when they are in their early teens. They eat a special food called *chanko-nabe* (chan-koe-nah-bay), engage in strenuous exercises and practice sessions several hours a day, and grow to huge sizes—usually between six and seven feet in height and weighing from 250 to 375 pounds.

The sport is controlled by the Japan Sumo Wrestling Association, which sponsors six 15-day tournaments a year—three in Tokyo (in January, May, and September) and one each in Osaka (March), Nagoya (July), and Fukuoka (November).

There are four grades of first-class or senior-class wrestlers. The highest is Grand Champion, or *Yokozuna* (Yoe-koe-zuu-nah), of which there may be several. Next are the Champions, or *Ozeki* (Oh-zay-kee). There are usually from two to four *Ozeki*. Then comes the *Sekiwake* (Say-kee-wah-kay) and *Komusubi* (Koe-muu-sue-bee) grades, with several wrestlers in each grade.

In the junior class, there are five grades: Juryo (Juu-rio), *Makushita* (Mah-kuussh-tah), *Sandame* (Sahn-dah-may), *Jo-ni-dan* (Joe-nee-dahn), and *Jo-no-kuchi* (Joe-no-kuu-chee). Altogether, there are several dozen junior-grade wrestlers.

The wrestlers belong to *beya* (bay-yah), or stables, that are usually owned and presided over by retired champions or grand champions. Altogether, there are 28 *beya* and around 700 wrestlers. The *beya* are divided into East and West camps for tournament purposes.

The bouts take place in large halls that have a raised, 14.9-square-foot ring in the center. The aim of *sumo* is for one wrestler to eject the other from the ring or to cause the other wrestler to touch the ground anywhere with anything other than his feet—by shoving, tripping, throwing, slapping, etc. in a prescribed and named move that all *sumo* fans know by heart. The action may be over in seconds, or it may last for several minutes. It is often dangerous, since wrestlers regularly get tossed completely out of the high ring.

To win promotion to a higher grade, wrestlers must win eight or more of their 15 bouts each tournament, and all except the grand champions are usually demoted if they do not consistently win the majority of their fights. The more bouts a *sumo* wins, the faster the promotions.

Wrestlers who win a tournament—by having no losses or the least number of losses—receive the Emperor's Cup and numerous other trophies and prizes, including money. Beginning in the late 1950s, David Jones, an American employee of Pan American Airways stationed in Tokyo, began presenting every tournament winner with a huge trophy and reading the winner's citation in the Japanese dialect of the district in which the tournament was held.

This extraordinary event, always shown on national television with the rest of the proceedings, became a traditional feature of *sumo* tournaments —and, of course, made Jones and Pan Am famous in Japan.

When an *Ozeki-class* wrestler wins two or three tournaments—especially in a row—he is usually promoted to grand champion. When lower ranked *sumo* win tournaments, they are generally jumped several grades in rank—only to be demoted, however, if they fall below eight wins in subsequent tournaments.

A *sumo* tournament is filled with pageantry and color. The huge wrestlers, wearing only stylized loincloths, go through a prescribed ceremony, including the throwing of salt, before each bout. There is also a traditional ceremony at the beginning and end of each tournament.

Sumo wrestlers, especially champions and grand champions, become national heroes, and, in recent decades, many of them have become wealthy. Some have gone on to successful careers in the movies, but most of the champions continue in the sport following retirement.

The most significant development in *sumo* in the history of the sport was the acceptance of several American "recruits" in the 1980s and 1990s, and the rise of several of them to champion rank. In 1993, Hawaiian Chad Rowan, wrestling under the name of Akebono, was promoted to Grand Champion after winning several tournaments, and for a number of subsequent tournaments was the only Grand Champion in the sport.

SUPERMARKETS / SUPA (Sue-pah)   In Japan, supermarkets are called superstores. There are 10 major superstore chains in the country. The largest is Daiei, followed by Ito-Yokado, Seiyu, Jusco, Nichii, Uny, Nagaskiya, Izumiya, Kotobukiya, and Chujitsu.

The primary merchandise lines in superstores are foodstuffs, clothing, sundries, household utensils, and miscellaneous.

SUPERSTITIONS / MEISHIN (May-e-sheen)   The Japanese, like most people, have their superstitions—perhaps more than most until recent times. Most Japanese superstitions concern numbers or dates and directions.

Unlucky days include the 4th and the 14th. The luckiest days of the month are the 15th and the 28th, and these are good days for beginning new projects and starting trips.

Unlucky ages are 19, 33, and 42. In the Zodiac, the Year of the Horse and Monkey are considered unlucky. With directions, the best are east and south. The unluckiest are north and northeast. Many people today are still concerned about which way their houses face and where the doors are.

Many Japanese give credence to divination and to such arts as palm reading and tea-leaf reading—but today probably no more so than do Americans or Europeans.

SUPREME COURT / SAIKO SAIBAN SHO (Sie-koe Sie-bahn Sho) There are 15 justices, including the chief justice, on Japan's Supreme Court. There are also some 20 judicial research officers assigned to the court. These officials, all qualified judges, help clarify disputed points on the basis of judicial theory and precedents (both Japanese and foreign). They are sometimes asked to state their opinions during trials and therefore play an important role in the court's work.

Japan's Court Organization Law requires that all Supreme Court justices be at least 40 years old and that at least 10 of them be judges, public prosecutors, lawyers, or professors of law. The remaining five are required to be persons of great insight with a knowledge of the law.

Most justices are around 60 years old when appointed; so the average age of the members of the court tends to be high.

SUSHI (Sue-she)   One of the most popular of all Japanese foods, *sushi* consists of slices or pieces of fish, shellfish, egg and (in one variety) a vegetable placed on top (or inside) a bun or roll of rice that has been flavored with vinegar, salt, sugar, and *mirin*, a sweet rice wine.

The individual pieces are generally dipped into soy sauce, in which a dab of grated horseradish has been mixed, just before eating.

There are some two dozen popular varieties of *sushi*, based on the species of fish, shellfish, or other delicacy that makes up the topping for the rice bun. Tuna and eel are two of the most popular.

Shops that serve only *sushi*—and there are thousands of them in Japan—are called *sushi-ya* (*sushi* shops). They are usually small, and often have only a counter, at which the customer sits and points to samples of whatever he or she wants.

A set lunch or dinner of *sushi* includes several varieties, including one or two that are generally eaten last to sharpen the palate. One of these, *nori-maki*, is a roll of rice wrapped in seaweed, with pieces of pickled radish on the inside.

Traditionally, *sushi* fans drank *sake* with their meals. Many now opt for beer.

Recommended reading: *The Book of Sushi*, by Kinjiro Omae and Yuzuru Tachibana (Kodansha International).

SWORDS / KATANA (Kah-tah-nah)   Like so many other things, the art of sword making was introduced into Japan from China and Korea in the early centuries. But, as usual, the Japanese modified and improved upon the imported technology.

Swords were to play an extraordinary role in the country's history, beginning with the mythology of its creation. The Sun Goddess, Amaterasu Omikami, is said to have given her grandson, Ninigi-no Mikoto, a sword when he was sent down to reign on earth. Swords made in the sixth and seventh centuries B.C. have been found in burial mounds.

The sword was the primary weapon of the Japanese from earliest times and sword making was developed to a higher degree of technical perfection than in any other country, before or since.

With the rise of the *samurai* warrior class in the tenth, eleventh, and twelfth centuries and the development of the code of *bushido*, swords became a virtual extension of the warriors' bodies. Eventually, they became objects of reverence—and even worship.

The sword was regarded as more than a physical weapon. It was imbued with a moral spirit of its own, and it was viewed as a means of achieving self-mastery and as a symbol of justice and of the triumph of good over evil. The most binding oath a Japanese *samurai* or noble could take was to swear on his sword.

The second, short sword, which became a part of the *samurai* uniform around the end of the fourteenth century, was used mainly for personal protection as opposed to regular battle.

Between the ninth and twelfth centuries, Japan's swords became wider across the base than across the tip and curved abruptly near the base. The art of sword making was hereditary by this time, and master makers began stamping their names onto their handiwork.

Other changes occurred in the thirteenth century, with the ascendancy of the *samurai* warriors, each of whom carried one long sword and one short one. The blade became broader, the breadth between the tip and base was reduced, and the tip was shortened and given a sharper angle.

This was the beginning of a golden age of Japanese swords. Special heating, forging, and hardening techniques made the swords incredibly tough and gave them a cutting edge that has never been equaled. The heyday of the art of sword making was the Kamakura Period (1192–1333), and the greatest swordsmith of all was Masamune Nyudo. The art was passed on from father to son, and the process of forging was surrounded by Shinto rituals that were meticulously followed.

It was believed that only the purest of heart, with the highest moral standards, could become a master swordsmith. Thus, those who mastered the art were honored and highly prized by their fief lords.

Practicing swordsmanship was one of the prime responsibilities of the *samurai*, because the development of skill was equated with the development of moral character and honor. As a class, the *samurai* thus became the most skillful swordsmen the world had ever seen.

Their greatest swordsmen developed a sixth sense that made them virtually unbeatable in even combat. There are records of single masters fighting several other swordsmen at the same time and killing them all.

Stories of great swordsmen abound in the chronicles covering the thirteenth to eighteenth centuries. Some are known to have confronted a dozen or more enemies at the same time and to have emerged victorious after battles that lasted for an hour or more.

This honing of extraordinary skill with the sword continued until 1868, when the last shogunate government fell. There are a few masters of the art in Japan today, and *kendo*, which is the practice of swordsmanship using a bamboo stave, is a widely practiced martial art in Japan.

The prowess of Japanese swordsmen of these early years is an important factor in the ongoing popularity of a genre of movie films known as *chanbara*, which tell stories about Japan's feudal *samurai* days.

Today Japanese swords made before the end of the sixteenth century are referred to as Old Swords, while those made since then are regarded as New Swords.

The best-known sword maker in Japan today is the Japan Sword Company in Tokyo. The ancient techniques and Shinto rituals of the early masters have been preserved by the swordsmiths at this company—and visitors are welcomed by appointment to view the key steps in forging a new sword.

Recommended reading: *The Samurai Sword*, by John M. Yumoto (Tuttle).

TACHIKAWA (Tah-chee-kah-wah)   A city of 140,000 about 30 minutes west of Tokyo's Shinjuku Station on the Chuo Line, Tachikawa is known to many foreigners, especially Americans, as the site of a major U.S. air force base following the end of World War II.

The original airfield was constructed there in 1922 by the Japanese Army.

Besides the airfield, which is still in operation, the city today is a thriving industrial and business center, as well as being a residential area for people who work in Tokyo.

TAIKUN (Tie-koon)   This is the title used by the Tokugawa *Shoguns* during their dealings with Americans and other foreigners from about 1854 to 1867. It means something like Great Leader. During the first years of their contact with Japan, Westerners believed that the *shogun* was the emperor and were shocked when they discovered otherwise.

The English word "tycoon" comes from *taikun*.

TAIRA, KIYOMORI (Tie-rah, Kee-yoe-moe-ree)   The glory of the Taira (Heike) clan lasted for only about 20 years, but it was one of the most extraordinary 20 years in Japan's history. By the middle of the twelfth century, the power of the famous Fujiwara clan, which had virtually controlled the country for over 300 years, had ebbed.

The provincial lords, mostly descended from noble rank, had begun to keep their own private armies as protection and to further their own ambitions at the expense of their neighbors and the central government.

Following the usual pattern, the profession of warrior had become hereditary, giving rise to a new class that were eventually to be called *samurai*, which literally means "to be on guard."

In the middle of the twelfth century, one of the most powerful and ambitious of these lords was Kiyomori Taira, head of the Taira clan, who became the governor of the province of Aki. The Tairas were descendants of the Emperor Kwammu (786–853) and were the blood enemies of the Minamoto clan, who were also descended from royalty. During the Hogen war (1156–1160), which came about when Emperor Shirakawa tried to wrest power from the Fujiwara family, whose regents had controlled the throne for several centuries, Kiyomori supported him and was victorious in the war.

As a result of this victory, Kiyomori became very powerful at court. He sent Yoritomo Minamoto, his arch rival, into exile and took Yoshitomo Minamoto's favorite concubine as his mistress.

In 1167, Kiyomori got himself appointed prime minister (*dajo daijin*) and immediately parceled out every important post in the country to his relatives. The following year, he came down with a strange, burning disease that was incurable—and is believed to have been responsible for some of his cruelty and arbitrary ways.

One of the stories about him is that he once assembled thousands of craftsmen in an attempt to build a temple in just one day in order to win a lady as his mistress.

Kiyomori died in 1181, one of the most disliked men in the realm. Kiyomori's son, Shigemori, on the other hand, was renowned for his loyalty to the emperor and for his prowess as a warrior. He tried to get support to build a canal from Lake Biwa to the sea but died prematurely in 1179. See HISTORY; MINAMOTO; SAMURAI.

TAKARAZUKA (Tah-kah-rah-zoo-kah)   Takarazuka refers to a famous resort spa, to an even more famous opera house, and to a form of theater that is one of the most popular attractions in the country—among young Japanese girls.

The resort spa of Takarazuka, located on the banks of the Muko River in the foothills, 24.8 kilometers from Osaka's Hankyu Station, is the most popular resort in the Osaka-Kobe area.

In addition to its dozens of *ryokan* inns along the banks of the Muko Gawa, the city has a large entertainment district known as Takarazuka Family Land.

The Family Land includes theaters, a health center, zoological and botanical gardens, a science amusement park, and an opera house that will seat 4,000 people.

It is this huge Takarazuka opera house, and its affiliated music school, that has made the spa nationally famous. The school accepts only female students. The operas presented in the theater—all musical renditions of Japanese and Western stories—feature only women performers, who play both male and female roles.

The female performers are divided into four troupes that take turns presenting the operas—at the theater in Takarazuka and at a branch Takarazuka Theater in the Hibiya district of Tokyo, across the street from the Imperial Hotel.

The Takarazuka operas are spectacular shows, and the stars attract huge numbers of young female fans.

TAKAYAMA (Tah-kah-yah-mah)   People who want to see and experience what much of old Japan used to look like are advised to go to the small city of Takayama, secluded in the moutains of Hida in the Japan Alps National Park, about two hours from Gifu on the Takayama Line.

Often called Little Kyoto, the streets of Takayama are built in the cross-bar pattern of Kyoto, and many of its houses and buildings are in the style of the Edo, or Tokugawa, Period (1600–1867).

Besides its nostalgia for history buffs, Takayama is also noted for the Hie Shrine and its annual Sanno Festival, held on April 14 and 15.

The festival is one of the largest and grandest in all of Japan, with 23 high-wheeled wagon floats (*yatai*), gorgeously decorated with gold and elaborate carvings, pulled through the streets by *sake*-fired, shouting young men.

Other cultural treasures in the city are the Kokubun Temple, founded in 1588, the Minzoku Kan or Folklore Museum, and the Shoren Temple, dating from 1504. Nearby are the famed Takahara Gorge and Hirayu hot springs spa.

TANEGASHIMA (Tah-nay-gah-she-mah)   This is a tiny island in the Satsunan group, lying just 200 miles south of Kyushu, which traditionally came under the influence and control of the lords of Kyushu. It is the place where three storm-tossed Portuguese, en route to Macau, became the first Westerners of record to set foot on Japanese soil, in August 1543.

Among the things these Portuguese drifters introduced into Japan were firearms, tobacco, and venereal disease. They were to be followed within a few years by a steady stream of traders, priests, and others who would alter the course of Japan's history and set the stage for one of the most dramatic and important periods in the lives of any people.

Tanegashima is 3–4 hours from Kagoshima by boat and 30 minutes by air. The Misaki Shrine on the southern end of the island, where the Portuguese landed, includes a memorial marking the event.

TANKA POETRY (Tahn-kah)   The *tanka* form of Japanese poetry has been popular since ancient times. Consisting of five lines of 5-7-5-7-7 syllables, it is a lyrical poetry primarily used to express emotion, especially stressing the beauty of life and nature.

The aim of the *tanka* poet is to express this yearning for beauty with such vivid power that all the most powerful emotions are intermingled in an elusive feeling referred to as *yojo* (yoe-joe).

Purists say that to be *tanka*, a poem must include the element of *yojo*.

TATAMI (Tah-tah-me)   The floors of traditionally styled Japanese rooms are covered with thick, rectangular straw mats called *tatami*. These mats measure approximately two inches thick, three feet in width, and six feet in length—and are the standard unit of measure in speaking of a Japanese room (four-mat room; six-mat room, etc.).

Tatami are made from tightly woven rice straw that is then covered with woven rush grass. The edges are bound with a band of sturdy cotton cloth, usually black or dark blue. The mats are firm but resilient and, when fresh, give off a delightful aroma that is part of their special attraction.

In earlier times, those who could afford it changed the *tatami* in their homes every spring.

Tatami floors are still the norm in older Japanese homes and in inns, and contemporary-built, Western-styled homes generally have one or more *tatami* rooms. Some meeting and athletic halls—some the size of huge auditoriums —have *tatami* floors.

The word *tatami* comes from *tatamu*, meaning "to fold," and the original *tatami* were floor cushions that were folded when not in use.

The *tatami* cushions survived until the Heian Period (794–1185), during which time they became more elaborate and began to be used to indicate graduations of rank among the aristocracy at the Imperial Palace. The higher the rank of the individual, the larger the *tatami* he or she sat on. The lowest ranking members of the court had to sit on the bare floor.

During the Muromachi Period (1333–1573), it became the custom to cover the entire floor with *tatami*, and the size and thickness was gradually standardized to what is used today.

The tightly woven rice straw, besides being soft and comfortable to sit or lie on, offers some other benefits as well. It absorbs and releases moisture, depending on the ambient humidity, and thus acts as a natural air-conditioner.

TAXES / ZEIKIN (Zay-e-keen)   There are two kinds of taxes in Japan, local and national. Local taxes include village, town, city, and prefectural taxes and account for about 30 percent of the revenue of local governments.

National taxes include income taxes, corporate taxes, and inheritance taxes —which are direct—along with gasoline taxes, liquor taxes, commodity taxes, stamp revenues, and taxes collected by the Japan Tobacco and Salt Corporation, which are all indirect.

Taxes in Japan currently amount to about 23 percent of per capita income.

TEA / CHA (Chah)   The custom of drinking tea was imported into Japan from China—where it originated, according to legend, some 5,000 years ago, when a Chinese emperor was sitting under a camellia tree, with a pot of boiling water in front of him. Leaves falling from the tree landed in the pot, sending out a fragrant aroma.

The emperor taste-tested the new brew and immediately named it Heavenly Dew.

Emperor Shomu (701–756) is credited with introducing tea drinking into Japan when Ganjin, a famous Chinese priest, brought him some medicines, among which was tea. This tea was called *tan-cha* (tahn-chah) and came in the form of steamed tea leaves pressed into bricks and dried, for either chewing or steeping in hot water.

During the Heian Period (794–1185), *matcha* (mot-chah), a tea made of steamed and dried green tea leaves ground into powder and stirred into hot water, became popular. It is the kind of tea used in the tea ceremony, still practiced today.

In the early decades, tea drinking was widespread only among priests, who used it to help fight off fatigue while they were studying. Because priests were the primary source of learning, the custom gradually spread among the general population.

Tea drinking was raised to an art form by Sen-no Rikyu (1521–1591), a famous Sakai (Osaka) merchant, who developed the tea ceremony as a way of countering the snobbery and pretension that existed among his rich fellow merchants. He stressed simplicity and spiritual tranquility and communion with nature in the *sado* (sah-doe), or tea ceremony.

Several types of tea that are popular in Japan, along with a number of tealike drinks that are made with something other than tea leaves.

The varieties of tea include *ban-cha*, the cheapest and one of the most common; *sen-cha*, a medium-priced tea that one usually serves to guests; and *gyokuro*, the highest and most expensive grade, reserved for special occasions.

Other popular kinds of tea are *hoji-cha*, which is *ban-cha* tea leaves that have been roasted (giving them a smoky flavor), and *genmai-cha*, which consists of tea leaves mixed with roasted and popped rice.

The nontea tea drinks are *mugi-cha*, made from roasted barley and usually served cool or chilled; *kobucha*, made from powdered seaweed (and tasting very much like salt soup); *habu-cha*, made from stinkweed seed; and *sakura yu*, which is made from salt-pickled cherry blossoms (for special ceremonial occasions).

The tea used in the famous tea ceremony, called *hiki-cha* or *mat-cha*, is made from young, tender leaves picked from aged tea plants, dried, and then ground in stone mortars.

Tea leaves are graded according to the way they are grown and picked. The best are the ones that are grown in shaded areas and picked when very young. They are kept green by steaming and heating to prevent oxidation.

The only Japanese tea that is sweetened is a summer drink made from powdered tea leaves.

TEA CEREMONY / CHANOYU (Chah-no-yuu)   The tea ceremony, a ritualized way of preparing and drinking tea, was perfected in the latter part of the sixteenth century by the famous Sen-no Rikyu. The *chanoyu* is an exercise in aestheticism and in the highest level of mental control and refined manners. It results in a state of serenity and right feeling.

The tea ceremony is Zen in spirit and was strongly influenced by the discipline and ideals of the *samurai* class. The main thing is the selfless spirit in which the tea is made and served, although the ritual manner of the ceremony is a vital part.

When the tea plant was first imported into Japan, it was primarily seen as a medicine which, according to early historians, was highly prized for its power to relieve fatigue, repair the eyesight, strengthen the will, and delight the soul. The Taoists in China used it in their immortality elixir, and the Buddhists used it to help them stay awake during their long hours of meditation.

The Buddhists of the Zen sect of southern China, who had adopted many Taoist concepts, developed tea drinking into a formalized ritual. These priests gathered in front of an image of Buddha and took turns drinking tea from a common bowl.

Tea drinking was a popular custom in Japan by the end of the seventh century. Emperor Shomu (who reigned from 724 to 749) once invited 100 Buddhist monks to the Imperial Palace for a tea party. But it was not until the fifteenth century that the tea ceremony, under the patronage of *Shogun* Yoshimasa Ashikaga, became a full-fledged independent aesthetic, spiritual, and philosophical ritual.

The teahouse, or *sukiya*, that developed along with the ceremony consists of a tearoom proper designed to accommodate a maximum of five guests; a service or wash room (*mizu-ya*), where the utensils are washed and readied; and a separate waiting room (*yoritsuki*), where guests wait until they are summoned to the the the tearoom.

The tearoom measures about 2.7 meters square and has two entrances—one for the host and another one for guests. The doorway for the guests is very low, requiring that they enter the room on their hands and knees (and thus humble themselves in preparation for the ceremony).

There are several tea ceremony schools, each of which has its own style. Some are very formal; others are rather casual and may include food. But in all cases, the purpose is the same—to exercise and sharpen the aesthetic sense, still the spirit, and develop harmony with the universe.

In the more formal schools, there is a main guest (*shokyaku*), and the ceremony takes up to three hours. The three most popular *chanoyu* schools today are the Ura-Senke, Omote-Senke, and Mushakoji.

There are several teahouses in Japan that are over 300 years old, some of which are registered as National Treasures. These include the Ginkaku, or Silver Pavilion, in Kyoto (designed by the Father of the Tea Ceremony, Shuko, in the fifteenth century), the Shokintei in the Katsura Imperial Villa in Kyoto (designed by Enshu Kobori, who lived from 1579 to 1647), the Kohoan and Shinjuan in Kyoto's Daitoku Temple, the Myokian in Kyoto (the residence of Sen-no Rikyu [1521–1591], one of the greatest of the tea masters), and the Rokusoan in the National Museum in Tokyo.

Basically, a ceremony begins when a host invites guests and then begins the preparations well before their arrival. The location may be inside or outside, but it should be a quiet room in which disruptions are unlikely. Devotees prefer a Japanese-style room or a separate cottage (in some exceptionally beautiful place) made especially for the ceremony.

The host takes great care to clean the room and utensils to be used, straightens up the garden or outside area, and prepares the special dishes to be served.

Any conversation before the ceremony begins should be light and calm and designed to enhance a contemplative, serene mood. Once the guests have all arrived, and the time is right, the host ladles powdered green tea into each guest's cup in turn, pours hot water over it, and then uses a whisk to stir it to a foam.

The taste of the tea is astringent. It is meant to stimulate the taste buds and help the person feel alive and at one with nature and the universe.

Once the tea is drunk, the guests take turns commenting on the beauty of the tea cups and expressing their appreciation to the host for the hospitality.

An essential part of the tea ceremony is scrutinizing and appreciating the utensils used—known as *dogu-haiken*, or inspection of the utensils. The various items are passed one at a time to each guest, who is expected to demonstrate both taste and refinement in commenting on and appreciating the beauty and artistry of the implements.

Genuine "teaists" look forward especially to the first tea ceremony of each new year, called *hatsu gama*, or first ceremony.

Today the tea ceremony is most popular among women—when they are young, as a way of developing good manners and a calm, harmonious attitude;

and as they grow older, as a way of sustaining the spirit and, along with their friends, communing with nature.

Recommended reading: *Cha-No Yu: The Japanese Tea Ceremony*, by A. L. Sadler (Tuttle); and *The Book of Tea*, by Kakuzo Okakura (Tuttle).

TELEPHONES / DENWA (Dane-wa)   Japan ranks second in the world, behind the U.S., in the number of telephones in use—well over 50 million—all of which are on automatic exchanges. Japan also has direct-dial telephone links with 83 countries and island groups around the world.

Telephone service in Japan dates from 1890, when a line was opened between Tokyo and Yokohama. It was 1899 before Tokyo was linked with Osaka and Kobe. In 1925, battery-operated phones were introduced into the country's six largest cities. Japan appears to have more outside public telephones than any other country—and they come in different colors and sizes. Regular-size public phones that are blue, pink, or red are for local calls. Calls are limited to three minutes per 10 yen coin. A chime sounds 30 seconds before the three minutes are up, and you must insert another coin to maintain the connection.

Large-size red phones will accept up to six coins at one time and return any that are unused. Yellow phones may be used for either local or long-distance calls—but unused coins or are not returned.

Japanese cities and the surrounding environs have their own area codes. See AREA CODES.

TELEVISION / TERUBI (Tay-rue-bee)   There are 1,502 VHF television broadcasting stations and 9,453 UHF stations in Japan. Of the former, 1,113 are owned by NHK—507 of them general and 506 of them educational. Forty-eight commercial companies own the other 489 VHF stations.

NHK is also the primary owner of UHF stations—altogether, 5,338, of which 2,699 are general and 2,639 are educational. Forty-six commercial companies own the remaining 4,115 commercial stations.

As for programming, Japanese TV devotes approximately 14 percent of its time to news, 25 percent to culture, 45 percent to entertainment, 12 percent to education, 2.5 percent to sports, and the balance to advertising and other subjects.

The types of programs on Japanese television are similar to those on American television. Japanese programmers have more leeway, however, in terms of the content, particularly regarding language and sex.

The *Yomiuri Newspaper's* famous Matsutaro Shoriki was instrumental in introducing television to Japan. Research into TV had been carried on by NHK in the 1930s, and, in 1939 and 1940, experimental broadcasting was open to the public. But all such activity ended with the beginning of the Pacific War. NHK opened its first TV station on February 1, 1953, followed by Shoriki's NTV on August 28, 1953. Radio Tokyo TV, now TBS, began operating on April 1, 1955.

Color television broadcasting began in Japan in September of 1960 by NHK and commercial broadcasters in Tokyo and Osaka. At that time, there were only 1,200 color TV sets in the whole country. The switch from black and white to color television in Japan was greatly accelerated by the Tokyo Olympic Games in 1964.

TEMPLE LODGINGS / SHUKUBO (Shuu-kuu-boe)   Inns for travelers have existed in Japan for hundreds of years, but long before they came along travelers were able to put up at night at many of the temples that dotted the countryside and urban areas.

The priests lodged travelers because of religious conviction and because they needed income for the upkeep of their temples.

This tradition continues in Japan today, although on a smaller scale. The accommodations are simple and rustic in most temples, and the food is usually vegetarian, but the cost is low and comes with an experience that in itself is valuable.

Many of those who take advantage of temple *shukubo* today are on temple pilgrimages, visiting a large number of noted temples during a single trip.

TEMPLE SCHOOLS / TERA KOYA (Tay-rah koya)   Shortly after the end of the Kamakura Period in 1333, a system of temple schools was developed throughout Japan, at which the children of *samurai* were taught religion, the Chinese *kanji* characters, and other subjects by Buddhist priests.

In later centuries, some of these temple schools were open to the children of common people, but they were not required to attend school and most did not. The *tera koya* continued in operation until 1868, when a modern school system was established.

TEMPURA (Tim-puu-rah)   One of the few Japanese dishes that Westerns like immediately, *tempura* is a variety of seafoods and vegetables dipped in a batter made of wheat flour mixed with egg and deep-fried in vegetable oil.

Tempura are best when hot, dipped in a sauce made of fish broth, sweet rice wine, and soy sauce, along with some grated ginger or radish.

A favorite variation is *tempura* placed on top of a bowl of noodles (*tempura soba* or *tempura udon*). *Soba* are small brownish noodles, and *udon* are large white noodles.

TENGU (Tane-goo)   The *tengu* are mythical, human-like creatures that are a popular part of Japanese folklore. They are usually depicted as having very long noses or a beak, long beards, and wings. They are said to live in groups in the mountains and to take special pleasure in kidnapping people, especially children.

When Westerners, with their long noses and beards, first began appearing in Japan, they were often compared to the *tengu*. In fact, it is possible that foreigners cast upon the shores of Japan in ancient times might have been responsible for the myth.

Japanese folklore traces the *tengu* to priests who were transformed by the powers of evil.

THUNDER GOD / RAIDEN (Rie-dane)   Visitors to Japan are often attracted to the statue of a large, red-faced demon that has two claws on each foot, carries several drums fastened to a rope, and reputedly loves to dine on human navels.

This is *Raiden*, the God of Thunder, and he is enshrined as a protection against lightning. Apart from his eating habits, he is a nice fellow to have around during thunderstorms.

TIPPING / CHIPU (Cheep-pu)   One of the special pleasures of living and traveling in Japan is that you do not have to tip taxi drivers, bartenders, waiters, and other service employees. The Japanese travel industry goes to great lengths to prevent the Western custom of direct tipping from spreading.

About the only people one is expected to tip directly in Japan are interpreters, guides, redcaps at airports and train stations, and taxi drivers who go out of their way to find an obscure location or are especially helpful with a carload of luggage.

Employees of hotels and the Japanese National Railways are instructed to refuse tips if offered, and this policy is strictly enforced.

Virtually no one tips at an ordinary restaurant. Tipping at special, exclusive restaurants is generally done in connection with entertaining special guests—and traditionally such tips are given before the meal, not afterward.

The rationale is that you are guaranteed good service by tipping in advance.

TOBACCO / TOBAKO (Toe-bah-koe)   Tobacco was first introduced into Japan in 1543, when a Portuguese ship ran aground on Tanega Island, south of Kyushu, during a storm. The smoking habit spread slowly at first. It was denounced by the shogunate authorities as an unhealthy and dangerous habit —particularly since Japanese homes and other wood and paper buildings were so susceptible to fire, but to no avail. Hundreds of thousands of Japanese were soon addicted smokers.

The Japanese developed a long-stemmed, tiny-bowled pipe called *kiseru* (kee-say-rue), adding to the popularity of the smoking habit. Today, the consumption of tobacco in Japan on a per capita basis among highest in the world.

The sale of tobacco in Japan was exclusively controlled by a government monopoly, the Japan Tobacco and Salt Corporation, until 1984, when it was turned over to a "private" company, Japan Tobacco Inc., which is still mostly owned by the government. About 60 percent of the revenue produced by tobacco sales goes to the national and regional governments. Annual sales are in excess of $12 billion.

Japan's 90,000 tobacco farmers are subsidized by the government, and the cost of raising tobacco in Japan is more than double the international average.

TOFU (Toe-fuu)   A favorite Japanese food that is rapidly becoming popular worldwide, *tofu* is a curd made of soybean paste. Soybeans are boiled and then made into a smooth pudding by adding bittern (what remains after sodium chloride is crystalized out of sea water).

Tofu is used as an ingredient in soups, *sukiyaki*, and numerous other dishes. It is eaten as is, boiled, and fried, with or without soy sauce. The protein content of *tofu* is very high (higher than that of meats), and it is easy to digest.

Recommended reading: *The Book of Tofu*, William Shurtleff and Akiko Aoyagi (Ten Speed Press).

TOGO, ADMIRAL HEIHACHIRO (Toe-go, Hay-e-hah-chee-roe)   One of Japan's greatest naval heroes, Admiral Heihachiro Togo (1847–1934) was in charge of the naval forces that defeated the Russian fleet in the Russo-Japanese war of 1904–1905. His flagship, the battleship *Mikasa*, is now a memorial in Yokosuka.

The large Togo Shrine in Tokyo's Harajuku district is dedicated to the admiral.

TOGU PALACE (Toe-guu)   The Togu Palace, located in the Aoyama district of Tokyo, a short distance southwest of the Imperial Palace grounds, is where The Crown Prince and Princess live. Built in a combination of Japanese and Western styles, the palace has over 40 hectares of floor space.

TOILETS / BENJO (Bane-joe)   The traditional Japanese-style toilet—a pit beneath the house, enclosed in a small room—is still common in Japan. At present, only about 35 percent of all households in the country are connected to sewage lines, but approximately half of all toilets are the flush-type.

The toilet pits are emptied periodically by sewage trucks equipped with suction pumps.

Extreme cleanliness has been a very important part of Japanese life since the country's history began. Rigorous sanitary conditions are required in all areas, particularly kitchens and toilets.

The Japanese traditionally equated cleanliness with cultural and spiritual standards.

TOKAIDO (Toe-Kie-Doe)   The Tokaido, which means "Eastern Seaway Road," was the most famous and most traveled of the seven great Do roads of feudal Japan, from the end of the twelfth century on. It began in Kyoto and traversed 15 old provinces to Edo (Tokyo). See ROADS.

The Tokaido was immortalized by woodblock-print master Hiroshige, who traveled the road in the early 1800s and then produced a print on each of the 53 stages of the famous highway. (Reproductions of the prints are available in gift shops in Tokyo, Kyoto, and other major cities.)

The Tokaido covered a distance of 323 miles from the Bridge of Japan (Nihon Bashi) in Edo to the center of Kyoto, through rice fields, along picturesque coastlines, over scenic mountains, and through dozens of rural towns and villages. It was traveled by peddlers, merchants, priests, entertainers, religious pilgrims, shogunate messengers, Imperial envoys, and clan lords and their retainers as they made their biannual trips to and from Edo to attend the *shogun's* court. See PROCESSIONS OF THE LORDS.

Most traffic on the Tokaido and Japan's other great highways was pedestrian, because only the nobility, ranking *samurai*, and official envoys or messengers were allowed to travel by palanquin or ride horses. Thus, there was a constant, colorful steam of people walking the highways, stopping over at roadside inns and fast-food restaurants at frequent intervals.

For nearly 250 years of the Tokugawa Shogunate, the Tokaido and other national highways of Japan were not only the political and economic lifelines of the country, they were also a central theme in the social life of Japan. See PROCESSIONS OF THE LORDS; TOKUGAWA.

TOKONOMA (Toe-koe-no-mah)   The *tokonoma* is a recessed alcove in the main room of Japanese homes and in the rooms of inns and other traditional Japanese buildings, which serves the purpose of displaying flower arrangements, hanging scrolls, or other art forms meant to be appreciated for their beauty and philosophical sentiments.

The Japanese are apparently the only people ever to make the deliberate, institutionalized appreciation of beauty an integral part of their life-style, and the universal *tokonoma* is one of the most important expressions of this traditional attitude.

The *tokonoma* itself is typically a work of art, with very special care taken in the selection of the materials used in its construction and in the artistry with which it is installed.

This special alcove originated as a Buddhist altar, in which an incense burner, flowers, and a Buddhist scroll were placed.

TOKUGAWA, IEYASU (Toe-kuu-gah-wah, E-eh-yah-sue)   Ieyasu Tokugawa, the founder of Japan's last great feudal house, the Tokugawa Shogunate, was born in 1543 to Hirotada Matsudaira, a warrior who was later to change his last name to Tokugawa.

The Matsudaira family was a minor clan that first appeared in history around 1400, when it was located in the foothills of what is now Aichi Prefecture near Nagoya. The clan was then headed by Chikauji Matsudaira. The family gradually extended its control over the surrounding territory and, by the mid-1500s, ruled most of the province.

In 1535, Kiyoyasu Matsudaira, then only 24, was killed and succeeded by his young son Hirotada as head of the clan. Hirotada allied himself with

Yoshitomo Imagawa, a powerful neighboring lord (*daimyo*). Twelve years later, the two had a falling out, and Hirotada was compelled to send his young son Takechiyo (later changed to Ieyasu) to Imagawa as a hostage.

En route to the Imagawa castle, the young boy was captured by another powerful warlord, Nobuhide Oda, who held him until his father was killed two years later and then sent him on to Imagawa. In 1560, Imagawa was killed in battle, and the 17-year old Ieyasu was allowed to return home.

The following year, as the head of his family, Ieyasu allied himself with Nobunaga Oda, Nobuhide's son. In 1567, he changed his name from Takechiyo Matsudaira to Ieyasu Tokugawa (an old ancestral name that had disappeared), to avoid conflicts with other members of the Matsudaira clan who coveted his role as head of the family.

Nobunaga Oda became the paramount power in Japan, and Ieyasu's fortunes rose with him. When Oda was killed and succeeded by his ablest general, Hideyoshi Toyotomi, Ieyasu became one of Hideyoshi's leading supporters.

Finally, when Hideyoshi died of natural causes in 1598, Ieyasu took up the fight against his enemies. His victory at the Battle of Sekigahara in 1600 made him the military master of Japan. In 1603, Emperor Yozei conferred the title of *shogun* on Ieyasu, thus formally recognizing his supremacy. Two years later, Ieyasu abdicated in favor of his 26-year old son, Hidetada, as a way of assuring that the position of *shogun* would remain in his family.

Ieyasu then retired to Shizuoka, midway between Edo and Nagoya, and, while he continued to direct the affairs of the country from behind the scenes, he also spent a lot of time studying literature and writing poetry.

In 1611, Ieyasu went to Kyoto in an attempt to heal the break between himself and the Toyotomi family by arranging a marriage between his granddaughter and Hideyori.

The family merger did not come off, however, and finally, in May 1615, Ieyasu's *samurai* troops stormed the Toyotomi's castle in Osaka and killed Hideyori and the rest of his family.

In 1615, Ieyasu further consolidated his shogunate by decreeing 13 articles (called *Buke-Shohatto*) that the feudal lords were required to obey. These articles controlled such matters as castle repairs, road repairs, and marriage.

The first two articles ordered the *samurai* to devote themselves to literature and arms and to refrain from debauchery. Articles 3–5 covered how the *daimyo* were to govern their fiefs. Articles 6–8 prohibited conspiracies or other activities by the *daimyo* against the shogunate. Articles 9–11 prescribed the clothing that each class was to wear, the vehicles that each could use, and the manners appropriate to each class. The last two articles called for *samurai* to live in a frugal manner and for the *daimyo* to promote their retainers on the basis of merit.

Thus, the *daimyo* were privileged to exercise absolute power in some areas within their domains—particularly the lives and fortunes of their subjects— but they were controlled in all areas of national interest by the laws of the *shogun* and could be removed or executed by the shogunate government.

The *daimyo* were divided into two groups—those who had supported Ieyasu before the Battle of Sekigahara, which assured his becoming *shogun*, and those who had not. Those who had allied themselves with him were known as *fudai* (fuu-die), or hereditary *daimyo*.

With the Tokugawa position secure, Ieyasu once again retired to Shizuoka, where he died in 1616 at the age of 74. See ADAMS, WILLIAM; TOYOTOMI, HIDEYOSHI; HISTORY.

There were to be 15 Tokugawa *shoguns* over the next 264 years, and the Tokugawa family was to grow into 20 different branches, including the main lineage that held the shogunate. This main lineage was known as *honke* (hone-kay), or the main family, while the others were called *bunke* (boon-kay), or branch families.

The primary branch families were the three established by the younger sons of Ieyasu, in Mito, Nagoya, and Wakayama. Later Tokugawa *shogun* were to establish other primary branch families in the seventeenth century.

The Tokugawa *Shoguns* and the dates of their rule were Hidetada (1616–1623), Iemitsu (1623–1651), Ietsuna (1651–1680), Tsunayoshi (1680–1709), Ienobu (1709–1712), Ietsugu (1713–1716), Yoshimune (1716–1745), Ieshige (1745–1760), Ieharu (1760–1786), Ienari (1787–1837), Ieyoshi (1837–1853), Iesada (1853–1858), Iemochi (1858–1866), and Yoshinobu (1866–1867).

During the Tokugawa Shogunate, the day-to-day government of cities and areas was in the hands of *bugyo* (boog-yoe), or magistrates, appointed directly by the *shogun*. The most important of these *bugyo* were those who were in charge of financial matters and supervising local governors and the people (*kanjo bugyo*); those who were responsible for legal affairs and running the cities (*machi bugyo*); and the ones who administered the affairs of temples, shrines, and priests (*jisha bugyo*).

The *machi bugyo* generally had a police sergeant and constable as assistants. The magistrates were rotated from one city to another on a monthly basis (to keep them from establishing power bases, no doubt) and were therefore frequent travelers on Japan's great walking roads.

One of the most popular TV programs in Japan during the 1970s, 80s, and 90s was a serial that recounted the road adventures of one of the most famous of the Tokugawa Shogunate magistrates and his assistants. They were always coming to the rescue of the oppressed and bringing the bad ones (usually *samurai* gone bad) to justice.

Ieyasu is revered in Japan as one of its greatest warriors and most skillful administrators. The system of government he devised and his descendants elaborated on was to give Japan one of its longest periods of peace and prosperity.

Of his 15 descendants who were to hold the position of *shogun*, only a few were of outstanding character or ability. Iemitsu (1623–1651), the third Tokugawa *shogun*, was the one who shut Japan's doors to the outside world, expelled the Christian missionaries, and originated the policy of having the *daimyo* spend every other year in Edo and leave their families there year-round. See PROCESSIONS OF THE LORDS.

The eighth Tokugawa *shogun*, Yoshimune (1716–1745), is ranked as the wisest, most humane, and ablest of Ieyasu's descendants. He was a patron of the arts, removed the ban on translating and reading European books; promoted trade between the provinces; and was active in improving medical treatment for the poor. He is also credited with having introduced the sweet potato to Japan.

Generally listed among the greatest families in Japanese history (the others being the Fujiwara, Minamoto, and Hojo), the Tokugawas are believed to have been descended from Yoshishige Nitta, the grandson of Yoshiie Minamoto (1041–1108).

TOKUSHIMA (Toe-kuu-she-mah)   The capital of Shikoku Island's Tokushima Prefecture, the city of Tokushima is noted today for its Awa Odori folk dances, puppet shows, cotton crepe fabrics, and wood furniture.

Situated on one of the channels of the Yoshino River, Tokushima began as the castle town of *Daimyo* Iemasa Hachisuka in 1586, and it is now one of the largest and most important cities on Shikoku.

Besides its nationally famous folk dances (which are performed in the streets each year from August 15 to 18) and its puppet dramas (staged between farming seasons by farmers traditionally skilled in the art), Tokushima is also known as the home of Wenceslao de Moraes, a Portuguese naval officer who came to Japan in 1893 in the consular service.

After retiring from the service, Moraes moved to Tokushima, the home of his Japanese wife, and devoted the rest of his life to studying and writing about things Japanese. He published 16 books—all in Portuguese—and today is often regarded as a Portuguese Lafcadio Hearn. See HEARN, LAFCADIO.

Special attractions in Tokushima include Tokushima Park, formerly the castle grounds of Lord Hachisuka and considered to be one of the finest examples of Momoyama period landscape gardening in the country; the ancient Nyorin Temple, headquarters of the Hoju-Shingon sect of Buddhism; and the cherry tree grove in Bizan Park, on the slopes of Otaki Hill, with its Peace Memorial Pagoda.

The house where Moraes lived is at the foot of Otaki Hill in Tokushima.

TOKYO   The only *To* (Toe), or Metropolitan District in Japan, Tokyo consists of 23 semi-autonomous wards (*ku*), 26 cities, seven towns, eight villages, the seven islands of Izu, and the Ogasawara Islands.

The site that is now Tokyo was first mentioned near the end of the twelfth century, when Taro Shigenaga Edo, the son of Shiro Shigetsu Edo of the Taira clan, was appointed political agent of the province of Musashi for *Shogun* Yoritomo Minamoto and gave his name (Edo) to a tiny fishing-farming village on an estuary at the head of a great bay (which came to be known as Edo Gulf).

Or it may have been the other way around. Since *edo* means estuary, which is what the area was, the Edos may have adopted it as their last name!

In 1457, Dokan Ota, a member of the Ogigayatsu Uesugi family, chose the site for a castle-fortress. Ota (1432–1486), also known as a poet, described the area around Edo in a famous poem:

Musahino wa	The wide plain
Tsuki no irubeki	of Musashi
Yama mo nashi	Has no hills at all
Kusa yori idete	Where the moon sets
Kusa ni koso ire	Over a sea of grass.

The area did not to change very much until 1590, when Ieyasu Tokugawa, the man who was to establish the Tokugawa Shogunate, Japan's last great feudal dynasty, was given the region as his fief and established his headquarters in the castle Dokan had built over 130 years earlier.

Edo grew quickly with the arrival of Ieyasu and his 70,000 retainers, and was to go through a second period of rapid growth three decades later when the Tokugawa Shogunate, as part of its military control of the land, required the more than 200 larger feudal lords throughout the country to build mansions in Yedo, leave their families there at all times, and themselves spend every other year in attendance at the *shogun's* court.

This policy resulted in a tremendous influx of people into Edo from all over the country—not only the lords and their families, but their retainers and servants, along with thousands of artisans, shopkeepers, merchants, priests, entertainers, and others to serve their needs. Within less than a decade, Edo was one of the most populous and sophisticated cities in the world.

With the downfall of the Tokugawa dynasty in 1868 and restoration of power to the emperor, Japan's Imperial capital was moved from Kyoto to Edo, and the name was changed to Tokyo, meaning Eastern Capital. Edo Castle became the Imperial Palace.

But the city never really became an integrated community. The Edo mansions of each of the clan lords tended to become the center of a separate community made up of the retainers of the lord and the various tradespeople from their fief who set up business there to serve them.

Thus, Edo was made up of a huge cluster of dozens of communities whose outlines are still recognizable in present-day Tokyo and some of whose names have been handed down in the form of the Cho and Machi that make up Tokyo area names. This is also one of the reasons why Tokyo's streets form such a maze.

In 1657, following a disastrous fire that destroyed much of the city, a serious attempt was made to widen and improve the main streets, but the effort was only marginally successful because people rebuilt their homes and shops as rapidly as possible in the same location.

By 1731, the population of Edo was nearly 600,000. Only 56 years later, it had passed 1,386,000, making it one of the largest cities in the world.

Most of the 26 cities that are within the jurisdiction of Tokyo-To are in the so-called Tama District, to the west of the city. These include Musashino, Mitaka, Koganei, Kokubunji, Kunitachi, Tachikawa, Hino, Hachioji, Fuchu, Chofu, Komae, Inagi, Tama, Machida, Hoya, Tanashi, Higashi Kurume, Kiyose, Higashi Murayama, Kodaira, Higashi Yamato, Musashi Murayama, Akishima, Fussa, Akigawa, and Ome.

Tokyo-To is administered by a governor elected by the residents and a Metropolitan Council of 125 members. Several satellite cities adjoin the metropolis, including Urawa, Omiya, Funabashi, and Chiba.

Tokyo's 23 wards make up the main metropolitan area of the city. These wards are Chiyoda, Chuo, Minato, Taito, Shinjuku, Bunkyo, Sumida, Koto, Shinagawa, Meguro, Ota, Setagya, Shibuya, Nakano, Suginami, Toshima, Kita, Arakawa, Itabashi, Nerima, Adachi, Katsushika, and Edogawa.

Downtown Tokyo is primarily located in the two wards of Chuo and Chiyoda, with portions of it extending over into Minato. Some of the more famous districts in Tokyo—each one virtually a city within itself—are the Ginza, Shimbashi, Kanda, Aoyama, Roppongi, Harajuku, Shibuya, and Shinjuku.

Metropolitan Tokyo now has a population in excess of 12 million and is one of the most cosmopolitan and colorful cities in the world, famous for its great department stores, dozens of huge shopping areas and entertainment districts, numerous theaters, and as many restaurants as are found in many well-known countries.

Central Tokyo, of which the Imperial Palace (formerly Edo Castle) is the hub, is divided into districts—one known as Uptown (Yamanote) and primarily residential, and the other known as Downtown (Shitamachi) and primarily commercial and industrial.

Practically speaking, the central area of Tokyo is made up of over a dozen centers, usually clustered around major commuter terminals, that are like cities within themselves. These include Yurakucho, the Ginza, Shimbashi, Shinagawa, Gotanda, Shibuya, Harajuku, Shinjuku, Ikebukuro, Ueno, Kanda, Nihonbashi, Akasaka, Roppongi, and Asakusa.

Although unbelievably crowded, Tokyo has one of the best transportation systems in the world, including loop-line trains, suburban railways, 12 subway lines, numerous bus lines, and several expressways. It also has several large taxi fleets that offer the most efficiently and courteously run taxi service in the world. See SUBWAYS.

The numerous transportation terminals that result from this system make up another primary characteristic of Tokyo—nearly 100 train and or subway stations, sometimes combined, that form population, commercial, and industrial centers. Among the largest of these centers are Shibuya and Shinjuku.

The Tokyo Metropolitan Government publishes a quarterly journal in English called *Tokyo Municipal News*, which covers the various problems, policies, and plans of the city and is available to interested foreigners.

TOKYO BUSINESS TODAY   An authoritative and respected monthly journal aimed at businesspeople and financiers, each issue of *Tokyo Business Today* contains a survey of a major industrial sector, along with news and analyses of political and economic issues. Contributors are leading Japanese scholars businesspeople, and foreign journalists.

The magazine is published by Toyo Keizai Shinposha Ltd. See OTHER SOURCES.

TOKYO CLIMATE   The weather in Tokyo is similar to that in Washington, D.C.—hot, humid summers, warm to cool falls, cool to cold winters, and cool to warm springs. During the spring rainy season, it is cloudy and rainy in Tokyo about three-fourths of the time. Throughout the rest of the year, it is cloudy and rainy about one-third of the time.

October is the wettest month in Tokyo because of fall typhoons, and December is the driest month. There are usually two or three light snowfalls in Tokyo every winter. A fairly heavy snowfall comes along only about once every 10 years. In earlier years, heavy snows were common in the city.

In August, the hottest month, temperatures range from 91 to 93 degrees F. Winter lows are 23–25 degrees F., but on the average it is above freezing.

Annual rainfall averages 1,503mm, or 63 inches. The weather is most likely to run to extremes in the winter—from sunny and dry to wet, windy, and cold.

TOKYO DISNEYLAND   Japan's Disneyland, usually referred to as the Tokyo Disneyland, but officially named the Magic Kingdom, opened May 15, 1983. Located six miles from downtown Tokyo on land reclaimed from Tokyo Bay, the 115-acre amusement park cost $650 million to build.

The Tokyo Disneyland is owned by the Oriental Land Company, which is owned in turn by the Keisei Railway Company and Mitsui Real Estate Development Company. Oriental Land Company bought the rights to use the Disneyland name and know-how from Walt Disney Enterprises in the U.S. and pays the American company a royalty of 10 percent of all admission fees and 5 percent of the revenue from restaurants and shops.

Among the attractions of the Magic Kingdom are a World Bazaar, which is the re-creation of a Victorian Era shopping center about the size of a baseball stadium and completely covered by a transparent roof, and Cinderella's Castle, which is as high a 13-story building.

Altogether, the park has 28 facilities for staging various shows, 25 restaurants, 34 boutiques, and hundreds of other shops and entertainment facilities. On the average, visitors are able to cover only about one-third of what the more Magic Kingdom has to offer during a one-day period. See DISNEYLAND.

TOKYO JOURNAL   A slick, monthly, English-language magazine founded in 1981 by Japanese entrepreneur Peter Y. Yamauchi and later sold to a real estate group, *Tokyo Journal* covers the entertainment and social scene and features a variety of human interest stories, some of them of a controversial nature, such as Japan's penal system and the treatment of prisoners.

In the early years, the primary circulation of *Tokyo Journal* was among the foreign community. It has since become popular with Japanese who have international backgrounds, and with Japanene students studying English.

TOKYO STATION / TOKYO EKI (Eh-kee)   The picturesque Tokyo Station Building and Hotel, designed by Kingo Tatsuno and completed in 1914, was virtually destroyed during World War II but was soon restored and in subsequent years greatly enlarged. The original three-story, red-brick building now constitutes the main west entrance to the station.

Tokyo Station is the main terminal of Japanese National Railways, where the famous Bullet Trains (Shinkan Sen) begin and end their journeys. It is also the home station for Tokyo's popular Yamanote Loop Line, which circles the heart of the city, the Chuo Line, and several others.

The station complex includes numerous offices and facilities and adjoins a number of important buildings, including the Japanese National Railways Building, the Japan Travel Bureau Building, the Tokyo Central Post Office, the Daimaru Department Store, and the Kokusai Kanko Kaikan (International Travel Building).

An underground shopping center on the Yaesuguchi side of the station extends over an immense area and has more than 400 stores and restaurants that cater to train travelers.

Although nearly two million passengers pass through Tokyo Station every day, it is still not the busiest station in the city. That distinction goes to Shinjuku Station, on the west side of town.

The Tokyo Station Hotel was a popular place before World War II, when it was hit by incendiary bombs and burned out. It reopened in 1950 and, for a while, recaptured some of the spirit of the old days. A number of famous people, including author Yasunari Kawabata, often stayed at the hotel.

TOKYO TOWER   Completed in December 1958 by the Nippon Television City Corporation, the 333-meter high, independent steel Tokyo Tower has been a conspicuous feature of Tokyo's skyline ever since.

Located near the southwest corner of Shiba Park, the tower has two observation platforms—one at the 150-meter level and the other 250 meters high—both providing a spectacular view of the surrounding city.

The tower is a major tourist attraction, drawing hundreds of thousands of people a year. It also houses the telecasting center of Tokyo's Channel 12.

TOKYO UNIVERSITY / TOKYO DAIGAKU (To-k-yoe Die-gah-kuu)   The ranking university in Japan, Tokyo University—or Todai, as it is often called—was founded in 1869 as a state university that grew out of a number of schools established during the last years of the Tokugawa Shogunate.

The campus area was formerly the estate of the Maeda family, one of Japan's largest and most powerful feudal clans. The only thing remaining on campus from the days of the feudal lords is the Aka Mon, or Red Gate, which stands near the main gate of the campus, facing the thoroughfare that is now called Hongo Avenue, from the name of the district.

The university is particularly noted for its medical, science, economics, literature, and law departments. It has long been noted for having what is almost a monopoly on placing graduates in the top government ministries and bureaus and for providing its graduates with an edge on employment with top corporations. This latter advantage appears to have diminished rather dramatically since the early 1980s, as many companies top-heavy with Todai graduates have been among the poorest performers in Japan.

As the most prestigious university in Japan, Todai's annual entrance examinations attract thousands of students competing for the limited number of openings. See RONIN; EXAMINATION HELL; STUDENTS.

In April 1985, the law faculty of Todai hired a foreign professor for the first time in its history. The foreign professor was Chinese-born Dr. Paul Heng-Chao Chen, a naturalized American citizen.

TOKYO WEEKENDER   A weekly English-language newspaper that is subtitled *A Forum for Foreigners in Japan*, the *Tokyo Weekender* was founded in 1969 by American journalist, raconteur, and jack-of-all-trades Millard (Corky) Alexander.

The *Weekender* covers entertainment, dining out, sports, travel information, and foreign-resident social news, in a spritely, sometimes clever, and often humorous approach that puts it several rungs above the average journalistic fare.

Several of Tokyo's most talented and unusual foreign residents are regular contributors to the *Weekender* and have helped make it must reading for the foreign community and large numbers of bilingual Japanese.

Many foreigners who leave Japan after several years' residence choose to subscribe to the *Tokyo Weekender* to keep up with the news. Address: Tuttle Building, 1-2-6 Suido, Bunkyo Ku, Tokyo, Japan 112.

TOUR COMPANION   A weekly tourist publication that covers events, shopping, dining, and nighttime entertainment in Tokyo, *Tour Companion* is a valuable aid for visitors in the city. It includes maps of the city, major shopping areas, and the subway system, along with all kinds of other information useful to tourists—from how to use the public telephones, postal rates, currency exchange rates, train timetables, and television programs in English, to tips on taxis, tipping, and otherwise staying out of trouble.

Tour Companion is available free in hotels, airline offices, and tourist shops.

TOURISM / KANKO (Kahn-koe)   Tourism is one of the best organized, and most efficiently run industries in Japan. But this is hardly surprising. Japan is one of the most scenic island countries in the world, and it has an endless array of historical sites and vacation spots. Thus, with an equally endless curiosity about everything, and travel traditions that go back centuries, the Japanese are inveterate sightseers and enjoy all forms of travel, especially within Japan.

The travel industry is organized on the highest level, with the Prime Minister's Office and the ministries of Transport, Foreign Affairs, Finance, and Health and Welfare all involved in coordinating and promoting international tourism. On the domestic side, there are even more government agencies and bureaus that play major roles in tourism.

In 1963, the Japanese government enacted a Basic Tourism Law that was designed to promote international friendship, the development of the national economy, and the adjustment of regional differences in social and economic conditions.

An Inter-Ministerial Liaison Council on Tourism was established in the Prime Minister's Office to coordinate policies on tourism, and a Department of Tourism was set up within the Ministry of Transport to supervise the tourism industry. This department has three divisions—Planning, Tourist Promotion, and Facilities.

The Department of Tourism supervises the activities of the Japan National Tourist Organization, conducts national examinations of tourist guides under the Guide-Interpreter Business Law, provides assistance to guides, and registers and supervises travel agents under the Travel Agency Business Law.

The Department is also responsible for the registration and supervision of inns and hotels, for tourism statistics, and for maintaining liaison and cooperation with all other domestic and international tourist bodies.

On the local level, each of Japan's 47 prefectures has its own tourist office that helps promote local tourism, as well as coordinating the industry with national and international bodies.

There are also two dozen other bureaus under the Ministry of Transport that have tourist offices in key cities and work closely with local tourism interests in a supervisory, as well as a liaison and support, capacity. See the JAPAN NATIONAL TOURIST ORGANIZATION.

TOURISTS IN JAPAN The first full-fledged tourist group arrived in Japan in 1860 aboard a passenger ship called the *Aden*, less than seven years after the arrival of Commodore Perry and his Black Ships and seven years before the fall of the Tokugawa Shogunate and the restoration of Imperial power. An American, Silas K. Burrows, is recorded as claiming to have been the first tourist in Japan in 1854, the same year Japan signed its first treaty with the outside world and ended its long centuries of isolation.

TOYAMA (Toe-yah-mah) Some 225 kilometers northwest of Gifu on the Japan Sea side of Honshu, the large port city of Toyama has a rather unusual claim to fame. In the seventeenth century, a physician from the province of Okayama visited Toyama and presented the ruling *daimyo*, Masatoshi Maeda, with some medicines prepared from old family recipes.

The *daimyo* was so impressed with the medicines that he ordered his retainers to set up a factory to manufacture the concoctions on a commercial scale and to market them as widely as possible.

The new enterprise established a network of peddler-salespeople who traveled to every corner of the country. Eventually, the medicines were sold in Korea, China, and Southeast Asia, helping to make the fief one of the richest in the country.

As one of the largest and richest of the *daimyo* during the Tokugawa period, Maeda took some 10,000 retainers with him when he made his biannual trip to Edo (Tokyo). See PROCESSIONS OF THE LORDS.

Still today, Toyama is a center for the manufacture of traditional, as well as modern, medicines, with its production valued well in excess of 85 billion yen a year.

TOYOTOMI, HIDEYOSHI (Toe-yoe-toe-me, He-day-yoe-she) Given the nature of society in feudal Japan, in which class more than anything else was the determining factor in the fortunes of men and women, it is an unending wonder that one of the country's greatest men was born a peasant and yet rose to become a leader of leaders.

The man history knows as Hideyoshi Toyotomi was born to a poor farmer named Yaemon in the village of Nakamura, in Owari Province, in the year 1536. Being peasants, the family did not have a last name, and the boy was called Hiyoshimaru. The little boy looked so much like a monkey that he was nicknamed Ko Zaru, or Little Monkey—and was to be called Saru-men Kwanpaku, or Monkey Face Prime Minister (behind his back), even after he had attained the highest office in the land.

Hiyoshimaru apparently behaved like a rowdy young monkey and caused so much trouble his parents couldn't control him. In desperation, they sent him to a temple where they thought the stern priests might be able to teach him gentler ways.

The priests also found Hiyoshimaru uncontrollable and unteachable, but because of the entreaties of his parents, they kept him until he was 12 years old. In the meantime, his father had died and his mother had married a retainer of Lord Nobunaga Oda, *daimyo* of the Omi Province.

His mother and stepfather apprenticed him several times, but each time he quit or was dismissed. Finally, after running away from the shop of a porcelain dealer, he set out for Okazaki to seek his fortune in the city.

While he was asleep alongside the road, a gang of robbers came by. One of them kicked the young boy just to have some fun with him. Angered by this, Hiyoshimaru jumped up, ready to fight the entire gang. A loud argument ensued, with Hiyoshimaru holding his own against the robber who had disturbed him.

The leader of the gang, Koroku Hachisuka, who was notorious in the area, was so impressed with Hiyoshimaru's courage and spirit—and the fact that he came from their own district—that he decided to take the boy along with the gang.

The gang leader later apprenticed Hiyoshimaru to a blacksmith and then a carpenter. While virtually uneducated, Hiyoshimaru had a natural intelligence and an incredibly quick mind that set him apart from other men. He also had an overwhelming ambition to achieve great things and, when he was in his twenties, managed to become the sandal-keeper to Lord Nobunaga Oda.

Although he was a nameless peasant so far below the lordly *samurai* that to address one of them in the wrong manner could mean instant death, Hiyoshimaru so impressed the great Nobunaga that he was put in charge of repairing Kiyosu Castle.

Completing the work in a far shorter time than expected, Hiyoshimaru was again promoted. Soon thereafter, he took advantage of his connections with the notorious robber Koroku Hachisuka, rounded up a gang of outlaws, and attacked one of Nobunaga's strongest enemies.

The attack was successful, and Hiyoshimaru was both promoted and given a new name, Hideyoshi Kinoshita, which was the equivalent of being elevated to the *samurai* class—a very rare event in Japan's history.

In 1570, Hideyoshi, by then the commander of an army of *samurai*, fought several successful battles against Yoshikage Asakura, another of Nobunaga's rivals. This time he was rewarded with an annual income of 30,000 *koku* (approximately 150,000 bushels) of rice, putting him on the level of a smaller *daimyo*.

Three years later, Hideyoshi attacked and captured the powerful Nagamasa Asai and his castle at Odani. Asai's fief, valued at 180,000 *koku* of rice a year, became Hideyoshi's property. Just one year later, he captured Nagahama Castle, on the shores of Lake Biwa, and kept it for himself. He also adopted a new family name, Hashiba.

Within five years, Hideyoshi had subjugated the five western provinces of central Honshu. By 1582, he was the leader of an army of 60,000 men. He then attacked the famous Takamatsu Castle, which was regarded as virtually impregnable. He engineered a way to flood the castle, and captured it easily.

While still in Takamatsu, Hideyoshi received the news that his benefactor, Nobunaga Oda, who was then the supreme military power in the country, had been assassinated by Mitsuhide Akechi, one of his own generals.

Hideyoshi immediately set out to avenge Nobunaga's death and prevent Akechi from usurping his power. He caught up with Akechi's army at Amagasaki, near Osaka, and destroyed it. Rather than face capture and execution, Akechi committed suicide.

This made Hideyoshi the supreme power in the country. In recognition of this, the Imperial Court gave him the title of lieutenant general. Later in the same year, he accepted the formal position of a privy councilor. He then had the magnificent Osaka Castle built and went there to live.

Hideyoshi had not yet achieved the success he craved. He still did not have an official surname, which identified him as being lowborn. He asked the last Ashikaga *shogun* to adopt him so he would have a proper name, but the *shogun* refused. He finally petitioned the emperor to allow him to officially take the name Toyotomi, which he made up, and his petition was granted.

In 1586, Hideyoshi was appointed *kwampaku* (prime minister), a position that had previously been held only by ranking Imperial nobles. This aroused more ire among the great *daimyo*, who resented Hideyoshi, and one of them, the Lord of Satsuma in Kyushu, challenged Hideyoshi. In 1587, Hideyoshi led a force of 150,000 men against the Satsuma clan and won a decisive victory.

The following year, in a further move to consolidate his power, Hideyoshi ordered all swords in the country not in the hands of approved *samurai* to be turned over to his military forces.

But two other leading clan lords, Ujimasa Hojo and Masamune Date, also refused to accept the supremacy of Hideyoshi. In 1590, he attacked and defeated them, which left him in total control of the country.

In 1591, Hideyoshi issued an edict establishing four distinct classes of people—*samurai*, farmers, artisans, and merchants (in that order), thus freezing social mobility in the country for the next 277 years—and making it impossible for anyone else to rise from peasant to prime minister, as he had done.

He then turned the position of prime minister over to his adopted son, Hidetsugu, and was given the title of *taiko*, or retired prime minister. Not content with having become the master of Japan, Hideyoshi began making preparations to invade and conquer Korea and China.

When ready, he dispatched an expedition of 150,000 men to Korea. Fierce fighters and well experienced in combat from their years of campaigning in Japan, Hideyoshi's armies began a successful march through Korea, killing huge numbers of Korean defenders (and collecting mountains of severed ears to prove it).

With victory in sight, Hideyoshi fell ill. When it became apparent that he was not going to survive, he ordered his generals to break off the attack and return to Osaka. He died, in 1598, before they returned.

Thus ended the life and career of one of the most remarkable men in Japan's long and colorful history—a man who is often compared to Napoleon in his skill as a general and as a great leader.

Recommended reading: *Toyotomi Hideyoshi*, by Walter Denning.

TRADE / BOEKI (Boe-aa-kee)   Despite its small size and lack of most vital raw materials, Japan is responsible for over 10 percent of the world's exports and approximately 8.5 percent of its imports.

Raw material supplies account for around 66 percent of Japan's imports, while its exports consist almost entirely of manufactured industrial products.

Japan's imports and exports are about evenly divided among developing and undeveloped nations. Major imports include fossil fuels, raw materials (textile raw materials, metallic raw materials, timber, and lumber), foodstuffs, machinery and equipment, and chemical products. Major exports are machinery and equipment (autos, electrical machinery, general machinery), nonmetallic minerals, textiles, and foods.

The United States, Japan's primary export market, takes well over 20 percent of its total exports, and Japan has a substantial imbalance of payments with the U.S. Some 12 percent of Japan's exports go to European countries, and approximately 5 percent go to Oceania.

TRADEPIA INTERNATIONAL   A well-written and edited quarterly magazine published by Nissho Iwai Corporation, *Tradepia International* covers trade issues, along with Japan's international political and economic relations, management and marketing in Japan, new technology, social issues, the economic outlook, and so on. See OTHER SOURCES.

TRADING COMPANIES/BOEKI GAISHA (Boe-a-kee guy-shah)   Japan's huge general trading companies have been world-famous since shortly after the turn of the century. Developed soon after industrialization began in 1868, the trading companies were closely tied in with the country's largest banks and with the top companies in each of the major industrial areas.

With access to capital and ties with the ranking manufacturing corporations, the trading companies enjoyed something of a national monopoly in all the key industries. The result of this was very rapid growth and tremendous power in the national economy.

When World War II ended, the huge *zaibatsu* combines, each of which had its own trading arm, were broken up. But soon after the end of the occupation of Japan by the Allied Powers in 1952, the groups came back together again in relatively loose federations. The breakup temporarily weakened the large trading companies and allowed several of the prewar medium-size companies to gain a substantial foothold in the country's import and export industries.

Despite the fact that several thousand small to medium-size Japanese manufacturers, particularly in consumer product fields, began to export directly in the 1950s, both the prewar and postwar trading giants were able to capture a significant percentage of the country's import-export trade.

Today Japan's nine largest trading companies account for over 50 percent of the nation's total import and export trade. They were able to achieve this because of their ability to arrange financing for both imports and exports, because of the expertize they developed in buying from and selling to foreign markets, and because they were able to arrange for product distribution, new manufacturing ventures, and reliable supplies of raw materials on a massive scale.

The Big Nine of Japan's general trading companies are Mitsubishi Shoji, Mitsui Bussan, Marubeni, Ito-Chu, Sumitomo Shoji, Nissho-Iwai, Toyo Menka, Kanematsu-Gosho, and Nichimen.

All of these companies have their own network of offices and related companies overseas, but the three largest, Ito-Chu, Mitsubishi, and Mitsui, are especially noted for the size and efficiency of their foreign networks. With offices in almost every country in the free world, they are able to supply a continuous stream of trade information to their headquarters that gives them a special advantage in this highly competitive world.

These huge, diversified trading companies are called Sogo Sho Sha (Soe-go Show Shah), or General Trading Companies (GTC).

One of the most important and significant functions of Japan's big GTC is their offshore trading activities—trading within and between other countries that does not involve Japan. In this category, the American branch of Mitsui & Company is the U.S.'s fourth largest trader. See MITSUI & COMPANY.

TRAINS / KISHA (Kee-shah)   Japan is world-famous for its trains—not only for their punctuality, efficiency, and speed, but also for the vast number of passengers they carry every day.

There are two train systems in Japan—one operated by the formerly government-owned Japanese National Railways, now privatized as the Japanese Railways Group (JR), and the other operated by independent private owners.

JR operates national, regional, and local lines, while the other private lines are limited to regional and local service. The smaller lines account for about 15 percent of Japan's passenger service and less than 1 percent of the freight transport.

The most famous of the JR trains are the so-called Bullet Trains of the Shin Kan Sen, or New Trunk Line, which began its first service on October 1, 1964. These trains leave Tokyo Central Station every few minutes—on the second.

Experimental work on magnetically levitated trains is well advanced in Japan. One example, developed by Japan Air Lines, was first demonstrated in April 1984. A futuristic looking vehicle called High-Speed Surface Train (HSST), it was tested at speeds up to 300 kilometers, or 188 miles, per hour.

Similar high-speed trains have been under development by the Japanese Railways Group since the early 1980s, and the first of them went into service in the mid-1990s.

TRAPPISTS IN JAPAN   Two of the most unexpected attractions in Hokkaido are a Trappist Convent about 20 minutes outside of Hakodate, near the famous Yunokawa hot spring spa, and a Trappist Monastery, also a short distance from Hakodate and just outside the town of Oshima-Tobetsu.

The monastery, founded in 1898 by eight French monks, is now operated by some 80 Trappistines divided into two groups—those who spend their time meditating and praying (and dress in white robes) and those who work at stock and dairy farming and make butter and candy. The working Trappistines wear brown robes.

Women are not allowed to enter the monastery buildings. Butter made at the monastery is available in some Tokyo shops.

TRAVEL / RYOKO (Rio-koe)   The Japanese are inveterate travelers and have been for generations. Perhaps because traveling within Japan—with some exceptions—was either prohibited or discouraged during most of the country's long history and was in fact not feasible for most Japanese until the mid 1960s, they developed an insatiable appetite for sightseeing and experiencing faraway places.

Another factor that encouraged traveling within Japan was the fact that the islands are incredibly scenic. The volcanic and mountainous nature of the terrain, the exceptionally long and varied coastlines, and the thousands of inlets and islands ringing the main islands like so many jewels have blessed the country with a variety and quality of scenery that is unsurpassed.

During the long, peaceful Tokugawa Period (1603–1868), Japan's great walking roads were crowded with gamblers, salespeople, priests, messengers, trades people, religious pilgrims visiting distant shrines and temples, wandering *samurai* who had lost their hereditary positions (the famous *ronin*), and entertainers. See ROADS.

With the tight security established by the Tokugawa Shogunate in the early 1600s, travel in Japan became much safer than it had been in earlier ages. Two special types of traveling became popular during the middle and latter years of the Tokugawa Period: *monomode* (moe-no-moe-day), or pilgrimages to famous shrines and temples around the country (of which there were thousands); and *yusan-tabi* (yuu-sahn-tah-bee), or sightseeing trips to scenic areas of the country, which are virtually endless.

Japan's most famous travel book series dates from the 1802–1822 period. Written by Ikku Jippensha and called *Tokai Dochu Hizakurige*, or *Traveling the Tokai Do by Shank's Mare* (on foot), the series chronicles the adventures of two men, Yajirobei and Hananosuke (later called Kitahachi), who prefer the perils and pleasures of the road to the carping of their wives.

The two typical Edo types get into just about every comic situation imaginable, and, in the process of telling their stories, Jippensha provides a vivid account of life, manners, and traveling in Japan during that era.

Recommended: *Shanks Mare* (Tuttle).

Soon after the Meiji Restoration in 1868, when the last Tokugawa *shogun* relinquished power to the emperor, school trips to different parts of the country were made a part of the educational system. This system continues, and, since the 1950s, various village and rural organizations have annually sponsored trips to major cities and scenic locations.

In addition, for decades it has been traditional for Japanese companies to take all their employees on company trips to beach or mountain resorts once a year. Altogether, the Japanese average over 130 million trips a year within Japan—or slightly more than one trip per person for the whole population.

Each year, some over 12 million Japanese travel abroad. Favorite destinations include Korea, Taiwan, Hong Kong, Thailand, Singapore, Guam, Hawaii, mainland U.S., and all the major countries of Europe.

TSU ISLANDS / TSUSHIMA (T'sue-she-mah)   Some 76 kilometers northwest of the northern tip of Kyushu, about halfway between Japan and Korea, Tsushima consists of two islands that acted as a link between the Asian mainland and the Japanese archipelago from earliest times.

The two islands—Kami (247 square kilometers) and Shimo (435 square kilometers)—are too mountainous to support much agriculture, and fishing is the main industry. The So clan ruled the islands from 1168 to 1860, and the ruins of their castle can be seen on the outskirts of the town of Izuhara. The islands are part of Nagasaki Prefecture. See MONGOL INVASIONS.

TSUKIJI HONGAN TEMPLE/TSUKIJI HONGAN JI (Ski-kee-jee hohn-ghan jee)   Founded in 1630, this is the Tokyo branch of the Nishi Hongan Temple of Kyoto, headquarters of the Jodo-Shinshu sect of Buddhism. A landmark in Tokyo since its founding, the temple has been destroyed by fire several times.

The present structure, built in ancient Hindu style in 1935, is both earthquake and fireproof. It will seat over 1,000 worshipers and includes a number of modern facilities not found in other temples in Japan.

It is frequently used for funeral services.

TSUKIJI WHOLESALE MARKET (Ski-jee)   One of 11 markets under the Central Wholesale Market of Tokyo, the Tsukiji Wholesale Market is one of the largest fish markets in the world and has become a national attraction.

The market was originally located in Nihonbashi, in the center of the city, and was one of the primary features of Edo and then Tokyo for nearly 300 years. In its present location just 10 minutes from the downtown area, the market handles 90 percent of the fish catch that arrives in Tokyo daily, along with meat, eggs, vegetables, and fruits.

There are several *sashimi* (raw fish) restaurants in the immediate vicinity of the market that attract customers from all over the country. Real *sashimi* lovers like to arrive at the restaurants before dawn in order to enjoy fish that was unloaded from ships that same night.

TUNNELS / TONERU (Toe-nay-rrue)   Being exceptionally mountainous, Japan's well-developed railroad and highway system led to the boring of many tunnels. One of the newest and most awe-inspiring of these tunnels is the Seikan (Say-e-khan) undersea railway tunnel, which connects the island of Honshu with Hokkaido, beneath Tsugaru Straits.

Begun in 1964 and completed in 1985, the Seikan tunnel is 33.49 miles long—making it the longest undersea tunnel in the world—and 787 feet below the sea.

The tunnel, built by the Japanese Railway Construction Corporation, was designed for Japan's famous high-speed Shinkansen Bullet Trains.

Other major tunnels in Japan include the one between the southern tip of Honshu and the island of Kyushu.

UENO (Way-no) In Taito Ward, just north of central Tokyo, Ueno has long been one of the most popular districts in Tokyo. The site of a major *daimyo* estate during the Tokugawa Shogunate (1603–1868), Ueno is now one of the city's primary shopping and entertainment districts. It is especially noted for Ueno Park, which has a number of the country's most important cultural facilities. See UENO PARK.

Ueno Station is the gateway for Japan Railway trains leaving for northern Honshu. It is crowded all the time, but especially in winter, when hundreds of thousands of Tokyoites flock to the ski resorts of north-central Honshu.

The station area and park are only about 15 train minutes from downtown Tokyo.

UENO PARK / UENO KOEN (Way-no koe-en) Formerly the estate of a *daimyo*, this 84 hectare (201.6-acre) site was taken over by the Tokugawa *Shogunate* in the early 1600s. The reigning shogun had a huge temple built on the grounds for the exclusive use of the Tokugawa family.

This temple was destroyed during the fighting that accompanied the Meiji Restoration in 1867. In 1878, the new Meiji government turned the grounds into a public park—now one of the largest and most popular in Tokyo—and a major cultural center.

Among the facilities and attractions in the park are the Tokyo National Museum, the Horyu Temple Treasure House, the Gallery of Eastern Antiquities, Tokyo Metropolitan Fine Art Gallery, National Science Museum, National Museum of Western Art, the Ueno Zoological Garden, the Japan Art Academy, Tokyo Metropolitan Festival Hall, several temples, the Ueno Library, the Toshogu Shrine, and an immense statue of Takamori Saigo, a hero of the Meiji Restoration. There are also a large pond and numerous walkways.

The main entrance to Ueno Park is a short walk from Ueno Station, the third busiest railway terminal in the city and the nucleus of a major shopping and entertainment district.

UENO ZOO / UENO DOBUTSU-EN (Way-no doe-boot-sue-inn) Regarded as one of the best zoos in the world, the Ueno Zoo was founded in 1882 by the Ministry of Agriculture. It was later transferred to the Imperial Household and finally turned over to the city of Tokyo in 1924.

Located on a 13 hectare (31.2-acre) site in Ueno Park (which altogether covers 84 hectares and was formerly the garden estate of a *daimyo* feudal lord), the zoo has over 813 species of animals and birds and sponsors numerous special events during the year.

It is open daily from 9:00 A.M. to 4:30 P.M., except from December 29 to 31.

UJI SHRINE / UJI JINJA (Uu-jee jeen-jah)   Founded in 313 A.D. on the site of the residence of Prince Wakiiratsuko Uji, this is one of Kyoto's oldest shrines. It is dedicated to Emperor Nintoku, the Prince's older stepbrother, and to his father, Emperor Ojin—both famous in Japanese history.

There are two shrines on the grounds, one of which was constructed in the tenth century and is said to be the oldest shrine building extant in Japan. Both shrines are registered as National Treasures.

A short distance from the Uji Shrine, on the slopes of Asahi Hill, stands the Koshi Temple, the first Buddhist temple of the Soto sect of Buddhism built in Japan (in 1233). See KOSHI TEMPLE.

UKIYO-E (Ou-key-yoe-eh)   One of the most famous of Japan's traditional schools of painting (at least among Westerners), *ukiyo-e*, or Paintings of the Floating World, first appeared in the early seventeenth century and primarily depicted the social life of the lower classes.

The first *ukiyo-e* were illustrations for storybooks, but they soon began to appear as independent prints. Iwasa Matabei (1578–1650) is sometimes named as the father of *ukiyo-e*, but his art was not aimed at the lower classes. The first great *ukiyo-e* master was Moronobu Hishikawa, who flourished from 1688 to 1704. He was followed by Harunobu Suzuki (1725–1770), Utamaro Kitagawa (1753–1806), Sharaku Saito (Toshusai), Toyokuni Utagawa (1769–1825), Hokusai Katsushika (1760–1849), and Hiroshige Ando (1797–1858).

Wood-block prints, or *hanga* (hahn-gah), had been produced in Japan since the Nara Period in the eighth century, but it was the genius of these *ukiyo-e* painters that brought them to the forefront of Japanese art. At first, the prints were largely ignored by artistic circles and the well-to-do, who considered them too plebeian, but when Western connoisseurs began to collect the *hanga* as masterpieces, their reputation soared.

The best-known *hanga* masters became famous for certain types of subject matter: Shunsho, Sharaku, and Toyokuni for portraits of actors; Harunobu, Kiyonaga, Eishi, Utamaro, and Toyokuni for pictures of beautiful women; and Hokusai and Hiroshige for landscapes.

Dutch traders stationed on the man-made island of Dejima in Nagasaki Bay from the early days of the Tokugawa Shogunate (1603–1867), sent the first *hanga* to Europe—sometimes as wrapping paper. It was not until the 1850s, however, when they were put on sale at a popular shop in Paris, that they really caught on in the West.

Several artists tried to introduce Western techniques into *hanga* during the late 1800s and early 1900s, but with little success. In 1931, the traditionalist theme was reaffirmed with the formation of the Nippon Hanga Kyokai (Neep-pone Hahn-gah K'yoe-kie), or Japan Woodblock-Print Association.

The art has evolved with the times, however, and the work of a number of contemporary *hanga* artists is now very popular.

The *ukiyo* style of painting and wood-block prints were associated with a style of literature that flourished during the Edo Period—and that came to be known as *ukiyo zoshi*, or Novels of the Floating World.

These novels were realistic depictions of Japanese society during this period, ranging from the highly formal and rigid life-style of the *samurai* to the loose, sensual, and often frivolous lives of the townspeople.

One of the best known of the writers who made this genre famous was Saikaku Ihara. See LITERATURE; WOOD-BLOCK PRINTS.

UMEDA and UMEDA UNDERGROUND CENTER (Uu-may-dah)   The area around Osaka Station is officially named Umeda, but it is popularly called Kita, or North. The city's primary transportation terminal for numerous train and bus lines, it includes a huge complex of office buildings, department stores, shops, restaurants, theaters, and nightspots.

Beneath much of the area is the immense Umeda Underground Center, which is like a small city within itself, with hundreds of stores and restaurants lining its passageways. The underground center links Osaka Station with many of the larger buildings in the district, as well as the Umeda Subway Station.

UNIONS / RODO KUMIAI (Roe-doe kuu-me-aye)   In Japan, unions are not organized on a craft, occupation, or job basis, as they are in the U.S. Instead, they are organized on a company basis—a difference that is of extraordinary importance to both management and labor.

While federated into national bodies, each union remains independent. All employees of a unionized company are automatically members of the union when they are hired. This means that all workers who advance to supervisory and management positions have had union experience and have often served as union leaders.

The relationship between Japan's company union members and management is, therefore, quite different from that in the U.S.—not only because of the nature of the union itself, but also because employees know that they will most likely work for the company until they retire and that they are not apt to find a comparable job elsewhere if they quit or if the company fails; and, in the case of many, because they expect to be promoted to management or to return to the folds of management when their term as union leader ends.

By the mid-1990s 24 percent of Japan's labor force was unionized. There are approximately 33,000 individual unions, most of which belong to one of several national federations.

The major national union federations are RENGO (the Japanese Trade Union Federation), which has a combined membership of approximately four million; ZENROREN (the National Confederation of Trade Unions), with some two million members; and ZENROKYO (the National Trade Union Council), with approximately 1.5 million members.

RENGO, previously known as SOHYO, is strongest in public sector unions (teachers, employees of Japan's six semiprivate railway companies, the post office and other government operated enterprises. In its earlier form RENGO generally opposed the long-ruling Liberal Democratic Party and supported Socialist platforms. But with both communism and socialism generally discredited worldwide, the federation has adopted a more pragmatic philosophy.

In addition to the Big Three union federations, there are half a dozen smaller union groups concentrated in specific industrial areas, which often cooperate with the Big Three in annual spring campaigns for salary increases.

Japan's unions continue to evolve as the economy matures and becomes more intimately linked with foreign economies. Most of the unions now approve to some extent the use of foreign labor in Japan, and a few comapny unions have programs that cover the few foreign workers legally employed in the country.

Approximately 75 percent of Japan's labor force works a five-day week.

In 1982, a new union federation, the All-Japan Council of Private Unions, or Zenminrokyo (Zen-meen-roe-k'yoe), was formed out of the amalgamation of 41 industrial unions with a combined membership of 4.25 million. The new federation's goals are to achieve unification of the labor front by bringing the majority of the private sector unions together.

To the Japanese way of thinking, the underlying philosophy of American unions is not only incompatible with the social nature of an enterprise, it is basically destructive. They say that American unions do not care if a company fails and goes out of business because of union demands. American unionism, they believe, is based on the idea that a company's primary obligation is to provide the level of working conditions and wages proposed by the union —and any company that cannot or will not do this does not deserve to survive.

UNIVERSITIES / DAIGAKU (Die-gah-kuu)   There are 93 national universities in Japan, 34 prefectural and municipal universities, and 319 private universities. In addition, there are 520 junior colleges in the country, plus a United Nations University, which was established in Tokyo by the UN in the 1970s.

Tokyo University (Tokyo Daigaku) is one of the oldest and most famous universities in Japan. Its predecessors, the Kaiseisho (Kie-say-e-sho) and Igakusho (Ee-gah-kuu-sho), were founded by the Tokugawa Shogunate. Todai, as the university is popularly known, dates from 1877, when these two *bakufu* schools were merged.

Other famous national universities include Kyoto University, Tohoku University, Kyushu University, Hokkaido University, Osaka University, and Nagoya University.

Among the most famous private universities are Keio and Waseda. Top-ranked Christian universities in Japan include Doshisha, Rikkyo, Sophia, Kwansei Gakuin, Kobe College, and Aoyama Gakuin. See individual listings and EXAMINATION HELL.

UNLUCKY NUMBERS   The two unluckiest numbers in Japan are four and nine. The Japanese word for "four"—*shi* (she)—is pronounced like the word that means "death." *Ku* (kuu), the word for "nine," suggests suffering. Thirteen is also an unlucky number (perhaps because it is unlucky in the West).

As a result of these superstitions, many hotels in Japan do not have rooms numbered four, nine, or thirteen.

UNZEN-AMAKUSA NATIONAL PARK   In a land blessed with scenery that often surpasses description, the Unzen-Amakusa National Park is a standout. The park covers 256 square kilometers, which includes a big portion of the Shimabara Peninsula near Nagasaki, the Ariake Sea on the east side of the peninsula, Chijiwa Bay on the west, and the Amakusa Islands to the south and east.

The park contains Mt. Unzen, which actually consists of three major mountain peaks and several lesser ones—all volcanic, plus Unzen Spa, which also consists of three different hot spring resorts, all at an altitude of over 700 meters in totally gorgeous surroundings. The park also has swimming and surfing beaches at Chijiwa, Obama, Kuzusa, and Shimbara, plus many other hot springs, geysers, *solfataras*, and *fumaroles*.

There are also mountain passes, Lake Shirakumo, waterfalls, campsites, the Tsukumo Isles off Shimabara Port (formed in 1792, when Mt. Maruyama, west of the city, erupted), the Shimabara Castle (at which nearly all the Christian converts in Japan were slaughtered in 1637), and the beautiful Amakusa Islands.

Lying south of Shimabara Peninsula, the Amakusa Islands (there are 70 in the group), are all mountainous and abound in one scenic spot after another—most of them with fantastic views of the surrounding seas.

The two largest of the islands—Amakusa Upper and Amakusa Lower—are connected by a drawbridge. Several of the other islands are also connected by bridges (completed in 1966 and all high enough to allow the passage of large ships beneath them).

Besides attracting vacationers and tourists, the islands are noted for their Amakusa dolls, camellia oil, pottery, and processed seafood.

URAGA (Uu-rah-gah)   Now a part of the port city of Yokosuka, on Miura Peninsula (where *Shogun* Ieyasu Tokugawa gave the English pilot Will Adams a fief), and known as the dockyard of the Uraga Heavy Industry Company, one of Japan's major shipbuilders, Uraga played a vital role in the history of Japan during the Tokugawa Period.

After establishing his shogunate headquarters in Edo (Tokyo) in 1603, Ieyasu made Uraga port the holding place for barges waiting for inspection before they could enter Tokyo Bay.

This is also the place where, in 1846, the American Commodore James Biddle and his two warships dropped anchor and gave the local shogunate officials a letter addressed to the emperor.

The officials took the letter but did not deliver it. Seven years later, Commodore Matthew C. Perry and his squadron of Black Ships showed up on the same mission—to get Japan to open its doors to the outside world. By that time, the situation in Japan had changed. Perry's letter was officially accepted at Kurihama, near Uraga, and delivered not to the emperor, but to the *shogun*, who was the real power in the country (a fact that the Western powers did not learn for several more years).

UTSUNOMIYA (Uut-sue-no-me-yah)   The prefectural capital of Tochigi, Utsunomiya is a large city 70 train minutes north of Tokyo on the way to Nikko. The castle town of the feudal lord of the province, Utsunomiya was also one of Japan's famous Post Stations, where the *Daimyo* Processions and other travelers of the Edo period put up at night.

In addition to being a thriving industrial and commercial center, Utsunomiya is also known for the Oya Temple, believed to have been founded by Kobo Daishi (774–835), who introduced the Shingon doctrines of Buddhism into the country. Part of the temple is inside a huge cave, the walls of which are decorated with the images of 10 Buddhas carved in relief.

This is the area where Frank Lloyd Wright got the soft brown stone (Oya stone) he used in building the famous (former) Imperial Hotel in Tokyo.

VACCARI, MR. and MRS. ORESTE   Oreste and Elisa Vaccari are well-known names to almost every person who has studied the Japanese language since the end of World War II—if not before.

An Italian who first went to Japan in the 1930s, Vaccari soon realized the need for a different kind of learning tool in the study of Japanese, and in 1939 he published the first edition of his *English-Japanese Conversation Dictionary*.

Over the next several decades, Vacarri and his wife turned out a steady stream of learning aides for both English and Italian students of the Japanese language.

Eventually, Vaccari and his wife established Vaccari's Language Institute in the Jingumae district of Tokyo's Shibuya Ward, to publish their works.

VIEWING FACILITIES   Cultural and recreational viewing facilities in Japan include 72 aquariums, 312 art museums, 93 botanical gardens, 2,085 movie theaters, 1,135 museums, 741 stage theaters, and 88 zoos (including safari parks).

VISAS / RYOKEN (Rio-ken)   There are over a dozen different types of visas for entering Japan, depending on the purpose. A transient visa (4-1-3) is good for 15 days; a tourist visa (4-1-4) is good for 90 days.

Other categories and periods of stay include businesspeople (4-1-5), three years; journalists (4-1-11), three years; students (4-1-6), one year; entertainers (4-1-9), 60 days; and teachers (4-1-7), three years.

The visas of government officials and those assigned to embassies and consular offices are good for the duration of their assignment, however long it might be. In most cases, term visas may be extended one or more times.

 Visas to enter Japan are available from the nearest Japanese Embassy or Consulate. Tourist visas are usually issued immediately on request. Commercial and other special category visas requiring documentation are generally sent to Tokyo for approval and take from several days to a few weeks to process.

Foreigners who are in Japan for whatever reason must have a new visa or a reentry permit if they leave the country and intend to return. Some visas,

512

such as tourist, are multiple-entry visas, meaning that the bearer can enter Japan any number of times during the valid period of the visa.

The citizens of more than 45 countries do not need visas to visit Japan because the nations involved have visa exemption agreements with Japan. The countries include the United States of America, Austria, Federal Republic of Germany, Ireland, Liechtenstein, Mexico, Switzerland, the United Kingdom, Argentina, Belgium, Canada, Denmark, France, Greece, Holland, Norway, Pakistan, Sweden, Turkey, and New Zealand.

VOLCANOES / KAZAN (Kah-zahn) Japan has about one-tenth of the world's active volcanoes and hundreds of inactive ones. The highest mountain in Japan—Mt. Fuji—is a dormant volcano that last erupted in the 1700s. See MT. FUJI.

WAKAYAMA (Wah-kah-yah-mah)   Less than an hour by train from Osaka, the city of Wakayama, on Kii Peninsula, has long been celebrated for its mild climate and scenic beauty and for its own special ambience that has made it a favorite with the Japanese, as well as foreign residents.

Another castle town that developed into a major city, Wakayama owes its early prominence to one of the most extraordinary figures in Japan's history, Hideyoshi Toyotomi, who ordered a castle built there in 1585.

During the long Edo era, Wakayama was of special importance because the *daimyo* of the province was a relative of the Tokugawa *shoguns*. Besides being the capital of Wakayama Prefecture, the city today is an industrial and commercial center, best known for its cotton flannel factories.

WAKKANAI (Wok-kah-nie)   Japan's northernmost city, Wakkanai is on the west shore of Soya Bay, near the tip of the Soya district of Hokkaido, which faces Sakhalin (Russia), just across the Soya Straits.

The warming Tsushima Current, which comes up through the Japan Sea from the South Pacific, keeps Wakkanai's port from freezing over in winter, and it is Hokkaido's top fishing port.

In earlier centuries, Wakkanai was the jumping-off point for Japanese explorers and travelers going to Sakhalin and the Kurile Islands.

Recommended reading: *Once a Fool—From Japan to Alaska by Amphibious Jeep*, by Boye Lafayette De Mente (Phoenix Books/Publishers).

WANDERING PRIESTS / KOMUSO (Koe-muu-soh)   One of the obligations of priests belonging to the Fuke sect of Zen Buddhism is to go on pilgrimages to collect alms. Soon after Zen Buddhism was introduced into Japan in the Middle Ages, such wandering priests became a common sight throughout the country.

Dressed in *kimono* robes and wearing large braided hats that covered their heads and hid their faces, the priests played long, five-hole bamboo flutes as they walked solemnly through villages and towns and along the great walking roads of the day.

Because of the dangers from road bandits, rogue *samurai*, and other unsavory types, the *komuso* also carried swords to protect themselves—and

514

they knew how to use them. Some *komuso* were, in fact, former *samuari* who had given up the way of the warrior for the way of the cloth and were expert at various martial arts.

During the turbulent periods in Japan's Middle Ages, it was common for *samurai* and others to disguise themselves as *komuso* in order to travel about the country without arousing suspicion. It was also common during years of turmoil for some *komuso*, especially ex-*samurai*, to be hired as spies by contending forces.

Many movies and television shows about that period make use of this theme. See KOMUSO.

WARRIOR MONKS   In 788, Emperor Kammu ordered the famous priest Saicho (767–822), later known as Dengyo Daishi, to establish a temple on the summit of Mt. Hiei to protect the new capital of Kyoto from evil spirits. The temple, named Enryaku, still is one of the most important temples in Japan.

Situated in a thick grove of cypress trees, the temple grew over the centuries into a great monastery, with thousands of priests. To protect themselves and the treasures of the massive temple complex, the priests took up the practice of military arts. Their favorite weapon was the halberd—a sword at the end of a long handle—which had developed in the early 1200s and was commonly used by the poorest of the *samurai*.

By the 1400s, the monks of Mt. Hiei had become fierce warriors, often raided sections of Kyoto in pursuit of enemies, and threatened the emperor. Finally, in the mid-1500s, Nobunaga Oda, then the supreme military power in Japan, declared war against the marauding monks and, in a number of battles, destroyed them.

WASEDA UNIVERSITY/WASEDA DAIGAKU (Wah-say-dah Die-gah-kuu) One of Japan's premier universities, Waseda was founded by Marquis Shigenobu Okuma in 1882 on grounds that were part of his estate, in what is now Shinjuku Ward.

Waseda is famous for a number of things besides its academic standing, including its baseball team, its rivalry with Keio University, and its success in placing graduates in leading newspaper companies.

It is also popular with foreign students.

WATER / MIZU (Me-zoo)   First-time visitors to Japan are often concerned about the quality of the drinking water—needlessly so. Tap water in Japan is perfectly safe to drink, and on the average it is better than that in most advanced countries.

At this time, approximately 95 percent of the households in Japan are provided with potable tap water.

WATER BUSINESS / MIZU SHOBAI   (Me-zoo show-bye) Mizu Shobai, literally Water Business, refers to Japan's nighttime entertainment trades—in particular, bars, cabarets, nightclubs, *geisha* houses, massage bathhouses, hot spring spas, and theaters—which employ a significant percentage of the working population.

Use of the term Water Business to describe this area of entertainment and recreation is typically Japanese—the connotation being that the various pleasures dispensed by these businesses is an ephemeral thing that evaporates like mist rising from a bath, or dew on the morning flowers. And, of course, hot baths have traditionally played a central role in Japan's Floating World of pleasure.

The use of the term Mizu Shobai has diminished in recent decades, but the industry is still very much a part of life in Japan. It is a vital part of virtually all business negotiations and transactions and especially important in the sales area.

(Old Japan-Hand Frank Kawahara often uses a Mizu Shobai analogy to help explain to Japanese the role of salespeople in the U.S. He compares American salespeople with hostesses who work in Japan's hundreds of thousands of cabarets. Their success often depends on their own personality and skill rather than the reputation of their employer or the product they sell, and when they leave a club they often take their best customers with them.) See CABARETS; HOSTESSES; NIGHTCLUBS.

Recommended reading: *Bachelor's Japan*, by Boye Lafayette De Mente (Tuttle); also, *Japan at Night*, by Boye Lafayette De Mente (Passport Books).

WAX FOOD MODELS   Several categories of Japanese restaurants use a very unusual and very effective method of promoting their food—they display wax models of the various dishes in windows or display cases.

The wax food models are incredibly lifelike, so much so that when I first saw them I thought they were real.

Signs giving the name of the dish—and usually the price—go along with the displays; so, in effect, you are able to see the menu before going inside.

The making of wax food models is a high art, and individual dishes cost up to several hundred dollars each. Two leading makers are Nippon Seiro, in the Kyobashi district of Tokyo; and the Rinrei Wax Company, in the Ginza area of Tokyo.

WEDDING CEREMONIES / KEKKON SHIKI (Keck-kone she-kee)   In earlier Japan, weddings were relatively simple affairs, many of them taking place in the bridegroom's home or at shrines or temples. When held at larger shrines or temples, they were more elaborate. Some of those held at Shinto shrines by the well-to-do were especially impressive.

Both the bride and the groom dressed in traditional clothing, the *kimono* and headdress of the bride being particularly elaborate. The highlight of

these ceremonies came when the couple exchanged tiny cups of *sake* nine times in a ritual that is called *san san ku do* (sahn sahn kuu doe).

Weddings in Japan today are very big business. Those who can afford it utilize specialized commercial wedding halls, the banquet rooms of leading hotels, or the banquet rooms of large restaurants.

Even ordinary working families go to considerable expense to stage impressive weddings that include full meals, drinks, and gifts for all the guests. The more affluent may have from 100 to 500 or more guests, all of whom are wined and dined in a very impressive manner—and given gifts.

The cost of such weddings ranges from several thousand dollars for a relatively modest affair to five or ten times that amount.

Fortunately, it is customary for everyone invited to attend a wedding reception to present the family of the bride or groom (whichever one they are connected to) with a money gift in a special envelope called *noshibukuro*—before the reception.

In today's weddings, the bride still wears the traditional wedding *kimono*, but the groom may opt for formal Western wear. Most ceremonies include the *san san ku do* exchange of sake cups, but some also have prayers by a Shinto or Buddhist priest.

Wedding receptions can be interminably long, with all the more important guests making speeches that cover just about every imaginable topic relating to the bride and groom. The matchmaker (*nakodo*) invariably leads off the program.

While dining recently at a large Chinese restaurant in Tokyo's Harajuku area, my host and I were treated to a very modern Japanese wedding. The couple marched in to the tune of "Here Comes the Bride." The bride was in the traditional *kimono*, the groom in a coat with tails.

A Shinto priest performed a sacred ritual and chanted prayers. The two exchanged *sake* cups. Then together they cut a huge Western wedding cake with a *samurai* sword.

WEIGHTS and MEASURES   Japan has been on the metric system since 1904 although the old, traditional Japanese system of weights and measures was commonly used in personal and cottage industry areas until well after 1945.

Even when you are just visiting, it helps to know a few of the most common weights and measures in the metric system. So if you are going to be visiting Japan, you might want to bone up a bit.

WINDS / KAZE (Kah-zay)   The Japanese and English monthly inflight magazine of Japan Air Lines, *Winds* covers travel destinations, food, life-styles, and other aspects of Japanese culture calculated to be of special interest to visitors. Its color features and insightful articles by well-known writers on Japan make it a popular subscription publication. See OTHER SOURCES.

WINE / BUDOSHU (Buu-doe-shuu)   Western-style wine is now consumed by many Japanese, and wine making is a growing industry. *Sake* is generally described as a rice wine, since it is fermented from rice. A sweetened version of *sake*, called *mirin*, also apparently qualifies as a wine.

One of the more popular Japanese wine brands is Akadama (Ah-kah-dah-mah), a sweet red wine.

WOMEN DIVERS / AMA (Ah-mah)   Japan has long been noted for its *ama*—women who dive for shellfish, agar-agar, and various other seafood. A traditional custom that goes back for uncounted centuries, the practice is still seen in several places around the islands, such as Hekura, Onjuku, Shirahama, and Wagu.

While the women do the diving, their husbands or menfolk handle the boats. There are a number of reasons given to explain why the women, instead of the men, do the diving—one being that women are better able to stand the chilly ocean waters.

The *ama* of Hekura are of special interest. Hekura is a small island 48 kilometers off the northern tip of Noto Peninsula, which juts out into the Japan Sea from Ishikawa Prefecture on Western Honshu.

Each summer, about 700 families leave the port city of Wajima on Noto Peninsula and go to the island of Hejima, where they spend the entire summer season, the women diving and the men taking care of their catch.

The annual migration is very systematically done, with the families accompanied by their children, teachers, doctors, and one or more police officers.

One of the largest communities of women divers is in Shirahama on Boso Peninsula, southeast of Tokyo. There some 1,500 women spend the summer months gathering shells and seaweed from the waters off the picturesque coast.

In the small fishing village of Onjuku, also on Boso Peninsula, there are 400 *ama* who practiced this ancient form of harvesting the ocean.

Wagu is the center of the *ama* divers on Shima Peninsula, near the famous Pearl Island and Toba, south of Nagoya. Here, much of the coastline is made up of picturesque cliffs and sheer rock islets just offshore, making this one of the most scenic of the areas noted for *ama*.

WOMEN'S ORGANIZATIONS   Given the tendency of the Japanese to form groups, it is not surprising to find that there are numerous national women's organizations in Japan—some of them quite powerful. A number of times in the 1950s and 60s, concerted action by some of these organizations resulted in new legislation concerning food standards and changes in consumer prices.

Among the leading general organizations are The League of Women Voters, Japanese Women's Democratic Club, Japan Housewives Association, National Women's Association of Agricultural Cooperation, the National Federation of Regional Women's Organizations, Japan Liaison Council for the National Congress of Mothers, Consumer Science Association, and the Lib Shinjuku Center.

There are several important vocational organizations, including the Medical Association of Japanese Women, Japan Midwives Association, Japanese Nursing Association, Women's Dentist Association, the National Federation of Women Teachers, and the Federation of Japanese Women's Organizations.

WOMEN'S RIGHTS   Article 14 of Japan's Constitution, promulgated in 1947, states: "All of the people are equal under the law and there shall be no discrimination in political, economic or social relations because of race, creed, sex, social status or family origin."

Laws have also been passed guaranteeing equal educational opportunities for the sexes, equal pay for the same work, and equal treatment in matters of inheritance (increasing the wife's share of an inheritance from one-third to one-half).

Changing economic and social circumstances have also drastically altered the options now open to Japanese women and the treatment they receive. On a practical basis, however, there is still considerable discrimination against women, but in more subtle ways than in the past (and similar to that found in the U.S.).

Some 53 percent of all office workers in Japan are women, some 43 percent of all technicians and specialists are female, and approximately 40 percent of the country's sales workers are women. On the managerial side, however, only about 7 percent are women.

Labor regulations in Japan provide paid maternity leaves for female employees, ban their employment for jobs requiring heavy lifting or involving physical danger, and guaranteeing them menstrual leave if they have painful monthly periods.

A labor union boss was recently quoted as saying, "Women are temporary, cheap, disposable labor." But this is now only partly true. In the 1960s, virtually all female employees left the work force when they got married or soon thereafter. Now some one-third of the labor force is made up of married women.

In the mid-1970s, the personnel director of IBM Japan Ltd. was quoted as saying that the only way a woman could advance into high-level management was to get a sex-change operation. By mid-1985, there were a significant number of female managers in the company, and 28 percent of the new entry-level employees hired by IBM Japan in 1985 were female, up from 10 percent just one decade earlier. The same personnel director now says that the quality of IBM's female workers is higher than that of the males.

Similar changes in attitude and practices are also vividly demonstrated in many Japanese companies, including Honda Motor Company, Nikko Securities, the Bank of Tokyo, and Toshiba.

As the end of the twentieth century draws near, however, only two Japanese women have ever had cabinet posts in the government, none has ever served as the governor of a prefecture, fewer than a dozen have ever been the president of a university, and none of the 1,065 firms on the Tokyo Stock Exchange has ever had a female president.

WOOD-BLOCK PRINTS / HANGA (Hahn-gah)   The first record of wood-block printing (*moku han*) in Japan occurred in 764, when Empress Koken ordered some sutras printed in this manner. The printing of the sutras, destined for distribution to temples around the country, was completed in 770.

For the next several hundred years, wood-block printing was used primarily for printing sutras and Buddhist pictures. The first book printed on *moku han* in Japan came out in 1346 (there is a copy preserved at the National Museum in Tokyo).

Thereafter *moku han* books became fairly popular, but it was the late 1600s before wood-block prints began to catch on. These first wood-block prints were in one color. The first multicolored print was produced in 1765 by Harunobu Suzuki.

Wood-block prints became increasingly popular following the appearance of full-color prints, and they were one of the first Japanese arts to attract interest in the West. Most of this popularity was due to the appearance of the great *hanga* artists Hokusai Katsushika and Hiroshige Ando, whose depictions of the everyday life of Japan, of actors and beautiful women in the entertainment trades, and of the scenic beauty of the country, heralded a golden age for wood-block prints.

The particular style developed by these famous *hanga* artists came to be known as *ukiyo-e* (uu-kee-yoe-eh), or Pictures of the Floating World.

Hokusai is especially noted for a series he painted depicting sights along the great Tokai Do walkway that connected Edo with Kyoto.

The names of wood-block print artists that end in *sai, ken,* or *an* originally referred to their studio, rather than to the artists themselves. Besides their real names, which are seldom, if ever, used, they also generally had professional names.

It is said that Europeans first became acquainted with Japanese woodblock prints because they were often used as wrapping paper on other items being shipped abroad. It wasn't too long thereafter that prints by the masters were much in demand, and commanded high prices.

Among the best-known wood-block print dealers in Tokyo are Kaigado, Uchida Art Company, Yokoyama, and Yoseido.

Recommended reading: *The Japanese Print—Its Evolution and Essence*, by Muneshige Narazaki, adapted by C.H. Mitchell (Kodansha International); *Utamaro*, by Tadashi Kobayashi, translated by Mark A. Harbison (Kodansha International); *Who's Who in Modern Japanese Prints*, by Frances Blakemore (Weatherhill); *The Japanese Print: A Historical Guide*, by Hugo Munsterberg (Weatherhill).

WOODEN CLOGS / GETA (Gay-tah)   One of two types of traditional Japanese footwear (the other being *zori*), *geta* are elevated wooden platform clogs that are traditionally worn on more formal occasions when one is dressed up.

The *geta* are cut out of single blocks of wood, with a front and back ridge left on the bottom to act as the sole. These ridges are of varying heights, depending on the purpose of the *geta*. The standard height is about two inches, but *geta* made to be worn in the rain (*amageta*) have sole ridges that are between three and four inches high.

Geta for men are made of plain wood, and the v-shaped thongs that hold the *geta* on the feet are usually black. *Geta* for women are often lacquered black or vermilion and have colorful thongs of velvet or silk.

WOODS BATHING / SHINRIN YOKU (Sheen-reen yoe-kuu)   The health movement in Japan has resulted in an age-old custom becoming institutionalized in a new way. People have known for ages that even a brief stay or walk in a forest was refreshing and regenerating.

In 1982, the Japanese Forestry Agency, in cooperation with the Environment Agency and local city governments, began promoting the health benefits of *shinrin yoku*, or "woods bathing," which has the connotation of submerging one's self in the essence of the forest and thereby relieving stress and fatigue.

The campaign was eminently successful, and hundreds of thousands of Japanese now make annual trips to well-known forests to bask in their invigorating aromas, sights, and sounds.

The health benefits of woods bathing have a scientific basis, according to Dr. Keizo Kamiyama, a professor at Kyoritsu Women's University, who is noted for his research on the effect of certain aromas on health.

WORD PROCESSING IN JAPANESE   The first Japanese language word processor was introduced into the market in 1978, and there are now over 30 companies offering similar machines to Japan's world of business. The first machine was priced at six million yen. Now they are available for well under half a million yen.

Business in Japan was traditionally hindered by the lack of modern typewriters that could handle the 3,000-plus Japanese *kanji* characters. The appearance of *kanji* word processors is a vital step in the automation of office work in Japan and will have a profound influence on work and labor in the future.

The leading personal computer maker in Japan is NEC, followed by Sharp, Hitachi, Oki, and Sord. Others rapidly coming up in the market are Fujitsu, Toshiba, Mitsubishi Electric, and Matsushita Electric Industrial Co.

WRAPPING CLOTH / FUROSHIKI (Fuu-roe-she-kee)   *Furoshiki* literally means "bath cloth," because it was originally used to sit on or to wrap one's clothes at a public bath, but over the centuries it gradually became a general wrapping and carrying cloth for anything and everything.

Now usually made of cotton, silk, or synthetic cloth, *furoshiki* are often decorated with artistic renditions of plants, flowers, or crests. While considerably less in evidence today because of the widespread availability of shopping bags and other kinds of bags, *furoshiki* are nevertheless still popular in Japan and a favorite gift item.

WRITING JAPANESE   Writing Japanese is a special challenge, because there are three sets of characters to learn—the well-known *kanji* (khan-jee) and the less well-known *hiragana* (he-rah-gah-nah) and *katakana* (kah-tah-kah-nah). The language can also be written with Roman letters, but this system is still not common, and the words cannot be read fluently by most Japanese.

Most nouns, root verbs, and adjectives are written in the more complicated *kanji* characters, which were borrowed from China in the sixth and seventh centuries. Because the characters were not totally adaptable to the Japanese language, Japanese scholars developed a series of phonetic characters, called *manyokana* (mahn-yoe-kah-nah), that were used to express the verb and adjective endings and the tenses.

In the ninth century, this phonetic system was further rationalized and divided into two sets of characters—*hiragana* and *katakana*—each with 46 symbols. Adverbs can be written in either *kanji* or *kana* characters.

By the beginning of modern times, the *hiragana* characters, which are soft and flowing, were widely favored over the *katakana* symbols, which are hard and static. It thereafter gradually became customary to use the *katakana* characters to write foreign words that were adopted into the Japanese language.

Japanese children learn the *hiragana* symbols first, often before they start to school.

In earlier years, Japanese was almost always written in vertical lines. Now there is a growing tendency for it to be written in a horizontal format. See CALLIGRAPHY; KANJI CHARACTERS.

YABUIRI (Yah-buu-ee-ree)   This word literally means "going back to the bush" and refers to the traditional practice of giving servants and apprentices holidays so they can return to their rural homes on January 16. In earlier times, it referred to wives visiting the homes of their parents, along with their husbands, after Obon in the summer to help cut wood and clear land.

Until well into this century, it was common for young boys to be apprenticed to tradesmen when they were as young as eight or nine and to live in the shops where they worked. Until they were 15, their masters would give them two days off a year at their convenience, but after they came of age, they were allowed to take their holidays during *yabuiri*.

The custom of *yabuiri*, called by different names in different parts of the country, is still practiced in Japan, but its old meanings have been virtually forgotten.

YAKITORI (Yah-kee-toe-ree)   This is chicken barbecued Japanese-style —cut up in tiny chunks and broiled over an open charcoal fire, along with pieces of such vegetables as onions and pimento.

The various pieces are impaled on metal or bamboo skewers, dipped in a sweetened barbecue soy sauce or sprinkled with salt (as the diner chooses), and then broiled.

Yakitori ya, or *yakitori* shops, abound all over Japan, especially in entertainment districts, as barbecued chicken is a popular evening and late-night snack. Many such shops have only a counter. Others are stand up-and-take-out places. Most are marked by a distinctive paper lantern called *chochin* (choe-cheen).

This is another typical Japanese dish that is immediately pleasing to the palates of most foreigners.

YAKUZA (Yah-kuu-zah)   The *yakuza* are Japan's professional criminal class, sometimes compared to the mafia. They have a long and somewhat honorable history in Japan.

The *yakuza* began as low-class gamblers and gangsters in Japan's early feudal days. Having to learn how to protect themselves from disgruntled victims, as well as from raids by the authorities, the *yakuza* eventually began

524

to use their skills to protect helpless citizens from marauders and *ronin* (masterless) *samurai*.

While continuing to function outside the law, the *yakuza* adopted their own codes similar to the ethics of the *samurai*, and some *yakuza* became folk heroes in their own time.

Today there are half a dozen major *yakuza* gangs in Japan—referred to as *kumi* (kuu-me) or *gumi* (guu-me), which is usually translated as "group," as in Yoshida Gumi or Tanaka Gumi—with a total of some 100,000 members.

Present-day *yakuza* gangs are involved in sports activities or in the entertainment business, running massage bathhouses, pachinko parlors, clandestine gambling dens, and other enterprises, including bars and nightclubs.

Newspaper stories linking leaders of the larger *Yakuza* gangs with powerful political figures and other rightist elements in Japan are commonplace. These stories say that politicians at the highest level regularly consult with *yakuza* bosses before making key decisions.

YAMAGUCHI CITY (Yah-mah-guu-chee) The capital of Yamaguchi Prefecture, which is on the southwestern tip of Honshu across from the southernmost main island of Kyushu, Yamaguchi City is old as a community, but it did not come into the limelight until the fourteenth century, when it was taken over by the Ouchi clan.

The Ouchis greatly expanded the economic activity of the city and built a large number of magnificent temples in imitation of those in Kyoto. In the sixteenth century, when Francis Xavier, the Spanish missionary, visited there, Yamaguchi was at the height of its glory. It was often called the Kyoto of the West at this time.

The province then came into the hands of the Mori clan, which fought on the losing side against Ieyasu Tokugawa in the Battle of Sekigahara in 1603.

The Mori Daimyo was exiled to Hagi, on the cold Japan Sea coast, and the fortunes of Yamaguchi declined.

When the movement against the Tokugawa Shogunate became intense in 1863, Yamaguchi became the base of its operations and again rose to prominence.

Today Yamaguchi is noted for its Yasaka Shrine, built in 1370; Kameyama Park, where the Ouchi Villa stood; and Yuda Spa.

YAMANASHI PREFECTURAL VISITOR CENTER   (Yah-mah-nah-she) Formerly the Fuji National Park Museum, the Yamanashi Visitor Center is near the shore of Lake Kawaguchi, one of the five lakes that ring the waist of Mt. Fuji and one that is popular both as a winter and a summer resort.

The Visitor Center, near the tollgate of the 29.5-kilometer Fuji Subarui Line that leads up to the fifth Station on one of the climbing trails of Mt. Fuji, contains numerous exhibits about the natural history of Mt. Fuji.

The Lake Kawaguchi area is a little over two train hours from Shinjuku Station in Tokyo. The north shore of the lake has been famous since ancient times for its fantastic view of Mt. Fuji, towering over the lake, as well as reflected in its waters.

YAMATO (Yah-mah-toe)   Yamato was a province in what is now Nara Prefecture, east of Kyoto, and was the location of the court of Japan's first fully documented ruler, Hatsukunishirasu Sumera-Mikoto, who later came to be known as Jimmu Tenno, or Emperor Jimmu.

At that time, the kingdom over which Hatsukunishirasu ruled was also known as Yamato, and for a long time thereafter that is what the Japanese called their country. See JAPAN.

The son of Emperor Keiko (71–130 A.D.) was named Prince Takeru Yamato, which indicates this may have been the name of the Imperial family.

YASUKUNI SHRINE / YASUKUNI JINJA (Yah-sue-kuu-nee Jeen-jah) This great shrine, on Kudan Hill on the northwest side of the Imperial Palace Grounds in Tokyo, is dedicated to Japan's national heroes—in particular, those who gave their lives in war.

When Shintoism was the state religion, from shortly after the Meiji Restoration in 1868 until 1945, Yasukuni Jinja was one of the most important shrines in the country and played a key role in the military-oriented affairs of government.

Today, Yasukuni Jinja is more like a national war memorial and is visited by large numbers of people throughout the year. Its entryway is marked by the largest granite *torii* in Japan and by a second colossal *torii* of bronze that is 22 meters high.

The shrine sponsors two major festivals every year—in the spring from April 21 to 23 and in the fall from October 17 to 19.

YELLOW PAGES   One of the most useful publications for foreign residents and business visitors in Tokyo, the *Yellow Pages* is just what it sounds like— a large telephone directory, primarily covering the Tokyo area, that lists in its Index Section emergency and public phones and provides detailed information about the phone system in Japan, the postal system, zip codes, public holidays and festivals, trade fairs and exhibitions, international conferences —and museums.

Section One lists airlines and travel businesses, hotels, nightclubs and cabarets, and restaurants. Section Two includes government agencies, followed by regular *Yellow Pages*-type listings under the appropriate product or service category.

Yellow Pages is published twice a year by Japan Yellow Pages Ltd., ST Building, 4-6-9 Iidabashi, Chiyoda-ku, Tokyo 102, Japan.

YEN / EN (Inn)   Japanese currency, the yen, is pronounced something like "inn" in Japanese. It was established as the legal currency of the land in 1871. It comes in 10, 50, 100, and 500 yen coins, and in 500, 1,000, 5,000, and 10,000 yen bills. See MONEY.

YOKOHAMA   One of the world's great port cities and the third largest city in Japan, Yokohama is on the west side of Tokyo Bay in Kanagawa Prefecture, 20 miles southwest of Tokyo.

Associated with trade and foreign residents since the last years of the Tokugawa Shogunate, Yokohama was a small fishing village in 1859, when it was designated as a foreign trade port city and open to residency by foreigners.

At that time, the town was divided into two sections—Kan Nai (Inside the Barrier) and Kan Gai (Outside the Barrier). Foreigners could live only Inside the Barrier, which faced the harbor and was walled off from the rest of the town. Foreign residents could leave their enclave only with permission on special occasions.

横 浜

The foreign residents of Yokohama, with their strange clothing and even stranger habits, were subjects of intense curiosity among the Japanese, and people traveled from distant areas in the hopes of getting a glimpse of the exotic-looking *Gaijin* (Outside People).

By 1889, when Yokohama was organized into a city, the population had exploded to 121,000. It was to continue to grow rapidly as the harbor and harbor facilities were improved, and the volume of foreign trade handled by the port increased at a remarkable rate. Much of the city was destroyed by the great earthquake of 1923, however, and again by firebomb raids during World War II, but it was quickly rebuilt each time.

Yokohama today is not only a great port but also is a major industrial center (automobiles, ships, chemicals, foodstuffs). The city is divided into 14 wards, and has its popular and distinctive entertainment, shopping, and residential districts—several of them with a foreign overlay that gives the area an attractive, cosmopolitan appearance.

There are also numerous shrines, temples, and other places of special interest in the city, including the Silk Center, Children's Country (Kodomo-no Kuni), China Town (which boasts 70 Chinese restaurants and two dozen shops selling Chinese foodstuffs and spices), Motomachi Shopping Street, and the Sankei En (Sankei Garden), which features a number of cultural properties moved there from various parts of Japan—including the villa of the Tokugawa family in Kii Province, which is the only remaining example of feudal lord villa architecture. Other attractions include a tea ceremony house built by the third Tokugawa *shogun* in the 1640s, a large farmhouse built in Gifu in the early 1700s without the use of nails or cramps, and a temple built by Hideyoshi Toyotomi for his mother in 1592 and originally in the courtyard of the Daitoku Temple in Kyoto.

YOKOSUKA (Yoe-kose-kah)   The largest city on the Miura Peninsula, a little over an hour southwest of Tokyo, Yokosuka has been famous as a naval base since World War I. It was the leading Japanese naval facility in eastern Japan until the end of World War II, when it was taken over by the U.S. Seventh Fleet and Japan's Maritime Self-Defense Force.

Since 1945, Yokosuka has developed into a major fishing and trade port and a gateway for sightseeing around the picturesque peninsula.

Besides being noted for its entertainment districts catering to naval personnel, Yokosuka is also famous as the final resting place of the Japanese battleship *Mikasa*, which was the flagship of Admiral Heihachiro Togo during the Russo-Japanese War in 1904–1905.

Embedded in concrete in 1961, the *Mikasa* is now a memorial that attracts large numbers of people annually. Also of special interest in the area are Tuskayama Park, where the English pilot Will Adams and his Japanese wife are buried (see ADAMS, WILLIAM); and Kinugasa Park, south of the city, which incorporates the grounds and ruins of Kinugasa Castle, headquarters of the Lord of Miura (destroyed in 1180).

YOMIURI LAND (Yoe-me-uu-ree)   A large recreational area on the banks of the Tama River, between Tokyo and Yokohama, Yomiuri Land was built by the giant Yomiuri Newspaper Company in the 1960s. It includes a fishing center, swimming pool, public golf courses, a roller skating rink, ski-jump platforms and slopes, an observation platform, and a parachute tower.

Other attractions include a marine aquarium, a jungle zoo, and a TV studio. A 2.5-kilometer-long monorail connects the various facilities.

YOMIURI NEWSPAPER / YOMIURI SHIMBUN (Yoe-me-uu-ree Shimboon)   One of Japan's Big Three national daily newspapers, the *Yomiuri* has a daily combined circulation of several million. It is printed in Osaka, Tokyo, Takaoka, and Sapporo. See NEWSPAPERS.

YOUTH HOSTELS   In 1958, the Japanese government instituted a policy of providing funds for the construction of modern, well-equipped, Western-style youth hostels around the country, in locations noted for their beauty or recreational facilities.

There are presently 600 hostels, most of which are managed by Japan Youth Hostels, Inc. (JYH). The hostels have bedrooms, dining rooms, showers, and central heating. Public kitchens are equipped with utensils that are for rent.

Japanese youth hostels are operated in accordance with international rules governing hostels. They offer simple but adequate accommodations that are neat, clean, and inexpensive. Their purpose is to promote wholesome travel by young people as a way of furthering good mental and physical health and strengthening international friendship.

Length of stay at individual hostels is three days, unless there are vacancies, in which case a guest may extend his or her stay for one or more nights. Directories of Japan's youth hostels are available from the Japan National Tourist Organization. See listing.

YOUTH TRAVEL VILLAGES / SEISHONEN RYOKO SON (Say-e-sho-nane Rio-koe Sone)   Another government-backed program, the Youth Travel Villages, located in popular resort areas, are aimed at providing young people with the opportunity to enjoy wholesome recreation at low cost.

Each Youth Travel Village is equipped with a clubhouse, campsites, lodging facilities (including some private accommodations), ball parks, and other outdoor sports facilities.

There are presently three dozen villages across the country—mostly used by Japanese groups.

YOSHINO (Yoe-she-no)   A small town on the crest of a ridge in the Yoshino Mountains, about an hour from Osaka, Yoshino is famous for its cherry trees, and, for two weeks out of the year, it is one of the most popular sightseeing destinations in Japan.

The area has four large groves containing some 100,000 cherry trees, first planted in the seventh century by Enno Ozuna, a Buddhist priest, who made nearby Mt. Sajogadake his headquarters.

The groves, gradually ascending the slopes of the mountain, blossom at different times, beginning in early April on the lowest level, and going on through late April. An annual cherry blossom festival is held on April 11 and 12.

There are several ancient temples and shrines in the Yoshino area and a number of places noted as good spots from which to view the cherry tree groves. The famous priest-poet-sage Saigyo (1118–1190) had a hermitage adjoining one of the groves—a spot now marked by the Kokeshimizu Shrine.

YOYOGI SPORTS CENTER (Yoe-yoe-ghee)   Adjoining the famous Meiji Shrine and just a short walk from Harajuku Station in Tokyo's Shibuya Ward, the Yoyogi Sports Center was built as the Olympic Village for the 1964 Tokyo Olympic Games.

Hundreds of thousands of Americans who spent time in Japan during the Occupation following World World War II would remember the location as Washington Heights, a major residential area for American dependents during that era.

Prior to being taken over by the U.S Occupation forces, the site was the Yoyogi Parade Grounds of the Imperial Japanese Army.

The primary structure in the sports center is the Kishi Memorial Gymnasium, which can accommodate 15,000 spectators for indoor events. An annex, housing a basketball gym, will seat 4,000.

A historical note: Yoshitoshi Tokugawa (1884–1963), a descendent of the Tokugawa *shoguns* (who voluntarily gave up power in 1868), made the first airplane flight in Japan on December 19, 1910, on this site. He flew for four minutes and gained an altitude of 70 meters.

The plane Captain Tokugawa flew is on display at the Transportation Museum in Kanda, Sudacho, Chiyoda Ward.

YUKATA (Yuu-kah-tah)   A thin, unlined cotton *kimono* that is worn as casual wear and often as a sleeping gown—especially in resort spas—the *yukata* is another distinctive feature of Japanese culture. Nearly all hotels and inns in Japan provide their guests with the handy, comfortable gown.

Yukata come with numerous design patterns, ranging from very conservative geometric motifs to elaborate scenes from nature. Those made for women tend to have more elaborate designs, as do those provided by resort inns for their guests.

The *yukata* provided by hotels are often so popular with guests that they sometimes take them home—unofficially. To help prevent this kind of loss, the management in some hotels have room signs advising their guests that the *yukata* may be bought in one of the hotel's arcade shops.

YUNOKAWA SPA (Yuu-no-kah-wah)   On Matsukawa River, seven kilometers southeast of the Hokkaido port of Hakodate, Yunokawa is one of the largest and reportedly the best-equipped hot springs spa in southern Hokkaido.

There are over 100 *ryokan* (inns) with hot spring baths clustered in the area of Yunokawa. The average temperature of the springs is 66 degrees centigrade. The spa has been popular since the mid-1600s.

YUSHIMA SEIDO (Yuu-she-mah say-e-doe)   Situated on a small rise facing Tokyo's Ochonomizu Station, on the north side of the Kanda River, the Yushima Seido, or Yushima Hall, is a shrine dedicated to Confucius, first erected in 1690 by Tsunayoshi Tokugawa, the fifth Tokugawa *shogun*.

Later, the hall became the center for the teaching of Confucianism under the patronage of the shogunate and the head of a government school called Shoheiko, where many of the famous scholars and statesmen of the shogunate received their Confucian education. (The Shoheiko was one of the forerunners of Tokyo University.)

During the Tokugawa era, the shrine burned down several times. The present buildings were constructed in 1935.

ZAIBATSU (Zie-bot-sue)   Following the Meiji Restoration, when the last of the Tokugawa *shoguns* relinquished power to Emperor Meiji in 1868, the new Japanese government took the lead in a crash program to industrialize the country.

Realizing that small, underfinanced companies would not be able to effect such a revolutionary change, the government provided financing and other help to a number of well-to-do families, which allowed them to establish industrial and financial conglomerates (*zaibatsu*) in all the key areas of business.

There were three types of *zaibatsu* established. Some combined financial and industrial enterprises (Mitsui, Mitsubishi, and Sumitomo); some were primarily in banking but used their resources to participate in industry (Yasuda, Nomura, etc.); and some were industrial (Asano, Okura, and Furukawa).

Each of these great conglomerates was controlled by a single holding company that owned all the shares in all the affiliated companies, with all power concentrated in the hands of the family head who was the sole owner of the holding company.

Each of the family-controlled *zaibatsu* maintained strong ties with the leading political parties. Each group worked independently to increase its market share and competitive power and to consolidate and strengthen its overall role in the nation's economy. Before the outbreak of World War II, Mitsui was the largest commercial organization ever seen, with over three million employees.

The *zaibatsu* were operated like independent feudal kingdoms, with their own house laws, and their owners were among the most powerful and wealthy men in the world.

Following World War II and the subsequent Military Occupation of Japan by the U.S., the *zaibatsu* were ordered to disband. Ostensibly, this was done, but in actuality the management simply went underground.

When the Occupation of Japan ended and soveriegn power was returned to the people and government, the *zaibatsu* reemerged in the form of industrial groups, but with some very important differences—the individual families that had once controlled them absolutely were no longer in power, and the various members of the groups operated semi-independently.

These newly reborn *zaibatsu*like conglomerates, played a seminal role in Japan's postwar economic miracle. The postwar years also saw the rapid development of several other major industrial groupings patterned after the new *zaibatsu*, including the Fuyo group centered around the Fuji Bank; the Sanwa group linked with the Sanwa Bank, and such manufacturing and processing groups as those headed by Nippon Steel, Toyota, Hitachi, and Matsushita.

There are over a dozen *zaibatsu*-type groups in Japan today. The six largest and best known are the Mitsubishi Group, the Mitsui Group, the Sumitomo Group, the Fuji Group, the Sanwa Group, and the Dai-Ichi Kangyo Group.

All of these groups are centered around a major bank and include companies that are among the leaders in their fields. The Mitsubishi Group, the largest and most powerful, is made up of 28 ranking companies centered around Mitsubishi Bank. Its coordinating body is called the Kinyobi Kai, or Friday Club, so named because that is the day the presidents of the various companies meet to discuss problems, policies, and mutual interests.

The Mitsui Group includes such giant corporations as Toyota Motor Company, Toshiba Machine, and Toray Industries, along with all the Mitsui companies, as well as several other firms, with a total of 23 in the main group.

The Sumitomo Group is regarded as the most cohesive of all the *zaibatsu* groupings. The principal organ of collaboration and coordination is the Hakusui Kai, or White Wednesday Club. Besides all the Sumitomo companies, this group includes Nippon Electric, Asahi Chemical Industry, Nippon Sheet Glass, and the automobile manufacturer Toyo Kogyo (Mazda)—a total of 16 companies (not counting subsidiaries and affiliated companies).

The Fuji Group, not as closely coordinated as the others, generally counts 29 major companies within its sphere of influence. The Sanwa Group lists 36 companies on its roster. The Dai-Ichi Kangyo Group has 44 members, making it the largest in number of affiliated companies.

The importance of these groups should not be ignored or minimized by any foreign company wanting to do business in or with Japan. While independent in most ways, the various companies are obligated to coordinate many of their activities with the group—which means, for example, that a trading company member may not take on a foreign product line for sale in Japan if one of its group members is involved in that line.

ZAIKAI (Zie-kie)   *Zaikai* translates more or less as "financial group" or "circle" and refers to a specific number of high-level, powerful executives who influence both economic and political policies in Japan by virtue of their financial clout.

The *zaikai* are not organized as such and do not present a common front. They make their influence felt through such business organizations as Keidanren and through their financial support of various politicians, the ruling party, and specific programs.

There is also a business publication called *Zaikai*, aimed at top-level businesspeople and government officials.

ZAO SKI RESORT (Zah-oh)   The largest ski resort in northeastern Japan, the Zao Spa and ski ground is in the Zao Quasi-National Park and is part of the Mt. Zao range of dormant volcanic peaks.

Accessible from Sendai by three scenic toll roads, the area is noted for its magnificient scenery in both summer and winter. It is a land of peaks, gorges, slopes, plateaus, and hot spring spas.

ZEAMI (Zay-ah-me)   Zeami Kanze (1363–1443), the son of Kanami Kanze, the man credited with establishing the foundations of modern *noh*, carried on his father's work and raised *noh* (which had previously been mostly juggling and acrobatics) to a classic fine art of music, dancing, and storytelling.

Under Zeami's tutelage, the essence of *noh* was subtlety (*yugen*), as was exemplified in the highly stylized beauty and grace of court nobles and their ladies. See NOH.

ZEMPUKU TEMPLE / ZEMPUKU JI (Zim-puu-kuu jee)   On one of Tokyo's main thoroughfares near Shiba Park and the Tokyo Tower, the Zempuku Temple was founded by the famed priest Kobo Daishi, who also founded the Shingon sect of Buddhism in the ninth century.

In 1859, the temple became the headquarters for the first American Minister in Japan and served as both the Consulate and the residence of Minister Townsend Harris.

The Zempuku, now the property of the Honganji school of the Jodo Shinshu sect of Buddhism, is a nostalgic landmark in the heart of modern-day Tokyo. See HARRIS, TOWNSEND.

ZEN (Zen)   Zen Buddhism was founded in the sixth century in India by a monk named Bodhidharma, who shortly thereafter left for China—apparently because he was unhappy with the dwindling of Buddhist adherents in his own country.

There is some conflict about the year of his arrival in China, but it appears to have been 520. In China, he ran afoul of a local Lord and was told to leave town. He traveled northward to a Shaolin Temple, where he sat facing a wall for nine years, meditating until he achieved enlightenment. At that time, he is said to have been so in tune with nature that he could hear the conversation of ants.

The word *Zen* comes from the Chinese *ch'an*, a corruption of the Sanskrit word *dhyana* and the Pali word *jhana*.

Introduced into Japan from China by the Buddhist priests Eisai (1141–1215) and Dogen (1200–1253), Zen taught salvation, self-control, and the development of inner powers through meditation and a regimen of strict

mental and physical discipline. A Zen adept is one whose thoughts are free of intellectual questioning and who is totally natural, spontaneous, and in tune with nature.

This new discipline was quickly adopted by the leaders of the shogunate government in Kamakura and the professional military families that were to become known as *samurai*.

Zen was part of the inspiration and a vehicle for much that came to be known as *bushido*, or the Way of the Warrior. Since the *samurai* were to become Japan's ruling class for the next 600 years, following the principles of Zen themselves, as well as establishing Zen-based standards for the common people to follow, the philosophy was to have an especially profound influence on the lives of all Japanese.

As the centuries passed, the Zen concepts of life and truth also became the spiritual guidelines for Japan's equally famous tea ceremony, flower arranging, and other aesthetic pursuits.

In Japan today, the philosophy of Zen has three main branches—Renzai, Soto, and Obaku. The main temple of the Rinzai sect is the Myoshin in Kyoto. The Mampuku Temple at Uji, south of Kyoto, is the headquarters of the Obaku sect of Zen. Soto Zen has two main temples, the Eihei, near Fukui, and the Soji, in the Tsurumi district of Yokohama.

The great Daitoku Temple in Kyoto is regarded as the true birthplace of Zen in Japan. It was founded in 1324 and has since been closely associated with some of the greatest figures in Japanese history.

Advocates of the Soto Zen sect believe in prolonged meditation to achieve enlightenment. The Rinzai sect believes in instant enlightenment, brought on by presenting the mind with a riddle (*koan*) that, if pursued persistently, results in breaking the mind free of its physical and intellectual restraints.

The goal of Soto practitioners is to perceive the truth in all things through direct personal experience, which they believe can be achieved by the rigorous and prolonged practice of *zazen* (zah-zen), or sitting in meditation.

Recommended reading: *Zen Flesh—Zen Bones*, by Paul Reps (Tuttle); *Zen Telegrams*, by Paul Reps (Tuttle); *Zen Dictionary*, by Ernest Wood (Tuttle); *The Zen Life*, by Koji Sato (Weatherhill); *Zen Mind, Beginner's Mind*, by Shunyu Suzuki (Weatherhill); *Zen Master Dogen*, by Yuho Yokoi (Weatherhill); *Zen Inklings*, by Donald Richie (Weatherhill); *Zen at Daitoku-ji*, by Jon Covell and Sobin Yamada (Kodansha International).

Today, many people practice *zazen* as a way to help them cope with the stress of modern life, as well as to clear and strengthen the mind for the pursuit of excellence in the arts, sports, business, and other endeavors.

Many of Japan's thousands of temples were founded by Zen priests, and many of these are still practicing centers for Zen Buddhism.

Zen advocates do not study scriptures or listen to lectures. They spend hours to years seated in silent meditation (with a fellow standing behind them with a stout stick in his hands to hit them on the shoulders if they nod off and to relieve tension that builds up in the shoulders).

In feudal days, the *samurai* turned to Zen to concentrate their thoughts and strength and to enhance their courage. The principles of Zen thought—austerity, simplicity, and oneness with nature—became the guiding principles of the tea ceremony, flower arranging, and landscape garden designing.

The state of spiritual enlightenment sought by Zen devotees is known as *satori* (sah-toe-ree). Once emancipated from worldly passions and at one with the universe, the Zen master's life is illuminated. He or she is able to discern the difference between reality and illusion, between the truth and falsehood.

There are dozens of famous Zen Buddhist temples in Japan, to which one may go to practice *zazen* under the watchful eyes of Zen masters.

In practicing *zazen*, one sits cross-legged, with the right foot resting on the left thigh and the left foot on the right thigh—a position that stops some would-be meditators right there! The neck and back should be perfectly straight. The hands should be cupped, with the right hand under the left hand, the thumbs just touching, and the hands resting in the lap.

During the practice of *zazen*, the eyes are slightly open—not closed, as one would ordinarily expect. The purpose of this is to help one concentrate on a single thing or thought and to avoid the jumble of thoughts that normally assails the mind when the outside world is closed off entirely.

The discipline in Zen temples is very strict; it is certainly not for the wishy-washy or faint-hearted. Just being able to complete several months of such training is a considerable accomplishment.

The famous riddles that Zen masters pose for their pupils—in an attempt to help them concentrate on one thing for several seconds, thereby strengthening their powers of concentration and understanding—are called *koan* (koe-ahn). They are described as intuitive dialogues between masters and disciples.

Zen Buddhist temples, called Zen-Dera, are divided into three structures —the place where the chief priest lives (*hojo*), the place where the master teaches (*hatto*), and the place where disciples practice *zazen* (*sodo*)

Other interesting books on Zen are *Zen Training Methods and Philosophy*, by Katsuki Sekida (Weatherhill); *A Zen Wave: Basho's Haiku and Zen*, by Robert Aitken (Weatherhill); and *Zen and Japanese Buddhism*, by Daisetsu Suzuki (Japan Travel Bureau).

Suzuki, who was over 90 when he died, was one of contemporary Japan's greatest Zen masters, ranking with many of the noted names of the past. He lived and taught in Kamakura, about an hour southwest of Tokyo, when I was working for JTB, his publisher.

ZEN FOOD   More and more people are getting interested in vegetarian dishes—*shojin ryori*-that have been standard fare in Zen temples since the fifteenth century. This popularity is likely to grow in the future as the result of the enterprise of two nuns at the Sanko Temple in the outskirts of Tokyo.

Soei Yoneda, abbess of the temple, who studied Zen cooking at another temple, and nun Koei Hoshino, have published a book called *Good Food From a Japanese Temple* (Kodansha), which gives recipes of 230 Zen dishes.

Said the abbess: "We are Zen nuns, but there is no reason why we should keep the secrets of Zen cooking to ourselves."

She added that the secret of good cooking is to retain and enhance the natural flavors of food and to prepare it with tender, loving care.

ZENI-ARAI BENTEN (Zay-nee-ah-rie bane-tane)   At Sasuke, a few minutes walk northwest of Kamakura Station, the Zen-Arai Benten is a shrine dedicated to doubling your money. Benten is the god of wealth, and Zen-Arai means Money-Cleansing. The idea is that money washed in the water of a spring from a cave on the grounds, on a zodiacal day of the Snake, will later double or even triple.

ZENIYA, GOHEI (Zay-nee-yah, Go-hay-e)   An important but tragic figure in the history of the Kaga clan, Gohei Zeniya (1773–1852) was a member of a wealthy shipping family who lived in Kanaiwa, near Kanazawa.

A terrible famine occurred in the early 1800s, bringing much suffering to the fief of the Kagas. Gohei was asked to advise the Kaga *Daimyo* on relief measures that could be taken. He suggested that the province begin trading with Korea and China, just across the Japan Sea—knowing that all trade except through the Dejima Dutch enclave in the port of Nagasaki was strictly forbidden by the Tokugawa Shogunate. See DEJIMA.

The Kaga *Daimyo* accepted Gohei's advice. Soon the trade was thriving, enriching both the *daimyo* and Gohei.

Eventually, the shogunate in Edo learned about the forbidden enterprise. To avoid retribution by the *shogun*, the *daimyo* and his chief retainers accused Gohei of poisoning the fish in Kahoku Lagoon and causing a plague. They imprisoned him and confiscated all of his property.

With Gohei in prison and penniless, the shogunate dropped its investigation. Gohei died in prison in 1852, just one year before Commodore Matthew Perry and his Black Ships arrived to open Japan to trade and diplomatic relations with the rest of the world.

ZENKOKU KINRO SEISHONEN HALL (Zen-koe-kuu keen-roe say-e-show-nane kie-khan)   Known in English as the All-Japan Working Youths Hall, and generally referred to as the Sun Plaza, this 21 -story building near Nakano Station in Tokyo is devoted to providing working youths with a place to study, exercise, and play.

The program is operated by the Employment Promotion Project Corporation, under the Ministry of Labor. The building includes study rooms, a theater, libraries, convention and ceremonial halls, hotel rooms, restaurants, a bowling alley, and gymnasium.

ZENKO TEMPLE / ZENKO JI (Zen-koe jee)   One of the most popular temples in Japan, the Zenko Temple occupies an area of 59,000 square meters on the northern edge of the city of Nagano. Founded in 642, the main hall was reconstructed in 1707 and is now registered as a National Treasure.

Bronze Buddhist statues in the temple are believed to have been presented to Japanese religious leaders by the king of the Paikche Dynasty of Korea in 552. Opponents of Buddhism tried to burn the images and then threw them into a canal in Naniwa (Osaka). They were recovered by a man named Yoshimitsu Honda in 602, who took them to his home village in Shinano Province and later built a small temple to house them.

Following numerous other adventures, the statues were restored to the Zenko Temple in 1598. The name of the temple comes from Yoshimitsu, which can also be read Zenko.

Administered by two groups, one made up of priests and the other of priestesses, the Zenko Temple attracts worshippers from all over Japan for its morning services. Many of them go hoping to get to touch the main statue while passing through the darkened tunnel where it is kept.

Services at the temple begin about half an hour after dawn, with the abbot and abbess waiting on the walkway to greet arrivals.

Nagano itself is one of the most spectacular prefectures in Japan. It is often called The Roof of Japan because of its location in the Japan Alps, the highest mountain range in the country, with 11 peaks that are over 3,000 meters high.

The city of Nagano is approximately three hours from Tokyo's Ueno Station by limited express on the Shinetsu Main Line.

ZENTSU TEMPLE / ZENTSU JI (Zen-t'sue jee)   Located at Zentsuji, some 38 kilometers from Takamatsu on the island of Shikoku, the famous

Zentsu Temple is the birthplace of Kobo Daishi and headquarters of the Shingon sect of Buddhism, which he founded.

The temple, which dates from 813, is on ground owned by Zentsu Saeki, Kobo Daishi's father. The temple complex consists of several buildings— the Main Hall, a pagoda, and a treasure house.

Two camphor trees on the grounds are said to have been growing since the temple was founded.

Zentsu is the 75th temple among Shikoku's Eighty-Eight Sacred Places —temples commemorating Kobo Daishi.

Recommended reading: *Japanese Pilgrimage*, by Oliver Statler (Morrow) —a chronicle of Statler's own pilgrimage on foot to the 88 Shikoku temples dedicated to Kobo Daishi. Statler will be remembered as the author of *Japanese Inn*, which told much of the history of the fabulous Tokugawa Shogunate from the viewpoint of an inn along the great Tokai Do walkway.

In *Japanese Pilgrimage*, Statler uses the same technique to tell much of the early history of Shikoku and Japan, along with present-day travel impressions.

ZODIAC / JUNI-SHI (Juu-nee-she)   Popular in Japan since ancient times, the *junishi* (10 animals, one bird, and a reptile) were imported into Japan from China, along with the Chinese lunar calendar. The signs cover a 12-year period, but the complete zodiac embraces 60 years—believed by the Chinese to be the end of man's ordinary life-cycle.

According to Chinese—and later Japanese—beliefs, people born in different year-cycles have different characters and personalities, some of which are compatible and some of which are not.

The *junishi* are *ne* (rat), *ushi* (ox), *tora* (tiger), *u* (hare), *tatsu* (dragon), *mi* (snake), *uma* (horse), *hitsuji* (sheep), *saru* (monkey), *tori* (cock), *inu* (dog), and *i* (wild boar).

One of the best-selling calendars in Japan is the Takashima Ekidan, an almanac based on the Chinese *Book of Changes* (*I Ching*). Besides giving all the signs of the zodiac and their various readings, the calendar covers lucky and unlucky days for traveling, getting married, breaking ground for a new building, launching a ship, burying the dead, and so on.

The story behind these zodiac animals is of special interest. They are the only ones, it is said, that hurried to the bedside of Buddha to express their sorrow when he died. The cat is not included in the group because it did not believe in the teachings of Buddha. The rat is first in the lineup because it played a trick on the ox, which was really the first to hurry to the Buddha's bedside.

The rat jumped on the ox's back and stayed there until it arrived at the Buddha's hut. It then jumped off of the cow and ran into the hut first.

ZOJO TEMPLE / ZOJO JI (Zoe-joe Jee)   On Hibiya Dori, the main avenue that runs through central Tokyo between the Imperial Palace Plaza and the Marunochi financial and business district (and near the Shiba Koen Subway Station), the Zojo Temple was founded in 1393. During the Tokugawa Shogunate (1603–1868) it was the family temple of the Tokugawas.

Today the Zojo Ji is the Kanto District headquarters of the Jodo sect of Buddhism. It is also a treasure trove of culturally important objects preserved from the past.

The huge red gate (*sam mon*) that faces Hibiya Avenue, built in 1605, is listed as an Important Cultural Property. The Hondo, or Main Hall, of the temple was destroyed during World War II. The present ferro-concrete structure was completed in 1974.

ZORI (Zoe-ree)   *Zori* are one of the traditional styles of Japanese footwear (others being *geta*, or wooden clogs, and *setta*, leather-soled sandals). *Zori* sandals were first made of straw. In more recent times, rubber *zori* were introduced. Now they are also made of plastic and other materials.

I happened to be one of the first to import rubber *zori* into the U.S., in 1952, but was unable to persuade the *zori*-makers of the Asakusa district in Tokyo to give me a realistic export price, and I soon gave up. Four years later, *zori* sales in the U.S. amounted to several million dollars a year.

ZUIGAN TEMPLE/ZUIGAN JI (Zuu-e-ghan jee)   On a small island in the famous Matsushima Bay (one of the Three Scenic Wonders of Japan), Zuigan Temple was founded in 828, and the present buildings were constructed in 1609 by order of Masamune Date, the leading *daimyo* of northeastern Japan.

All the buildings are registered as National Treasures and contain many important cultural properties, including sliding screens in the main hall that were painted by the Kano School masters of the day.

In the beautiful Peacock Room is a seated, one-eyed statue of Masamune Date in full armor. He lost the eye in one of his many battles.

Japanese cedars and many caves line the approach to the temple. The caves were used by traveling priests for shelter, as well as places in which to meditate in early times. The temple is about an hour from Sendai.

ZUIRYU HILL (Zuu-e-ree-yuu)   A short distance from Mito, headquarters of the famous Mito clan during the Tokugawa Period, Zuiryu Hill is the cemetery for the House of Mito and contains the tombs of 13 lords of Mito.

It is situated on a slope densely forested with pines and cedars. See MITO.

ZUISEN TEMPLE / ZUISEN JI (Zuu-e-sen Jee)   In Kamakura, about one kilometer east of the Kamakura Shrine, in a secluded vale, the Zuisen Temple was founded in 1327 by Muso Kokushi, one of the period's most celebrated Zen priests.

The temple was renovated by Motouji Ashikaga (1340–1367), brother of the second Ashikaga *shogun*, while he was governor of the Kanto District. A few decades later, it was designated as the second most important of the 10 Rinzai temples in the Kanto area by Emperor Gokameyama.

The Founder's Hall, listed as an Important Cultural Property, includes a wooden statue of Kokushi.

The garden of the temple is regarded as one of the most beautiful Zen-inspired gardens in Japan. It is especially popular for its plum blossoms in February and its golden maple leaves in November.

ZUSHI (Zuu-she)   On the Sagami Bay side of the Miura Peninsula, south of Yokohama, Zushi is a popular seaside resort and residential area for affluent commuters who work in Yokohama and Tokyo. It is situated between Kamakura (which was the shogunate capital of Japan from 1192 until 1333) and Hayama, to the south. The latter is the location of the Imperial Villa, where Emperor Hirohito spent so much time studying the sea life in the area.

OTHER ENGLISH-LANGUAGE SOURCES

American Chamber of Commerce in Japan
(Zainichi Beikoku Shoko Kaigi Sho)
Fukide Building #2
4-1-21 Toranomon, Minato-ku, Tokyo 105 Japan
Publications: *The Journal of the American Chamber of Commerce in Japan*
                Living in Japan

Asahi Evening News
7-8-5 Tsukiji, Chuo-ku, Tokyo 104 Japan
Publications: *The Asahi Evening News*

Asahi Shimbun
5-3-2 Tsukiji, Chuo-ku, Tokyo 104 Japan
Publications: *The Japan Quarterly*

Assn. for International Cooperation of Agriculture & Forestry
(Kokusai Noringyo Kyoryoku Kyokai)
19 Ichiban-cho, Chiyoda-ku, Tokyo 100 Japan
Publications: *Japan's Agricultural Review*

Assn. for Research of Economic & Foreign Affairs
(Keizai Gaiko Kenkyu Kai)
Seno Building
3-14-9 Roppongi, Minato-ku, Tokyo 106 Japan
Publications: *Statistical Survey of Japan's Economy*

Assn. of Agriculture & Forestry Statistics
(Norin Tokei Kyokai)
Publications: *Abstract of Statistics on Agriculture,*
                Forestry and Fisheries
                Monthly Statistics of Agriculture, Forestry and Fisheries
                Statistical Yearbook of the Ministry of Agriculture, Forestry and
                  Fisheries

Automotive Herald Co. Ltd.
Shinto Building #3
5-21-5 Shinbashi, Minato-ku, Tokyo 105 Japan
Publications: *Japan Automotive News*

Bank of Japan
(Nihon Ginko)
2-2-1 Hongoku-cho, Nihonbashi, Chuo-ku, Tokyo 103 Japan
Publications: *Balance of Payments Monthly*
                 Economic Statistics Annual
                 Economic Statistics Monthly
                 Monthly Economic Review
                 Price Indexes Annual
                 Price Indexes Monthly
Sales Agent: Japan Publications Trading Co., Ltd.

Business Intercommunications, Inc. (BII)
C.P.O. Box 587, Tokyo 100-91 Japan
Publications: *Directory of Foreign Capital Affiliated Enterprises in Japan*
                 A Wage Survey of Foreign Capital Affiliated Enterprises in Japan
                 White Paper on the Japanese Economy

Center for Japanese Social and Political Studies
(Nihon Shakai Shiso Kyenkyu Sho)
9-29-12 Seijo, Setagaya-ku, Tokyo 157 Japan
Publications: *The Japan Interpreter*

Charles E. Tuttle Co., Inc.
1-2-6 Suido, Bunkyo-ku, Tokyo 112 Japan
U.S. address: 28 S. Main St., Rutland, Vt. 05701
Publications: *Numerous books on Japan*

Chemical Economy Research Institute
(Kagaku Keizai Kenkyu Sho)
1-13-7 Uchikanda, Chiyoda-ku, Tokyo 101 Japan
Publications: *Chemical Economic and Engineering Review*

Daiwa Securities Co., Ltd.
Research Department
2-6-4 Otemachi, Chiyoda-ku, Tokyo 100 Japan
Publications: *Analysts' Guide*

Defense Agency of Japan
Public Information Division
9-7-45 Akasaka, Minato-ku, Tokyo 107 Japan
Publications: *Defense Bulletin*

Dempa Publications, Inc.
(Dempa Shimbun Sha)
1-11-15 Higashi Gotanda, Shinagawa-ku, Tokyo 141 Japan
Publications: *Japan Electronics Almanac*
                 Japan Electronics Buyers Guide
                 Journal of Asia Electronics Union
                 Journal of Electronic Engineering
                 Journal of Electronics Industry

Dentsu, Inc.
Publications Department
1-11 Tsukiji, Chuo-ku, Tokyo 104 Japan
Publications: *Dentsu Japan Marketing/Advertising*

Diamond Lead Co., Ltd.
1-4-2 Kasumigaseki, Chiyoda-ku, Tokyo 100 Japan
Publications: *Diamond's Economic Journal INDUSTRIA*
Diamond's Japan Business Directory

East Publications, Inc.
3-19-7-101 Minami-Azabu, Minato-ku, Tokyo 106 Japan
Publications: *The East*

Economic Planning Agency
3-1-1 Kasumigaseki, Chiyoda-ku, Tokyo 100 Japan
Publications: *Annual Report on National Life*
Economic Outlook Japan
Monthly Economic Report
Outlook and Basic Policy for the
National Economy
Sales Agent: Government Publications Service Center

Far East Reporters, Inc.
1 Fl., Palace Nishi Azabu Building
3-17-40 Nishi Azabu, Minato Ku
Tokyo, Japan 106
Publications: *Far East Traveler Magazine*

Farming Japan Co., Ltd.
1-11-13 Uchikanda, Chiyoda-ku, Tokyo 101 Japan
Publications: *Farming Japan*

Federation of Bankers Associations of Japan
(Zenkoku Ginko Kyokai Rengo-Kai)
1-3-1 Marunouchi, Chiyoda-ku, Tokyo 100 Japan
Publications: *Banking System in Japan*

Foreign Press Center of Japan
Nippon Press Center Building
2-2-1 Uchisaiwaicho, Chiyoda-ku, Tokyo 100 Japan
Publications: *About Japan Series*
Diplomatic Bluebook
Sales Agent: Government Publications Service Center

Government Publications Service Center (GPSC)
(Seifu Kankobutsu Service Center)
1-2 Kasumigaseki, Chiyoda-ku, Tokyo 100 Japan
Sales agent for numerous government publications

Hitachi, Ltd.
Advertising Department
Nippon Building
2-6-2 Otemachi, Chiyoda-ku, Tokyo 100 Japan
Publications: *Hitachi Review*

Honda Motor Co., Ltd.
Overseas Public Relations Dept.
6-27-8 Jingumae, Shibuya-ku, Tokyo 150 Japan
Publications: *News from Honda*

Industrial Bank of Japan Ltd.
(Nihon Kogyo Ginko)
1-3-3 Marunouchi, Chiyoda-ku, Tokyo 100 Japan
Publications: *IBJ Monthly Report*
                Japanese Finance & Industry: Quarterly Survey

Industrial News Agency
(Kogyo Jiji Tsushin Sha)
3-10 Kanda Ogawa-cho, Chiyoda-ku, Tokyo 101 Japan
Publications: *Industrial News Weekly*

Institute for Financial Affairs, Inc.
(Kinyu Zaisei Jijo Kenkyu Kai)
19 Minami Moto-machi, Shinjuku-ku, Tokyo 160 Japan
Publications: *Handbook of the Japanese Bond Market*

Institute of Administration Management
(Gyosei Kanri Kenkyu Center)
3-1-1 Higashi Ikebukuro, Toshima-ku, Tokyo 170 Japan
Publications: *Organization of the Government of Japan*

Institute of Energy Economics
(Nihon Enerugi Keizai Kenkyu Sho)
Mori Building #10
1-18-1 Toranomon, Minato-ku, Tokyo 105 Japan
Publications: *Energy in Japan*

Institute of Labor Administration
(Romu Gyosei Kenkyu Sho)
1-4-2 Higashi-Azabu, Minato-ku, Tokyo 106 Japan
Publications: *Labor Laws of Japan*

Intercontinental Marketing Corp.
C.P.O. Box 971, Tokyo 100-91
Publications: *Japan English Books in Print*
                Japan English Magazine Directory
Sales agent for many books, publications on Japan

International Management Assn. of Japan, Inc.
(Sekai Keiei Kyogi Kai)
Mori Building #10
1-18-1 Toranomon, Minato-ku, Tokyo 105 Japan
Publications: *Management Japan*

International Society for Educational Information, Inc.
(Kokusai Kyoiku Joho Center)
2-7-8 Shintomi, Chuo-ku, Tokyo 104 Japan
Publications: *Understanding Japan*

International Trade & Industry Statistics Assn.
(Tsusan Tokei Kyokai)
6-15-2 Ginza, Chuo-ku, Tokyo 104 Japan
Publications: *Statistics on Japanese Industries*

Japan Air Lines Co., Ltd. (JAL)
2-7-3 Marunouchi, Chiyoda-ku, Tokyo 100 Japan
Publications: *Winds*
                Japan Unescorted
                JAL Shopping & Dining Guide to Tokyo

Japan Atomic Industrial Forum, Inc.
(Nihon Genshi-ryoku Sangyo Kaigi)
Yasudakasai Otemachi Building
1-5-4 Otemachi, Chiyoda-ku, Tokyo 100 Japan
Publications: *Atoms in Japan*

Japan Automobile Manufacturers Assn. Inc.
(Nihon Jidosha Kogyo Kai)
1-6-6 Otemachi, Chiyoda-ku, Tokyo 100 Japan
Publications: *Motor Vehicle Statistics of Japan*

Japan Chamber of Commerce & Industry
(Nihon Shoko Kaigi Sho)
Overseas Publishing Department
World Trade Center Building
2-4-1 Hamamatsu-cho, Minato-ku, Tokyo 105 Japan
Publications: *Japan Commerce & Industry*
                JCCI Business Guide
                New Products & Marketable Commodities
                Standard Trade Index of Japan

Japan Commerce, Ltd.
(Kaiun Boeki Tsushin Sha)
Tanaka-Yaesu Building
1-5-15 Yaesu, Chuo-ku, Tokyo 103 Japan
Publications: *The Japan Commerce—Iron & Steel (Daily)*

Japan Echo, Inc.
2-10-2 Nagato-cho, Chiyoda-ku, Tokyo 100 Japan
Publications: *Japan Echo*

Japan Economic Journal
(Nihon Keizai Shimbun Sha)
1-9-5 Otemachi, Chiyoda-ku, Tokyo 100 Japan
Publications: *Industrial Review of Japan*
The Japan Economic Journal

Japan Economic Research Center
(Nihon Keizai Kenkyu Center)
Nikkei Building
1-9-5 Otemachi, Chiyoda-ku, Tokyo 100 Japan
Publications: *A Five-Year Economic Forecast*
Long-Term Economic Forecast Series
Quarterly Forecast of Japan's Economy

Japan Economic Review, Ltd.
1-5-8 Nishi-Shinbashi, Minato-ku, Tokyo 105 Japan
Publications: *Japan Economic Review*

Japan External Trade Organization (JETRO)
(Nihon Boeki Shinko Kai)
JETRO Building
2-2-5 Toranomon, Minato-ku, Tokyo 105 Japan
Publications: *Access to Japan's Import Market*
China Newsletter
Exporting to Japan
Facts and Finds Series
Focus Japan
Japan Industrial & Technological Bulletin
JETRO Marketing Series
Update
White Paper on International Trade
Your Market in Japan
Available from JETRO's overseas offices

Japan Foreign Trade Council, Inc.
(Nihon Boeki Kai)
World Trade Center Building, 6th Floor
2-4-1 Hamamatsu-cho, Minato-ku, Tokyo 105 Japan
Publications: *JFTC News*

Japan Institute of International Affairs
(Nihon Kokusai Mondai Kenkyu Sho)
Mori Building #19
1-2-20 Toranomon, Minato-ku, Tokyo 105 Japan
Publications: *Project 80s: Foreign Policy Guidelines of Japan*
White Papers of Japan

Japan Institute of Labor
(Nihon Rodo Kyokai)
1-7-6 Shiba Koen, Minato-ku, Tokyo 105 Japan
Publications: *Japan Labor Bulletin*
                Japanese Industrial Relations Series
Sales Agent: Overseas Courier Service Co. (OCS)

Japan International Social Security Assn.
(Nihon Kokusai Shakai Hosho Kyokai)
1-2-2 Kasumigaseki, Chiyoda-ku, Tokyo 100 Japan
Publications: *Outline of Social Insurance in Japan*

Japan Iron & Steel Federation
(Nihon Tekko Renmei)
Keidanren Kaikan
1-9-4 Otemachi, Chiyoda-ku, Tokyo 100 Japan
Publications: *Japan Steel Bulletin*
                The Steel Industry of Japan
                Monthly Iron & Steel Statistics

Japan Iron & Steel Journal Co., Ltd.
Ohki-Sudacho Building, 6th Floor
1-23 Kanda, Sudacho, Chiyoda-ku, Tokyo 101 Japan
Publications: *Japan Steel Journal*

Japan Management Association
JMA Building
3-1-22 Shiba Koen, Minato-ku, Tokyo, 105 Japan
Publications: *Numerous books, newsletters, and papers*
                published on business and management
                subjects; some in English.
                Contact International Department for catalog.

Japan Newspaper Publishers and Editors Assn.
(Nihon Shimbun Kyokai)
Nippon Press Center Bldg.
2-2-1 Uchisaiwaicho, Chiyoda-ku, Tokyo 100 Japan
Publications: *The Japanese Press*

Japan Petroleum Consultants, Ltd.
Sanwa Building #3
4-5-4 Iidabashi, Chiyoda-ku, Tokyo 102 Japan
Publications: *Japan Petroleum & Energy Weekly*
                Japan Petroleum & Energy Yearbook

Japan Petroleum Institute
(Nihon Sekiyu Gakkai)
3-27-12 Nishi-Ikebukuro, Tomshima-ku, Tokyo 171 Japan
Publications: *Journal of the Japan Petroleum Institute*

Japan Publications Trading Co., Ltd.
(Nihon Shuppan Boeki)
1-2-1 Sarugaku-cho, Chiyoda-ku, Tokyo 101 Japan
I.P.O. Box 5030, Tokyo 100-31 Japan
Exporters and sales agents for numerous publications

Japan Statistical Association
(Nihon Tokei Kyokai)
95 Wakamatsu-cho, Shinjuku-ku, Tokyo 162 Japan
Publications: *Annual Report on the Consumer Price Index*
                 Annual Report on Family Income and Expenditure Survey
                 Annual Report on Labor Force Survey
                 Annual Report on Retail Price Survey
                 Annual Report on Unincorporated Enterprise Survey
                 Employment Status Survey
                 Establishment Census of Japan
                 Family Saving Survey
                 Housing Survey of Japan
                 Japan Statistical Yearbook

Japan Tariff Association
(Nihon Kanzei Kyokai)
Jibiki Building #2
4-7-8 Kojimachi, Chiyoda-ku, Tokyo 102 Japan
Publications: *Customs Tariff Schedules of Japan*
                 Export Statistical Schedule
                 Import Statistical Schedule
                 Japan Exports and Imports (commodity by country)
                 Japan Exports and Imports (country by commodity)
                 Japan Laws and Regulations Concerning
                     Customs Duties and Customs Procedures
                 Summary Report: Trade of Japan

Japan Times, Ltd.
4-5-4 Shibaura, Minato-ku, Tokyo 108 Japan
Publications: *The Japan Times (daily newspaper)*
                 The Japan Times Weekly
                 Defense of Japan
                 Economic Survey of Japan
And various popular books

Japan Trade & Industry Publicity, Inc.
(Tsusan Seisaku Koho Sha)
Toranomon Kotohira Kaikan
1-2-8 Toranomon, Minato-ku, Tokyo 105 Japan
Publications: *Digest of Japanese Industry & Technology MITI Handbook*

Japan Yellow Pages, Ltd.
ST Building
4-6-9 Iidabashi, Chiyoda-ku, Tokyo 102 Japan
Publications: *Yellow Pages—Japan Telephone Book*

Japanese National Commission for UNESCO
C/O Ministry of Education
3-2-2 Kasumigaseki, Chiyoda-ku, Tokyo 100 Japan
Publications: *Crosscurrents*

Japanese National Committee of the World Petroleum Congresses
Kasahara Building
1-6-10 Uchikanda, Chiyoda-ku, Tokyo 101 Japan
Publications: *The Petroleum Industry in Japan*

John Weatherhill, Inc.
7-6-13 Roppongi, Minato-ku, Tokyo, Japan
U.S. address: 6 E. 39th St., New York, NY 10016
Publications: Numerous books on Japan

Keidanren (Federation of Economic Organizations)
(Keizai Dantai Rengo Kai)
Keidanren Kaikan
1-9-4 Otemachi, Chiyoda-ku, Tokyo 100 Japan
Publications: *Keidanren Review on Japanese Economy*

Keizai Koho Center
(Japan Institute for Social and Economic Affairs)
Otemachi Building
1-6-1 Otemachi, Chiyoda-ku, Tokyo 100 Japan
Publications: *Economic Eye*
                Japan: An International Comparison (updated annually)
                Speaking of Japan

Kodansha International
2-12-21 Otowa, Bunkyo-ku, Tokyo, Japan
U.S. address: Harper & Row Bldg.
10 E. 53rd St., New York, NY 10022
Publications: Numerous books on Japan

Local Government Research & Data Center
(Chiho Jichi Kenkyu Shiryo Center)
4-6-2 Minami-Azabu, Minato-ku, Tokyo 106 Japan
Publications: *Local Government Review in Japan*

Look Japan Ltd.
Kawate Building
2-2 Kanda, Ogawa-cho, Chiyoda-ku, Tokyo 101 Japan
Publications: *Look Japan*
                Report on the Present State of Communications in Japan

Mainichi Newspapers
(Mainichi Shimbun Sha)
1-1-1 Hitotsubashi, Chiyoda-ku, Tokyo 100 Japan
Publications: *Mainichi Daily News*
                Japan Statistical Yearbook

Ministry of Finance
(Okura Sho)
Printing Bureau
2-4-2 Toranomon, Minato-ku, Tokyo 105 Japan
Publications: *Annual Report on Business Cycle Indicators*
                Indicators of Science and Technology
                Japanese Economic Indicators
                An Outline of Japanese Taxes
                Polls on Preferences in National Life
                Quality of the Environment in Japan
Sales Agent: Government Publications Service Center

Ministry of Foreign Affairs
(Gaimusho)
Public Information and Cultural Affairs Bureau
2-1-2 Kasumigaseki, Chiyoda-ku, Tokyo 100 Japan
Publications: *Information Bulletin*
Sales Agent: GPSC

Ministry of International Trade & Industry (MITI)
(Tsusansho)
Information Office
1-3-1 Kasumigaseki, Chiyoda-ku, Tokyo 100 Japan
Publications: *Background Information*
                Japan Reporting
                News from MITI

Mitsubishi Corporation
Corporate Communications Office
2-6-3 Marunouchi, Chiyoda-ku, Tokyo 100 Japan
Publications: *Tokyo Newsletter*

Mitsui & Co., Ltd.
Corporate Planning Division
Public Relations Department
1-2-1 Otemachi, Chiyoda-ku, Tokyo 100 Japan
Publications: *Mitsui Trade News*

National Diet Library
(Kokuritsu Kokkai Toshokan)
1-10-1 Nagata-cho, Chiyoda-ku, Tokyo 100 Japan
Publications: *National Diet Library Newsletter*

Nihon Boeki Shimbun Sha
(Japan Foreign Trade Newspaper Co.)
1-7-2 Otemachi, Chiyoda-ku, Tokyo 100 Japan
Publications: *Japan Foreign Trade Journal*

Nihon Kogyo Shimbun
(Japan Industrial Newspaper)
1-7-2 Otemachi, Chyoda-ku, Tokyo 100 Japan
Publications: *Business Japan*

Nikkeiren (Japan Federation of Employers' Assns.)
(Nihon Keiei Sha Dantai Renmei)
1-4-6 Marunouchi, Chiyoda-ku, Tokyo 100 Japan
Publications: *Report of the Committee for the Study of Labor
                 Questions*

Nippon Steel Corporation
(Shin Nippon Seitetsu)
Secretary's Office, Public Relations Section
2-6-3 Otemachi, Chiyoda-ku, Tokyo 100 Japan
Publications: *Nippon Steel News
                 Japan-The Land and its People*

Nissho Iwai Corporation
Public Relations Center, Editorial Office
2-4-5 Akasaka, Minato-ku, Tokyo 107 Japan
Publications: *Tradepia International*

Nomura Research Institute
(Nomura Sogo Kenkyu Sho)
1-1 1-1 Nihonbashi, Chuo-ku, Tokyo 103 Japan
Publications: *NRI Quarterly Economic Review*

Overseas Courier Service Co., Ltd. (OCS)
(Kaigai Shimbun Fukyu)
2-9 Shiba-ura, Minato-ku, Tokyo 108 Japan
Overseas distributor for numerous publications
See local offices

Overseas Electrical Industry Survey Institute, Inc.
(Kaigai Denryoku Chosa Kai)
1-4-2 Uchisaiwaicho, Chiyoda-ku, Tokyo 100 Japan
Publications: *Electric Power Industry in Japan*

PHP Institute International, Inc.
(Kokusai PHP Kenkyu Sho)
Mori Building #32, 6th Floor
3-4-30 Shiba Koen, Minato-ku, Tokyo 105 Japan
Publications: *PHP*

Prime Minister's Office
Statistics Bureau
95 Wakamatsu-cho, Shinjuku-ku, Tokyo 162 Japan
Publications: *Statistical Handbook of Japan
                 White Papers on Japan
                 Etc.*
Sales Agent: Japan Publications Trading Co., Ltd.

Publishers Association for Cultural Exchange
(Shuppan Bunka Kokusai Koryu Kai)
1-2-1 Sarugaku-cho, Chiyoda-ku, Tokyo 101 Japan
Publications: *Guide to Publishers & Related Businesses in Japan*

Research & Training Institute of the Ministry of justice
(Homu Sogo Kenkyu Sho)
1-1-1 Kasumigaseki, Chiyoda-ku, Tokyo 100 Japan
Publications: *Summary of the White Paper on Crime*

Research Institute for Peace and Security
(Heiwa Anzen Hosho Kenkyu Sho)
Roppongi Denki Building
6-1-20 Roppongi, Minato-ku, Tokyo 106 Japan
Publications: *Asian Security*

Research Institute of International Trade & Industry
(Tsuho Sangyo Chosa Kai)
6-15-2 Ginza, Chuo-ku, Tokyo 104 Japan
Publications: *Industrial Statistics Monthly*

Sangyo Horei Center, Inc.
Sakata Building
3-4-3 Iidabashi, Chiyoda-ku, Tokyo 102 Japan
Publications: *The Japan Business Law Journal*

Sangyo Press, Ltd.
Toei Building, 8th Floor
4-2 Nihonbashi Muromachi, Chuo-ku, Tokyo 103 Japan
Publications: *Japan Metal Bulletin*

Sanwa Bank, Ltd.
International Department
1-1-1 Otemachi, Chiyoda-ku, Tokyo 100 Japan
Publications: *Sanwa Bank Economic Letter*

Shufunotomo Sha
1-6 Kanda Surugadai, Chiyoda-ku, Tokyo 101 Japan
Publications: *Eating Cheap in Japan*
                 P's & Ques for Travelers in Japan
                 Other titles

Social Insurance Agency
(Shakai Hoken Cho)
1-2-1 Kasumigaseki, Chiyoda-ku, Tokyo 100 Japan
Publications: *Guide to Social Insurance Systems in Japan*

Sumitomo Corporation
Public Relations Department
C.P.O. Box 1524, Tokyo 100-91 Japan
Publications: *Sumitomo Corporation News*

Telecommunications Association
(Denki Tsushin Kyokai)
New Yurakucho Building, 11th Floor
1-12-1 Yuraku-cho, Chiyoda-ku, Tokyo 100 Japan
Publications: *Japan Telecommunications Review*

Three "I" Publications, Ltd.
Kamakura-cho Parking Building
1-5-16 Uchikanda, Chiyoda-ku, Tokyo 101 Japan
Publications: *Cement Technology and Plant Engineering*
                Oil Substituting Energy and Energy-Saving Technology
                Solar Heating, Cooling and Hot Water Supply Systems

Tokyo Metropolitan Government
International Communications Division, Bureau of
Citizens and Cultural Affairs
2 Nishi Shinjuku, Shinjuku-Ku, Tokyo 160, Japan
Publications: *Tokyo Municipal News*

Tokyo News Service, Ltd.
5-3-3 Tsukiji, Chuo-ku, Tokyo 104 Japan
Publications: *Shipping & Trade News*

Toyo Keizai Shimpo Sha
(The Oriental Economist)
1-4 Hongoku-cho, Nihonbashi, Chuo-ku, Tokyo 103
Japan
Publications: *Japan Company Yearbook*
                Japan Economic Yearbook
                The Oriental Economist (monthly)

Toyota Foundation
Shinjuku Mitsui Building, 37th Floor
2-1-1 Nishi Shinjuku, Shinjuku-ku, Tokyo 160 Japan
Publications: *The Toyota Foundation Annual Report*
                The Toyota Foundation Occasional Report

Toyota Motor Sales Co., Ltd.
2-3-18 Kudan-Minami, Chiyoda-ku, Tokyo 102 Japan
Publications: *The Motor Industry of Japan*
                The Wheel Extended

Trust Company Association of Japan
(Shintaku Kyokai)
Nippon Building
2-6-2 Otemachi, Chiyoda-ku, Tokyo 100 Japan
Publications: *Trust Banks of Japan*

Union of Japanese Scientists and Engineers (JUSE)
Nihon Kagaku Gijutsu Renmei)
5-10-11 Sendagaya, Shibuya-ku, Tokyo 151 Japan
Publications: *Reports of Statistical Applicate Research*

Universal Media Corporation
C.P.O. Box 46, Tokyo 100-91 Japan
Publications: *Bulletin of the Japanese Market (BOJAM)*

University of Tokyo Press
7-3-1 Hongo, Bunkyo-ku, Tokyo 113 Japan
Publications: Various titles on Japan

World Trade Center of Japan
2-4-1 Hamamatsu-cho, Minato-ku, Tokyo 105 Japan
Publications: *World Traders*

Yohan (Yosho Hambai)
3-14-9 Okubo, Shinjuku-ku
Tokyo 169 Japan
Publications: *Shopping Your Way Around Japan*
                 Pioneer American Merchants in Japan
                 The Emperor's Islands
                 America and Japan—The Twain Meet
                 The Japanese
                 More About the Japanese
                 Inside Japan, Inc.
                 Japan: The Coming Social Crisis
                 Japan: The Coming Economic Crisis
Other titles

Yomiuri Newspaper
(Yomiuri Shimbun)
1-7-1 Otemachi, Chiyoda-ku, Tokyo 100 Japan
Publications: *The Daily Yomirui*

Zaikei Shoho Sha
1-2-14 Higashi-Shinbashi, Minato-ku, Tokyo 105 Japan
Publications: *Guide to Japanese Taxes*

About the Author

An ex-"very low-level spook," journalist, editor, adventurer, lecturer, and the author of more than 20 books on Japan, Boye Lafayette De Mente was born in southern Missouri in 1928, moved to St. Louis in 1940, joined the U.S. Navy in 1946, was trained as a cryptographer and served in the Pacific, Panama, and Washington, D.C.

In 1948 De Mente switched from Naval intelligence to the Army Security Agency (ASA) and was assigned to Tokyo, Japan, as an intelligence processor. In 1950 he founded and became the editor of the weekly newspaper *The ASA Star*, which eventually became the official newspaper of ASA Pacific.

Returning to the U.S. in 1952, De Mente attended the American Graduate School of International Management (then The American Institute for Foreign Trade), and went back to Tokyo in 1953. For the next four years, he worked for a succession of newspapers and magazines, including *Today's Japan* and *The Japan Times*, and was co-founder and the first editor of *Far East Traveller* magazine. At the same time he earned a degree in Japanese and economics from *Jochi University* in Tokyo.

In May 1957 De Mente joined Australian adventurer Ben Carlin on an amphibious jeep called *Half-Safe* and made a 4-month-long crossing of the Pacific Ocean (which he later recounted in a book appropriately called *Once A Fool—From Japan to Alaska by Amphibious Jeep*). Details of the crossing are in the *Guinness Book of World Records*.

After spending the winter in Phoenix, Arizona, recuperating from his adventurous ordeal, De Mente returned to Tokyo in the spring of 1958 to assume editorship of *The Importer Magazine*, the leading English-language journal featuring Asian products for world markets. He covered Japan, Korea, Taiwan, Hong Kong, Thailand, Malaysia, Singapore, and the Philippines for the publication.

In 1959 De Mente wrote his first book, *Japanese Etiquette & Ethics in Business*. A pioneer work in its field, it was an immediate best-seller "everywhere except in the U.S." He quickly followed with *Bachelor's Japan* and *How to Do Business With the Japanese*, both of which also broke new ground and were successful enough that he was able to retire from salaried employment in 1962.

De Mente remained in Japan with his wife Margaret Warren ("imported from California") until 1964, averaging two new books a year. He then moved to Honolulu, did a book on Hawaii, and finally settled in Paradise Valley, Arizona ("a haven between Phoenix and Scottsdale").

While commuting to the Orient up to five times a year on research, writing, and consulting projects, De Mente wrote several books on Arizona and Mexico, began publishing, founded the very successful Arizona Authors' Association, and taught a course on "How to Do Business in Japan" at the American Graduate School of International Management.

In 1975 De Mente became executive advisor to East Asia Publishing Company in Tokyo and Hong Kong, and in the early 1980s became re-associated with the *Far East Traveller* magazine in Tokyo as consultant to the publisher and senior editor. From 1986 to 1988 he served as associate publisher of the *Japan Journal* based in Tokyo. Concurrently he was also adviser to the president of Kodansha International, Japan's largest English-language book publisher.

De Mente's most recent books for NTC are *Behind the Japanese Bow: An In-Depth Guide to Understanding and Predicting Japanese Behavior* and *NTC's Dictionary of Japan's Cultural Code Words*.